# Focus on Behavior Analysis in Education

## Achievements, Challenges, and Opportunities

Edited by

William L. Heward
Timothy E. Heron
Nancy A. Neef
Stephanie M. Peterson
Diane M. Sainato
Gwendolyn Cartledge
Ralph Gardner III
Lloyd D. Peterson
Susan B. Hersh
*The Ohio State University*

Jill C. Dardig
*Ohio Dominican University*

PEARSON

Merrill
Prentice Hall

Upper Saddle River, New Jersey
Columbus, Ohio

**Library of Congress Cataloging-in-Publication Data**

Focus on behavior analysis in education : achievements, challenges, and opportunities /
    edited by William L. Heward . . . [et al.].
       p. cm.
     Includes bibliographical references.
     ISBN 0-13-111339-9
     1. Behavioral assessment—Congresses. 2. Children with
disabilities—Education—Congresses. I. Heward, William L., 1949-

LB1060.2.F63 2005
370.15'28—dc22
                                       2004044405

**Vice President and Publisher:** Jeffery W. Johnston
**Acquisitions Editor:** Allyson P. Sharp
**Editorial Assistant:** Kathleen S. Burk
**Production Editor:** Linda Hillis Bayma
**Production Coordination:** Linda Zuk, WordCrafters Editorial Services, Inc.
**Design Coordinator:** Diane C. Lorenzo
**Cover Designer:** Keith Van Norman
**Production Manager:** Laura Messerly
**Director of Marketing:** Ann Castel Davis
**Marketing Manager:** Autumn Purdy
**Marketing Coordinator:** Tyra Poole

This book was set in Garamond Light by Pine Tree Composition, Inc. It was printed and bound by
R.R. Donnelley & Sons Co. The cover was printed by Coral Graphic Services, Inc.

Cartoons on pages 212, 213, 215, 217, and 227 from *The Big Box of Art 615,000,* 2002, Gatineau, Quebec:
Hemera Technologies Inc. Copyright 1997-2002 by Hemera Technologies Inc.

---

Pearson Education Ltd.
Pearson Education Singapore, Pte. Ltd.
Pearson Education Canada, Ltd.
Pearson Education—Japan

Pearson Education Australia PTY, Limited
Pearson Education North Asia Ltd.
Pearson Educación de Mexico, S.A. de C.V.
Pearson Education Malaysia, Pte. Ltd.

10 9 8 7 6 5 4 3 2 1
ISBN 0-13-111339-9

*To John O. Cooper,*
*behavior analyst,*
*precision teacher,*
*colleague,*
*and friend*

# Contributors

Sheila R. Alber
The University of Southern Mississippi

Saul Axelrod
Temple University

Donald M. Baer
The University of Kansas

David F. Bicard
Hawthorne Country Day School
Hawthorne, NY

Judy Cameron
University of Alberta

Judith J. Carta
Juniper Gardens Children's Project
The University of Kansas

John O. Cooper
The Ohio State University

Tina Covington
Hawthorne Country Day School
Hawthorne, NY

Sayaka Endo
Hawthorne Country Day School
Hawthorne, NY

Summer J. Ferreri
The Ohio State University

Roland Good III
University of Oregon

Charles R. Greenwood
Juniper Gardens Children's Project
The University of Kansas

Beth A. Harn
University of Oregon

Gregory F. Harper
State University of New York—Fredonia

Timothy E. Heron
The Ohio State University

William L. Heward
The Ohio State University

Kelly A. Hobbins
Headsprout, Seattle, WA

Robert H. Horner
University of Oregon

Edward J. Kame'enui
University of Oregon

Laura Lacy-Rismiller
The Ohio State University

T. V. Joe Layng
Headsprout, Seattle, WA

Larry Maheady
State University of New York—Fredonia

Barbara Mallette
State University of New York—Fredonia

Richard W. Malott
Western Michigan University

Catherine Maurice
Association for Science in Autism Treatment

Christopher S. McDonough
Hawthorne Country Day School
Hawthorne, NY

Deborah Meinberg
Hawthorne Country Day School
Hawthorne, NY

April D. Miller
Texas Woman's University

Nancy A. Neef
The Ohio State University

Janet S. Nelson
The University of Southern Mississippi

Lloyd D. Peterson
The Ohio State University

Stephanie M. Peterson
The Ohio State University

Amos Rolider
Emek Yezreel College, Israel

Ilene S. Schwartz
University of Washington

Trina D. Spencer
Hawthorne Country Day School
Hawthorne, NY

Greg Stikeleather
Headsprout, Seattle, WA

George Sugai
University of Oregon

Bridget A. Taylor
Alpine Learning Group

Matthew J. Tincani
University of Nevada, Las Vegas

Janet S. Twyman
Headsprout, Seattle, WA

Renée K. Van Norman
The Ohio State University

Dale Walker
Juniper Gardens Children's Project
The University of Kansas

Jo Webber
Texas State University—San Marcos

# Preface

This book is a collection of papers developed from presentations delivered at The Ohio State University's *Third Focus on Behavior Analysis in Education Conference,* which took place in September 2002. The three-day program included 80 invited addresses, research papers, and posters—many by the most prominent behavioral educators in the world. Scholars from Canada, Iceland, Israel, and Japan made the conference an international event. (Videotapes of 11 of the invited addresses may be viewed on the Internet; see page xiv for details.)

Like its predecessors from the first two OSU Focus Conferences (Gardner et al., 1994; Heward, Heron, Hill, & Trap-Porter, 1984), this book covers a wide range of topics and issues. Collectively, the contributing authors present literature reviews, conceptual analyses, and data from several original studies; they describe advancements in curricula, classroom and school-wide interventions, and teacher training programs; and they offer personal perspectives on the current status and future directions of behavior analysis in education.

## Organization of This Text

The book's 19 chapters are organized into four parts. Part I, "Achieving Improvements in the Lives of Children with Autism," includes two chapters on the role of applied behavior analysis in the lives of children with autism and their families. The late Don Baer, one of the founding fathers of applied behavior analysis, describes the required features of applied behavior analysis as an educational treatment and its critical value to all children who depend on systematic instruction to learn useful skills. Catherine Maurice and Bridget Taylor discuss challenges and opportunities for educators, therapists, and parents who want to provide effective help for children diagnosed with autism. Maurice and Taylor offer reflections and recommendations gleaned from a decade of direct action, research, and publishing; interactions with parents, teachers, therapists, and children; and observations of the political forces at play in the world of autism intervention.

Part II, "Recent Developments, Continuing Challenges, and Emerging Opportunities," begins with two chapters outlining recent contributions by behavior analysis to curriculum design and assessment for beginning reading instruction. Janet Twyman, Joe Layng, Greg Stikeleather, and Kelly Hobbins describe Headsprout Reading, a commercially available online reading program that combines behavior analysis, instructional design, usability testing, and an organizational systems approach. Ed Kame'enui, Roland Good, and Beth Harn examine a school-wide model for preventing beginning reading failure that is based on early and frequent measures of specific reading behaviors as a reliable predictor of reading risk.

George Sugai and Rob Horner provide a rationale, examples, and guidelines for building a preventive continuum of positive behavior support that extends behavioral interventions and practices to the school and district levels. Charlie Greenwood, Judy Carta, and Dale Walker provide clear examples of how indicators for early communication, movement, social interaction, and adaptive behavior can be used as important measures for early childhood growth and development.

Stephanie Peterson, Nancy Neef, Renée Van Norman, and Summer Ferreri critically examine the research literature on assessment of choices and the factors that influence choice making in educational settings. They propose a model for conceptualizing and assessing choice making and describe its implications for teaching children to make beneficial choices.

The five chapters in Part III, "Training, Supporting, and Learning with Measurably Effective Teachers," examine various issues and approaches to preservice teacher preparation and the professional development of practicing teachers. Larry Maheady, Gregory Harper, and Barbara Mallette describe the development, implementation, and ongoing evaluation and refinement of a teacher preparation program grounded in the beliefs that highly effective teachers engage in a systematic and recursive process—planning–instructing–reflecting–responding—while teaching and that they adjust their instructional practice in response to ongoing measures of pupil performance. Jo Webber describes how cooperative learning techniques and field experiences can help preservice teachers learn to manage difficult student behavior by applying ABA principles. Sheila Alber and Janet Nelson describe how student teachers and their mentor teachers can work collaboratively to conduct classroom research. The authors present this approach as one method for decreasing the research-to-practice gap by transforming preservice teachers and their mentor teachers from passive consumers of research to active change agents.

Chris McDonough, Tina Covington, Sayaka Endo, Deborah Meinberg, Trina Spencer, and Dave Bicard address the question, What does it mean to be a behavioral school? These authors outline the philosophy, instructional methods, and outcome measures that they believe define behavioral schooling, and they describe how these measures are applied to five distinct groups of learners at the Hawthorne Country Day School: students, teachers, teaching assistants, supervisors, and parents.

In the final chapter in Part III, Dick Malott describes a behavioral-systems approach for teaching behavior analysis that he and his students have developed and refined at Western Michigan University. Malott's approach integrates goal-directed systems design, behavioral systems engineering, performance management, and a skills-training model of education.

Part IV, "Perspectives on the Current and Future Functions of Behavior Analysis in Education," consists of seven chapters examining the current and future role of applied behavior analysis in education. Ilene Schwartz presents a framework for describing meaningful educational outcomes for all children in inclusive settings, and she makes recommendations for the role of applied behavior analysis in helping educators achieve those outcomes.

Lloyd Peterson and Laura Lacy-Rismiller suggest that a critical element of a school's effectiveness is having all members of a school's community focus on building positive, prosocial student behaviors rather than suppressing inappropriate behaviors. They address the challenges of changing the views of teachers, administrators, parents, and/or students who might otherwise support a punishment-based climate in the school to one that supports reinforcement.

Tim Heron, Matt Tincani, Stephanie Peterson, and April Miller use Plato's allegory of the cave as a metaphor for examining the present educational system and the standard of best practice by which it should operate. In their revised allegory, teachers imprisoned by the false promises of novel, untested, and ill-defined instructional ideas can be released from the bondage of their chains by turning to fundamental principles and key contributions of behavior analysis.

Amos Rolider and Saul Axelrod describe the results of a study showing that the public's acceptance of behavioral interventions increases significantly when those interventions are described in conversational language followed by an explanation of the intended outcome of the prescribed interventions. Purely technical descriptions of behavioral interventions correlate with a perception by the public that those interventions were less understandable and less compassionate.

John Cooper compares the research traditions of applied behavior analysis and precision teaching and concludes that both approaches produce applied research important for advancing the science of behavior and educational practice. He notes that, although the steady-state experimental logic used in applied behavior analysis is well suited to the discovery of functional relationships, the measurement and charting conventions used by precision teachers are appropriate for investigating questions about behavioral dynamics.

Judy Cameron debunks the widely held notion in education that rewards and reinforcement undermine an individual's intrinsic motivation to learn. Cameron describes the original studies in social psychology used as evidence for the negative effects of rewards and summarizes the results of several reviews and meta-analyses of that literature that show that the argument against the use of rewards is an overgeneralization based on a narrow set of circumstances. She suggests that the so-called negative effects of rewards have been used to reject the science of behavior, its principles, and its programs.

In the book's final chapter, Bill Heward contends that achieving significant improvements in education will require reducing the disparity between what behavioral research has discovered about effective teaching practices and the curriculum and instruction experienced by most students. He suggests some reasons why applied behavior analysis is well suited to contribute to educational reform, identifies a competing list of reasons that impede the acceptance and adoption of behavioral interventions in education, and offers some suggestions to those who wish to see applied behavior analysis play a more meaningful role in education.

## Who Can Use This Text?

As co-editors, we hope this book becomes a useful resource for three groups: (1) educators seeking information and resources on measurably effective instructional tools; (2) students of behavior analysis wishing to learn about its applications, accomplishments, and future research needs in education; and (3) anyone—preservice education major, in-service teacher, school administrator, parent, or consumer—who has heard about the "behavioral approach" and wonders what it is all about. We believe this book provides readers from all three groups with an accessible, accurate, and representative account of the relevance and the potential of applied behavior analysis in education.

## ACKNOWLEDGMENTS

Publication of this book would not have been possible without the support and contributions of many talented people at the Merrill Education group at Prentice Hall. We are especially grateful to Jeff Johnston, Vice President and Publisher, and to Allyson Sharp, Editor; their decision to publish this book is further evidence of their sustained commitment to making information on evidence-based practices available to educators. We thank Production Editor Linda Bayma for her skillful handling of the numerous steps required to turn a large pile of manuscript pages into a handsome bound book. The copyeditor, Patsy Fortney, did a laudable job of tightening up the text; and Linda Zuk, our Production Coordinator, pulled it all together in a timely, efficient, and cheerful manner. A special note of appreciation goes to Keith Van Norman who, in addition to designing the logo and program for the Focus Conference, designed the cover for this book.

We thank all of the chapter authors for their contributions. A list of contributing authors is given on pages v and vi. We also pay special tribute to five authors—other than OSU faculty—who have contributed chapters to all three volumes in the *Focus on Behavior Analysis in Education* series: Donald M. Baer, Judy J. Carta, Charles R. Greenwood, Richard W. Malott, and Dale Walker.

The study questions and follow-up activities for each chapter were prepared by two-person teams of Ohio State graduate students in special education and applied behavior analysis. We are grateful to the following students for their important contributions to the book: Natalie J. Allen, Michelle A. Anderson, Gwen A. Dwiggins, Summer J. Ferreri, Theresa L. Hessler, Jamie M. Hughes, Madoka Itoi, Tabitha J. Kirby, Laura Lacy-Rismiller, Brandon E. McCord, Corinne M. Murphy, Shobana Musti-Rao, Michele M. Nobel, Mary D. Salmon, Susan M. Silvestri, Renee K. Van Norman, Donna M. Villareal, Charles L. Wood, and Amanda J. Yurick.

Finally, we thank Mike Sherman, Director of the School of Physical Activity and Educational Services, and Donna Evans, Dean of the College of Education, both at Ohio State, for their ongoing support of our Special Education and Applied Behavior Analysis programs and our students.

*William L. Heward*
*Timothy E. Heron*
*Nancy A. Neef*
*Stephanie M. Peterson*
*Diane M. Sainato*
*Gwendolyn Cartledge*
*Ralph Gardner III*
*Lloyd D. Peterson*
*Susan B. Hersh*
*Jill C. Dardig*

## REFERENCES

Gardner III, R., Sainato, D. M., Cooper, J. O., Heron, T. E., Heward, W. L., Eshleman, J., & Grossi, T. A. (Eds.). (1994). *Behavior analysis in education: Focus on measurably superior instruction*. Monterey, CA: Brooks/Cole.

Heward, W. L., Heron, T. E., Hill, D. S., & Trap-Porter, J. (Eds.). (1984). *Focus on behavior analysis in education*. Columbus, OH: Merrill.

**Note:** All royalties generated from sales of this book will be deposited in the ABA Program Development Fund at The Ohio State University, which is used to support future conferences and other activities that advance the application of behavior analysis in education.

# Discover the Companion Website Accompanying This Book

## THE PRENTICE HALL COMPANION WEBSITE: A VIRTUAL LEARNING ENVIRONMENT

Technology is a constantly growing and changing aspect of our field that is creating a need for content and resources. To address this emerging need, Prentice Hall has developed an online learning environment for students and professors alike—Companion Websites—to support our textbooks.

In creating a Companion Website, our goal is to build on and enhance what the textbook already offers. For this reason, the content for each user-friendly website is organized by topic and provides the professor and student with a variety of meaningful resources. Common features of a Companion Website include:

## FOR THE PROFESSOR—

Every Companion Website integrates **Syllabus Manager™**, an online syllabus creation and management utility.

- **Syllabus Manager™** provides you, the instructor, with an easy, step-by-step process to create and revise syllabi, with direct links into Companion Website and other online content without having to learn HTML.
- Students may logon to your syllabus during any study session. All they need to know is the web address for the Companion Website and the password you've assigned to your syllabus.

- After you have created a syllabus using **Syllabus Manager™**, students may enter the syllabus for their course section from any point in the Companion Website.
- Clicking on a date, the student is shown the list of activities for the assignment. The activities for each assignment are linked directly to actual content, saving time for students.
- Adding assignments consists of clicking on the desired due date, then filling in the details of the assignment—name of the assignment, instructions, and whether it is a one-time or repeating assignment.
- In addition, links to other activities can be created easily. If the activity is online, a URL can be entered in the space provided, and it will be linked automatically in the final syllabus.
- Your completed syllabus is hosted on our servers, allowing convenient updates from any computer on the Internet. Changes you make to your syllabus are immediately available to your students at their next logon.

## FOR THE STUDENT—

- **Overview and General Information**–General information about the topic and how it will be covered in the website.
- **Web Links**–A variety of websites related to topic areas.
- **Content Methods and Strategies**–Resources that help to put theories into practice in the special education classroom.

- **Reflective Questions and Case-Based Activities**–Put concepts into action, participate in activities, examine strategies, and more.

- **National and State Laws**–An online guide to how federal and state laws affect your special education classroom.

- **Behavior Management**–An online guide to help you manage behaviors in the special education classroom.

- **Message Board**–Virtual bulletin board to post and respond to questions and comments from a national audience.

To take advantage of these and other resources, please visit the *Focus on Behavior Analysis in Education* Companion Website at

**www.prenhall.com/heward**

# EDUCATOR LEARNING CENTER: AN INVALUABLE ONLINE RESOURCE

Merrill Education and the Association for Supervision and Curriculum Development (ASCD) invite you to take advantage of a new online resource, one that provides access to the top research and proven strategies associated with ASCD and Merrill— the Educator Learning Center. At **www.EducatorLearningCenter.com** you will find resources that will enhance your students' understanding of course topics and of current educational issues, in addition to being invaluable for further research.

## How the Educator Learning Center Will Help Your Students Become Better Teachers

With the combined resources of Merrill Education and ASCD, you and your students will find a wealth of tools and materials to better prepare them for the classroom.

### Research

- More than 600 articles from the ASCD journal *Educational Leadership* discuss everyday issues faced by practicing teachers.
- A direct link on the site to Research Navigator™ gives students access to many of the leading education journals, as well as extensive content detailing the research process.
- Excerpts from Merrill Education texts give your students insights on important topics of instructional methods, diverse populations, assessment, classroom management, technology, and refining classroom practice.

### Classroom Practice

- Hundreds of lesson plans and teaching strategies are categorized by content area and age range.
- Case studies and classroom video footage provide virtual field experience for student reflection.
- Computer simulations and other electronic tools keep your students abreast of today's classrooms and current technologies.

## Look into the Value of Educator Learning Center Yourself

A four-month subscription to Educator Learning Center is $25 but is **FREE** when used in conjunction with this text. To obtain free passcodes for your students, simply contact your local Merrill/Prentice Hall sales representative, and your representative will give you a special ISBN to give your bookstore when ordering your textbooks. To preview the value of this website to you and your students, please go to **www.EducatorLearningCenter.com** and click on "Demo."

# Invited Addresses Available Online

Video presentations of 11 invited addresses from The Ohio State University's *Third Focus on Behavior Analysis in Education Conference* can be viewed online at the following URLs:

- Letters to a Lawyer—Donald M. Baer (paper read by Elsie Pinkston)
  http://streaming1.osu.edu:7070/ramgen/media/behavioranaly02/baer.rm

- The Rewards and Intrinsic Motivation Controversy—Judy Cameron
  http://streaming1.osu.edu:7070/ramgen/media/behavioranaly02/cameron.rm

- What I Have Learned from My Collection of 2,067 Standard Celeration Charts: Behavior Dynamics in Applied Research and Speculations on Teaching Academic Skills—John O. Cooper
  http://streaming1.osu.edu:7070/ramgen/media/behavioranaly02/cooper.rm

- Beginning Reading Failure and the Quantification of Risk: Behavior as the Supreme Index—Edward J. Kame'enui
  http://streaming1.osu.edu:7070/ramgen/media/behavioranaly02/kame-enui.rm

- Developing, Implementing, and Maintaining a Responsive Teacher Preparation Program for Preservice General Education Teachers—Larry Maheady
  http://streaming1.osu.edu:7070/ramgen/media/behavioranaly02/maheady.rm

- Teaching Behavior Analysis—Richard W. Malott
  http://streaming1.osu.edu:7070/ramgen/media/behavioranaly02/malott.rm

- Inclusion: What It Is, What It Isn't, And How Behavior Analysts Can Help—Ilene S. Schwartz
  http://streaming1.osu.edu:7070/ramgen/media/behavioranaly02/schwartz.rm

- Remediation and Prevention of Aggression: Effects of Behaviorally-Based Early Intervention at 25 Years—Phillip S. Strain
  http://streaming1.osu.edu:7070/ramgen/media/behavioranaly02/strain.rm

- Schoolwide Positive Behavior Support: Beyond Classroom and Behavior Management—George Sugai
  http://streaming1.osu.edu:7070/ramgen/media/behavioranaly02/sugai.rm

- A Nonlinear Approach to Curriculum Design: The Role of Behavior Analysis in Building an Effective Reading Program—Janet S. Twyman
  http://streaming1.osu.edu:7070/ramgen/media/behavioranaly02/twyman.rm

- Teaching ABA to Preservice Personnel: A Cooperative Field-Based Approach—Jo Webber
  http://streaming1.osu.edu:7070/ramgen/media/behavioranaly02/webber.rm

# Brief Contents

## PART I

### Achieving Improvements in the Lives of Children with Autism     1

CHAPTER 1     LETTERS TO A LAWYER     3
*Donald M. Baer*

CHAPTER 2     EARLY INTENSIVE BEHAVIORAL INTERVENTION FOR AUTISM: CHALLENGES AND OPPORTUNITIES     31
*Catherine Maurice and Bridget A. Taylor*

## PART II

### Recent Developments, Continuing Challenges, and Emerging Opportunities     53

CHAPTER 3     A NONLINEAR APPROACH TO CURRICULUM DESIGN: THE ROLE OF BEHAVIOR ANALYSIS IN BUILDING AN EFFECTIVE READING PROGRAM     55
*Janet S. Twyman, T. V. Joe Layng, Greg Stikeleather, and Kelly A. Hobbins*

CHAPTER 4     BEGINNING READING FAILURE AND THE QUANTIFICATION OF RISK: READING BEHAVIOR AS THE SUPREME INDEX     69
*Edward J. Kame'enui, Roland Good III, and Beth A. Harn*

CHAPTER 5     SCHOOLWIDE POSITIVE BEHAVIOR SUPPORTS: ACHIEVING AND SUSTAINING EFFECTIVE LEARNING ENVIRONMENTS FOR ALL STUDENTS     90
*George Sugai and Robert H. Horner*

CHAPTER 6     INDIVIDUAL GROWTH AND DEVELOPMENT INDICATORS: TOOLS FOR ASSESSING INTERVENTION RESULTS FOR INFANTS AND TODDLERS     103
*Charles R. Greenwood, Judith J. Carta, and Dale Walker*

CHAPTER 7    CHOICE MAKING IN EDUCATIONAL SETTINGS    125
*Stephanie M. Peterson, Nancy A. Neef, Renée K. Van Norman,*
*and Summer J. Ferreri*

## PART III

### Training, Supporting, and Learning with Measurably Effective Teachers    137

CHAPTER 8    DEVELOPING, IMPLEMENTING, AND MAINTAINING A RESPONSIVE
EDUCATOR PROGRAM FOR PRESERVICE GENERAL EDUCATION TEACHERS    139
*Larry Maheady, Gregory F. Harper, and Barbara Mallette*

CHAPTER 9    TEACHING APPLIED BEHAVIOR ANALYSIS TO PRESERVICE PERSONNEL:
A COOPERATIVE FIELD-BASED APPROACH    154
*Jo Webber*

CHAPTER 10    COLLABORATING WITH PRESERVICE AND MENTOR TEACHERS
TO DESIGN AND IMPLEMENT CLASSROOM RESEARCH    173
*Sheila R. Alber and Janet S. Nelson*

CHAPTER 11    THE HAWTHORNE COUNTRY DAY SCHOOL: A BEHAVIORAL APPROACH
TO SCHOOLING    188
*Christopher S. McDonough, Tina Covington, Sayaka Endo, Deborah Meinberg,*
*Trina D. Spencer, and David F. Bicard*

CHAPTER 12    BEHAVIORAL SYSTEMS ANALYSIS AND HIGHER EDUCATION    211
*Richard W. Malott*

## PART IV

### Perspectives on the Current and Future Functions of Behavior Analysis in Education    237

CHAPTER 13    INCLUSION AND APPLIED BEHAVIOR ANALYSIS: MENDING FENCES
AND BUILDING BRIDGES    239
*Ilene S. Schwartz*

CHAPTER 14    BUILDING BEHAVIORS VERSUS SUPPRESSING BEHAVIORS: PERSPECTIVES
AND PRESCRIPTIONS FOR POSITIVE SCHOOLWIDE POSITIVE BEHAVIOR
CHANGE    252
*Lloyd D. Peterson and Laura Lacy-Rismiller*

CHAPTER 15    PLATO'S ALLEGORY OF THE CAVE REVISITED: DISCIPLES OF THE LIGHT
APPEAL TO THE PIED PIPERS AND PRISONERS IN THE DARKNESS    267
*Timothy E. Heron, Matthew J. Tincani, Stephanie M. Peterson,*
*and April D. Miller*

CHAPTER 16    THE EFFECTS OF "BEHAVIOR-SPEAK" ON PUBLIC ATTITUDES TOWARD
BEHAVIORAL INTERVENTIONS: A CROSS-CULTURAL ARGUMENT
FOR USING CONVERSATIONAL LANGUAGE TO DESCRIBE BEHAVIORAL
INTERVENTIONS TO THE GENERAL PUBLIC    283
*Amos Rolider and Saul Axelrod*

CHAPTER 17    APPLIED RESEARCH: THE SEPARATION OF APPLIED BEHAVIOR ANALYSIS
AND PRECISION TEACHING    295
*John O. Cooper*

CHAPTER 18    THE DETRIMENTAL EFFECTS OF REWARD HYPOTHESIS: PERSISTENCE
OF A VIEW IN THE FACE OF DISCONFIRMING EVIDENCE    304
*Judy Cameron*

CHAPTER 19    REASONS APPLIED BEHAVIOR ANALYSIS IS GOOD FOR EDUCATION
AND WHY THOSE REASONS HAVE BEEN INSUFFICIENT    316
*William L. Heward*

# Contents

## PART I

### Achieving Improvements in the Lives of Children with Autism        1

CHAPTER 1        LETTERS TO A LAWYER        3
*Donald M. Baer*

Introduction *by William L. Heward*        3
Letters to a Lawyer *by Donald M. Baer*        5
Case 1        5
Case 2        14
Case 3        17
Case 4        21
*References*        29
*Study Questions and Follow-Up Activities*        30

CHAPTER 2        EARLY INTENSIVE BEHAVIORAL INTERVENTION FOR
                 AUTISM: CHALLENGES AND OPPORTUNITIES        31
*Catherine Maurice and Bridget A. Taylor*

Introduction *by Jill C. Dardig*        31
Part I. Political and Philosophical Reflections on the Treatment of Autism
    *by Catherine Maurice*        32
Part II. Some Critical Components of Autism Treatment
    *by Bridget A. Taylor*        39
*References*        46
Appendix: Resources for Behavioral Intervention for Autism
    *by Catherine Maurice*        48
*Some Books on Autism or ABA or Both*        49
*Study Questions and Follow-Up Activities*        51

## PART II

### Recent Developments, Continuing Challenges, and Emerging Opportunities        53

CHAPTER 3        A NONLINEAR APPROACH TO CURRICULUM DESIGN:
                 THE ROLE OF BEHAVIOR ANALYSIS IN BUILDING
                 AN EFFECTIVE READING PROGRAM        55
*Janet S. Twyman, T. V. Joe Layng, Greg Stikeleather, and Kelly A. Hobbins*

Nonlinear Instructional Design        57
The Nonlinear Programming Process        57

Conclusion    65
*References    66*
*Study Questions and Follow-Up Activities    67*

CHAPTER 4    BEGINNING READING FAILURE AND THE QUANTIFICATION
OF RISK: READING *BEHAVIOR* AS THE SUPREME INDEX    69
*Edward J. Kame'enui, Roland Good III, and Beth A. Harn*

Reading: A Complex Cognitive Construct    70
The Need for Early Identification    73
A Model of Reading Prevention    75
Substantive Presuppositions of a Prevention Model    81
Conclusion    86
*References    86*
*Study Questions and Follow-Up Activities    88*

CHAPTER 5    SCHOOLWIDE POSITIVE BEHAVIOR SUPPORTS: ACHIEVING
AND SUSTAINING EFFECTIVE LEARNING ENVIRONMENTS
FOR ALL STUDENTS    90
*George Sugai and Robert H. Horner*

What School Challenges Call for a Schoolwide Positive Behavior Support
Approach?    92
How Is Schoolwide Positive Behavior Support Defined?    92
What Guiding Principles Characterize the Implementation of Schoolwide
Positive Behavior Support?    94
What Does Schoolwide Positive Behavior Support Look Like?    94
What Do Schools Say About Schoolwide PBS Approaches?    96
How Do Schools Establish Effective, Efficient, and Relevant Schoolwide
Positive Behavior Support Systems?    97
What Is Needed to Enhance and Sustain the Systemic Use of Schoolwide
Positive Behavior Support?    97
Conclusion    98
*References    99*
*Study Questions and Follow-Up Activities    101*

CHAPTER 6    INDIVIDUAL GROWTH AND DEVELOPMENT INDICATORS:
TOOLS FOR ASSESSING INTERVENTION RESULTS
FOR INFANTS AND TODDLERS    103
*Charles R. Greenwood, Judith J. Carta, and Dale Walker*

Purpose    105
The Research and Development Approach: General Outcome
Measurement    105
Case Example for Infants and Toddlers    106
Central Features of General Outcome Measurement    108
Additional Features of General Outcome Measurement    109
Individual Indicators of Growth and Development for Infants
and Toddlers    110

Principles Guiding Development     110
Conclusion     119
*References*     *121*
*Study Questions and Follow-Up Activities*     *124*

CHAPTER 7     CHOICE MAKING IN EDUCATIONAL SETTINGS     125
*Stephanie M. Peterson, Nancy A. Neef, Renée K. Van Norman,*
*and Summer J. Ferreri*

Overview of Choice in Behavior Analysis     126
Choice as an Intervention     126
Choice as a Dependent Variable in the Assessment of Preference     128
Conclusion     132
*References*     *133*
*Study Questions and Follow-Up Activities*     *136*

PART III

Training, Supporting, and Learning with Measurably Effective Teachers     137

CHAPTER 8     DEVELOPING, IMPLEMENTING, AND MAINTAINING
A RESPONSIVE EDUCATOR PROGRAM FOR PRESERVICE
GENERAL EDUCATION TEACHERS     139
*Larry Maheady, Gregory F. Harper, and Barbara Mallette*

Guarded Optimism     140
Historical Perspectives: From RARE to REP     141
NCATE and the Responsive Educator Program     143
So Where Are We Today?     147
Where Do We Go from Here?     148
Sustaining a Responsive Educator Program: Preservice Teacher Preparation
     for General Educators Is Not for the Meek!     148
Look on the Bright Side of Life     149
Where Do We Hope to Be in 2013?     149
Conclusion     150
*References*     *150*
*Study Questions and Follow-Up Activities*     *151*

CHAPTER 9     TEACHING APPLIED BEHAVIOR ANALYSIS TO PRESERVICE
PERSONNEL: A COOPERATIVE FIELD-BASED APPROACH     154
*Jo Webber*

Course Description     155
Cooperative Organization     158
Course Outcomes     164
Limitations     168
Conclusion     170
*References*     *170*
*Study Questions and Follow-Up Activities*     *171*

CHAPTER 10     COLLABORATING WITH PRESERVICE AND MENTOR
               TEACHERS TO DESIGN AND IMPLEMENT CLASSROOM
               RESEARCH                                                     173
*Sheila R. Alber and Janet S. Nelson*

The Research-to-Practice Gap     174
Obstacles     184
Conclusion     185
*References     185*
*Study Questions and Follow-Up Activities     186*

CHAPTER 11     THE HAWTHORNE COUNTRY DAY SCHOOL:
               A BEHAVIORAL APPROACH TO SCHOOLING                           188
*Christopher S. McDonough, Tina Covington, Sayaka Endo,
Deborah Meinberg, Trina D. Spencer, and David F. Bicard*

History of the Hawthorne Country Day School     188
What Is a Behavioral School?     190
Why Take a Behavioral Approach to Schooling?     190
Students in a Behavioral School     192
Teacher Training in a Behavioral School     195
The Role of the Behavior Analyst in a Behavioral School     199
Parent Education in a Behavioral School     201
Is Behavioral Schooling Effective?     202
Conclusion     206
*References     206*
*Study Questions and Follow-Up Activities     209*

CHAPTER 12     BEHAVIORAL SYSTEMS ANALYSIS AND HIGHER
               EDUCATION                                                    211
*Richard W. Malott*

Prolog     211
Critique     212
Recommendations     214
The Behavior Analysis Training System: An Example of a Behavioral Systems
   Approach to Higher Education     221
Conclusions and Implications     227
Addendum: A Dialogue on Responsibility in Higher Education
   *by Richard W. Malott and Nancy A. Neef*     228
*References     234*
*Study Questions and Follow-Up Activities     236*

## PART IV

**Perspectives on the Current and Future Functions of Behavior Analysis in Education**     237

CHAPTER 13     INCLUSION AND APPLIED BEHAVIOR ANALYSIS:
               MENDING FENCES AND BUILDING BRIDGES                          239
*Ilene S. Schwartz*

What Is Inclusive Education?     239

What Is Applied Behavior Analysis?    240
Inclusion Missteps    241
ABA Missteps    244
Defining Outcomes for All Children    246
Conclusion    249
*References*    *249*
*Study Questions and Follow-Up Activities*    *251*


CHAPTER 14    BUILDING BEHAVIORS VERSUS SUPPRESSING BEHAVIORS:
PERSPECTIVES AND PRESCRIPTIONS FOR POSITIVE
SCHOOLWIDE POSITIVE BEHAVIOR CHANGE    252
*Lloyd D. Peterson and Laura Lacy-Rismiller*

Overview of Past and Present Behavior Change Programs    252
Structure of Schools    254
Important Considerations for Schoolwide Positive Behavior Change    255
Case Example of Schoolwide Positive Behavior Change Program    256
Conclusion    264
*References*    *265*
*Study Questions and Follow-Up Activities*    *266*


CHAPTER 15    PLATO'S ALLEGORY OF THE CAVE REVISITED: DISCIPLES
OF THE LIGHT APPEAL TO THE PIED PIPERS
AND PRISONERS IN THE DARKNESS    267
*Timothy E. Heron, Matthew J. Tincani, Stephanie M. Peterson,*
*and April D. Miller*

The Revised Allegory    269
Applied Behavior Analysts as Disciples Who Have Seen the Light    271
Key Contributions of Behavior Analysis to Effective Instruction    273
The Continuum of Effective Instruction Practice    276
Conclusion    277
*References*    *278*
*Study Questions and Follow-Up Activities*    *281*


CHAPTER 16    THE EFFECTS OF "BEHAVIOR-SPEAK" ON PUBLIC ATTITUDES
TOWARD BEHAVIORAL INTERVENTIONS: A CROSS-CULTURAL
ARGUMENT FOR USING CONVERSATIONAL LANGUAGE
TO DESCRIBE BEHAVIORAL INTERVENTIONS TO
THE GENERAL PUBLIC    283
*Amos Rolider and Saul Axelrod*

Method    285
Results    288
Conclusion    289
*References*    *292*
*Study Questions and Follow-Up Activities*    *293*

CHAPTER 17     APPLIED RESEARCH: THE SEPARATION OF APPLIED
                         BEHAVIOR ANALYSIS AND PRECISION TEACHING               295
*John O. Cooper*

Researchers Can Be Experimental Without Asking Questions
    About Functional Relationships     296
A Search for Functional Relationships: The Defining Feature of Applied
    Behavior Analysis     298
The Experimental Analysis of Behavior Began as an Investigation
    of Behavior Dynamics: The Focus of ABA Became Steady State     299
The Separation of Applied Behavior Analysis and Precision Teaching:
    PT Asks Questions About Behavior Dynamics, Not Functional Relations     300
Conclusion     301
*References     302*
*Study Questions and Follow-Up Activities     303*


CHAPTER 18     THE DETRIMENTAL EFFECTS OF REWARD HYPOTHESIS:
                         PERSISTENCE OF A VIEW IN THE FACE
                         OF DISCONFIRMING EVIDENCE                           304
*Judy Cameron*

Research on Rewards and Intrinsic Motivation     305
Meta-Analytic Reviews of the Research     308
Persistence of the Detrimental Effect of Reward Hypothesis     310
Historic Context of the Rewards and Intrinsic Motivation Literature     311
Conclusion     312
*References     313*
*Study Questions and Follow-Up Activities     314*


CHAPTER 19     REASONS APPLIED BEHAVIOR ANALYSIS IS GOOD
                         FOR EDUCATION AND WHY THOSE REASONS
                         HAVE BEEN INSUFFICIENT                            316
*William L. Heward*

The Knowledge-to-Practice Gap     316
Twelve Reasons ABA Is Good for Education     319
Why ABA Has Had a Limited Impact on Education     324
Reconciling the Opposing Reasons     336
*References     340*
*Study Questions and Follow-Up Activities     347*


NAME INDEX                                                                 349

SUBJECT INDEX                                                              355

# PART I

## Achieving Improvements in the Lives of Children with Autism

Chapter 1      Letters to a Lawyer
               *Donald M. Baer*

Chapter 2      Early Intensive Behavioral Intervention for Autism: Challenges
               and Opportunities
               *Catherine Maurice and Bridget A. Taylor*

# Letters to a Lawyer

*Donald M. Baer*

## INTRODUCTION
*William L. Heward*

A chapter by Donald M. Baer enhances immensely the legitimacy and value of any book that claims to be about applied behavior analysis and education. To say that Don Baer was an important figure in applied behavior analysis is akin to saying that Babe Ruth was a pretty good baseball player. After receiving his PhD in 1957 from the University of Chicago, Don took a teaching position at the University of Washington, where he and Sidney Bijou established the "behavior analysis" approach to child development (Bijou & Baer, 1961, 1965). In 1965 Don moved to the University of Kansas, where he and his colleagues, Montrose Wolf and Todd Risley, formally founded the discipline of applied behavior analysis and the *Journal of Applied Behavior Analysis* (Baer, Wolf, & Risley, 1968).

Don published more than 200 articles, chapters, and books on an amazingly wide range of topics: experimental methods and design; inter-vention research in early childhood education, developmental disabilities, chronic aberrant behavior, and the generalization of treatment outcomes; basic and applied research on imitation, language development, self-regulation, and social development; and professional issues such as training practitioners and the role and acceptance of behavior analysis in society. The experimental data and conceptual analyses contained in this body of work provide significant contributions to our knowledge of how "behavior works" and how to build and use a technology that takes advantage of that knowledge for the betterment of society.[1]

Don had an unparalleled ability to speak extemporaneously about any topic in behavior analysis and to do so with words that were not only conceptually sound and empirically current, but socially important and practical as well.

---

1. To learn more about Don Baer's contributions, as both a scholar and a teacher, to behavior analysis and to education, see Budd and Stokes (2003), Cataldo (2002), and Sherman (2002).

Because Don's words always possessed both scientific validity and human value, he was often asked to share them. As Cataldo (2002) noted, the first thing that any group planning a conference or meeting always said was, "Let's see if we can get Don Baer" (p. 320). That is exactly what my colleagues and I did when planning each of The Ohio State University Focus on Behavior Analysis in Education conferences. Don gave the opening address at the first Focus conference in 1982 (Baer & Fowler, 1984), he was a keynote speaker at the second Focus conference in 1992 (Bushell & Baer, 1994), and he was the first person we invited to speak for the 2002 conference.

"Letters to a Lawyer" is an original manuscript compiled by Don in the fall of 2000 for students enrolled in my seminar, Contemporary Issues in Special Education. Scholars at other universities provide the content for the seminar by assigning several of their published papers. Each class session features a 90-minute teleconference via speakerphone in which students discuss papers assigned by that week's "guest faculty" member. On three occasions spanning three decades Don graciously served as Distinguished Guest Faculty for this course. To read some of the highlights of those seminars with Don, see Heward and Wood (2003).

"Letters to a Lawyer" is a collection of affidavits made by Don as an expert witness for the plaintiffs in court cases in which parents were suing schools or Medicaid agencies to provide applied behavior analysis services for their children with autism. "Letters to a Lawyer" is a plain-English description of the requirements and potential of applied behavior analysis as an educational treatment for children with autism and pervasive disabilities. In Don's words, the paper is "my best estimate of how to be clear to nonbehaviorists."

Because "Letters to a Lawyer" contained so many important insights about applied behavior analysis and its critical value to all children who depend on systematic instruction to learn useful skills, my colleagues and I invited Don to make the manuscript the basis for the opening address at the third OSU Focus conference planned for September 2002.

In a letter to me dated February 22, 2002, Don wrote:

> My contribution to the OSU conference] in September will be the chapter, Letters to a Lawyer, which you and your students have already seen. Experience since then has shown me ways in which I would like to enlarge it, a little. Is that all right?
>
> The same experience has shown me how to make it much more engaging to a listening audience. Thus, I now propose a (slightly longer) chapter, and an hour's talk, and they are not identical in topography even though I think they serve the same function. Will it be all right to offer the talk to the conference and the chapter to the book?

I do not know what Don wanted to add to the original manuscript. His death occurred before he could share the new insights his additional experiences had shown him. With the exception of some light copyediting, we have published "Letters to a Lawyer," perhaps Don's last published work, in nearly verbatim form.

Although Don's paper speaks directly to the pointed questions and difficult issues often raised in court cases with respect to the relevance, need, and risks and benefits of intensive behavioral treatment of young children with autism, "Letters to a Lawyer" transcends the topic of autism by its relevance to fundamental questions about teaching and learning such as the following:

- Is society morally, ethically, and legally responsible to provide effective education to children?

- How do we know when education is effective?

- Why are curricular decisions and lesson planning so critical to effective instruction?

- How does the direct and frequent measurement of student learning inform teaching, and what is likely to happen in its absence?

- What are the necessary components of effective teaching, irrespective of student characteristics, curriculum, or setting?

- How are applied behavior analysis and responsible teaching similar?

## LETTERS TO A LAWYER
*Donald M. Baer*

**Donald Merle Baer (1931–2002)**
Photo taken by Jack Michael on May 23, 1997, at the annual convention of the Association for Behavior Analysis

Increasingly, parents of children with autism know that something called applied behavior analysis (ABA) can do remarkably good things for their children, in stark contrast to all the other programs they have encountered. Many parents ask schools or Medicaid agencies either to provide ABA for their children or to pay for the parents' securing it on their own. These agencies often refuse, sometimes claiming that ABA is one of the many things they already do. Increasingly, parents sue these agencies. Their lawyers tell them they will need expert witnesses. People like me are asked to testify, sometimes in person, more often by affidavit.

What follows is an edited collection of some of the affidavits I have composed. I do not claim that these affidavits are correct or incorrect, or effective or ineffective; they are my best opinion and my best estimate of how to be clear to nonbehaviorists. My purpose in collecting them is to cause readers to consider their own testimonies, if asked these questions—an increasingly likely event.

It should be remembered that the audience for these affidavits is first a lawyer and, subsequently perhaps, a hearing officer, a judge, and a jury. For this reason, I have sometimes used connotational terms, even though denotational terms are preferred within the discipline of behavior analysis and are far superior in establishing unambiguous meanings. My judgment was that this audience had neither the time nor the tolerance for a course in the scientific terminology of behavior analysis. I see the irony in this: Behavior analysis is a discipline insistently built on denotational rather than connotational terms; that insistence has always been one of its definitive attributes.

## CASE 1

The first case is one in which a single mother of a 7-year-old autistic boy asked the state Medicaid agency to pay for the ABA home program she had secured for him. The mother had very little income; she could not possibly pay for this program herself. The agency at first paid, but then refused. The mother sued. Her lawyer, a public defender, asked me a series of questions, to which I replied as follows.

Dear [Lawyer]:
Please use all or any part of what follows as the affidavit you need from me. Please call me with any suggestions for changes or additions you think would help the case; if I do not agree, I will try to create a different statement useful to the case and agreeable to me.

*1. You asked whether this child's severe autism constitutes a "medical necessity" for ABA.* The child's severe autism, if untreated, will almost surely bar him from a near-normal adult life. Autism makes it very difficult to change the behavior of such children—too difficult for the ordinary procedures used in most special education classrooms found in today's schools. Such children need the most powerful techniques known to behavioral science, applied intensively and extensively to the most shrewdly chosen sequence of behaviors that should be changed, often in conjunction with carefully chosen behavior-relevant medications. Only such a protocol will give children with autism their best chance at an adult life in mainstream society, either independently or with the moderate assistance of group home living. Current research shows that the intense application of ABA, pursued correctly for 30 to 40 hours per week throughout early childhood and perhaps into adolescence, can give children like this boy about a 50% chance of a mainstreamed adult life. Absent such an intense application to accomplish most of that shrewd sequence of behavior changes by adulthood, the probability that children like him will require intensive services and supports as an adult, often in the form of maximum institutionalization, has been estimated at 90% to 95% (Bristol et al., 1996). Maximum institutionalization typically results in behavioral regressions, lethargy, and excessive self-stimulatory and self-injurious behaviors. All of these outcomes are obviously bad from a medical point of view. ABA is the best chance of avoiding them. Thus, in my opinion, ABA is a medical necessity for a child with autism.

You did not ask if this child's autism constitutes a legal necessity for ABA, and of course that is your province, not mine. I only note that the federal Individuals With Disabilities Education Act (IDEA of 1997, P.L. 105-17) seems to promise every child with disabilities a "free and appropriate public education." I ask, rather than argue: If an intensive, extensive ABA program is the child's only realistic chance for an independent adult life (which, indeed, is my professional opinion), then how can its absence from a child's education be "appropriate"?

*2. You asked why ABA is the distinctive treatment for autism.*   ABA is the discipline that has most consistently studied and refined teaching techniques to their maximal effectiveness. It has also most consistently considered the problem of what behavior changes, made in what order

and by what techniques, will confer the maximal benefit to the child. ABA acknowledges from the outset of each case that each child with autism requires a unique sequence of behavior changes made by different procedures to maximize his or her chances of achieving the best outcome possible. ABA is, as far as I know, the only approach that has always measured its outcomes objectively, reliably, and validly. Approximately 500 published studies show that one or a few of the many behavior changes children with autism require can be made by ABA programming. True, perhaps 300 of those 500 studies lacked a convincing experimental design and formal evidence of reliable measurement, but the other 200 replicated their results and extended them with good measurement and convincing designs. ABA is, as far as I know, the only approach that has evaluated outcomes in well-controlled clinical trials (one of them, the Lovaas [1987] study, was exceptionally well controlled; another four were not so thoroughly controlled). ABA has produced unprecedented good results—an approximately 50% chance for an independent adult life. No other approach has proved that it can do nearly as well, as far as I know.

*3. You asked whether effective ABA requires a large university center and massive funding.* Very few of the U.S. centers that offer effective ABA to children with autism began with thorough federal or state agency funding. The others began as, and most remain, very small operations, yet many of them are very effective. These small operations usually were started and maintained by small groups of parents of children with autism who had learned two things: (a) ABA offered their children their best chance for a reasonable adult life, and (b) ABA was not available in their local schools or clinics.

Small-scale ABA can be very effective. The essential requirement for effectiveness is to hire a director thoroughly trained and experienced in ABA for children with autism. Such a director can do all of the following:

- Design procedures and choose the sequences of behavior changes that each child requires, and change those sequences as progress dictates.

- Teach parents and carefully chosen paraprofessionals to use the chosen techniques for programming in home, clinic, classroom, or daycare settings.

- Supervise parents and paraprofessionals, and ensure the accuracy and intensity of their work through feedback, retrainings, or refinements of prior trainings.

- Teach parents and paraprofessionals how to record and graph every instance of their work and the results in the child's behavior.

- Monitor graphs daily to see when progress is satisfactory and when it is not.

- When progress is satisfactory, choose the next best behavior changes.

- When progress is not satisfactory, analyze experimentally why the current procedures are failing and decide what other procedures would prove better.

- Train parents and paraprofessionals in new procedures, monitor their uses of them, and monitor the progress the child makes—or fails to make—with new procedures, then repeat the cycle until satisfactory progress is achieved.

A director's premise is always that satisfactory progress can be achieved with every child, and that a humane way can be found to make the desired behavior changes. The better trained and experienced the director, the more likely the director will be to find that humane way soon.

Given a properly trained and experienced director, no special equipment or special space of any great cost is necessary, and no further personnel of high qualifications are necessary. A *very* effective small center can proceed with major costs only for the director's annual salary and the hourly wages of the paraprofessionals.

Many of the current small but effective ABA treatment centers for autism came about in this way and continue in this way.

*4. You asked about the usual behavior changes ABA chooses for children with autism.* The highest priority often is teaching communication skills, preferably spoken communication, to give the child more control of the social environment. The next priority is teaching social skills, to make the child endearing to parents and acceptable to others, and again to give the child more control of the social environment. The next priority is teaching self-care skills to make the child increasingly independent. The last priority is teaching intellectual skills: the concepts of same–different, more–less, sequence, and the like.

*5. You asked why these are the usual priorities.* These skills seem most likely to give the child the best possible chance for an independent or semi-independent life in mainstream society. They are not chosen to mimic the usual developmental sequences of typically developing children; they are chosen to help the child proceed steadily from the current setting to a better one and, in general, to help the child proceed from more restrictive settings to less restrictive settings.

*6. You asked if the priority of teaching communication skills requires speech professionals to conduct the program.* Applied behavior analysts without professional speech certifications have been developing selected language and communication skills in children with severe developmental delays in language and communication for more than 30 years. Applied behavior analysts developed some of the first comprehensive language-training programs meant to take a child from minimal competence to rudimentary social conversation that would expand thereafter. The issue should not be whether the ABA director is a certified language teacher. Rather, the director should be able to determine what communication skills would serve each child best and what the next situation should be once the child's communication skills have improved.

The director should also know how those communication skills should be taught. Training in ABA targets both skill classes: targeting the most useful behaviors to change and techniques for achieving the desired changes in behavior.

Parents of autistic children must continue to teach their children at home and be fierce advocates regarding access to the proper but difficult-to-acquire remedial treatments elsewhere in society. The conventional psychopathic measures of parent–child relationships (e.g., "bonding") are irrelevant. The key is for parents never to give up on their child. A shrewd behavior analyst who found any hint that parents were starting to give up on their child would probably prescribe teaching the child various ways of telling the parents, with feeling, that the child loves them. This simple social-communicative skill can cement parents into a permanent dedication to their child.

7. *You asked whether an effective ABA program can be accomplished by teaching its techniques to an autistic child's present classroom teachers.* No. The child with autism needs teachers who know much more than a few techniques such as contingent approval and soft drinks, star charts, sign boards, and time-out. The effectiveness of applied behavior analysis depends on *analysis.* When teaching techniques fail, which often happens with autistic children, that failure should be detected within a few days and analyzed to find whether any of the following have happened:

- The child's rewards have lost their power.
- The child is being taught something for which the child does not yet know the prerequisite skills.
- The new situation brings out past errors incompatible with learning the new skill.
- A more supportive technique is needed.
- The teacher has lost some of the necessary precision of technique and timing.
- The child is ill or tired.

Knowing ABA means knowing how to test for each of these possibilities and knowing an extensive variety of ways to remedy them.

Many teachers believe that the way they were taught to teach is the correct way. Even when the child is not learning, they believe that the best response is to continue teaching in what they still consider to be the correct way. That strategy is the very opposite of analysis.

I have seen special education teachers produce videotapes to demonstrate that they are impeccably conducting what they call "discrete trial training" (DTT), which they (and their administration) argue constitutes ABA. They also produce graphs to show that they are in constant touch with their students' progress. But those graphs often show no progress over many months of teaching. In ABA, a graph showing no progress in the last 2 weeks is always a powerful indicator of a need for analysis and changes in teaching technique reflecting that analysis. If those changes produce progress in the next 2 weeks, then the new techniques are continued; if those changes do not produce progress in the next few weeks, then a new analysis is conducted based on the original failure and the previous ineffective analysis. Now, with twice as much information, the next analysis has a higher probability of being correct. If it is not, the one after has an even higher probability of being correct. Failure is always informative in the logic of behavior analysis, just as it is in engineering. This constant reaction to lack of progress—a definitive hallmark of ABA—is conspicuously absent from the vast majority of classrooms I have observed.

Teachers cannot be taught all the skills necessary to conduct that kind of analysis in a few workshops. Children with autism need to attend a center directed by the kind of ABA director I have described; or such an ABA director needs to be hired to teach in the public school. Because children spend 30 hours per week in school (and remember that the evidence prescribes 40 hours per week of intensive, extensive ABA programming to maximize children's chances at an independent adult life), schools should offer effective programming.

An ABA director can and should teach certain ABA techniques to the parents of an autistic child, but the director must be available to monitor, analyze, and alter the parents' efforts as the child's progress, or lack of progress, dictates.

*8. You say that the Medicaid agency has consulted local education officials, who say that autism is an educational problem with which they can and do deal, and that the Medicaid agency cites that as evidence that autism is not a medical problem. You asked if I agree.* I do not agree. The Medicaid agency's education consultants say that the special education program currently offered by the school can make children "more knowledgeable, compliant, and attentive." Of course it can, but only if the children already have enough rudimentary knowledge, compliance, and attention skills to enter a teaching paradigm based on the presence of those skill classes. Children must understand what is being said and done, do what is asked, and draw conclusions. Autistic children often cannot do those things well enough to make progress in public school special education classrooms. Most children with severe and pervasive disabilities need a classroom that will start at their unique skill levels. The children need to learn numerous and diverse behavior changes, probably different in each of their cases, that, cumulatively, would enable each child to enter and benefit from the general curriculum. To assign children with autism who do not possess those skills to the usual public school classroom is to assign them to regression.

*9. You said that the Medicaid agency's education consultant argued that public school special education classrooms could deal with autistic children as long as they were free of any "dangerous" aggressive or self-destructive tendencies, and that freeing them of such behaviors is a pediatric or psychiatric task. The education consultant also argued that "undesirable behaviors that interfere with learning but are not physically dangerous can be addressed by teachers." You asked me to comment.* Children with autism rarely are free of dangerous or self-destructive behaviors in programs other than ABA. The research and application literature of ABA contains hundreds of cases in which "dangerous" behaviors were reduced, quickly and thoroughly. Psychiatrists or medical doctors were not needed at all for those reductions. In fact, in virtually all of those studies, a medical doctor had authorized the behavior analytic program as a promising alternative to a medication regimen. The research and application literature of ABA also contains hundreds of cases in which undesirable behaviors that interfered with learning but were not physically dangerous were not only addressed, but solved, by ABA practitioners. Thus the education consultant's distinction of two kinds of disruptive behavior has no relevance in this autistic child's case. All the behavior changes needed can be achieved more efficiently and durably with ABA than by a typical public school program.

*10. You say that the Medicaid agency and its education consultant argue that the "so-called" ABA techniques are not distinctively ABA, but instead are found in many other approaches to teaching and therapy and are always accompanied by many other techniques not thought of as ABA techniques. The Medicaid agency and its education consultant believe that these techniques should be accompanied by many others because reliance on a small set of techniques must be less effective than reliance on a large number of techniques. They argue that the far preferable method always is to "blend" a great variety of techniques. They criticize the ABA practice they have seen in this child's case as a constant "picking and choosing" among a very small set of techniques, rather than the "obviously" more desirable uniform programming of a constant large number of techniques. You asked if I agree.* No. The behavior change techniques known and used in ABA are not unknown in other approaches to therapy and teaching. Behavioral teaching techniques are often borrowed by other approaches, but without the underlying behavior analytic principles that explain their effectiveness and show how to extend their effectiveness to new or unusually difficult problems.

The ABA practitioner is always individualizing every child's treatment program to that child's current skill deficits and that child's destructive, aggressive, and self-destructive behavior. Such individualization is always done in the context of what has yielded progress in the recent past and what has not. The ABA practitioner *should* appear to be "picking and choosing"; that is exactly what autistic children's problems require.

The argument that many techniques must be "blended" for the most effective outcome is based on the precedent that each of these techniques has seemed to be of some educational benefit to (normal) children in the past, and that the techniques should therefore be of some educational benefit to children with autism. But the fact is that empirical measures of the present child's current progress, rather than precedent or belief about effectiveness, prove that many traditional teaching procedures are ineffective for children with autism. The apparent restriction of ABA to a small set of techniques is not based on ideology, tradition, or belief. It is based on the effectiveness of these techniques, which are measured constantly for their effectiveness in teaching the child at hand; they are "picked and chosen" only according to that measurement.

An analogy will not prove this argument, of course, but may help to clarify it: In treating an infection, a very large, repeated dose of an antibiotic is far more effective than a small dose of antibiotic blended with aspirin, acupuncture, massage, and chicken soup. ABA has proven effectiveness in helping children make the behavior changes crucial to ameliorating autism, whereas the other techniques have no proof of effectiveness. Diminishing the use of a *proven*

*effective* technique in order to blend it with techniques not proven effective is unreasonable.

*11. You say that the education consultant has argued that the school's special education teachers use "discrete trial training" (DTT) and "contingent restraint," which is all that ABA or Lovaas uses, and so there is no need to pay more for the same services under another name. DTT and contingent restraint are and always have been available to this child in the special education classrooms of the public school. Thus, there is no need for any additional "ABA" programs. You asked if I agree.* The discrete trial method of teaching, or DTT, is as old as teaching and much older than education. It can be described as follows:

1. The teacher prepares a set of problems to present to a student one at a time.

2. This sequence is usually in an optimum order for teaching and learning, to the best of the teacher's ability.

3. The student responds or fails to respond to each problem.

4. The teacher responds to each of the student's responses or nonresponses, rewarding or acknowledging correct responses; ignoring, correcting, or reproving incorrect responses; and either ignoring or prompting responses after nonresponses.

5. The cumulative effect of this teaching is to impart a new set of integrated facts, a concept, or a skill.

The discrete trial training method is the method whereby children learn games and parents teach children language. It is commonly used in school classrooms for teaching any subject matter. DTT is the method of Socratic dialogue, it is often how law students are taught their most useful skills, and it is often how medical interns are taught clinical and diagnostic skills.

The discrete trial method of teaching has no intrinsic worth. Like any teaching method, it can be done on a continuum from very well to very badly, and no doubt is done at every point on that continuum somewhere in our society.

Teachers often misuse DTT in three ways: (a) they do not know how, or are unwilling, to vary the content and timing of trials when the student is not learning (as argued earlier in this affidavit); (b) they do not know how, or are unwilling, to add something to their acknowledgments of correct responses—a treat, a special brief activity, a hug, a song, always individualized to fit the tastes of the child being taught—that would make the trials delightful to the child; and (c) they use unnecessarily harsh consequences when the child does not respond or responds incorrectly. ABA teachers are trained to recognize and analytically understand such behaviors as indications of ineffectiveness and to avoid them.

Teachers also often misuse contingent restraint in four ways:

1. They use methods of restraint that are too severe.

2. They use restraint inconsistently.

3. They use restraint to encourage behavior changes that could have been accomplished by positive techniques. (Children offered desirable activities rarely need restraint.)

4. They persist in using restraint when it is not succeeding. (When restraint succeeds, it of course becomes obsolete. When there is no longer any behavior that requires restraint, no more restraint will occur.)

The fourth abuse is common among people not trained to measure the effects of restraint and graph those measures every day. ABA practitioners are taught to always measure the effects of their teaching, to graph those measures, to examine the graphs every day to see when progress is satisfactory and when it is not, and to change techniques when they do not produce good results.

Further, and very important to your question, ABA does not rely exclusively on DTT and con-tingent restraint in its programs; it also uses teaching procedures usually labeled preference assessment, incidental teaching, errorless programming, stimulus fading, stimulus shaping, chaining, and others.

*12. You asked about the usual extent of an ABA program for a child with autism. Must it start in the first 3 or 4 years of the child's life?* To give an autistic child the best chance at an independent adult life, ABA should start as early as possible, be conducted intensively, and continue until all the behavior changes (skills taught, undesirable behaviors eliminated) deemed essential to an independent adult life have been made. In children who have relatively many skills to begin with and start early in life, the program may need only a few years of 10 hours of treatment per week, perhaps only in a clinic or in the child's home. Considering the severity of most cases of autism and the frequent late start of treatment, the usual treatment program operates both at home and in a clinic or classroom for 30 to 40 hours per week until the child has reached the late teen years. Such a program is necessary to achieve all the behavior changes needed for an independent adult life.

There is no intrinsic limit to how much time is needed for an intervention to be effective. In the case of severe autism, many behavior changes are needed, and they are difficult to make quickly. The later a program starts, the less time it has to effect the necessary changes before adulthood is reached, and the more time the child has been practicing undesirable behaviors. The laws of behavior do not change with age; only the amount of time available for their practical application does.

Intensive programs produce many positive benefits, even when they do not accomplish an independent adult life. The child-become-adult is very likely to be free of bizarre or intense forms of aggression, destruction, self-destruction, and self-stimulation. The adult will most likely have learned to be socially oriented, or at least perfectly tolerant of living with other people; to have effective communication skills, even if they are considered somewhat strange in everyday life settings; to have the necessary everyday self-care skills of washing, cleaning house, dressing appropriately, cooking and eating in a healthy way, and cleaning up after meals; to be able to use public transportation; and to have a skill that can be sold in our society. This adult may very well require an after-work and weekend life in a group home or supported living arrangement. But even so, this adult has many freedoms, some hobbies, and some friends. Such an adult costs society very little, especially compared to adults with autism who were untreated as children and must be provided intensive supports in all aspects of their lives.

*13. You report that the Medicaid agency says that its consultants have assessed this boy and find him too reactive to the ordinary stresses and frustrations of the classroom to be a fruitful student; he becomes angry and aggressive and self-stimulates. Therefore, there is no medical necessity to pay for a treatment that clearly will fail. You ask if I have any reply to this claim.* Stress, frustration, and anger are the predicted responses of *all* organisms to failures to control their environment. Such failures lead to losses of their accustomed reinforcement (rewards) and to punishment and pain, which are the immediate evocative events for frustration and anger. Too much frustration and anger for too long create stress. Most of us are taught to suppress these responses. Fortunately, most of us also learn a variety of skills that control our environments so that we do not often feel frustration and anger, especially not severe forms of them. Autistic children, by contrast, have had little or no teaching about how to suppress frustration and anger, and they have very few of the skills needed to control their environment in socially acceptable ways. Their usual pattern is to retreat into the simplest environment available, do nothing in that environment except self-stimulation (which may be about all they know how to

do), and punish anyone who tries to complicate that environment or take them out of it, no matter how good the interferer's motives.

ABA programs make heavy use of techniques that require very small changes in behavior, especially at first, so that the child experiences mainly reinforcement, yet is always learning something new. Changing behavior with very few failures or mistakes and consequent loss of reinforcement requires an extensive knowledge of ways to effectively reinforce specific behaviors, especially as the child's tastes change over time, and of how to program a seamless sequence of behavior changes without significant or protracted failures. (At issue are not behavioral failures but reinforcement failures. The successful ABA practitioner knows how to reinforce often, yet not reinforce the wrong behavior. This skill requires knowledge and practice.) In particular, a good program uses techniques such as differential reinforcement, or shaping, stimulus fading, stimulus transformation, reinforcement scheduling, errorless teaching, and generalization programming. Control over children's behavior is steadily transferred from the teacher to naturally occurring events the children encounter and eventually to the children themselves, but only when they are ready.

Any less sophisticated treatment program will create many gaps in the ongoing frequency of reinforcement, and each of these gaps will evoke, especially from a child with autism, anger, self-stimulation, aggression, or self-injury. Enough of such displays may cause the unsophisticated teacher to cancel the program, which marks the end of the child's chance at an independent adult life or one close to it.

Yet it is eminently possible to offer a child with autism a diverse set of tasks; manage the difficulty of these tasks so as to create a steady flow of reinforcement, always for correct responses; use that as a baseline for teaching compliance with the teacher's instructions of what task to do each time; and then deliberately and carefully introduce an occasionally more difficult task and use the child's response to that difficulty as an occasion to teach him communication skills that secure help and to label his feelings as angry. Enough of that should mean that future failures result in progressively less and less anger and more and more constructive responses that undo the failure and recover the frequent reinforcement. My point here is that when we have a baseline of responding for dependable reinforcement we can interrupt it to teach any additional useful skills.

This strategy means ignoring the developmental progressions shown by normal children and abandoning the conventional methods for teaching developmentally appropriate behavior. Educators often see that as heretical. The strategy I have described is indeed fundamentally different from conventional education practice. But my best understanding of this child's case, and of cases like his, is that those standards must be abandoned if he is to make any progress.

*14. You ask if this boy's problems are not simply a result of his low IQ.* His many problems are probably not a result of his low IQ; most likely, his low IQ is a result of his many problems. It is important to understand that an IQ test is a collection of the kind of facts, things to label, tasks, and problems that the average child has learned to solve by age 3; of other problems the average child has learned to solve by age 4; of other problems the average child has learned to solve by age 5; and so on. If a given child has not learned what the average child of his age has learned, the child is considered less able to learn than the average child and is assigned a correspondingly lower IQ.

The original intent of IQ test designers was to measure something they thought of as the child's "ability to learn." Because they could not see how to measure that directly, they argued instead that the ability to learn must be obvious in what a child *has* learned by a given age, compared to other children. So the IQ tests very largely reflect how much of a certain set of common labels, facts, tasks, and problems a child

has learned, compared to what other children of that age have learned.

One interpretation—the one most educational psychologists use—is that this child did not learn as much as other children his age have learned because his genes and his illnesses have taken from him some of his ability to learn. But another interpretation—a typical ABA interpretation—is that his illnesses and their accompanying behavior changes have kept him from the opportunities to learn what other children his age have had ample opportunities to learn. Perhaps if he had had their opportunities, he too would have learned what they have learned.

The ABA home program this child encountered shows that he quickly learned everything it programmed. That suggests that he can indeed learn, given the optimum opportunity. It can be said that the task of an ABA program is to understand and create that optimum opportunity to learn.

*15. You say that several psychologists have given this child several labels implying progressive physiological deterioration of his behavior. The Medicaid agency sees that as reason not to fund an eventually useless treatment. You asked if I agree.* It is interesting that the Medicaid agency cannot secure a medical or biological verification of these labels. Perhaps they are only behavioral. If this child's behavior is not changed steadily in an ever more habilitative manner, he will indeed be vulnerable to a variety of behavioral deteriorations. These may well attract diagnostic labels implying mental illness. The various labels of mental illness tend to lose accuracy when the person diagnosed has very few behavioral skills, so they may well not be accurate if this boy is unfortunate enough to lose the programming that can keep him from those labels. Whether the labels will be accurate or not in his case seems trivial; what seems important is to keep him in a program that will steadily give him more and more skills that will correspondingly make those labels unlikely and unnecessary.

ABA acknowledges that autism and pervasive developmental disabilities have an organic basis as well as a basis in societal deprivation and distortion. In either case, the result is a person who needs the most powerful behavior change techniques known to behavioral science, applied to a shrewdly chosen sequence of behavior changes that will steadily allow that person to enter and live in steadily less restrictive environments.

*16. You say that some psychologists see ABA as a surface intervention, rather than an intervention into this boy's "personality" and "emotional life," and that this may seem to make ABA unworthy of funding. You asked if that is an accurate view of ABA.* The discipline of ABA conceptualizes personality as a psychological construct. Its underlying premise is that the behaviors of a person can fall into groups that operate much the same and into patterns of different groups. When that happens, it lets us describe people not by all the behaviors they have and the stimuli that occasion each of those behaviors, but by lumping many behaviors (and many stimuli) into very global labels. Thus we like to say that a given person is perhaps characteristically anxious in social situations, or characteristically authoritarian in work and family situations, or characteristically lazy when there is work to be done, or characteristically reckless with money, or characteristically insensitive to the opposite sex, and so on.

The key elements in labeling people are the word *characteristically* and the choice of global terms to lump together many different responses (e.g., "lazy") and many different stimuli (e.g., "opposite sex"). ABA knows how to organize separate behaviors into groups such that all the behaviors in the group operate similarly. It also knows how to organize separate stimuli into groups such that every stimulus in the group affects behavior in the same way. But ABA also knows how difficult it is to do either of those things *permanently* and how easy it is to undo such groupings. Consequently, *personality* is a

readily understood term for ABA theorists, but not a useful term for ABA practitioners. We cannot depend on its predictions proving stable when we begin programming.

Behavior analysis, like most psychological theories, shows mixed opinions about how to define emotions so that they can be distinguished from everything else. A majority view might well be that emotions are special kinds of responses that are experienced by the person having them as either gratifying or aversive. If emotions are recruited carefully and sophisticatedly, they can enhance behavior change programs. If they are not recruited in careful and sophisticated ways, they can interfere with and sometimes nullify behavior change programs. A well-designed behavior change program usually evokes only a mild emotion of pleasure, and a long-running, effective program often evokes no evidence of emotion in its students or clients, either positive or negative.

This child needs programming that does not evoke his negative emotions. Everything I have described as typical ABA programming does not evoke negative emotions.

## CASE 2

In this case, a 7-year-old girl with autism had been treated for 18 months with a sophisticated ABA program located within a public school—a very rare event. She made many valuable advances in those 18 months. The parents had taken her there because they believed that would happen, but they felt they could not afford to stay much longer. They returned the girl to their home school district, accepting its assurances that its special education program could do just as well. Within a year that special education program had lost every one of the girl's behavioral advances and taught her some undesirable escape behaviors as well. The parents protested that they had not been informed of the girl's losses during that year, and they protested the losses as well. The parents' protests produced nothing more than a blizzard of graphs from the school purporting to show that the girl was learning. The parents sued the school district, asking it either to hire qualified ABA professionals or to pay for the girl's schooling elsewhere. In the process I was asked by the parents' lawyer to evaluate those graphs.

Dear [Lawyer]:

I evaluated a set of 89 graphs given to your clients by their child's public school. These graphs purport to summarize the child's performance in 32 skills being taught at school. These graphs span time periods ranging from a few months to one year of instruction. I assume the school made these graphs to inform your clients about their child's progress. I know that your clients had complained that their child had regressed under the school's instruction, and that the school had kept them from realizing that until much damage had been done.

I evaluated how well these graphs could inform any parents and how well they could inform any professional trying to evaluate this child's school program. For either purpose, these graphs have several very severe shortcomings.

Sixteen of the 89 graphs were copied incorrectly: Their margins no longer contained the words describing the skill being taught and the numbers quantifying the child's progress. Since there is no uniformity of format across most of these graphs, any viewer would be mystified.

The skills being graphed were identified by only a word or a very brief phrase on each graph—for example, *Eyes, Ears, On, Off, Big, Little, Single Step Commands, Navigate B1d., Circle Match, 3 Color Sort,* and so forth. Some of these are a jargon neither the parents nor I understand. All are too brief for the parents or me to understand exactly what skill their child was being taught, or to judge whether it was an important or a trivial skill for their child, or to know how to support that new skill at home.

Rarely, some presumably relevant events or changes are indicated on these graphs, but only by a word or a very brief phrase—for example, *Scd, no spoon food, met, Base-2 week absence,*

*no self correct, yes-self corrected, 2nd opportunity,* and so forth. These notes by themselves cannot clearly inform the parents of what is happening and how it affects the teaching program or why the teaching program is being changed at those points.

You also asked me to evaluate the child's Individualized Education Program (IEP). How each of the skills being graphed relates to the child's IEP is not explained. Each graph should list the IEP item served by the teaching results being graphed. The IEP has the same five characteristic flaws I have seen in the IEPs of almost every case I have been asked to evaluate:

1. The behavioral advance specified is vague and subject to very different interpretations by different observers.

2. The conditions under which the behavioral advance is to be tested are never specified.

3. The amount of behavior change proposed as annual goals could be accomplished with a sophisticated ABA program in 1 to 2 weeks.

4. The behavioral advances proposed are almost exclusively academic rather than communication, social interaction, or daily living skills—all of which should have much higher priority than academic skills in most autistic children's curricula.

5. The IEP is not individualized: It closely resembles every other IEP this school program produces for children of any form or level of developmental disability.

The parents say that when they met with school personnel to help make the IEP, it was simply printed out by the school's computer. All of their attempts to individualize it to their child's case were resisted by the school personnel, who assured the parents that this form would fit their child very well.

Most of the graphs do not indicate what level the child's response must achieve to be considered mastered. A few of these graphs show that the skill had been taught to mastery in the course of a few months, yet teaching continued beyond that point without explanation. What skill ought to be taught next is not indicated.

Most troubling to me is that most of the graphs show that the child is not mastering the skills being taught, yet teaching continues, usually with no changes noted in teaching methods or, rarely, with changes that failed to produce an improvement. A basic principle of behavioral science and education is that the more an error is practiced, the more difficult it will be to correct it and to prevent it from reemerging in the future. These graphs show that this child is very often made to practice errors, sometimes for months, sometimes for a year. Each such graph testifies not merely to no progress, but, worse, to more and more difficulty in any future teaching that assumes that the present skills have been learned, or in trying to undo these errors. Yet this kind of mounting future difficulty is avoidable by the analytic use of ABA, as I have explained elsewhere in these affidavits.

A constant objective of ABA is to prevent the practice of errors. A common technique is to begin with a skill the child can do perfectly and steadily and gradually transform that skill into the new skill to be taught. This technique demands some sophistication by the teacher, but it has been shown effective in dozens of research studies for reducing and preventing the practice of errors. Errorless teaching is described in the professional literature of education and of ABA, and it is routinely taught to ABA students. These graphs show that this child would profit greatly from it. The frequency with which these graphs show very slow or no progress means that, in fact, the child requires errorless teaching if future teaching is to become easier rather than progressively more difficult.

These graphs do not show how each skill is being taught. That knowledge is necessary to understand when progress is seen and when it is not (as it usually is not). Without a brief description on each graph of the teaching procedures and contingencies, it is impossible to evaluate the educational significance of what this child is being taught, as shown in these 89 graphs. Each graph should include a brief note in plain language that says what the teacher presents to the student, what the teacher says, what the teacher does if the student responds correctly, what the teacher does if the student responds incorrectly, and what the teacher does if the student does not respond in time. An example might be as follows:

> Teacher shows card with a large square and a small square. Teacher says, "Point to [either "large" or "small"]." Correct point by student within 5 seconds produces excited approval, clapping, and edible treat from teacher. Next card is offered immediately with different-sized large and small circles than the previous card and in different positions on the card than were the squares of the prior card. No student response within 5 seconds causes teacher to withdraw the card, wait 5 seconds, and then present yet another card. Incorrect point by student within 5 seconds produces quiet "No," 5-second pause, and "This is [either "large" or "small," whichever is correct]; point to it" from teacher. Correct subsequent point by student causes teacher to present the next card immediately.

This example, which could usefully be labeled, "large–small discrimination teaching: generalized across figures," shows how brief the explanation of teaching procedures can be and still allow a reader to evaluate the significance of what is being taught. By constrast, the following example (unfortunately, typical of the teaching I have observed in this school), is admirably clear—clear enough to show that nothing worthwhile is being taught:

> Teacher shows card with a large square and a small square. Teacher says, "Point to [either "large"' or "small"]." Correct point by student within 5 seconds produces quiet "Yes" from teacher. Same card is offered again immediately. No student response within 5 seconds causes teacher to withdraw the card, wait 5 seconds, and then present it again. Incorrect point by student within 5 seconds produces quiet "No," 5-second pause, and "This is [either "large" or "small," whichever is correct]; point to it" from teacher. Correct point by student produces quiet "Yes" and causes teacher to present same card again immediately.

In this example, the student need not learn anything about relative size to gain the teacher's praise and edible treat. The student need not listen to any of the teacher's words. The student need only wait for noise from her and then point to whatever was pointed to last time. This cannot fairly be labeled as anything but "point training." As such, it has little if any educational significance.

In my opinion, only 17 of the 89 graphs show good progress by the student. The remaining graphs show ongoing failure or success achieved so slowly that a damaging and largely avoidable practicing of errors happened. That much ongoing practicing of errors means that teaching this student in the future will become steadily more and more difficult.

In my opinion, 64 of these 89 graphs show teaching of skills that, guessing from their very brief and arcane labels, are probably trivial for this student's best future. This student, like most students with developmental disabilities, needs ongoing teaching in four skill areas: communication, social interaction, daily living, and academics. Of these, the first three are crucial to her prospects for a semi-independent adult life; without them, the academic skills will not contribute to that outcome. Yet the relatively few skills listed in these 89 graphs that seem to name communication, social interaction, and daily living skills show very little progress and protracted practicing of errors; only some of the more numerous ones that seem to label academic skills show good progress. In my opinion, this is a serious misbalance in the student's curriculum.

The fact that this student diagnosed with autism is progressing at the pace shown in these graphs is very disturbing. Autistic children are very difficult to teach; steady success is seen only when the most powerful teaching methods are used in a systematic program. The difficulty of teaching them means that a large number of the basic skills necessary to an independent adult life have not been learned when they should have been; that is what brings these children to remedial programs. In those remedial programs, autistic children have to be taught almost everything. Recent well-controlled studies show repeatedly that, if the most powerful teaching is begun early in autistic children's lives and continued for 30 to 40 hours per week, the children will have approximately a 50% chance of learning enough of these many skills quickly enough to have an independent, self-sustaining adult life at the end of their adolescence. Autistic children not given this kind of intensive programming have perhaps a 5% chance of achieving a semi-independent adult life. Thus, every instance of insufficient, slow, inefficient, and unsuccessful teaching—especially teaching that allows much practice of errors—reduces that 50% chance downward toward to a mere 5% chance.

In short, this child cannot afford the level of teaching these graphs reveal. The society that will pay for her lifelong maintenance if she does not achieve some degree of independence should not have to, either, especially if it knows how to achieve that 50% chance of independent living.

## CASE 3

Dear [Lawyer]:

For several days I observed the teaching applied to your clients' child by three different teachers at her school. During that time, these three teachers, one at a time, tried to teach the child many very elementary intellectual skills (e.g., color names, identifying body parts, very simple picture puzzles); very few, very primitive communication skills (e.g., picture exchanges for pretzels and soft drink); very few, very minimal peer-interaction skills (e.g., being at recess with the other children on the playground, joining in the standardized gestures of some children singing a song, joining a line of children going to lunch); some skills probably aimed at improving her sensory integration (e.g., doing a picture puzzle while lying on and presumably balancing a very large ball; digging out picture-puzzle pieces buried in a large container of what seemed to be birdseed, and making the puzzle; rolling and pinching putty); and very few daily living skills (e.g., being taken to the toilet and then washing her hands, eating in the school cafeteria with the other children, returning her empty tray).

The teachers were warm, even-tempered, and, with one brief exception, gentle. They were working hard in the ways that they had been taught; they would be tired at the end of their teaching day.

Their teaching practices could not be seen as ABA. They used rewards that probably were not rewards, and they misused these supposed rewards. They taught in a variety of ways recognized in ABA not only as ineffective, but also as damaging mistakes, as follows:

**1.** Their statements meant to reward correct performance—"good," "right," "good girl," and the like—were not more animated, more dramatic, louder, or longer than their statements about anything else, nor did any distinctive facial expressions or body language accompany these supposed rewards. This child, who so far has very few language skills, could not know when she was correct and when she was not. From her point of view, she was asked to do many things and was offered what I can only call "patter" when she was correct, when she was incorrect, and when she was not engaged in the skill being taught. That she discriminated one kind of patter from another is very unlikely.

To be more specific: If she did not make the subtle discriminations between events such as "Good, [Name], that was right," "No, [Name], not that one," "All right, [Name], let's get back to work," and "Well, [Name], you'll like this," all offered in the same tone of voice, the same pace, for the same length of time, then she was living in a world of "Blah, [Name], blah blah blah" when she was correct, when she was incorrect, and when she was not engaged. No child with extremely limited language skills could learn much under those noncontingencies. If being spoken to by these teachers was in itself a re-

ward for her, then she was being rewarded equally for being correct, for being incorrect, and for being unengaged. Indeed, as I will explain later, she was being rewarded more often and perhaps more powerfully for being incorrect or unengaged than for being correct.

The definitive proof of the child's failure to discriminate among the teachers' various patters would require a diagnostic experiment. However, the teachers' graphs of the child's behavior during this "teaching" showed no progress at all by the child; that is strong evidence that she did not discriminate the teachers' attempts to reward her correct responses from the rest of their patter.

Teachers using ABA when teaching children with autism usually offer very clear-cut, dramatic, loud, animated, lengthy displays of their pleasure and delight when their students are correct, and they are very nearly silent at other times during a series of teaching trials. Thus the distinction between correct and incorrect responses is unmistakable to the student, and if the teacher's attention is a good reward for the student, a very extravagant form of that attention has been offered for correct responding, and only for correct responding. Students as difficult to teach as autistic children often require very extravagant rewards to learn—extravagant rewards that cannot be gained any other way.

**2.** The teachers often responded to a series of the child's mistakes by offering her what they considered the best reward they had, explaining to her (almost certainly without her comprehension) that she could have this best reward if only she would get the next try correct. If the offer and display of the reward was itself a reward for her (as they assumed it was), then she was often being rewarded for having been incorrect many times consecutively—exactly the wrong thing to reward. ABA teaches teachers to always analyze what behaviors are being rewarded and what behaviors are not, so that the intended behaviors are learned.

**3.** The child was not usually asked to discriminate between two things, only to point to one thing over and over. She might be asked to point to her mouth again and again or, later, to an orange again and again. This did not teach her the word *mouth* or the word *orange;* it only taught her that at this moment the teacher wanted her to repeatedly put her finger to the lower part of her face and, at another time during the day, to repeatedly put her finger on the object in the teacher's hand, which happened to be orange. But on both those occasions, she could satisfy the teacher and maximize the teacher's approval (if she could discriminate it from the constant teacher patter in which she lived) without having learned the word *mouth* or the word *orange.*

This fact would explain many of her graphs, which show responses never being perfectly mastered over months of teaching, yet seeming to be largely correct. This teaching method would almost guarantee that every day she would be asked to point to the orange, have no idea what the teacher wanted, be shown by the teacher to point to what the teacher had in her hand, do that for the next five trials without having to learn that it was an orange (just put her finger on the teacher's hand when the teacher made a noise), and be scored as correct on five of every six trials every day. The resulting graph would show that she never perfectly mastered the orange skill, yet seemed to make progress because her responses were well above the chance level.

ABA teaches teachers to require a discrimination between at least two things, such as "point to your mouth" on some trials and "point to your nose" on other intermixed trials, or presenting both an orange and a green object and saying "Point to orange" on some trials and "Point to green" on other intermixed trials. There would be many errors at first, but soon the child would have learned what the words *mouth* and *nose* and *orange* and *green* actually mean.

**4.** The teachers seemed to try to prevent the child from making too many errors and thereby probably systematically failed to teach. The teachers often responded to an error by taking the child's hands in theirs and gently creating a correct response, which they then approved of, meanwhile explaining why it was correct and why her previous response was incorrect. If their patter and their handling of the child were both rewards, then the child was better rewarded when she was incorrect (she got longer patter and handling) than when she was correct (she got only brief patter).

**5.** The child often spontaneously made a clearly intelligible and correct or appropriate spoken response. The teachers uniformly reacted to this as tolerable but not relevant to what they were teaching at the time—they made some brief, quiet patter about returning to the task at hand. Yet spoken communication is perhaps the most important skill the child must learn. On those occasions, an ABA practitioner would have instantly shouted approval, clapped and danced, and then acted on the content of what the child had said—giving her what she asked for, taking her where she wanted, changing from this task to the one she said she wanted to do, and so on—as if to teach her that when she spoke clearly, the world was hers for a few moments. The fact that she had spoken spontaneously would have made the importance of immediate, extravagant rewards even higher.

**6.** Occasionally on the playground during the morning recess periods, in the groups of students singing songs while waiting to go to lunch, and at lunch, another (nondisabled) child made an initiation to interact with this child. She did not respond to these initiations. Yet becoming acceptable to peers is probably the second most important set of skills for her to learn. An ABA practitioner would have been watching for those incidents and would have extravagantly rewarded the (nondisabled) child making those initiations to the autistic child, and then would have prompted the child with autism to react to the typical child if she did not, and would have extravagantly rewarded that reaction, if at all acceptable. Indeed, an ABA practitioner would have prompted (and later rewarded) a number of other children to make those initiations to the autistic child every day in each of those settings so the teacher would be sure to have multiple opportunities to teach the autistic child useful social skills. None of that was done. The teachers only put the child in these settings and watched to see that she was safe.

**7.** A picture-exchange system (PECS) of communication in ABA is used to begin teaching communication that can quickly be transformed into spoken language. Its rationale is that the child with few language skills can easily learn to present pictures of what she wants to her teachers, who can easily understand the child's communication and reward it appropriately. With that as a start, the teachers are supposed to use the child's ability to imitate sounds and teach the child the spoken words that go with each picture, rewarding the child's use of those words even more powerfully than the child's use of the pictures. If that is done consistently, the child will soon use the words as well as the pictures and then use the words instead of the pictures, which the teachers should reward most powerfully of all.

This child's PECS teacher merely said the word for whatever picture the child presented to her and never asked the child to imitate that word. The child had no reason even to listen to the teacher's model, let alone imitate it. On several occasions during the picture-exchange teaching, the child spoke clearly about what she wanted, and her teacher reacted with brief, uninterested patter and insisted on returning to more picture exchanges. The real point of the picture exchange was being dismissed.

This practice will commit the child to a world of picture-exchange communication, which is not readily useful in the real world, rather than the spoken communication, which is. In fact, the child is being taught some picture exchanges for words she already knows how to speak and does speak, but without clear rewards for doing so in this classroom. (The teacher said she had been to a workshop on PECS, but had not read the definitive article on its rationale and application [Bondy & Frost, 1994].)

**8.** Two of the three teachers I observed showed an unfortunate systematic tendency: The more consistently the child attended to her task of the moment and responded correctly to its trials, the less enthusiastic and reliable was the teacher's approval. When the child then made an error or her attention wandered, the teachers again became more emphatic and more consistent in their next approvals, until the child once again became consistently attentive and consistently correct, whereupon the pattern would be repeated. In effect, these two teachers were teaching the child not to be consistently attentive or correct by offering her fewer rewards when she was consistent and more rewards when she erred or wandered.

An ABA practitioner would have become even more extravagant with praise and other rewards as the child became consistently attentive or consistently correct in every skill being taught. In effect, the ABA practitioner would teach the child that *steady, long-lasting* attention and correct performance are the best rewarded of all her performances.

**9.** One teacher I observed sometimes displayed a lovely smile, but never as part of her reward for the child's correct response. Instead, she smiled at the child when the child was unengaged, as a way of recalling the child to the task at hand. If that smile was a reward for the child, it was being used to teach the child disengagement: The way to be smiled at was to go off task.

In summary, the teachers I observed tried (and usually failed) to teach only a few of, and often unimportant examples of, the most important three skill classes the child required (communication, social interaction, and daily living), spending their time instead on the least important academic skills; did not use many different rewards in that teaching; were not sure that what they offered as rewards were powerful rewards; in various ways misused the rewards they assumed were rewards, most obviously by offering essentially the same rewards for correct, incorrect, and unengaged behaviors by the child; missed many opportunities to teach valuable, important skills; inadvertently untaught some previously taught skills; and if the rewards they used were strong ones, inadvertently taught some seriously undesirable habits.

---

## CASE 4

### Part A

A consortium of families with autistic children sued the level of their government that determined the education and health care of their children, claiming that the government's failure to provide ABA was damaging to their children and hence illegal. They cited the Lovaas studies as evidence. I was asked to evaluate the credibility of the Lovaas studies (Lovaas, 1987; McEachin, Smith, & Lovaas, 1993).

Dear [Lawyer]:
I am writing in evaluation of two studies on the treatment of childhood autism published by Dr. Ivar Lovaas, sometimes with other colleagues (referenced later). In what follows, I will refer to the research team simply as Lovaas.

In 1987 Lovaas reported using an ABA program in the treatment of childhood autism. At the time, it was not the conventional treatment that was applied to autistic children by medical doctors, psychologists, or educators. Lovaas had recruited two groups of children with autism, 19 children in each group. One group of children received a program of intensive, one-to-one behavioral programming for 40 hours each week for a period of 2 years or more until they reached age 4. The other group received those conventional treatments the parents could find in the metropolitan area of Los Angeles, California.

The results were dramatic: Approximately half (9 of 19 children) of the group receiving the ABA program showed marked improvements, and most of the remainder showed considerable improvement. By contrast, the children of the other group showed virtually no valuable improvements.

None of the many previous conventional attempts to treat autism reported in the scientific literature had achieved anything close to such positive results. Long-term observations of children with autism have established that only 5% of untreated autistic children show any improvement.

In 1993 Lovaas described those two groups of children 5 to 6 years after treatment. The children who had received the ABA program and had done well in 1987 had maintained those gains in 1993. Particularly remarkable and unprecedented was the finding that eight of the nine "best outcome" children were enrolled and doing well in regular class where they were essentially indistinguishable from typical children on tests of intelligence and adaptive behavior. The children of the other group had not progressed any further.

In clinical science, most reports of unprecedented success attract skepticism, as they should. This is especially true when the disorder being treated has almost perfectly resisted all prior attempts at treatment, even intensive ones, and shows a very poor prognosis when untreated. Some of the resultant skepticism of Lovaas's studies was standard scientific caution, and, in my opinion, some was not. I will discuss some major instances of both.

The nonstandard skepticism of the Lovaas studies often reduced to a mistaken exercise in logic. Some critics assumed that this newcomer, ABA, simply could not improve autism because it was so different from prior, conventional attempts at therapy for autism. They argued that the children who had improved under ABA must not have been autistic; they argued that the prior diagnoses of these children as autistic must have been mistaken.

The premise that ABA could not improve autism was a poor one. An autistic child needs many, many behaviors to be changed if the child is to have an independent adult life. Yet the behavior of these children is classically resistant to all but the most deeply analytic, perfectly designed, and intensively pursued attempts to change it. It is exactly in ABA that we find such deeply analytic, perfectly designed, and intensively pursued techniques.

More to the point, the behavioral literature preceding Lovaas's work contained many reports of improving some single behavior from that list of the many that needed to be changed if the autistic child was to have a chance for an independent adult life. Throughout my professional career, I have been a student of and occasional contributor to that literature, which dates from the late 1950s to the present. I estimate that if we accept all the simple, often impressionistic case histories reported in that literature, as well as the carefully measured, carefully designed experimental analyses, the reported number of successful autism-relevant behavior changes is approximately 500. If we exclude the merely impressionistic, nonexperimental case histories, the reported number of successful autism-relevant behavior changes is approximately 200. Each study (of the 500 or the 200) typically targeted and reported on only one successfully managed behavior change; but taken as a whole, the literature reported a wide diversity of the behavior changes we would list as cumulatively crucial to a subsequent independent adult life for an autistic child.

With these precedents, it was natural that someone like Lovaas would ask if it was possible to assemble many of these behavior change techniques into a long-term, integrative, extensive, intensive, self-analytic, and self-correcting treatment program. The experimental question would be: Could that program accomplish, integrate, and maintain enough cumulative behavior changes to confer an independent life to the child with autism? The answer appeared to be yes, in the results Lovaas reported in 1987 and 1993.

A second criticism of these studies centered on how the children were assigned to its two groups. Ideally, to compare the effectiveness of any two therapies, participants should be assigned at random to each group (i.e., to each therapy). The point of random assignment is to prevent a biased assignment of disproportionately more of the easy-to-cure cases to one therapy and disproportionately more of the difficult-to-cure cases to the other. Such a bias could make the first therapy seem more effective than the second, even if it were in fact no more effective, or even less effective.

In the Lovaas studies, random assignment was proposed at first, but was not used, on ethical and humane grounds. Instead, Lovaas accepted for the ABA program all the autistic children referred to him, *if* he had the treatment resources available for the child's treatment at the time the child was referred. The ABA treatment program required a great deal of time by many highly trained people. Often, autistic children were referred for treatment at times when too many of these people were fully engaged in the treatment of previously referred children. In that case these children were referred to the other group.

That is not random assignment according to the technical definition of the procedure. But I cannot see that it is biased assignment: The children accepted into the ABA program were accepted because treatment resources were available, not for any other reason. The subsequent ease or difficulty of a given child's case could not affect whether these treatment resources were available at the time the child was referred. Thus, I think this method of assigning cases to the two groups, although not random, nevertheless allowed a fair comparison of the two therapies. In my published critique of the studies (Baer, 1993), I referred to it as "quasi-random." I believe the subsequent comparison of outcomes was not biased or misleading and can be accepted at face value.

In my professional opinion, psychologists cannot accurately predict which cases of autism in young children will subsequently prove easy or difficult to treat. Our best, but very imperfect, prediction is that the earlier in life children encounter the program, the better they will do in it (because we will have more time to make the many necessary behavior changes). Thus, I do not believe that it was possible to assign only the easy cases to the behavioral program, or even a disproportionate set of them, even if anyone wanted to try. I have known Lovaas and his work for 40 years; I do not believe he wanted to try. I am certain that he wanted only the true answer to his comparison of the two therapies.

Furthermore, Lovaas applied many conventional standardized tests of ability and clinical disposition to both groups prior to the program. According to those tests, his necessity-driven method of assigning children to the groups produced two groups that were essentially similar. The major exception was that the group receiving the ABA program contained a few more of the slightly older children than did the other group. So, whatever quite imperfect prediction of treatment success can be derived from an age difference favored the nonbehavioral group, not the one receiving the behavioral program. Yet it was the group receiving the ABA program that showed the dramatic, unprecedented improvements.

The same standardized tests are used by many clinicians, behavioral and otherwise, to identify and characterize cases of autism. Some arguments are heard in the field that different tests should have been used: If different tests had been used, perhaps not all the children would have been labeled autistic. In that case, Lovaas's results, although admirable, might not all be about autism.

Unfortunately, psychologists still do not always agree on which of the very many tests available are ideal for any given diagnostic purpose. Thus, some may argue that Lovaas's results might have been different if he had used other tests. In psychology, if an argument is possible, it will occur. However, the tests that Lovaas used were numerous, conventional, and to a considerable degree overlapping and redundant in their probable sensitivities to the children's abilities and clinical status. Thus, Lovaas had been very careful and conservative in assessing the children

as autistic and as seriously disabled. Moreover, although some of the tests he used are not every professional's favorite, each of them is the favorite of many, many professionals.

In summary, I cannot see any choice but to accept that Lovaas's results are what they seem to be: an experimental proof that applied behavior analysis, when pursued in a systematic, constantly measured, self-analytic, self-correcting, and integrated way, as it was in the Lovaas program, can be extraordinarily effective in the long-term treatment of children with autism and can give them a previously unprecedented chance at an independent adult life.

## Part B

In the same case brought by the consortium of families, I was asked to comment on affidavits secured by the other side from two experts in education and psychology, including one who has published extensively in the ABA literature. I have used the pseudonyms Professor Echt and Professor Wassermilch to refer to the plaintiff's expert witnesses.

Dear [Lawyer]:
You asked for a response to the affidavit written by Professor Echt, whose comments were being used by the medical and education agencies resisting your clients' suit for government provision of ABA programs for their autistic children.

Echt's claim that ABA is not a medical treatment is arbitrary. The definition of medical treatment presumably is whatever cures illness. Increasingly, the major causes of death are illnesses of the cardiovascular system, respiratory system, diabetes, sleep apnea, and so on. All these are most directly attributable not to the classical medical events of infection and trauma, but instead to "lifestyle," meaning almost always a habitually poor diet, a habitual lack of exercise, and the habitual abuse of various substances. The treatment of lifestyle is inherently behavioral: to eat differently, to exercise regularly, and to abstain from the use of various substances. Increasingly, medical doctors maintain, prescribe, and bill for the relevant behavioral services for patients with such illnesses. In other words, behavioral treatment has become medical treatment.

When children with autism are referred to pediatricians for treatment, their modern recourse is the same as for the lifestyle diseases: to prescribe the appropriate behavioral programs. The essence of autism is a lack of the basic and secondary skills essential to communication, social interaction, daily living, and academics and other forms of intellectual endeavor. The ongoing absence of those skills will result in a lifetime of institutionalization and the various debilitations secondary to that life; in effect, institutionalization is a very undesirable and quite unhealthy lifestyle. The remedying of these lacks in childhood will allow, according to present data, perhaps a 50% chance at an independent adult life, and thus the avoidance of institutionalization and its psychological and biologically unhealthy consequences.

Echt acknowledges that applied behavior analysis is the treatment of choice for autism. He argues that Lovaas used one class of teaching procedures from ABA, called discrete trial training (DTT). He argues that although DTT is a part of ABA, there is so much more to ABA that reliance only on DTT is grounds for criticism.

Three answers are required in response to Echt's argument:

**1.** Echt is incorrect to claim that DTT is only a small part of ABA. DTT is instead a very large portion of its procedures. It is the oldest and most ubiquitous of all teaching methods and is used in countless variations. All it means is that the teacher has prepared some relevant materials or events to present to the student and is prepared to answer correctly any possible response the student may make to them so that the result is the behavior change the teacher targeted. DTT is essentially only the teacher's careful preparation of what is to be taught and learned today. It

can range from the rote drudgery of memorization to the most abstract forms of Socratic dialogue. Whether DTT is drudgery or sublimely informative depends not on its format, but on how skillfully the teacher has prepared what the student will encounter and how skillfully the teacher can answer whatever response to the encounters the student may make.

**2.** The list of ABA procedures used to teach children with autism, which are not always called DTT, usually includes (a) the various techniques of stimulus control, such as fading, transformation, and superposition; (b) the related practice of errorless discrimination; (c) the uses of the behavioral momentum concept; (d) the Premack principle; (e) the response deprivation methods; (f) the incidental teaching methods; (g) the use of stimulus equivalence principles; and others. But analysis shows that each of these is procedurally based on and reducible to DTT. Each is an example of using the three-term contingency that Echt correctly acknowledges is at the heart of ABA. (Incidentally, this last decade has required that the three-term contingency be renamed the $N$-term contingency, to acknowledge that our analyses now deal with more complex relations than before.) In application, the three-term contingency is almost always a matter of discrete trials.

In short, those procedures not called DTT are, for the most part, DTT. Consider, for example, incidental teaching, which sometimes is superficially categorized as "not using trials." In incidental teaching, the teacher waits for an incident that reveals that the child intensely wants something in the setting. The teacher uses that incident to require the child to practice some useful skill (perhaps talk about what is wanted) and uses the intensely wanted object or activity to reinforce that practice. But incidental teaching is efficient only when the teacher has made the setting rich in the materials and activities the child is likely to want, so that one apparently child-initiated trial follows another at a rapid rate. It is true that the teacher does not present each trial. Instead, the teacher "salts" the environment with materials and activities that will almost surely catch the child's interest. The teacher then merely waits for these salted events to exert their appeal for the child. In effect, the teacher *has* presented the teaching trials by making them so abundant that they are unavoidable. Thus, the method is best seen as still another variation of the basic DTT format. (Incidentally, teachers not skilled in this salting make very slow progress with their students.)

**3.** Whether DTT is a small or a very large part of ABA is not relevant to the present case. The crucial question is whether DTT is a *powerful* part of ABA. The great majority of the techniques that have proven powerful and efficient in teaching children with autism were indeed one form or another of DTT. Done correctly, DTT is among the most powerful methods known to the discipline. The crucial point is not that the Lovaas team relied very heavily on DTT, but rather that the team used DTT well. The data of their studies, and of many studies derived from theirs, clearly show that these DTT procedures were unprecedentedly powerful for teaching useful skills to children with autism. All other techniques reported in the literature come nowhere close to that achievement.

Echt also argues that the absence of true random assignment in the Lovaas studies is fatal to their credibility. He argues that assignment is either random or not. That is, of course, tautologically correct, and so it has only the importance that any tautology does. The truly important point is not whether the Lovaas team religiously adhered to a textbook canon of good experimental design; the crucial point is whether the children assigned to the experimental group were systematically easier to treat, or systematically were starting from more favorable baselines of skill, than the children assigned to the nontreated group. If the favorable cases could be systematically assigned to the experimental group, that would of course misleadingly make the experimental procedures seem very effec-

tive. If the favorable cases could be systematically assigned to the other group, that would of course misleadingly make the experimental procedures seem dysfunctional. The crucial question is not whether assignment was random, but whether it was conducive to systematically getting the favorable cases into one group rather than the other.

True, random assignment is one way of avoiding that misleading bias, but it is not the only way. Lovaas's studies report that children were assigned to one group or another on the basis of whether the personnel and other resources needed for the experimental treatment were available when the children were referred for treatment and participation in the studies. The momentary availability of the experimental personnel and resources can hardly have any relation to whether the child referred at the moment was a favorable or an unfavorable case. Hence I have argued that assignment in these studies was quasi-random, in that it was not random but it prevented the kind of misleading bias that random assignment also prevents. The point is not the label, but the avoidance of that bias.

As a nonessential but possibly heuristic issue, I point out that if legal decisions and social policy had to be based only on the kind of experiments that Echt demands before ceding credibility to the Lovaas team's results, the United States would not be distributing billions of dollars in damages from tobacco companies. A huge amount of data supports the conclusion that smoking causes cancer, but none of it rises to the textbook standard that Echt cites (except in the case of laboratory animals), a fact that has been exhaustively argued in U.S. courts for years. Indeed, by that textbook standard, the Lovaas team's studies are better proof that their model of ABA is extraordinarily valuable to children with autism than are the myriad nonexperimental studies asserting that smoking causes cancer.

Echt also argues that Lovaas and his colleagues responded "defensively" to the criticisms applied to their studies. I point out that the essence of science is always to routinely attack all new and important discoveries to see exactly how robust they are and so learn whether to develop them further or abandon them. We assume that the truth, and what to do next, will best emerge from ongoing cycles of attack and defense. The correct stance for the science audience is to attack, and the correct stance for the science presenter is to defend, for very many cycles. There is no merit in assigning scientists the task of defense and then criticizing them for being defensive.

Echt argues further that the Lovaas team should have done much more in their treatment method because autism is so severe that it ought to have everything possible applied to it. Unfortunately, autism has indeed had every possible method applied to it for the past 30 years, to almost no avail. The significance of the Lovaas team's method is that it successfully placed an unprecedented number of autistic children into everyday society. When a carefully controlled, extensively measured treatment succeeds, it is scientific folly to argue that it should not be adopted yet because it *seems* to do less than the severity of the problem *seems* to require. Facts are more important here than preconceptions about the necessary mechanisms. By way of analogy, this argument might have derided penicillin as impossible to have cured serious infections because it was, after all, only bread mold.

Furthermore, the impression that the Lovaas method does not do as much as the severity of the problem would seem to require is indeed only an impression. The Lovaas method teaches very, very many skills that were carefully chosen and sequenced for the child's best outcome; and teaching is done 40 hours per week, every week, year after year by a variety of people concurrently in the child's classrooms and home. Labeling it DTT may seem to make it just one thing, but in fact it is a wide and integrated spectrum of procedures, personnel, and settings.

Echt then argues (surprisingly, considering his prior arguments) that the Lovaas team's method

actually is promising, but that its application should be delayed until many more studies have been done. This is a reasonable argument in many cases, especially those in which a new treatment might do harm that could otherwise be avoided. But in the case of autism, this argument seems hurtful.

Autism untreated is extraordinarily harmful. It means a life of institutionalization and self-isolation and all the psychological and biological debilitations shown to be a consequence of that kind of life. That outcome represents a great expense of human spirit and of the wealth of a society. ABA, in the form Lovaas has developed for this problem, or any other form widely applied at present, is indeed expensive—but it can do no harm to the child, especially compared to the harm that waits inevitably for that child despite any other extant treatment. The rhetorical question might be stated in this way: How many autistic children, half of whom we could have given a better life, should we doom to the most miserable of existences while we wait for the lengthy studies that will satisfy Echt's textbook standards?

Those studies will be lengthy (15 to 20 years) because the basic question is whether a childhood-long intervention can achieve some degree of an independent adult life. Very few, if any, researchers would undertake such studies largely because they now seem ethically improper, not to mention exceptionally expensive. Yet we do have the six less-than-textbook-perfect studies replicating the Lovaas teams' findings cited by Echt (Anderson, Avery, DiPietro, Edwards, & Christian, 1987; Birnbrauer & Leach, 1993; Fenske, Zalenski, Krantz, & McClannahan, 1985; Harris, Handleman, Gordon, Kristoff, & Fuentes, 1991; Kohler, Strain, & Shearer, 1992; Scheinkopf & Siegel, 1998).

Each of these studies used procedures strikingly similar to those of the Lovaas team, even if DTT terminology was not used to describe what they did; and all of them seemed to show the same extraordinary effectiveness of the Lovaas team's studies, albeit with less convincing research designs. Given that, why should we wait? It seems to me indefensible to wait, necessarily at great length, for the outcomes and level of proof Echt demands. To wait will do great harm to the children; to proceed will do no harm except to certain agencies' budgets. Does the law allow us to damage children because it is expensive not to damage them?

Echt argues that the Lovaas team treated autism by changing the behaviors characteristic of it, yet without determining the cause of those behaviors; he sees that as a criticism. To this I have three answers:

**1.** If we were always forbidden to cure any diseases before we know their causes, very many more of us would be dead or debilitated. One of the standard cautionary stories of medical science is the case of Dr. Ignasz Semmelweis, a Viennese physician of the 19th century. He discovered that most of the many women who died of puerperal fever after childbirth could be saved if their physicians would merely wash their hands in a chlorine solution before examining these women. He proved twice that this practice dramatically reduced the death rate attributable to puerperal fever, first in one clinic he managed, then in a second. The physicians of his day rejected his discoveries, despite his repeated dissemination of his findings, because those findings did not fit the prevailing theory about puerperal fever (which was that it resulted from bad air or "humors"). Many women continued to die unnecessarily. The story is routinely taught to modern medical students in the hope that their generation will not kill their patients just because the proven salvation does not conform to current theory.

It is to the credit of the Lovaas team's method, not its discredit, that it achieves its striking effectiveness without knowing the formal causes of the behaviors and behavioral deficits it had to remedy. Such a finding testifies to the power of the technique, not its irrelevance.

**2.** It is a truism in behavioral science that the original cause of a behavior may be strikingly different from its present cause, which in turn may be strikingly different from its cause in the near future. It is not always cost-effective to spend time looking for original or current causes when we can simply override them, whatever they are. The Lovaas team's method, in effect, simply overrides the causes of the behaviors and behavioral deficits it must change because it can, and because it is urgent to do so now.

**3.** The word *cause,* or its modern substitute, *functional analysis,* is prone to semantic rather than real significance. At the level of semantics, the Lovaas team's systematic approach to treatment and its evaluation has indeed achieved a functional analysis of the many behaviors and behavioral deficits it must remedy: Those behaviors and deficits are the results of this form of teaching not having been applied earlier. In short, the fundamental cause of ignorance often is simply the prior lack of effective teaching. In that case, the truly "functional" remedy is to supply some effective teaching. That is exactly what ABA does. Pragmatically, there is no need to know why the effective teaching methods were not applied earlier; if we can apply them now, we should.

Dear [Lawyer]:

You asked for my comment on the affidavit by Professor Wassermilch. I believe I have answered many of Professor Wassermilch's arguments in my response to Professor Echt's affidavit. However, some additional arguments may be relevant and useful.

Wassermilch does not accurately characterize ABA when he equates it to nothing more than DTT. That is because he relies on what he has read about it rather than on extensive years of experience in building the discipline and practicing it. It also is because he has not read enough about it. I estimate that the cost of knowing well the basic principles and paradigms of the theoretical and experimental aspects of behavior analysis would require about 2,000 pages and some laboratory experience. ABA shares the same basic principles with the theoretical and experimental branches of behavior analysis and adds to them an even larger number of secondary principles, strategies, and tactics for making those basic principles work in the real world as they do in the laboratory. ABA also adds a set of principles about ethical and humane practice, prominent among which is the need to be certain, through constant and extensive measurement and experimentation, that the particular case at hand is going well and will continue to go well—because it will change as it progresses. The cost of knowing all that is, I estimate, about 3,000 pages of reading and several years of supervised practical experience.

Wassermilch reduces ABA to DTT, and then labels DTT a mere formula; that lets him claim that a disability as severe as autism deserves all formulas—not just ABA. Unfortunately for his argument, the alternatives he cites as enriching practices, which he argues would be preempted by exclusive reliance on DTT (i.e., on ABA), are merely other instances of ABA, all reducible to DTT. Wassermilch does not seem to realize that the alternatives he cites so approvingly (and quite a few other techniques he might have named but did not) are all described in modern comprehensive ABA textbooks as ABA and as trials-based teaching. The fact that they are given distinctive labels (incidental teaching, naturalistic teaching, errorless teaching, individualized teaching, stimulus equivalence, behavioral momentum, stimulus control, shaping, fading, and more) should not conceal their membership in ABA.

Finally, it should be noted that Wassermilch and Echt should not have offered the Lovaas methods as a formula describable in less than a page, or even a handful of such formulas. If read in its entirety, the Lovaas team's program, developed over these past 35 years, comprises the following 11 categories of strategies, tactics, and procedures, not one of which is as simple as a formula:

1. A program, not a recipe, of applied behavior analysis.

2. An extremely detailed set of procedures for teaching any skill to the most difficult to teach child with autism.

3. A thorough description of how to shorten, soften, abbreviate, or transform—in short, how to individualize—these procedures for less difficult to teach cases (because time is of the essence, and it cannot be wasted on teaching skills that do not require teaching).

4. A thoroughly specified curriculum of the particular communication, socialization, daily living, and academic/intellectual skills to teach the most difficult to teach child, and in what order, so as to achieve a decent probability of an independent adult life.

5. A thorough description of how to shorten, soften, abbreviate, or transform—in short, how to individualize—this curriculum for less difficult to teach, more developed children (because time is of the essence, and it cannot be wasted on teaching skills of little use to this particular case).

6. An exhortation and set of procedures to transfer teaching of these skills, as they are mastered, to naturalistic settings and natural teachers, suitable to the individual case.

7. An exhortation and set of procedures to program the generalization of these skills, as they are mastered, so that other skills of the same class will emerge and be maintained without direct teaching (because time is of the essence, and it cannot be wasted on directly teaching every member of what should be a generalized class of skills).

8. A set of procedures to guarantee the maintenance of previously taught skills and their proper generalizations as the program proceeds (because time is of the essence, and it cannot be wasted by having to reteach what was taught earlier).

9. The warning that proper application of the program to achieve all its potential benefits requires not just reading but supervised practicum trainings (because time is of the essence, and it ought not be wasted by inefficient treatment personnel).

**10.** An acknowledgment that more and better variations of these methods will surely be developed in the future, but that only experimental proof, not any form of orthodoxy, is the criterion for replacing any present, already proven method by any future method.

**11.** The reminder that 35 years of experimentation has shown that these methods do work remarkably well compared to their current alternatives.

These 11 categories, of which the last 2 are perhaps the most important, are not formulas; they are titles of book chapters or of books.

---

## REFERENCES

Anderson, L. T., Avery, D. L., DiPietro, E. K., Edwards, G. L., & Christian, W. P. (1987). Intensive home-based early intervention with autistic children. *Education and Treatment of Children, 10,* 353–366.

Baer, D. M. (1993). Quasi-random assignment can be as convincing as random assignment. *American Journal of Mental Retardation, 97,* 373–374.

Baer, D. M., & Fowler, S. A. (1984). How should we measure the potential of self-control procedures for generalized educational outcomes. In W. L. Heward, T. E. Heron, D. S. Hill, & J. Trap-Porter (Eds.), *Focus on behavior analysis in education* (pp. 145–161). Columbus, OH: Merrill.

Baer, D. M., Wolf, M. M., & Risley, T. R. (1968). Some current dimensions of applied behavior analysis. *Journal of Applied Behavior Analysis, 1,* 91–97.

Bijou, S. W., & Baer, D. M. (1961). *Child development: Vol. 1. A systematic and empirical theory.* New York: Appleton-Century-Crofts.

Bijou, S. W., & Baer, D. M. (1965). *Child development: Vol. 2. Universal stage of infancy.* New York: Appleton-Century-Crofts.

Birnbrauer, J. S., & Leach, D. J. (1993). The Murdoch early intervention program after 2 years. *Behaviour Change, 10,* 63–74.

Bondy, A. S., & Frost, L. A. (1994). The picture exchange communication system. *Focus on Autistic Behavior, 9* (3), 1–18.

Bristol, M., Cohen, D., Costello, J., Denckla, M., Eckberg, T., Kallen, R., Kraemer, H., Lord, C., Maurer, R.,

McIlvane, W., Minshew, N., Sigman, M., & Spence, M. (1996). State of the science in autism: Report to the National Institute of Health. *Journal of Autism and Developmental Disorders, 26,* 121–154.

Budd, K. S., & Stokes, T. (Eds.). (2003). *A small matter of proof: The legacy of Donald M. Baer.* Reno, NV: Context Press.

Bushell, D., Jr., & Baer, D. M. (1994). Measurably superior instruction means close continual contact with the relevant outcome data. Revolutionary! In R. Gardner III, D. M. Sainato, J. O. Cooper, T. E. Heron, W. L. Heward, J. Eshleman, & T. A. Grossi (Eds.), *Behavior analysis in education* (pp. 3–10). Pacific Grove, CA: Brooks/Cole.

Cataldo, M. F. (2002). A tribute to Don Baer. *Journal of Applied Behavior Analysis, 35,* 319–321.

Fenske, E. C., Zalenski, S., Krantz, P. J., & McClannahan, L. E. (1985). Age at intervention and treatment outcome for autistic children in a comprehensive intervention program. *Analysis and Intervention in Developmental Disabilities, 5,* 49–58.

Harris, S. L., Handleman, J. S., Gordon, R. Kristoff, B., & Fuentes, F. (1991). Changes in cognitive and language functioning of preschool children with autism. *Journal of Autism and Developmental Disorders, 21,* 281–290.

Heward, W. L., & Wood, C. L. (2003). Thursday afternoons with Don: Selections from three teleconference seminars on applied behavior analysis. In K. S. Budd & T. Stokes (Eds.), *A small matter of proof: The legacy of Donald M. Baer* (pp. 293–310). Reno, NV: Context Press.

Kohler, F. W., Strain, P. S., & Shearer, D. D. (1992). The overtures of preschool social skill intervention agents: Differential rates, forms, and functions. *Behavior Modification, 16,* 525–542.

Lovaas, O. I. (1987). Behavioral treatment and normal educational and intellectual functioning in young autistic children. *Journal of Consulting and Clinical Psychology, 55,* 3–9.

McEachin, J. J., Smith, T., & Lovaas, O. I. (1993). Long-term outcome for children with autism who received early intensive behavioral treatment. *American Journal in Mental Retardation, 97,* 359–372.

Scheinkopf, S., & Siegel, B. (1998). Home-based behavioral treatment for young autistic children. *Journal of Autism and Developmental Disorders, 28,* 15–23.

Sherman, J. A. (2002). A tribute to Donald M. Baer. *Journal of Applied Behavior Analysis, 35,* 315–318.

## STUDY QUESTIONS AND FOLLOW-UP ACTIVITIES

1. Conduct a mock debate between a Medicaid or school district official who isn't convinced that an ABA-based intervention is needed and worth the money and a parent who demands ABA services for her child.

2. Baer states, "ABA is a medical necessity for a child with autism." Do you agree with this statement? Why or why not?

3. What does the author mean by "denotational" and "connotational" terms? Provide examples of each from the text, and then rephrase each example in the other form.

4. Based on Baer's review of student programs, list and describe several quality indicators of ABA services that parents should look for and teachers should ensure.

5. How does the Individuals with Disabilities Education Act of 1997 (IDEA) define or describe "free, appropriate public education (FAPE)"? How would you improve this definition or description? Examine rulings from the U.S. Supreme Court to determine how FAPE has been interpreted.

Study questions and follow-up activities prepared by Susan M. Silvestri and Charles L. Wood.

6. Baer writes, "This strategy means ignoring the developmental progressions shown by normal children and abandoning the conventional methods of teaching developmentally appropriate behavior." How do you reconcile this statement with guidelines for developmentally appropriate practices?

7. Suppose you attend an IEP meeting in which members of the team recommend full inclusion of a young child with autism into their general education preschool program. Suppose you have worked with this child and believe she would benefit from attending a local center-based program that uses ABA. Outline your reasons for supporting the center-based program, and your strategy for trying to sway the IEP members, as the most appropriate placement for the child with autism.

8. Baer evaluated graphs for one of the affidavits he prepared. Design a classroom-based template for graphing that incorporates the important elements to which Baer refers.

9. Discuss Baer's statement "The discrete trial method of teaching, or DTT, is as old as teaching, and much older than education." Compare and contrast DTT and ABA.

10. Identify three common misunderstandings about ABA, as evidenced by the lawyers' questions. Provide clarifications or responses for each misunderstanding you list.

### CHAPTER 2

# Early Intensive Behavioral Intervention for Autism
## Challenges and Opportunities

*Catherine Maurice*      *Bridget A. Taylor*

## INTRODUCTION
*Jill C. Dardig*

I first heard Catherine Maurice speak at the Association for Behavior Analysis convention in San Francisco in 1996. I immediately bought her book, *Let Me Hear Your Voice: A Family's Triumph Over Autism,* and read it cover to cover on the plane from San Francisco to Columbus. I literally could not put it down. Those of you who have read this book will agree, I am sure, that it is a gripping story sensitively and artfully told by a mother faced with the extreme challenge of having two children with autism.

*Let Me Hear Your Voice* not only deals with applied behavior analysis (ABA) treatment for children with autism, but also addresses many issues faced by families with a child with a disability. These issues include finding an accurate diagnosis, marital and sibling interactions, relationships with professionals, access to financial and other resources, family support systems, selection of intervention options, and susceptibility to quackery and unscientific "miracle cures."

*Let Me Hear Your Voice* also introduces us to Bridget Taylor, then a graduate student, who provided intensive ABA intervention for Catherine's children. When Catherine introduces Bridget on page 70, she tells us that Bridget was "twenty-three years old, long blond hair, blue jeans, high-top leather sneakers. She was finishing her master's degree at Teachers College, Columbia University. She looked like a kid. I distrusted her instantly. What did this person, just barely into adulthood, know about children, let alone autistic children? I grilled her. She answered all my questions with a serious, reserved politeness. She was neither friendly nor hostile, but seemed just comfortable with who she was and what she knew."

But, despite her relative newness to the field and Catherine's suspicious reception, and in contrast to some of the other providers the Maurice family encountered, Bridget demonstrated competence, sensitivity, and professionalism. She was a top-notch therapist and would emerge as an outstanding role model for teachers and others in the field.

For these reasons, I decided to use *Let Me Hear Your Voice* as the textbook for a parent–teacher collaboration course I teach at Ohio Dominican University. I assign three chapters of this book per week, and students are under strict orders not to read ahead so that we are all on the same page for class discussions. Despite my warnings, many students do read ahead. When I catch them doing this, their defense is that they couldn't help themselves and just had to keep reading. *Let Me Hear Your Voice* is so engaging and on target that students cannot put it down. In 27 years of college teaching, no matter what textbook I've used for a class, I have never had to tell students *not* to read ahead. It's usually the opposite case of having to encourage or even force students to keep up with the reading.

But Catherine Maurice has done far more than share the powerful and moving personal story of her children's recovery from autism. She has become a tireless advocate and resource provider on behalf of all parents who seek access to effective, scientifically based treatments for autism. Her books include, in addition to *Let Me Hear Your Voice* (Maurice, 1993), *Behavioral Intervention for Young Children with Autism: A Manual for Parents and Professionals* (Maurice, Green, & Luce, 1996), and *Making a Difference: Behavioral Intervention for Autism* (Maurice, Green, & Foxx, 2001). Catherine is also a founder of the Association for Science in Autism Treatment (ASAT).

Catherine's children's therapist, Bridget Taylor, went on to receive her PhD in psychology from Rutgers and later cofounded the Alpine Learning Group, a New Jersey treatment center for children with autism. Dr. Taylor has authored articles and book chapters on autism treatment and is a regular presenter at national and international conferences.

When Catherine Maurice received her PhD in French Literature, I'm sure she probably did not imagine that her professional life would go in a different direction entirely. We in the field are fortunate that her efforts, along with those of Bridget Taylor, have made such a positive difference.

# PART I. POLITICAL AND PHILOSOPHICAL REFLECTIONS ON THE TREATMENT OF AUTISM
*Catherine Maurice*

When Bill Heward asked me to contribute to this work, I was honored. But I was also somewhat hesitant. I knew that I could offer some political and philosophical reflections on how we treat autism in this country, having observed "the autism wars" for over 14 years. But I felt that there was another, more urgent matter that should be addressed: What are the essential elements of a good ABA intervention program for a child with autism? I turned to someone I knew to be highly qualified to address that question, Bridget Taylor, and invited her to collaborate with me on this chapter.

I first met Bridget in 1987, when she appeared, the answer to a prayer, on my doorstep in response to an advertisement I had placed at Teachers College, Columbia University. My 2-year-old daughter had just been diagnosed with autism, and in the panic and confusion that followed, my husband and I had made one highly uncertain decision. We had read about work with autistic children at UCLA, by Dr. Ivar Lovaas, and we thought that the intervention model used by Lovaas's clinic was worth serious consideration, even if the name by which we heard it described at the time, *behavioral intervention,* seemed cold. Nevertheless, the results that the UCLA people had managed to obtain with very young children were unprecedented and filled us with hope at a time when hope seemed very dim. We had decided that we needed to try this type of therapy with our daughter. Consequently, the house was becoming crammed with books and papers, anything we could get our hands on that would help us understand what this therapy was, how it worked, and how we could access it.

We could not get into the UCLA project, which was why we sought behavioral therapists in New York City. Nor could we find a single program in New York that embraced a behavioral intervention model for children with autism. What we did find, in our early days, were three primary strains of thought regarding treatment.

First, there were many vestiges of a psychodynamic approach: The predominant way of thinking about autism ever since it was identified in 1948 was that it was an emotional disturbance, a disorder of attachment between parent and child, and thus supposedly amenable to intervention that stressed psychological nurturing, intuitive understanding, and emotional connecting. These ideas, championed by people such as Bruno Bettelheim, who wrote *The Empty Fortress,* and Virginia Axline, who wrote *Dibs in Search of Self,* gave rise to intervention models based on psychoanalysis (always a trick with a nonverbal child), "play therapy," and therapeutic nurseries (which amounted to little more than surrogate parent programs). Unfortunately, these ideas and interventions failed to help children with autism, who learned nothing and often grew worse as therapists followed them around the room trying to connect with them more lovingly than Mommy and Daddy. Moreover, as we all know now, these therapeutic models caused great suffering for parents, who were accused of having caused their children's autism in the first place.

Second, I was told about biological interventions: drugs that might help suppress self-injury in some autistic children. However, the psychiatrist I consulted about these pharmacological approaches told me that his field had so far not been successful in identifying any drug that would significantly increase language or socialization in autistic children. He did not recommend putting my daughter on anything, and I was grateful for his candor.

Third, we immediately encountered a multitude of "alternative treatments," miracle cures, wonderful new interventions, at the rate of one every 6 months, it seemed. These treatments were touted in the popular press, then later on the Internet, always accompanied by much passion, many heartfelt testimonials, and anger at anyone who voiced caution.

The Autism Society of America (ASA), to whom I turned for treatment information, was perhaps in part responsible for this endless parade of "breakthrough" cures. I contacted them soon after my daughter's diagnosis, and they sent me an outdated reading list that included not only the standard parent-bashing treatises (e.g., *Dibs in Search of Self*) and various monuments to hopelessness (e.g., *Autism: Nightmare Without End*), but also a great many books and articles featuring home-grown treatments for autism. In the ASA newsletter as well, I found a dizzying assortment of testimonials, anecdotes, and advertisements about treatments. No mention of scientific assessment, outcome measures, reliable data, or objective verification appeared in the information they sent to me. Nor was there any mention at all of Early Intensive Applied Behavior Analysis, an intervention model that was then beginning to create a stir in professional circles. In fact, when I called ASA again to ask about behavioral treatment for children with autism, they were among the first to dismiss it out of hand. "Child abuse," their spokesperson informed me: "robot training."

Today—after how many years?—the ASA Web site does include a paragraph on behavioral intervention, which they describe in rather inaccurate terms. (ABA is described as a "theory," and the therapy itself is described as 30 to 40 hours a week of discrete trial teaching, with no mention of incidental teaching, functional analysis, or generalization.) You can find this paragraph alongside their discussions of facilitated communication, vitamin therapy, dolphin therapy, and so on, but frankly, ABA winds up sounding less appealing than any of these. In fact, ABA is still presented as potentially damaging to children's emotional health:

> Some practitioners feel it is emotionally too difficult for a child with autism, that the time requirement of 30 to 40 hours a week is too intensive and intrusive on family life; and that while it may change a particular behavior, it does not prepare a child with autism to respond to new situations. (www.autism-society.org)

Why such continued antipathy toward behavioral intervention? And perhaps even more perplexing, why such persistent promotion of pseudoscience? In 1995, perhaps under pressure from mounting criticism, the ASA board of directors adopted the following statement, defending their policy of making no evaluation of any treatment claim. The board justified this policy through the highly seductive rhetoric of *parent choice:*

> ASA embraces an overall philosophy which chooses to empower individuals with autism, their parents or caregivers, to make choices best suited to the needs of the person with autism. At the very core of the parent choice philosophy is the belief that no single program or treatment will benefit all individuals with autism. Furthermore, the recommendation of what is "best" or "most effective" for a person with autism should be determined by those people directly involved—the individual with autism, to the extent possible, and the parents or family members. (www.autism-society.org)

Let's see. My child is diagnosed with cancer, he's 3 years old, and I am going to leave it up to him, his father, and me to determine whether he should have radiation, shark cartilage, apricot pits, multivitamins, or chemotherapy. If he does elect to have chemotherapy, he, his dad, and I will determine which of several powerful drugs are appropriate for his form of cancer. Why not? Isn't this all about "empowerment"?

Unfortunately, the ASA position of treating all options as equally worthy of consideration dominates much of the political and Internet discussions surrounding autism today. Any discussion of the scientific basis (or lack thereof) for any treatment becomes immediately sidetracked into this debate about parental choice, about "the empowerment of people with autism." But this is not about choice or empowerment. ASA is an organization whose mission is supposed to be about guidance. ASA claims to be, and many still rely on it as, "the leading source of information and referral on autism" (www.autism-society.org).

Parents are free to choose whatever treatments they want, research based or not, and autistic people should have every opportunity to participate in decisions regarding their care. But organizations that purport to inform, guide, and instruct a vulnerable public, as well as the press, have a responsibility to elucidate those choices, to educate people as to what constitutes reliable information. This "philosophy" is a large part of the reason treatments like facilitated communication are able to endure, in spite of study after study exposing the exaggerated claims of that particular fad. This politically correct *democracy of therapies* enabled the *New York Times* to run articles extolling the virtues of dolphin therapy, which, we are informed, "can improve autistic children's auras" (Specter, 1997). This try-anything/how-can-it-hurt? approach encourages us to subject our children to megadoses of vitamins, hormone injections, radical diets, physical manipulations, weighted vests, marathon holding sessions, drum therapy, "rebonding therapy," sensory stimulation or deprivation, and on and on. The ASA position is polite, egalitarian, and nonoffensive. Unfortunately, a glance at the history of autism treatment in this country is enough to let us know that all treatment choices are not equal and that many families and children have been harmed, emotionally and financially, by this steady stream of nonsense.

But the Autism Society was not the only source of misinformation for us and other parents. Back in the late 1980s, the major teaching hospitals we consulted in New York City echoed that other given: ABA is bad for children. Again and again we heard behavioral intervention

dismissed and denigrated. "Morally reprehensi-
ble," was the way one psychiatrist described this
intervention to me. When I asked another authority what she thought of the Lovaas study
(Lovaas, 1987), she grew livid and sputtered that
"everyone knew" that Lovaas had preselected
only high functioning children who weren't really autistic to begin with and, besides, they
were still very autistic at the end of treatment.
Although this statement struck me as a logical
impossibility, I said nothing. It seemed useless
to argue. Besides, my first priority was not to
change their minds; it was to help my daughter

This virulent distrust of what was called "behavior modification" was widespread in the late
1980s. Unable to find any treatment program
using applied behavior analysis, we decided,
after much agony of indecision, to set up our
own program at home—quite a challenge, considering that at the time we knew nobody who
was doing such a thing and there were very few
published resources to guide us. But, as I
watched our team of therapists work lovingly
with my daughter and witnessed the wonderful
progress she was making, it disturbed me profoundly to know that other kids were being denied access to this treatment and instead
shuffled into the same useless therapeutic nurseries that had already proved so inadequate. As
I kept hearing about the abusiveness of behavioral intervention, I thought it was all a matter of
misunderstanding. I thought that those psychiatrists, social workers, and educators who were
so adamantly opposed to behavioral intervention had simply been ignorant, like me, about
what a quality behavioral program looked like,
what it could accomplish. I thought people
were turned off by the name *behavior modification,* with its intimations of Pavlov's dogs, robot
training, and the like. I felt that if they could see
with their own eyes how much my child was
learning and how alive and engaged and happy
she became during the teaching sessions
they would understand that, whatever their
intellectual or philosophical differences with
Skinner or Lovaas or whomever, the actual inter-

vention could be very loving and humane, to
say nothing of effective.

I think I was naïve about the willingness of
people who have a vested interest in something
to change their minds. Whether it's a question of
income, status in the field, the fear of saying "I
was wrong," people just have a hard time
changing their views about anything. For the
purveyors of therapeutic nurseries, play therapy,
relationship therapy, or any other model on
which they had built their reputations, it was
just too much to admit that behavioral intervention was actually capable of taking children with
autism further than had ever been possible before. I think it has to be parents who make the
leap into new territory, because what matters is
not their reputation or the income they are making from any particular type of therapy. What
matters is whether their child is learning,
whether their son or daughter is becoming more
independent, more capable, and more connected to them.

You can sustain the latest miracle cure only
as long as the media buzz lasts. You can sustain
play therapy only as long as something more effective is not available. But when something
more effective is available, no amount of furious
tirades against it will blur the truth of the matter,
which is this: ABA is not a panacea; it is the
most effective intervention we have at the current time. ABA does not offer answers as to why
autism happens; it offers a practical means of
helping children who are autistic. ABA is not a
biological intervention, although it may have a
concrete impact on a developing nervous system. ABA will not recover all kids from autism,
but it will recover some. ABA does not solve all
our problems, and I hope that something easier
to administer and cheaper will come along
sometime soon—but for the moment, ABA offers all children with autism, every one of them,
a real opportunity to learn.

So here we are, almost 14 years after Bridget
Taylor first knocked at my door, and what has
changed? Well, there's good news and bad. The
bad news is that antibehavioral sentiment still

runs deep in certain quarters. Many still denigrate behavioral treatment, painting it as a coercive training of skills, rather than as a caring and evolving teaching technology.

Bruno Bettelheim, who built his career out of blaming parents for autism, wrote a horrific description of what he called "operant conditioning":

> Here I wish to comment on current efforts to deal with infantile autism through operant conditioning—that is, by creating conditioned responses through punishment and reward. Temporarily this breaks down the child's defenses . . . and arouses him to some actions. But the actions are not of his devising. They are those the experimenter wants . . . autistic children are reduced to the level of Pavlovian dogs. . . . Conditioned response regimes may turn autistic children into more pliable robots. . . . (Bettelheim, 1967, p. 410)

Bettelheim's dark caricature was very powerful: It influenced generations of professionals—unfortunately all the way up to the present.

In 1998 a special educator, Shirley Cohen, published a book in which she purported to give an overview of everything known about autism. Her description of behavioral intervention could have come straight from Bettelheim:

> In programs derived from the Lovaas Young Autism Project [this is how Cohen describes behavior intervention programs] intrusion begins immediately. . . . Directions are often given in a loud voice. Physical guidance is used to ensure that the child follows the adult's directions, with food or other rewards used to reinforce the child's compliance. Some young children cry and try to escape . . . for days or even weeks as they are initiated into treatment programs. . . . The adult directs . . . the child responds with imitation and compliance. (Cohen, 1998, p. 638. Words in brackets added.)

Cohen's description is flawed not so much in what it says as in what it does not say. Her skewed portrayal is analogous to describing a surgical operation by concentrating exclusively on the fact that someone is drugged to oblivion, strapped to a table, and assaulted with scalpels. Without a full understanding of the context and the purpose, the process and the results, no-body in his or her right mind would ever consent to such an act.

Fortunately, most parents today are ignoring these negative descriptions and taking the time to see behavioral intervention in action so that they can make the decision for themselves. The problem with such one-sided presentations of behavioral programs is that they tend to influence the policy makers who control where the money goes. As long as politicians and agencies are influenced by people who don't like behavior analysis, public funding for this treatment will remain scarce, and families who cannot afford it will suffer from a lack of equal access.

Finally, the bad news is that the parade of quick fixes does not stop; each blazes onto national headlines before giving way to the next craze. Whoever proposes a new treatment is very popular because new treatments equal new *hope*. Whoever questions the scientific veracity of these treatments bears the heat of anger because to question means to deprive people of hope.

I understand all too well why these treatments survive. I'm a mother. During those first weeks and months after diagnosis, I embraced anyone who offered me hope, no matter how weak the evidence. When your child's future is threatened, there is a very powerful impetus to believe whatever gives you hope—even to the point of accepting theories and claims that we might otherwise reject on the basis of reason or logic alone. What I don't understand are the psychologists, educators, and other professionals who so readily buy into these claims. Are they not trained to look for credible evidence? Do they not know what constitutes solid research? I was astounded at the ease, for instance, with which many in the professional communities accepted the preposterous claim that nonverbal autistic children could suddenly communicate through "facilitated communication." If ever there was reason to be skeptical, surely it was in the face of that sensational "breakthrough." Suddenly, profoundly impaired, heretofore completely nonverbal children were said to be revealing their innermost thoughts and feelings when their hands were manipulated around a keyboard by a "facilitator." (Don't question *how*—that would indicate your lack of faith in the facilitator's magical powers.)

But what about the hope, the search for new treatments? Should we not all be open-minded to other interventions, especially given that ABA is not the be-all and the end-all answer? Of course we should. But there is a difference (well described by people more scientifically knowledgeable than myself) between responsible exploration and testing of new treatment hypotheses and irresponsible claims of effectiveness long before any compelling data are in. In the years that I have been observing autism politics, I have seen far too many magic bullets marketed too aggressively to a vulnerable population without care or caution for the kind of rigorous testing and retesting that good science demands. These miracle cures are costly and time consuming, and they turn energy and funds away from the real research that is so desperately needed in autism. They will not go away until the people who promote them become more cautious about their claims (unlikely) and the people who buy into them become more discriminatory about what distinguishes hype from hope.

How do we nonscientists develop such discriminatory thinking? That is the crucial question. The good news is that some progress has occurred on several fronts.

First, we now have some respected organizations, not just a few beleaguered individuals, willing not only to guide parents and professionals through the evidence behind various treatments, but, more important, to help them determine the quality of the evidence. For example, in 1999 the New York State Department of Health convened an independent panel of experts from multiple disciplines to develop early intervention guidelines for children with autism. The panel adopted a rigorous methodology, established by the Agency for Health Care Policy and Research (AHCPR), to help them assess the evidence behind various interventions. To review their own work, the panel then consulted with a national advisory group of experts in early intervention, who provided feedback on both the methodology and its guidelines (New York State Department of Health, 1999). Their resulting report was notable for its objectivity in evaluating the kind and degree of scientific support behind many proposed treatments for autism. Moreover, the document did not shy away from making recommendations "based on the best scientific evidence about 'best practices,' for assessment and intervention for young children with autism" (New York State Department of Health, 1999)—something that had heretofore been so challenging for parents to sort out on their own. This position was clearly a break from the dominant ASA philosophy, which had specifically repudiated any role in making such recommendations.

Also in 1999 the Maine Administrators of Services for Children With Disabilities published a report of its Autism Task Force. This report offered a detailed analysis of methods for educating children with autism. The analysis focused, like the New York State report, "on the scope and quality of scientific research which substantiates or fails to substantiate each method's effectiveness." The report represents another invaluable tool for anyone trying to navigate the maze of treatment options for autism.

Second, parents and professionals are beginning to work together to form advocacy organizations whose missions go beyond support and sharing, as important as these types of groups may be. New organizations have been formed that focus on the dissemination of reliable information, on fostering and funding research, and on educating the public about certain standards of evidence and care. Two such groups are as follows:

- **ASAT, the Association for Science in Autism Treatment,** an organization founded to provide science-based, credible information to any parent, teacher, therapist, or professional who needed it. Since its founding, ASAT has had several major conferences featuring respected researchers and clinicians from both the behavioral and the biological sphere. In addition, ASAT publishes a newsletter, *Science in Autism Treatment,* that seeks to provide factual information on any subject related to autism and its treatments.

- **NAAR, the National Alliance for Autism Research.** Founded in 1994, NAAR seeks to "fund and otherwise accelerate biomedical research in autism." If I had a child who still had autism, I would want to know that every avenue was being explored. NAAR's mission provides an important source of hope that one day we will identify the causes and potential biological cures for autism.

It is critically important, however, that *both* avenues of research—the behavioral and the biological—be supported by the other side and that both receive adequate funding. While seeking to find the cure of tomorrow, we must take care of the children who are alive today. I am disturbed to read the demeaning characterizations of behavioral intervention that some of the more biologically oriented people continue to disseminate to the public, on Web sites, or in public conferences: "Training for compliance and imitation," "Treating the symptoms only, and not the cause." Why undermine an approach that at present represents the most effective treatment we have for autistic children? Besides, who knows what "systemic" effects behavioral intervention may have on a developing nervous system? Maybe, to a certain degree in some children, ABA *can* cause some kind of rerouting of brain function or compensatory neurological development. Stroke victims can sometimes learn to talk through environmental stimulation, or reeducation, and nobody understands exactly what happens in those cases. It would not surprise me to learn one day that intensive behavioral intervention, especially in very young children, can help to restore neuro-

logical function. In any case, the bottom line is that we need to support ABA treatment and research programs *and* biological research into the causes and potential cures for autism.

Third, significant progress has been made toward the certification of behavior analysts. Less than a decade ago, there was almost no way of telling who was qualified to deliver behavioral intervention. It seemed that anyone who had attended a workshop or two given by anyone remotely connected to a behaviorally based program somewhere could be designated a behavior therapist. Now, the critically important Behavior Analyst Certification Board (www.BACB.com) has raised the standards for all of us.

Fourth, specific, science-based information about behavioral intervention and its application to autism is much more readily available through books, symposia, conferences, and Web sites. For a good overview of this type of information, I recommend the Cambridge Center for Behavioral Studies (www.behavior.org).

The appendix to this chapter contains additional resources that may be helpful to people who suddenly find themselves in a position in which a child's future demands that they make these critical distinctions. These authors and organizations will not tell anyone what to do: They just try to give people the tools to make informed decisions themselves.

Also in the appendix is a reference to Dr. Lovaas's *The Me Book,* and I would like to say a word about that: I believe in giving credit where credit is due. Today, it is generally understood that since *The Me Book* was published, over 20 years ago, applied behavior analysis has significantly evolved. Even when my children were in treatment, we took teaching programs from *The Me Book* that seemed appropriate for us and ignored those that did not. We invented some of our own teaching programs, and we went to the ABA community to discover other intervention strategies and ideas. In other words, we were not wedded to one model, one researcher, or one book. But I believe that some of the infighting that goes on in the ABA/autism community would be alleviated if both parents and professionals learned to give credit where credit is due. Dr. Lovaas's *The Me Book* is very important in the history of autism treatment and should be acknowledged as such. One can express differences of opinion about what constitutes "the best" form of ABA for any particular child without diminishing the work of other legitimate scholars and researchers.

By the same token, as consumers of applied behavior analysis we need to guard against too much belief in any one practitioner or researcher. Ten years ago I saw people forming camps around this clinician or that. Today I see people engaging in the same behavior around new personalities, new ideologies, and what they think are brand-new forms of ABA. A French father recently e-mailed me, asking, "I am hearing about this new ABA, called Verbal Behavior. Is this something worth pursuing, or is it more useless infighting?" My response was, "Yes, it is definitely worth pursuing. Any advance in knowledge about how to increase verbal communication in children with autism is worth pursuing. But is it a 'new form' of ABA? The teaching of language, the shaping of verbal communication has been an important part of every ABA program, I have observed." My therapists, my husband, and I used principles of ABA to teach our own children to talk—really *talk,* as in dynamic, interactive, reciprocal, conversational communication—without ever hearing or using the term *verbal behavior.*

In other words, in behavioral circles, as in every professional field, some generously advance their discipline, acknowledging those who have gone before and making no claim about reinventing the wheel. Others get caught up in promoting and defending their brand name of ABA, allowing or encouraging others to believe that they have invented something out of whole cloth. Or perhaps it is parents who begin to think of one provider as

having all the answers, when that could simply never be. What one person could ever possibly understand the needs of all children with autism? As someone who benefited from the work of *many* ABA researchers and clinicians when my own children were in treatment, I suggested to this father that he do the same—that he read widely within that discipline, that he draw from the work of many, and that he ignore any "useless infighting" within behavioral or other circles.

In the next section Dr. Bridget Taylor—who has helped not only my children, but so many others—will discuss some of the specific program components that scholars and clinicians have identified over the past decade as essential for educating children with autism.

## PART II. SOME CRITICAL COMPONENTS OF AUTISM TREATMENT
*Bridget A. Taylor*

As Catherine Maurice has well demonstrated, the field of behavioral treatment for children with autism has undergone significant transformation. To the continued benefit of children, parents, and clinicians, the last decade has witnessed burgeoning growth in the availability and provision of early behavioral intervention for children with autism. This growth is both fueled by and reflected in increased demand for behaviorally based services. The concomitant expansion in both the breadth and depth of services has led to an emerging—if still evolving—consensus regarding the essential components of behavior analytic interventions for children with autism. In this section, drawing on my own work as cofounder and director of Alpine Learning Group (a school for children with autism) and the research base supporting that work, I will highlight some of those critical components and reflect on challenges with which the autism treatment community—both privately and publicly funded—must still contend.

## Early Intervention

Intervention for children with autism must begin early in a child's development—ideally, immediately upon diagnosis. Research in the area of normal brain development suggests that the brain is highly receptive to environmental input from birth through age 8 to 9 (Shore, 1997). Further, some studies in the behavioral treatment of children with autism indicate that better outcomes—transition to mainstream classes, gains in language functioning, for example—are achieved when treatment commences prior to age 5 (Fenske, Zalenski, Krantz, & McClannahan, 1985; Harris & Handleman, 2000). Although arguments that early intensive behavioral intervention can actually alter the neuroanatomy of a child's brain remain speculative, it seems reasonable that if we are to effect change of this nature, behavioral intervention should be introduced as soon as a sound diagnosis can be provided (Green, 2001).

For many children with autism, however, there are significant delays in securing behavioral treatment (Jacobson, 2000a). In most states, funding for special education begins at age 3 and in some cases, age 5; this is clearly incompatible with, and arguably antithetical to, a mandate for early intervention. Although it is promising that some states have issued guidelines recommending that behavioral intervention begin as soon as a child is diagnosed (e.g., MADSEC, 1999; New York State Department of Health, 1999), more—and more comprehensive—legislation is needed to make early behavioral intervention a national standard. Alongside increased advocacy and legislation, continued research is required to evaluate the efficacy of specific behavioral procedures for this increasingly younger population. These data must then be used to promote standardization in treatment and to bolster the argument that even toddlers with autism benefit from behavioral intervention (Green, Brennan, & Fein, 2002).

## Intensive Intervention

Intervention should be intensive. Research indicates that children with autism require near immersion in behavioral instruction; Lovaas's 1987 study, for one, demonstrated that children require at least 40 instructional hours per week to enter first grade at a level of intellectual and social functioning indistinguishable from their typical peers. Intensity, unsurprisingly, remains a *relative* term and one open to debate. What is clear, however, is that children need significantly more intervention than previously thought. The considerable learning challenges of children with autism necessitate exposure to many successive learning opportunities to master very simple responses—often in a one-to-one teaching format. Thus, skill deficits and behavioral challenges alike require instructional remediation far exceeding the typical 9-to-3 school day and a lower teacher-to-student ratio than that typically provided in most special education classes—particularly if children are to "catch up" to the continuing progress of typical peers.

This creates several challenges for the autism treatment community and for public special education in particular. First, typical special education programs do not have sufficient staff to support a one-to-one teaching model and are thus unable to provide the recommended intensity of instruction. Second, most publicly funded early intervention programs provide only a limited number of hours of early intervention services prior to age 3; moreover, the typical special education school day may end at noon (for preschoolers) or 3 o'clock (after age 5). Although debate continues among professionals regarding the number of hours of behavioral instruction required for children to make measurable gains (Sheinkopf & Siegel, 1998), behavior analysts must be closely involved in not only the advocacy for intensity, but also the *determination* of intensity: identifying individual strengths and weaknesses that may necessitate a prescribed number of treatment hours or increased one-to-one instruction.

Children enrolled in Alpine Learning Group, for example, receive 5½ hours of instruction per day across a 12-month program, excluding the typical breaks for summer vacation and holidays (Meyer, Taylor, Levin, & Fisher, 2001). Some children—particularly those that present with significant behavioral challenges—have required more instruction to prevent regression in performance. At different times and in different cases, extension of the school day beyond 3 o'clock dismissal and even extension of the school year to include services during vacation weeks have been warranted. Advocacy for these children involved supporting the family's request for services from their funding school district with documentation of improved performance at school and home following additional treatment hours. Intensity of services may vary and change over time according to the individual needs of the child; nonetheless, intensity of instruction per se—and beyond that, *early* intensive instruction—has consistently proven to be an essential component of successful behavioral treatment.

## High-Quality Intervention

Intensity—even when presented in great quantity—is not the only strong predictor of successful treatment. In the end, quantity and intensity of treatment depend on the *quality* of the intervention—that is, the extent to which instruction is scientifically based and systematically applied. Traditional special education in the public sector provides an instructive example. For years, children with autism have received roughly 25 hours of instruction per week in "generic" or more eclectic special education public school classrooms with minimal documentation of measurable gains. In contrast, be-

haviorally based education programs—using a systematic, research-based pedagogy—have generated documented successes within a comparable treatment window (Eikeseth, Smith, Jahr, & Eldevik, 2002; Fenske et al., 1985). Quality in early intensive behavioral intervention can then be defined as active engagement in experimentally validated teaching approaches. More simply: Children must be involved *in active learning*—involving consistent, repeated opportunities to respond to stimuli and to respond, in turn, to the corresponding consequences (Green, 1996). Systematic behavioral teaching techniques (e.g., discrete trial teaching, incidental teaching, procedures to teach conditional discriminations) maximize the *quantity* of treatment time by infusing it with instruction of a more rigorous *quality*.

## Individualized Programming

Children with autism display a markedly heterogeneous array of skill deficits and unique learning styles; consequently, both treatment goals and instructional strategies must be developed in the context of individualized treatment programs. Individualization should include a number of different factors: baseline assessment of present functioning, examination of personal interest and motivation, analysis of skill deficits and behavioral excesses, observation of responses to various teaching interventions, and incorporation of family and community priorities. Thus, formulaic instructional recommendations within a behavioral treatment program—such as those that privilege one type of strategy or intervention over another—inherently fail to view each child as an individual and, in doing so, may undermine the very goals targeted by the program.

Consider a child who has not yet developed functional language skills and demonstrates an extremely high rate of stereotypy in the form of playing with string and little interest in age-appropriate toys or activities. A naturalistic treatment paradigm favoring child-directed learn-ing and incidental teaching with the aim of in-creasing language targets may have little impact because of the child's limited interests and the persistence of the stereotypic behavior. A pro-gram incorporating teacher-directed interven-tions, on the other hand (e.g., blocking access to self-stimulatory behavior, systematically ma-nipulating establishing operations to increase motivation to engage in teaching interactions, and using discrete trial teaching), *along with* naturalistic techniques may accelerate progress by aggressively addressing problematic behavior and responding to the unique behavioral profile of the child. In the case of another child—one with similarly low language skills, but demon-strated interest in toys and activities—using nat-uralistic techniques *along with* teacher-directed interventions may harness the momentum of the child's own interests and thus fuel treatment. In-dividualization demands more than an under-standing of the strengths and limitations of procedures that may strengthen particular skills; it also—and more critically—demands the ability to identify target objectives and match proce-dures to a child's unique behavioral and learn-ing profile.

## Comprehensive Programming

In a similar sense, behavioral treatment must also be comprehensive in both its aims and pro-cedures. Clinicians must strive to address the en-tire spectrum of skills that will enable the individual with autism to participate fully in family and community life. Teaching proce-dures, to be fully comprehensive, must similarly address a full range of treatment concerns, in-cluding generalization and maintenance of skills and reduction of problem behaviors. Behavioral treatment, then, does not merely include identi-fication of specific language targets and skills that lead to academic functioning; goals relevant to family life must also be identified. As such, preprescribed curricular agendas may not be consistent with a family's priorities and objec-tives. A program focusing on the acquisition of specific academic skills, for example, will only partially serve a family for whom a more imme-diate objective is involving their child in public religious services.

Rosales-Ruiz and Baer (1997) described the development of behavior across the life span in terms of behavioral cusps: "Cusps are behavior changes, sometimes simple, sometimes complex, that systematically cause other, further, not for-mally programmed behavior changes" (p. 537). Drawing on the behavioral cusp model, Bosch and Fuqua (2001) proposed a set of guidelines for identifying potential targets of behavior change, including access to new reinforcers, contingencies, and environments; social validity; generativeness; competition with inappropriate responses; and number and relative importance of people affected. The multivalent nature of be-havioral cusps itself may provide both an incite-ment to and a containing framework for comprehensive and targeted interventions.

## Parent Training and Education

Successful behavioral treatment programs part-ner with parents in both designing and carrying out interventions. In addition to the assessment of priorities, successful partnering with families should include training in the implementation of procedures and regular follow-up sessions (Mc-Clannahan, Krantz, & McGee, 1982). A special education program providing parents with a di-dactic lecture and sporadic home visits, al-though undoubtedly well intentioned, fails to support an individualized approach to parent training and education. Parent training must be flexible enough to provide a family with as many visitations as necessary to identify and im-plement relevant programs. It must also define participation and participants broadly, including siblings, extended family members, baby-sitters, and nannies. Finally, high-quality training pro-grams will demonstrate sensitivity to families as unique and dynamic entities. Family participation, for example, may vary depending on multiple factors: the family's financial circumstances; the severity of the child's disability; the rate of the child's progress; the size and composition of the immediate family; and the changing needs of not only the child with autism, but each individual family member.

Extending such individualized parent training to the public sector—where the hours of the school day and week are legislated, and teachers' time is contracted—is not without challenge. The appellation *special* must be applied not only to the targeted population of students and curriculum, but to the structure and implementation of the educational services themselves. Matching the administration of services to student and family needs will require a redefinition of the school day and the school grounds and a reconceptualization of the scope of instruction.

## Programming for Generalization

If learned skills are to generalize for children with autism, intervention must incorporate specific procedures that will promote the durability of skills across novel settings, materials, and people. Generalization, however, presents particularly complex methodological challenges (Stokes & Baer, 1977). Fostering the generalization and durability of skills, for example, often requires highly technical and creative teaching skills: establishing multiple exemplars, presenting different sets of stimuli, using varied teaching spaces and settings, and envisioning possible configurations of future environments. Training programs must incorporate generalization planning and programming from the outset, along with ongoing supervision. In my experience as a trainer I have come to learn that teachers, like all other students, rarely assimilate lessons through verbal instruction alone; behavior analytic programs must follow teacher training with ongoing prompts and ample supervision in implementation of procedures.

## Procedures to Address Problem Behavior

Proper identification and implementation of procedures to reduce problem behavior present still more challenges. The current pedagogical emphasis on teaching basic skill sets—language skills and readiness skills, for example—often supercedes the necessary attention to problem behavior. Problem behavior can be exceedingly complex and idiosyncratic. Tantrum behavior or aggression, for example, may be maintained by multiple consequences; stereotypy may prove persistent in the absence of social contingencies and may be inherently reinforced by properties of the behavior itself. For these reasons, teaching alternative skills may prove insufficient in the absence of systematic functional analyses and the subsequent development of procedures directed toward a given behavior's function (Iwata, Dorsey, Slifer, Bauman, & Richman, 1982, 1994). To offer an example, a child may acquire functional language skills and a host of other academic skills, yet still engage in severe tantrum behavior that limits involvement in family and community activities. However successful this child's academic curriculum may have been, the overall treatment program remains negligent unless the underlying function of the tantrum behavior is identified and addressed through an appropriate procedure.

Further, for procedures such as differential reinforcement programs or punishment strategies (e.g., response cost or time-out) to be successful, procedures must be implemented systematically and consistently. Thus, treatment programs must provide comprehensive, ongoing training and supervision in the implementation of behavior-reductive procedures. Such training and supervision should include interobserver agreement on the operational definitions of responses, treatment integrity, and the data collection procedures used to monitor progress. Rarely, however, in the public sector is such supervision and accountability provided. Inclusion of these practices requires not only greater individualization of procedures, but also the availability of personnel to provide training and supervision in functional analyses and the proper implementation of procedures once they are established.

## Data-Based Evaluation and Decision Making

Learner performance can vary from day to day, across skills, and over extended time spans. As such, data collection procedures must be sensitive to these fluctuations and play an integral role in programming decisions within a behavioral treatment program. At the same time, data systems need to be simple and flexible enough to be used effectively by teachers and parents. Cumbersome observation and data collection procedures that are difficult to use or that interfere with critical teaching interactions can compromise the important story that the data can relate about performance both before and after treatment and over time. Behavior analysts must continue to develop and refine data collection systems that maintain the integrity of the science and that are also efficient and likely to be implemented.

## Ongoing Supervision and Evaluation of Staff

Comprehensive treatment also necessitates the ongoing evaluation of a child's learning styles, needs, and performance and ongoing supervision of the subsequent treatment plan. This evaluation should include regularly scheduled meetings with all relevant treatment providers. At Alpine, all learners participate in weekly or monthly clinical meetings with parents, teachers, and supervisors to review objective data, troubleshoot teaching programs with which the learner may be experiencing difficulty, reprioritize objectives, and establish new or different instructional procedures. During such clinics, teachers, supervisors, and in some cases parents take turns working with the learner across a variety of programs. Regular contact among

all those participating in treatment provides both ongoing assessment of learner performance and additional opportunities to supervise instructional staff in the implementation of procedures; further, such interaction encourages collaboration in the development of treatment objectives and strategies. Regularly scheduled clinical meetings, of course, require considerable time and resources. In the private sector, these demands—although incorporated in the program's design—may translate into additional costs; in the public sector, they may not translate at all as a result of legal, financial, and contractual restrictions.

## Programming Across the Life Span

Although the focus of this chapter has been *early* behavioral intervention, research indicates that at best about 50% of children with autism successfully mainstream to public school classes (e.g., Fenske et al., 1985; Lovaas, 1987). Therefore, behavioral treatment must be conducted with an eye toward the future needs of learners with autism. Such a long-term perspective requires attention to personal and social contexts across many developmental stages and across the individual's entire life span. Alpine's oldest learner, for example, is now 20 years old. In the last 5 years of his treatment—and in anticipation of his entrance into the school's adult vocational program—the ability to work in the absence of immediate adult supervision emerged as a critical instructional goal. Our efforts to prepare this learner for the workplace have prompted us to teach more and younger students this essential skill. Programming developed during childhood must in a sense be visionary, both addressing immediate concerns and anticipating skills that may become necessary in the future.

## Considerations for the Future

For all their complexity, these many issues and challenges may be collected under two simple rubrics: quality and availability. Not surprisingly, future directives and initiatives for the autism treatment community also address these two fundamental and enduring concerns. Although it may seem a truism to advocate further research, continued collection and analysis of data serve as an indisputable cornerstone of quality services. Research must be conducted with a view not only to generating new behavioral techniques or new applications of established theories, but also as a means of evaluating extant behavioral approaches and concepts—particularly those that seize public attention and achieve a sort of "vogue" before their long-term implications can be assessed. The field must also confront the challenge of integrating research and practice; research pertinent to clinical practice must be made more accessible to all communities it has the potential to impact—not only clinicians and behavior analysts, but also special education teachers and parents. Ongoing empirical investigation into the applicability and durability of specific behavioral procedures as well as the effective translation of research into practice will doubtlessly improve the quality of services offered to children with autism.

Even the highest standards of quality are rendered all but meaningless if services are not readily available to those who require them. Although many children with autism and their families are much better off today than they were 15 years ago, the autism community is still struggling with the availability of services. Limited availability affects autism treatment in both private and public sectors; private institutions have accrued impossibly long waiting lists, and public schools have barely begun to develop behaviorally based autism programs. The provision of quality behavioral treatment by the public schools could effect a transformation in the availability of services; it remains to be seen, however, whether the comprehensive provision of behaviorally based intervention is structurally feasible within the public education system (Jacobson, 2000b). This is not to say that decisive steps cannot be taken toward that goal in the present even as the future remains hypothetical and systemic issues daunting.

Teacher training may prove to be the most viable point of departure. In fact, several universities (such as Ohio State University, Penn State University, the University of North Texas, and the University of Reno Nevada) already offer specializations in autism and/or applied behavior analysis within their special education or psychology programs. However, these programs reach relatively few preservice teachers, and my own experience hiring special education teachers suggests that most candidates lack the skills and training necessary to provide even standard behavior analytic services, let alone specialized instruction for children with autism.

In addition to expanding and improving the skills of teachers, such comprehensive training in applied behavior analysis and autism treatment may facilitate the acceptance and integration of behavior analytic methodology at an institutional level. It is therefore incumbent on behavior analysts to participate actively in the development of teacher training curricula at the university level. Additionally, proponents of certification in behavior analysis must advocate for policy changes that would recognize ABA certification as a viable teaching credential within the public education system. The corollary follows: The fields of both educational administration and special education must begin to recognize ABA certification and must solicit the involvement of the behavior analytic community in public schools and classrooms.

Perhaps the most powerful tool for maintaining standards of quality and increasing availability of services is collaboration both *within* the field of behavior analysis and *between* the private and public sectors. Collaboration within the field may assume a number of forms, such as joint publications and cooperative research efforts among practitioners and applied researchers and, further, between basic and applied researchers. In addition to fostering a collegial atmosphere, collaborative efforts within the field may promote consistency in services provided and increase standardization in practice. Improved consistency and standardization would, in turn, positively affect the perception and reception of behavior analysis in both the public education system and the public at large.

In beginning to foster collaborative relations between private and public sectors, private specialized schools serving children with autism must serve as models to public schools and—using the principles of shaping—must systematically reinforce public schools' attempts to educate children with autism within a behavior analytic framework. Modeling in this sense is anything but static: Private schools must function as open resources, allowing not only visitation but also interactive inquiry; they must consult in the development of public school programming for children with autism; and they must assist in teacher training. The role of public educators and public institutions in such a collaborative effort would be receptive, but in no way passive: Restrictions and limitations must be communicated and then challenged; support—both financial and administrative—must be given, and given generously.

Such collaboration is in many ways the logical continuation of the growth of a field in which teaching and learning overlap and inform one another; it may also be the logical continuation of the growth of a field in which helping the widest population most effectively will always remain the ultimate and essential goal. What is logical, however, is not a foregone conclusion or fait accompli. The momentum that has propelled early intensive behavioral intervention this far must be maintained and actively harnessed in the service of children with autism and their families.

# REFERENCES

Bettelheim, B. (1967). *The empty fortress: Infantile autism and the birth of self.* New York: The Free Press.

Bosch, S., & Fuqua, W. (2001). Behavioral cusps: A model for selecting target behaviors. *Journal of Applied Behavior Analyis, 34,* 123–125.

Cohen, S. (1998). *Targeting autism: What we know, don't know, and can do to help young children with autism and related disorders.* Berkeley: University of California Press.

Eikeseth, A., Smith, T., Jahr, E., & Eldevik, S. (2002). Intensive behavioral treatment at school for 4- to 7-year-old children with autism: A 1-year comparison controlled study. *Behavior Modification, 26,* 49–68.

Fenske, E. C., Zalenski, S., Krantz, P. J., & McClannahan, L. E. (1985). Age of intervention and treatment outcome for autistic children in a comprehensive intervention program. *Analysis and Intervention in Developmental Disabilities, 5,* 49–58.

Green, G. (1996). Early behavioral intervention for autism: What does research tell us? In C. Maurice (Ed.), G. Green, & S. Luce (Co-Eds.), *Behavioral intervention for young children with autism: A manual for parents and professionals* (pp. 29–44). Austin, TX: Pro-Ed.

Green, G. (2001, February). *Does behavioral intervention change the brain?* Invited address to the annual meeting of the California Association for Behavior Analysis, Redondo Beach, CA.

Green, G., Brennan, L, & Fein, D. (2002). Successful intensive behavioral treatment for a toddler at high risk for autism. *Behavior Modification, 26,* 69–102.

Harris, S. L., & Handleman, J. S. (2000). Age and IQ at intake as predictors of placement for young children with autism: A four- to six-year follow-up. *Journal of Autism and Developmental Disorders, 30,* 137–142.

Iwata, B. A., Dorsey, M. F., Slifer, K. J., Bauman, K. E., & Richman, G. S., (1982/1994). Toward a functional analysis of self-injury. *Journal of Applied Behavior Analysis, 27,* 197–209.

Jacobson, J. W. (2000a). Early intensive behavioral intervention: Emergence of a consumer-driven service model. *The Behavior Analyst, 23,* 149–171.

Jacobson, J. W. (2000b). Converting to a behavior analysis format for autism services: Decision making for educational administrators, principles, and consultants. *Behavior Analyst Today, 1* (3), 6–16. Available online at www.behavior.org

Lovaas, O. I. (1987). Behavioral treatment and normal intellectual and educational functioning in autistic children. *Journal of Consulting and Clinical Psychology, 55,* 3–9.

Maine Administrators of Services for Children With Disabilities (MADSEC). (1999). *Report of the MADSEC autism task force-revised edition.* Manchester, ME.

Maurice, C. (1993). *Let me hear your voice: A family's triumph over autism*. New York: Fawcett Columbine.

Maurice, C., Green, G., & Foxx, R. M. (2001). *Making a difference: Behavioral intervention for autism*. Austin, TX: PRO-ED.

Maurice, C., Green, G., & Luce, S. C. (1996). *Behavioral intervention for young children with autism: A manual for parents and professionals*. Austin, TX: PRO-ED.

McClannahan, L. E., Krantz, P. J., & McGee, G. G. (1982). Parents as therapist for autistic children: A model for effective parent training. *Analysis and Intervention in Developmental Disabilities, 2,* 223–252.

Meyer, L. S., Taylor, B. A., Levin, L., & Fisher, J. R. (2001). Alpine Learning Group. In J. Handleman & S. Harris (Eds.), *Preschool education programs for children with autism* (pp. 135–155). Austin, TX: Pro-Ed.

New York State Department of Health. (1999). *Clinical practice guideline: The guideline technical report—Autism/pervasive developmental disorders, assessment and intervention*. Albany: Early Intervention Program, New York State Department of Health.

Rosales-Ruiz, J., & Baer, D. M. (1997). Behavioral cusps: A developmental and pragmatic concept for behavior analysis. *Journal of Applied Behavior Analysis, 30,* 533–544.

Sheinkopf, S. J., & Siegel, B. (1998). Home-based behavioral treatment of young autistic children. *Journal of Autism and Developmental Disorders, 28,* 15–24.

Shore, R. (1997). *Rethinking the brain: New insights into early development*. New York: Families and Work Institute.

Specter, M. (1997, August 4). Dolphins study war no more (they mend nerves). *The New York Times,* p. A4.

Stokes, T. F., & Baer, D. M. (1977). An implicit technology of generalization. *Journal of Applied Behavior Analysis, 10,* 349–367.

U.S. Department of Health and Human Services. (1999). *Mental Health: A report of the surgeon general*. Rockville, MD: U.S. Department of Health and Human Services, Substance Abuse and Mental Health Services Administration, Center for Mental Health Services, National Institutes of Health, National Institute of Mental Health.

# Resources for Behavioral Intervention for Autism
*Catherine Maurice*

Behaviorally based programs are ideally structured around each individual child's needs. No generic model is applicable to every child with autism. Many clinicians and scholars can be helpful when a parent or teacher is seeking strategies to help children learn communicative language. If a parent chooses ABA for a child, it is probably wise not to get caught up in "the autism wars" (bickering about whose treatment model is "the best)," but rather to learn as much as possible from a variety of sources within the ABA literature.

A few of those resources are listed here, especially for those who cannot easily access a quality behavioral program for a child. I highly recommend, however, checking the various Web sites for more titles and leads. The list is not meant to be exhaustive.

## TREATMENT GUIDELINES: REPORTS OF MULTIDISCIPLINARY PANELS

*Clinical Practice Guideline: Report of the Recommendations.* Autism/Pervasive Developmental Disorders, Assessment and Intervention for Young Children (Age 0–3 Years). 5″ × 8″, 322 pages. 1999 Publication No. 4215. Call the New York State Department of Health at 518-439-7286 to order.

*Clinical Practice Guideline: Quick Reference Guide.* Autism/Pervasive Developmental Disorders, Assessment and Intervention for Young Children (Age 0–3 Years). 5″ × 8″, 108 pages. 1999 Publication No. 4216. Call the New York State Department of Health at 518-439-7286 to order.

*Report of the Autism Task Force.* (1999). Maine Administrators of Services for Children with Disabilities, www.madsec.org.

## AGENCIES DEDICATED TO AUTISM ADVOCACY, AND/OR THE DISSEMINATION OF INFORMATION ABOUT AUTISM, AND/OR APPLIED BEHAVIOR ANALYSIS

Association for Science in Autism Treatment (ASAT), www.asatonline.org See: *Science in Autism Treatment,* ASAT's newsletter.

The Cambridge Center for Behavioral Studies, www.behavior.org.

The Association for Behavior Analysis, www.abainternational.org.

See especially "Guidelines for Consumers of Applied Behavior Analysis Services to Individuals with Autism," published by the Autism Special Interest Group of the Association for Behavior Analysis. Access it also through www.asatonline.org.

Autism Biomedical Information Network, www.autism-biomed.org. Good source of information about proposed biological treatments for autism.

Web site of the U.S. Surgeon General. See especially "Mental Health: A Report of the Surgeon General." Chapter 3: "Autism," www.surgeongeneral.gov/library/mentalhealth/images/mast.gif.

NAAR, National Alliance for Autism Research, www.NAAR.org. Mission: To "fund and otherwise accelerate biomedical research in autism."

American Association of Mental Retardation, www.aamr.org. See especially "Behavioral Consultants:

Who Are They and How Do I Find the Right One?" (Click on the Psychology Divisions page.)

## SOME BOOKS ON AUTISM OR ABA OR BOTH

See the resource lists on the various Web sites noted already, or check out the bibliographies of the works cited here for many more titles. This list is not meant to be exhaustive.

Cooper, J. O., Heron, T. E., & Heward, W. L. (in press). *Applied behavior analysis* (2nd ed). Upper Saddle River, NJ: Merrill/Prentice Hall. An introductory textbook in applied behavior analysis.

Latham, G. (1997). *Behind the schoolhouse door: Eight skills every teacher should have.* Logan, UT: P&T Ink.

Lovaas, O. I. (1981). *Teaching developmentally disabled children: The me book.* Austin, TX: Pro-Ed.

Maurice, C., Green, G., & Luce, S. C. (1996). *Behavioral intervention for young children with autism—A manual for parents and professionals.* Austin, TX: Pro-Ed.

Maurice, C., Green, G., & Foxx, R. M. (2001). *Making a difference: Behavioral intervention for autism:* Austin, TX: Pro-Ed.

McClannahan, L. E., & Krantz, P. J. (1999). *Activity schedules for children with autism: Teaching independent behavior.* Bethesda: MD: Woodbine.

Princeton Child Development Institute (PCDI) Research, www.pcdi.org/biblio.htm.

Sulzer-Azaroff, B., & Mayer, G. (1991). *Behavior analysis for lasting change.* Atlanta: Wadsworth.

Sundberg, M. L., & Partington, J. W. (1998). *Teaching language to children with autism or other developmental disabilities.* Pleasant Hill, CA: Behavior Analysts.

### Guidelines for Discriminating Between Science and Pseudoscience

1. Tables reprinted from www.quackwatch.org with permission of Stephen Barrett, MD, who runs the site. The following tables are part of an article by Dr. Rory Cocker, MD.

| *Science* | *Pseudoscience* |
| --- | --- |
| Their findings are expressed primarily through scientific journals that are peer-reviewed and maintain rigorous standards for honesty and accuracy. | The literature is aimed at the general public. There is no review, no standards, no pre-publication verification, no demand for accuracy and precision. |
| Reproducible results are demanded; experiments must be precisely described so that they can be duplicated exactly or improved upon. | Results cannot be reproduced or verified. Studies, if any, are always so vaguely described that one can't figure out what was done or how it was done. |
| Failures are searched for and studied closely, because incorrect theories can often make correct predictions by accident, but no correct theory will make incorrect predictions. | Failures are ignored, excused, hidden, lied about, discounted, explained away, rationalized, forgotten, avoided at all costs. |
| As time goes on, more and more is learned about the physical processes under study. | No physical phenomena or processes are ever found or studied. No progress is made; nothing concrete is learned. |
| Convinces by appeal to the evidence, by arguments based upon logical and/or mathematical reasoning, by making the best case the data permit. When new evidence contradicts old ideas, they are abandoned. | Convinces by appeal to faith and belief. Pseudoscience has a strong quasi-religious element: it tries to convert, not to convince. You are to believe in spite of the facts, not because of them. The original idea is never abandoned, whatever the evidence. |

| Does not advocate or market unproven practices or products. | Generally earns some or all of his living by selling questionable products (such as books, courses, and dietary supplements) and/or pseudoscientific services. |

2. Pseudoscientific Therapies: Some Warning Signs

I have not been able to identify the author of these warning signs. This list may have originally appeared on a brochure published by the American Arthritis Foundation, but an Internet search of that Foundation's publications, as well as a more extended Internet search, yielded no information about the origin of the list. Nevertheless, I find the warning signs so valuable that I would like to include them here, with all credit to whoever wrote them.

High "success" rates are claimed.

Rapid effects are promised.

The therapy is said to be effective for many symptoms or disorders.

The "theory" behind the therapy contradicts objective knowledge and sometimes common sense.

The therapy is said to be easy to administer, requiring little training or expertise.

Other, proven treatments are said to be unnecessary, inferior, or harmful.

Promoters of the therapy are working outside their area of expertise.

Testimonials, anecdotes, or personal accounts are offered in support of claims about the therapy's effectiveness, but little or no objective evidence is produced.

Catchy, emotionally appealing slogans are used in marketing the therapy.

Belief and faith are said to be necessary for the therapy to "work."

Skepticism and critical evaluation are said to make the therapy's effects evaporate.

Promoters resist objective evaluation and scrutiny of the therapy by others.

Negative findings from scientific studies are ignored or dismissed.

Critics and scientific investigators are often met with hostility and are accused of persecuting the promoters, being "close-minded," or having some ulterior motive for debunking the therapy.

3. Publications

Green, G. (1996). Evaluating claims about treatments for autism. In C. Maurice, G. Green, & S. C. Luce (1996). *Behavioral intervention for autism: A manual for parents and professionals*. Austin, TX: Pro-Ed.

www.quackwatch.org.

Thaler Singer, M, & Lalich, J. *Crazy therapies: What are they? Do they work?* (1996). San Francisco: Jossey-Bass.

4. Useful Thoughts

"The scientific process [can be defined] . . . as comprehending probability, the experimental method and hypothesis testing . . . we need to teach that science is not a database of unconnected factoids but a set of methods designed to describe and interpret phenomena, past or present, aimed at building a testable body of knowledge open to rejection or confirmation." (From "Smart People Believe Weird Things" by Michael Schermer, publisher of *Skeptic* magazine, www.skeptic.com.)

5. Behavior Analyst Certification

Information about behavior analyst certification and the registry of board-certified behavior analysts can be found at the Behavior Analyst Certification Board web site: www.bacb.com.

## STUDY QUESTIONS AND FOLLOW-UP ACTIVITIES

1. Name and describe three primary early theories regarding the cause and treatment of autism.

2. Catherine Maurice encountered many professionals who were negative about the use of ABA or behavior modification with children with autism. State possible reasons why non-ABA professionals may hold these negative opinions. (See Chapters 15, 16, 18, and 19 in this text for possible reasons.)

3. There is often a substantial time difference between the discovery of new knowledge and its application in daily life. Give examples of premature and delayed applications of new technology in other fields (e.g., medicine, engineering), and state how consumers were affected. Next, describe the danger in applying new treatments in autism without accumulated scientific data.

4. How do the reports of the New York State Department of Health and the Maine Administrators of Services for Children with Disabilities cited by the author contribute to the advancement of autism treatment?

5. What have ASAT and NAAR contributed to the field of autism? Describe those contributions.

6. Do you think there may be a biological basis for autism? Why or why not?

7. Why does Bridget Taylor state that *early* intervention is necessary in the treatment of autism?

8. Because public funding for special education is limited, the development of intensive, quality programs for young children with autism may suffer. What are some methods that a school district could employ to jump-start scientifically based and systematically applied early intervention strategies for children with autism even in a hostile funding environment?

9. Frequent data collection, coupled with skillful interpretation of data trends, is at the core of applied behavior analysis. Assume that you are the teacher for a group of 10 preschool children (half of whom are diagnosed on the autism spectrum and half of whom are developing typically) with two teaching assistants. Describe a data collection system and procedures that you could use efficiently and effectively to document behavior change in that setting.

10. How can a parent or consumer evaluate the quality of a behavioral program?

11. What are the "naturalistic techniques" referred to by Taylor? Give an example of how a naturalistic technique can be used in conjunction with an ABA technique for a child with autism.

12. The authors indicate that programs for children with autism must be visionary in nature not only to address the student's immediate needs, but also to anticipate those skills that will be necessary in the future. Describe several of the skill requirements that are essential to ensuring that the student be able to participate actively and meaningfully within the family and the community.

13. Describe the roles of incidental teaching, functional analysis, and programming for generalization in ABA.

14. Describe several "autistic" behaviors that might require reductive techniques. State how a least restrictive alternative approach should be applied to select the method to reduce these behaviors.

---

Study questions and follow-up activities prepared by Mary D. Salmon and Amanda L. Yurick.

**15.** The authors recommend more comprehensive legislation to make high-quality behavioral interventions available to all families. What do you see as barriers to this type of legislation occurring at the national and local levels? What might early intervention specialists do to facilitate the adoption of state and national guidelines that recommend or require early intensive behavioral intervention?

**16.** Explain Taylor's views on collaboration between ABA and non-ABA professionals and between public and private schools that serve children with autism. What successful collaborations have you observed?

**17.** Effective interventionists must possess an understanding of the strengths and limitations of procedures that change behavior and strengthen skills as well as be able to identify target objectives and match procedures to students' unique needs. Reflect on your own preservice teacher education program and describe its strengths and weaknesses in preparing you to meet these goals.

# PART II

# Recent Developments, Continuing Challenges, and Emerging Opportunities

Chapter 3     A Nonlinear Approach to Curriculum Design: The Role of Behavior Analysis in Building an Effective Reading Program
*Janet S. Twyman, T. V. Joe Layng, Greg Stikeleather,* and *Kelly A. Hobbins*

Chapter 4     Beginning Reading Failure and the Quantification of Risk: Reading Behavior as the Supreme Index
*Edward J. Kame'enui, Roland Good III,* and *Beth A. Harn*

Chapter 5     Schoolwide Positive Behavior Supports: Achieving and Sustaining Effective Learning Environments for All Students
*George Sugai* and *Robert H. Horner*

Chapter 6     Individual Growth and Development Indicators: Tools for Assessing Intervention Results for Infants and Toddlers
*Charles R. Greenwood, Judith J. Carta,* and *Dale Walker*

Chapter 7     Choice Making in Educational Settings
*Stephanie M. Peterson, Nancy A. Neef, Renée K. Van Norman,* and *Summer J. Ferreri*

# A Nonlinear Approach to Curriculum Design
## The Role of Behavior Analysis in Building an Effective Reading Program

*Janet S. Twyman*     *T. V. Joe Layng*
*Greg Stikeleather*     *Kelly A. Hobbins*

Whether teaching reading is rocket science may be debated, but clearly, teaching it effectively, efficiently, and across a variety of learners *is* learning science. In this congressionally recognized "Decade of Behavior" (see www.APA.org), it is becoming increasingly clear that if U.S. education is going to improve, we will have to begin applying principles and procedures derived from the learning sciences directly to teaching. This trend toward recognizing the critical importance of a scientifically informed approach to teaching is indicated by the new federal requirements for scientifically based instruction and in positions such as those represented in the U.S. Department of Education's (1993) publication, *Toward a New Science of Instruction: Programmatic Investigations in Cognitive Science and Education*.

Headsprout is an Internet-based learning sciences company whose initial product is Headsprout Early Reading. The program is composed of two parts, Headsprout Reading Basics and Headsprout Reading Independence. Whereas Reading Basics focuses on decoding and beginning comprehension and is ideal for Pre-K as well as beginning K-1 learners, Reading Independence has a focus on reading fluency and comprehension. Headsprout has not only applied the principles derived from the scientific study of learning to the teaching of fundamental reading skills, but has also turned the process of building such a program into a science itself, with valid, empirical, replicable results. With over 40% of the nation's fourth-grade students failing to demonstrate basic reading skills (National Center for Education Statistics, 2004), the need for such a program has become increasing clear in the past few years (see Layng, Twyman, & Stikeleather, in press).

But what do we mean when we talk about turning the process of building such a program into a science itself? For that matter, what do we mean by *science*? This chapter will describe our approach to science and its application to the development, not just the testing, of instructional programs.

Science is not simply a collection of facts, observations, interpretations, or theories (Brownowski, 1956). Science is the *process* by which we develop and test our interpretations or theories. Science is a process of searching for fundamental and universal principles that can offer parsimonious accounts of how observed changes in one set of conditions can result in changes in another set of conditions. The process involves building, testing, and connecting *falsifiable accounts* to describe, explain, and often predict phenomena (Brownowski, 1956; Kitchner, 1982; Sidman, 1960). The scientific method often includes inferences, repeatable experiments, and observations that select one set of inferences over others, and the positing of new inferences (Platt, 1964). The prime criterion in determining the usefulness of an inference is the extent to which the inference correctly makes predictions or explains phenomena verifiable by independent observers and stands up to tests of falsifiability (after Goldiamond & Thompson, 1967 [revision by Andronis, in press]; Popper, 1968). Specifically:

*Inferences must be falsifiable.* There must be a way to prove the inference wrong. If we can't prove it wrong, it is not a scientific theory. This idea of an inference being falsifiable is one of the most important aspects of science.

*Inferences must be able to predict.* All scientific inferences must have some predictive value or generality. Prediction can come from the ability to control relevant variables or from the likelihood of a match between predicted and obtained observations. The greater the extent to which predictions hold under a variety of conditions, the greater the generality.

*Inferences must be economical.* An inference must provide an account of the observed relations that is as complete as possible with the simplest set of principles or axioms possible. In other words, the inference must be parsimonious.

*Inferences must be replicable.* It is not acceptable that only one person, or only one group, can obtain results that support the inference.

Anyone using proper procedures must be able to achieve the same results.

*Inferences must engender confidence.* We have degrees of confidence in inferences. Scientists have confidence in inferences that remain intact after repeated attempts at falsification and fit with other inferences and observations (Kitchner, 1982). Although strong confidence in an inference is sometimes warranted, it can never be absolute.

The scientific method can be applied to designing good instruction. *Inferences* about what and how to teach are developed from the current knowledge base. Instructional procedures are designed, tested, evaluated, revised, and retested until a highly *predictable* result is obtained. *Falsified,* or ineffective, strategies are modified or discarded. Patterns of behavior change are identified and connected, with the most effective and simplest strategies for producing the change retained (*parsimony*). Finally, the effects of the instructional methods are verified across a variety of individual learners in different contexts, even across time and space (*replication* and *confidence*).

Headsprout's inferences about how to build a reading repertoire fit within the scientific process. Headsprout used data from more than 30 million responses, across more than 10,000 learners, in a scientific approach to the design of its early reading program. Through the application of single-subject experimental design (Johnston & Pennypacker, 1993; Neuman & McCormick, 1995, 2002; Sidman, 1960), some of our inferences were falsified, whereas others were repeatedly supported by the data. These data allowed us to predict other behavior–environment relations and to replicate them over the project's large scale. However, the process from where we began to the current design did not follow a straight path. As is often true of laboratory research, our approach was (and still is) nonlinear, circuitous, and replete with continuous evaluation and revision.

**Figure 3-1.**
Numbers 1–4 indicate the steps followed in typical linear instructional design.

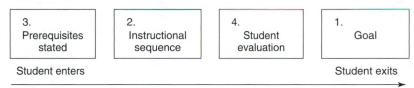

## NONLINEAR INSTRUCTIONAL DESIGN

We use the term *nonlinear* in two ways. The first applies to the overall development strategy. The sequence of design and development (see Figures 3-1 and 3-2) did not proceed in a step-by-step, linear manner. The second sense of nonlinear is borrowed from Israel Goldiamond (1975, 1979, 1984) to refer to occasions in which the "behavior of interest" (the target behavior, the terminal behavior, etc.) is not simply a function of the occasion and consequences (and their history) that immediately surround it, but of the occasions and consequences of alterna-tive behavior patterns (and their history) as well. We will first consider the former meaning.

## THE NONLINEAR PROGRAMMING PROCESS

One typical approach to instructional design is to apply a top-down process (see Figure 3-1). The goal is identified, broken down into smaller steps, and checked for "social agreement" (do experts, or at least those with some familiarity, think it's reasonable?); the program is then writ-ten in its entirety and tested with students. At times, designers will take data, note if their

**Figure 3-2.**
Numbers 1–6 indicate the nonlinear steps adapted from Markle and Tie-mann's (1967) programming process.

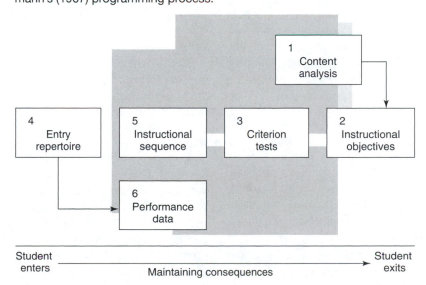

students fail, and redo some portion of the program. This often occurs in the context of field testing with groups of learners. If the overall group tends to meet the goal (often judged by consensus and learner emotional reaction), then the product is considered finished. Many designers and curriculum publishers fail to perform the last two steps of minimal test and revision. Such a program may purport to present content that is derived from scientific principles, but the program itself does not meet the criteria for a scientifically developed program. The program may even provide a better outcome than some alternative approach against which it is compared, but still the program cannot be considered scientifically developed.

Markle and Tiemann (1967) described a different instructional programming process. They noted that the entire instructional design process determines whether an instructional product will fulfill its vision. Markle and Tiemann took the position that a rigorous scientific control–analysis system is necessary for successful instructional design. Nevertheless, that recommendation has seldom been followed (Cook, 1983; Markle, 1969, 1990). One reason may be that there are few examples of its application on a large scale that can serve as a guide to others who are interested in producing quality instructional materials. Another, perhaps greater, obstacle is the time and expertise required to fully implement all elements of a scientific instructional design process. Markle and Tiemann's programming process can be slightly updated and summarized as follows (see Figure 3-2):

1. Perform a content analysis. Content is examined and classified as to the type of learning involved (e.g., strategy, principle, concept, verbal repertoire, sequence or algorithm, multiple discrimination, paired associate, kinesthetic repertoire, chain or motor response).

2. State the objectives. Clear, measurable objectives are developed that reflect the content analysis and the overall goal of the program.

3. Determine the criterion tests. Tests are constructed against a standard that often involves both accuracy and frequency criteria. The tests are developed for each teaching activity or routine within a lesson segment, for each lesson, for blocks of lessons, and finally for the program.

4. Establish the required entry behavior. Given what is to be learned, determine the skills needed to progress through the program. Entry behaviors are the specific prerequisites skills needed for success, not simply prerequisite experiences (such as taking a "prerequite" course without actually acquiring the behaviors identified in the course).

5. Build the instructional sequence. The content analysis and the criterion tests are used as a guide to produce instruction that will result in learner behavior that meets specified criteria.

6. Use performance data to continually adjust the instructional sequence (5) until it meets the objectives (2).

7. Build in maintaining consequences, an additional step in the process that was added from Goldiamond (1974). Plan for the different types of motivation that will be required, both program extrinsic and intrinsic (Goldiamond, 1974).

The learner begins at 4 (entry repertoire), goes to 5 (instructional sequence), and is evaluated at 3 (criterion tests) to determine if 2 (instructional objectives) has been reached. As is evident, the student does not progress through a sequence in the same way as the program was built. Nor is the program written in its entirety before it is tested. In this approach the learners' behavior shapes the program until nearly all learners meet the specified criteria.

Headsprout has based its development on this nonlinear, scientific instructional design approach. In the next section we describe the progression through this design process, as well as the revision cycles and phases of empirical testing. We also describe how the "other" meaning of nonlinear (Goldiamond, 1975, 1979, 1984) is critical to the Headsprout approach.

## Step 1: Content Analysis

First, we decided what our program would be about: Program design usually begins with at least a general statement of goals. Goals are often accomplishment based and are general statements of what is to be achieved (Mager, 1997). Our goal was to teach reading and decoding skills at the mid-second-grade level in 24 instructional hours.

We studied the existing literature base. We did a thorough analysis of early reading skills—what skills research determined were essential, what skills interfered with or hampered instruction, and what was currently occurring in reading instruction. In the scientific method, we build our inferences from within a coherent framework of the existing knowledge base—from empirical studies and outcomes that have weathered the test of replication. Headsprout founders spent over a year reviewing the literature and determining areas of instruction, levels of instruction, and types of instruction. Using a constructional approach (after Goldiamond, 1974), we asked, What needs to be established, what repertoire needs to be built, where do we begin? In general, we found that research on effective reading instruction focused on these critical skills (as identified by the National Institute of Child Health and Human Development, 2000): phonemic awareness, phonics, fluency, vocabulary development, and text comprehension.

These skills were analyzed into their constituent elements. The types of learning (kinetic, simple cognitive, complex cognitive, etc.) (Tiemann & Markle, 1991), the hierarchy of skills, and the relation of one skill set to another were determined. The final objectives and the criterion tests for each objective were derived from this analysis. A more complete description of these skills and strategies as analyzed by Headsprout can be found in Layng and colleagues (in press).

## Step 2: Instructional Objectives

Based on the content analysis and identification of critical areas for reading success, we identified larger "composite" skills that we knew our learners should be taught. For example, we knew that phonics, or the relation between the letters (graphemes) of written language and the sounds of written language (phonemes), involved the ability to rapidly identify print in the presence of sound, or to reliably produce sound in the presence of print. Table 3-1 provides the sample composite skills and types of discriminations we determined students would need to read and decode at the mid-second-grade level.

These skills involved multiple subsets of skills and behavior sequences, which needed to be broken down into their constituent parts. For example, what does it mean to recognize that sounds make words, words make sentences, and sentences make stories? What behaviors comprise that repertoire? What does the learner actually do to demonstrate the skill? To answer those questions, we needed to determine exactly what *component,* or basic, skills made up our *composite* skills. We needed to identify "pinpoints" that would serve as our learning objectives and the "learning channels" (Haughton, 1980) under which our learners would operate. Pinpoints are considered the relevant behaviors that indicate skilled performance, whereas learning channels are the active portion of a behavioral objective. In the instructional design literature, the term *channel* refers to how stimuli are perceived ("input" behavior, which is usually identified by one of the five senses—see, hear, touch, smell, and taste) and how the learner subsequently demonstrates "knowledge" ("output" behavior, or what the learner does).

With Headsprout Early Reading, for example, we examined this composite behavior: "The learner will recognize that there is a one-to-one correspondence between sounds [phonemes] and print [graphemes]." We then broke it down into its component or "tool" skills. What were the minimal behaviors needed to establish a

**Table 3-1**
Sample Composite Skills

| Composite Skill | Type of Learning |
| --- | --- |
| Recognize that there is a one-to-one correspondence between sounds (phonemes) and print (graphemes) | Paired associates, multiple discriminations |
| Recognize that sounds make words, words make sentences, and sentences make stories | Limited range concepts |
| Identify the beginning, middle, and ending sounds of words | Multiple discriminations, algorithms |
| Segment words into sounds | Psychomotor chains, multiple discriminations |
| Use letter-to-sound correspondence to sound out new words | Principle applying, psychomotor chains |
| Fluently blend sounds to read hundreds of new words | Principle applying, practice |
| Use a repertoire of basic word families and patterns to read new words | Principle applying, algorithm following, strategies |
| Read frequently occurring words automatically and confidently | Paired associate, multiple discrimination practice |
| Read irregularly spelled words and words containing diphthongs, special vowel spellings, and common word endings | Paired associate, multiple discrimination, principle applying |
| Self-correct reading mistakes | Principle applying |
| Independently read aloud early stories with at least 90% word recognition accuracy | Verbal repertoire |
| Recognize and use the cues of punctuation when reading, including commas, periods, question marks, and quotation marks | Principle applying |

single letter–sound relationship for a learner? Some of our conclusions are presented in Table 3-2. A live, interactive sample of how a learner would experience this sequence may be found online at www.headsprout.com/aol/teachers.cfm.

## Step 3: Criterion Test

Next, we built our criterion-based measures of learning—what we would use to test for mastery, fluency, and application. In one sense, our computer-based Internet delivery made the identification of the response topography easy—we were not using voice recognition, so all we had was a mouse click. A mouse click

worked well for the task of hearing a sound and then clicking on the correct letters representing that sound. We were, however, faced with the challenge of using mouse clicks to indicate the proper blending of sounds, saying words, and reading sentences. We developed strategies reminiscent of psychophysical indicator response methodology (Goldiamond, 1958, 1962). That is, we devised activities whose correct response (a mouse click in this case) required another unrecorded response to occur. For example, after sounding out a word, a learner might be asked to listen to three different pronunciations of a word by three different Headsprout cartoon characters and to click on

**Table 3-2**
Sample Minimal Behaviors to Establish Letter–Sound Relationships

| Pinpoint (objective) | Skill Hierarchy | Learning Channel (input/output) |
|---|---|---|
| Listen to pairings of auditory and visual presentations of a phonetic element | Paired associate | [See/(Hear), then Hear/(See)] |
| Make observing response to element | Paired associate, psychomotor responding | See • Hear/Click element |
| Select examples of a phonetic element from example/ nonexample array | Multiple discrimination | Hear element • See elements/Click element heard |

the character that said the sound "like you did."

The typical method of building a test to determine what a student has learned after an existing instructional sequence is designed or used is not sufficient to provide the moment-to-moment data required to develop a program scientifically. Every response was recorded and any error was evaluated to determine what was responsible for the error. It was never assumed that errors indicated a lack of ability on the part of the learner; instead, they indicated that a change was required in the program. In addition to moment-to-moment response evaluations, tests were built into the sequence in the form of terminal exercises for each particular teaching activity. Furthermore, episodic tests were designed to test the cumulative effect of an entire lesson, and additional tests were designed to determine overall student performance once they finished the entire sequence.

We observed more than 500 children in our on-site laboratory as they engaged with the program. We measured their vocal responding, overall affect, attention to the program, and approach or escape behaviors, as well as empirical data on performance (accuracy of responding, rate, latency, error patterns, etc.). All learners were videotaped, and the tapes were used to evaluate the developing sequences along with the recorded "click" data.

## Step 4: Entry Repertoire

We also needed to determine what skills our students needed to bring to the learning interaction for the instruction to be effective. For example, we had to determine the required current relevant repertoire, or entry behavior. Answers were provided through the content analysis and literature reviews, and by further analyzing component skills, probing actual learners, and using tryout and revision cycles. We determined that the language skills of a typical 4-year-old child; the psychomotor skills necessary to move and click a mouse; and a rudimentary concept of "first," "next," "last," and "not" were all that was required. A mouse practice program was developed that included practice on all these elements as they applied to Headsprout Reading. If a child can successfully navigate this program, it is highly likely that the child has the entry skills needed to learn to read with Headsprout.

## Step 5: Instructional Sequence

We had determined both what we thought needed teaching and how we thought we would know if students had learned it. We then had to determine how to teach it. We needed an instructional sequence designed to take learners from their entry repertoire to the terminal outcome. We were alternately hampered and aided by our choice to have all instruction delivered entirely over the Internet. Unlike books, the Internet allows for direct interaction with the learner's behavior. However, unlike face-to-face instruction, no person would be available to mediate and provide contingent feedback. Continuous online delivery, though not completely foreign to us, presented unique challenges. As noted earlier, not only were we unable to rely on the presence of an adult for instruction, but also we wouldn't be able to hear a word our learners said—and yet we were teaching oral reading.

The guiding principles of our design were nonlinear and systemic. We analyzed the immediately or directly visible contingencies, as well as alternative sets. We did this with the primary behaviors of interest, as well as with the matrices of behaviors that made up the repertoire.

### Nonlinear Analysis

A nonlinear approach involves analysis of (a) the contingency of which the target behavior is a member (the direct or linear relations); (b) alternative sets, or matrices, of consequential contingencies, of which the target behavior and currently available alternative patterns are members; and (c) the contingencies or relations that can potentiate the matrices (the nonlinear relations). This analysis is applied to gain an understanding of the patterns of observed learner behavior, which occur as a result of the interaction of these matrices.

In a science of instruction, there is no such thing as a student not learning. Errors are treated as the rational outcome of the current program contingencies (i.e., the response requirements on certain occasions and their consequence) and their alternatives, including the learning history of the learner. Consider an example of this approach as it pertains to reading instruction: A learner is faced with the task of, upon hearing the spoken phonetic unit /ip/, selecting a printed letter pair, such as "ip" from a set of alternative letters representing other phonetic units. This is commonly referred to as a condi-

tional discrimination. We might observe that when the learner hears /ip/, the learner selects "ip" on 90% of the occasions; thus we feel quite comfortable that the conditional discrimination is well established. Upon closer examination, however, we might discover that the learner has learned to reject the other stimuli presented and select "ip" by exclusion, thereby getting it correct. Alternatively, he or she might have learned to choose "ip" when it is surrounded by one set of stimuli (a discrimination based on one set of nonexemplars), and select "ip" by exclusion when surrounded by other sets. In this scenario, hearing /ip/ and seeing "ip" may guide only some of the correct responses, whereas other responses considered correct may be occasioned by seeing sets that are something other than "ip." These two different contingencies may combine to produce a 90% correct rate, but may not truly represent that the target discrimination was learned (Sidman 1980, 1992).

Furthermore, when ambiguous conditions are present, a history with the consequences of calling something an example when it is not (a false alarm), or of failing to call something an example when it is (a miss), can be as influential as the consequences of selecting the example (Robbins, Layng, & Karp, 1995). These and other contingencies (see, for example, Blough, 1972) may act together to determine any given response at any given point in time. It is the job of the learning scientists and instructional designers to consider these factors when designing instruction, testing program segments, revising sequences, and interpreting learner data. It is important, therefore, to carefully control and vary how stimuli are presented, their sequence of presentation, the salience of the stimuli, the learner's history of responding to the alternatives, how the response request to the learner is made, and the consequences of responding to all alternatives (see Ray, 1969; Ray & Sidman, 1970).

The analysis can be more complex because the instructional problem presented is not always the problem to be solved. Learner failure in a particular sequence might not be the result of the design of that particular sequence, but of the design of preceding sequences, their order of presentation, or the amount of practice. Accordingly, a *systemic* analysis (after Goldiamond, 1984) that goes beyond the sequence where the problem is observed (a *topical* analysis) is often required.

Practice is an important part of the instructional sequence as well. Well-designed "guided" practice firms the skills and leads to learner fluency. Guided practice is not simple repetition; it often involves models, confirmations, and corrections. Practice follows the establishment of components so that they will be readily available for recombination with other equally firm components (Johnson & Layng, 1992, 1994), and is often timed. Timing allows for the greatest number of response opportunities in the shortest period of time and can have properties in its own right that assist in the retention and application of skills. The timed practice and the basic instructional sequence are intertwined, one building on another.

## Step 6: Performance Data

Each element of the program had to be continuously tested with new users *during* development; it was not sufficient to simply test for outcomes after the program was developed. No matter how well thought out any sequence might be, learners will show where the analysis, design, or both went wrong. Very systematic tryout and revision cycles are required. Data must be used to track changes and evaluate the various versions tested. Fortunately, computer-based instruction enables the collection of data that can be used to adapt the program to the learner's responses and helps ensure mastery of the material. Data on the percentage of correct responses, albeit helpful, are not sufficient. We also closely examine the frequency of correct versus incorrect responses (after Lindsley, 1997).

In addition, Headsprout's on-site user test laboratory allowed us to record, observe, or probe for behaviors that the computer could not

detect. If a student could not perform the terminal exercise for an instructional episode or sequence within an episode, the episode or sequence was revised until the student met the exit criteria. Additional testing of outcomes was performed outside the program to further validate that valid criterion measures were, in fact, built into the program. Once the program sequences and episodes were verified, tests were administered to determine if the sequence itself met the criterion. Changes were made in the program until 90% of the learners met the exit criteria. This process has resulted in over 10,000 data-based program revisions to date.

The process involved (and still involves) constant testing, revision and recycle, and retesting. This process is referred to as "formative evaluation" by Scriven (1974), and as "developmental testing" by Markle (1967), and involves the consensus of best practices, experience, and point of view. The design is initially based on previous research, can come from a variety of disciplines, and may be based on elements implemented in the program and not on the program itself. All elements of the program are tested for effectiveness, and if the criteria are not met, alternative strategies are built and tested. The process iterates until all criteria are met, with performance always measured against a set of standards. The sequencing of program steps and their relation to the learner's behavior is explicitly identified, thereby generating new knowledge—about both the program and the behavior. This process continues and becomes aggregated as the "chunks" of the program units change in size (e.g., for Headsprout, a segment of a lesson, a lesson, groups of lessons, and the program). The research is based on individuals and therefore can be generalized to individuals (Layng et al., in press; Sidman, 1960).

As a result of the developmental testing process, our instructional objectives have been further refined, with skills added and others removed from the sequence. This process was incorporated in three distinct stages of testing (Markle, 1967): developmental testing (conducted in-house, in the user test laboratory); validation testing (conducted as a beta release of the program, in controlled remote locations); and field testing (conducted via public launch of the program).

These three phases of empirical testing (developmental, validation, and field testing), identified by Markle (1967) and implemented by Headsprout, are briefly summarized within the following guidelines (see also Johnson, Twyman, & Hobbins, 2001).

### Developmental Testing

In the developmental testing phase, the goal is to develop a workable instructional program. For Headsprout, this occurred in our on-site user test laboratory. The instructional designers observed and interacted individually with students while the students used the program. Learners progressed through initial drafts of the program and were encouraged to speak out loud their "reasons" for doing what they were doing (after Markle, 1967); they were often questioned about their behavior.

Developmental testing data were collected on a wide variety of general and precise performance and affective measures, both quantitative and qualitative. The cycle is tryout, revision, tryout, revision, and so on, and always begins with the leanest possible design that might achieve the instructional objective (Gilbert, 1962; Markle, 1990). In developmental testing, the learner's behavior determines what needs to be added to the program. Our motto was that instruction is like salt: It's easier to put in than take out! Data-based program interventions included software debugging; improving the writing, graphics, layout, or motivational variables; and, most important, improving the instructional variables to achieve program objectives.

### Validation Testing

In the validation testing phase, the goal is to obtain a precise description of performance characteristics as they occur when learning with the entire product. It focuses less on product development and more on the outcomes of systematic replications across learner demographics. Validation testing occurs in various settings and for Headsprout included both schools and the homes of our learners. Ongoing, moment-by-moment (click-by-click) data were collected, as well as learner performance on various criterion-referenced tests. This enabled us to answer questions such as, Who does or doesn't learn? How much is learned? and In how much time? Data were analyzed to determine the extent and limit of program effectiveness and to make further refinements in the program.

### Field Testing

The goal of the field testing phase is to monitor the use of the product "in the field." The product is compared to other products, used with a new population or setting, or used under different circumstances. Field testing settings vary widely and with Headsprout included thousands of learners. With Headsprout, moment-by-moment (click-by-click) data were collected in real time, and criterion-referenced and norm-referenced outcome measures were used. Data provided more information about the extent and limit of the program's effectiveness and are still being used to refine the program. As of this writing, randomized control group studies are being conducted to further ascertain the effectiveness of Headsprout's reading program.

All three testing phases are employed in the development of Headsprout programs. Although very expensive and time consuming, this commitment to user testing is necessary to build instruction that is truly scientifically based (for more information, see Layng et al., in press). The Internet, although presenting challenges, also presents opportunities. Almost every learner response to the program can be collected and analyzed. As the number of users grows, so too does the ongoing field-test database. When the program is revised, all learners immediately receive the revision.

## Step 7: Maintaining Consequences

As with any instructional sequence, we needed contingencies that would maintain the individual learner's behavior throughout the program. Without human delivery, potent consequential contingencies had to be built into every step of the program (Goldiamond, 1974). This is done by (a) ensuring that the learner is successful and makes visible progress in the program; (b) carefully placing extrinsic consequences such as verbal praise, fun sounds, and brief animations; and (c) ensuring that the skills being learned will be useful (the program-intrinsic consequences obtained from reading). While developing this early reading program, we carefully balanced the instructional (and practice) sequences with the type, frequency, and duration of consequences that would maintain or increase the desired behavior.

## CONCLUSION

Teaching involves the coordination of a complex set of teacher and student repertoires. A host of complex interlocking consequential contingencies must be carefully analyzed, sequenced, and arranged. Given the importance of effective reading instruction to America's future, we believed it was necessary to base our beginning reading program not only on the most up-to-date scientific literature, but also on state-of-the-art scientific control–analysis methodology in its design. This effort necessitated a nonlinear approach to both overall program design and the analysis of each response, its occasion, and consequence.

How large a scale was the project that produced the initial Headsprout beginning reading program? It took over 25 people, 3 years, and

over $4 million to produce the initial 40-episode program and its underlying generative learning technology. The next 40 episodes took an additional year. The team included learning scientists, instructional designers, prototype programmers, copyeditors, creative writers, graphic artists, animators, sound engineers, system architects, system administrators, and Web software engineers. The efforts of all of these individuals had to be coordinated and synchronized as part of an iterated product development system—a nonlinear metasystem, informing and being informed by the nonlinear instructional design system. The result was not only a program that effectively teaches beginning reading, but also a unique, patented instructional technology (Layng et al., 2003).

We have demonstrated that it is possible to develop a complex cumulative repertoire over the Internet (see Johnson & Layng, 1992, 1994), in which component behaviors are systematically established and brought together to make larger behavioral units called composite repertoires. These composites can then combine with other components or composites to make yet other composites. Whereas many approaches to computer-based instruction may appear to limit what a learner experiences, our nonlinear approach frees the learner to respond in ways not typically thought possible for computer-based instruction. Indeed, as described in Layng and colleagues (in press), we can actually engineer successful "discovery learning." We can teach our young speakers to be their own listeners who often correct themselves, and we can reliably teach our learners to make correct articulation of sounds and words without the need for expensive, often cumbersome voice recognition hardware and software. We have provided a highly effective and reliable teaching system that can be easily implemented and maintained. There are few limits on the ultimate scalability of the Headsprout beginning reading program. (For more information on how to access the Headsprout curriculum, visit www.headsprout.com.) We hope that the Headsprout effort will serve as a model for other large-scale projects whose goals are not only the design and deployment of instruction based on scientifically based principles, but also instruction that is itself a product of a scientific approach to design.

# REFERENCES

Blough, D. S. (1972). Recognition by the pigeon of stimuli varying in two dimensions. *Journal of the Experimental Analysis of Behavior, 18,* 345–367.

Brownowski, J. (1956). *Science and human values.* New York: Harper and Row.

Cook, D. A. (1983). CBT's feet of clay: Questioning the informational transmission model. *Data Training 3* (12), 12–17.

Gilbert, T. F. (1962). Mathetics: The technology of education. *Journal of Methetics, 1,* 70–73.

Goldiamond, I. (1958). Indicators of perception: I. Subliminal perception, subception, unconscious perception: An analysis in terms of psychophysical indicator methodology. *Psychological Bulletin, 55,* 373–411.

Goldiamond, I. (1962). Perception. In A. Bachrach (Ed.), *Experimental foundations of clinical psychology* (pp. 28–340). New York: Basic Books.

Goldiamond, I. (1974). Toward a constructional approach to social problems: Ethical and constitutional issues raised by applied behavior analysis. *Behaviorism, 2,* 1–84.

Goldiamond, I. (1975). Alternative sets as a framework for behavioral formulations and research. *Behaviorism, 3,* 49–86.

Goldiamond, I. (1979). Behavioral approaches and liaison psychiatry. *Psychiatric Clinics of North America, 2,* 379–401.

Goldiamond, I. (1984). Training parent trainers and ethicists in nonlinear analysis of behavior. In R. F. Dangle & A. Polster (Eds.), *Foundations of research and practice* (pp. 504–545). New York: Gilford Press.

Goldiamond, I., & Thompson, D. (1967 [revision edited by P. T. Andronis, in press]). *The functional analysis of behavior.* Cambridge, MA: Cambridge Center for Behavioral Studies.

Haughton, E. C. (1980). Practicing practices: Learning by activity. *Journal of Precision Teaching, 1,* 3–20.

Johnson, K. R., & Layng, T. V. J. (1992). Breaking the structuralist barrier: Literacy and numeracy with fluency. *American Psychologist, 47,* 1475–1490.

Johnson, K. R., & Layng, T. V. J. (1994). The Morningside model of generative instruction. In R. Gardner III et al. (Eds.), *Behavior analysis in education: Focus on measurably superior instruction* (pp. 173–197). Pacific Grove, CA: Brooks/Cole.

Johnson, K., Twyman, J. S., & Hobbins, K. (2001, May). Using learner performance to improve a Web-based beginning reading program. Paper presented in G. Bruce (Chair), *Evaluate learning efficiency to design learning efficient programs,* at the 27th annual conference for the Association for Behavior Analysis, New Orleans, LA.

Johnston, J. M., & Pennypacker, H. S. (1993). *Strategies and tactics of behavioral research* (2nd ed.). Hillsdale, NJ: Erlbaum.

Kitchner, P. (1982). *Abusing science: The case against creationism.* Cambridge, MA: MIT Press.

Layng, T. V. J., Johnson, K., Twyman, J. S. Ford, V., Layng, M. P., Gilbert, M., & Stikeleather, G. (2003). *U.S. Patent No. 6,523,007.* Washington, DC: U.S. Patent and Trademark Office.

Layng, T. V. J., Twyman, J. S., and Stikeleather, G. (in press). Selected for success: How Headsprout Reading Basics teaches beginning reading. In D. J. Moran & R. Malott (Eds.), *Empirically supported educational methods.* St. Louis, MO: Elsevier.

Lindsley, O. R. (1997). Precise instructional design: Guidelines from Precision Teaching. In C. R. Dills & A. J. Romiszowski (Eds.), *Instructional development paradigms* (pp. 537–554). Upper Saddle River, NJ: Educational Technology Publications.

Mager, R. F. (1997). *Making instruction work* (2nd ed.). Atlanta, GA: CEP.

Markle, S. M. (1967). Empirical testing of programs. In P. C. Lange (Ed.), *Programmed instruction: Sixtysixth yearbook of the National Society for the Study of Education: 2* (pp. 104–138). Chicago: University of Chicago Press.

Markle, S. M. (1969). *Good frames and bad: A grammar of frame writing* (2nd ed.). New York: Wiley.

Markle, S. M. (1990). *Designs for instructional designers.* Champaign, IL: Stipes.

Markle, S. M., & Tiemann, P. W. (1967). Programming is a process [Slide/tape interactive program]. Chicago: University of Illinois.

National Center for Education Statistics. (2004). Percentage of students, by reading achievement level, grade 4: 1992–2003. Retrieved January 14, 2004, from http://nces.ed.gov/nationsreportcard/ reading/results2003/natachieve-g4.asp

National Institute of Child Health and Human Development. (2000). *Report of the National Reading Panel. Teaching children to read: An evidence-based assessment of the scientific research literature on reading and its implications for reading instruction: Reports of the Subgroups* (NIH Publication No. 00-4754). Washington, DC: U.S. Government Printing Office.

Neuman, S. B., & McCormick, S. (1995). *Single-subject experimental research: Applications for literacy.* Newark, DE: International Reading Association.

Neuman, S. B., & McCormick, S. (2002). A case for single-subject experiments in literacy research. In M. L. Kamil, P .B. Mosenthal, P. D. Pearson, & R. Barr (Eds.), *Methods of literacy research* (pp. 105–118). Mahwah, NJ: Erlbaum.

Platt, J. R. (1964). Strong inference. *Science, 146,* 347–353.

Popper, K. R. (1968). *The logic of scientific discovery.* London: Hutchinson.

Ray, B. A. (1969). Selective attention: The effects of combining stimuli which control incompatible behavior. *Journal of the Experimental Analysis of Behavior, 12,* 539–550.

Ray, B. A., & Sidman, M. (1970). Reinforcement schedules and stimulus control. In W. N. Schoenfeld (Ed.), *The theory of reinforcement schedules* (pp. 187–214). New York: Appleton-Century-Crofts.

Robbins, J. K., Layng, T. V. J., & Karp, H. (1995). Ambiguity and the abstract tact: A signal detection analysis. *The Analysis of Verbal Behavior, 12,* 1–11.

Scriven, M. (1974). Evaluation perspectives and procedures. In J. W. Popham (Ed.), *Evaluation in education: Current application.* Berkeley, CA: McCutchan.

Sidman, M. (1960). *Tactics of scientific research: Evaluating experimental data in psychology.* Boston: Authors Cooperative.

Sidman, M. (1980). A note on the measurement of conditional discrimination. *Journal of the Experimental Analysis of Behavior, 33,* 285–289.

Sidman, M. (1992). Adventitious control by the location of comparison stimuli in conditional discrimination. *Journal of the Experimental Analysis of Behavior, 58,* 173–182.

Tiemann, P. W., & Markle, S. M. (1991). *Analyzing instructional content.* Champaign, IL: Stipes.

U.S. Department of Education. (1993). *Toward a new science of instruction: Programmatic investigations in cognitive science and education.* http://www.ed.gov/pubs/InstScience/

## STUDY QUESTIONS AND FOLLOW-UP ACTIVITIES

1. Examine research from a reading curriculum publisher (e.g., Houghton Mifflin, McGraw-Hill). Determine whether the curriculum meets the criteria for a scientifically developed program.

2. Select a composite skill to teach a student. Conduct a component/composite analysis to determine the necessary component skills to teach. Plan a fluency-building lesson in which your student practices the component skills.

3. Create a list of composite skills you would like to teach. Match each composite skill with a type of learning as described in Table 3-1.

4. Select a teaching objective and describe the pinpoint, skill hierarchy, and learning channel. Use Table 3-2 as a guide.

5. Explain to a teacher the advantages of using frequency measures of correct and incorrect student performance compared to percentages of correct performance to guide instruction.

6. Review the research base on one of the following: a published reading curriculum (e.g., Four Blocks, SRA's Direct Instruction), computer-based instruction, or toylike reading instruction tools (e.g., Leapfrog). Compare and contrast these findings with Headsprout's research base.

Study questions and follow-up activities prepared by Charles L. Wood and Susan M. Silvestri.

7. Consider this statement: "It was never assumed that errors indicated a lack of ability on the part of the learner; instead, they indicated that a change was required in the program." What are the implications of this statement for classroom instruction?

8. What are the prerequisite skills for most beginning reading programs? How do they compare to Headsprout's prerequisite language and motor skills?

9. Go to Headsprout's Web site and sample a few lessons. Write a description of the lessons that you could use to explain the structure and benefits of the program to the parent of a child who needs supplemental reading instruction.

10. Stage a mock debate between proponents of scientifically developed instructional programs and program developers who think science is of little value.

### CHAPTER 4

# Beginning Reading Failure and the Quantification of Risk
## Reading *Behavior* as the Supreme Index

*Edward J. Kame'enui*          *Roland Good III*          *Beth A. Harn*

The current national commitment to beginning reading, as evidenced by the federal law No Child Left Behind (2002) and, in particular, the Reading First Initiative, is the result of at least three well-established considerations: (a) 37% of all fourth-grade students in the United States do not read well enough to complete grade-level assignments (National Assessment of Educational Progress, November, 2003); (b) reading trajectories are established early in the K–3 "learning-to-read" phase (National Center to Improve the Tools of Educators, 1998) and are difficult to change once established, particularly during the "reading-to-learn" phase (Good, Simmons, & Kame'enui, 2001); and (c) a substantial and compelling body of scientifically based reading research (commonly referred to as SBRR) (Adams, 1990; National Reading Panel, 2000; National Research Council, 1998) is currently available to inform practitioners on how to improve practice in schools (Simmons, Kame'enui, Good, Harn, Cole, & Braun, 2002). These considerations have ostensibly shaped the program of prevention research designed explicitly to intervene early, systematically, differentially, and intensively (Simmons, Kame'enui, Stoolmiller, Coyne, & Harn, 2003; Torgesen, 2000) to decrease the incidence and prevalence of children who experience reading difficulties.

The national investment in the prevention of reading difficulties in the early grades is predicated on the now unremarkable assumption that reading in an alphabetic writing system, although a gallantly complex cognitive and linguistic process, is learned and therefore must be taught (Kame'enui, 1998; Liberman & Liberman, 1990; National Reading Panel, 2000; National Research Council, 1998; Shaywitz, 2003; Wolf & Katzir-Cohen, 2001). As plain and conspicuous as this point now appears, such a proposition was at the epicenter of a rancorous historical,

*Author Note:* Preparation of this chapter was supported in part by Project CIRCUITS, Grant No. H324X010014, OSEP, U.S. Department of Education. This material does not necessarily represent the policy of the U.S. Department of Education, nor is the material necessarily endorsed by the federal government.

professional, and epistemological quarrel for more than a decade (Adams, 1990). Bower (1992) further asserted that such a debate has haunted the field of reading for more than 100 years. Such public debates are invariably cast in broad and vulgar dichotomies (e.g., whole language vs. phonics; direct instruction of reading vs. literature-based, student-centered teaching; phenomenology vs. behaviorism) that are often pitched in bold and blunt terms (Kame'enui, 1995, 1999).

Naturally, blunt arguments fail at nuance and subtlety, especially when complex symbolic and cognitive systems such as reading are invoked. At the very heart of this nettlesome debate is whether beginning reading should be taught systematically or permitted to develop naturally. This debate has largely taken place among researchers and thinkers in the "academy" rather than by the public at large who entrust schools with their children. However, researchers and those in the academy would be wise to note the fundamental tenet that reading, particularly for children in the early formative years of learning, is important to the social, psychological, and educational health of the nation (No Child Left Behind, 2002). These complex cognitive events, although naturally private because they take place inside the neural circuitry of the brain, require, by virtue of their social and political significance, *a prominent and trustworthy public index* of these valued cognitive events. Such an index must be observable, measurable, reliable, repeatable, scalable, viable, and valid as an indicator or marker of a distinct cognitive process. For behavior analysts, this index is rather obvious: It is reading behavior itself, however defined or scaled. For others unimpressed by behavioral views on learning, focusing on behavior as the primary index of cognition simply misses the point; after all, calling attention to the behavior itself "misses the underlying structures that make the behavior possible" (Searle, 1995, p. 5). Focusing on the behavior, the argument goes, simply trivializes the essence of constructing meaning from printed words (Kame'enui, 1998). After all, reading, writ large, is not about an alphabetic writing system or about observ-

able reading behavior; it's about human emancipation and human agency (Kame'enui, 1995).

In this chapter we focus on reading behavior as the supreme index for gauging the reading success or failure of children. In doing so, we first describe the complexity of reading in an alphabetic writing system and offer a theoretical and conceptual framework of prevention as a context for thinking about this complexity. We also describe a three-tier prevention model designed to prevent reading difficulties or reading disabilities. In addition, we discuss three substantive presuppositions of this prevention model with examples of results obtained from our work in a specific school district, the Bethel School District in Eugene, Oregon.

## READING: A COMPLEX COGNITIVE CONSTRUCT

Reading behavior is complex. In fact, as Shaywitz (2003) eloquently observed, reading is "an extraordinary ability, peculiarly human and yet distinctly unnatural. It is acquired in childhood, forms an intrinsic part of our existence as civilized beings, and is taken for granted by most of us" (p. 3). This extraordinary ability that is peculiarly human and distinctly unnatural is also an unwieldy, developmental construct with numerous dimensions, including, for example, phonemic, perceptual, visual, alphabetic, orthographic, semantic, syntactic, linguistic, morphographic, syllabary, conceptual, audile, oral, contextual, phonological, psychological, memorial, intellectual, social, emotional, neural, and behavioral dimensions. To index reading requires identifying the behavioral dimensions of reading with the most predictive power for determining later reading risk. Moreover, such an index must be tethered to a theoretically, conceptually, and scientifically sound model of reading prevention.

### The Quantification of Reading Behavior

A historical analysis of different methods of measuring the complex skills related to proficient reading is beyond the scope of this chapter. However, over 30 years of research on the effectiveness of formative evaluation in improving educational decision making and outcomes for students is worthy of serious consideration (Deno, 1985; Fuchs, Fuchs, & Hamlett, 1989; Shinn, 1989, 1998). Formative evaluation involves the recurring assessment of progress toward a long-term goal or objective (Salvia & Ysseldyke, 2004). The purpose of this kind of assessment is to provide teachers objective information to evaluate students' responses to instruction in a timely manner so that proactive midcourse corrections can be made (Howell & Nolet, 2001).

Historically, most measures of reading development were informal, nonrepeatable, and time consuming to administer and score and lacked research demonstrating their efficacy (Fuchs, Deno, & Mirkin, 1984). The most commonly reported assessment method teachers have used in the past has been informal observations of students' reading. According to Deno (1985), the goal of such measurement was to provide teachers with evaluation procedures to improve the timeliness and validity of instructional decision making. However, informal observations of students' reading were often irrelevant to classroom instruction. In addition, they also lacked objectivity and specificity. Thus, Deno and colleagues suggested a scientific method to increase the objectivity of these observations by creating a standardized 1-minute sample of the observable reading behavior of oral reading fluency.

### Oral Reading Fluency

The most commonly used methods of formative evaluation of reading performance are the procedures related to oral reading fluency (ORF). The standardized ORF procedures were developed at the University of Minnesota Institute for the Research on Learning Disabilities (IRLD) between 1977 and 1983 as part of a range of formative evaluation methods designed to assess reading, math, spelling, and written expression. Such formative evaluation methods are often more commonly known as curriculum-based

measurement (CBM; Deno, 1985) or general outcome measurement (Deno, Espin, & Fuchs, 2002). ORF procedures require a student to read a grade-level passage orally for 1 minute. The number of words read correctly is counted and serves as the primary metric or index of a child's reading ability. Typically, this metric produces a rate of accuracy (defined as the number of words encountered in the passage that are read correctly per minute) or fluency (defined as the ease, speed, and accuracy of a child's ability to read connected text). Such measures have become well-established predictors of reading comprehension (Fuchs, Fuchs, Hosp, & Jenkins, 2001). For a complete account of these practices, the reader is referred to Deno (1985), Shinn (1989, 1998) and more recently to Fuchs and colleagues (2001).

For a measurement procedure to be viewed as acceptable, it must be reliable, valid, easy to administer, cost and time efficient, and sensitive to small, incremental changes in student performance over time. The need for repeatable, time efficient, and skill-sensitive measurement is essential because such data must be employed within time-series analyses to examine students' rate of progress in response to classroom instruction. These measures can be administered daily with results graphed to enable a teacher to discern if the instructional program is responsive to students' learning needs. As Deno (1992) observed, the "conceptual roots of CBM are also found in the observational and analytical methodology of applied behavior analysis" (p. 9). Although this formative measurement approach had been commonly employed in evaluating intervention effectiveness with students displaying overt behavioral difficulties, the application of this approach to evaluating educational interventions was revolutionary.

These established criteria (brief, repeatable, easy to administer, sensitive to instruction) specified what the measures should look like. However, the assessment of such a complex skill as reading, especially given that few issues in education are as contentious as beginning reading, has invoked a range of philosophical, pedagogical, psychometric, and methodological issues that required careful analysis (Adams, 1990; Bower, 1992; Kame'enui, 1998). Thus, attempting to quantify such a complex, symbolic process in a time efficient and repeatable manner has been an ambitious task. It is essential to remember that the researchers suggesting the use of ORF as a measure of reading skill were not attempting to assess the entire domain of reading. After all, reading is a rather unwieldy theoretical and operational construct that means different things to different folks or, more fashionably, to different discourse communities. Instead, these researchers were attempting to identify an efficient *indicator* of reading proficiency that was reliably correlated with other established (yet less efficient) reading measures. Traditional reading achievement measures (published norm-referenced tests), although useful for some purposes, were simply not sensitive to changes in growth and development of skill performance over time. Moreover, they lacked treatment utility (Good & Jefferson, 1998; Messick, 1989). Deno (1985) characterized the intent of researchers to measure reading skill as an effort to create measures that served as "vital signs" of reading development and well-being, analogous to using a person's temperature as a vital sign or general indicator of overall health. Although a person's body temperature does not represent all aspects of a person's health, it is a highly predictive indicator of a person's general health and may indicate a need for further diagnosis.

Relying on reading research developed at the time, coupled with general psychometric principles, researchers created and evaluated reading measures that required students to perform five different kinds of reading tasks: (a) read words in isolation (word lists); (b) read underlined words in context (i.e., read specific words underlined in passages); (c) read stories aloud counting words read correctly (e.g., oral reading fluency); (d) generate missing words in a passage (i.e., within a given story, words would be deleted and students had to provide an appropriate choice for the passage); and (e) define

words from a given story. Each of these tasks had empirical support as an essential skill related to overall reading achievement (Deno, 1985; Fuchs et al., 2001; Marston, 1989). For each of these measures, variations in test administration were investigated systematically (e.g., examining the differences among measures administered for 30, 60, and 90 seconds) and examined within a program of research involving reliability and validity studies (Deno, Mirkin, & Chiang, 1982; Marston, 1989).

Criterion validity studies have been conducted on the relation of each of the five reading tasks to published norm-referenced standardized measures of reading achievement (see Marston, 1989, for a summary). With the exception of the task that required students to define words, all measures correlated strongly (i.e., .75 to .95) with the criterion measures of word reading and reading comprehension. However, the average correlation of ORF (i.e., .91) to the criterion measures was significantly higher than those of all the other reading tasks.

Criterion validity studies notwithstanding, the development of measures that were sensitive to changes in skill performance over time was still necessary. Measures that were sensitive to changes in growth and the development of skill performance were considered critical to evaluating the effects of instructional interventions. When comparing the nature of the five reading measure procedures, ORF was found superior in discriminating between skilled and low-skilled readers and representing changes in individual skill performance over time (Deno, 1985). Deno (1985) characterized ORF as a "simple datum" of the number of words a student reads correctly in 1 minute that "reliably and validly discriminates growth in reading proficiency throughout the elementary school years" (p. 224). The extensive use of ORF over the past three decades in educational settings (Good, Simmons, & Kame'enui, 2001; Howell & Nolet, 2001; Shinn, 1998) and in intervention research (Fuchs et al., 2001) demonstrates how a 1-minute unadorned sample of reading behavior can help provide assessment data and set the occasion for instruction that is more responsive to student performance (Fuchs, Fuchs, & Hamlett, 1989).

## THE NEED FOR EARLY IDENTIFICATION

Oral reading fluency is a robust measure for assessing reading development from the end of first grade into middle school (Shinn, 1998). However, we now know that reading risk emerges before the end of first grade and can be identified as early as preschool and kindergarten through measures of phonological awareness and letter knowledge (Good, Simmons, & Smith, 1998; National Research Council, 1998; Stanovich, 2000). Students who perform below criterion levels on these foundational skills can be readily identified to receive effective, systematic, and explicit intervention (Juel, 1988; Stanovich, 2000). Because the measures commonly used with kindergarteners and first-graders were not designed to regularly monitor and evaluate early intervention efforts, the absence of such measures motivated researchers at the Early Childhood Research Institute on Measuring Growth and Development at the University of Oregon to develop the Dynamic Indicators of Basic Early Literacy Skills (DIBELS). Specifically, Good and Kaminski (2003) developed DIBELS using the same scientific method employed in the development of ORF; that is, they created brief, repeatable, valid, reliable, and formative measures of early literacy skills for use in a prevention model (Good, Simmons, & Kame'enui, 2001).

An essential difference between the DIBELS measures and curriculum-based measures (CBM) is that DIBELS has research-based goals and time lines for each measure. In contrast, CBM is used to measure overall reading growth and development in relation to teacher- or school-determined goal levels. The established goal for each DIBELS measure provides an objective standard of performance that students are expected to

demonstrate on essential skills that are predictive of later reading proficiency (Good, Simmons, & Kame'enui, 2001). Areas identified for measurement development were derived from the convergence of research on the foundational skills related to later reading proficiency, including phonological awareness, alphabetic understanding, vocabulary development, reading comprehension, and fluency and accuracy with connected text (National Reading Panel, 2000; National Research Council, 1998).

In the next section we summarize the two domains assessed and the DIBELS measures used for early identification and intervention: measuring phonological awareness and the alphabetic principle. For more information, including full reliability and validity information, the reader is referred to Good and Kaminski (2003) and to the official DIBELS Web site, where the measures can be viewed and downloaded (http://dibels.uoregon.edu).

## Measuring Phonological Awareness

Phonological awareness is the ability to hear and manipulate the sounds within spoken language (Yopp, 1992). For example, a child with phonological awareness would understand that in the word *ball* there are three sounds (phonemes), /b/ /a/ /l/, and if asked, he or she could substitute the sound /m/ for /b/ to create the new word *mall*. Phonological awareness includes a continuum of skills ranging from splitting words into syllables, rhyming, identifying pictures beginning with a specific sound, isolating sounds in a given word, and segmenting the constituent sounds in a word, to substituting specific sounds within a word. However, the research has identified that isolating, blending, and segmenting words at the phoneme level are essential skills in later reading proficiency (Smith, Simmons, & Kame'enui, 1998). There are two different DIBELS measures designed to assess phonological awareness: initial sound fluency (ISF) and phoneme segmentation fluency (PSF).

## Initial Sound Fluency

The ISF measure assesses a child's ability to recognize and produce the initial sound in an orally presented word (Kaminski & Good, 1996, 1998). The examiner presents four pictures to a child, names each picture, and then asks the child to identify (i.e., point to or say) the picture that begins with the sound the examiner produced orally. For example, the examiner says, "This is sink, cat, gloves, and hat. Which picture begins with /s/?" The student then points to the correct picture. The child is also asked to produce orally the beginning sound for an orally presented word that matches one of the pictures. The examiner calculates the amount of time taken to identify or produce the correct sound and converts the score into the number of initial sounds identified and produced correctly in a minute. This measure is typically used in preschool and the beginning of kindergarten with the criterion performance or goal (i.e., a score of 25 or more) on this measure established at the middle of kindergarten. Students meeting the goal in the middle of kindergarten are highly likely (i.e., the odds are 80% or greater) to meet the end-of-kindergarten goal specified on the next measure of phonological awareness (Good, Simmons, & Kame'enui, 2001).

## Phoneme Segmentation Fluency

A more complex measure of phonological awareness employed from the middle of kindergarten throughout first grade is phoneme segmentation fluency (PSF). The PSF measure assesses the ability to fluently segment three- and four-phoneme words into their constituent individual phonemes. The PSF measure has been found to be a good predictor of later reading achievement (Kaminski & Good, 1996). The PSF task is administered by the examiner orally presenting words of three to four phonemes. The student must produce verbally the individual phonemes for each word. For example, the examiner says "sat," and the student says "/s/ /a/ /t/" to receive a point for each correct phoneme produced. After the student responds,

the examiner presents the next word. The behavior counted is the number of correct phonemes produced in 1 minute, which determines the final score. This measure is typically given in the middle of kindergarten with the criterion performance goal represented by a score of 35 or more at the end of kindergarten. Students meeting this goal are more likely (i.e., the odds are greater than 80%) to be proficient readers by the end of first grade (Good, Simmons, & Kame'enui, 2001).

## Measuring the Alphabetic Principle

The alphabetic principle relates to a learner's ability to associate sounds (phonemes) with letters (graphemes) and use these sounds to read a word (Moats, 1999). Juel (1988) found that the primary difference between good and poor readers was the student's skill in using knowledge of letter sounds and then blending those sounds to decode or read a word. Because English is alphabetic, decoding is an essential strategy to reading words. There are simply too many words in the English language to rely on memorization as a primary word identification strategy (Bay Area Reading Task Force, 1997).

Correspondingly, the DIBELS measure developed to assess this essential skill is nonsense word fluency (NWF). With this measure the student is presented a sheet of paper with randomly ordered VC and CVC nonsense words (e.g., *sij, rab, ov*) and asked to produce verbally the individual letter sound of each letter or simply read the nonsense word. For example, if the stimulus word is *vaj*, the student could say "/v/ /a/ /j/" or the word /vaj/ to obtain a total of three correct letter sounds. The student is allowed 1 minute to produce as many individual letter sounds or to read as many nonsense words as possible. The behavior counted is the number of correct letter sounds produced in 1 minute. This measure is typically given in the middle of kindergarten with the criterion performance goal represented by a score of 50 or more by the middle of first grade. Students meeting this goal are more likely (i.e., the odds are greater than 80%) to be proficient readers by the end of first grade (Good, Simmons, & Kame'enui, 2001).

Following in the footsteps of CBM, the DIBELS measures provide a downward extension of dynamic and formative assessment to identify students at risk for later reading difficulties. Identifying and quantifying behavioral dimensions of early reading skills is an essential component for evaluating the effectiveness of the systems-level prevention model discussed in the next section.

## A MODEL OF READING PREVENTION

The theoretical and conceptual framework we employ for the prevention of reading difficulty is drawn from the public health domain and literature (Caplan & Grunebaum, 1967, cited in Simeonsson, 1994). This framework is comprised of three individual levels of prevention: *primary prevention, secondary prevention,* and *tertiary prevention* (Kame'enui, Simmons, Good, & Chard, 2002). In this framework, the concept of prevention is defined in two different ways: as an action that stops an event from happening and as an action that "reduces" a problem or condition that has already been identified.

In the following definitions of primary, secondary, and tertiary prevention, these two meanings are evident. At a systems level, *primary prevention* is concerned with *reducing the number of new cases (incidence) of a potential problem* (e.g., reading difficulties, learning disabilities, reading disabilities) in the population. Thus, primary prevention directs the sources of information and resources (e.g., instructional and curricular programs, strategies, procedures, and approaches in beginning reading) at the school and child level to ensure that the needs of all learners are addressed *before* reading difficulty crystallizes, takes hold, and stabilizes. The primary focus of this strategy is to minimize the number of students requiring more intensive resources. In preventing reading diffi-

culties, primary prevention begins in kindergarten and first grade and involves implementing scientifically based practices to decrease the likelihood of students' developing reading difficulties.

In contrast to primary prevention, *secondary prevention* is concerned with *reducing the number of existing cases (prevalence) of an already identified condition or problem* in the population. According to the Committee on the Prevention of Reading Difficulties of the National Academy of Science, secondary prevention "involves the promotion of compensatory skills and behaviors . . . . The extra effort is focused on children at higher risk of developing reading difficulties but before any serious, long-term deficit has emerged" (National Research Council, 1998, p. 16).

Finally, *tertiary prevention* is concerned with *reducing the complications associated with an existing and identified problem or condition.* According to the National Research Council (1998), "Programs, strategies, and interventions at this level have an explicit remedial or rehabilitative focus. If children demonstrate inadequate progress under secondary prevention conditions, they may need instruction that is specially designed and supplemental—special education, tutoring from a reading specialist—to their current instruction" (p. 16).

The three levels of prevention are depicted in Figure 4-1. As indicated, the level of information, resources, and specialization of support services increases for students demonstrating reading difficulty. The focus of the three-tier primary prevention model is to intensify instruction systematically in kindergarten and first grade in response to student performance that is predictive of later reading difficulties, which should prevent students from needing additional support after first grade. The goal of secondary and tertiary prevention is to provide additional instructional support for students as needed after first grade.

We base the features of primary prevention on our collective research and professional

**Figure 4-1.**
Three-tier prevention model.

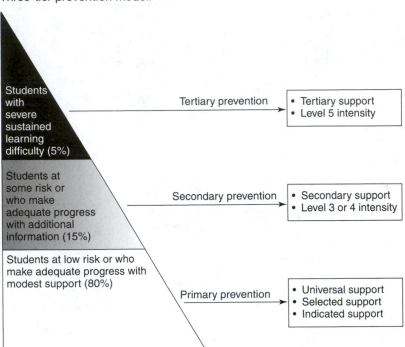

development efforts over the past several years to scale up, implement, and document *schoolwide systemic strategies and processes for effectively reforming a school's efforts to prevent reading difficulties for* all *readers* (Good, Simmons, & Kame'enui, 2001; Kame'enui & Simmons, 2002; Simmons et al., 2002). Although the educational community realizes the necessity of systems-level prevention research, there is no agreed-on approach or metric for evaluating what constitutes an effective prevention model. As Zins, Heron, and Goddard (1999) discussed, no experimental studies of such a prevention model (i.e., random assignment to treatment and control groups) have been conducted, and the nonexperimental studies completed often do not have as their dependent variable student academic outcomes. Thus, the best method to evaluate these intervention efforts has yet to be determined. We propose that one effective method for evaluating these efforts on the read-

ing performance of students is to use DIBELS on a systems-wide level within a three-tier prevention model. This is the approach we have taken in our research. In the next section we discuss specifically how this approach can be implemented on a systems-wide level.

## DIBELS and the Three-Tier Prevention Model

The DIBELS measures are administered to all children in each school in the district three times per year to determine their reading performance in relation to established goals. Within the prevention model, data representing a student's performance on these measures are aggregated and compared to the DIBELS database (containing the performance measures of almost 800,000 students nationwide), and a level of risk for that student is determined. This level of risk specifies one of three types of support (i.e., benchmark, strategic, intensive) a student will need. Instructional recommendations for each level of risk are provided at each DIBELS administration.

### Benchmark

Students given a *benchmark* instructional recommendation are considered on track and at low relative risk, which means that the odds are in their favor (i.e., 80% or greater) of achieving the next early literacy goal if they continue to receive their current effective instructional support.

### Strategic

Students given a recommendation of *strategic* instructional support are at increased relative risk. The odds of achieving the next goal are neither in their favor nor strongly against them.

### Intensive

Students given *intensive* instructional recommendations have the odds against them for reaching the next literacy goal unless substantial additional instructional support is provided immediately, explicitly, and repeatedly.

Within our prevention model, the instructional recommendations parallel Simeonsson's (1994) three levels of primary prevention: (a) universal, (b) selected, and (c) indicated. At each level, students who are at increased relative risk as a result of individual characteristics and current levels of performance are provided increasing levels of instructional support. To prevent reading difficulties, instruction is intensified for students demonstrating the lowest levels of early reading performance.

## Universal/Benchmark Instructional Support: Low Risk Status

The intent of universal support is to implement a schoolwide reading program that emphasizes the essential components of scientifically based reading research (SBRR) to support the needs of all kindergarten through first grade students in acquiring essential early reading skills. In our

schoolwide reading program, all students in the school receive effective, research-based reading instruction. Table 4-1 shows the recommended instructional level of support matched with seven "alterable variables" within the teacher's or school district's control. For instance, the instructional intensity needed at the universal/benchmark instructional support level is not high. Students who are in the benchmark instructional recommendation range on the DIBELS measures are on track, and the assessment and formative data would indicate that they are benefiting from the typical research-based curriculum that is being delivered by the general education teacher. Because these students are on track, assessment with the DIBELS is completed only three times per year (i.e., at the beginning, middle, and end of the year) to ensure that students at this benchmark level maintain learning rates predictive of later reading proficiency. However, students at the selected/strategies and indicated/intensive levels require and receive increasingly more support and attention across the alterable variables; thus the DIBELS assessment is completed more frequently.

In our conceptualization of a systems-level primary prevention model, the universal instructional level represents the *core* curricular and instructional reading programs and strategies implemented at the school level. Primary prevention at the universal instructional level is designed to accommodate the majority of students in a school or approximately 80% of K–3 students enrolled. More important, it is designed to *prevent* children from becoming at risk for reading problems. Therefore, the *core* reading programs and strategies represent the primary prevention investments of the K–3 teachers, paraprofessionals, parents, and administrators. Primary prevention also involves a formative assessment system (DIBELS) that provides practitioners with timely and important information on the reading performance of all students, as well as the effectiveness of the core instructional investments. In summary, the following six essential features characterize primary prevention:

**Table 4-1**

Alterable Variables for Reading Instruction in Kindergarten and First Grade: Primary Prevention of Later Reading Difficulties

| Alterable Variable | Level of Recommended Instructional Support | | |
| --- | --- | --- | --- |
| | Universal/Benchmark | Selected/Strategic | Indicated/Intensive |
| Curriculum | Research-based core reading program emphasizes the five essential areas of beginning reading instruction | Research-based core reading program with strategic enhancements on identified areas of instructional need or specific targeted supplemental programs | Research-based reading program with supplemental or accelerated/intervention programs on identified areas of instructional need |
| Teacher-Guided Instruction | Provided throughout the school day | Additional opportunities to practice embedded throughout the day Increased explicitness of instruction and focus Increased opportunities to review skills | Additional opportunities to practice embedded throughout the day Increased explicitness of instruction and focus Increased opportunities to review skills |
| Highly Qualified Instructor | General education teacher | General education teacher with additional general education support | General education teacher with additional general education or specialized support |
| Grouping (Opportunities to Learn) | Mainly large group with some small-group arrangements | A mixture of large and small-group instruction with strategic selection of skills targeted for small-group instruction | Mainly small-group instruction with strategic selection of skills targeted for large group instruction |
| Allocated Time | A minimum of 90 minutes allocated to the range of literacy skills | A minimum of 90 minutes allocated to the range of literacy skills Time specifically set aside to supplement or enhance essential skill development in small groups | A minimum of 90 minutes allocated to the range of literacy skills Time specifically set aside to enhance essential skill development in small groups; additional 20 to 30 minutes per day provided in a small-group settings |
| Instructional Setting | General education classroom | General education classroom | General education classroom with push-in or pull-out instructional support |
| Frequency of Assessment | Assess at the beginning, middle, and end of the year | Assess 1-2 times per month | Assess 2-4 times per month |

**Increasing Instructional Intensity** →

1. Effective, research-based core curriculum and instruction

2. A system of additional interventions and supports

3. Interventions that can be arranged on a continuum of instructional intensity

4. Meaningful and important goals representing reading health

5. A brief, repeatable, valid formative assessment of reading progress toward goals that is sensitive to intervention

6. Adequate time allocated to reading instruction and judiciously protected

## Selected/Strategic Instructional Support: Increased Risk Status

The intent of the selected or strategic level of instructional support at the primary prevention level is to identify groups of students with increased relative risk status of not becoming proficient readers. This increased relative risk can be operationalized by recommendations of strategic or intensive instructional support on the DIBELS assessments.

Figure 4-2 illustrates how a student can be identified at the beginning of the school year in kindergarten as needing additional instructional support to increase the likelihood of the student achieving the middle-of-the-year early literacy goals. In the fall of the kindergarten year increased relative risk on DIBELS is identified by low performance on initial sound fluency (ISF) or letter naming fluency (LNF) or both. A "cutoff score" of 7 on ISF is illustrated in Figure 4-2, which is intended to illustrate the decision-making process. The specific cutoff may be modified or refined based on additional research and evidence, but a cutoff of 7 has been found to be reasonably accurate and reliable (Good, Simmons, Kame'enui, Kaminski, & Wallin, 2002). If this decision is made in the fall of first grade, different measures and different cutoff scores are employed, but the logic of the decision would be the same. In the fall of first grade, similar figures use a cutoff of 35 on phoneme segmentation fluency (PSF) and 24 on nonsense word fluency (NWF), for example.

Because the DIBELS measures are brief and efficient (i.e., 1 minute long), and because the children being assessed are typically very young and variable in their behavior, it is desirable to have provisions for being reasonably confident of increased risk status (selected/strategic status). Thus, we often administer alternative forms

**Figure 4-2.**
Criteria to identify children with low initial early literacy skills for *selected* status on initial sounds. (a) Student performance does not meet criteria for selected/strategic status; (b) student performance meets the criteria for selected/strategic instructional support status in the fall of kindergarten.

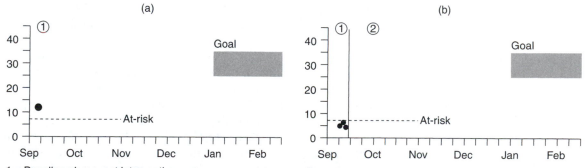

1 = Baseline phase, not intervention.
2 = An intervention phase is required because child's performance is at risk.

of the DIBELS ISF measure to the student on different days and under different conditions (e.g., familiar examiner) to ensure an accurate measure of skill performance. A pattern of consistently low performance on multiple samples of behavior, over multiple days, under multiple conditions provides a reasonable degree of confidence in decisions of selected status (see student b in Figure 4-2). When a student has been identified as requiring more intensive instructional support, instructional variables are altered or intensified to increase learning rates, prevent continued early reading failure, or both.

Table 4-1 indicates that students needing selected/strategic instructional support may need some small-group instruction, with increased specificity and explicitness, and additional opportunities to practice and review essential early reading skills. Because these students are at risk and we are allocating additional instructional resources, we need to ensure that the students are benefiting from the instruction. Thus, their learning is monitored more often using the DIBELS measures. Their instructional program can then be modified as data warrant.

Because of individual child variation in learning to read in an alphabetic writing system and the reality that one program is not likely to meet the needs of all children, schools must develop and implement a range of reading programs and strategies. "One size does not fit all" is a pedagogical and instructional reality in almost all schools. Therefore, selected/strategic instructional support involves programs, strategies, and procedures designed and employed to *supplement, enhance, and support* the core reading program for children identified with marked reading difficulties. Selected or strategic instructional support is akin to a second level of intervention designed to both maintain and stabilize the primary prevention efforts and to prevent the need for more intensive intervention. Selected or strategic instructional support typically accommodates approximately 15% of the K–3 students who are not benefiting fully from the typical core instruction.

## Indicated/Intensive Instructional Support: High-Risk Status

Students needing indicated/intensive instructional support demonstrate both low skills and low progress when provided additional attention, focus, and support by the general education teacher within the general education setting. Students needing indicated/intensive instructional support require significantly more instructional resources delivered with greater specificity than students needing selected/strategic support. Instructional adjustments may include selecting a curricular program that is more explicit, providing many opportunities to practice active student responses (Heward, 1994), reviewing essential skills, and delivering instruction in a small group setting to accelerate learning rates. Students receiving this level of instructional support may have the program delivered by educational personnel with greater specialization, as well as receive more reading instruction throughout the school day to maximize learning. To ensure that this intensive instructional program is meeting the needs of these at-risk students, data are collected at least every 2 to 4 weeks to evaluate learning rates in a more timely and sensitive manner.

Figure 4-3a illustrates a student who demonstrates adequate progress when provided with additional attention, focus, and support (selected/strategic support) within the classroom. Figure 4-3b illustrates a student who does not make adequate progress when provided with the same level of support. The student in Figure 4-3b would need indicated/intensive instructional support to beat the odds of not making the next early reading goal. If data continued to indicate limited learning, changes to the instructional program would be warranted.

Indicated or intensive instructional support represents reading instruction that is *specifically designed and customized* for students with marked difficulties in reading or reading disabilities who have not responded to other intervention efforts. Indicated or intensive instructional

**Figure 4-3.**
Criteria to identify children who are not making adequate progress for *indicated* status.

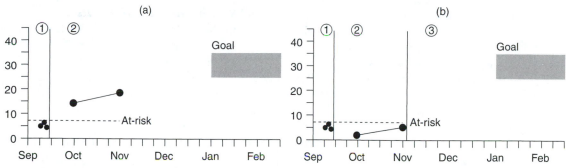

1 = Baseline phase, not intervention.
2 = An intervention phase is required because child's performance is at risk.

support is typically required for 5% of students with marked difficulties learning to read and is customized to the individual reading and literacy needs of each student. Often the instruction is delivered by personnel with specialized training (i.e., Title 1 special education reading specialists) employing specially designed instructional materials (i.e., intervention or acceleration programs). In summary, the essential features of selected and indicated levels of instructional support in the prevention model include the following:

1. Integrated, flexible general and special education service delivery systems positioned to provide intervention of increasing intensity

2. Decision rules and operational procedures that are reliable and valid and designed to mobilize intensive prevention resources early, before reading difficulty and failure takes hold

3. A schoolwide process that directs the school resources necessary to address the three-tier prevention needs

## SUBSTANTIVE PRESUPPOSITIONS OF A PREVENTION MODEL

A primary prevention model is predicated on at least three substantive presuppositions that have both epistemological and ontological standing.

First, we *know* something about the condition, problem, or target behavior (e.g., reading risk or reading disability) that we consider to be true based on the best available scientific evidence. This scientific truth does not invoke certainty, but it does require a set of publicly announced criteria for adjudicating the scientific evidence and determining the findings, however tentative. Second, the condition, problem, or target behavior actually *exists* in ways that permit verifiability or falsifiability (Searle, 1995). Finally, the scientific evidence is both *accessible* and *usable* for practitioners who must treat the condition, problem, or target behavior. In the next section these three substantive presuppositions of a prevention model are delineated with some examples from our collaborative efforts working with a specific school district, the Bethel School District in Eugene, Oregon, over the past 5 years.

## Knowability of the Problem: Reading Risk Is Identifiable

The first presupposition is that reading risk and reading disabilities are knowable and identifiable using reliable and verifiable measures. Further, when a defined risk condition has been identified and potential risk factors are targeted, a comprehensive preventive strategy can be implemented to slow and ultimately reverse the risk, thereby improving the well-being of children (Simeonsson, 1994). For example, at the primary prevention level, children who do not attain a specified criterion level of performance on an early reading task (e.g., being able to segment the sounds in words at a rate of 35 phonemes per minute) by a designated time (e.g., the end of kindergarten) would likely be identified or "selected" (Simeonsson, 1994) to receive a targeted intervention to prevent them from becoming new cases of reading disabilities.

Our research on DIBELS (Good & Kaminski, 2003) and the DIBELS data system (Good, Kaninski, Smith, Simmons, Kame'enui, & Wallin, 2003) enables us to examine a fairly robust data set on early reading performance and risk. For example, the DIBELS data system permits us to examine school and student performance involving approximately 1,125 school districts, more than 3,734 schools, and approximately 800,000 students across 44 states participating in the DIBELS data system during the 2003–2004 academic year (Good et al., 2003).

Based on our analysis of the DIBELS data for the 2001–2002 academic year, our research suggests that students should have an established awareness of the initial sounds in words as indicated by a score of 25 or more on the initial sounds fluency (ISF) subtest in the middle of kindergarten. In addition, students in the middle of kindergarten who score 27 or more on the letter naming fluency (LNF) subtest, 18 or more on the phoneme segmentation fluency (PSF) subtest, and 13 or more on the nonsense word fluency (NWF) subtest have the odds (i.e., 88% or greater) strongly in favor of achieving end-of-kindergarten reading goals *and* are not likely to experience serious difficulty with phonemic awareness skills at the end of kindergarten. In contrast, students who score below 10 on ISF, below 15 on LNF, below 7 on PSF, and below 5 on NWF are considered at risk for serious reading problems and do not have odds (e.g., 14%) in their favor of achieving the goal of being readers (i.e., reading at least 40 correct words per minute) at the end of first grade unless they receive intensive instructional support (Good et al., 2003).

### Bethel School District Application

Our work with the staff of the Bethel School District in Eugene, Oregon, provides examples of how schools are using the DIBELS data to identify students needing additional instructional support. In the fall semester of kindergarten, all students are assessed with two measures from the DIBELS assessment system: initial sounds fluency (ISF) and letter naming fluency (LNF). It takes approximately 3 minutes to screen each student. The data are then entered into the DIBELS data system, an online Web server that organizes and analyzes the data to identify students at risk for reading difficulties and needing additional instructional support. One of several reports available to the schools is a histogram that provides a frequency count of students performing at different levels.

For example, Figure 4-4 displays beginning-of-the-year phonological awareness performance (as measured by ISF) for all kindergartners at one of the Bethel elementary schools. Research with DIBELS indicates that students performing below 4 on ISF are at risk for not meeting the midyear goal of 25 or more on the ISF measure. At this school, 13% of students are performing in the at-risk range, 25% are at some risk, and 62% are at low risk of not meeting the midyear goal. The school uses these data to determine which students need more intensive instructional support.

At most schools, students indicating selected/strategic instructional support receive additional small-group reading instruction on essential reading skills, and progress is monitored at least monthly. Students demonstrating either significantly low levels of early literacy skills or students who have not responded positively to the selected/strategic level of instructional support are targeted for indicated/intensive instructional support. Students identified for more intensive instructional support receive an additional 30 minutes of small-group reading instruction, in

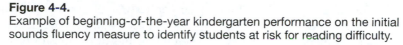

**Figure 4-4.**
Example of beginning-of-the-year kindergarten performance on the initial sounds fluency measure to identify students at risk for reading difficulty.

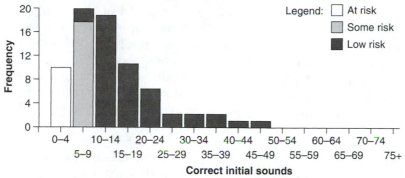

addition to the half-day kindergarten instructional time, with an intervention program designed explicitly to accelerate learning of essential early literacy skills. The program and reading growth of students receiving the most intensive support are monitored with the ISF measure at least twice a month.

According to our analysis of the DIBELS data, coupled with a compelling convergence of research evidence (Foorman & Torgesen, 2001; Lovett, Lacerenza, & Borden, 2000; O'Connor, 2000; Torgesen et al., 1999; Vellutino et al., 1996), reading risk as a condition in the population is clearly identifiable. However, the identification of reading risk is complex, and it must be conducted within a broader conceptual and technical framework that permits the valid and reliable use of assessment tools and systems.

## Existence of the Problem: Reading Risk Is Preventable

The second presupposition about a prevention model is that the target condition of reading risk and reading disability exists but is preventable. If reading risk is identifiable and not an organic, immutable characteristic of the learner or learning, then it can be prevented; that is, we can actually design prevention systems and strategies to prevent reading risk. However, determining with ample confidence that a particular preven-

tive system or strategy was indeed responsible for preventing the particular target condition (e.g., reading difficulties or reading disabilities) is not easy, conceptually or experimentally (Zins, Heron, & Goddard, 1999). This is especially true when complex symbolic systems are invoked that are the primary (if not exclusive) province of complex organizations such as schools.

The efficacy of a prevention system requires (a) a longitudinal evidentiary basis in which a group or cohort of children is identified as at risk of reading difficulties in kindergarten, (b) the random assignment of students to either a treatment condition (e.g., a schoolwide prevention of reading problems model) or a comparison condition (e.g., a schoolwide traditional reading model), and (c) the tracking of students for an extended period of time (kindergarten to the end of third grade) to determine the long-term experimental effects of either of these conditions in *actually preventing* reading difficulties for children in the early years of reading development. To determine the efficacy of a schoolwide prevention model, the evidence for this kind of experimental, longitudinal intervention program of research must also address the following questions:

1. How many children must benefit from a prevention program, treatment, or strategy before it is deemed preventive? Specifically, is

prevention an all-or-nothing proposition? That is, must the schoolwide prevention system actually prevent *all* participants in the study from acquiring the condition of reading difficulty or disability?

2. How long must prevention last (i.e., the absence of the risk condition) before the problem or condition is considered to have been prevented, and periodic intervention is no longer required?

3. What criterion levels of performance or benchmarks—on what reading skills, at what points in time, under what assessment conditions (e.g., timed vs. untimed), and on what reading assessment measures (e.g., Woodcock Reading Mastery Test-Revised, DIBELS)—are required to consider prevention effective?

4. What is the extant research evidence on the effectiveness of preventing reading difficulties or reading disabilities in children in kindergarten through third grade?

### *Bethel School District Application*

Although our research with the Bethel School District did not employ causal experimental research designs, some of the accomplishments are noteworthy and may assist other researchers when designing and conducting future studies. Prior to the districtwide implementation of the primary prevention model of schoolwide reading improvement, the district average referral rate of students identified with reading difficulties or disabilities to special education was 15%. After 3 years of implementation, the average referral rate has been approximately 5% over the past 2 years. These data provide a level of evidence that the research-based practices being implemented beginning in kindergarten and first grade are reducing the numbers of students identified with reading disabilities. Additionally, during the first year of implementing the prevention model (1998–1999), 21% of district third-graders did not meet the standard on the Oregon Statewide Assessment Test (OSAT). In contrast, by the end of the 2002–2003 school

year, only 10% of third-graders in the Bethel School District did not meet this same standard. The ORF results at the end of first grade are represented in Figure 4-5, which reports the percentage of students reading at the different reading risk levels across the 5 years of the prevention model implementation. Although we and the district continue to strive for less than 1% risk cases, increasing the percentage of students ending first grade at low risk for later reading difficulties (i.e., reading more than 40 words correctly on ORF) from 28% in the first year of implementation to 64% 5 years later is a step in the right direction.

### Addressing the Problem: Research Based on Prevention Is Substantial, Accessible, and Usable

The third substantive presupposition of a prevention model is that a trustworthy and substantial research base in beginning reading is available for immediate application in schools. The term *prevention* permeates virtually every large-scale national report (e.g., National Research Council, 1998, *Preventing Reading Difficulties in Young Children*) and is readily embraced by practitioners (American Federation of Teachers, 1999; Learning First Alliance, 1998), researchers (Adams, 1990; Foorman & Torgesen, 2001), and policy makers alike (No Child Left Behind, 2002). Moreover, there appears to be good reason for this apparent convergence of professional commitment to the prevention of reading difficulties. In the last 10 years, there have been three federally funded, substantive analyses of the research on beginning reading (Adams, 1990; National Reading Panel, 2000; National Research Council, 1998), and each of these reports points to a clear and compelling convergence on the importance of several "big ideas" in beginning reading that are now part of the federal law, No Child Left Behind (2002), including (a) phonological awareness, (b) alphabetic insight and understanding, (c) automaticity and fluency with connected texts, (d) vocabu-

**Figure 4-5.**
Monitoring prevention efforts: End-of-year first-grade reading proficiency in Bethel School District.

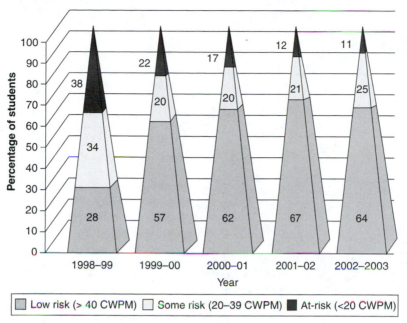

lary development, and (e) reading comprehension (Kame'enui, Carnine, Dixon, Simmons, & Coyne, 2002; National Reading Panel, 2000).

In addition, the research convergence makes particularly plain that reading does not come naturally, but must be taught systematically, explicitly, and diligently (Liberman & Liberman, 1990; Shaywitz, 2003). As the Committee on the Prevention of Reading Difficulties in Young Children observed, "Most reading difficulties can be prevented" (National Research Council, 1998, p. 13). Moreover, they asserted, "The critical importance of providing excellent reading instruction to all children is at the heart of the committee's recommendation. Accordingly, our central recommendation characterizes the nature of good primary reading instruction" (p. 5).

The impact of these major reports is currently being demonstrated in the substantive changes and improvements publishers have made in the most recent versions of commercially available core reading programs. Improving the quality of the tools we provide all educators by making

the research usable and accessible will support our national efforts in preventing students from the compounding consequences of early reading difficulties.

### Bethel School District Application

One of the major goals of our work with the Bethel School District was to build the capacity within the schools and district to independently implement and sustain the effective reading practices within the prevention model (Simmons et al., 2002). In each school in Bethel, a research-based core reading program is being implemented for at least 90 minutes per day 5 days per week, small-group reading instruction is being provided to students requiring additional instructional support, and a range of instructional programs or resources is available to accelerate learning rates for all children. An integral component of this success was a usable and accessible formative evaluation system (DIBELS) implemented by all school personnel to provide timely feedback to teachers and administrators on the quality of instructional practices and the growth and development of all K–3 students. The district's commitment to meeting the needs of all of its students is displayed in the professional and compassionate work that administrators, teachers, educational assistants, and parents provide every day.

## CONCLUSION

Although teaching beginning reading is complex, employing an objective, repeatable, and valid behavioral indicator of performance (e.g., number of correct phonemes, letters, or word per minute) provides schools the information to evaluate the effectiveness of their prevention efforts in meeting the needs of all students. The three-tier prevention model provides schools with the organizational structure and logic needed to support the instructional needs of the full range of learners. The model is predicated on reading research that makes plain the essential importance of identifying at-risk students early in their reading development and the power of systematically and differentially providing instruction to alter the course of later reading development. Because a child's reading growth and development is not in equal units per unit of time (Bloom, 1964), schools must use an objective and formative evaluation system that reliably and validly demonstrates that a child is displaying the essential reading behaviors predictive of later reading proficiency.

## REFERENCES

Adams, M. J. (1990). *Beginning to read: Thinking and learning about print.* Cambridge, MA: MIT Press.

American Federation of Teachers. (1999). *Building on the best, learning from what works: Seven promising reading and English language arts programs.* Washington, DC: Author.

Bay Area Reading Task Force. (1997). *A reading-writing-language source book for the primary grades.* San Francisco: University School Support for Educational Reform.

Bloom, B. S. (1964). *Stability and change in human characteristics.* New York: Wiley.

Bower, B. (1992). Reading the code, reading the whole: Researchers wrangle over the nature and teaching of reading. *Science News, 141* (9), 138–141.

Deno, S. L. (1985). Curriculum-based measurement: The emerging alternative. *Exceptional Children, 52,* 219–232.

Deno, S. L. (1992). The nature and development of curriculum-based measurement. *Preventing School Failure, 36,* 5–10.

Deno, S. L., Espin, C. A., & Fuchs, L. S. (2002). Evaluation strategies for preventing and remediating basic skill deficits. In M. R. Shinn, H. M. Walker, & G. Stoner (Eds.), *Interventions for academic and behavior problems II: Preventive and remedial approaches* (pp. 213–242). Bethesda, MD: National Association of School Psychologists.

Deno, S. L., Mirkin, P., & Chiang, B. (1982). Identifying valid measures of reading. *Exceptional Children, 49,* 36–45.

Foorman, B. R., & Torgesen, J. (2001). Critical elements of classroom and small-group instruction promote reading success in all children. *Learning Disabilities Research & Practice, 16* (4), 203–212.

Fuchs, L. S., Deno, S. L., & Mirkin, P. K. (1984). Effects of frequent curriculum-based measurement on pedagogy, student achievement, and student awareness of learning. *American Educational Research Journal, 21,* 449–460.

Fuchs, L. S., Fuchs, D., & Hamlett, C. L. (1989). Effects of alternative goal structures within curriculum-based measurement. *Exceptional Children, 55,* 429–438.

Fuchs, L. S., Fuchs, D., Hosp, M., & Jenkins, J. R. (2001). Oral reading fluency as an indicator of reading competence: A theoretical, empirical, and historical analysis. *Scientific Studies of Reading, 5,* 239–256.

Good, R. H., & Jefferson, G. (1998). Contemporary perspectives on Curriculum-Based Measurement Validity. In M. R. Shinn (Ed.), *Advanced applications of curriculum-based measurement* (pp. 61–88). New York: Guilford.

Good, R. H., & Kaminski, R. A. (2003). *DIBELS: Dynamic indicators of basic early literacy skills* (6th ed.). Longmont, CO: Sopris West.

Good, R. H., Kaminski, R. A., Smith, S., Simmons, D. S., Kame'enui, E. J., & Wallin, J. (2003). Reviewing outcomes: Using DIBELS to evaluate kindergarten curricula and interventions. In S. R. Vaughn & K. L. Briggs (Eds.), *Reading in the classroom: Systems for observing teaching and learning* (pp. 221–266). Baltimore: Paul H. Brookes.

Good, R. H., Simmons, D. C., & Kame'enui, E. J. (2001). The importance and decision-making utility of a continuum of fluency-based indicators of foundational reading skills for third-grade high-stakes outcomes. *Scientific Studies of Reading, 5* (3), 257–288.

Good, R. H., Simmons, D. C., Kame'enui, E. J., Kaminski, R. A., & Wallin, J. U. (2002). *Summary of decision roles for intensive, strategic, and benchmark instructional recommendations in kindergarten through third grade* (Technical Report No. 11). Eugene, OR: University of Oregon.

Good, R. H., Simmons, D. C., & Smith, S. (1998). Effective academic interventions in the United States: Evaluating and enhancing the acquisition of early reading skills. *School Psychology Review, 27,* 45–56.

Heward, W. L. (1994). Three "low tech" strategies for increasing the frequency of active student response during group instruction. In. R. Gardner, J. O. Cooper, T. E. Heron, W. L. Heward, J. Eshleman, & D. Sainato (Eds.), *Behavioral analysis in education: Focus on measurably superior instruction* (pp. 283–320). Monterey, CA: Brooks-Cole.

Howell, K., & Nolet, V. (2001). *Curriculum-based evaluation: Teacher and decision making* (3rd ed.). New York: Wadsworth.

Juel, C. (1988). Learning to read and write: A longitudinal study of 54 children from first through fourth grades. *Journal of Educational Psychology, 80,* 437–447.

Kame'enui, E. J. (1995). Response to Deegan: Keep the curtain inside the tub. *The Reading Teacher, 48* (8), 700–703.

Kame'enui, E. J. (1998). The rhetoric of all, the reality of some, and the unmistakable smell of mortality. In J. Osborn & F. Lehr (Eds.), *Literacy for all: Issues in teaching and learning* (pp. 319–338). New York: Guilford.

Kame'enui, E. J. (1999). The National Research Council report on the prevention of reading difficulties in young children, and the process of dubitation. *Journal of Behavioral Education, 9* (1), 5.

Kame'enui, E. J., Carnine, D. W., Dixon, R., Simmons, D. C., & Coyne, M. D. (2002). *Effective teaching strategies that accommodate diverse learners* (2nd ed.). Upper Saddle River, NJ: Prentice Hall.

Kame'enui, E. J., & Simmons, D. C. (2002). From an "exploded view" of beginning reading toward a schoolwide beginning reading model: Getting to

scale in complex host environments. In R. Bradley, L. Danielson, & D. P. Hallahan (Eds.), *Identification of learning disabilities: Research to practice* (pp. 163–172). Mahwah, NJ: Erlbaum.

Kame'enui, E. J., Simmons, D. C., Good, R., III, & Chard, D. (2002). *Focus and nature of primary, secondary, and tertiary prevention: CIRCUITS model.* Unpublished manuscript.

Kaminski, R. A., & Good, R. H., III (1996). Toward a technology for assessing basic early literacy skills. *School Psychology Review, 25* (2), 215–227.

Kaminski, R. A., & Good, R. H., III (1998). Assessing early literacy skills in a problem-solving model: Dynamic indicators of basic early literacy skills. In M. R. Shinn (Ed.), *Advanced applications of curriculum-based measurement.* New York: Guilford.

Learning First Alliance. (1998). Every child reading: An action plan of the Learning First Alliance. *American Educator, 1–2,* 52–63.

Liberman, I. Y., & Liberman, A. M. (1990). Whole language vs. code emphasis: Underlying assumptions and their implications for reading instruction. *Annals of Dyslexia, 40,* 51–76.

Lovett, M. W., Lacerenza, L., & Borden, S. L. (2000). Putting struggling readers on the PHAST Track: A program to integrate phonological and strategy-based remedial reading instruction and maximize outcomes. *Journal of Learning Disabilities, 33* (5), 458–476.

Marston, D. (1989). Curriculum-based measurement: What is it and why do it? In M. R. Shinn (Ed.), *Curriculum-based measurement: Assessing special children* (pp. 18–78). New York: Guilford.

Messick, S. (1989). Validity. In R. L. Linn (Ed.), *Educational measurement* (3rd ed., pp. 13–103). New York: Macmillan.

Moats, L. C. (1999). *Teaching reading is rocket science: What expert teachers of reading should know and be able to do.* Washington, DC: American Federation of Teachers.

National Assessment of Educational Progress (Authors: Grigg, W. S., Daane, M. C., Jin, Y., & Campbell, J. R.). (2003). *The nation's report card: Reading 2002.* Washington, DC: National Center for Education Statistics. Available: http://nces.ed.gov/pubsearch/pubsinfo.asp?pubid=2003521.

National Center to Improve the Tools of Educators. (1998). *Learning to read/reading to learn information kit.* Washington, DC: American Federation of Teachers.

National Reading Panel. (2000). *Teaching children to read: An evidence-based assessment of the scientific research literature on reading and its implications for reading instruction: Reports of the subgroups.* Bethesda, MD: National Institute of Child Health and Human Development.

National Research Council. (1998). *Preventing reading difficulties in young children.* Washington, DC: National Academy Press.

No Child Left Behind, 2002, Title I, Part B, Student Reading Skills Improvement Grants, Subpart 1, Reading First.

O'Connor, R. (2000). Increasing the intensity of intervention in kindergarten and first grade. *Learning Disabilities Research & Practice, 15* (1), 43–54.

Salvia, J., & Ysseldyke, J. (2004). *Assessment in special and inclusive education* (9th ed.). New York: Houghton Mifflin.

Searle, J. R. (1995). *The construction of social reality.* New York: The Free Press.

Shaywitz, S. (2003). *Overcoming dyslexia: A new and complete science-based program for reading problems at any level.* New York: Knopf.

Shinn, M. R. (1989). *Curriculum-based measurement: Assessing special children.* New York: Guilford.

Shinn, M. R. (1998). *Advanced applications of curriculum-based measurement.* New York: Guilford.

Simeonsson, R. J. (1994). Promoting children's health, education, and well-being. In R. J. Simeonsson (Ed.), *Risk, resilience, & prevention* (pp. 3–11). Baltimore: P. H. Brookes.

Simmons, D. C., Kame'enui, E. J., Good, R. H., III, Harn, B. A., Cole, C., & Braun, D. (2002). Building, implementing, and sustaining a beginning reading improvement model school by school and lessons learned. In M. Shinn, G. Stoner, & H. M. Walker (Eds.), *Interventions for academic and behavior problems II: Preventive and remedial approaches* (pp. 537–569). Bethesda, MD: National Association of School Psychologists.

Simmons, D. C., Kame'enui, E. J., Stoolmiller, M., Coyne, M. D., & Harn, B. (2003). Accelerating growth and maintaining proficiency: A two-year intervention study of kindergarten and first-grade children at risk for reading difficulties. In B. Foorman (Ed.), *Preventing and remediating reading difficulties: Bringing science to scale* (pp. 197–228). Timonium, MD: York Press.

Smith, S. B., Simmons, D. C., & Kame'enui, E. J. (1998). Phonological awareness: Instructional and curricular basics and implications. In D. C. Simmons & E. J. Kame'enui (Eds.), *What reading research tells us about children with diverse learning needs: Bases and basics.* Mahwah, NJ: Erlbaum.

Stanovich, K. E. (2000). *Progress in understanding reading: Scientific foundations and new frontiers.* New York: Guilford.

Torgesen, J. K. (2000). Individual differences in response to early interventions in reading: The lingering problem of treatment resisters. *Learning Disabilities Research & Practice, 15* (1), 55–64.

Torgesen, J. K., Wagner, R. K., Rashotte, C. A., Rose, E., Lindamood, P., Conway, T., & Garvan, C. (1999). Preventing reading failure in young children with phonological processing disabilities: Group and individual responses to instruction. *Journal of Educational Psychology, 91* (4), 579–593.

Vellutino, F. R., Scanlon, D. M., Sipay, E. D., Small, S. G., Pratt, A., Chen, R., & Denckla, M. B. (1996). Cognitive profiles of difficult-to-remediate and readily remediated poor readers: Early intervention as a vehicle for distinguishing between cognitive and experiential deficits as basic causes of specific reading disability. *Journal of Educational Psychology, 88* (4), 601–638.

Walker, H. M., Horner, R. H., Sugai, G., Bullis, M., Sprague, J. R., Bricker, D., & Kaufman, M. J. (1996). Integrated approaches to preventing antisocial behavior patterns among school-age children and youth. *Journal of Emotional and Behavioral Disorders, 4,* 194-209.

Wolf, M., & Katzir-Cohen, T. (2001). Reading fluency and its intervention. *Scientific Studies of Reading, 5* (3), 211–239.

Yopp, H. K. (1992). Developing phonemic awareness in young children. *Reading Teacher, 45* (9), 696–703.

Zins, J. E., Heron, T. E., & Goddard, Y. L. (1999). Secondary prevention: Applications through intervention assistance teams and inclusive education. In C. R. Reynolds & T. B. Gutkin (Eds.), *The handbook of school psychology* (3rd ed., pp. 800–821). New York: John Wiley & Sons.

## STUDY QUESTIONS AND FOLLOW-UP ACTIVITIES

1. You have been asked to serve on a committee to choose the reading curriculum for your school

Study questions and follow-up activities prepared by Natalie J. Allen and Shobana Musti-Rao.

district. After reading this chapter, what components of an effective reading curriculum will you include in your recommendation? How will you know that the curriculum that you recommend is actually designed to teach what it advertises?

2. Administer the oral reading fluency (ORF) measure of the DIBELS assessment to an elementary student (K–3). Administer another measure of reading fluency to the same student (e.g., a running record). Score the two measures and compare and contrast their respective utility as measures of current performance and as predictors of future progress. State what measures you would use as a teacher. Explain why.

3. After having conducted the DIBELS test during the early part of kindergarten, your analysis shows that two students have scores less than 4 on initial sounds fluency and less than 10 on letter naming fluency. Prepare a dialogue for a parent–teacher conference in which you will discuss the DIBELS testing and the steps you intend to take to assist these two students to get "on track" in their reading ability prior to the end of the year.

4. Establish a panel of two to four participants to debate the issue of direct instruction of reading versus a literature-based or whole-language approach. In preparing remarks, each panelist should write a one- to two-page paper articulating his or her position on the approach. Support for respective positions must be based on relevant literature. (Chapter 15 contains some background on direct instruction and a whole-language approach.)

5. Think back to how you learned to read. Ask a member of your family about the approach that was used. Reflect on the different activities that were involved and list the different factors that affected you in becoming a better reader.

6. Interview a respected general education teacher at a local elementary school with regard to the reading curriculum that is currently being implemented. Next, evaluate to what extent the reading curriculum encompasses and emphasizes the "big ideas" of reading.

7. You are appointed as a reading consultant to a neighborhood elementary school. The fall semester benchmark scores of the DIBELS assessments reveal that 15 out of 40 first-graders have been identified as being at risk for reading failure. Using Table 4-1 as your guide, develop a plan of action for preventing reading failure considering the three levels of prevention discussed in the chapter.

8. Assume that you are a parent advocate. Further assume that a parent has come to you because she is concerned about her child's progress in second-grade reading. How would you advise this parent to respond to a teacher who stated, "When he's ready to learn to read, he will. Don't worry about it."

9. As a teacher, list different formal, informal, and criterion-referenced reading assessment measures that you have used in your classroom. Describe the skills that you intended to measure using these instruments and protocols. To what extent were these assessments valid and reliable? Would you consider using the DIBELS protocol? Explain your position.

10. Ms. Dixon is a first-grade teacher. The midyear benchmark assessment results indicated that four of her first-graders need intensive intervention and are at risk for reading failure. With only 5 more months before the end of the academic year, she does not know how she can provide individualized attention to these students given that she has 20 other students in the class. What advice do you have for Ms. Dixon as to how she can help her students?

11. Your cousin is the curriculum director in a local elementary school. She is searching for a reading program that promises a "balanced literacy" approach to beginning reading instruction. She believes that explicit phonics instruction impairs children's "enjoyment of reading." Write a dialogue in which you and your cousin discuss her goals and concerns for beginning reading instruction. Your part in the dialogue should include descriptions of critical elements from this chapter and other key citations mentioned in the chapter that focus on the primary area of prevention and how your cousin might implement them in her school.

### CHAPTER 5

# Schoolwide Positive Behavior Supports
## Achieving and Sustaining Effective Learning Environments for All Students

*George Sugai*     *Robert H. Horner*

Schools are told to improve outcomes, be more accountable for their efforts, provide for the educational needs of all students, and create safer learning and teaching environments (e.g., Safe Schools, Reading First, No Child Left Behind, Individuals With Disabilities Education Act). However, meeting these demands is challenging because of shrinking resources and budgets, multiple competing and overlapping initiatives, fewer qualified personnel, and less time. One of the greatest challenges is responding effectively and efficiently to the range of problem behaviors (e.g., defiance/insubordination, disruptions, aggression, harassment, property destruction) that take place in classrooms, in hallways, on playgrounds, on buses, and in cafeterias and that interrupt and disrupt teaching and learning environments. When occurrences of problem behaviors become excessive and intense, the social culture of schools often becomes reactive and oppressive, and the delivery of effective instruction is hindered.

The immediate and seductive solution is to react with "get tough" policies and procedures in which punishment and exclusionary practices are emphasized, especially for individual students. For example, when rates of problem behavior begin to rise, teachers increase their use of verbal reprimands, office discipline referrals, and loss of privileges. When the occurrence of problem behavior becomes widespread, schools increase their adoption of "zero tolerance" policies; surveillance cameras, metal detectors, and security personnel; in-school detention and out-of-school suspension consequences; and referrals to more restrictive alternative programs (Skiba & Peterson, 1999, 2000).

Although this reactive, get-tough approach often is associated with immediate decreases in displays of problem behaviors, research indicates that results are short-term in effect and, more disturbingly, associated with increases in future occurrences of antisocial behavior, devaluation of teacher–student relationships, and decreases in academic success (Barriga et al., 2002; Bowditch, 1993; Hyman & Perone, 1998; Kellam et al., 1998; Mayer, 1995; Walker, Colvin, & Ramsey, 1995).

In addition, an erroneous assumption exists that students who display problem behaviors are inherently bad and will "learn" more appropriate ways of behaving by being punished and carefully monitored. The reality is that students are not born, for example, with words of profanity in their vocabulary and acts of aggressive behavior in their behavioral repertoire, and they do not learn to manage anger and solve conflicts by repeatedly being sent to the office for administrative consequences. Problem behaviors are learned and shaped by social, familial, and school experiences. Like academic skills, appropriate social behaviors and skills must be taught directly and positively reinforced contingently if meaningful improvements in problem behaviors are to be realized.

The literature is clear that a better way of improving the social culture and academic outcomes in schools is to adopt a sustained, positive, preventive, and instructional approach to schoolwide discipline and behavior management (Colvin, Kame'enui, & Sugai, 1993; Dwyer, Osher, & Hoffman, 2000; Horner, Sugai, Todd, & Lewis-Palmer, in press; Mayer, 1995; Mayer & Butterworth, 1979; Metzler, Biglan, Rusby, & Sprague, 2001; Nelson, 1996; Nelson, Martella, & Galand, 1998; Safran & Oswald, 2003; Sulzer-Azaroff & Mayer, 1986, 1994). This approach gives priority to teaching and positively reinforcing prosocial schoolwide behavioral expectations and increasing school capacity to support the sustained use of evidence-based practices. Emphasis is placed on practices and curricula that prevent the development and occurrence of antisocial behavior by neutralizing or eliminating risk factors and enhancing protective factors (Gottfredson, 1997; Gottfredson & Gottfredson, 1996; Gottfredson, Gottfredson, & Hybl, 1993; Grossman et al., 1997; Guerra & Williams, 1996; Hawkins, Catalano, Kosterman, Abbot, & Hill 1999; Loeber, 1990).

Although addressing problem behavior continues to be challenging, attempts to utilize evidence-based technologies are short-term and inconsistent. Thus, the goal has shifted to establishing host environments that support the adoption and sustained use of evidence-based practices (Zins & Ponti, 1990). This goal, however, is easier said than accomplished. Biglan (1995) described the challenge in the following way: "We know a great deal about what can be done, but we have not yet translated our knowledge into widespread changes in the incidence of antisocial behavior or the proportion of children who engage in antisocial behavior" (p. 480). We must (a) increase the availability, adoption, and sustained use of validated practices and (b) use what we know about the science of human behavior to affect school systems and organizations (Biglan, 1995; Carnine, 1997; Gilbert, 1978; Gilbert & Gilbert, 1992; Morrison, Furlong, & Morrison, 1997; Peters & Heron, 1992; Zins & Ponti, 1990). Horner (2001) further reminded us that we must stay close to our behavioral roots when we take a systems or organizational perspective:

1. "Organizations do not 'behave': individuals behave."

2. "An organization is a group of individuals who behave together to achieve a common goal."

3. "Systems are needed to support the collective use of best practices by individuals in an organization."

The purpose of this chapter is to encourage the adoption of practices, policies, and systems that give schools the capacity to establish and sustain positive and effective school climates for all students. Specifically, schoolwide positive behavior support (PBS) is suggested as an approach by which this purpose can be realized (Lewis & Newcomer, 2002; Lewis & Sugai, 1999; Luiselli, Putnam, & Handler, 2001; Safran & Oswald, 2003; Sugai et al., 2000; Sugai & Horner, 2002; Sugai, Horner, & Gresham, 2002; Tolan, Gorman-Smith, & Henry, 2001). Achieving the goal of creating and sustaining safe and productive learning environments (i.e., effective and efficient host environments) for all students is linked to four key messages.

First, *investments must be made in early prevention*. The most effective and efficient way to improve the social climate of schools is to commit to a sustained and focused investment in early prevention. Like the Reading First and Early Reading initiatives, schoolwide PBS is an example of that type of investment.

Second, *behavior support must be made available to all students*. Schools need a continuum of programs and systems to support those children with the most intense problem behaviors. These programs are particularly important early in the development of antisocial behavior patterns because they can change the behavioral trajectory of children. However, they must be effective, efficient, and relevant and, most important, supported by a solid proactive schoolwide system of PBS. This range of support options must include highly efficient systems that link educational, family, and behavioral supports.

Third, faculty must learn to *work smarter, not more*. Policy makers, administrators, educators, and family members must invest in and give high priority to systems and practices that facilitate a "working smarter" approach. This approach gives schools the capacity to (a) do less, but better; (b) invest in the long term; (c) give priority to what works; and (d) focus on clear and measurable outcomes.

Fourth, educators, administrators, and school decision makers must *rely on evidence-based practices*. A science of behavior, prevention, and effective behavioral interventions has existed for over 60 years, yet this knowledge is not overtly considered and applied in many classrooms and schools. Schoolwide PBS offers a process for giving priority to what works.

## WHAT SCHOOL CHALLENGES CALL FOR A SCHOOLWIDE POSITIVE BEHAVIOR SUPPORT APPROACH?

The adoption and sustained use of a schoolwide PBS approach is not a simple matter because many systemic challenges hinder progress. The following challenges must be addressed directly in a schoolwide approach to PBS:

1. Schools are being asked to "do more with less" because of (a) multiple competing and overlapping initiatives; (b) rapidly diminishing fiscal and personnel resources; and (c) increasing number of students who look more different from each other than similar with respect to their behavioral, emotional, social, and learning characteristics.

2. Reactive, intolerant, structural, and exclusionary practices are overused when responding to and managing norm- and rule-violating problem behavior.

3. Processes for problem solving and systems change are inefficient and ineffective.

4. Effective instructional and social change practices are poorly adopted, implemented, and sustained.

5. The capacity to provide specialized behavioral interventions that are individualized, function-based, and sustained for students who display the most challenging problem behaviors is systemically underdeveloped or lacking.

6. Professional development and system change efforts are based on a "train and hope" perspective.

## HOW IS SCHOOLWIDE POSITIVE BEHAVIOR SUPPORT DEFINED?

To address the challenges just listed, schoolwide PBS combines a broad range of systemic and individualized strategies for achieving important social and learning outcomes while preventing problem behavior in all students (Sugai et al., 2000). PBS is an integration of valued social and academic outcomes, a science of human behavior, validated instructional practices, and a systems approach to change (OSEP Center on Positive Behavioral Interventions and Supports, 1999). The goal of PBS is to enhance the capacity of schools to educate all students, especially students with challenging social behaviors, by establishing an effective and full continuum of instructional and behavioral supports.

PBS is not another curriculum or program that is added to what is already occurring in schools. Schools cannot afford to keep adding new initiatives whenever a new problem occurs, or implementing existing efforts with low fidelity or accuracy. Instead PBS schools are asked to consider ways of "working smarter by doing less, but harder" (Kame'enui & Carnine, 2002): (a) "do less, but what you do, do better"; (b) "do it once, but for a long time"; (c) "invest in clear outcomes"; and (d) "invest in a sure thing."

The implementation of PBS involves a balanced consideration of (a) clearly specified academic and social behavior student outcomes, (b) evidence-based practices that maximize student outcomes, (c) systems that support the sustained school use of evidence-based practices, and (d) data that specify school behavior–related outcomes, practices, and systems (see Figure 5-1).

**Figure 5-1.**
Four defining elements of schoolwide positive behavior support.

Social competence &
academic achievement

Outcomes

Supporting
staff behavior

Systems

Data

Supporting
decision
making

Practices

Supporting
student behavior

*Source:* Sugai, G., & Horner, R. H. (2002). The evolution of discipline practices: School-wide positive behavior supports. *Child & Family Behavior Therapy 24*(1/2): Figure 1, p. 30. Article copies available from The Haworth Document Delivery Service: 1-800-HAWORTH. E-mail address: docdelivery@haworthpress.com

From a behavior analytic perspective, schoolwide PBS has six guiding principles. First, *technologies that are more effective, efficient, and relevant than reactive practices must be adapted and selected.* If alternative interventions require more effort, produce less socially important change, and are contextually irrelevant than more intrusive and aversive interventions, we would expect the use of these interventions to continue. Second, *formal opportunities to teach and practice evidence-based technologies must be arranged.* If implementers of a technology do not have the competence and fluency with a new evidence-based practice, we would expect outcomes to be affected and acceptance of the intervention to drop.

Third, *conditions that occasion and maintain undesirable practices must be removed or weakened.* The adoption and continued use of contraindicated or nonsupported interventions is likely to continue as long as the ease with which undesirable practices can be implemented is higher. Fourth, *conditions that occasion and maintain desirable practices must be increased.* The continued and generalized use of an evidence-based practice must be prompted by clear antecedent factors and maintained by an overt and contextually appropriate schedule of positive reinforcement.

Fifth, *aversive stimuli that inhibit the adoption and durable use of desirable practices must be removed or weakened.* If the use of an evidence-based practice is followed by the presentation of an aversive consequence, the occurrence of this practice would be expected to decrease. Sixth, *learning and teaching environments and routines that support a continuum of positive behavior supports must be established and redesigned.* All students should have access to PBS practices and systems; however, the intensity and frequency of use of these practices and systems are affected by the support provided by the environment and by the nature of the environments in which they are expected to be implemented.

## WHAT GUIDING PRINCIPLES CHARACTERIZE THE IMPLEMENTATION OF SCHOOLWIDE POSITIVE BEHAVIOR SUPPORT?

The outcomes, practices, data, and systems of schoolwide PBS are guided by the following principles (Horner et al., in press; Lewis, 2001; Lewis & Sugai, 1999; Sugai & Horner, 2002; Walker et al., 1996):

1. *Promote prevention.* Prevention has three important levels: (a) teaching and encouraging social competence in all students; (b) reducing the number of students who are at risk of learning and displaying problem behaviors; and (c) reducing the intensity, complexity, and frequency of chronic problem behaviors displayed by some students.

2. *Integrate academic and behavioral programming.* The application of evidence-based behavioral practices and systems promotes academic engagement and achievement, and the use of evidence-supported instructional practices and systems promotes displays of prosocial student behavior and creates safe classroom and school settings.

3. *Consider all students.* All students in a school should have access to positive, preventive, structured, and ongoing opportunities to learn, practice, and be acknowledged for displays of prosocial schoolwide and individual social skills.

4. *Use evidence-based practices and systems.* The adoption, implementation, monitoring, and sustained use of evidence-based practices and systems of behavior support must be given highest priority.

5. *Use data.* Information must be used to guide understanding, analysis, intervention, evaluation, and decision making.

6. *Work as a team.* Problem solving, action planning and implementation, and schoolwide leadership must be guided by a team of individuals.

7. *Establish a continuum of support.* As the intensity of behavioral challenges increases, the intensity and specialization of prevention and intervention strategies likewise must become more intensive and specialized (see Figure 5-2).

8. *Focus on outcomes.* Measurable and relevant outcomes must be used to guide the effective and efficient identification, implementation, evaluation and sustainability of behavioral practices and systems.

9. *Emphasize a systems approach.* If the use of effective practices and interventions is to be accurate and durable, teachers, family members, administrators, and other support staff must have access to implementation supports that are ongoing, relevant, and efficient.

## WHAT DOES SCHOOLWIDE POSITIVE BEHAVIOR SUPPORT LOOK LIKE?

Schools that successfully adopt and sustain schoolwide PBS systems and practices have outcomes, appearances, and operations that cause them to be characterized as competent and positive learning and teaching communities. A walk through these schools would reveal the following observations (Horner et al., in press; Safran & Oswald, 2003):

1. More than 80% of students (and adults!) can name the three to five schoolwide positive expectations (e.g., respect, responsibility, cooperation, safety) and give behavioral examples for each.

2. Formalized lessons are in place for directly teaching, regularly practicing, actively supervising, and frequently acknowledging behavioral displays of these schoolwide expectations.

3. Positive adult-to-student interactions exceed negative interactions by a ratio of at least five to one in classroom and nonclassroom settings throughout the school.

**Figure 5-2.**
Continuum of schoolwide positive behavior support.

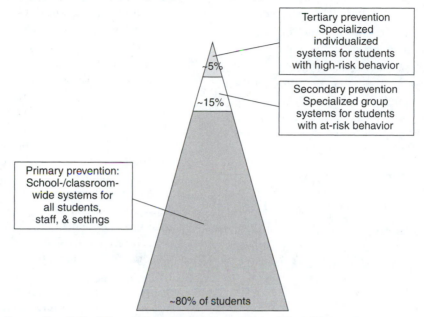

Tertiary prevention
Specialized
individualized
systems for students
with high-risk behavior

~5%

~15%

Secondary prevention
Specialized group
systems for students
with at-risk behavior

Primary prevention:
School-/classroom-
wide systems for
all students,
staff, & settings

~80% of students

*Source:* Sugai, G., & Horner, R. H. (2002). The evolution of discipline practices: School-wide positive behavior supports. *Child & Family Behavior Therapy* 24(1/2): Figure 2, p. 38. Article copies available from The Haworth Document Delivery Service: 1-800-HAWORTH. E-mail address: docdelivery@haworthpress.com

4. Understanding the purpose or function of displays of problem behavior is used as the basis for preventing future occurrences of the problem behavior and teaching and encouraging displays of socially appropriate and desirable behaviors (i.e., functional assessment-based behavior intervention planning).

5. Problem solving, action planning, and intervention implementation are data- and team-based. Information is used to guide decision making, and leadership teams are in place to maximize implementation efforts and outcomes.

6. Administrators are active participants in that they proactively lead teams and school staff, maintain implementation focus and priority, use school data to guide decision making, provide encouragement and constructive feedback, and maintain systems of accountability.

7. A full continuum of behavior support is available to all students and their families. This continuum provides for increasingly specialized interventions and supports as the intensity of problem behavior increases and becomes more complex.

8. Academic programming and schoolwide PBS are integrated, implemented concurrently, and seen as mutually enhancing.

9. School-specific information (e.g., behavior incident rates, types of problem behavior, location of behavior incidents) is used on a monthly and quarterly basis to determine the status of the school climate and inform school improvement action planning.

10. Professional development activities are on-going, targeted, and naturally occurring within the school and classroom context.

11. Families and community members are active participants in school activities.

12. Every student is considered within the context of his or her individual strengths and challenges, and every effort is made to provide an individualized, appropriate, and normative learning and teaching environment.

## WHAT DO SCHOOLS SAY ABOUT SCHOOLWIDE PBS APPROACHES?

When schools adopted a schoolwide positive and preventive approach to behavior support, a variety of outcomes are possible. Following are some examples:

1. In a middle school of 550 students, office discipline referrals were decreased by more than 45% in the first year and have been maintained 5 years later (Taylor-Greene et al., 1997; Taylor-Greene & Kartub, 2000).

2. The rates of observed moderate problem behaviors were decreased by approximately 50% in the hallways of five middle schools (Horner et al., in press).

3. During a 5-year period, over 80% of students in an elementary school of 500 students have received no office disciplinary referrals. In addition, over the same time period, a total of four students have required formal behavioral supports outside the school (Colvin & Fernandez, 2000).

4. On an elementary school playground each day, supervisors "catch" students who are engaging in prosocial behaviors at least 10 times more often than they respond to students who violate rules (D. Forsheim, personal communication, April 15, 2000).

5. In one year an elementary school decreased its office discipline referrals from 600 to 100 and its days of suspension from 80 to 35. These improvements translated into 19 days of time saved by the administrator and 72 student-days of instructional time reclaimed in the classroom (Barrett & Scott, 2001).

6. A school district established a districtwide continuum of positive behavior support in which (a) a common approach to proactive discipline is emphasized in all schools, (b) all schools have school climate leadership teams that meet on a monthly basis, (c) administrators provide active leadership, (d) individual student behavior intervention plans are monitored on a regular basis, and (e) a districtwide behavior support leadership team gives guidance and support to individual schools (Nersesian, Todd, Lehmann, & Watson, 2000; Sadler, 2000).

7. A school district has established a 5-year school improvement plan in which priority and maximum visibility are given to three initiatives: (a) early reading and literacy, (b) positive behavior supports, and (c) family involvement (C. Dickey & C. Cole, personal communication, May 21, 2000).

8. More than 80% of students in a middle school can state the schoolwide expectations (respect yourself, respect others, respect the environment, respect learning) and can give and show at least one behavioral example for each expectation.

9. A special education student who was being considered for an out-of-school placement because of chronic problem behaviors is succeeding in a general education classroom after adjustments were made in his behavior intervention plan. Changes involved increased opportunities for receiving positive feedback about his behavior and arranging supports for staff to ensure accurate and durable implementation of the behavioral interventions (E. R. Fernandez, personal communication, February 11, 2003).

10. Over the past 4 years in an elementary school of 390 students, family attendance at

the annual "Family Fun Night" has steadily grown from 400 to over 900 family participants (E. R. Fernandez, personal communication, March 2, 2003).

11. A school district uses data on outcome and implementation efforts to guide its development of objectives and activities for annual action planning (Nakasato, 2000).

## HOW DO SCHOOLS ESTABLISH EFFECTIVE, EFFICIENT, AND RELEVANT SCHOOLWIDE POSITIVE BEHAVIOR SUPPORT SYSTEMS?

Although the "look" or details of specific schoolwide discipline practices, classroom management strategies, and individual student interventions will vary, the process for achieving effective, efficient, and relevant schoolwide behavior support systems has nine important ingredients (Sugai & Horner, 2002):

1. Secure active leadership and participation of administrator.
2. Establish and maintain a schoolwide leadership team that has status, priority, authority, and resources.
3. Secure commitments and agreements to the effort from a majority of the staff members (e.g., >80%).
4. Conduct regular self-assessments to identify the status of existing practices and processes and to narrow new action plan targets.
5. Invest in practices and processes that give priority to teaching prosocial skills and preventing the development and occurrence of problem behavior.
6. Invest in establishing specialized behavioral support competence within the school.
7. Establish behavior-related information systems that enable timely and easy decision making (data collection, summarization, and display).

8. Monitor the impact and outcomes of existing efforts on a continual basis.
9. Give priority to arranging learning environments so that implementers of schoolwide behavior support practices will be successful and positively reinforced for their efforts and actions.

## WHAT IS NEEDED TO ENHANCE AND SUSTAIN THE SYSTEMIC USE OF SCHOOLWIDE POSITIVE BEHAVIOR SUPPORT?

Establishing and sustaining effective schoolwide PBS practices and supports requires more than "one-shot" training seminars, packaged curricula, and administrative mandates. Vaughn, Klingner, and Hughes (2000) suggested that many factors contribute to the likelihood that a research-based practice will be sustained—for example, who is affected by a failed implementation, who is in control of implementation, the degree of improvement, who is the target of the practice, and the amount of empirical support for a practice. Latham (1988) further warned that many school initiatives are adopted with good intentions but are not maintained for more than 2 to 4 years. This failure to maintain might be attributed to a "train-and-hope" approach (Stokes & Baer, 1977) to school reform and professional development. This ineffective approach involves the following pattern:

1. A problem or need is identified.
2. A practice or curriculum is identified to address the problem.
3. An expert is selected and hired to train the school staff on the use of the practice (usually in a workshop format).
4. The expert leaves after the training is completed.
5. Everyone assumes that the practice will be adopted, implemented with accuracy, and sustained over time and locations.

6. School staff members wait until another problem or need arises.

Given this train-and-hope approach, a behavior analyst would predict an incomplete, inaccurate, and short-lived implementation because staff members (a) are not trained to mastery, (b) do not practice to fluency, (c) do not receive corrective feedback and meaningful positive reinforcement, (d) are not given multiple examples and nonexamples with which to practice, and (e) are not trained in the natural context. In addition, the expertise of the trainer is not developed within the school staff to fill the void when the trainer departs (i.e., extinction occurs).

A more important factor may be a failure to consider carefully the redesign of the environments in which a new practice must be applied. As indicated in Figure 5-1, school change efforts should (a) use data to identify and characterize the problem or need, (b) specify what the measurable outcome (objective) should be, (c) identify an evidence-based practice that has a high probability of achieving the outcome, and (d) establish the systems that would enable staff to implement the practice accurately and durably. The essential elements of an effective in-service training approach, especially in PBS, have been identified (Dunlap et al., 2000). Thus, in contrast to the train-and-hope approach, an enhanced process might be considered:

1. Organize a team to lead the process and develop training and coaching capacity.

2. Review data to identify the need or problem.

3. Analyze, describe, and prioritize the need or problem within the appropriate context.

4. Specify a measurable outcome (objective).

5. Select an evidence-based practice.

6. Select a trainer or process for the adoption and adaptation of the practice.

7. Involve the team in the training of the practice.

8. Provide supports for accurate, sustained adoption and implementation.

9. Monitor practice implementation and progress toward the outcome.

## CONCLUSION

The purpose of this chapter is to encourage the adoption of practices, policies, and systems that give schools the capacity to establish and sustain positive and effective school climates for all students. Specifically, schoolwide PBS is suggested as an approach by which this purpose can be realized. However, much more needs to be done to verify the features of this approach, increase the efficiency with which it is implemented over time, and ensure that it represents the best that behavior analysts can provide. For example, Greenwood, Delquadri, and Bulgren (1993) suggested that behavior analysts must conduct studies that demonstrate the "large-scale, high quality implementation and sustained use of effective educational practices" (p. 401).

To conclude, we suggest that a number of next steps might be considered. First, we must demonstrate how to *take PBS "to scale."* Mechanisms and supports must be dedicated to and given high priority for taking PBS "to scale" at the state, regional, district, and school levels. Second, we must *expect evidence-based practices.* Schools must be given the capacity to identify, adopt, and sustain the use of existing empirically supported and demonstrated PBS practices. Third, we must *support a program of research* that validates, replicates, enhances, and extends the features and processes of schoolwide PBS.

Fourth, we must *demonstrate success at all levels of the continuum of behavior support.* Successful and sustainable demonstrations of schoolwide PBS must be established to show others what is possible and to model what effective implementation looks like. Fifth, we must *integrate instructional and behavioral support practices and systems* and show the benefits of such an integration on achieving meaningful academic and behavioral outcomes. Sixth, we must *engage in meaningful professional development* to increase the capacity of administrators, educators, and student support personnel to build and sustain host environments that are effective, efficient, durable, and relevant for all students. Train-and-hope approaches must be discouraged. Seventh, we must *increase meaningful and functional collaborations* among educators, mental health workers, juvenile justice personnel, family support agents, and so on, to maximize academic and behavioral outcomes for all students. Finally, we must *support, educate, and protect all students*. Policy makers must maintain protections for all students that maximize and guarantee access to schoolwide PBS practices, procedures, and systems.

## REFERENCES

Barrett, S., & Scott, T. (2001). *The costs of office discipline referrals and suspensions.* Unpublished manuscript. Eugene, OR.

Barriga, A., Doran, J., Newell, S., Morrison, E., Barbetti, V., & Robbins, B. (2002). Relationships between problem behaviors and academic achievement in adolescents: The unique role of attention problems. *Journal of Emotional and Behavioral Disorders, 10,* 233–240.

Biglan, A. (1995). Translating what we know about the context of antisocial behavior into a lower prevalence of such behavior. *Journal of Applied Behavior Analysis, 28,* 479–492.

Bowditch, C. (1993). Getting rid of troublemakers: High school disciplinary procedures and the production of dropouts. *Social Problems, 40,* 493–507.

Carnine, D. (1997). Bridging the research-to-practice gap. *Exceptional Children, 63,* 513–521.

Colvin, G., & Fernandez, E. (2000). Sustaining effective behavior support systems in an elementary school. *Journal of Positive Behavior Interventions, 2,* 251–253.

Colvin, G., Kame'enui, E. J., & Sugai, G. (1993). Schoolwide and classroom management: Reconceptualiz-

ing the integration and management of students with behavior problems in general education. *Education and Treatment of Children, 16,* 361–381.

Dunlap, G., Hieneman, M., Knoster, T., Fox, L., Anderson, J., & Albin, R. W. (2000). Essential elements of inservice training in positive behavior support. *Journal of Positive Behavior Interventions, 2,* 22–32.

Dwyer, K. P., Osher, D., & Hoffman, C. C. (2000). Creating responsive schools: Contextualizing early warning, timely response. *Exceptional Children, 66,* 347–365.

Gilbert, T. F. (1978). *Human competence: Engineering worthy performance.* New York: McGraw.

Gilbert, T. F., & Gilbert, M. B. (1992). Potential contributions of performance science to education. *Journal of Applied Behavior Analysis, 25,* 43–49.

Gottfredson, D. C. (1997). School-based crime prevention. In L. Sherman, D. Gottfredson, D. Mackenzie, D. Eck, P. Reuter, & S. Bushway (Eds.), *Preventing crime: What works, what doesn't, what's promising.* College Park, MD: Department of Criminology and Criminal Justice.

Gottfredson, G. D., & Gottfredson, D. C. (1996). *A national study of delinquency prevention in schools: Rationale for a study to describe the extensiveness and implementation of programs to prevent adolescent problem behavior in schools.* Ellicott City, MD: Gottfredson Associates.

Gottfredson, D. C., Gottfredson, G. D., and Hybl, L. G. (1993). Managing adolescent behavior: A multiyear, multischool study. *American Educational Research Journal, 30,* 179–215.

Greenwood, C. R., Delquadri, J., & Bulgren, J. (1993). Current challenges to behavioral technology in the reform of schooling: Large-scale, high-quality implementation and sustained use of effective educational practices. *Education and Treatment of Children, 16* (4), 401–404.

Grossman, D. C., Neckerman, H. J., Koespsell, T. D., Liu, P., Asher, K. N., Beland, L., Frey, K., & Rivara, F. P. (1997). Effectiveness of a violence prevention curriculum among children in elementary school: A randomized controlled trial. *Journal of the American Medical Association, 277,* 1605–1612.

Guerra, N. G., & Wiliams, K. R. (1996). *A program planning guide for youth violence prevention: A risk-focused approach.* Boulder, CO: Center for the Study and Prevention of Violence, University of Colorado.

Hawkins, J. D., Catalano, R. F., Kosterman, R., Abbott, R., & Hill, K. G. (1999). Preventing adolescent health-risk behaviors by strengthening protection during childhood. *Archives of Pediatrics & Adolescent Medicine, 153,* 226–234.

Horner, R. H. (2001). School-wide positive behavior support. Presentation at 2001 Annual Convention of the Council for Exceptional Children. Kansas City, MO.

Horner, R. H., Sugai, G., Todd, A. W., & Lewis-Palmer, T. (in press). School-wide positive behavior support: An alternative approach to discipline in schools. In L. Bambara & L. Kern (Eds.), *Positive behavior support.* New York: Guilford Press.

Hyman, I. A., & Perone, D. C. (1998). The other side of school violence: Educator policies and practices that may contribute to student misbehavior. *Journal of School Psychology, 36,* 7–27.

Kame'enui, E. J., & Carnine, D. W. (2002). *Effective teaching strategies that accommodate diverse learners* (2nd ed.). Upper Saddle River, NJ: Merrill.

Kellam, S. G., Mayer, L. S., Rebok, G. W., & Hawkins, W. E. (1998). The effects of improving achievement on aggressive behavior and of improving aggressive behavior on achievement through two prevention interventions: An investigation of causal paths. In B. Dohrenwend (Ed.), *Adversity, stress, and psychopathology* (pp. 486–505). Oxford: Oxford University Press.

Latham, G. (1988). The birth and death cycles of educational innovations. *Principal, 68* (1), 41–43.

Lewis, T. J. (2001). Building infrastructure to enhance schoolwide systems of positive behavioral support: Essential features of technical assistance. *Beyond Behavior, 11* (1), 10–12.

Lewis, T. J., & Newcomer, L. L. (2002). Examining the efficacy of school-based consultation: Recommendations for improving outcomes. *Child and Family Behavior Therapy, 24,* 165–181.

Lewis, T. J., & Sugai, G. (1999). Effective behavior support: A systems approach to proactive schoolwide management. *Focus on Exceptional Children, 31* (6), 1–24.

Loeber, R. (1990). Development and risk factors of juvenile antisocial behavior and delinquency. *Clinical Psychology Review, 10,* 1–41.

Luiselli, J. K., Putnam, R. F., & Handler, M. W. (2001). Improving discipline practices in public schools: Description of a whole-school and district-wide model of behavior analysis consultation. *The Behavior Analyst Today, 2* (1), 18–26.

Mayer, G. (1995). Preventing antisocial behavior in the schools. *Journal of Applied Behavior Analysis, 28,* 467–478.

Mayer, G. R., & Butterworth, T. (1979). A preventive approach to school violence and vandalism: An experimental study. *Personnel and Guidance Journal, 57,* 436–441.

Mayer, M. J., & Leone, P. E. (1999). A structural analysis of school violence and disruption: Implications for creating safer schools. *Education and Treatment of Children, 22,* 333–358.

Metzler, C. W., Biglan, A., Rusby, J. C., & Sprague, J. R. (2001). Evaluation of a comprehensive behavior management program to improve school-wide positive behavior support. *Education and Treatment of Children, 24,* 448–479.

Morrison, G. M., Furlong, M. J., & Morrison, R. L. (1997). The safe school: Moving beyond crime prevention to school empowerment. In A. Goldstein & J. Cooley (Eds.), *The handbook of violence prevention.* New York: Guilford.

Nakasato, J. (2000). Data-based decision making in Hawaii's behavior support effort. *Journal of Positive Behavior Interventions, 2,* 247–251.

Nelson, J. R. (1996). Designing schools to meet the needs of students who exhibit disruptive behavior. *Journal of Emotional and Behavioral Disorders, 4,* 147–161.

Nelson, J. R., Martella, R., & Galand, B. (1998). The effects of teaching school expectations and establishing a consistent consequence on formal office disciplinary actions. *Journal of Emotional and Behavioral Disorders, 6,* 153–161.

Nersesian, M., Todd, A., Lehmann, J., & Watson, J. (2000). School-wide behavior support through district-level system change. *Journal of Positive Behavior Interventions, 2* (4), 244–247.

OSEP Center on Positive Behavioral Interventions and Supports (1999). *Applying positive behavioral support and functional behavioral assessment in schools.* Eugene, OR: University of Oregon.

Peters, M. T., & Heron, T. E. (1992). When the best is not good enough: An examination of best practice. *Journal of Special Education, 26,* 371–385.

Sadler, C. (2000). Effective behavior support implementation at the district level: Tigard-Tualatin school district. *Journal of Positive Behavior Interventions, 2* (4), 241–243.

Safran, S. P., & Oswald, K. (2003). Positive behavior supports: Can schools reshape disciplinary practices? *Exceptional Children, 69,* 361–373.

Skiba, R. J., & Peterson, R. L. (1999). The dark side of zero tolerance: Can punishment lead to safe schools? *Phi Delta Kappan, 80,* 372–382.

Skiba, R. J., & Peterson, R. L. (2000). School discipline at a crossroads: From zero tolerance to early response. *Exceptional Children, 66,* 335–347.

Stokes, T. F., & Baer, D. M. (1977). An implicit technology of generalization. *Journal of Applied Behavior Analysis 10* (2), 349–367.

Sugai, G., & Horner, R. H. (2002). The evolution of discipline practices: School-wide positive behavior supports. *Child and Family Behavior Therapy, 24,* 23–50.

Sugai, G., Horner, R. H., Dunlap, G. Hieneman, M., Lewis, T. J., Nelson, C. M., Scott, T., Liaupsin, C., Sailor, W., Turnbull, A. P., Turnbull, H. R., III, Wickham, D., Reuf, M., & Wilcox, B. (2000). Applying positive behavioral support and functional behavioral assessment in schools. *Journal of Positive Behavioral Interventions, 2,* 131–143.

Sugai, G., Horner, R. H., & Gresham, F. (2002). Behaviorally effective school environments. In M. R. Shinn, G. Stoner, & H. M. Walker (Eds.), *Interventions for academic and behavior problems: Preventive and remedial approaches* (pp. 315–350). Silver Spring, MD: National Association of School Psychologists.

Sulzer-Azaroff, B., & Mayer, G. R. (1986). *Achieving educational excellence: Using behavioral strategies.* New York: Holt, Rinehart & Winston.

Sulzer-Azaroff, B., & Mayer, G. R. (1994). *Achieving educational excellence: Behavior analysis for achieving classroom and schoolwide behavior change.* San Marcos, CA: Western Image.

Taylor-Greene, S., Brown, D., Nelson, L., Longton, J., Gassman, T., Cohen, J., Swartz, J., Horner, R. H., Sugai, G., & Hall, S. (1997). School-wide behavioral support: Starting the year off right. *Journal of Behavioral Education, 7,* 99–112.

Taylor-Greene, S. J., & Kartub, D. T. (2000). Durable implementation of school-wide behavior support: The high five program. *Journal of Positive Behavior Interventions, 2,* 233–245.

Tolan, P., Gorman-Smith, D., & Henry, D. (2001). New study to focus on efficacy of "whole school" prevention approaches. *Emotional and Behavioral Disorders in Youth, 2* (1), 5–7.

Vaughn, S., Klingner, J., & Hughes, M. (2000). Sustainability of research-based practices. *Exceptional Children, 66,* 163–171.

Walker, H., Colvin, G., & Ramsey, E. (1995). *Antisocial behavior in public school: Strategies and best practices.* Pacific Grove, CA: Brookes/Cole.

Walker, H., Horner, R. H., Sugai, G., Bullis, M., Sprague, J., Bricker, D., & Kaufman, M. J. (1996). Integrated approaches to preventing antisocial behavior patterns among school-age children and youth. *Journal of Emotional and Behavioral Disorders, 4,* 194–209.

Zins, J. E., & Ponti, C. R. (1990). Best practices in school-based consultation. In A. Thomas and J. Grimes (Eds.), *Best practices in school psychology—II* (pp. 673–694). Washington, DC: National Association of School Psychologists.

## STUDY QUESTIONS AND FOLLOW-UP ACTIVITIES

1. Why might future increases in antisocial behavior be associated with using a reactive, or "get-tough," approach to discipline?

2. Describe each of the four keys to creating and sustaining productive learning environments.

3. Describe the potential problems with continually adopting new and underresearched disciplinary practices schoolwide.

4. Name three specific procedures that can enable timely and easy decision making in terms of behavior-related information systems.

5. Consider that the school leadership team has determined that social skills training needs to be implemented in the classrooms. Discuss and contrast how this identified need would be addressed through a "train-and-hope" procedure compared to an "enhanced process" approach.

6. Name and describe three ways that educators and administrators could "work smarter." What would be the first steps to implement these procedures in the classroom or school district?

7. The authors discuss a train-and-hope method of professional development. Have you experi-

Study questions and follow-up activities prepared by Amanda L. Yurick and Natalie J. Allen.

enced this type of in-service training? What was your frustration level following this training? What are some ways that you could influence more meaningful training in your school?

8. Name two ways you could increase your level of implementation of behavioral support across all three areas (primary, secondary, and tertiary) of support. What steps would you need to take to implement each of them?

9. What do the authors mean when they say we need to "take PBS to scale"? How could you do this at your level?

10. What are some of the problems associated with get-tough or zero tolerance policies? How can you avoid these pitfalls in your classroom or building?

11. What prompted the development of the zero tolerance policy? What is the current debate in the literature regarding this policy?

12. The authors mention that one of the key messages is that educators, administrators, and school decision makers must rely on evidence-based practices. If you are a teacher, what cur-

rent curriculum are you using in your classroom? Does this curriculum meet the standard for being an evidence-based practice? If not, what steps can you take to implement a program that would meet those guidelines?

13. What do the authors mean by the statement that "PBS is not another curriculum or program that is added to what is already occurring in schools"?

14. One of the guiding principles of PBS is that "conditions that occasion and maintain undesirable practices must be removed or weakened." After identifying a practice that is undesirable or does not meet the criteria for being evidence-based, what can you do to weaken the contingencies that are maintaining this particular practice?

15. Using a behavior analytic perspective, how might school administrators motivate and engage their school staff to embrace and implement PBS? How would the motivation be sustained? How would effectiveness be measured and evaluated? What steps could be taken if desired results were not achieved?

### CHAPTER 6

# Individual Growth and Development Indicators
## Tools for Assessing Intervention Results for Infants and Toddlers

*Charles R. Greenwood*       *Judith J. Carta*       *Dale Walker*

Appropriate, sensitive tools for planning and measuring early intervention results are imperative in today's early childhood policy context and its heightened expectations for accountability (e.g., young children's "readiness for school"; National Educational Goals Panel, 1999). Federal and state mandates for young children including those at sociodemographic risk (i.e., Early Head Start) and with developmental delays and disabilities (i.e., IDEA, Parts B and C) require accountability for results.

Early childhood educators and early interventionists need tools specifically designed and validated to carry out three critical missions central to early intervention results (Meisels, 1996; Preator & McAllister, 1995). First, we must identify children who may need early intervention (Carta, Schwartz, Atwater, & McConnell, 1991). There is currently a sense that too many children are identified late and thus fail to receive maximal benefit from early intervention services. Second, we need to monitor an individual child's growth and developmental progress over time (McConnell, 2000). This information is cen-tral to guiding and altering intervention decisions. Information is needed describing the specific conditions of early intervention under which an individual child is making progress and those under which the child is not making progress. Third, it is imperative to evaluate the effectiveness of early intervention programs and services provided to individuals and groups of children (Carta & Greenwood, 1997; Meisels, 1996).

For young children with developmental delays, the critical characteristics and recommended practices of assessment were described in the Council for Exceptional Children, Division of Early Childhood's report, *Recommended Practices: Indicators of Quality in Programs for Infants and Young Children With Special Needs and Their Families.* Recommended assessment practices cited in this report were those that (a) point to behavioral objectives for change that are judged important and acceptable, (b) guide change in treatment activities, (c) incorporate several instruments and scales including observation and interviews, (d) incorporate input from parents, and (e) can be used on multiple occasions (Neisworth, 1993, 2000).

Unfortunately, early childhood educators and early interventionists lack sufficient, appropriate tools for informing practice because most existing measures lack these and other salient features of concept, technical adequacy, and practicality (Bagnato & Neisworth, 1991). Many current measures are based on conceptual frameworks that do not account for the role of the environmental context in general and early intervention in particular. Consequently, a murky relationship often exists between measurement results and the actions to be taken by early childhood educators in providing programs and services (Greenwood, Luze, Cline, Kuntz, & Leitschuh, 2002). For example, many measures of children's motor abilities are based on conceptual frameworks that posit growth in the neuromuscular or the central nervous system (Burton & Miller, 1998) to the exclusion of the environment and early experience, which are the factors under the control of the early interventionist. Thus, the utility of this information in guiding design and changing early intervention is low. And, because the evidence supporting growth in many of these central nervous system abilities is weak (Burton & Miller, 1998), the utility of this information is of little value to early interventionists.

Too many existing measures require highly trained professionals with specialized expertise to administer and interpret them (e.g., occupational or physical therapists); they are not intended for use by early interventionists. The majority of existing measures require more time to administer than is typically available to early interventionists, and once administered, these measures may not be readministered frequently enough to assess short-term progress (e.g., sooner than 6 months) without violating standardization procedures. Consequently, these measures do not generate timely information that early interventionists can act on by manipulating the factors that they have most control over, for example, child- and home-care routines.

The vast majority of measures are not explicitly designed to be sensitive to the rate of growth and development over time. Normative-based and criterion-based measures address growth in terms of the discrepancy between a child's performance and the norm for children of this age (e.g., mental, developmental, or skill domain age scores). For example, results from such measures may reveal that a child has a mental or developmental age score of 23 months of age (compared to norms) when the child's chronological age is 25 months. In this case, the child's development is 2 months behind the normative group at this age. These scores may also be extended to reflect a child's status in skill domains (e.g., cognitive, motor, social/emotional, etc.). With this knowledge, the early interventionist knows that the child is behind expectation. However, the child's scores provide little information to inform intervention decision making or to gauge how long and under what circumstances this child will need to catch up to the developmental norm.

Too few traditional measures are designed and tested for treatment validity—the demonstration that the measure is sensitive to early intervention effects (Greenwood, Dunn, Ward, & Luze, 2003; Greenwood, Luze, & Carta, 2002). In the absence of this information for individuals and groups of young children, it is unclear whether the measure will show improved results as a function of intervention.

Another issue is that very few traditional measures are designed to be readily understood by early interventionists and parents. Many existing measures actually make communications with caregivers difficult and confusing rather than understandable and helpful because of their complicated conceptual frameworks, technical complexity, or both. Measures are needed that improve communication and support the strategic participation of caregivers and parents in the delivery of early intervention.

The lack of measures expressly designed for use by early interventionists is certainly true for children 5 years of age and younger, *but even more so for children 3 and younger* (Kagan,

Moore, & Bredekamp, 1995; Kagan, Rosenkoetter, & Cohen, 1997). Relatively little attention has yet been paid to identifying the developmental domains of very young children as compared to the academic/curricular domains of older children on which to base accountability systems (Priest et al., 2001). A particularly important illustration is recent efforts to discover the precursors of *school readiness* in increasingly younger children, preschoolers, toddlers, and infants.

The failure to be ready for school is defined as an impairment of ability that severely restricts competence, adaptive function, and quality of life (Whitehurst & Lonigan, 2001). The most important and essential ingredient of school readiness is readiness to learn to read. Because reading competence is a keystone for future success, failure to learn to read is an educational and a public health problem.

The prevalence of significant reading disability is estimated at 17% to 20% of children (one in five), and more than 33% of children (one in three) experience difficulties learning to read (Whitehurst & Lonigan, 2001). The proportion of children entering school who are not ready is unknown; however, the children at highest risk are poor children, minority children, non-native speakers of English, and children whose parents do not read.

Empirical knowledge currently identifies the precursors of reading with key skill elements in (a) early oral language, (b) emerging literacy, (c) self-regulation of behavior, and (d) social competency. Thus, the ability to promote school readiness and ameliorate problems before school entry through early intervention in the preschool and in the home rests squarely on the availability and use of sensitive, technically adequate, and practical measures of results that can guide interventions and programs.

## PURPOSE

The purpose of this chapter is to describe a line of work seeking to develop and validate measurement tools specifically designed and validated for use by early interventionists serving children from *birth to 3 years of age*. This effort was part of a larger coordinated effort to develop measurement tools for children birth through age 8 (Early Childhood Research Institute on Measuring Growth and Development, 1998b; McConnell et al., 1996). We discuss the approach, progress to date, and ongoing work with what we call *individual growth and development indicators (IGDIs)* for infants and toddlers.

## THE RESEARCH AND DEVELOPMENT APPROACH: GENERAL OUTCOME MEASUREMENT

Excellent models for the kind of tools sought in this work are evident in existing measures designed specifically for progress monitoring and measurement of intervention results: (a) growth charts used by pediatricians in well-child visits, (b) the "celeration" charts used by behavior analysts to monitor behavior change progress, (c) growth charts used by early interventionists to monitor progress acquiring early literacy skills, and (d) fluency charts used by elementary educators to monitor progress in learning basic academic skills. Each of these existing applications uniquely overcomes the problems of concept, technical adequacy, and practicality that plague many of the existing measures previously discussed. For example, the conceptual frameworks underpinning these approaches embrace the fact that intervention and environmental contexts are expected to influence measurement outcomes. For the pediatrician, the intervention may be parents implementing a prescribed nutritional regimen plus medication. For the behavior analyst, the intervention may be parents implementing a home-based program of prompting and reinforcing a child's movements to strengthen locomotion skills. For the preschool or kindergarten teacher, the intervention may be implementing phonemic awareness training to improve children's ability to segment words by their sounds. For the elementary reading teacher, the intervention may be implementing a peer tutoring reading program. In each of these cases, interventions play a critical role by supplying a treatment process whose results are expected to accelerate the rate of progress toward a socially desired outcome—a thriving infant of normal physical weight (for the pediatrician); a standing and walking toddler (for the behavior analyst); a kindergartener skilled in manipulating the sound structures in spoken language (for the kindergarten teacher); and a fluent, comprehending reader (for the elementary educator). In addition to being designed to be administered by interventionists, these measures are explicitly designed to guide intervention decision making and intervention problem solving by indicating a lack of progress and thus the need to change an intervention that is no longer effective (Deno, 2002). These measures also indicate when a child is making expected progress (in which case no change is needed).

## CASE EXAMPLE FOR INFANTS AND TODDLERS

A case example is illustrative. Alyrique, a 24-month-old female, is one of 32 young children in the Headlands Early Head Start program. As do all of the children in this program, she receives an IGDI, the early communication indicator. The early communication indicator involved Alyrique and her home visitor playing with a toy house for 6 minutes while a staff member recorded the frequency of occurrence of her gestures, vocalizations, single words, and multiple word utterances (the key skill elements) identified in prior research as important indicators of a child's expressive communication (Carta et al., 2002; Greenwood, Luze, Cline, et al., 2002).

Growth in her early communication was assessed every quarter coordinated with her birthday. The information was used to monitor program results and to determine whether her growth in acquiring early communication profi-

ciency was delayed and in need of early intervention. The early communication indicator was graphed in a standard chart to allow comparison of Alyrique's proficiency to normative proficiency, just like the pediatrician's height and weight chart. This information on individual progress was aggregated to reflect the mean progress of all children in the program and thus the effectiveness of the entire EHS program.

The general strategy for using this assessment information to improve intervention results for all children is shown in Figure 6-1. Its major steps are to (a) monitor progress over time, (b) identify and validate lack of progress, (c) explore potential solutions and implement one as an intervention, (d) evaluate whether the intervention is working, and (e) evaluate whether the problem has been solved. Additional assessment and information gathering may be needed to identify specific details of what a child can and cannot yet do and thus needs to learn, and to identify the suitable intervention agents, settings, and procedures to be used. Potential solutions may also seek to rule out medical problems such as hearing or vision problems, involve parents in delivering an intervention, and eliminate failure to implement the solution to a level of fidelity (Greenwood, Luze, & Carta, 2002). An intervention is then implemented and progress is monitored to determine whether performance is accelerated as a consequence.

Alyrique's home visitor reported that her Early Communication chart showed a delay for her age compared to the norms (Luze et al., 2001). This was a concern because communication is a general outcome of early childhood and plays a critical role in cognitive and social development. Alyrique primarily used gestures and vocalizations to communicate with her parents and the home visitor in the assessments. She used only a few words regularly and, according to Mom, had not yet put words together in sentences. The home visitor confirmed these patterns of communication at home with Alyrique's mother.

**Figure 6-1.**
Growth charts inform intervention decision making.

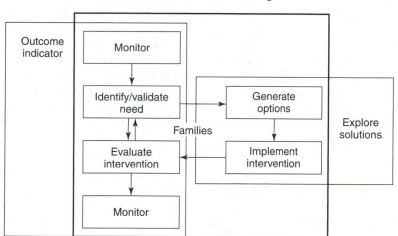

In the first assessment, Alyrique produced only 5 communicative behaviors per minute, and all were prelinguistic gestures and utterances. Because the growth chart contained a benchmark mean level of 13 communication behaviors per minute (the average for similarly aged children), it was clear that Alyrique's skills were below age expectancy.

The home visitor decided to implement strategies based on Incidental Teaching and Responsive Interaction (Hart & Risley, 1978, 1995). She did so by explaining, modeling, and teaching Mom to carry out these procedures. Mom was shown how and learned to follow Alyrique's lead during interactions, ask more open-ended questions, expand on her utterances, and use a delay to encourage Alyrique to fill in missing words; for example, when singing a familiar song, she would pause and let Alyrique complete the phrase. The intervention was implemented during eating and snack times and other daily care routines and evaluated again 3 weeks later, and then every month, using the early communication indicator.

These results showed that Alyrique had made progress toward the goal of 13 communications per minute; in fact, she had nearly matched the goal and was now using many more words.

Mom reported that she felt comfortable continuing the intervention and could see noticeable improvement in her communications at home in addition to the increases shown in Alyrique's chart. The home visitor and Mom planned to continue the intervention for an additional 6 weeks and with additional monthly progress-monitoring assessments. These assessments, when graphed, continued to show improvement. At this point, the additional strategies were introduced to support the use of multi-word utterances, and the frequency of assessment dropped from monthly to quarterly.

In contrast, Sierra, also a 24-month-old female, who attends the Unlimited Futures Early Head Start program in her community, receives an annual test of early receptive and expressive communication, the Preschool Language Scale for children 0–5 years (Zimmerman, Steiner, & Pond, 1992). The home visitor was not qualified to administer this test, which is composed of a parent interview and direct child observation, so it was scheduled to be given by the program's contracted psychologist. After administration and scoring was completed, the psychologist explained the findings to the home visitor, who in turn discussed the results with Mom. Like Alyrique, Sierra's communication appeared delayed for her age compared to the test norms. Sierra primarily used gestures and vocalizations to communicate and was not using words regularly. Based on these results, the home visitor decided to teach the mom to use a language tool kit, a set of evidenced-based strategies for supporting a child's early communication skills adopted by the Early Head Start program. This was completed over the next two home visits and a follow-up visit 2 months later. A year later, the Preschool Language Scale was readministered. Unfortunately, although Sierra had made some progress according to her mother, her scores still reflected a delay compared to the test norms.

As this example illustrates, frequent progress monitoring provides a formative, rather than summative, evaluation of the growth in a young child's proficiency. *Formative* refers to collecting information while learning is occurring, whereas *summative* refers to collecting progress information at a later set point in time (e.g., once per year). The advantage of a formative approach is that early interventionists can use the information to change their programming and children's early experiences to help speed progress. Summative approaches fail to provide this kind of support.

## CENTRAL FEATURES OF GENERAL OUTCOME MEASUREMENT

An approach to progress monitoring using growth charting is general outcome measurement (GOM). It is an increasingly well understood framework for developing and validating measures designed for use by interventionists interested in measuring intervention results (Deno, 1997). In discussing the approach, it is helpful from the outset to differentiate among the general outcome, the outcome indicator, and the general outcome measure or protocol.

The *general outcome* is a socially validated statement of the general ability or goal of interest. For example, outcome statements such as "Child solves problems that require reasoning about objects, concepts, situations, and people" or "Child moves in a fluid and coordinated manner to play and participate in home, school, and community settings" reflect desired cognitive and movement competencies that are relevant for children and youth across a wide age range (Priest et al., 2001). A distinguishing feature of a general outcome statement is that it is broadly relevant to individual competence. A second feature is that it is socially valid; that is, a group has evaluated it and concluded that it is important and desired. Social validity underpins the relevance and value of the general outcome of interest (Wolf, 1978). Linking measurement to socially valid outcomes is critically important to gaining broad acceptability of an individual or group accountability system. Socially valid outcomes are different from instructional or developmental goals and objectives desired by parents, early interventionists, the curriculum, or others. A third feature of a general outcome statement is that it is not a measure or a score in and of itself; rather it is a general statement of competence.

The *outcome indicator* is comprised of one or more *key skill elements* selected to measure progress toward proficiency in attaining the general outcome. For example, the key skill elements we selected after systematic research for use as an indicator of infants' and toddlers' proficiency in movement were change in position, horizontal and vertical locomotion, roll/trap, and throw/catch. The growth rate of these combined skills per minute during a standard play situation serves as a single individual growth and development indicator (IGDI) for movement (Greenwood, Luze, Cline et al., 2002). Like other leading indicators (e.g., growth in weight or oral reading fluency over time) of other general outcomes (e.g., healthy physical growth, growth in literacy), an outcome indicator is designed to reflect increasing proficiency. However, indicators are not designed to be comprehensive with respect to all skills to be learned, as discussed next.

*General outcome measures* are typically short probes designed to quickly gauge skill fluency in terms of rate of response per minute. The general outcome measure for infants and toddlers is the actual protocol of procedures used to make a 6- to 10-minute assessment of a situation in which a familiar caregiver plays with a young child using a nondirective style of interaction and a standard set of toys. An observer records the frequency of occurrence of each key skill guided by specific behavioral definitions using a standard recording form.

## ADDITIONAL FEATURES OF GENERAL OUTCOME MEASUREMENT
### Selection of Key Skill Elements

In general outcome measurement, the indicator of progress toward the general outcome is selected to be representative of the skill set of an age range or grade level but not to be exhaustive. For example, the skills measured on a second-grade math general outcome measurement will be drawn from the second-grade math curriculum in order to represent proficiency at this age or grade level. Items drawn from the entire year's skill set are placed on 1-minute probes and administered repeatedly (weekly). Thus, each probe samples the entire year's expectation using alternate, equivalent forms. Alternate, equivalent forms of the measure are used to eliminate the effects of memory, practice, and patterned responding unrelated to skill learning. Because the same key skills are tested each time in this example (i.e., the year's skill set), growth is a reflection of the child's increasing proficiency or fluency. Similarly for children birth to 3 or 3 to 5 years, key skills to be measured as an indicator are drawn from those known to represent the general outcome domain of interest (e.g., communication, movement, etc.) expected of typically developing children within the age range of interest.

Therefore, the developmental continuity in progress toward a general outcome for young children is demonstrated by evaluating new key skill elements at a few important age ranges. The general outcome remains the same at all ages, but the indicators change to reflect greater proficiency. Take, for example, the following general outcome: "The child uses gestures, sounds, words, or sentences to convey wants and needs or to express meaning to others."

- For children ages 0 to 3, the key skills measured as indicators are gesture, vocalization, and single-word and multiple-word fluency, which reflect the fact that children are making the transition from prelinguistic to spoken communication as infants and toddlers.

- For children ages 3 to 5, a key skill is rapid picture naming fluency, a skill that reflects the fact that preschoolers are advancing in spoken vocabulary knowledge.

- For children ages 5 to 8, word use and word description fluencies are key skills reflective of these children's even greater sophistication in spoken vocabulary and ability to communicate the meaning of words.

Within each of these age ranges, rate of growth remains the indicator of progress; across age ranges, changes in the key skills actually measured take into account age-appropriate expectations for performance relative to the general outcome. Desirable across the entire developmental continuity (e.g., birth to 8 years old) are predictive links among adjacent indicators measured at the same points in time. Such evidence confirms that they are measuring the general outcome (Good, Gruba, & Kaminski, 2002; Good, Simmons, & Kame'enui, 2001).

### Growth Versus Mastery

Another distinguishing feature of general outcome measurement is the idea of *partial attainment* in the acquisition and display of proficiency indexed by rate of growth. Partial attainment is evident in behavioral assessment wherein individual progress is indexed by growth in frequency, rate, or fluency. The success of intervention is considered to be progress toward a desired outcome. Conventional forms of measurement in early childhood are most often either *full attainment/mastery* or *terminal skill* measurement (Priest et al., 2001).

*Full attainment* is defined as achieving high-level performance (90% accuracy) on one or more skill domains. For example, most criterion-referenced assessment approaches embrace the concept of mastery of a skill set or domain of content knowledge. Intervention success is defined by the child achieving close to 100% accuracy. Many behavioral assessment approaches embrace the concept of *terminal skill attainment,* which is linked to performing a skill that represents the end-point goal within a hierarchy of subskills.

Although full attainment and terminal skill attainment are clearly important and sound approaches to measuring intervention results, the logic supporting these approaches is that important skills are taught and learned one at a time.

A problem arises when we don't know all these skills or the order for teaching them. In that case measurement of these skills must await their identification and articulation in task analyses and research.

When applied to the growth and development of young children, the *partial attainment* idea reflects progress toward a socially desired general outcome, rather than acquisition of any one end-point skill or mastery of a large skill class. (For a comprehensive discussion of these differences between general outcome and other approaches, see Fuchs & Deno, 1991.)

In summary, the advantages of the general outcome measurement approach over other traditional assessment approaches for young children are its conceptual, technical adequacy and practical features designed specially for use by early interventionists in their work with children and families. This approach represents advances in that it (a) combines social validity information with evidence of sensitivity and criterion validity and (b) focuses on standardized, replicable procedures that enable development of a common database for use in building norms and thus norm-based identification decisions for children needing interventions, as well as intervention decision making and problem solving designed to improve intervention results. Collectively, these features give GOMs the assets needed for large-scale use in individual- and program-level accountability systems. We now turn to a discussion of a line of research and development designed to produce GOMs for infants and toddlers (Early Childhood Research Institute on Measuring Growth and Development, 1998b, 1998c).

## INDIVIDUAL INDICATORS OF GROWTH AND DEVELOPMENT FOR INFANTS AND TODDLERS

Developing and validating IGDIs for infants and toddlers required multistudy and multiyear sets of activities designed to create and validate general outcomes and their indicators; test and improve the indicators; and ensure that they addressed the desired criteria of concept, practicality, sensitivity, and technical adequacy.

## PRINCIPLES GUIDING DEVELOPMENT

Guiding the development of these measures for infants and toddlers were the following principles initially used by Deno, Mirkin, and Chaing (1982):

1. Measures should assess key skill elements representative of an important general outcome.

2. Measures should identify child behaviors in natural settings. Behaviors characteristic of natural settings are particularly important for infants and toddlers because they are less able and willing to perform specific skills on demand than older children are. When asked to interact with unfamiliar people in unfamiliar situations, young children are even less likely to engage in desired

behaviors. However, when young children are given an opportunity to engage in typical behaviors in familiar environments, a much more accurate representation of skills can be obtained (e.g, Neisworth, 1993).

3. Measures should be standardized and replicable to ensure that the data from separate administrations are comparable.

4. Measures must be sensitive to growth over a short period of time so they can be used to evaluate intervention effectiveness.

5. Measures must meet the requirements of technical adequacy, including interobserver agreement, and reliability of alternate forms to provide accurate information that can be interpreted and used for decision making.

6. Measures should be efficient and economical so that early interventionists can gather repeated measurements that are usable for decision making without adding to their workload.

7. Measures should be sensitive to intervention and intervention effects.

Directed by these principles, researchers over the past 6 years sought to develop five general outcome measures for infants and toddlers.

## Issue 1: Create and Socially Validate the General Outcomes

An initial study was devoted to creating and socially validating a comprehensive set of general outcome statements (Early Childhood Research Institute on Measuring Growth and Development, 1998c; Priest et al., 2001) to be used to guide subsequent research and to develop indicators for measuring proficiency in attaining the general outcome. The first step included reviewing the early childhood literature and existing measures as a basis for writing and refining a comprehensive but parsimonious set of initial general outcome statements from across the five traditional developmental domains: communication, cognition, motor, social/emotional, and adaptive.

The second step in creating and socially validating the general outcomes involved a national survey of parents of young children with disabilities and the professionals and educators who serve those children. In the survey, parents and professionals were asked to rate each general outcome statement according to three levels of importance in a child's successful development: *critically important, very important,* or *somewhat important.* The parents and professionals surveyed were encouraged to provide suggestions and recommendations for improving the content and clarity of each general outcome statement. To ensure that parents receiving the survey in fact had had recent experiences with young children, only those indicating that they had a child 12 years or younger were asked to complete and return a survey. The overall return rates of completed surveys were 351 parents (32%) and 672 professionals (53%).

A list of 15 general outcome statements developed in the initial study (two to four general outcomes per domain) was evaluated as to their importance by parents and professionals (Priest et al., 2001). From these results, the infant and toddler development team selected one general outcome statement per domain to guide their work in developing a comprehensive but parsimonious set of growth and development indicators (one indicator per domain). Because all were highly rated, selection was a judgment call wherein relative critical importance, breadth, and the unique age range of 0 to 3 years were considered. Reported in this chapter are the research and development results for four of the five completed infant and toddler IGDIs; the fifth IGDI (self-help/adaptive) remains to be completed.

The general outcomes selected to guide work in developing individual growth and development indicators are reported in Table 6-1 along with the percentage of parents and professionals rating each as *critically important* and *very important.* As seen in Table 6-1, importance percentages for communication, movement, social, problem solving, and self-help/adaptive general

**Table 6-1**
General Outcomes Social Validation Findings for Children 0–8 Years

| Outcome | Outcome Statement | Percentage of Importance (Very and Critically) | |
|---|---|---|---|
| | | Parents | Professional |
| Communication | The child uses gestures, sounds, words, or sentences to convey wants and needs or to express meaning to others. | 100 | 100 |
| Movement | The child moves in a fluent and coordinated manner to play and participate in home, school, and community settings. | 96 | 72 |
| Social | The child interacts with peers and adults, maintaining social interactions and participating socially in home, school, and community. | | |
| Problem Solving | The child solves problems that require reasoning about objects, concepts, situations, and people. | 93 | 84 |
| Self-Help/ Adaptive | The child engages in a range of basic self-help skills, including but not limited to skills in dressing, eating, toileting/hygiene, and safety/identification. | 99 | 97 |

Note: Percentage based on ratings that were *critically important* and *very important*.

outcomes statements were generally above 84%, ranging from 100% (for communication) to 72% (for movement). Based on these results, parents and professionals most agreed on the critical importance of communication (parents: 100%; professionals: 100%) and diverged most on the critical importance of movement (parents: 96%; professionals: 72%).

## Issue 2: Identify Key Skill Elements and Create Definitions and Observational Measurement Procedures

A literature review and small-scale testing were undertaken to identify, refine, and test a set of key skill indicators that could be used to mark a child's progress across the 0 to 3 age range toward attaining the general outcomes: early communication indicator, early movement indicator, early social indicator, and early problem-solving indicator. A single skill for a single indicator was sought. Secondarily, a composite indicator was created based on a few skill elements whose combination and incremental attainment over

time would reflect increasing proficiency (Deno, 1997; Fuchs & Deno, 1991).

For example, this literature review for the early social indicator indicated that the function of social interaction is to achieve a response from another person ranging from proximity, to simple reciprocity, to coordinated action to achieve a common outcome, to friendship and acceptance of peers (Eckerman, 1996; Warren, Yoder, & Leew, 2002). Clearly, social interaction in infants develops first with adults and second with peers (Didow & Eckerman, 2001; Eckerman, Davis, & Didow, 1989).

Based on the literature review, a social skills/ competence conceptual framework for infants and toddlers was constructed for young children developing typically through the 0 to 3 age range. This framework separated positive social behaviors from negative social behaviors with acceleration in positive nonverbal behaviors (i.e., smiles, gestures) posited over time, along with accelerating frequencies of positive verbal social behavior (i.e., use of words in greetings, bids to play, etc.). These positive nonverbal and verbal social behaviors are also posited to be differentially directed to adults, then to peers with increasing age and skill, and then to more than a single person in a play situation (nondirected). From this framework, detailed behavioral definitions were developed for observational recording. Work next focused on creating behavioral definitions of these key skill elements, selecting an observational measurement procedure for testing in subsequent pilot and longitudinal studies (Carta, Greenwood, Luze, Cline, & Kuntz, in press). Similar reviews and logical analyses of key skill elements, definitions, and measurement procedures were carried out for each IGDI in development (Greenwood, Luze, Cline et al., 2002; Luze, 2001; Luze, Greenwood, Carta, Cline, & Kuntz, 2002; Luze et al., 2001).

The four individual growth and development indicators (IGDIs) and their associated key skill indicators are shown in Table 6-2. While each IGDI was purposely planned to uniquely reflect increasing proficiency toward its general outcome, the final form of each was different. For example, the work on the problem-solving indicator returned a single key skill, *functions*, which was defined as using a toy in a way consistent with its purpose. This indicator proved most valid and sensitive to growth across the total infant–toddler age range. The other three IGDIs were best served by key skill element composites. In the case of the social indicator, the most parsimonious, sensitive, and valid composite was

*total positive verbal*. In the case of the movement indicator, a composite of five key skill elements was used (see Table 6-2). In the case of the communication indicator, research indicated that none of the key skills uniformly reflected growth over the age range; in fact, gestures and vocalizations declined in 2- and 3-year-olds, while at the same time single- and multiple-word communications were growing. Consequently, to form a single indicator sensitive to growth over the age range, we weighted these skills in a composite (gestures and vocalizations = 1 per occurrence, single words = 2, multiples words = 3).

## Issue 3: Identify Toys That Readily Evoke the Key Skill Elements

In addition to identifying key skills and creating definitions and an observational recording procedure, we sought to develop a standard play testing situation for each IGDI. Each situation would include a familiar adult and toy sets with a high potential of evoking the key skill elements in the young children of interest. Initial efforts in this work compared the frequencies of key skill elements occurring in natural classroom play situations versus those in our standard play (analogue) situation with a familiar caregiver and select toy sets (Greenwood, Luze, Cline et al., 2002). Comparison of the data for the same children measured in both natural and analogue situations typically indicated that the natural

**Table 6-2**

Indicators and Key Skill Elements for Infants and Toddlers 0–3 Years

| Name | Indicator | Key Skill Elements | | | | |
| --- | --- | --- | --- | --- | --- | --- |
| | | 1 | 2 | 3 | 4 | 5 |
| Early Communication | Total weighted communication | Gesture | Vocalization | Single words | Multiple words | |
| Early Movement | Total movement | Transition in position | Grounded locomotion | Vertical locomotion | Roll/trap | Throw/catch |
| Early Social | Total positive verbal | To peer | To adult | Nondirected | | |
| Early Problem Solving | Problem solving | Functions, when toy use follows function | | | | |

classroom situation was unsatisfactory because children received systematically fewer or more variable counts of key behaviors (e.g., Luze, 2001). The occurrence of key skill elements in natural settings was too often influenced by natural variations in equipment, toys, and ongoing teacher–student interaction within centers in the classroom—the natural situations present for evoking behaviors. Thus, the more structured situation comprised of familiar adult and selected toy sets was selected for use in subsequent research and development studies for each IGDI (see Greenwood, 2002; Luze et al., 2001).

Considerable effort went into the final selections of toys to be used. Initially, for each IGDI logically appropriate toys thought best likely to evoke the key skill elements of interest were screened for function. A subset was selected based on the observed potential of the toys for engaging the interest of infants and toddlers and evoking the key skills of interest (Luze, 2001). Additional criteria guiding this selection were considerations of safety, developmental appropriateness, and availability in typical child-care settings.

Some of the toys ranked in demonstrated ability to evoke the children's *social skill elements* were Tub of Toys (TT), Window House (WH), and Kitchen With Dishes (KD), with enhancements added to each, including squeaky food items, blocks that pop together, and the

Fun Sounds Garage (FSG). Cut from this list were toys such as the Fire Engine, Ball Tower, Car Mat, and Blocks, which had failed to engage children for the entire session or promoted parallel play or imitation of the adult's behavior instead of the key social skill elements.

Toys passing this screening were tested further with a small sample of children stratified across the first, second, and third years of life. We used the observational recording protocol (previously described) to test each individual toy's equivalence in evoking social behaviors (alternate forms).

From these several small-scale studies testing and revising toy items, we were able to generate toys and toy sets from which to create alternate forms. These were employed in subsequent studies of sensitivity to growth over time and technical adequacy. Thus, toy situations were refined for each IGDI's set of key skill elements. For example, the House and Barn, each containing related objects such as furniture or animals, provided a situation highly evocative of interpersonal communication between the child and caregiver. Blocks/Balls and the Window House, on the other hand, were highly evocative of active movement and play between the child and the caregiver (see Table 6-3).

The final validated toy forms for each validated IGDI are displayed in Table 6-3. For all but the early problem-solving indicator (EPSI), single toys were identified that, with minor

**Table 6-3**
Alternate Toy Forms for Infants and Toddlers

| Indicator | Equivalent Toy Forms | | |
|---|---|---|---|
| | **A** | **B** | **C** |
| Early Communication | House | Barn | — |
| Early Movement | Blocks/Balls | Shopping Cart | Window House |
| Early Social | Tub of Toys | Window House | Kitchen w/Dishes |
| Early Problem Solving | Pop-up Dinos | Pop-up Pets | — |
| | Stacking Cups (Square) | Stacking Cups (Round) | — |
| | Dome (Drop 'n' Catch) | Dome (Pull 'n' Pop) | — |
| | Gazebo (6 items) | Gazebo (another 6 items) | — |
| | Sound Puzzle (Animals) | Sound Puzzle (Bears) | — |

exceptions, (i.e., the movement indicator— Shopping Cart) evoked nearly equivalent rates of performance (Greenwood, Luze, Cline et al., 2002). In the case of the problem-solving indicator, five parallel toy sets were used consisting of similar toys within a set. For example, pop-up dinosaurs and pop-up pets were different but similar toy forms with highly similar functions.

## Issue 4: Longitudinal Studies of Sensitivity to Growth and Technical Adequacy

Longitudinal studies were conducted to test each IGDI's sensitivity to growth, validity with respect to criterion measures, and reliability of measurement. The general design called for collecting criterion-validity measures of each outcome (i.e., communication, movement, social, problem solving) before and after nine monthly repeated measures using the IGDI. Because of time limitations, however, this time line was accelerated for the movement indicator and the problem-solving indicator. In the case of the movement indicator, data were collected every 3 weeks. In the case of the problem-solving indicator, data were collected on only five rather than nine occasions, and only one criterion testing wave was conducted after the collection of the IGDI data.

In each of the four longitudinal studies, purposive sampling of child-care centers and children in each center was used. Because of the frequent and intensive measurement in each study, it was not economically possible to recruit large representative samples at this stage in research and development. Thus, purposive sampling was used to obtain small samples composed of participants widely ranging in SES, cultural and linguistic diversity, and inclusion of children with disabilities [i.e., with Individual Family Service Plans (IFSPs)]. For example, the number of child-care centers participating in each longitudinal study ranged from two to five, with children sample sizes ranging from 27 to 57 (see Table 6-4). In each case, the participating sample of children was racially and socioeconomically diverse and included children with disabilities.

### IGDI Test Administration Procedures.

A standard administration protocol was used to ensure that each IGDI was administered in an equivalent way on each occasion by each assessor. The general setup involved an individual toy-play activity in a controlled, quiet setting with a familiar adult. Each testing session lasted for only 6 minutes (10 minutes for the problem-solving indicator). The adult assessor's role was to facilitate play and follow the child's lead. Additional duties included timing the session duration and ending the session after exactly 6 minutes. The assessor was also responsible for selecting and setting up the testing situation and, following the session, cleaning up and putting away all the toys and equipment used. A second adult was responsible for video taping the child's

**Table 6-4**
Longitudinal Study Samples for Infants and Toddlers 0–3 Years

| Indicator | Child Care Centers | Total Children | Gender M/F% | Racially Diverse | With Disabilities | SES |
|---|---|---|---|---|---|---|
| Early Communication (ECI) | 5 | 50 | 52/48 | Yes | Yes | Lo, Mid, Hi |
| Early Movement (EMI) | 2 | 34 | 52/48 | Yes | Yes | Lo, Mid, Hi |
| Early Social (ESI) | 5 | 57 | 56/44 | Yes | Yes | Lo, Mid, Hi |
| Early Problem Solving (EPSI) | 2 | 27 | 50/50 | Yes | Yes | Lo, Mid, Hi |

Note: Abbreviations are as follows: M = male, F = female, Lo = low, Mid = middle, Hi = high, SES = Socioeconomic status behavior for later observational recording. Observational recording of the child's performance was guided by definitions of key skill elements developed for each IGDI, for example, like those of the movement indicator in Table 6-5.

### Do the IGDIs Measure Growth Over Time?

For each infant and toddler IGDI, it proved possible to identify an indicator based on key skill elements that was sensitive to growth over the 0 to 3 age range (Greenwood, Carta, & Walker, 2002, October; Greenwood, Luze, Cline et al.,

2002; Luze, 2001; Luze et al., 2001; Luze et al., 2002). For example, we reported that both mean intercepts (levels) and slopes for each IGDI used in each longitudinal study of young children were positive in magnitude and significantly greater than zero.

The mean growth trajectories for each IGDI are displayed in Figure 6-2. Each trajectory and growth chart is bounded by a +1.0 and −1.0 standard deviation trajectory. As can be seen, each chart portrays growth over time. Linear trajectories proved to best reflect the pattern of

**Table 6-5**
Movement Indicator: Movement Key Skill Element Definitions

| Key Skill Element | Definition | Example Behaviors |
|---|---|---|
| Transitional Movement | Transitional movements are motions used by a child to achieve a new position within a posture or to a new posture. This can include movement within a stable posture (changing the primary weight-bearing surface) or moving from one distinct posture (lying supine or prone, sitting, kneeling, stooping, standing) to another. An episode begins when a child begins moving from a stable position to a new position. The episode ends when the child has regained a stable position or begins locomotion. | Rolling to stomach from back, rolling to back from stomach, moving in and out of sitting position, standing up, kneeling down resting on knees. |
| Grounded Locomotion | Locomotion involves movements that transport the body forward, backward, sideways, or upward from one point in space to another. Grounded locomotion is movement horizontal to the ground; it does not include upright postures when moving. | Moving on belly from one location to the next, either forward, backward, or sideways (pivot in prone). Thrusting arms forward and then subsequently flexing them in a movement that results in a slight forward or backward movement. |
| Vertical Locomotion | Vertical locomotion is movement in an upright position that moves the child forward, backward, or sideways. | Cruising is walking while holding onto furniture for support. Walking involves alternating feet; one foot is always on the floor. |
| Throwing/ Rolling | Throwing is propelling an object through the air. Rolling is pushing a circular object so that it rolls away from the child's body. | Throwing an object using an overarm, underarm, or sidearm throw. Rolling an object toward a person. |
| Catching/ Trapping | Catching is bringing an airborne object under control using hands and arms. Trapping is stopping a moving object (moving through the air or rolling on the ground) with hands, arms, legs, or body. | Catching an object with one's hands or arms or trapping it against the body. |

**Figure 6-2.**
Growth charts for the early communication indicator (ECI: upper left panel), early movement indicator (EMI: upper right panel), early social indicators (ESI: lower left panel), and early problem solving indicators (EPSI: lower right panel).

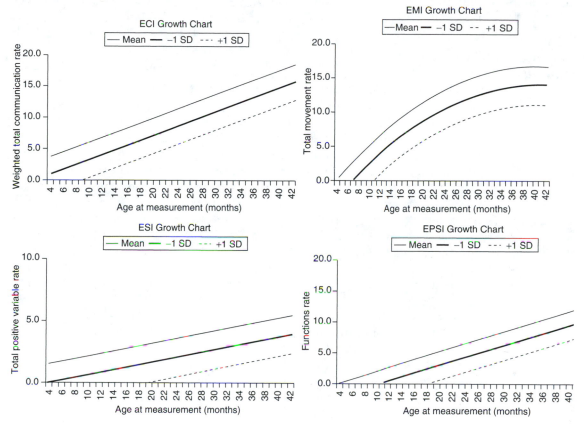

growth for three of the four IGDIs; however, curve-fitting tests indicated that the movement indicator growth pattern was best represented by a curvilinear model. As can be seen, after a rapid increase in the early months of life, the movement indicator growth trajectory became negatively accelerating with comparatively slower growth for 2- to 3-year-old children than for children from birth to 2. Mean growth parameters were Slope = 0.40 responses per minute per month for the communication indicator, Slope = 0.56 and Acceleration = −0.013 responses per minute per month for the movement indicator, Slope = 0.31 responses per minute per month for the problem-solving indicator, and Slope = 0.61

responses per minute per month for the social indicator. Like the pediatrician's growth charts, these IGDI charts reflect sample mean and variability in growth trajectories.

Additionally, we reported that IGDI growth was a function of child cohort defined by age at the start of each longitudinal study. For example, Cohort 1 = 0–12, Cohort 2 = 13–24, and Cohort 3 = 25–36 + months. Tests demonstrated that age cohort accounted for significant differences in mean level for the communication indicator, movement indicator, social indicator, and problem-solving indicator, as would be expected. (Younger compared to older children produced significantly less behavior.) For the movement indicator, these tests also indicated significant differences in slope; in this case, older cohorts had smaller slopes compared to younger cohorts, reflecting the negatively accelerating, curvilinear pattern of this IGDI over the age range.

### Do the IGDIs Measure What They Are Supposed to Measure—Criterion Validity?

For each infant and toddler IGDI, it proved possible to demonstrate significant, positive correlations with commonly used and recognized criterion measures. The criterion measures used for each IGDI are listed in Table 6-6. They were selected because they measure the developmental domain of interest, cover the age range 0 to 3, and are widely used in the assessment of young children. With the exception of the problem-solving indicator, criterion measures included two different measures, each administered by different test agents (i.e., a professional observer, a tester versus a parent).

These criterion validity correlations were highest in the case of the movement indicator (ranging from 0.77 to 0.86), showing that the movement indicator measured movement in ways similar to the ways professionals and parents measured (see Table 6-7). Similarly, the communication indicator was correlated 0.62 and 0.51 to professional- and parent-administered measures of early communication, respectively. The social indicator was similarly positively correlated although much more so to the Vineland measure than to the Howes direct observation measure (see Table 6-7). Lastly, the early problem-solving indicators correlated 0.48 to the Bayley MDI.

### Are the IGDIs Reliable?

Each IGDI produced reasonable indicators of interobserver agreement and measurement reliability (i.e., split half, alternate forms). Interobserver reliability estimates on each indicator ranged from 90% (for the communication indicator) to 95% (for the problem-solving indicator), indicating that observers could agree on key skill definitions and record similar frequencies of behavior (see Table 6-7). Measurement reliability indices were also respectable. Split-half, odd–even observation waves produced relative equal frequencies of behavior with correlations ranging from 0.85 (for the social indicator) to 0.89 (for the communication indicator), indicating similar estimates for one set of observations (odd waves) versus the other set (even waves).

Alternate form estimates also produced respectable estimates within IGDI forms and across IGDIs. These ranged from a low of 0.57

**Table 6-6**

Criterion Validity Measures Employed 0–3 Years

| Indicator | Measure | Citation |
| --- | --- | --- |
| Early Communication (ECI) | Preschool Language Scale—3 (PLS-3) | Zimmerman, Steiner, & Pond, 1992 |
| | Caregiver Communication Measure (CCM) | Walker, Hart, Linebarger, & Parsley, 1998 |
| Early Movement (EMI) | Peabody Developmental Motor Scales (PDMS-2) | Folio & Fewell, 2000 |
| | Caregiver Assessment of Movement Skills—Gross Motor | Kuntz, 2001 |
| Early Social (ESI) | Vineland Social—Emotional Scales | Sparrow, Balla, & Cicchetti, 1998 |
| | Howes Peer Play Scale | Howes, 1980 |
| Early Problem Solving (EPSI) | Bayley Scales of Infant Development | Bayley, 1993 |

**Table 6-7**
Validity and Reliability Statistics, 0–3 Years

| | | Criterion Validity | Reliability | | |
|---|---|---|---|---|---|
| Indicator | Criterion Measure | Pearson *r* | Interobserver Agreement | Split Half | Alternate Form |
| Early Communication (ECI) | PLS-3 (Zimmerman, Steiner, & Pond, 1992) | 0.62 | 90% | 0.89 | 0.72 |
| | CCM (Walker et al., 1998) | 0.51 | | | |
| Early Movement (EMI) | PDMS-2: Locomo (Folio & Fewell, 2000) | 0.86 | 93% | 0.88 | 0.84–0.91 |
| | PDMS-2: Station (Folio & Fewell, 2000) | 0.77 | | | |
| | CAMS-GM (Kuntz, 2001) | 0.85 | | | |
| Early Social (ESI) | Vineland-Interpersonal (Sparrow, Balla, & Cicchetti, 1998) | 0.65 | 92% | 0.85 | 0.57–0.71 |
| | Vineland-Play/Leisure (Sparrow, Balla, & Cicchetti, 1998) | 0.62 | | | |
| | Howes-Simple Social Play (Howes, 1980) | 0.47 | | | |
| | Howes-Composite (Howes, 1980) | 0.34 | | | |
| Early Problem Solving (EPSI) | Bayley (MDI) (Bayley, 1993) | 0.48 | 95% | 0.88 | 0.90 |

Note: Abbreviations are as follows: PLS-3 = Preschool Language Scale (ver. 3), CCM = Caregiver Communication Measure, PDMS-2 = Peabody Developmental Motor Scale (ver. 2), CAMS-CM = Caregiver Assessment of Movement Skills—Gross Motor, MDI = Mental Development Index.

on the social indicator to a high of 0.90 on the problem-solving indicator (see Table 6-7). Taken together, these findings indicate acceptable levels of sensitivity, validity, and reliability.

## Issue 5: Sensitivity to Intervention (Treatment Validity)

Treatment validity is an experimental demonstration that a measure is sensitive to intervention and, in fact, reveals intervention effects. As of this date, the treatment validity of the infant and toddler IGDIs has only been investigated with the communication indicator in single-case, single-subject design studies (Greenwood et al., 2003; Kosanic, 2000; Murray, 2002). In these studies, several interventions were employed ranging from a relatively simple "warm-up" pro-

cedure prior to administering the communication indicator (Greenwood et al., 2003) to caregiver training in the milieu and responsive intervention teaching (Kosanic, 2000; Murray, 2002).

## CONCLUSION

In this chapter we described a line of work developing and validating general outcome measures for use by early interventionists serving infants and toddlers (birth to 3 years). Specific progress developing individual growth and development indicators (IGDIs) for early communication, movement, social competence, and problem solving was reported. Each early indicator was shown to (a) be sensitive to chronological age and growth over time (construct validity); (b) measure the developmental domain it was designed to measure (criterion validity); (c) meet high standards of interobserver agreement (accuracy); (d) be reliable (test–retest and alternate forms reliability); (e) meet standards of practicality and cost reasonable to early interventionists (utility); and, in the case of the early communication indicator, (f) be sensitive to intervention effects (treatment validity).

IGDIs are superior to traditional measures and measurement approaches used with infants and toddlers because they posit a strong role for intervention decision making and environmental influence in the conceptual framework, can be used by early interventionists to guide intervention services and arrange experiences that they have control over for young children, can be administered in a reasonable amount of time, are sensitive to growth over chronological age and time, use metrics linked to the time needed to achieve proficiency rather than to chronological age, and improve communications with parents. The IGDIs are also consonant with the Division of Early Childhood's recommended assessment practices in that they can be used to guide change in treatment activities, help locate behavioral objectives for change that are judged important and acceptable, and incorporate input from parents in the overall decision-making model. Also, they are designed for use on multiple, frequent occasions (Neisworth, 1993, 2000).

With respect to what is now known about the early precursors of school readiness and reading, the IGDIs (early communication, problem solving, and social competence) appeared to provide excellent tools for future investigations of precursors. For example, preliminary evidence of a positive, moderately large association between early communication fluency for children 2.5 to 3.5 years old exists with a measure of rapid picture naming fluency (early vocabulary) at two time points, $r = .41$ and $.39$ with total communication fluency, and even larger at $r = .66$ and $.65$ with the early communication indicator key skill element, multiple word fluency. These findings are suggestive of the early communication indicator's

predictive validity with respect to later communication and emerging literacy skills in older children. McConnell and colleagues reported that picture naming fluency was strongly correlated with both the Peabody Picture Vocabulary Test and the Preschool Language Scale (Version 3) in children older than 3 years, both of which are standard measures of early communication (McConnell, Priest, Davis, & McEvoy, 2002).

Of particular importance in this work was the development of measures with both the technical and practical features needed to construct large-scale accountability systems for individual children and early intervention programs. The implications of this work at this point are several. First, these several measures comprise a comprehensive but parsimonious set of measures for use by early childhood educators and early interventionists in the early identification, progress monitoring, and evaluation of infants and toddlers. Second, these IGDIs provide early educators a new set of measures supported by evidence of technical soundness and practicality that they can use to address a range of "accountability" needs (e.g., Early Childhood Research Institute on Measuring Growth and Development, 1998a). Third, the IGDIs are uniquely designed to work in the context of early intervention to make decisions about intervention needs, plans, effectiveness, and intervention change over time. Fourth, the IGDIs provide a unique opportunity to interventionists interested in designing and testing the effects of new interventions.

Although the IGDI development progress described here was substantial, its present rigor and breadth best support the assertion that general outcome measures for infants and toddlers are feasible and appear highly promising. Limiting the work and setting the stage for future research, however, are several needs:

1. Continuing refinements in toy forms, key skill elements, and other details of IGDI procedures are needed, particularly for the movement and problem-solving indicators.

2. Data collected on larger, population-representative samples are needed to convincingly define "normative" growth rates.

3. Replications demonstrating the beneficial effects of early interventions for individuals and programs in terms of effect sizes as a function of specific interventions are needed.

4. A need exists to use each IGDI in the context of clinical treatment decision making, demonstrating intervention cases. Particularly important will be intervention cases in which child-care workers and parents have been trained and act as implementers of treatment shown to be effective by the use of IGDIs. Such work with infants and toddlers needs to parallel similar clinical intervention work with pediatricians using height and weight charts to make decisions, behavior analysts using celeration charts to make decisions, and elementary- and secondary-level educators using curriculum-based measurement fluency charts to make decisions (Fuchs & Deno, 1991).

5. The use of IGDIs in program evaluations is needed to demonstrate their contribution to accountability and program improvement.

6. Similarly, there is a need to use IGDIs in intervention research and model development, in ways that demonstrate their utility and importance in improving child results and program quality.

7. A need exists to develop training for assessors and program directors in the theoretical underpinnings and practical applications of IGDIs for infants and toddlers. Such an effort could be supported by the development of specific materials and Web sites wherein such information can be made readily accessible and usable (e.g., http://www.lsi.ku.edu/jgprojects/ igdi/).

Consequently, we believe that the feasibility of IGDIs for infants and toddlers has been sufficiently demonstrated. IGDIs are ready for experimental trial in child-care centers, Early Head Start programs, and other birth to 3 programs serving children in homes or centers. Similar measures have been developed for children 3 to 5 years (McConnell, Priest, Davis, & McEvoy, 2002) and children 5 to 8 years (Good & Kaminski, 1996, 2000; Kaminski & Good, 1996). Additionally, the approach merits systematic replication designed to refine and expand these measures in ways thought to make them more sensitive to growth, more practical, more accessible, and easier to use. Lastly, the training of early interventionists to use IGDIs, which is clearly relevant and highly important, has yet to be addressed.

# REFERENCES

Bagnato, S. J., & Neisworth, J. T. (1991). *Assessment for early intervention: Best practices for professionals*. London: Guilford.

Bayley, N. (1993). *Bayley Scales of Infant Development* (2nd ed.). New York: Psychological Corporation.

Burton, A. W., & Miller, D. E. (1998). *Movement skill assessment*. Champaign, IL: Human Kinetics.

Carta, J. J., & Greenwood, C. R. (1997). Barriers to the implementation of effective educational practices for young children with disabilities. In J. W. Lloyd, E. J. Kame'enui, & D. Chard (Eds.), *Issues in the education of students with disabilities* (pp. 261–274). Mahwah, NJ: Erlbaum.

Carta, J. J., Greenwood, C. R., Luze, G. J., Cline, G., & Kuntz, S. (in press). Developing a general outcome measure of growth in social skills for infants and toddlers. *Journal of Early Intervention*.

Carta, J. J., Greenwood, C. R., Walker, D., Kaminski, R., Good, R., McConnell, S., et al. (2002). Individual growth and development indicators (IGDIs): Assessment that guides intervention for young children. *Young Exceptional Children Monograph Series, 4* (15–28).

Carta, J. J., Schwartz, I., Atwater, J. B., & McConnell, S. R. (1991). Developmentally appropriate practice? Appraising its usefulness for young children with disabilities. *Topics in Early Childhood Special Education, 11,* 11–20.

Deno, S. L. (1997). Whither thou goest . . . Perspectives on progress monitoring. In J. W. Lloyd, E. J. Kame'enui & D. Chard (Eds.), *Issues in educating students with disabilities* (pp. 77–99). Mahwah, NJ: Erlbaum.

Deno, S. L. (2002). Problem solving as "best practice." In A. Thomas & J. Grimes (Eds.), *Best practices in school psychology IV* (pp. 37–56). Washington, DC: National Association of School Psychologists.

Deno, S. L., Mirkin, P. K., & Chaing, B. (1982). Identifying valid measures of reading. *Exceptional Children, 49* (1), 36–45.

Didow, S. M., & Eckerman, C. O. (2001). Toddler peers: From nonverbal coordinated action to verbal discourse. *Social Development, 10* (2), 170–188.

Early Childhood Research Institute on Measuring Growth and Development. (1998a). *Accountability system for children birth through age eight* (Technical Report No. 1). Minnapolis: Center for Early Education and Development, University of Minnesota.

Early Childhood Research Institute on Measuring Growth and Development. (1998b). *Research and development of individual growth and development indicators for children birth to age eight* (Technical Report No. 4). Minneapolis: Author.

Early Childhood Research Institute on Measuring Growth and Development. (1998c). *Theoretical foundations of the Early Childhood Research Institute on Measuring Growth and Development: An early childhood problem solving model* (Technical Report No. 6). Minneapolis: Center for Early Education and Development.

Eckerman, C. O. (1996). Early social-communicative development: Illustrative developmental analyses. In R. B. Cairns & G. H. J. Elder (Eds.), *Developmental science: Cambridge studies in social and emotional development* (pp. 135–167). New York: Cambridge University Press.

Eckerman, C. O., Davis, C. C., & Didow, S. M. (1989). Toddlers' emerging ways of achieving social coordination with a peer. *Child Development, 60,* 440–453.

Folio, M.R., & Fewell, R. R. (2000). *Peabody Developmental Motor Scales (PDMS-2)* (2nd ed.). San Antonio, TX: The Psychological Corporation.

Fuchs, L. S., & Deno, S. L. (1991). Paradigmatic distinctions between instructionally relevant measurement models. *Exceptional Children, 57,* 488–500.

Good, R. H., Gruba, J., & Kaminski, R. A. (2002). Best practices in using dynamic indicators of basic early literacy skills (DIBELS) in an outcomes-driven model. In A. Thomas & J. Grimes (Eds.), *Best practices in school psychology* (4th ed., pp. 699–720). Washington, DC: National Association of School Psychologists.

Good, R. H., & Kaminski, R. A. (1996). Assessment for instructional decisions: Toward a proactive/prevention model for decision making for early literacy skills. *School Psychology Quarterly, 11,* 1–11.

Good, R. H., & Kaminski, R. (2000). *Dynamic indicators of basic early literacy skills (DIBELS)*. [Online], from http://dibels.uoregon.edu.

Good, R. H., Simmons, D. C., & Kame'enui, E. J. (2001). The importance and decision-making utility of a continuum of fluency-based indicators of foundational reading skills for third-grade high-stakes outcomes. *Scientific Studies of Reading, 5* (3), 257–288.

Greenwood, C. R. (March 2002). *Development of a general outcome measure of growth in movement for infants and toddlers.* Paper presented at the Conference on Research in Early Intervention, San Diego, CA.

Greenwood, C. R., Carta, J. J., & Walker, D. (2002, October). *Individual growth and development indicators (IGDIs): Practitioner's tools for assessing intervention results for infants and toddlers.* Paper presented at the Institute for Child Development, University of Kansas Medical Center, Kansas City, KS.

Greenwood, C. R., Dunn, S., Ward, S. M., & Luze, G. J. (2003). The Early Communication Indicator (ECI) for infants and toddlers: What it is, where it's been, and where it needs to go. *The Behavior Analyst Today, 3* (4), 383–388.

Greenwood, C. R., Luze, G. J., & Carta, J. J. (2002). Assessment of intervention results with infants and toddlers. In A. Thomas & J. Grimes (Eds.), *Best practices in school psychology IV* (Vol. 2, pp. 1219–1230). Washington, DC: National Association of School Psychology.

Greenwood, C. R., Luze, G. J., Cline, G., Kuntz, S., & Leitschuh, C. (2002). Developing a general outcome measure of growth in movement for infants and toddlers. *Topics in Early Childhood Special Education, 22* (3), 143–157.

Hart, B., & Risley, T. R. (1978). Promoting productive language through incidental teaching. *Education in Urban Society, 10,* 407–429.

Hart, B., & Risley, T. R. (1995). *Meaningful differences in the everyday experience of young American children.* Baltimore: Brookes.

Howes, C. (1980). Peer play scale as an index of complexity of peer interaction. *Developmental Psychology, 16* (4), 371–372.

Kagan, S. L., Moore, E., & Bredekamp, S. (1995). *Reconsidering children's early development and learning: Toward common views and vocabulary*. Washington, DC: National Education Goals Panel.

Kagan, S. L., Rosenkoetter, S., & Cohen, N. (1997). *Considering child-based results for young children: Definitions, desirability, feasibility, and next steps*. New Haven, CT: Yale Bush Center in Child Development and Social Policy.

Kaminski, R. A., & Good, R. H. (1996). Toward a technology for assessing basic early literacy skills. *School Psychology Review, 25,* 215–227.

Kosanic, A. Z. (2000). *Toward a technology for monitoring growth in the expressive communication of infants and toddlers*. Unpublished master's thesis, University of Kansas, Lawrence, KS.

Kuntz, S. (2001). *Caregiver assessment of movement skills-Gross Motor*. Kansas City, KS: Juniper Gardens Children's Project, University of Kansas.

Luze, G. J. (2001). *Pilot investigations towards developing a social general outcome measure for infants and toddlers*. Kansas City, KS: Early Childhood Research Institute on Measuring Growth and Development, Juniper Gardens Children's Project, University of Kansas.

Luze, G. J., Greenwood, C. R., Carta, J. J., Cline, G., & Kuntz, S. (2002). *Developing a general outcome measure of growth in social skills for infants and toddlers*. Kansas City, KS: Early Childhood Research Institute on Measuring Growth and Development, Juniper Gardens Children's Project, University of Kansas.

Luze, G. J., Linebarger, D. L., Greenwood, C. R., Carta, J. J., Walker, D., Leitschuh, C., et al. (2001). Developing a general outcome measure of growth in expressive communication of infants and toddlers. *School Psychology Review, 30* (3), 383–406.

McConnell, S. R. (2000). Assessment in early intervention and early childhood special education: Building on the past to project into the future. *Topics in Early Childhood Special Education, 20,* 43–48.

McConnell, S. R., McEvoy, M. A., Carta, J. J., Greenwood, C. R., Kaminski, R., Good, R. I., et al. (1996). *Early childhood research institute on program performance measures: A growth and development approach*. Minneapolis: University of Minnesota. Proposal funded by the Early Education Programs for Children with Disabilities, Office of Special Education and Rehabilitation Services, U.S. Office of Education.

McConnell, S. R., Priest, J. S., Davis, S. D., & McEvoy, M. A. (2002). Best practices in measuring growth and development for preschool children. In A. Thomas & J. Grimes (Eds.), *Best practices in school psychology IV* (Vol. 2, pp. 1231–1246). Washington, DC: National Association of School Psychologists.

Meisels, S. J. (1996). Charting the continuum of assessment and intervention. In S. J. Meisels & E. Fenichel (Eds.), *New visions for the development and assessment of infants and young children* (pp. 27–52). Washington, DC: Zero to Three.

Murray, A. (2002). *Implementing a language intervention in a childcare setting using prelinguistic language-teaching techniques*. Unpublished master's thesis, University of Kansas, Lawrence, KS.

National Educational Goals Panel. (1999). *The National Education Goals report: Building a nation of learners, 1999*. Washington, DC: U.S. Government Printing Office.

Neisworth, J. T. (1993). Assessment. In *DEC recommended practices: Indicators of quality in programs for infants and young children with special needs and their families* (pp. 11–16). Reston, VA: Division for Early Childhood.

Neisworth, J. T. (2000). Assessment. In *DEC recommended practices in early intervention/early childhood special education* (pp. 11–16). Longmont, CO: Sopris West.

Preator, K. K., & McAllister, J. R. (1995). Best practices assessing infants and toddlers. In A. Thomas & J. P. Grimes (Eds.), *Best practices in school psychology III* (Vol. 3, pp. 775–788). Bethesda, MD: National Association of School Psychologists.

Priest, J. S., McConnell, S. R., Walker, D., Carta, J. J., Kaminski, R. A., McEvoy, M. A., et al. (2001). General growth outcomes for children: Developing a foundation for continuous progress measurement. *Journal of Early Intervention, 24* (3), 163–180.

Sparrow, S. S., Balla, D. A., & Cicchetti, D. V. (1998). *Vineland Social Emotional Early Childhood Scales*. Circle Pines, MN: American Guidance Service.

Walker, D., Hart, B., Linebarger, D., & Parsley, K. (1998). *Caregiver communication measure (CCM)*. Kansas City, KS: Juniper Gardens Children's Project, University of Kansas.

Warren, S., Yoder, P. J., & Leew, S. V. (2002). Promoting social-communicative development in infants and toddlers. In H. Goldstein, L. Kaczmarek, & K. English (Eds.), *Promoting social communication: Children with developmental disabilities from birth to adolescence* (Vol. 10, pp. 121–149). Baltimore, MD: Brookes.

Whitehurst, G. J., & Lonigan, C. J. (2001). Emergent literacy: Development from prereaders to readers. In S. B. Neuman & D. K. Dickinson (Eds.), *Handbook of early literacy research* (pp. 11–29). New York: Guilford Press.

Wolf, M. M. (1978). Social validity: The case for subjective measurement or how applied behavior analysis is finding its heart. *Journal of Applied Behavior Analysis, 11,* 203–213.

Zimmerman, I. L., Steiner, V. G., & Pond, R. V. (1992). *Preschool Language Scale—3.* San Antonio, TX: The Psychological Corporation.

## STUDY QUESTIONS AND FOLLOW-UP ACTIVITIES

1. Results of norm-referenced and criterion-referenced assessments may indicate that a child is behind age expectations, but offer little information to inform intervention decision making. Describe the environmental, social, and instructional factors that are critical to determining optimal program components for a child with disabilities.

2. Many special educators complain about the lack of time for frequent student assessment and intervention planning and evaluation. How might use of an assessment instrument such as that proposed by the authors benefit educators and their students?

3. Describe arguments that may be raised when adaptation of Individual Growth and Development Indicators (IGDIs) is proposed in a school setting, and provide supporting statements for their use in individual- and program-level accountability systems.

4. Outcome measurement is intended to be an indicator of progress toward a general outcome and is selected to be representative of the skill set of an age range or grade level. Because it is not intended to be an exhaustive measure of progress, the practitioner must be well versed in normal child development to effectively use this information to individualize the educational program for a child with special needs. Reflecting on your own preservice teacher preparation program, describe what changes must occur to better prepare teachers (and subsequently their students) to benefit from IGDIs.

5. A parent of a preschool child with severe disabilities dreads quarterly progress reports because her child appears to make little progress based on the premise of full attainment or mastery of goals. Assuming a shift toward indicators of general outcomes, describe the benefits to the parent as well as the student and teacher.

6. Describe how IGDIs may make program planning and decision making more precise since they are linked to the time needed to achieve proficiency rather than to the chronological age of the student.

7. Quality and quantity of early intervention services have been linked to positive outcomes for students with special needs. Discuss the advantages and disadvantages of using IGDIs in assessing the outcomes of specific interventions and programs.

8. What are the key disadvantages and limitations of using yearly measures of children's motor abilities as the basis for guiding early intervention and program design?

9. Make a table to compare and contrast the assessment procedures used for the examples of Alyrique and Sierra. Discuss these results in terms of the goals of the individual growth and development indicators (IGDIs).

10. The authors give examples of models for the indicators that they are trying to develop (e.g., growth charts, celeration charts, fluency charts). Prepare examples of these charts to share with colleagues, a parent group, or a group of early childhood educators. Script what you would say to explain the advantages of each of these examples and how each has contributed to the development of the IGDIs.

11. How might IGDIs be useful in other fields of education? Provide specific examples.

12. Measuring the social validity of interventions is important. Make a plan for determining the social validity before, during, and after an intervention that uses IGDIs.

13. Go to the Juniper Gardens Children's Project Web site and write a summary of the information you find about IGDIs.

Study questions and follow-up activities prepared by Mary D. Salmon and Donna M. Villareal.

### CHAPTER 7

# Choice Making in Educational Settings

*Stephanie M. Peterson*     *Nancy A. Neef*
*Renée K. Van Norman*     *Summer J. Ferreri*

Making choices pervades daily human activity. In fact, most behavior can be viewed as choice to the extent that it involves doing one thing to the exclusion of doing something else. In the area of education for children with disabilities, choice is an important consideration in planning interventions because it can lead to improved functioning, more social approval, increased learning, increased reinforcement, and adaptive behaviors consistent with societal norms.

Because choice has important implications for a broad spectrum of human behavior, it has received a great deal of attention in both basic and applied behavioral research (see Fisher & Mazur, 1997, and Lancioni, O'Reilly, & Emerson, 1996, for reviews). Some research has focused on choice as an intervention or independent variable. For example, studies have examined the effects of making particular options available on the subsequent problem behavior of individuals with behavior disorders (e.g., Gardner, Cole, Berry, & Nowinski, 1983; Munk & Repp, 1994).

Other research has examined variables that influence choices, including factors that affect whether an individual will choose to engage in undesirable behavior or a more socially appropriate behavior alternative (e.g., Horner & Day, 1991; Peck et al., 1996). In these studies, the focus is on assessment of the variables that influence choice, and choice serves as the dependent variable.

The purpose of this chapter is to critically examine the literature on choice in educational settings and its implications for intervention planning. First, we consider issues of how choice is conceptualized. Second, we discuss the conceptual and methodological difficulties of investigations of choice as an intervention or independent variable. Third, we examine research on the assessment of choices and the factors that influence them. Finally, we illustrate the utility of the proposed conceptualization and

We would like to extend our deep appreciation to John O. Cooper and Diane M. Sainato for their comments on earlier drafts of this manuscript. Their assistance and commitment to excellence on our behalf, in spite of tight time lines, were remarkable.

assessment of choice with applications that promote beneficial choices.

## OVERVIEW OF CHOICE IN BEHAVIOR ANALYSIS

In behavior analysis, a choice occurs when a person is "confronted with a variety of alternatives and selects one alternative to the exclusion of the others" (McDowell, 1988, p. 96). Sometimes alternatives are arranged. For example, a teacher might give a student the option of working on a math assignment or a reading assignment. But even when options are not arranged, the child may still demonstrate choice. For example, a child who is given an instruction to complete a math worksheet might begin to work on it, he might choose to ignore the instruction and continue what he is doing, or he might do something else. Each response alternative is associated with different consequences. When behavior can alternate among response alternatives and there are consequences for choosing each alternative, a concurrent schedule of reinforcement exists (McDowell, 1988). The implications of various recommendations and approaches to intervention can be evaluated according to this conceptualization.

One approach to intervention is to make certain options available. A frequent recommendation is to infuse opportunities for making choices into daily instructional activities (e.g., Brown, Apple, Corsi, & Wenig, 1993; Kohn, 1993; Shevin & Klein, 1984). In these situations, choice is treated as an intervention. One reason often cited for providing opportunities for choices is that it is consistent with social values such as self-determination and empowerment. The options likely to be offered, however, are those that are deemed acceptable by others. For example, the teacher might give the student opportunities to choose among assignments, task materials, or sequences; however, a choice to engage in disruptive or aggressive activities in lieu of assignments would not be considered acceptable. Whether the student chooses to en-

gage in one of the options presented or another behavior altogether depends on his or her sensitivity to the consequences associated with each of the possible response alternatives (i.e., concurrent schedules of reinforcement).

We argue that consideration of concurrent schedules is important to understanding and predicting the effects of providing opportunities for choices. We also maintain that we can best "empower" students by arranging conditions to promote choices that benefit the student and by helping students to recognize the factors that can influence their choices.

Recommendations to provide opportunities for choices are, in addition, often made on empirical grounds. Some research on choice as an independent variable suggests that making particular options available is associated with increased task compliance, decreased task avoidance, and less problem behavior (see Bannerman, Sheldon, Sherman, & Harchik, 1990). However, other research has yielded mixed results. Because researchers have sometimes conceptualized choice as an intervention, we provide an overview of this research in the following section. We describe methodological issues affecting interpretation of the research and argue that choice requires consideration of preference. Specifically, when an individual makes a choice, he or she is expressing preference for particular reinforcers relative to others.

Fortunately, behavior analysts have developed effective technologies for assessing preference and the variables that affect preference. These technologies, the effects of various dimensions of reinforcement, and the implications these dimensions of reinforcement have for understanding choice are the focus of this chapter.

## CHOICE AS AN INTERVENTION

Early research on the effects of choice as an independent variable suggested that providing options might yield a number of benefits (see Bannerman et al., 1990). For example, individuals may prefer situations in which certain response options are available, which may in turn enhance task performance. In addition, structured choice opportunities have been associated with increased task compliance, decreased task avoidance, and less problem behavior. Dyer, Dunlap, and Winterling (1990) reported the potential positive effects of providing choice opportunities. This study compared a choice condition (in which participants chose among a variety of work tasks) to a no-choice condition (in which the same tasks were assigned to the participants). All three participants demonstrated lower levels of problem behavior during the choice condition as compared to the no-choice condition. No consistent differences in rate of correct responding occurred across conditions, indicating that increases in problem behavior in the no-choice condition were not attributable to the difficulty of these tasks.

Dyer and colleagues and others (e.g., Dunlap et al., 1994; Koegel, Dyer, & Bell, 1987; Mason, McGee, Farmer-Dougan, & Risley, 1989) suggested that providing structured opportunities for choice can produce reductions in problem behavior. However, conclusions about the effects of providing choice opportunities must be made with caution. Much of the early research in this area did not occur in applied settings (e.g., Champlin & Karoly, 1975; Corah & Boffa, 1970; Devine & Fernald, 1973; Geer, Davison, & Gatchel, 1970; Geer & Maisel, 1972; Glass, Singer, & Friedman, 1969; Kanfer & Grimm, 1978; Perlmuter & Monty, 1973; Stotland & Blumenthal, 1964; Wright & Strong, 1982; Zuckerman, Porac, Lathin, Smith, & Deci, 1978); thus, generality of such findings to individuals with disabilities in naturalistic settings was unknown (Bannerman et al., 1990). Although applied behavior analysts studied the effects of providing structured opportunities for choice on socially significant behaviors (e.g., problem behavior, task engagement), the choice condition was often confounded with other variables. For example, in the Dyer and colleagues (1990) study, the teacher selected the tasks during the no-choice condition. The students might not have preferred the task at the time of teacher selection. Therefore, the researchers were unable to isolate the effects of the act of choosing from the reinforcing value of the tasks selected.

In an effort to control for the effects of preference, some within-subject analyses have yoked the stimuli used in the no-choice condition to those in the choice condition. For example, Dunlap and colleagues (1994) evaluated the effects of providing structured opportunities for choice on task engagement. To control for preference, the researchers used the activities selected in the choice condition in the no-choice condition. When the same stimuli were used, problem behavior increased and task engagement decreased in the no-choice condition relative to the choice condition.

Although the yoking procedure used by Dunlap and colleagues represented a methodological improvement, preferences can change rapidly. Thus, it could be argued that yoking stimuli in choice and no-choice conditions does not control for preference because what was preferred earlier may no longer be preferred later. Having access to preferred stimuli can change the motivating operation (Laraway, Snycerski, Michael, & Poling, 2003).

Specifically, access to preferred stimuli prior to subsequent choice opportunities can serve as an abolishing operation that decreases the likelihood that these stimuli will be preferred in the future. Thus, studies that control for preference by yoking stimuli in choice and no-choice conditions are still confounded by potential abolishing effects and resulting momentary shifts in preference.

The momentary shifts in preference might account for the mixed or equivocal effects of other investigations of the influence of choice on problem behavior (e.g., Bambara, Ager, & Koger, 1994; Kennedy & Haring, 1993; Lerman et al., 1997; Parsons, Reid, Reynolds, & Bumgarner, 1990; Smith, Iwata, & Shore, 1995; Vaughn & Horner, 1997; Waldron-Soler, Martella, Marchand-Martella, & Ebey, 2000). For example, Bambara and colleagues (1994) conducted preference assessments for three adults with severe disabilities and identified high- and low-preference tasks. On-task behavior was measured across three conditions: (a) assignment of low-preference tasks, (b) assignment of high-preference tasks, and (c) choice between high- and low-preference tasks. Similar levels of on-task behavior occurred in the assigned high-preference task and choice conditions. On-task behavior was lowest when low-preference tasks were assigned. In a follow-up analysis, the authors examined on-task behavior when low-preference tasks were assigned, and when participants were allowed to choose among low-preference task alternatives. On-task behavior in the choice condition was only slightly higher than that in the no-choice condition.

The previously discussed studies suggest that relative preference plays a key role in the effectiveness of choice as an intervention. To the extent that preference is at least, if not more, influential than the act of choosing, it is important to consider the variables that affect preference, and therefore choices. This requires examination of research on the assessment of choice, in which choice is the dependent variable.

# CHOICE AS A DEPENDENT VARIABLE IN THE ASSESSMENT OF PREFERENCE

## Assessment of Preference

Given the importance of accommodating an individual's preferences in treatment and service delivery, a great deal of research has addressed the role of choice in the assessment of preference (e.g., DeLeon & Iwata, 1996; Faw, Davis, & Peck, 1996; Hanley, Piazza, Fisher, Contrucci, & Maglieri, 1997; Higbee, Carr, & Harrison, 1999; Newton, Ard, & Horner, 1993; Parsons & Reid, 1990; Piazza, Fisher, Hanley, Remick, Contrucci, & Aiken, 1997; Reid, Parsons, & Green, 1998). "The purpose of a reinforcer assessment is to evaluate stimuli that have been identified as being preferred to identify whether they actually function as reinforcers" (Fisher & Mazur, 1997, p. 396). Although caregiver opinion is often so-

licited as a means of identifying an individual's preferences (e.g., Hutchins & Renzagli, 1998), research has shown that such information is not necessarily a valid predictor of preference (e.g., Green, Middleton, & Reid, 2000; Parsons & Reid, 1990). Therefore, research has focused on direct assessment of preferences (particularly with individuals with more severe disabilities). This is typically accomplished by observing an individual's choices (e.g., pointing to pictures; duration of interaction with, or approach vs. avoidance toward, available materials) when stimulus options are presented concurrently. However, choice as an expression of preference, like any behavior, is subject to environmental influence. Thus, a valid assessment of preference requires acknowledgement of those influences.

## Alteration of Preference via Motivating Operations

Certain events can alter the effectiveness of consequences and thereby affect the occurrence of behaviors that are followed by those consequences. These events have been termed "motivating operations" and consist of (a) establishing operations, and (b) abolishing operations, which increase and decrease the effectiveness of consequences, respectively (Laraway et al., 2003). For example, if asking for a glass of water is reinforced by access to water, eating salty foods may be an establishing operation that increases the value of water as a reinforcer. This, in turn, may increase the likelihood of a request for water. If a request for food is maintained by access to food, eating a large meal may be an abolishing operation that decreases the effectiveness of food as a reinforcer, and thereby also the likelihood of a request for food.

Some have suggested that making choices provides individuals with control over reinforcement—in other words, it allows individuals to adjust reinforcer delivery relative to ongoing fluctuations in motivating operations (Catania, 1998). When an individual chooses one behavior over another, it can produce variety in the reinforcers obtained, thereby mitigating abolishing operations. Presession access to potential reinforcers has been found to differentially affect responding during test conditions in which the same reinforcers are presented contingent upon a target behavior (e.g., Ayllon & Azrin, 1968; Berg et al., 2000; O'Reilly, 1999; Vollmer & Iwata, 1991). Some studies have shown that presession access to potential reinforcers serves as an abolishing operation and decreases the effectiveness of those reinforcers in subsequent sessions (e.g., Berg et al., 2000; O'Reilly, 1999; Vollmer & Iwata, 1991). Other research has shown that presession access that allows brief sampling of potential reinforcers can serve as an establishing operation that increases the effectiveness of those reinforcers in subsequent sessions (Ayllon & Azrin, 1968). Whether presession access to potential reinforcers serves as an establishing or abolishing operation may depend on the amount or duration of exposure.

Gottschalk, Libby, and Graff (2000) found that preference assessment results were greatly influenced by prior access to or deprivation of the stimuli evaluated. Specifically, when participants were provided with access to stimuli previously identified as highly preferred, preference for those stimuli decreased during subsequent preference assessments. Likewise, for some participants the value of previously identified low-preference stimuli increased when the participants were deprived of access to them prior to the preference assessment. Thus, stimuli may lose or gain reinforcing value at certain points in time, depending on whether access to them was available previously.

Graff and Libby (1999) and Bowman, Piazza, Fisher, Hagopian, & Kogan (1997) suggested that stimulus variation can improve the effectiveness of reinforcement. Participants in the Graff and Libby study chose between interventions that (a) provided reinforcer selection before the session or (b) provided reinforcer selection throughout the session. In the latter intervention, individuals selected different reinforcers throughout the session as preferences changed within the session. When both interventions were concurrently available, all participants selected the intervention that provided within-session reinforcer choice more frequently than the intervention that produced only presession reinforcer choice.

Bowman and colleagues (1997) provided participants with a choice of sitting in one of three different chairs. Selecting one chair produced no reinforcement, selecting another chair produced high-quality reinforcement, and selecting the third chair produced slightly lower quality stimuli than the high-quality chair, but the stimuli changed with each selection response (i.e., varied reinforcement). Four of the seven participants consistently chose varied reinforcement over consistent reinforcement; two participants chose consistent, high-quality reinforcement over varied reinforcement; and one participant's choices alternated between consistent and varied reinforcement. The results of these studies suggest that "allowing individuals to choose from arrays of preferred stimuli provides them with a mechanism for adjusting reinforcer delivery in accordance with momentary fluctuations in preference or motivation" (Bowman et al., p. 456).

## Reinforcer Dimensions

The choices an individual makes are affected by dimensions of the competing response options and their consequences, such as the rate, quality, immediacy, and delay to reinforcement. Individuals tend to allocate their choices in proportion to the various dimensions of reinforcement obtained from response options (with respect to the rate, duration, immediacy, or amount of reinforcement, or some combination of those dimensions) and the amount of effort required to obtain reinforcement. For example, research by Martens and his colleagues (Martens, 1990; Martens, Halperin, Rummel, & Kilpatrick, 1990; Martens & Houk, 1989; Martens, Lochner, & Kelly, 1992) showed that student engagement in on-task versus competing problem behavior occurred in approximate proportion to the relative amount of teacher attention associated with those behavior alternatives.

Neef, Mace, Shea, and Shade (1992) examined how three special education students allocated their responding across two concurrently available math tasks that differed with respect to the rate of reinforcement, quality of reinforcement, or both. Students were presented with choices between two sets of math problems, and they could select a math problem from either set at any point in time. Points exchangeable for prizes were awarded for correct completion of math problems on different variable interval (VI) schedules, such that performance of math problems selected from one set (A) was reinforced more often than performance of math problems from the other set (B). When the prizes for which points could be exchanged were equal for the two math problem alternatives, the students performed more problems from the set that produced a higher rate of reinforcement. However, when the two sets of math problems also differed with respect to the quality of reinforcement (i.e., prizes that could be earned with the points obtained), the students spent more time completing the problems associated with the more preferred rewards (set B) even though they received less frequent reinforcement for those problems. For these students, then, the quality of reinforcement influenced their choices more than the rate of reinforcement did.

Neef and colleagues used a similar methodology to examine the relative influence of immediacy of reinforcement (Neef, Mace, & Shade, 1993); response effort (Mace, Neef, Shade, & Mauro, 1996); and the interactive effects of reinforcer rate, quality, delay, and response effort (Neef, Shade, & Miller, 1994; Neef & Lutz, 2001a). Because choices in everyday situations are likely to involve response options that differ on a number of dimensions, understanding how these dimensions combine to influence choices can be useful in understanding, predicting, and managing behavior. Therefore, Neef and Lutz (2001a, 2001b) used the previously discussed method in-

volving concurrent response options in the development of a brief computer-based assessment that evaluated the sensitivities of individuals with learning and behavior difficulties to particular reinforcer dimensions. The assessment involved the presentation of two task options in each of six conditions. In each condition, the task options competed on a different dimension. For example, in the effort versus quality condition, the choices were between easy tasks associated with less preferred reinforcers and difficult tasks associated with highly preferred reinforcers. Competing dimensions were counterbalanced across the six conditions of the initial assessment, and the conditions resulting in the most and least time allocated to one task alternative relative to the other were then replicated. The results showed that participants demonstrated differential responsiveness to the various reinforcer dimensions and that the influence of each dimension varied across students.

## Applications of Assessment Results to Promote Beneficial Choices

Bannerman and colleagues (1990) noted, "All people have the right to eat too many donuts" (p. 86). Yet we can take steps to encourage choices of low-fat entrees (e.g., Mayer, Heins, Vogel, Morrison, Lankester, & Jacobs, 1986) and make less preferred (but more beneficial) options more attractive. Understanding how reinforcer dimensions affect an individual's choices can enable us to manipulate those dimensions to promote choices that favor desirable versus less desirable choices.

Neef and Lutz (2001b) used the information derived from the assessment of the influence of different reinforcer dimensions described earlier to develop and evaluate interventions for classroom problem behaviors of individual students. For example, preferred rewards contingent on low levels of disruptive behavior were compared with less preferred rewards for meeting the established criterion with a student for whom quality of reinforcement had been identified as the most influential reinforcer dimension. The results of a reversal design showed that, for each student, interventions based on favorable levels of the dimension that had been identified as influential in the preceding assessment were differentially effective in treating the student's problem behavior.

Horner and Day (1991) also demonstrated how reinforcer dimensions could affect choices among competing adaptive and problem behaviors. The results of their study showed that three individuals with severe disabilities chose to engage in functional communication rather than problem behavior when the communication alternative was made less effortful (Experiment 1), yielded a higher rate of reinforcement (Experiment 2), or produced more immediate reinforcement (Experiment 3).

Other investigations have demonstrated that, by increasing the quality of reinforcement produced by appropriate behavior, appropriate behavior increased and inappropriate behavior decreased (Peck et al., 1996; Piazza et al., 1997). Peck and colleagues demonstrated how this approach could be advantageous when the use of extinction for undesirable behaviors is untenable. One of the participants in the study engaged in life-threatening self-injurious behavior (SIB; pulling and chewing on his central-venous line) when he was left alone, which necessarily produced attention from adults. The reinforcer that maintained his SIB (attention) could not be withheld because engaging in the behavior was potentially life threatening. The authors therefore designed an intervention to make a communicative response a more preferred option than SIB. They provided higher quality and a longer duration of attention for appropriate communication (enthusiastic praise for 2 minutes) than for problem behavior (neutral redirection that lasted only a few seconds). After only a few training sessions, the child engaged almost exclusively in appropriate communication rather than SIB.

Hanley, Iwata, and Lindberg (1999) evaluated the preferences of individuals with disabilities for daily activities. One of the participants in the study often chose lounging in the living room over completing household chores. However, when preferred alternative reinforcement (edibles and music) was made available while chores were being completed, the participant began to choose and engage in chore completion more frequently than lounging. The Peck and colleagues (1996) and Hanley and colleagues (1999) studies demonstrate that preference can be affected by altering the dimensions of reinforcement associated with more socially desirable responses.

This strategy can also be useful in situations in which problem behavior is maintained by automatic reinforcement. When the behavior itself directly and immediately produces the reinforcer (e.g., sensory stimulation), it is often difficult to prevent. Zhou, Goff, and Iwata (2000) demonstrated how the manipulation of response effort could be used to promote adaptive choices in four individuals with profound developmental disabilities whose self-injurious hand-mouthing appeared to be automatically reinforcing. Although during baseline participants were given free access to preferred leisure items (identified by the length of time they manipulated the items in a preceding preference assessment), they continued to engage in high levels of hand-mouthing. In an effort to promote choosing a competing response (leisure item manipulation) over hand-mouthing, the experimenters had participants wear soft, flexible sleeves that increased resistance for elbow flexion (and thus the effort to engage in hand-mouthing). The results of mixed multiple baseline and reversal designs showed that increasing the response effort for hand-mouthing produced an increase in choices of object manipulation relative to hand-mouthing for all participants. The study is notable because it suggests that preferences can be altered to favor adaptive choices (leisure item manipulation) by altering the dimensions of the less desirable but initially preferred response option (hand-mouthing).

Another area in which it is helpful to understand how reinforcer dimensions affect choices among competing response options is the area of self-control. Behavioral researchers have defined self-control as choosing to wait longer periods of time to have access to larger, higher quality reinforcers (e.g., forgoing purchase of a small item in favor of saving money for a more valued item at a later point in time). Impulsivity, on the other hand, can be defined as choosing immediate access to smaller, lower quality reinforcers (Ainslie, 1974; Rachlin & Green, 1972; Schweitzer & Sulzer-Azaroff, 1988). Basic research with both humans and nonhumans has demonstrated that specific histories of reinforcement can influence the development of choices that demonstrate self-control (e.g., Ferster, 1953; Mazur & Logue, 1978; Schweitzer & Sulzer-Azaroff, 1988).

Neef, Bicard, and Endo (2001) established self-control with three students with attention deficit hyperactivity disorder (ADHD) by manipulating various reinforcer dimensions to compete with reinforcer immediacy. A brief assessment of the influence of various reinforcer dimensions had revealed that each of the student's task choices was influenced principally by the immediacy of reinforcement (reflecting impulsivity). Self-control training involved arranging for the task associated with the delayed reinforcement to be associated with another influential dimension identified by the assessment (higher rate or quality of reinforcement). The delay to reinforcement for that task was minimized and then progressively increased. This procedure resulted in the students choosing to engage in that task option the majority of the time, despite delays to delivery of reinforcement for up to 24 hours. These findings were encouraging considering prevailing viewpoints that children with ADHD are deficient in the capacity for their behavior to be governed by temporally remote contingencies (Barkley, 1997).

Similarly, Dixon, Hayes, Binder, Manthey, Sigman, & Zdanowski (1998) evaluated the effects of a self-control training procedure using concurrent schedules of reinforcement on the choices and task engagement of three adults with mental retardation who did not engage in the target tasks and whose choices were shown to be impulsive. The self-control training procedure began with offering a choice between the small and large reinforcers with no work requirement or delay for either choice. The purpose of this phase was to establish choice for the larger reinforcer. When this had been accomplished, the authors progressively increased the delay to obtain the larger reinforcer. That is, participants could choose between a smaller, immediate reinforcer with no work requirement and a larger, delayed reinforcer with a small work requirement (which slowly increased over time as the participants consistently chose this response option). Within several sessions, all three of the participants consistently chose the larger, more delayed reinforcer and engaged in the target behavior for the total amount of time required.

## CONCLUSION

Although some authors have suggested that the provision of options has therapeutic benefits, it may be that the act of choosing is effective only to the extent that it permits access to preferred reinforcers. We posit that assessment of the variables that affect preference contributes to efforts to promote choices that are beneficial. Research using a concurrent reinforcement schedules approach has demonstrated the role of motivating operations (i.e., establishing and abolishing operations) and various dimensions of reinforcement on preference and choice. Relative sensitivities to reinforcer dimensions or contingencies associated with response options affect an individual's choice to engage in one behavior or another at any given point in time. In this sense, individuals do not need to be taught to make choices; behavior reflects choice (J. O. Cooper, personal communication, December 1, 2003).

It may be helpful to teach individuals how to communicate their preferences when specific choice opportunities are provided or to communicate preferences in a socially desirable way. There is an abundance of research on teaching functional communication skills. However, teaching communication skills is not teaching choice. Choice already exists in the repertoire of the behaving individual. As demonstrated by Horner and Day (1991), even when appropriate communication skills are taught, individuals may choose problem behavior as opposed to communication responses if the reinforcement contingencies associated with problem behavior are more favorable than those associated with communication responses. Thus, we must be mindful of the contingencies of reinforcement that operate for concurrent response options. Choice does not give power to reinforcement. Rather, reinforcement gives power to choice (J. O. Cooper, personal communication, December 1, 2003).

## REFERENCES

Ainslie, G. W. (1974). Impulse control in pigeons. *Journal of the Experimental Analysis of Behavior, 21,* 485–489.

Ayllon, T., & Azrin, N. H. (1968). Reinforcer sampling: A technique for increasing the behavior of mental patients. *Journal of Applied Behavior Analysis, 1,* 13–20.

Bambara, L. M., Ager, C., & Koger, F. (1994). The effects of choice and task preference on the work performance of adults with severe disabilities. *Journal of Applied Behavior Analysis, 27,* 555–556.

Bannerman, D. J., Sheldon, J. B., Sherman, J. A., & Harchik, A. E. (1990). Balancing the right to habilitation with the right to personal liberties: The rights of people with developmental disabilities to eat too many doughnuts and take a nap. *Journal of Applied Behavior Analysis, 23,* 79–89.

Barkley, R. A. (1997). *ADHD and the nature of self-control.* New York: Guilford.

Berg, W. K., Peck, S., Wacker, D. P., Harding, J., McComas, J., Richman, D., & Brown, K. (2000). The effects of presession exposure to attention on the results of assessments of attention as a reinforcer. *Journal of Applied Behavior Analysis, 33,* 463–477.

Bowman, L. G., Piazza, C. C., Fisher, W. W., Hagopian, L. P., & Kogan, J. S. (1997). Assessment of preference for varied versus constant reinforcers. *Journal of Applied Behavior Analysis, 30,* 451–458.

Brown, F., Apple, C., Corsi, L., & Wenig, B. (1993). Choice diversity for people with severe disabilities: *Education and Training in Mental Retardation, 28,* 318–326.

Catania, A. C. (1998). *Learning* (4th ed.). Upper Saddle River, NJ: Prentice Hall.

Champlin, S. M., & Karoly, P. (1975). Role of contract negotiation in self-management of study time: A preliminary investigation. *Psychological Reports, 37,* 724–726.

Corah, N. L., & Boffa, J. (1970). Perceived control, self observation, and response to aversive stimulation. *Journal of Personality and Social Psychology, 16,* 1–4.

DeLeon, I. G., & Iwata, B. A. (1996). Evaluation of a multiple-stimulus presentation format for assessing reinforcer preferences. *Journal of Applied Behavior Analysis, 29,* 519–532.

Devine, D. A., & Fernald, P. S. (1973). Outcome effects of receiving a preferred, randomly assigned, or nonpreferred therapy. *Journal of Consulting and Clinical Psychology, 41,* 104–107.

Dixon, M. R., Hayes, L. J., Binder, L. M., Manthey, S., Sigman, C., & Zdanowski, D. M. (1998). Using a self-control training procedure to increase appropriate behavior. *Journal of Applied Behavior Analysis, 31,* 203–210.

Dunlap, G., dePerczel, M., Clarke, S., Wilson, D., Wright, S., White, R., & Gomez, A. (1994). Choice making to promote adaptive behavior for students with emotional and behavioral challenges. *Journal of Applied Behavior Analysis, 27,* 505–518.

Dyer, K., Dunlap, G., & Winterling, V. (1990). Effects of choice making on the serious problem behaviors of students with severe handicaps. *Journal of Applied Behavior Analysis, 23,* 515–524.

Faw, G. D., Davis, P. K., & Peck, C. (1996). Increasing self-determination: Teaching people with mental retardation to evaluate residential options. *Journal of Applied Behavior Analysis, 29,* 173–188.

Ferster, C. B. (1953). Sustained behavior under delayed reinforcement. *Journal of Experimental Psychology, 45,* 218–224.

Fisher, W. W., & Mazur, J. A. (1997). Basic and applied research on choice responding. *Journal of Applied Behavior Analysis, 30,* 387–410.

Gardner, W. I., Cole, C. L., Berry, D. L., & Nowinski, J. M. (1983). Reduction of disruptive behaviors in mentally retarded adults: A self-management approach. *Behavior Modification, 7,* 76–96

Geer, J. H., Davison, G. C., & Gatchel, R. I. (1970). Reduction of stress in humans through nonveridical perceived control of aversive stimulation. *Journal of Personality and Social Psychology, 16,* 731–738.

Geer, J. H., & Maisel, E. (1972). Evaluating the effects of the prediction-control confound. *Journal of Personality and Social Psychology, 23,* 314–319.

Glass, D. C., Singer, J. E., & Friedman, L. N. (1969). Psychic cost of adaptation to an environmental stressor. *Journal of Personality and Social Psychology, 12,* 200–210.

Gottschalk, J. M., Libby, M. E., & Graff, R. B. (2000). The effects of establishing operations on preference assessment outcomes. *Journal of Applied Behavior Analysis, 33,* 85–88.

Graff, R. B., & Libby, M. E. (1999). A comparison of presession and within-session reinforcement choice. *Journal of Applied Behavior Analysis, 32,* 161–173.

Green, C. W., Middleton, S. G., & Reid, D. H. (2000). Embedded evaluation of preferences sampled from person-centered plans for people with profound multiple disabilities. *Journal of Applied Behavior Analysis, 33,* 639–642.

Hanley, G. P., Iwata, B. A., & Lindberg, J. S. (1999). Analysis of activity preferences as a function of differential consequences. *Journal of Applied Behavior Analysis, 32,* 419–435.

Hanley, G. P., Piazza, C. C., Fisher, W. W., Contrucci, S. A., & Maglieri, K. A. (1997). Evaluation of client preference for function-based treatment packages. *Journal of Applied Behavior Analysis, 30,* 459–473.

Higbee, T. S., Carr, J. E., & Harrison, C. D. (1999). The effects of pictorial versus tangible stimuli in stimulus-preference assessments. *Research in Developmental Disabilities, 20,* 63–72.

Horner, R. H., & Day, M. D. (1991). The effects of response efficiency on functionally equivalent competing behaviors. *Journal of Applied Behavior Analysis, 24,* 719–732.

Hutchins, M. P., & Renzaglia, A. (1998). Interviewing families for effective transition to employment. *Teaching Exceptional Children, 30,* 72–78.

Kanfer, F. H., & Grimm, L. G. (1978). Freedom of choice and behavior change. *Journal of Consulting and Clinical Psychology, 46,* 873–878.

Kennedy, C. H., & Haring, T. G. (1993). Teaching choice making during social interactions to students with profound multiple disabilities. *Journal of Applied Behavior Analysis, 26,* 63–76.

Koegel, R. L., Dyer, K., & Bell, L. K. (1987). The influence of child-preferred activities on autistic children's social behavior. *Journal of Applied Behavior Analysis, 20,* 243–252.

Kohn, A. (1993). *Punished by rewards: The trouble with gold stars, incentive plans, A's, praise, and other bribes.* Boston: Houghton Mifflin.

Lancioni, G. E., O'Reilly, M. F., & Emerson, (1996). A review of choice research with people with severe and profound developmental disabilities. *Research in Developmental Disabilities, 17,* 391–411.

Laraway, S., Snycerski, S., Michael, J., & Poling, A. (2003). Motivating operations and terms to describe them: Some further refinements. *Journal of Applied Behavior Analysis, 36,* 407–414.

Lerman, D. C., Iwata, B. A., Rainville, B., Adelinis, J. D., Crosland, K., & Kogan, J. (1997). Effects of reinforcement choice on task responding in individuals with developmental disabilities. *Journal of Applied Behavior Analysis, 30,* 411–422.

Mace, F. C., Neef, N. A., Shade, D., & Mauro, B. C. (1996). Effects of problem difficulty and reinforcer quality on time allocated to concurrent arithmetic problems. *Journal of Applied Behavior Analysis, 29,* 11–24.

Martens, B. K. (1990). A context analysis of contingent teacher attention. *Behavior Modification, 14,* 138–156.

Martens, B. K., Halperin, S., Rummel, J. E., & Kilpatrick, D. (1990). Matching theory applied to contingent teacher attention. *Behavioral Assessment, 12,* 139–156.

Martens, B. K., & Houk, J. L. (1989). The application of Herrnstein's laws of effect to disruptive and on-task behavior of a retarded adolescent girl. *Journal of the Experimental Analysis of Behavior, 51,* 17–27.

Martens, B. K., Lochner, D. G., & Kelly, S. Q. (1992). The effects of variable-interval reinforcement on academic engagement: A demonstration of matching theory. *Journal of Applied Behavior Analysis, 25,* 143–151.

Mason, S. A., McGee, G. G., Farmer-Dougan, V., & Risley, T. R. (1989). A practical strategy for ongoing reinforcer assessment. *Journal of Applied Behavior Analysis, 22,* 171–179.

Mayer, J. A., Heins, J. M., Vogel, J. M., Morrison, D. C., Lankester, L. D., & Jacobs, A. L. (1986). Promoting low-fat entree choices in a public cafeteria. *Journal of Applied Behavior Analysis, 19,* 397–402.

Mazur, J. E., & Logue, A. W. (1978). Choice in a "self-control" paradigm: Effects of a fading procedure. *Journal of the Experimental Analysis of Behavior, 30,* 11–17.

McDowell, J. J. (1988). Matching theory in natural human environments. *The Behavior Analyst, 11,* 95–109.

Munk, D. D., & Repp, A. C. (1994). The relationship between instructional variables and problem behavior: A review. *Exceptional Children, 60,* 390–401

Neef, N. A., Bicard, D. F., & Endo, S. (2001). Assessment of impulsivity and the development of self-control in students with attention deficit hyperactivity disorder. *Journal of Applied Behavior Analysis, 34,* 397–408.

Neef, N. A., & Lutz, M. N. (2001a). A brief computer-based assessment of reinforcer dimensions affecting choice. *Journal of Applied Behavior Analysis, 34,* 57–60.

Neef, N. A., & Lutz, M. N. (2001b). Assessment of variables affecting choice and application to classroom interventions. *School Psychology Quarterly, 16,* 239–252.

Neef, N. A., Mace, F. C., & Shade, D. (1993). Impulsivity in students with serious emotional disturbance: The interactive effects of reinforcer rate, delay, and quality. *Journal of Applied Behavior Analysis, 26,* 37–52.

Neef, N. A., Mace, F. C., Shea, M., & Shade, D. (1992). Effects of reinforcer rate and reinforcer quality on time allocation: Applications of matching theory to educational settings. *Journal of Applied Behavioral Analysis, 25,* 691–699.

Neef, N. A., Shade, D., & Miller, M. S. (1994). Assessing influential dimensions of reinforcers on choice in students with serious emotional disturbance. *Journal of Applied Behavior Analysis, 27,* 575–583.

Newton, J. S., Ard, W. R., Jr., & Horner, R. H. (1993). Validating predicted activity preferences of individuals with severe disabilities. *Journal of Applied Behavior Analysis, 26,* 239–245.

O'Reilly, M. F. (1999). Effects of presession attention on the frequency of attention-maintained behavior. *Journal of Applied Behavior Analysis, 32,* 371–374.

Parsons, M. B., & Reid, D. H. (1990). Assessing food preferences among persons with profound mental retardation: Providing opportunities to make choices. *Journal of Applied Behavior Analysis, 23,* 183–195.

Parsons, M. B., Reid, D. H., Reynolds, J., & Bumgarner, M. (1990). Effects of chosen versus assigned jobs on the work performance of persons with severe handicaps. *Journal of Applied Behavior Analysis, 23,* 253–258.

Peck, S. M., Wacker, D. P., Berg, W. K., Cooper, L. J., Brown, K. A., Richman, D., McComas, J. J., Frischmeyer, P., & Millard, T. (1996). Choice-making treatment of young children's severe behavior problems. *Journal of Applied Behavior Analysis, 29,* 263–290.

Perlmuter, L. C., & Monty, R. A. (1973). Effect of choice of stimulus on paired-associate learning. *Journal of Experimental Psychology, 99,* 120–123.

Piazza, C. C., Fisher, W. W., Hanley, G. P., Remick, M. L., Contrucci, S. A., & Aitken, T. A. (1997). The use of positive and negative reinforcement in the treatment of escape-maintained destructive behavior. *Journal of Applied Behavior Analysis, 30,* 279–298.

Rachlin, H., & Green, L. (1972). Commitment, choice and self-control. *Journal of the Experimental Analysis of Behavior, 17,* 15–22.

Reid, D. H., Parsons, M. B., & Green, C. W. (1998). Identifying work preferences among individuals with severe multiple disabilities prior to beginning supported work. *Journal of Applied Behavior Analysis, 31,* 281–285.

Schweitzer, J. B., & Sulzer-Azaroff, B. (1988). Self-control: Teaching tolerance for delay in impulsive children. *Journal of the Experimental Analysis of Behavior, 50,* 173–186.

Shevin, M., & Klein, N. (1984). The importance of choice-making skills for students with severe disabilities. *Journal of the Association for Persons with Severe Handicaps, 9,* 159–166.

Smith, R. G., Iwata, B. A., & Shore, B. A. (1995). Effects of subject- versus experimenter-selected reinforcers on the behavior of individuals with profound developmental disabilities. *Journal of Applied Behavior Analysis, 28,* 61–71.

Stotland, E., & Blumenthal, A. L. (1964). The reduction of anxiety as a result of the expectation of making a choice. *Canadian Journal of Psychology, 18,* 139–145.

Vaughn, B. J., & Horner, R. H. (1997). Identifying instructional tasks that occasion problem behaviors and assessing the effects of student versus teacher choice among these tasks. *Journal of Applied Behavior Analysis, 30,* 299–312.

Vollmer, T. R., & Iwata, B. A. (1991). Establishing operations and reinforcement effects. *Journal of Applied Behavior Analysis, 24,* 279–291.

Waldron-Soler, K. M., Martella, R. C., Marchand-Martella, N. E., & Ebey, T. L. (2000). Effects of choice of stimuli as reinforcement for task responding in preschoolers with and without developmental disabilities. *Journal of Applied Behavior Analysis, 33,* 93–96.

Wright, R. M., & Strong, S. R. (1982). Stimulating therapeutic change with directives. *Journal of Counseling Psychology, 29,* 199–202.

Zhou, L., Goff, G. A., & Iwata, B. A. (2000). Effects of increased response effort on self-injury and object manipulation as competing responses. *Journal of Applied Behavior Analysis, 33,* 29–40.

Zuckerman, M., Porac, J., Lathin, D., Smith, R., & Deci, E. L. (1978). On the importance of self-determination for intrinsically motivated behavior. *Personality and Social Psychology Bulletin, 4,* 443–446.

## STUDY QUESTIONS AND FOLLOW-UP ACTIVITIES

1. You are the teacher in a self-contained special education classroom. Jerry, a student in your classroom, exhibits physical aggression during transitions between classroom tasks. For example, Jerry typically bites you when you instruct him to put his math sheets in his desk and go to reading group. You think he does this behavior to escape or avoid completing the task (i.e., you think escape from tasks is a reinforcer for Jerry). How could you make use of influential dimensions of reinforcers (e.g., Neef & Lutz, 2001a, 2001b) to develop an effective intervention to address Jerry's aggression during these transitions?

2. When given a choice, Roderick consistently selects previously mastered spelling drills over spelling drills with new words. Roderick's teacher is concerned that he is not receiving sufficient practice on new spelling words. How might Roderick's teacher influence Roderick's choices by altering aspects of the two different sets of spelling drills?

3. In your own words, offer an interpretation of the following statement: "Choice does not give power to reinforcement. Rather, reinforcement gives power to choice" (J. O. Cooper, personal communication, December 1, 2003).

4. During recess, Lisa almost exclusively chooses to play jump rope and listen to rap music. Lisa's teacher would like to see improvements in Lisa's on-task behavior during math instruction (which occurs *immediately following* recess). Lisa's teacher decides to offer Lisa a choice of reinforcers for staying on task during math. What should the teacher consider before selecting rope-jumping and rap music as Lisa's only activity choices? What alternative strategies might the teacher follow in identifying activities that could be offered to Lisa as reinforcers in this case?

5. Michael is a 5-year-old boy diagnosed with autism. When given a choice for leisure time, he typically chooses to play on the computer alone rather than participate in group activities with his peers. Michael's teacher is concerned that Michael rarely interacts with his peers. What can Michael's teacher do to encourage Michael to choose group activities with his peers more frequently than isolated computer time?

6. Explain the relationship between and interactions among antecedent variables (e.g., motivating operations) and consequence variables (i.e., dimensions of reinforcement) and how they affect choice (as an indicator of preference).

7. In the past, Cal's teacher has successfully reinforced Cal's completion of clean-up activities following leisure time by providing him with contingent access to a portable CD player. However, Cal has begun to discard the CD player when it is given to him, and its effects as a reinforcer are waning. Based the research of Gottschalk, Libby, and Graff (2000) and Graff and Libby (1999), what might the teacher do to increase the effectiveness of the CD player as a reinforcer for Cal?

8. Explain how the use of concurrent schedules of reinforcement in applied research has good external validity in terms of analyzing choice responding.

9. What is a potential drawback to relying on information from caregivers in determining a student's preferences? What are two potential alternative methodologies for identifying preferences?

10. Explain what abolishing operations are and the impact they might have on the effectiveness of edible reinforcers during classroom work following lunch.

---

Study questions and follow-up activities prepared by Brandon E. McCord, Tabitha J. Kirby, and Jamie M. Hughes.

# PART III

## Training, Supporting, and Learning with Measurably Effective Teachers

Chapter 8    Developing, Implementing, and Maintaining a Responsive
             Educator Program for Preservice General Education Teachers
             *Larry Maheady, Gregory F. Harper, and Barbara Mallette*

Chapter 9    Teaching Applied Behavior Analysis to Preservice Personnel:
             A Cooperative Field-Based Approach
             *Jo Webber*

Chapter 10   Collaborating with Preservice and Mentor Teachers to Design and
             Implement Classroom Research
             *Sheila R. Alber and Janet S. Nelson*

Chapter 11   The Hawthorne Country Day School: A Behavioral Approach
             to Schooling
             *Christopher S. McDonough, Tina Covington, Sayaka Endo,
             Deborah Meinberg, Trina D. Spencer, and David F. Bicard*

Chapter 12   Behavioral Systems Analysis in Higher Education
             *Richard W. Malott*

# Developing, Implementing, and Maintaining a Responsive Educator Program for Preservice General Education Teachers

*Larry Maheady*  *Gregory F. Harper*  *Barbara Mallette*

Approximately 10 years ago, we raised a number of questions regarding preservice general education teachers' knowledge of behavior analysis principles and procedures. We asked, for example, how familiar future classroom teachers were with basic behavioral concepts such as positive and negative reinforcement, punishment, and extinction and, more important, how well versed they were in the actual use of behavior analytic practices. The results at that time were quite pessimistic. We noted, for example, that many professionals felt that applied behavior analysis had played a very limited role in preservice teacher preparation, particularly within general education (e.g., Axelrod, 1991; Cuban, 1988; Deitz, 1994; Hall, 1991; Kohler & Strain, 1992). Moreover, our personal experiences with general educators revealed little interest in, contact with, or understanding of behavior analysis. Unfortunately, a decade later we must conclude that little has changed since our initial assessment, although there does appear to be reason for more optimism this time around.

Here we provide a brief rationale to support our optimism and describe a *different* preparation program for preservice general educators—one that has integrated behavior analysis principles and practices into its course work and applied field experiences over the past 10 years. We begin with a brief historical perspective on the development of the Reflective and Responsive Educator (RARE) program and its transformation into the Responsive Educator Program (REP), paying particular attention to those factors that have promoted or inhibited programmatic change. We then discuss three specific programmatic changes that have been used to incorporate behavior analytic strategies into the instructional repertoires of our preservice general education teachers. In particular, we describe how we prepare them to implement evidence-based teaching practices, collect and use direct and frequent measures of student performance, and engage in data-based professional reflections. We conclude with a discussion of how a variety of programmatic factors, internal and external, have worked to either inhibit or sustain REP implementation. We offer this analysis within the broader context of preservice teacher preparation in the United States today.

## GUARDED OPTIMISM

Singer-songwriter Bob Dylan once wrote, "the times they are a changing." This sentiment clearly reflects the substantive changes occurring within contemporary teacher education. As behaviorists and empiricists, we believe that such changes provide a more favorable climate for those interested in extending applied behavior analysis practices within general education settings. In the recent Dewitt Wallace-Reader's Digest Distinguished Lecture, for example, Slavin (2002) argued that education is on the brink of a scientific revolution that may profoundly transform policy, practice, and research. The nature of this revolution emanates from monumental *evidence-based* policies such as No Child Left Behind (U.S. Congress, 2001) and Comprehensive School Reform (i.e., Southwest Educational Research Laboratory, 2002) as well as recent shifts and trends in research funding policies. To Slavin's knowledge, this marked the first time in history that federal education policy and funding were linked *directly* to evidence of instructional effectiveness.

Similarly, recent reform efforts within teacher accreditation have taken on a much more behavior-friendly tone. The National Council for the Accreditation of Teacher Education (NCATE), for example, in its most recent standards document (NCATE, 2002) articulated the following important ideas: (a) new teaching standards should focus on what new teachers *know* and *can do;* (b) institutions of higher education (IHEs) must assume a *systematic* approach to teaching, learning, and learning to teach; (c) standards must focus on *performance-based outcomes* and *continuous monitoring* of performance; and (d) IHEs must collect *more data*—particularly data examining the impact of teacher candidates' instruction on pupil out-

comes. Few, if any, behavior analysts would be troubled by such important and measurable educational goals. Indeed, Greenwood and Maheady (1997) suggested earlier that *change in pupil performance as a function of teacher instruction* should serve as "the gold standard for making judgments concerning effective instruction" (p. 266).

Evidence-based educational policies would be important at any time in our history, but they may be particularly salient today given the rise in professional accountability (Slavin, 2002). State and national governments, for example, are asserting greater control over local education by establishing school-based consequences that are tied to state-level academic assessments. Although the accountability movement has been dominant for decades and many problems exist when using year-to-year changes as indicators of schooling quality (e.g., Linn & Haug, 2002), the general notion of holding IHEs and teachers accountable for teacher candidate and student progress makes good sense to behavioral researchers and educators. Behavior analysts can provide the proven instructional strategies to help teachers and teacher educators reach their educational goals while simultaneously providing the evaluation and design procedures necessary to document functional instructional effects.

A fourth contributor to the changing nature of contemporary teacher education stems from the recent assaults on "traditional" teacher preparation programs and certification practices. In July 2002, for example, the U.S. secretary of education issued a report titled *Meeting the Highly Qualified Teacher's Challenge.* This document essentially called for the dismantling of traditional teacher education systems and the redefining of teacher qualifications to include little preparation for teaching (Darling-Hammond & Youngs, 2002). In refuting many of the secretary's claims, the authors noted that the report itself failed to meet its own standards for the use of scientifically based research to formulate policy. Similarly, the Abell Foundation (2001), a private foundation dedicated to improving the quality of life in Baltimore and Maryland, issued a report titled *Teacher Certification Reconsidered,* in which they stated, "Maryland's requirement that individuals must complete a prescribed body of coursework before teaching in a public school is deeply misguided" (p. iii). The possible threat of losing the right to prepare teachers is moving many IHEs and educational reformers to examine innovative practices that can *directly* document their instructional effects on teacher candidates and schoolchildren alike.

Finally, Greenwood (2002) argued persuasively that recent advances in behavioral research can address some *major* problems confronting 21st-century schools. As such this should provide increased demand for behavioral services. He cited, for example, the explicit teaching of independence skills, prevention of discipline problems, effective literacy and academic skill instruction, and the conduct of research that is more relevant to teachers and parents (e.g., bridging the research-to-practice gap) as shining examples of what applied behavior analysis has to offer general educators.

It is within this context of new performance standards for teachers, increased calls for evidence-based policies and practices, greater educational accountability, and accumulating reports of major behavioral successes that the Responsive Educator Program (REP) has evolved at SUNY Fredonia. Here we provide a brief historical perspective on its development and implementation.

## HISTORICAL PERSPECTIVES: FROM RARE TO REP

Over a decade ago, the New York State Department of Education (NYSDOE) mandated systemic reforms in teacher preparation. The state, in effect, asked teacher preparation programs to improve the quality of their programs by making future educators more responsive to the changing needs of a new and substantially different population of learners. NYSDOE directed

teacher educators, more specifically, to develop professional programs that would prepare future educators to *work more effectively* with students from different cultural and linguistic backgrounds; students with specific learning and behavioral challenges; and those from poverty, neglect, and abuse environments.

Initially, we used this state mandate as an opportunity to infuse behavior analysis principles and procedures throughout our preservice general education program. We integrated behavioral content into basic curriculum requirements for *all* teacher candidates (i.e., elementary and secondary); included more direct and highly structured instructional opportunities; promoted the use of evidence-based teaching practices; provided increased levels of systematic feedback (instructor and peer); and adopted an outcomes-based, decision-making model for evaluating and adapting existing teaching practices. The result was the development of the Reflective and Responsive Educator (RARE) program (see Maheady, Harper, Mallette, & Karnes, 1993, 1994, for a more complete program description).

The RARE program included a "core" of four years of developmentally sequenced, highly structured field-based experiences, the majority of which were provided in high-need local school districts. These applied teaching experiences began in the freshman year and occurred throughout each year of the program. RARE teacher candidates learned to use evidence-based teaching practices (e.g., response cards, graphic organizers, guided notes, Classwide Peer Tutoring, and Numbered Heads Together) through the use of in-class modeling and role-playing, and then applied their strategies within selected field-based assignments. Teacher candidates were prepared directly in peer collaboration skills through the use of partner pairings, cooperative learning groups, and specific peer coaching assignments, and they were introduced to a conceptual framework that emphasized reflective decision making and lifelong learning.

In general, the RARE program appeared to be quite successful. RARE graduates passed national-and state-level certification exams at high levels (e.g., 97%–99%) from AY1993–2000, and the vast majority (i.e., 80%) either entered graduate school or found full-time teaching positions within 2 years. Moreover, independent social validity assessments indicated that employers were extremely pleased with the instructional performance of RARE graduates (Harper, 2001), and program enrollment continued to increase every year since initial implementation.

The development and implementation of the RARE program followed a recursive process of initial planning, gradual and systematic implementation, and evaluation and refinement of *separate* program components. Individual programmatic components were refined primarily in response to candidate and pupil performance, as well as to ongoing feedback from our partner schools. Initial implementation and evaluation took place in EDU 250, Introduction to the Exceptional Learner, the second required field-based experience for RARE candidates. Teacher candidates completed course work on meeting the needs of children with learning and behavioral challenges and were required to simultaneously tutor such youngsters over an 8- to 10-week field experience.

The Pair Tutoring Program, an after-school program for students with special needs, was established in two high-need partner schools (i.e., Dunkirk [New York] Elementary School #3 and Dunkirk, [New York] Middle School). The after-school tutoring experience was designed to be mutually beneficial. On one hand, teacher candidates provided a source of much needed individualized instructional assistance for pupils. In return they received direct opportunities to instruct (and learn about teaching) students who had learning and behavioral challenges. Teacher candidates worked in pairs (2:1) twice a week for 1-hour sessions to provide basic literacy and content area instruction. They then met in teaching assistance teams on campus to discuss their instructional efforts and to plan subsequent teaching activities. Initial evaluations of the Pair Tutoring Program showed that teacher candi-

dates provided almost 2,700 hours of individualized tutoring services over the course of two semesters (spring and fall, 1994), a total that exceeded 4,000 hours during AY 2001–2002. In addition, student outcome measures (i.e., curriculum-based assessments) revealed noticeable improvements in oral reading fluency and comprehension for *selected* pupils as a function of their tutoring experience and high levels of consumer satisfaction from pupils, classroom teachers, and teacher candidates (Maheady, Mallette, & Harper, 1996).

Programmatic refinements were extended next to a course called Introduction to Contemporary Education, during the subsequent academic year. This course also included an 8- to 10-week field experience that was titled the Instructional Assistants Program (IAP). The IAP consisted of a multifaceted instructional package that (a) clearly delineated instructional roles and responsibilities for teacher candidates (i.e., via teaching/learning contracts), (b) included partner pairings and cooperative learning groups to serve as vehicles for linking theory and practice, and (c) used progress monitoring scales and consumer satisfaction surveys to evaluate teacher candidate outcomes. Initial program evaluation indicated that teacher candidates provided over 4,000 hours of in-class assistance to classroom teachers over two semesters (AY 1993–1994), and that approximately 90% of candidates' assigned duties were instructional (as opposed to noninstructional) in nature (Maheady, Harper, Karnes, & Mallette, 1999). Moreover, consumer satisfaction surveys revealed that pupils, classroom teachers, and teacher candidates rated program goals, procedures, and outcomes very favorably. In fact, 115 out of 117 teacher candidates reported that they preferred taking this course with the zero credit field-based component even though it entailed substantially more work on their part.

Additional critical events in the evolution of the RARE program included (a) the development, implementation, and evaluation of the third, early field-based experience in EDU 305,

Cultural and Linguistic Diversity (AY 1993–1994); (b) the development and implementation of EDU 227, Literacy and Technology (AY1994–1995); (c) a reconfiguration of the professional year (AY 1995–1996); (d) an Expert Practitioner study (AY 1997–1998); (e) the formation of the Professional Educational Council (AY 1999–2000); and (f) an initiation of NCATE reform activities (AY 2000–2001).

# NCATE AND THE RESPONSIVE EDUCATOR PROGRAM

In AY 2000–2001, SUNY Fredonia initiated contact with NCATE to seek accreditation for its early childhood, childhood, and adolescence education programs. New accreditation was sought primarily because the Regents of the State University of New York, who had been recognized by the U.S. Department of Education as an accrediting agency, was getting out of the accreditation business by February 2004, and New York State institutions had to seek other national accreditation options. Therefore, the School of Education at SUNY Fredonia selected NCATE, and the process of reexamining the RARE program in light of new 2002 performance standards was undertaken.

For the most part, we believe that the RARE program already included many programmatic components mandated by NCATE 2002 standards. We had, for example, already adopted a programmatic focus on what teacher candidates knew and could do and had established a fairly systematic approach for preparing them to do so. Moreover, we had collected data on teacher candidate and pupil outcomes that were, in turn, used to inform and refine program implementation. Yet our NCATE-related deliberations revealed a number of other ways that the RARE program could be improved. Here we cite three specific programmatic changes (i.e., adopting and infusing a new conceptual framework, aligning instructional practices and outcomes with this framework, and adopting an ongoing

monitoring system to facilitate data-based decision making across all programmatic levels) that should greatly enhance the quality of our teacher preparation program.

## Adopting and Infusing a New Conceptual Framework

One of the initial NCATE-related requirements was the development of a conceptual framework or a *shared vision* for the professional educational unit (PEU) (i.e., all college faculties involved in teacher preparation). This particular framework must be clearly written, logically coherent, and consistent with existing professional standards in teaching, learning, and learning to teach. SUNY Fredonia adopted a conceptual framework that is organized around three central features: (1) the process of responsive instruction (represented by the acronym PIRR), (2) the four pillars of understanding on which this process is grounded, and (3) the steps of validation and support.

The first organizational feature, PIRR, represents the process of responsive instruction, comprised of planning, instructing, reflecting, and responding (PIRR). These stages, taken together, represent a recursive process that all effective professionals engage in when providing best teaching practice. When this process is guided by formative measures of learner performance, it can provide the basis for the ongoing validation and self-correction of one's teaching practice (Greenwood & Maheady, 1997).

This dynamic process, in turn, is informed by the four pillars of understanding—knowledge, pedagogy, diversity, and professionalism, which comprise the *shared knowledge bases* of responsive educators. Professional education unit faculty believe that the foundation for best teaching practice includes (a) a thorough understanding of curricular content, instructional context, and human development; (b) a theoretical and empirical grounding in pedagogy; (c) sensitivity and responsiveness to individual difference and diversity; and (d) explicit standards of professionalism. We argue further that each pillar of understanding must be supported by (a) information gleaned from trustworthy educational research, (b) contextual influences that directly affect instructional delivery (e.g., economic, social, and legal factors), and (c) existing and evolving teaching and learning standards (e.g., NY State Learning Standards, NCATE, INTASC, and NBPTS).

A widely accepted model for responsible professional practice in the teacher education literature is that of a reflective practitioner (Schon, 1983, 1987). Reflective practitioners monitor, analyze, and presumably adjust their instructional behavior as a function of both its underlying rationale and its impact on pupil performance. To date, however, two aspects of the reflective practitioner model have remained underevaluated: (a) the relationship between professional reflection and teaching practice and (b) the resultant impact of changes in teaching practice on important pupil outcomes (Howey, 1996; Maheady & Huber, 2002). In other words, to what extent do professionals' reflections influence what and how they teach? And, perhaps more important, what impact do any subsequent changes in instructional practice (as a result of professional reflection) have on pupil performance? We believe that reflection without responsiveness or instructional responsiveness in the absence of improved learner performance is unacceptable at any level of educational reform. Therefore, questions regarding the relationships among professional reflection, instructional practice, and pupil outcomes serve as the foundation for the basic evaluation components of the Responsive Educator Program.

## Aligning Instructional Practices and Outcomes with the New Conceptual Framework

Perhaps the most significant impact of the NCATE accreditation process is that it has required us to align our teaching and evaluation

practices with our shared vision and in so doing to extend the generality of our teacher preparation model. In our earlier commentary (Maheady et al., 1993), we noted that not all faculty members participated in the program restructuring and delivery. As such, some RARE components were implemented with high degrees of fidelity, whereas others were left to the discretion of individual faculty members. In effect, there was no mandate or incentive for some faculty members to adjust their teaching or evaluation methods in the RARE program. NCATE-related planning, however, has provided both the mandate and the incentive for everyone to "get on board."

To facilitate faculty involvement, we also adopted a multiparadigmatic perspective on teaching, learning, and learning to teach (Kromrey, Hines, Paul, & Rosselli, 1996). A multiparadigmatic perspective recognizes the unique and valuable contributions that individuals (e.g., liberal arts and science and school of education faculty, classroom teachers, and teacher candidates) bring to the conceptualization process. In practice, this perspective has increased the breadth and depth of our professional dialogue surrounding programmatic reform by allowing individuals to contribute to the identification and measurement of specific teaching practices and learning outcomes. At the same time, however, our multiparadigmatic approach is guided first and foremost by what works best for students (i.e., promotes student learning) and second by theoretical perspective—a position that Shulman (1986) labeled "disciplined eclecticism." If selected learner outcomes improve as a function of a specific instructional approach, then the practice (irrespective of its theoretical base) is deemed effective in this particular instance and as such would be retained in teacher candidates' instructional repertoires. As Kromrey and colleagues (1996) observed, "future work needs to be guided by a perspective capable of sorting out the differences and contributions of theoretically diverse forms of educational research; and where possible, integrating their effective ingredients and components" (p. 97).

Three specific instructional practices and evaluation methods have been developed and adopted by professional education unit faculty and are currently being piloted to assess their impact on teacher candidate and pupil performance: (a) teaching/learning projects, (b) data-based case studies, and (c) instructional support projects.

### Teaching/Learning Projects

All sections of EDU 105, Introduction to Contemporary Education, now require teacher candidates to teach a minimum of two formal lessons during their first applied teaching experience (i.e., Instructional Assistants Program). Within each lesson, teacher candidates must collect both pre- and postteaching assessments of their pupils' performance (e.g., short objective quizzes, curriculum-based assessment measures, K-W-L) and engage in the recursive (PIRR) teaching process inherent in our conceptual framework. To facilitate this process, all teacher candidates are given a teaching/learning project protocol (available from the authors on request) to guide their efforts and to structure their written responses. In addition, teacher candidates must use at least one evidence-based teaching practice (e.g., response cards, Classwide Peer Tutoring, graphic organizers, guided notes, Numbered Heads Together) in one of their two formal lessons. In-class modeling and role-playing within small cooperative learning groups allow candidates to acquire specific teaching practices. Direct observations in field placements by partners using procedural checklists permit us to assess candidates' accuracy in using specific evidence-based practices. In the spring of 2003, our EDU 105 teacher candidates conducted a total of 84 formal lessons. (The nature and outcomes of these sample lessons are available in graph form from the authors.)

In general, teacher candidates presented a wide variety of formal lessons and used multiple evidence-based practices. The most frequently selected innovative practices were response cards ($n$ = 21), Numbered Heads Together ($n$ = 14), Think-Pair-Share ($n$ = 9), graphic organizers ($n$ = 7), and guided notes ($n$ = 4). In addition, direct observations revealed that candidates implemented evidence-based teaching practices with a high degree of accuracy (X fidelity ratings across five practices = .88). For the most part, pupils appeared to benefit from candidates' lessons (i.e., 53 of 84 candidate lessons presented data that showed a noticeable change in pupil performance), and most candidates were able to "reflect and respond" appropriately to their pupils' performance. One teacher candidate commented, for example, that "students' performance increased greatly as a result of our teaching. Pretest scores averaged 9% correct and the average on the posttest was 78.7%. We also noticed that 25 out of 28 pupils earned passing grades on the posttest." Another noted, "The graphic organizer was really helpful; it made the pupils give more in-depth answers than when we just asked questions orally. I am not making any changes with these practices because the results were great and the students enjoyed learning in this way." There were, however, some logistical issues associated with the use of these activities with such large groups of teacher candidates that will be discussed later. The PIRR teaching protocols are currently being used in other early field experiences and are being adapted for our new student teaching assessments.

### Data-Based Case Studies

A second set of instructional activities that require teacher candidates to engage in the PIRR process while simultaneously deriving useful information from the pillars of understanding are data-based case studies. These projects are being piloted in Developmental and Educational Psychology courses. Teacher candidates are assigned initially to small cooperative learning groups and are provided with detailed case studies that are augmented with sample data sets (e.g., initial baselines of pupil performance).

Instructional teams are then required to plan and describe their instructional lessons for each case. Lesson plans and teaching practices are then assessed in terms of their appropriateness and/or responsiveness to presented data (i.e., did candidates include and respond to initial measures of pupil performance when formulating lessons and selecting preferred teaching practices?). After lessons are presented following the required format, the instructor then provides a second data set to depict pupil outcomes following prescribed lessons (i.e., data sets that depict accelerating, decelerating, or no trends in pupil performance).

Teacher candidates reflect on these data (using a series of stimulus questions) and then formulate a revised set of lesson plans and descriptions of their instructional delivery formats. Once again, instructors assess candidates' reflections and responses in light of presented pupil outcomes. Basically, do teacher candidates continue to use instructional practices that result in accelerating performance rates? Do they discard or adapt existing practices when no change or decelerating data patterns are presented? What rationales do they provide to support their instructional decision making? The process is repeated for a third time prior to the end of the semester. Fundamentally, we have attempted to assess and guide the instructional decision making of our teacher candidates by focusing their attention primarily on the outcomes of their proposed teaching practices. Once more, teacher candidates were quite capable of recognizing when pupils were doing better or worse in a very general way, and they were able to maintain or adjust their planned instruction as a result.

Using analogue procedures in these required, non-field-based courses has allowed us to engage teacher candidates in the PIRR teaching process while requiring them to draw on relevant information from developmental and educational psychology. Similarly, logistical demands were greatly reduced via the use of simulated data, and we were able to exert much more control over the types of outcomes that were presented, reflected on, and responded to by teacher candidates.

### Instructional Support Projects

The hiring of two new special educators, one of whom has a strong behavioral background, has allowed us to extend our instruction and evaluation of the PIRR process to the Pair Tutoring Program within a course called Introduction to the Exceptional Learner. Unlike the aforementioned activities in which sample pre- and postassessments or simulated data were used, instructional support projects require teacher candidates to collect, analyze (reflect on), and respond to ongoing measures of pupil performance. Within the context of their 8- to 10-week after-school tutoring experience, teacher candidates are required to collect curriculum-based assessment measures at the end of each tutoring session. They are then required to co-plan, co-teach, and co-evaluate each lesson using pupil data as one source of progress monitoring. Again, they are provided with a series of instructional decision-making questions and guidelines to address each week, and they must turn in their data samples and written reflections and responses three times during the semester. Instructors then evaluate and respond to teacher candidates' reflections and responses in terms of their clarity, thoroughness, and appropriateness with regard to the outcomes they had collected.

Ongoing small group instructional time is also used for modeling and role-playing the use of a variety of evidence-based teaching practices. Teacher candidates are strongly encouraged to implement and evaluate selected instructional practices within their tutoring sessions, and they earn bonus points for their critical assessments and accuracy in responding to ongoing measures of pupil performance. Beginning in the fall semester of 2003, teacher candidates were required to meet preestablished training criteria (i.e., 85% fidelity without instructor assistance) in the use of a selected number of evidence-based practices prior to using such strategies in their tutoring experience.

Collectively, the aforementioned instructional activities represent our initial attempts to get teacher candidates to use evidence-based practices, to get them to collect and use direct and ongoing measures of pupil performance, and to engage them in data-based decision-making activities.

## Adopting an Ongoing Monitoring System to Facilitate Data-Based Decision Making

To assess the effects of REP on teacher candidates' development, the PEU formally adopted a multi-gated assessment model (MGAM). This particular model provides for a level of uniformity among various programs (e.g., early childhood, childhood, and adolescent education) with regard to professional expectations and programmatic outcomes. The MGAM also allows us to monitor candidate progress through the professional program and includes follow-up evaluations. In addition, the model guides candidates in the development of their professional portfolios. These portfolios, in turn, serve as professional development tools and allow candidates to document their mastery of New York State and NCATE standards. The portfolios also generate data that are used in the formative evaluation of candidates and can be aggregated at the program level to assess REP efficacy.

The multi-gated assessment model requires teacher candidates to meet programmatic standards at five points: program entry; end of the first, second, and third years; and program completion. Candidates must successfully pass through each "gate" as a condition for admission to the succeeding level. The REP also provides for remediation in the event that candidates have not met the criteria established at each gate. The model assumes that effective teachers are prepared best through a combination of solid educative experiences and ongoing constructive evaluations. The gated assessment

model addresses mastery of content, performance in field-based experiences, and the demonstration of behaviors and attitudes (dispositions) appropriate to a professional educator.

Candidates must provide concrete evidence in the form of papers, projects, journals, or candidate ratings at each gate. These become the foundation of their professional portfolio. We plan to systematically collect, and in some cases sample, data from these portfolios to document candidates' mastery of major programmatic outcomes. The outcomes were derived from NCATE Unit Standards, New York State teacher preparation standards, and our conceptual framework. Outcome data will be used at two levels, program and unit. At the program level, we will examine the impact of our course work, field experiences, and other preprofessional experiences on candidates' performance. Patterns of candidate outcomes can be analyzed to determine areas of relative strength and weakness in professional preparation. At the unit level, we will document the PEU's efficacy in meeting unit standards established by NCATE and New York State.

## SO WHERE ARE WE TODAY?

In general, we have developed a preservice teacher preparation program for general educators that infuses many basic behavior analysis concepts and practices (e.g., active student engagement, ongoing and direct monitoring of pupil performance, and use of evidence-based teaching practices) throughout the program. Our teacher candidates have behaved professionally both on campus and in the public schools. They have brought a mixture of enthusiasm, individualized attention and instruction, and emerging teaching competence to large numbers of students. Most preservice general educators like our behavioral principles and practices. Many, in fact, view them as welcome alternatives to the more general recommendations they receive from competing instructional models. They particularly value the explicitness of our methods, the evidence-based arguments to support their use, and the potentially empowering effects that such methods can have on them as future classroom teachers.

We have also established a functional infrastructure built around applied practice and service in predominantly high-need school systems that all teacher candidates are now required to complete. This infrastructure has proved functional, albeit strained, even when delivering instruction to the large numbers of teacher candidates that occupy our classes. It is rewarding, however, to review graduating candidates' résumés and find three or more direct teaching experiences in high-need school systems among the regular entries. Finally, we have begun to collect more representative and direct samples of our teacher candidates' instructional practice and decision making, while trying to do the same with pupil outcomes. This has become time consuming and arduous. Although we are aware of the fact that many of our methods and measures can be refined substantially, we have not always found the time and energy to do so.

## WHERE DO WE GO FROM HERE?

Obviously, a considerable amount of work must still be completed on the Responsive Educator Program. We need, for example, more and better measures of candidates' instructional practices as well as additional tools to capture important pupil outcomes. In particular, we must identify ongoing measures of pupil performance that teacher candidates can use routinely in their instructional planning for entire classrooms of children. We must also develop more systematic ways of teaching our candidates to implement evidence-based instructional practices (i.e., beyond small samples of teaching practice in restricted curriculum areas). Although teacher candidates have done a good job of acquiring such competence through in-class modeling and role-playing, it has become obvious that they need additional opportunities

to learn how to apply such practices on a more generalized basis. Currently, we are working on a model in which preestablished training criteria will be used in conjunction with "out of class" direct preparation activities in selected teaching practices.

We must also do a better job of examining the relationships among our own teaching practice and that of our teacher candidates and to extend these analyses to their impact on candidate and pupil outcomes. Which components of the Responsive Educator Program, for example, are responsible for noticeable improvements in teacher candidates' instructional practice? Which teaching practices produce the most significant impact on pupil learning? What are the generalized and long-term effects of our preparation program on candidates' performance following graduation?

Finally, we must also learn how to leverage more resources to maintain program quality and integrity. As seen in our concluding paragraphs, we have been fighting an unending battle to maintain program quality in the midst of budget reductions, competing institutional priorities, and mixed messages from state and national policy makers.

## SUSTAINING A RESPONSIVE EDUCATOR PROGRAM: PRESERVICE TEACHER PREPARATION FOR GENERAL EDUCATORS IS NOT FOR THE MEEK!

Although many of us have bemoaned our own institution's lack of support, we're not sure that anything can prepare one for the harsh realities of preservice teacher preparation in general education. Soaring enrollments, significant understaffing, and administrative willingness to capitalize on these and related factors have produced the venerable "cash cow" on many college and university campuses across this nation (e.g., Forsyth, 1989; Twombley & Ebmeier, 1989). If this country is serious about the need to reform teacher preparation practices, then significant changes must occur both in terms of the institutional importance and prestige attached to teacher education and the conditions under which it is practiced on many campuses. SUNY Fredonia has been affected by what has become a far too common and unacceptable practice in teacher education—*increasing enrollment and decreasing human resources.* Since AY 1991–1992 (the advent of the RARE program), for example, we have experienced a 63% increase in our undergraduate early childhood and childhood enrollment (i.e., 573 to 916). Graduate enrollment within the School of Education has also increased from 67 to 201 students (i.e., +300% increase) over the past 6 academic years, whereas participation in our adolescence education programs has increased by approximately 46% during that same time period. In spite of such enormous increases in both undergraduate and graduate enrollments, full-time faculty positions have actually *decreased* throughout the decade. We presently have one fewer full-time faculty member than we did over a decade ago when we had over 500 fewer teacher candidates. To compensate, part-time faculty positions have soared. In AY 2001–2002, for example, we had 54 part-time faculty members in the School of Education (compared to 17 full-timers). Instructional workloads typically include 12-hour teaching assignments each semester with an average of about 140 students per instructor. Given the substantial data collection responsibilities associated with our new program's implementation, we must find more effective and efficient ways to monitor pupil, teacher candidate, and program performance.

## LOOK ON THE BRIGHT SIDE OF LIFE

If we have learned anything over the past decade or two, it is how to survive and find joy in what we have been doing. Most recently, we have been able to recruit and hire a highly qualified core of colleagues within the School of Education. We have also learned how to engage our institutional leaders in a dialogue about the need to support teacher education at the highest levels. In response, we have received the campus's lion's share of new full-time faculty lines (although this only brings us back to where we were a decade ago). We have also managed to move many of our more effective part-time faculty members into full-time instructional lines and have provided them and a growing number of full-time graduate assistants with systematic training and continuing support to align their practice with the REP goals and expectations. These training activities have included the development of adjunct faculty professional handbooks; coteaching assignments with full-time faculty members; and the alignment of course goals, procedures, and outcomes. We have also developed an enrollment management plan for the School of Education that is tied to institutional resource allocation plans for the next 5 to 7 years. Whether such institutional responsiveness flows from sincere intentions, the persuasiveness of our advocacy efforts, or from the "fear of NCATE" factor is difficult to assess. In any event, we appreciate the increased institutional support and will do whatever we can to sustain its flow.

## WHERE DO WE HOPE TO BE IN 2013?

By 2013 we hope to be presenting once again to our friends and colleagues at the Annual Focus Conference at The Ohio State University. By then the Buckeyes will have won 154 straight football games and 11 consecutive national championships. We hope the Responsive Educator Program will be equally successful—a well-recognized and replicated model for preparing general education teachers to work effectively with our most challenged learners. Our graduates will maintain and extend their instructional competence by becoming self-regulated and lifelong learners. They will view themselves as good teachers but even better pupils of teaching. Many more behavior analysts from other academic programs (e.g., psychology and behavioral medicine) will work either within or in collaboration with teacher preparation programs in their respective institutions. They will identify mutually beneficial professional goals and forge meaningful relationships with those who prepare teachers. Additional recognition and support will accrue to teacher education as a function of its ability to provide the necessary "evidence" to support its practice and importance to children and youth.

## CONCLUSION

The purpose of this chapter was to introduce readers to a preservice preparation program for general education teachers that integrates behavior analysis principles and practices into its coursework and applied field experiences. We provided a historical overview of the development and implementation of the Responsive Educator Program and highlighted three specific programmatic changes that are being used to teach preservice teachers to use behavioral strategies in their daily interactions with school children. By preparing them to implement evidence-based teaching practices, to use direct and frequent measures of pupil performance, and to engage in data-based professional reflections, we hope to prepare a cadre of classroom teachers who are well equipped to meet the instructional challenges confronting them in 21st century classrooms.

To date, our preservice teachers have brought enthusiasm, individualized assistance, and a sampling of evidence-based teaching practices to large numbers of children enrolled primarily in high-need school districts. We found that our preservice teachers generally like behavior analysis practices and are empowered by the notion that they can monitor and change the effects of their own instruction on important student outcomes. Obviously we have a great deal of work to do with regard to refining our instructional and evaluation methods, increasing the fidelity with which the REP is implemented, and replicating our effects using more systematic and rigorous research designs. Moreover,

we must identify and elicit institutional support to *sustain* this rather labor-intensive program in the midst of soaring enrollments, dwindling resources, and increased calls for professional accountability. The analysis of how to do this is not yet complete, yet the knowledge and desire to do so remain intact.

## REFERENCES

The Abell Foundation. (2001, October). *Teacher certification reconsidered: Stumbling for quality.* Baltimore: Author. Available from http://www.abell.org.

Axelrod, S. (1991). The problem: American education. The solution: Use behavior analytic technology. *Journal of Behavioral Education, 1,* 275–282.

Cuban, L. (1988). Why do some reforms persist? *Educational Administration Quarterly, 24,* 329–336.

Darling-Hammond, L., & Youngs, P. (2002). Defining "high qualified teachers": What does "scientifically-based research" actually tell us? *Educational Researcher, 31* (9), 13–25.

Deitz, S. M. (1994). The insignificant impact of behavior analysis on education: Notes from a Dean of Education. In R. Gardner III, D. M. Sainato, J. O. Cooper, T. E. Heron, W. L., Heward, J. Eshleman, & T. A. Grossi (Eds.), *Behavior analysis in education: Focus on measurably superior instruction* (pp. 33–41). Belmont, CA: Brooks/Cole.

Forsyth, P. (1989). *National Conference for Professors of Educational Administration (NCPEA) and the University Council for Educational Administration (UCEA): Converging missions.* ERIC Document No. 319114.

Greenwood, C. R. (2002, May). *The Juniper Gardens Children's Project documented reasons to hope that public schools can provide quality education.* Paper presentation at the annual meeting of the Association for Behavior Analysis, Toronto, Canada.

Greenwood, C. R., & Maheady, L. (1997). Measurable change in student performance: Forgotten standard in teacher preparation. *Teacher Education and Special Education, 20,* 265–275.

Hall, R. V. (1991). Behavior analysis and education: An unfulfilled dream. *Journal of Behavioral Education, 1,* 305–316.

Harper, G. F. (2001). *2001 survey of graduates of the elementary and early childhood education graduates of the School of Education at the State University of New York at Fredonia.* Unpublished report, School of Education, SUNY Fredonia, New York.

Howey, K. (1996). Designing coherent and effective teacher education programs. In J. Sikula, T. J. Buttery, & E. Guyton (Eds.), *Handbook for research on teacher education* (pp. 143–169). New York: Macmillan.

Kohler, F. W., & Strain, P. S. (1992). Applied behavior analysis and the movement to restructure schools: Compatibilities and opportunities for collaboration. *Journal of Behavioral Education, 2,* 367–390.

Kromrey, J. D., Hines, C. V., Paul, J. L., & Rosselli, H. (1996). Creating and using a multi-paradigmatic knowledge base for restructuring teacher education in special education: Technical and philosophical issues. *Teacher Education and Special Education, 19,* 87–101.

Linn, R. L., & Haug, C. (2002). Stability of school-building accountability scores and gains. *Educational Evaluation and Policy Analysis, 24* (1), 29–36.

Maheady, L., Harper, G. F., Karnes, M., & Mallette, B. (1999). The Instructional Assistants Program: A potential entry point for behavior analysis in education. *Education and Treatment of Children, 22,* 447–469.

Maheady, L., Harper, G. F., Mallette, B., & Karnes, M. (1993). The Reflective and Responsive Educator (RARE): A training program to prepare pre-service general education teachers to instruct children and youth with disabilities. *Education and Treatment of Children, 16,* 474–506.

Maheady, L., Harper, G. F., Mallette, B., & Karnes, M. (1994). "Mainstreaming" applied behavior analysis principles and procedures into a preservice training program for general education teachers. In R. Gardner III, D. M. Sainato, J. O. Cooper, T. E. Heron, W. L., Heward, J. Eshleman, & T. A. Grossi (Eds.), *Behavior analysis in education: Focus on measurably superior instruction* (pp. 43–56). Belmont, CA: Brooks/Cole.

Maheady, L. & Huber, M. (2002). *The Responsive Educator Program: A conceptual framework.* Unpublished manuscript, School of Education, SUNY, Fredonia, New York.

Maheady, L., Mallette, B., & Harper, G. F. (1996). Pair tutoring: A potentially replicable early field-based experience for pre-service general educators. *Teacher Education and Special Education, 19,* 277–297.

NCATE (2002). *Professional standards for the accreditation of schools, colleges, and departments of education.* Washington, DC: Author.

Schon, D. (1983). *The reflective practitioner.* New York: Basic Books.

Schon, D. (1987). *Educating the reflective practitioner: Toward a design for teaching and learning in the professions.* San Francisco: Jossey-Bass.

Shulman, L. S. (1986). Paradigms and research programs in the study of teaching: A contemporary perspective. In M. C. Wittrock (Ed.), *Handbook of research on teaching* (3rd ed.). New York: Simon & Schuster Macmillan.

Slavin, R. E. (2002). Evidence-based education policies: Transforming educational practice and research. *Educational Researcher, 31* (7), 15–21.

Southwest Educational Research Laboratory. (2002). *CSRD database of schools.* Retrieved from http://www.sedl.org/csrd/awards.html.

Twombley, S., & Ebmeier, H. (1989). *Educational administration programs: The* cash cow *of the university? Improving the preparation of school administrators. Notes on reform no. 4.* ERIC Document No. 314828.

U.S. Congress. (2001). No Child Left Behind Act. Washington, DC: Author.

## STUDY QUESTIONS AND FOLLOW-UP ACTIVITIES

1. Descriptions of the REP program include many of the "catch phrases" used in general education today (e.g., *responsive teaching, pedagogy, diversity,* and *literacy education*) and very few technical behavioral terms. Terms such as *responsive teaching* are used to describe data-based decision making. Why do you think the authors chose to avoid technical terminology? Think about the audience and their possible histories of reinforcement. What are some advantages of using such terminology to promote this program to general education teachers? What are some advantages of this type of marketing for ABA? Can you think of any potential disadvantages of using nontechnical language? (See Chapter 16 for additional discussion regarding the use of nontechnical language.)

---

Study questions and follow-up activities prepared by Michelle A. Anderson and Theresa L. Hessler.

2. The authors state, "although teacher candidates have done a good job of acquiring such competence through in-class modeling and role-playing, it has become obvious that they need additional opportunities to learn how to apply such practices on a more generalized basis." Consider proven strategies for promoting generalized outcomes and develop a list of additions or modifications that could be made to the REP program to increase the likelihood of skills generalizing to new situations, settings, or students.

3. Once preservice teachers graduate from their university programs and enter the schools, they often abandon what they have learned in favor of the predominant teaching methods used by teachers in their new schools. Develop a follow-up plan that could be used after an REP graduate leaves the program to monitor the maintenance of her newly acquired skills. If you found that the teachers were not maintaining their skills, what type of "booster" program would you recommend for recapturing those skills?

4. If more teacher preparation programs followed the gated system that the REP program uses (i.e., students must pass certain competencies before advancing in the program), do you think student enrollment in preservice education programs would be affected? If so, what effect do you think this would have on the already existing teacher shortage in some fields of education? What can we do to increase the number of qualified, motivated teachers while simultaneously increasing the requirements to obtain teacher certification or licensure?

5. Compare and contrast the REP teacher education program to the program you attended or know about. How do the criteria for graduation differ? Which program do you think would produce more qualified teachers, and why? What aspects, if any, of the REP program do you wish your program had included? What aspects, if any, are you glad your program did not include?

6. Select a graph from a recent issue of a behavioral journal (e.g., *Journal of Applied Behavior Analysis, Journal of Behavioral Education*) showing the effects of a behavioral intervention with an individual student. With a partner, role-play a parent–teacher conference in which you discuss the behavior of that student as illustrated by the graph. Take turns being the teacher and explaining the behavior change to the parent without the use of jargon or technical terms. The parent should ask questions for clarification whenever necessary.

7. Using the ERIC database, find and review four articles written about the No Child Left Behind Act of 2002 that address various aspects of it. Summarize the controversy about this legislation, and then write a one- to two-page outline of the implications for practice in your area of interest. Be sure to include the potential negative and positive implications.

8. The REP program participants learned to use evidence-based practices such as response cards, graphic organizers, and Classwide Peer Tutoring. Another evidence-based practice is choral responding. Choose any one of these practices and develop a list of topics, subjects, or skills that could be covered (e.g., functional skills in a class of students with severe disabilities or academic content in four core subjects for students with learning disabilities). For each topic, subject, or skill, briefly explain how you would use the evidence-based practice that you chose. Refer to relevant, refereed journals for ideas or develop your own.

9. Compare and contrast the course as described in Chapter 9 with the Responsive Educator Program. Use either a table or narrative format. Review the similarities and determine whether the preservice education program that you are most familiar with contains any of these characteristics. Draft a letter to the dean that supports the inclusion of the missing characteristics, especially those common to both. Consider citing pertinent information from these two chapters.

10. Request the teaching/learning project protocol from the authors and use it to develop a formal lesson plan in your area of interest. Include a component for collecting pre- and postteaching assessments of your pupils' performances. Seek out an opportunity to teach this lesson; then engage in the PIRR, the recursive teaching process central to REP/RARE framework and explained by the authors in this chapter.

**11.** If you were to ask people to list the qualities of a "good" teacher, the answers would vary and might include such vague (i.e., difficult to objectively measure) characteristics such as creative, fun, strict, or rapport builder. Based on this and other chapters of this book, create a list of *behaviors* that an effective teacher exhibits. List those teacher behaviors that are most important to student achievement. Describe how you would measure them.

### CHAPTER 9

# Teaching Applied Behavior Analysis to Preservice Personnel
## A Cooperative Field-Based Approach

*Jo Webber*

The general failure of school personnel to apply principles of applied behavior analysis (ABA) in the practices of instruction and behavior management despite its proven effectiveness is well documented and lamented (Carnine, 2000; Deitz, 1994; Hall, 1991; Kauffman, 2002; Kohler & Strain, 1992; Sugai & Horner, 1999; Walker, Colvin, & Ramsey, 1995). Even special education teacher preparation programs that include ABA competencies fail to promote generalization of skills (Dietz, 1994; O'Reilly, Renzaglia, & Lee, 1994). Several hypothesized reasons for the dearth of effective ABA school practices include (a) no universal appreciation for outcome data, (b) little preference for ABA techniques in favor of progressive education, and (c) less emphasis on instruction in general (specifically, effective instruction), in favor of law and administrative structures (Dietz, 1994; Kauffman, 2002). Furthermore, it is assumed that teacher educators are guilty of either not adequately training ABA skills and knowledge or not providing opportunities to practice the skills in applied settings with prompts and feedback (Dietz, 1994; O'Reilly et al., 1994).

Perhaps as a result of despair over the fact that preservice training has not resulted in effective behavior management practices, a current approach to embedding ABA techniques into school practices promotes an in-service, rather than preservice, model (Scott & Nelson, 1999; Sugai & Horner, 1999; Todd, Horner, Sugai, & Sprague, 1999). Positive Behavioral Support (PBS) or Effective Behavioral Support (EBS) training, based in ABA, proposes a systems and team approach to management of challenging behavior in schools with functional behavioral assessments (FBA) and related planning. The emphasis is on prevention through antecedent manipulations and positive reductive techniques. The PBS model presents ABA skills during in-service programs with in-class coaching and feedback. Schoolwide, classwide, and individual data and outcome analyses are encouraged. Definitive data showing widespread school applications of ABA competencies resulting from such in-service training are eagerly awaited.

At Texas State University—San Marcos (Texas State), we have developed a preservice model with PBS components for the purposes of teaching ABA principles as they apply to managing challenging behavior for special education students. Many of the strategies recommended by others to better ensure the acquisition and generalization of ABA competencies by school personnel have been included. For example, Mallott (1984) outlined 55 specific recommendations for teaching ABA to university students using an ABA model, and Maheady and his colleagues (1994) specified an ABA curriculum and instructional strategies for general education preservice teachers. Common to these recommended strategies are systematic training in peer collaboration, problem solving, and decision making; meaningful and successful field-based experiences; teaching for generalization; and frequent opportunities for active responding. Additionally, Dietz (1994) argued the merits of natural or functional reinforcers inherent in field-based learning. The Texas State course uses a cooperative learning structure to promote peer collaboration, problem solving, and decision making and a field-based behavior management project to encourage the successful application of ABA strategies in typical school settings.

## COURSE DESCRIPTION

Classroom and Behavior Management Strategies for Students with Disabilities (SPED 5375) is a postgraduate special education course required for special education certification and for a master's degree in special education. The course is also required for graduate students seeking licensure in school psychology. Thus, students in this class may be certified teachers seeking a master's degree (in-service); postgraduates seeking initial certification, some of whom may be teaching on emergency permit (preservice); and school psychology majors. The course is sometimes chosen as an elective by general education, child development, therapeutic recreation, and communication disorders majors. For these students, this course is typically the first, and

often the only, ABA course in their graduate and certification plans.

This course primarily addresses basic ABA principles as they apply to managing challenging behavior in public schools. ABA principles covered in this course include (a) definitions of operant conditioning and PBS terminology; (b) the efficacy of and strategies for conducting functional behavioral assessments (FBAs); (c) choosing replacement behavior and writing goals and objectives; (d) observational recording techniques and graphing; (e) a summary of research design; (f) principles of and strategies for applying reinforcement; (g) writing behavioral intervention plans; and (h) principles of and strategies for applying differential reinforcement, extinction, and punishment techniques. Additionally, students gain experience on a behavior management team; apply various ABA techniques in public schools; and practice data collection, graphing, and reporting. Table 9-1 provides a list of ABA and PBS principles covered in this course, and Table 9-2 depicts a semester time line to illustrate how the information is covered.

The principles covered in this course provide enough information for teachers and school psychologists to view behavior as a function of antecedent and consequent stimuli, ascribe to the application of PBS, conduct brief FBAs and formative assessment, and develop sound behavior intervention plans based on their assessment findings. The field research is generally limited to an AB design, and intervention is limited to antecedent manipulations and differential reinforcement. Assignment deadlines are typically flexible because of naturally occurring obstacles (e.g., sick or expelled subjects, school schedules, miscommunication between Texas State students and school personnel). In these cases, students are encouraged to present solutions to the professor and to reschedule their deadlines. The course textbooks are *Applied Behavioral Analysis for Teachers* (Alberto & Troutman, 2002) and *CHAMPS: A Proactive and Positive Approach to Classroom Management* (Sprick, Garrison, & Howard, 1998).

**Table 9-1**
ABA and PBS Principles Covered in the SPED 5375 Course

1. Definitions (e.g., learning, teaching, curriculum, instructional strategies, classical and operant condition-ing, setting events, direct antecedents, positive reinforcement, negative reinforcement, extinction, re-sponse-cost, time-out, presentation of aversives, differential reinforcement, token reinforcement, stimulus control, discriminative stimuli, functional behavioral assessment and analysis)
2. Preferred classroom antecedents (classroom organization, routines, rules, expectations, effective instruc-tion, noncontingent attention, enthusiasm)
3. FBA (assumptions, process, data collection methods both indirect and direct, writing summary state-ments and hypothesized functions, simple hypothesis testing, competing behavior paths)
4. Writing goals and objectives [choosing replacement and alternate behavior, formats for writing objec-tives, levels of learning, task analysis, writing behavior intervention plan (BIP), components and formats]
5. Data collection (anecdotal reports, permanent product recording, observational recording systems, relia-bility, graphing conventions, line graphs, developing aim lines, classwide data collection techniques)
6. Research design (rationale, summary of basic designs)
7. Increasing behavior (positive reinforcement, types of reinforcers, selecting effective reinforcers, token re-inforcement and point cards, reinforcement schedules, negative reinforcement, group and classroom contingencies, cautions about level systems, classwide motivations systems)
8. Decreasing behavior (differential reinforcement techniques, extinction, removing desirable stimuli, pre-senting undesirable stimuli, cautions, classwide correction procedures)
9. Teaching students to manage their own behavior (self-recording and evaluation, self-instruction)

*CHAMPS* is composed of a series of in-service modules addressing typical classroom antece-dents and setting events such as scheduling, fur-niture arrangement, attention signals, routines, teaching expectations and rules, and manage-ment of student work. Additionally, the modules present easy ways to collect data on student and teacher behavior and to set up classwide and in-dividual reward-based structures. This content was recently added to the course for the purpose of better connecting ABA principles to popular PBS content and to better illustrate and apply the notions of antecedent manipulation and stimulus control.

Because this is a one-semester course, only selected ABA principles are targeted for mastery. The main purpose of the course is to familiarize students with the practice of ABA for behavior management purposes, convince them that these practices will greatly assist them as teachers, and illustrate the effectiveness of ABA for children's well-being. The course content stresses vocabu-lary and definitions, but direct application for behavior management purposes takes prece-dence. Major concepts include the following:

- Behavioral excesses are related to the context and to behavioral deficits.

- Management of behavioral excesses requires a comprehensive instructional approach rather than a singular punishment intervention.

- Student behavior usually changes as a result of altered teacher behavior.

- Reinforcement is a powerful motivator; pun-ishment is typically misapplied.

- It is often reinforcing to punish and punish-ing to reinforce.

- Effective instruction requires accountability for choosing appropriate goals and objectives and for monitoring student progress.

Lectures, class discussions, and video presen-tations provide general information for skill acquisition. A cooperative learning structure, field-based project, and teacher–student meet-ings address skill fluency and application.

**Table 9-2**
Semester Time Line

| Week | Topics | Readings to Be Assigned | In-Class Activities |
|------|--------|------------------------|---------------------|
| 1 | Introduction<br>Behavioral deficits and<br>    excesses<br>ABA history<br>Review course requirements | Chapter 1;<br>Alberto & Troutman<br>Module 1, 2<br>CHAMPS (vision,<br>classroom organization) | Brainstorm common<br>    problems and causes |
| 2 | Theories of human development and<br>    behavior<br>Merits of ABA<br>ABA terminology<br>Classroom organization | Chapter 6, text<br>Module 3, CHAMPS | Video of Module 2<br>    CHAMPS<br>Quiz 1, Chapter 1 |
| 3 | Positive behavioral supports classwide<br>    and individual interventions<br>Functional behavioral assessment:<br>    definition, purpose, process, examples of<br>    indirect and direct methods of data<br>    collection (e.g., O'Neill et al., 1997) | Module 5, CHAMPS | |
| 4 | Classwide PBS techniques: expectations<br>    and motivation strategies<br>Functional analysis (developing a<br>    hypothesis, summary statements, quick<br>    tests to verify)<br>Components of a BIP | Chapter 2, text | Videos of Modules 3, 5<br>Quiz 2, Chapter 6 |
| 5 | Choosing replacement behaviors, writing<br>    goals and objectives | Chapter 3, text | Take home quiz 3 over<br>    Chapter 2 |
| 6 | Counting specific behaviors: observational<br>    recording techniques | Chapters 4, 5<br>Module 6, CHAMPS | Video practice<br>Graphing practice |
| 7 | Graphing<br>Summary of research design | | First group meetings all<br>    week for review of actual<br>    FBAs and hypotheses |
| 8 | Midterm<br>Summarize classwide data collection<br>    strategies | Chapter 7<br>Module 8, CHAMPS | Video of Module 6:<br>    monitor and revise |
| 9 | Reinforcement: define, types, choosing,<br>    token systems, point cards | | Review midterm<br>    Class time to plan rein-<br>    forcement systems |
| 10 | Reinforcement<br>Classwide systems and schedules | Chapter 8 | Video of Module 8: class-<br>    wide motivation |
| 11 | Differential reinforcement; extinction and<br>    punishment (define, examples, preferred<br>    uses) | Module 7, CHAMPS | Quiz 4: reinforcement 2nd<br>    group meetings all week<br>    (baseline and interven-<br>    tion plan) |

*(continued)*

**Table 9-2**
Semester Time Line *(continued)*

| Week | Topics | Readings to Be Assigned | In-Class Activities |
|------|--------|-------------------------|---------------------|
| 12 | Extinction, response-cost, time-out, aversives, overcorrection (define, examples, cautions, preferred practices) | Chapter 11 | Discussion of ramifications of misuse of punishment<br>Video of Module 7: corrective procedures |
| 13 | Teaching students to manage their own behavior: self-monitoring, evaluation, reinforcement | | |
| 14 | Review for final<br>Students present brief summaries of their projects | | Projects due |
| 15 | Final | | Return graded projects |

## Cooperative Learning

Cooperative learning is an instructional method for arranging the curriculum and students to promote interdependent, rather than individualistic or competitive, learning (Johnson, Johnson, & Holubec, 1993). Dietz (1994) promoted the merits of student-centered learning strategies such as cooperative learning for instructing educators in ABA. He stated that cooperative learning promotes teamwork and leadership skills and that "behavior analysis could gain more influence in education if they were to construct systems that incorporated these concepts and furthered these skills" (p. 37).

Cooperative learning requires face-to-face supportive interaction, such as sharing, helping, teaching and encouraging, and individual and group accountability (Johnson et al., 1993). Furthermore, cooperative learning proposes to promote interpersonal and small group skills such as leadership, decision making, trust building, communication, and conflict management—all useful skills in teaching and collaboration. Cooperative learning also allows for group processing about progress and effectiveness, certainly skills compatible with ABA principles. Finally, cooperative learning facilitates teams working for shared goals, mutual benefit, and

the celebration of each member's accomplishments (Johnson et al., 1993). Since federal law requires that most instructional decisions, including those addressing challenging behaviors, be determined by teams, conducting a behavior management project as part of a team makes sense. This team approach seems to work particularly well when the teams are composed of practicing special education teachers, teachers-to-be, and school psychologists.

## COOPERATIVE ORGANIZATION

Cooperative groups typically consist of three people and are predicated on the assumption that each member must depend on all other members to achieve a goal. Cooperative learning organization consists of several components: (1) structuring a group goal; (2) identifying an interdependence model; (3) structuring contingencies and rewards; (4) assigning group membership; (5) promoting individual accountability and social skills; and (6) promoting interdependence, processing, and celebration (Johnson & Johnson, 1991).

### Structuring a Group Goal

The group goal for this behavior management class is to conduct a single-subject (typically an AB design) behavior management project.

Specifically, students are to develop and implement a behavior management plan for a target special education student referred because of challenging behavior and to report the results. Each ABA component is taught prior to application. The students themselves obtain subjects if they are working in schools, or the professor approaches special education directors in search of challenging students. We ask to work with subject(s) presenting the most difficulties who are likely to remain in school for 4 to 5 months. Subjects may be found in elementary, middle, or high schools. Sometimes subjects are very young (3 to 4 years old). Many of the subjects are students with emotional and behavioral disorders, and some have mental retardation or autism; often subjects have been diagnosed with ADHD. The professor obtains Texas State internal review board (IRB) committee approval for this course project each semester.

## Identifying an Interdependence Model

In structuring cooperative learning situations, there are three main interdependence models from which to choose: resource interdependence, role interdependence, and task interdependence (Johnson & Johnson, 1991). Resource interdependence creates member dependence on each other for the necessary resources to achieve a goal. Each group member receives a portion of the necessary resources, information, or materials for task completion. Members are compelled to share in order to reach their goal. Role interdependence requires that each person perform a role (e.g., reader, recorder, checker) and only that role in order to obtain a goal. This prevents one member from doing all the work or any member from not doing work and facilitates each member assisting another with his or her task. In task interdependence, each member is given a portion of a task to perform; all members must complete their portions for the entire goal to be achieved. Group members are motivated to assist each other with individually assigned tasks because everyone will benefit from reaching the goal.

Task interdependence is the model chosen for the ABA behavior management course. For the purposes of this course, the behavior management project was task analyzed and arranged into three sections, one for each group member. Table 9-3 is a list of these project components.

Group members are randomly assigned a number from 1 to 3. For example, the group member whose name is closest to the front of the alphabet is number 1. After reviewing the three sections, if group members have a good reason to trade assignments, they may do so. Usually, trading occurs as a result of time commitments. For example, one student who was pregnant did not want to commit to the last section as assigned because she was afraid she would not be available to finish it after giving birth. Group member 1 tasks are usually best completed by someone *not* currently teaching. This section includes several types of assessments so that students may practice obtaining progressively more detailed information. Practicing teachers often have difficulty finding that amount of observation time.

## Structuring Contingencies and Rewards

Cooperation typically will not occur unless contingencies and rewards are arranged to encourage it (Johnson & Johnson, 1991). In this case, each member of the group receives the grade on the group project. Because the written project is worth 75 of 200 points, motivation to produce a quality product is usually high. Additionally, the group is required to meet with the professor twice during the semester—once after assessment is completed and again after a plan is formulated based on assessment and baseline data (see Table 9-3). During these meetings each member must answer questions about the tasks assigned and completed prior to that meeting. Each meeting is worth 10 points, 5 of which reflect responses to these questions and the quality of work to date. Thus, the member who completed the tasks is motivated to teach and share information with fellow members to

**Table 9-3**
Task-interdependent project components

---

**Group Member 1 Tasks: Background and Assessment**

---

1. Obtain background information on the subject. Include age, type of disability, achievement levels, history of the problem, etc. Use no names. You can obtain this information by interviewing the teacher. Complete a functional assessment interview (FAI) (O'Neill et al., 1997) with one or more teachers and/or the parent. Try to be as thorough as possible. You will be able to obtain very useful information from this form.
2. Describe the problem behavior in behavioral terms. Be as specific as possible.
3. Complete at least *one anecdotal recording* (20–30 minutes) and an *ABC chart* pertaining to the problem behavior for at least a half-hour observation.
4. Observe the student for two additional days (observations) recording targeted behaviors on a *scatter plot* or the *functional assessment observation (FAO)* form (Horner, Albin, Sprague, & Todd, 2000). Describe what you found about the following:
   a. What seems to contribute or cue the problem behavior?
   b. What consequences typically follow the behavior?
   c. What purpose does the behavior seem to serve (positive or negative reinforcement, communication, sensory feedback)?
5. Write summary statements based on assessment data and your hypothesis about the function(s) of the targeted behavior.
6. Conduct any other assessments that might help explain why the behavior is occurring (e.g., vision, hearing, academic diagnosis, medication check, receptive language).
7. *Test the hypotheses.* You might observe the student under different conditions or change the antecedents to see if the behavior decreases, or you might give the rewards that you think are maintaining the behavior to see if the problem behavior increases. Record the hypothesis conditions on the scatter plot or FAO form completed previously. Settle on hypotheses and describe them in the correct narrative format.
8. Inform your group members of all of the findings. They should be able to answer any question I ask about these tasks at the meeting. *Set up a meeting with me to review these tasks.*

**Group Member 2 Tasks: Targeting Behavior and Obtaining a Baseline**

---

1. Target a behavior that needs decreasing based on the assessment information. Choose at least one replacement behavior using appropriate criteria.
2. Justify why you picked those behaviors to target. It must be in the best interest of the student to alter his or her behavior.
3. Write a goal and at least one objective indicating what you intend the student to learn. Use *correct format* (Alberto & Troutman, 2002).
4. Choose a research design for your project and justify choosing that design. An AB design is acceptable.
5. Develop a behavioral observation form and conduct a baseline count of *both* the maladaptive and replacement behaviors over 5 days.
6. Describe the conditions in the classroom during each observation (type of class, type of lesson, student behaviors). What were the other students doing? What were the consequences for the inappropriate behavior? Choose another student in the class who does not display challenging behavior and count the same behaviors for each of the five observations. Compare the target student's behavior to the comparison student.
7. Conduct a reliability check once during the baseline on *all* targeted behaviors. Compute. Reliability must be sufficient, or you will need to conduct your observations again.
8. Compute an average of the baseline count and display on a graph.
9. Graph the baseline and include all pertinent information.

*(continued)*

**Table 9-3**
Task-interdependent project components

---

### Group Member 3 Tasks: Intervention

1. Develop a behavior intervention plan (BIP) based on the assessment and baseline information. Include strategies to change antecedents and to teach and reinforce replacement behaviors. For this project, avoid punishment strategies.
2. Develop a token system. State the behavior(s) to be reinforced. List available reinforcers (at least 10) based on a reinforcer survey. Develop point cards, reinforcement menus, and contracts as necessary (e.g., Alberto & Troutman, 2002; Sprick et al., 1998). Decide how you will teach the system to the target student.
3. *Set up a meeting with me to present all of Group Member 2's tasks and your BIP.*
4. Apply the intervention.
5. Count and graph the target behaviors for 10 days. Conduct one reliability check and plot on the graph for all behaviors. Continue to count the comparison student's behavior. *Construct a progress aim line.*
6. Describe the conditions of the intervention:
   - How you manipulated antecedents
   - How you taught the replacement behavior and reinforcement system
   - Where the tokens were stored as the student earned them
   - When the student exchanged tokens
   - What lessons you presented during the intervention phase
   - Examples of what the student did and said
   - Which reinforcers were chosen by the subject
   - How many tokens were earned each day

   Attach point cards, contracts, reinforcement menus, and work samples.

### Group Members 1, 2, and 3 Tasks: Conclusion

---

1. *Describe the results.* Interpret the data and state what happened to the behavior during intervention. Compare baseline and intervention data. Describe any variance in data across conditions. Include averages in each condition.
2. Draw conclusions about the entire project. Speculate about why the subject's behavior changed or did not change. Do not draw conclusions that your data do not support. Discuss how to thin the reinforcement schedule and facilitate generalization.
3. Each member needs to write a rough draft of the project report.
4. Choose the report to be turned in for a grade. Assure that this report is typed in the correct format with appropriate attachments. The report to be graded should be clearly marked as such.

---

enhance performance during the meetings, and all members are motivated to help with the tasks to ensure high-quality ratings.

An optional contingency is to assign bonus points to group members for certain predesignated group test averages. For example, the members of each group that averages an A on the midterm will receive extra points toward the semester grade. It's important to be aware of students who are poor test takers and who may bring group averages down, not for lack of trying and not for lack of group help and support. In these cases, this option may not be a good one.

At the conclusion of each meeting, members rate themselves and each other anonymously regarding the level of cooperation. The average of the ratings (from 1 to 5) for each student results in additional points. The point totals for each member's knowledge and for the assignment (group points) plus individual points for cooperative skill ratings could total 10 points for each student for each meeting. Individual points are also received for a draft report. To ensure that all students understand each component and can produce a report, each member is required to turn in a draft report for 5 points along with the report to be graded. These draft reports do not need to be finished products, but they need to convince the professor that the individual has learned key concepts, understands all aspects of the project, and can summarize the findings. Individual points are also given for midterm and final exams and four quizzes.

## Assigning Group Membership

Typically, cooperative groups are formed to ensure a mix of member ability, ethnicity, and gender (Johnson & Johnson, 1991). This can be accomplished by compiling three piles of student names; for example, one pile with high achievers, one pile with ethnic minorities, and one pile with all men. Picking a name from each pile to form a group would result in a high achiever, an ethnic minority, and a man in each group. At Texas State, the main consideration for group membership is geography. Students at Texas State reside or work in a 140- by 70-mile corridor. Thus, students must be grouped so they can easily access a particular school.

Second, students are grouped according to a preference for secondary or elementary environments. Third, when possible, school psychology majors are spread across groups so that each group has a mix of school psychology and special education majors, simulating common public school disciplinary team membership. Since students who are currently teaching would not be free to visit other schools, nonteaching students are assigned to their group. This facilitates the acquisition of project subjects because the practicing teachers can locate students with problem behaviors and clear access to those students with their principals. The professor collects an information form during the first class period and assigns group membership the fol-

lowing week. Membership problems can be addressed at that point. Typical problems involve work schedules and driving time. Sometimes individual students live so far away that no other class members could reasonably travel to that location. These students must conduct the project individually. For students who prefer *not* to work in a group, the option of conducting an individual project is available provided that choice is announced during the second class period. However, the project is constructed to emphasize the benefits of working in a group. Few students choose to conduct projects alone. Once groups are formed, students are discouraged from dropping out for any reason. Sometimes, because groups are formed by geography, the group consists of only two members. It is better to have a group of two than a group of four to ensure that each member has an adequate number of tasks (Johnson & Johnson, 1991). In two-member groups, number 2 tasks are divided between the members.

The first 15 minutes of every class are devoted to group meetings. Groups are encouraged to meet outside of class time to discuss project progress and to plan and adjust group actions. Sample projects from previous semesters are provided during meeting times so that the students can review the desired product. No access to schools is allowed until principals sign consent forms and return them to the professor. This is usually accomplished within a week.

Occasionally during the semester group members complain about one student who is not adequately contributing to the process and product. Usually, students are encouraged to talk to the recalcitrant member about the effect of his or her behavior on their performance. Learning to communicate with team members who do not complete assigned tasks is a functional skill for both school psychologists and special educators. However, if direct dialogue does not work, the professor meets with the target student, the group, or both to identify the problem. If it is obvious that group members will suffer because of one member's performance deficit, that member is pulled from the group and told to complete the project alone, usually with another subject. Since these are postgraduate and graduate students, this type of problem rarely occurs.

## Promoting Individual Accountability and Social Skills

Targeting individual accountability and social skill attainment is a main goal of cooperative learning (Johnson et al., 1993). The ABA class promotes individual accountability for learning course content through quizzes, individual questioning in class, and tests. Individual accountability is also checked during group meetings with the cooperative skills rating and on the draft report. Over half the semester points are obtained individually: quizzes (25 points), tests (75 points), draft report (5 points), and cooperative skills rating (10 points). Observation of group meetings during class time also provides information about individual participation.

The course syllabus lists the social skills necessary to participate successfully in the group project (adapted from Johnson et al., 1993):

1. Use effective collaboration skills such as making a commitment to other group members and the product; participating regularly; criticizing ideas, not people; listening actively; and extending and sharing information

2. Complete your part of the project in a timely manner and strive for a quality product. Your group members are depending on your performance. The expectation is that you will be a productive member of the group.

Social skill ratings are reflected in two cooperative skills ratings completed by group members on themselves and their partners. Surprisingly, some postgraduate students need to be taught how to collaborate. Some have come from professions in which collaboration was not expected, and many have failed in previous professions because of social skills deficits. Cooper-

ative learning provides a good opportunity for the professor to identify those students needing such instruction.

Social skills instruction occurs in a one-to-one conference in which the professor outlines group member complaints and asks the student what might be done to correct the situation. In most cases, students acknowledge their communication or commitment problems. Typically this is not the first time they have had this type of feedback. If they are aware of their own behaviors, the conference becomes an opportunity to suggest other ways to say things, time management strategies, assertiveness skills, or methods for solving personal problems. If students resist recognizing their own problem behavior, the conference becomes more directive with specified behavioral expectations, time lines, and a contingency (e.g., they will have to complete the project alone) if problems persist. The vast majority of students have no trouble performing in collaborative groups.

## Promoting Interdependence, Processing, and Celebration

As described earlier, interdependence is promoted through group contingencies. It is also promoted through the two group meetings and the nature of the group project. Because the project is conducted in public schools, naturally occurring problems arise. For example, a subject may be sent to a juvenile justice facility, hospitalized, or suspended before the intervention can take place. A subject may receive some other intervention independent of the Texas State project that reduces the problem behavior. In these cases, the group must develop solutions and present possibilities to the professor. Sometimes groups must find a new subject, in which case the project is abbreviated. Sometimes the group must target a new behavior or work with the same subject in a different setting. Groups are warned at the beginning of the semester that the project will require them to solve common public school problems. Semester deadlines need to be flexible to accommodate such occurrences, in some cases allowing a grade of "incomplete" until the project is completed. If this occurs, students must sign a contract with the professor delineating a date for project completion. Most students are very motivated to complete the course in a timely fashion.

Group members are encouraged to reinforce fellow members for task completion, cooperation, initiative, resourcefulness, and effective instruction. Large group discussions a few times during the semester address individual perceptions of the cooperative process and sharing of project progress. The report itself is a product achieved through interdependence, and high grades are always a call for group celebration.

## COURSE OUTCOMES

Outcomes for this ABA course are reflected in the quality of the projects themselves and testimony from students after entering the teaching profession. Furthermore, student evaluations reflect social validity (consumer satisfaction and probability of continued applications) of the course content (Daly & Cooper, 1993). Two typical group projects will be discussed to illustrate quality.

The first project involved David, a high school special education student with mild mental retardation served in a resource class, who was reported to yell, disrupt class, and get out of his seat without permission. A functional behavioral assessment showed that he was off task; out of his seat; and interrupting the teacher during lectures, independent work, and group work. It was hypothesized that he did these behaviors to obtain teacher and peer attention, which was happening on a variable schedule. The group chose to target interruptions and replace this behavior with hand-raising. Baseline data showed that the subject interrupted the teacher an average of 15 times during five 30-minute observations and never raised his hand. This was compared to another student in the class who

interrupted an average of 0.8 times during that period and also did not raise his hand.

The intervention consisted of a token system rewarding David for each instance that he raised his hand and waited for the teacher to call on him and for every 5 minutes that he did not interrupt the teacher or yell in class. David was able to use the tokens to buy small boxes of candy or games or to save for a desired wallet. Figure 9-1 depicts the project graph as submitted by the cooperative group. Note that the aim line and average lines are missing. Nevertheless, the intervention is notable for its simplicity and apparent effectiveness, both of which are desirable in special education classrooms.

The second example involves Matthew, a 7-year-old boy with autism and mental retardation who was reported to roll his head, bite his hand, and make high-pitched vocalizations. An FBA showed that hand-biting was the most frequently occurring of these behaviors and was at its worst during lunch. The group determined that Matthew, who had extremely low language ability, was probably trying to communicate about what he wanted to eat by biting his hand. They decided to replace hand-biting with card-handing as a communication method. Baseline data showed that he averaged 26 hand-bites per lunch period over 5 days.

The group used a changing conditions design to depict teaching Matthew to recognize and hand the teacher each of three picture cards to obtain desired foods (pizza, chocolate milk, ketchup). A different card was taught under each of the first three conditions. The fourth condition included a token system whereby Matthew obtained a star for each 3 minutes during lunch that he did not bite his hand. Group member 3 taught Matthew the card-handing procedure using a trial-by-trial format (Fovel, 2002; Scheuermann & Webber, 2002). The teacher gave a discriminative stimulus ("What do you want?"), prompted the student to hand the card, and reinforced him with what was depicted on the card. Figure 9-2 illustrates Matthew's rapid acquisition of card-handing in

**Figure 9-1.**
Project graph of David's interrupting behaviors and hand-raising.

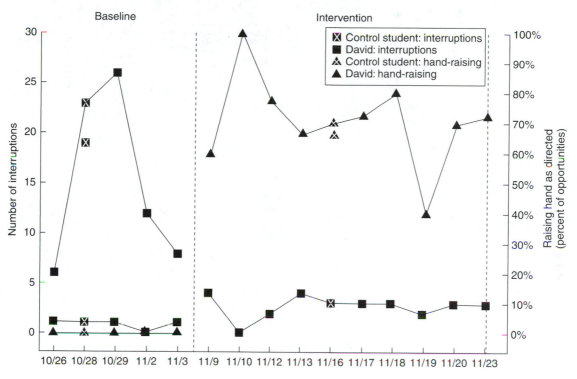

response to a verbal cue ("What do you want?") by the teacher. Figure 9-3 is a graph of Matthew's hand-biting incidents, which reduced to an average of two per lunch period in condition 4 (the entire project spans 10 days).

Both of the projects were apparently successful, as most are, which results in reinforcement for all group members for their thoughtful, hard work. Project success is defined by the students themselves in the behavioral objectives they must develop. Mastery criteria are written into the objectives, which are developed for a 10-day intervention. Aim lines are constructed to show that progress toward mastery is on track. If students are making expected progress or have reached the designated criterion, the project is considered successful. Grades, however, are not based on project success, but on the performance of the designated tasks. The two meetings with the professor facilitate project success by allowing a time to solve potential problems and create plans that are likely to succeed.

Sometimes, after completing the course, students contact the professor about behavior management successes or with questions or comments pertaining to effective or ineffective interventions. Such testimony might be construed to indicate the generalizability of ABA skills. Some examples of such testimonies follow. Although the first example does not guarantee generalized application, the student's positive attitude toward ABA is noteworthy. Testimonies from the three practicing teachers appear to indicate content generalization.

**Figure 9-2.**
Project graph of Matthew's card-handing over four conditions.

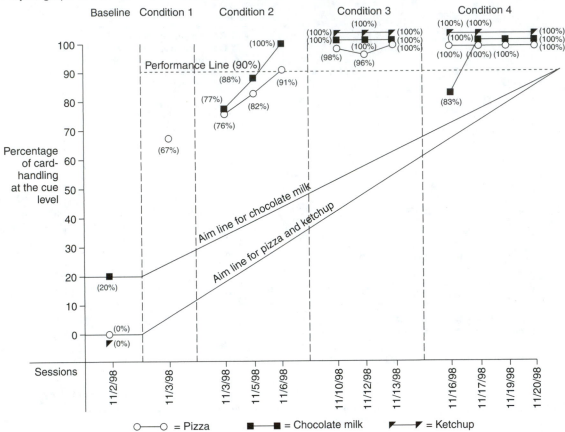

From a previous semester practicum special education student:

Hello,

Here is some good news about the behavior project we did last semester for your class. I was talking to BW's special education teachers, the ladies I am doing my practicum with, and they were talking about BW's behavior. They stated that BW's behavior last semester has changed 180 degrees for the good. He is now doing great in school and acting wonderful [sic] for all his teachers. In fact, the day I was meeting with my practicum special education teachers, I heard BW over the intercom giving the daily announcements. Later I talked to him and told him that I heard him over the intercom and I was very proud of him. I asked him how he was able to get permission do this. BW

told me that his homeroom teacher recommended him for this honorable privilege because of how much his behavior has improved. So, two special education teachers, BW's homeroom teacher and the principal, all thought that BW's behavior was miraculously improved for the better.

More proof that ABA really works. Thanks a lot for teaching me all this great stuff. I had no idea what an effect it would have on my students for changing their behavior so much. Wow.

Good Day,

Betti Jo (Elizabeth) Hobbs (e-mail communication, February 12, 2002)

From a former student finishing his first year teaching students in inclusion and resource settings in a middle school:

**Figure 9-3.**
Project graph of Matthew's hand-biting over four conditions.

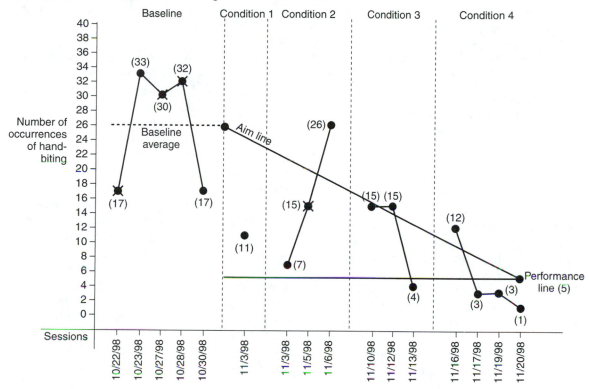

A basic tool I incorporated in my daily routine was to focus on three basic strategies, which included getting familiar with the students, having minimal distractions in their academic settings, and actually teaching students positive behaviors to replace existing negative behaviors. It was important to support this effort with something tangible that the students could see and feel. Point sheets targeting 4 desirable behaviors were utilized on a daily basis with a reward system. I also used a reinforcement survey to discover what each student would prefer. Another important strategy that I have utilized is one of context and how it relates to and can be modified for successful learning. Many problem behaviors occur because of something (structure of the classroom) or someone (seating arrangement) affecting the student in a negative way.

David Martinez (written correspondence, April 2003)

From a former student beginning his eighth year as a high school special education resource teacher:

If I had not started at Texas State, I would not have survived this long. That is a fact. When my kids act up, I have skills to deal with it. I am very proud of the fact that "office referral" has been dropped from my teacher vocabulary. It is not all easy, but the behavioral tools I derived from your program help me every day.

Jimmie Smith (e-mail correspondence, August 17, 2003)

From a former student completing her first year as a high school resource teacher:

A classroom out of control was what I feared most about teaching and what I had to contend with the first few months because of my lack of consistency. I started out the year with a well thought-out and clearly posted behavior management plan with positive reinforcement. However, my rules were too general and I was not consistent in following through with consequences. After rewriting my rules, rewarding good behavior and ignoring undesired behavior, and enforcing the rules consistently, things got much better! I also added a visual warning system. Students are learning more, and I hardly ever cry on my way home from work!

Jessica Cohen (written correspondence, May 2003)

Student perceptions of ABA were obtained, with a questionnaire adapted from Daly and Cooper (1993), which was administered at the course's conclusion. Table 9-4 depicts the results of this survey for two semesters. Of the 30 students completing the questionnaire in 2002-2003, 28 indicated that ABA was worth learning about. Eighteen of the students considered ABA very compatible with their work styles, 11 indicated that it was fairly compatible, and 1 indicated that it was not compatible with her work style. Many students reported using ABA techniques in the schools, one of whom also used a reinforcement system with her boyfriend for cleaning the apartment 2 hours a week! Twenty-two students felt they had learned enough about FBAs to be able to implement these techniques in a useful manner, and five thought they had almost acquired such skill but not quite. Eighteen students indicated that the group project was very helpful in their understanding of ABA. Only eight students indicated that the cooperative group structure was helpful, but the objective for that structure is primarily to facilitate collaborative and cooperative skills in addition to facilitating learning of ABA content. Finally, one student wrote:

This class was very helpful. I feel much more comfortable working in the schools, and I felt the techniques learned will be a great help. Before this semester I had reservations about ABA techniques—now I feel that I understand how they can be used in an ethical manner to help children suc-

ceed in school/life. This class was extremely valuable, and I feel I learned how to apply the techniques discussed after completing the project. Overall, I had a great experience. (Anonymous)

If we can assume that individuals who perceive ABA principles in a positive light are likely to use those techniques and that demonstration of appropriate use of the techniques enhances generalization, then this scant data might indicate that a cooperative field-based approach to teaching ABA techniques has some merit. Actual testimony from three practicing teachers substantiates that claim.

Although projects produced by a group are not always of higher quality than those produced by individuals, group interventions have historically been more creative and group assessments more carefully conducted and analyzed than those by individuals. Groups that included members from different academic disciplines who bring different strengths to the project tend to have the most thorough projects. The cooperative structure allows opportunities to formulate supportive relationships and to practice interpersonal skills. It also allows the professor to check students' interpersonal skills and instruct students who lack them. Finally, because the project is conducted in school settings, real-world problems arise and must be solved. Working with particularly challenging students also alters perceptions about what constitutes a behavior problem. As one general education student recently said, "Working in that ED classroom was a real eye-opener. My algebra class is a piece of cake!"

## LIMITATIONS

One significant limitation to the cooperative group structure is that not all students practice all project components. Even with contingencies in place, it is often obvious that not all group members understand each step. Some of this content can be retaught and included on

**Table 9-4**
Frequency of student responses to course survey

| Question | Gen Ed n = 1 | Ed Psych n = 16 | Preservice SPED n = 4 | SPED Masters n = 9 | Total n = 30 |
|---|---|---|---|---|---|
| To me, the application of ABA is | | | | | |
| Very compatible | | 11 | 1 | 6 | 18 |
| Fairly compatible | 1 | 5 | 2 | 3 | 11 |
| Not compatible | | | 1 | | 1 |
| I learned enough about FBA to implement it in a useful manner. | | | | | |
| Yes | | 13 | 4 | 7 | 22 |
| No | | | | 1 | 1 |
| Almost, but not quite | 1 | 3 | | 1 | 5 |
| I used the following ABA techniques for preventing and managing problem behavior | | | | | |
| FBA | | 6 | 1 | 5 | 12 |
| Antecedent manipulation | | 4 | 1 | 6 | 11 |
| Teaching replacement behaviors | | 4 | 1 | 6 | 11 |
| Differential reinforcement | | 3 | | 4 | 7 |
| Data collection | | 3 | 1 | 4 | 8 |
| Token system | | 4 | | 5 | 9 |
| Level system | | | 1 | 1 | 2 |
| Research design | | 3 | 1 | | 4 |
| The teaching techniques that were most helpful in my understanding of ABA were | | | | | |
| The textbook | | 5 | 1 | 4 | 10 |
| The CHAMPS modules | 1 | 3 | 2 | 2 | 8 |
| The CHAMPS videos | 1 | 3 | | 2 | 6 |
| Studying with other students | | 3 | 1 | | 4 |
| Class lectures | | 10 | 3 | 7 | 20 |
| The cooperative group structure | | 4 | 2 | 2 | 8 |
| The class project | | 12 | 3 | 3 | 18 |
| Time spent in the schools | | 5 | 1 | 2 | 8 |
| Group meetings with professor | | 2 | 2 | 4 | 8 |
| Handouts | | 4 | 2 | 5 | 11 |
| In my opinion, ABA was | | | | | |
| Worth learning about | 1 | 14 | 4 | 9 | 28 |
| Not significantly worth learning about | | 1 | | | 1 |
| Not worth learning about at all | | | | | 0 |

quizzes and tests, but vigilance is required to prevent the acquisition of only partial knowledge. A second limitation is that of weak groups. Geography often results in a group of students, all of whom are struggling to grasp the content, who cannot write and organize information well, and who may not give the time and commitment required. This phenomenon requires more time from the professor and should be avoided whenever possible. Mixed-ability groups are preferred (Johnson et al., 1993) so that stronger students can help teach complicated content to weaker students.

In groups whose members have no experience in the schools, the tasks of hypothesizing, testing methods, analyzing, and developing reinforcement systems often reflect less creativity. Because of their lack of experience with children and youth, they are not as adept at analyzing causes of behavior and choosing effective reinforcers. The professor will need to do more teaching in the group meetings in these instances, directly providing ideas. Finally, there is the ever-present limitation of generalization once the student is out teaching. Some former students have been found to resort to punishment systems rather than functional and instructional interventions once they are teaching. Presumably, they are overwhelmed by curricular demands and find no positive models or support in their teaching positions. Many of the ABA students, however, go on to develop effective behavior management systems and conduct FBAs on a regular basis. Judging which students will generalize their ABA knowledge is difficult and should be a subject of further research.

## CONCLUSION

Teaching ABA to preservice and in-service school personnel so that they can effectively use the principles in their profession has thus far been elusive. For various reasons, school personnel typically shun ABA applications or apply them incorrectly (e.g., punishment). Despite re-

search supporting the positive effects of functional behavioral assessments, differential reinforcement systems, antecedent manipulations and stimulus control, and data-based accountability systems for instructional and behavior management purposes, too few preservice programs include the training, and too few students generalize those skills that are taught. Teaching ABA with cooperative learning structures and field-based projects may increase the likelihood that students will be reinforced by applying the principles, learn additional collaboration and problem-solving competencies, and ultimately master the content so that they can apply it successfully and actually do so in their new professions. This, in turn, may result in more school applications of ABA.

## REFERENCES

Alberto, P., & Troutman, A. (2002). *Applied behavioral analysis for teachers* (6th ed.). Columbus, OH: Merrill.

Carnine, D. (2000). *Why education experts resist effective practices and what it would take to make education more like medicine.* Washington, DC: Fordham Foundation.

Daly, P. M., & Cooper, J. O. (1993). Persuading student teachers and inservice teachers to use precision teaching after the course is over. *Education and Treatment of Children, 16* (3), 316–325.

Dietz, S. M. (1994). The insignificant impact of behavior analysis on education: Notes from a dean of education. In R. Gardner, D. M. Sainato, J. O. Cooper, T. E. Heron, W. L. Heward, J. Eshleman, & T. A. Grossi (Eds.), *Behavioral analysis in education* (pp. 33–41). Pacific Grove, CA: Brooks/Cole.

Fovel, J. T. (2002). *The ABA program companion: Organizing quality programs for children with autism and PDD.* New York: DRL Books.

Hall, R. V. (1991). Behavior analysis and education: An unfulfilled dream. *Journal of Behavioral Education, 1,* 305–316.

Horner, R. H., Albin, R. W., Sprague, J. R., & Todd, A. W. (2000). Positive behavior support. In M. E. Snell & F. Brown (Eds.), *Instruction of students with severe disabilities* (5th ed.; pp. 207–244). Upper Saddle River, NJ: Merrill.

Johnson, D. W., & Johnson, H. (1991). *Learning together and alone: Cooperation, competition, and individualization* (3rd ed.). Englewood Cliffs, NJ: Prentice Hall.

Johnson, D. W., Johnson, R. T., & Holubec, E. J. (1993). *Cooperation in the classroom* (6th ed.). Edina, MN: Interaction Book Company.

Kauffman, J. M. (2002). *Education reform: Bright people sometimes say stupid things about education.* Lanham, MD: Scarecrow Press.

Kohler, F. W., & Strain, P. S. (1992). Applied behavior analysis and the movement to restructure schools: Compatibilities and opportunities for collaboration. *Journal of Behavioral Education, 2,* 367–390.

Maheady, L., Harper, G. F., Mallette, B., & Karnes, M. (1994). "Mainstreaming" Applied Behavior Analysis principles and procedures into a preservice training program for general education teachers. In R. Gardner, D. M. Sainato, J. O. Cooper, T. E. Heron, W. L. Heward, J. Eshleman, & T. A. Grossi (Eds.), *Behavior analysis in education: Focus on measurably superior instruction* (pp. 43–56). Belmont, CA: Brooks-Cole.

Malott, R. W. (1984). In search of human perfectability: A behaviorial approach to higher education. In W. L. Heward, T. E. Heron, D. S. Hill, & J. Trap-Porter (Eds.), *Focus on behavior analysis in education* (pp. 218–245). Columbus, OH: Merrill/Prentice Hall.

O'Neill, R. E., Horner, R. H., Albin, R. W., Sprague, J. R., Storey, K., & Newton, J. S. (1997). *Functional assessment and program development for problem behavior: A practical handbook* (2nd ed.). Pacific Grove, CA: Brooks/Cole.

O'Reilly, M. F., Renzaglia, A., & Lee, S. (1994). An analysis of acquisition, generalization and maintenance of systematic instruction competencies by preservice teachers using behavioral supervision techniques. *Education and Training in Mental Retardation, 29* (1), 22–33.

Scheuermann, B., & Webber, J. (2002). *Autism: Teaching DOES make a difference.* Belmont, CA: Wadsworth.

Scott, T. M., & Nelson, C. M. (1999). Universal school discipline strategies: Facilitating positive learning environments. *Effective School Practices, 17* (4), 54–64.

Sprick, R., Garrison, M., & Howard, L. (1998). *CHAMPS: A proactive and positive approach to classroom management.* Longmont, CO: Sopris West.

Sugai, G., & Horner, R. (1999). Discipline and behavioral support: Practices, pitfalls, and promises. *Effective School Practices, 17* (4), 10–22.

Todd, A. W., Horner, R. H., Sugai, G., & Sprague, J. R. (1999). Effective behavior support: Strengthening school-wide systems through team-based approach. *Effective School Practices, 17*(4), 23–37.

Walker, H. M., Colvin, G., & Ramsey, E. (1995). *Antisocial behavior in schools: Strategies and best practice.* Pacific Grove, CA: Brooks/Cole.

## STUDY QUESTIONS AND FOLLOW-UP ACTIVITIES

1. You have been asked to consult in the development of an intervention plan for a student with autism who is demonstrating high rates of calling out and noncontextual speech in a general education second-grade classroom. Describe the components of the plan and who you would include in the training program. Be sure to include those who will do the coaching and those who are to be trained. Include provisions for ensuring that the plan will be maintained over time.

2. This chapter focused on how to develop skill repertoires in teacher trainees. Give three examples of activities that would provide preservice teachers with the opportunities to engage in situations they will likely encounter in the field. Define the skills that would be honed with these activities. Outline the possible interventions that peers, mentors, and supervisors could use to help students who struggle developing those skills.

3. List three contingencies based on the principles of reinforcement that could promote the acquisition and maintenance of behavioral strategies by teachers in the classroom. State who would create, organize, and provide these contingencies.

4. Outcome measures and accountability are a major focus with the passage of the No Child Left Behind Act of 2002. How can applied behavior analysts facilitate increased accountability and improved outcomes?

Study questions and follow-up activities prepared by Theresa L. Hessler and Gwen A. Diggins.

5. Teachers often want to focus on eliminating an unwanted behavior instead of increasing or improving a desired behavior. List five common undesirable classroom and home-related behaviors. Suggest corresponding desirable replacement behaviors that could be taught instead. Provide a rationale for why the replacement behaviors are in the best interest of the student.

6. Choose one of the behaviors from Question 5 and develop a comprehensive plan, including how and where you would teach the replacement behavior and what reinforcement strategy you would use to establish and maintain the behavior. Include a complete, concise, objective definition of the behavior, including criteria for successful implementation of the plan.

7. One of the reasons teachers give for not applying behavioral strategies in their classrooms is the difficulty of collecting data while teaching. Choose a common classroom behavior, either undesired (e.g., talk-outs) or desired (e.g., problem solving), and design a simple data collection strategy, including a data collection sheet.

8. Design a strategy that an in-service teacher could implement to increase his or her praise statements to students. Include a data collection form.

9. Design a token reinforcement system for a fourth-grade class that has low rates of seatwork completion and high rates of miscellaneous off-task behavior. Assume the work is relevant and appropriate. Include individual and group contingencies. Be specific about how tokens are to be earned, exchanged, and withdrawn.

10. The author outlines how the group members are to conduct a functional assessment observation (FAO). Conduct an FAO on a student and write a summary based on your observation(s), including your hypothesis about the function of the behavior. Think about what other assessments should be conducted that might help explain the function of the behavior (e.g., a hearing test for a student who is often seen not paying attention). List those possible assessments. Share the information with the student's teacher(s).

11. Compare and contrast the program described in Chapter 8 with the course work outlined in this chapter. Use either a table or narrative format. Review the similarities and determine if the pre-service education program that you are most familiar with contains any of these characteristics. Draft a letter to the dean that supports the inclusion of course work that would develop those characteristics. Use pertinent information from these two chapters to develop your argument.

# Collaborating with Preservice and Mentor Teachers to Design and Implement Classroom Research

*Sheila R. Alber*        *Janet S. Nelson*

The use of empirically validated instruction in the classroom has long been an important goal for teacher educators, researchers, school personnel, and policy makers. That goal became a mandate when President Bush signed into law the No Child Left Behind Act (NCLB) of 2001 (U.S. Department of Education, 2002). This law requires that K–12 public schools be held accountable for improving the academic performance of all students and stresses the implementation of instructional approaches that have been validated through scientifically based research. To that end, evidence-based practice and ongoing assessment are mandated, and classroom teachers are expected to make instructional decisions based on reliable evidence that the program is effective.

Researchers in the field of education have produced an impressive body of findings documenting effective instructional programming. Unfortunately, applied research has had little impact on instructional practice (Cuban, 1993; Fuchs & Fuchs, 2001; Gersten, Morvant, & Brengelman, 1995; Greenwood & Abbot, 2001; Sin-

delar & Brownell, 2001). The approach most widely used for attempting to bridge this research-to-practice gap has been staff development, which typically takes the form of brief lectures or workshops with little or no support or follow-up. Although such activities are intended to keep teachers current with the advances of their practice, the carryover into classrooms has unfortunately been minimal (Fuchs & Fuchs, 2001; Joyce & Showers, 1995; Lieberman & Miller, 1991; Purvis & Tice, 1996; Wood & Thompson, 1993).

Clearly, we cannot look to staff development as the only vehicle for bringing empirically sound practices into the classroom. Rather, we should begin addressing this concern more substantively at the preservice level. The success of teacher education programs can be determined by the extent to which graduates of the program are equipped with the skills necessary to affect student learning (Greenwood & Maheady, 2001). To that end, exposure to validated teaching practices during preservice training is a necessary step. However, such exposure is not enough to make a long-term difference in public education. To truly have an effect on classroom instruction, graduates of teacher education programs must continue to use validated practices throughout their careers.

One way to transform the current research-to-practice gap into a continuum is for teacher preparation programs to instill in preservice teachers a respect for the importance of field-based research and to empower them to become consumers, producers, and disseminators of validated teaching practices (Greenwood & Maheady, 2001). However, preservice teachers may not actually believe in the value of field-based research if teacher educators simply tell them that it is important. If, on the other hand, preservice teachers actually participate in and witness the outcomes of such research, they may begin to view themselves as agents of change in the classroom (Greenwood & Maheady, 2001). That is, they may see themselves as having the power to really affect student learning. Just as important, preservice teachers may realize that they can make important contributions to the teaching profession when they are involved in research dissemination activities. Continued professional development is a likely outcome of the rewards derived from sharing research.

In this chapter we first summarize the literature examining reasons for the research-to-practice gap. We then present a step-by-step process for involving preservice teachers in initiating, designing, implementing, assessing, and disseminating the results of collaborative research. We illustrate this process with an example of a classroom research project in which the research team consisted of two student teachers, a mentor teacher, and two university faculty members.

## THE RESEARCH-TO-PRACTICE GAP

To address the research-to-practice gap, teacher educators must first understand the reasons for the discrepancy between research and practice

and then clearly communicate those reasons to preservice teachers (Greenwood & Maheady, 2001). For example, one reason for the gap is that researchers often target problems and plan interventions that may be of little relevance, accessibility, and usability to teachers (Abbot, Walton, Tapia, & Greenwood, 1999; Gersten, Vaughn, Deshler, & Schiller, 1997; Greenwood & Abbot, 2001). Additionally, although a goal of research is to produce knowledge that is applicable to a wide range of teaching situations, teachers want information that they can use in their own classrooms. Given these disparate goals, it is no wonder that teachers are critical of educational research. For example, teachers have described research as abstract, erroneous, and inconsistent. Further, they view research as out of context with the real world and inapplicable to their own individual teaching situations (Malouf & Schiller, 1995). Given these negative opinions, it is not surprising that teachers have traditionally not been consumers of research (Kaestle, 1993; Viadero, 1994).

To make empirically sound instructional methodology more relevant to teachers, researchers must identify problems and target specific interventions that are important to practitioners and then evaluate the effects of the interventions on student outcomes (Greenwood, Delquadri, & Bulgren, 1993). Further, if teachers are directly involved in implementing selected interventions in their own unique teaching situations and collecting data to assess student outcomes, they will see firsthand what works. Beyond seeing the impact on their own classrooms, teachers would also have the opportunity to contribute to the teaching profession by disseminating their findings to other teachers. As teachers may well be more likely to trust a fellow teacher than a university researcher, they might then see empirically validated interventions as more relevant, accessible, and usable in the context of their own school culture. By alleviating some of the skepticism and mistrust teachers may have for applied research, teacher-to-teacher dissemination could thus be very influential in bridging the research-to-practice gap.

The above benefits cannot accrue, however, if the research and practice communities continue to be as separate as they have been traditionally. This separation has contributed to the research-to-practice gap in that opportunities for practitioners and researchers to communicate and collaborate with one another have been very infrequent (Carnine, 1997; Greenwood & Abbot, 2001). Collaborative research efforts, then, have the potential to ameliorate the research-to-practice gap. We believe that, ideally, preservice teachers should also be involved in such research so they would be more likely to see its value. Therefore, during preservice teacher preparation, future teachers should receive formal opportunities to engage in collaborative research and to disseminate their findings. For these practices to continue beyond graduation, teacher educators should encourage future teachers to continue seeking opportunities to collaborate with researchers, thereby helping to identify best practices throughout their teaching careers (Greenwood & Maheady, 2001).

Collaborative research projects should involve student teachers as well as university faculty and mentor teachers. Such a research team would bring the traditionally separate research and practice communities together and allow team members to investigate the accessibility, usability, and relevance of jointly identified research questions. Thus, the student teaching experience has the potential to serve as a bridge that connects the research and practice communities. Collaborative research projects, however, need not be limited to the student teaching experience. When possible, university faculty should attempt to involve any undergraduate practicum students, graduate students, and practicing teachers who are inclined to participate. The following sections describe the steps that a collaborative research project would typically include. These steps can be applied to all configurations of university and school district research teams.

We illustrate the collaborative research process using our own project in which two student teachers were members of the research team.

## Assembling the Research Team

Project collaboration should begin at least a couple of months prior to the anticipated starting point of data collection. Sufficient time must be set aside for assembling the research team, obtaining the necessary permissions from the school and the university, and beginning the planning of the research. We believe that all members of the team should be volunteers so that the project is truly collaborative. In our experiences, few student teachers were willing to volunteer once they understood the amount of time and effort required. However, it is best to not exclude any student who is interested. If faculty members are not equipped to supervise the number of student teachers who want to participate, doctoral students can be recruited to take the lead in supervising additional collaborative research projects.

Once the research team is assembled, it is important to ensure that certain members do not take the lead throughout the project. One way to do this is to discuss varying levels of knowledge, experience, and interest specific to the different stages of planning and implementation. The lead role would then change across the project stages, with certain members taking the lead and others assisting at different times.

In our project, one of the university faculty members assumed the lead role for assembling the research team. She recruited students from a teaching methods class that they typically take the semester before student teaching. She also contacted local school districts to identify teachers who wanted to be involved. After assembling the team, we had to first obtain informal approval from the office of field experiences, the district level administrator, and the school principal. After we had our project planned and ready to implement, we then had to get formal permission from the school board and the university's human subjects review board.

## Identifying Target Students and Their Critical Learning Needs

Once the research participants are assembled, they should have a meeting to identify student needs that can be addressed in the research project. The mentor teacher, university researchers, and student teachers should first brainstorm to generate a list of the specific difficulties the students are experiencing in the classroom. After identifying the students' critical learning needs, the team members should rank those needs in order from most important to least important. The most important needs are those that are functional, frequently required in the classroom, and necessary for student success. The needs that are selected as most critical should be addressed as the first area for possible research; the remaining items on the list may be saved for possible future research projects.

In our project, the mentor teacher took the lead role in this discussion because she was in the best position to identify and prioritize the needs of her individual students. The student teachers also contributed classroom information that informed the decision making; the university faculty merely facilitated the process. The mentor teacher identified reading proficiency as the most critical goal for almost all her students. She also identified four students with the most severe reading problems to be the target students for this project. The research team therefore decided to plan a project that would target reading accuracy and proficiency for four second-graders with learning disabilities.

## Gathering More Information

Prior to planning an intervention, the research team must gather more information on the student characteristics, classroom schedules, and the time frame for implementing the research project. The project should fit into the existing schedules of the students, mentor teacher, and student teachers.

In our project, the mentor teacher identified the part of the day that was most workable for the intervention, a period during which second-grade students with learning disabilities attended her special education resource room. She identified four students with reading difficulties and described the reading program that was currently in place. During these discussions, the mentor teacher had some concerns that the experiment might take up too much time and cut into her existing instructional schedule.

## Working around Time Constraints

One of the most challenging aspects of collaborative research is planning the project in the context of the time available to the research team. The research team must be prepared for this challenge and be willing to modify the plan when time constraints are presented. For example, student teachers in our special education program are required to complete two 8-week placements, one elementary and one secondary. Because 8 weeks is not enough time to plan and implement an experiment, we arranged for pairs of student teachers to work as a team across the two halves of the semester. Specifically, while one student teacher was in an elementary classroom, the other was placed in a high school special education classroom adjacent to the elementary school. This arrangement allowed both student teachers to be involved in both classrooms throughout the semester. The student teacher in the high school setting was excused for a small part of the school day a couple of times each week to help with interobserver agreement (IOA) and procedural reliability.

## Identifying Possible Interventions

Once the research team has identified the students, their critical learning needs, and the schedules of the team members, they can begin to collaboratively identify possible interventions.

Interventions should be selected based on the teacher's comfort level with the approach and the feasibility relative to classroom resources and scheduling. Interventions should be relatively simple, be low cost in terms of time and effort, and revolve around what the team members are willing to do. This increases the likelihood that the intervention will be implemented as consistently as possible.

During this stage of our project, the university faculty took the lead in generating ideas for interventions, the student teachers took the lead in researching them, and the mentor teacher took the lead in determining their feasibility. Our team selected systematic error correction and repeated readings from several possible interventions to increase reading accuracy and fluency. Additionally, we decided that a student teacher would work individually for about 5 or 6 minutes each day with the student participants to implement the intervention.

## Developing Research Questions

Once the general direction of the experiment is decided on, it is time to develop specific research questions. Because of their expertise and experience with classroom research, university researchers will typically guide this process. Because other members of the team may not have much experience with data collection, the research questions should be written carefully so as to guide every aspect of the experiment. The research questions should include the independent variables (the conditions manipulated by the experimenters), the dependent variables (the behaviors the experimenters are attempting to influence), and the population of students on whom the effects of the intervention will be assessed.

We decided that our independent variables would be systematic error correction and repeated readings, the dependent variables would be words read correctly per minute and words read incorrectly per minute, and the students would be four second-graders with learning dis-

abilities. The research questions we developed were as follows:

1. What are the effects of systematic error correction on the number of words read correctly per minute by second-graders with learning disabilities?

2. What are the effects of systematic error correction on the number of words read incorrectly per minute by second-graders with learning disabilities?

3. What are the combined effects of systematic error correction and repeated readings on the number of words read correctly per minute by second-graders with learning disabilities?

4. What are the combined effects of systematic error correction and repeated readings on the number of words read incorrectly per minute by second-graders with learning disabilities?

## Measuring Dependent Variables

The next step for the research team is to decide how the dependent variables will be measured. After the dependent variables have been defined with precise specificity, an appropriate recording instrument should be designed. The measurement system should be direct, consistent, and accurate. For many experiments, permanent product measures may be more feasible to assess than direct observation of ongoing behavior and will be easier to check for accuracy.

Because we were assessing oral reading rate, we decided to use direct observation. We could have used tape recorders, but we were concerned about inaccuracy of data collection as a result of possible audiotape distortions. Reading rate was measured by timing each student for 1 minute as he or she read a passage and then counting the number of words read correctly and incorrectly. A word was counted as correct if the student independently pronounced the word correctly within 3 seconds without prompting from the student teacher. A word was counted as incorrect if it was pronounced incorrectly, mis-cued, omitted, or not stated within 3 seconds. Additionally, self-corrects within 3 seconds were counted as correct.

Although the university faculty took a leader-ship role in the process of defining the depen-dent variables, the student teachers were actively involved. For example, their question, "How should we count the word if the student corrects himself?" reminded us to address that issue in the definitions. With respect to developing a form that was functional for recording the data, one of the student teachers, with some input from a faculty member, took the lead role. The collection of interobserver agreement (IOA) data was also a point of discussion. A faculty mem-ber pointed out that during several sessions another team member must be present to inde-pendently and simultaneously record data. The faculty member explained that assessing IOA would add to the believability of the findings and therefore strengthen the experiment.

### Selecting an Experimental Design

When designing an experiment, the research team must take into consideration the schedules, teaching routines, and school calendar to help make data collection consistent. Ideally, data should be collected at the same time each day and in the same setting. This reduces the possi-bility of confounding variables—that is, vari-ables other than those directly related to the intervention influencing the data. Taking these factors into account, the research team should select an appropriate experimental design. Among others, the following examples of de-signs may be selected for collecting individual student data: reversal, multiple baseline, or alternating treatments (see Cooper, Heron, & Heward, 1987).

After a discussion of the possible experimen-tal design options, we decided that a multiple baseline across students design would be most appropriate and most feasible. A multiple base-line across students design would require the in-terventions to be implemented with one student at a time. If each student's baseline data re-mained stable and his or her performance changed when and only when the intervention was implemented, there would be evidence of a functional relationship of the intervention and student performance. The multiple baseline across students design was most appropriate be-cause we would not have to withdraw the inter-vention and attempt to return the students' reading proficiency back to their baseline per-formance. This design also allowed us the flexi-bility of adding new conditions if necessary.

### Specifying Experimental Procedures

When designing experimental procedures, re-searchers must be very specific to increase the likelihood of consistency. Experimental control does not always ally with ongoing instructional decisions made by teachers, so it is important for the university researchers to take a leader-ship role and to emphasize the importance of following the experimental procedures the same way and in the same sequence for every experi-mental session. Consistent implementation of experimental procedures will increase the likeli-hood that the results can truly be attributed to intervention. The research team should collabo-ratively decide on the procedures or steps for implementing the interventions and then de-velop a step-by-step checklist for each experi-mental condition. Prior to the beginning of data collection, the student teacher and others re-sponsible for implementing the intervention and measurement should practice implementing the procedural steps and recording data. During these practice sessions, the student teacher should receive ongoing feedback from univer-sity faculty until mastery is attained.

After considerable discussion among univer-sity faculty and student teachers as well as ap-proval from the mentor teacher, our research team decided on the procedures for implement-ing each intervention. Table 10-1 shows the pro-cedures for each condition of our investigation.

**Table 10-1**
Experimental Procedures for Each Condition

| | |
|---|---|
| Baseline | 1. The student will read a selected passage to the teacher for 5 minutes. |
| | 2. Each time the student makes a reading error, the student teacher will say the correct word. |
| | 3. After the 5-minute reading period, the student teacher will ask the student to reread the passage and time the student for 1 minute. |
| | 4. The student teacher will record words read correctly and words read incorrectly per minute. |
| Systematic Error Correction | 1. The student will read a selected passage to the teacher for 5 minutes. |
| | 2. Each time the student makes an error, the student teacher will say the correct word, and the student will repeat the correct word and reread the sentence. |
| | 3. At the end of the 5-minute reading period, the student teacher will review all the words the students pronounced incorrectly by pointing to the word and asking the student to read it. |
| | 4. If the student makes an error during the review, the student teacher will state the correct word, and the student will repeat it. |
| | 5. After the reading period, the student teacher will ask the student to reread the passage and time the student for 1 minute. |
| | 6. The student teacher will record words read correctly and incorrectly per minute. |
| Systematic Error Correction plus Repeated Readings | 1. The student teacher will follow the same procedures for the error correction condition, except that the student will read for 3 minutes (instead of 5). |
| | 2. After the 3-minute period, the student teacher will conduct three 1-minute timings (the student will start from the beginning of the passage for each timing). |
| | 3. The student teacher will record the number of words read correctly and incorrectly per minute during the last timing. |

After the procedures were decided on and written, they were used as a guide by the student teacher implementing the intervention, and they were also used to assess procedural reliability. A second observer was present to assess procedural reliability for as many experimental sessions as possible. About 20% to 25% of the sessions should be enough to determine that the intervention was implemented consistently throughout the duration of the experiment. However, because of scheduling conflicts within our research team, we were able to assess procedural reliability for only about 10% of the sessions. The low percentage of reliability checks was a limitation of our investigation. Despite this limitation, peer reviewers of a special education journal recommended acceptance of this paper for publication because they believed that this investigation made a contribution to the literature.

## Deciding Who Will Be Responsible for Each Task

As stated before, the lead roles and responsibilities for each task should remain flexible, changing across stages according to differing levels of knowledge. Once our research design was in place, we still had several more tasks to do before we could begin data collection. Those tasks were as follows: completing the paperwork for school board approval, completing the paperwork for the human subjects review board, obtaining parent permission for the students to participate, and obtaining the reading materials used in this experiment. We also had to decide who would implement the experimental procedures, complete the IOA assessments, observe for procedural reliability, and graph the data.

Both university faculty members took responsibility for completing the paperwork for the school board and the university human subjects review board. Both institutions, which only met once a month, had to give their permission before we were allowed to go forward with this project. We ended up losing about 6 weeks of data collection time while we waited for permission from the university and school district. During this 6-week time period, the mentor teacher took responsibility for obtaining permission from the students' parents, and the student teachers and university faculty members obtained the reading materials.

Clarifying in writing, in the form of an agreement, the tasks for which each team member is responsible is helpful. We recommend that each team member sign the agreement and receive a copy. This might help to prevent some confusion later. For example, at one point in our project, one of the faculty members said, "Didn't you say that you would do the paperwork for the human subjects review board?" and the other faculty member responded, "I probably did say that, but I don't remember."

## Selecting Instructional Materials

The research team must put careful thought into selecting the materials that will be used in the investigation. The materials should be appropriate for the students, relevant to practice, and relatively free of any variables that might confound the experiment. Our team decided that we could not use the reading materials that were currently being used by the mentor teacher because doing so would confound the results of the experiment. Previous exposure to the reading materials used in our investigation would then be an alternate explanation for any results we obtained. Using a different reading series served as a control for this possible confounding variable. We selected another widely available reading series,

one with a controlled vocabulary. Nevertheless, the progression in difficulty from one passage to another was not as gradual as we had anticipated; this was a distinct disadvantage. We elected to use this series anyway. Our rationale was twofold. First, we reasoned that if the effects of the intervention were robust enough, the students would continue to make substantial gains despite the increasing difficulty of the reading passages. Second, most basal reading programs used in regular classrooms gradually increase in difficulty, and we decided that this variable might have important implications for the practical application of our intervention.

## Staying Flexible

When all of the preparations for the investigation are complete and a firm plan is in place, the research team must be prepared for the likelihood that their roles may have to change. For example, by the time we received approval from the human subjects review board and the school board, we were already in the second 8 weeks of the student teaching experience. So, the student teacher assigned to the mentor teacher's classroom during the second 8 weeks was responsible for implementing the experimental procedures. The student teacher who was assigned to that placement during the first 8 weeks (and was now in an adjacent high school setting) was responsible for collecting IOA data. She had to get permission from her other mentor teacher to be excused for a short time period a couple of times each week to perform this task. The two university faculty members assessed procedural reliability, and one of the faculty members took responsibility for graphing the data. The mentor teacher was unable to take part in the IOA or procedural reliability checks because she was teaching the other students in the class during data collection sessions. Ideally, mentor teachers involved in collaborative research should also assist with implementing interventions, and university faculty should encourage this type of participation. However, in our project, we were grateful to find a volunteer mentor teacher who did in fact participate in other substantive ways. Our recommendation for university faculty is to encourage the mentor teacher to participate as much as possible, but be willing to accept less.

## Having Regular Meetings

Throughout the duration of the experiment, the research team should have regular meetings to review the ongoing data and make collaborative decisions about what to do next. Ideally, these meetings should take place at the school for the convenience of the mentor teacher. Because finding the time to meet regularly can be difficult, the team should make use of technology. Once the planning stage is over and data collection has begun, team members can communicate through e-mail and call an in-person meeting only when necessary.

Because our experiment employed a multiple baseline across students design, the team had to meet and examine the data regularly to determine when and for whom we would implement the next phase change. We based these decisions on the examination of the stability of each student's data. Regular meetings are also important opportunities for discussing any unforeseen problems that might influence the data. For example, during the third phase of the experiment (error correction plus repeated readings), the student teachers reported that the reading materials were becoming much too difficult for the students, which seemed to influence their motivation. We decided to implement a fourth condition, error correction plus repeated readings with materials the students had previously read. We expected big leaps in the data because the reading material was easier, but the data in this condition were not as robust as we expected. Based on informal feedback from student and mentor teachers, we identified some possible reasons for this outcome. The last 2 weeks of data collection proved to be very difficult because it was the end of the school year and

many school activities (e.g., field day, awards day) sometimes conflicted with data collection. Also, student and mentor teachers believed that with summer vacation coming soon, the students seemed to lose their motivation for schoolwork in general.

## Analyzing the Data

When data collection is complete, the team should meet and analyze the data to determine if the variables are functionally related and, if so, to what extent. Additionally, the team can identify the limitations of the experiment and decide how the experiment can be improved for future systematic replications. The results we obtained in our project are as follows.

Figure 10-1 shows the number of words read correctly and incorrectly per minute in all 33 sessions, and Table 10-2 shows the mean number of words read correctly and incorrectly (errors) per minute by each student in each condition. During baseline, the mean number of words read correctly ranged from 35.78 wpm (Daniel) to 57.38 wpm (Alex), and the mean number of errors ranged from 3.50 (Wesley) to 9.00 (Daniel). Wesley was the only student who substantially increased his reading rate in the error correction condition, but all four students made fewer errors per minute ranging from a mean of 1.64 (Mary) to 3.38 (Daniel). When repeated readings were added to the error correction condition, the mean number of words read per minute ranged from 66.00 (Daniel) to 77.40 (Wesley). Wesley made the greatest gains in the final condition with a mean of 81.00 words read correctly per minute and 0.75 errors per minute. Over the course of this study, all four students increased their reading rate by a mean of 12.29 to 29.02 more words read correctly per minute and had a mean of 2.75 to 6.2 fewer errors. Our team decided that the differences in the students' performance were substantial considering that experimental sessions lasted only 6 minutes and the reading materials continued to become progressively more difficult.

**Figure 10-1.**
Number of words read correctly and incorrectly per minute by each student in each condition.

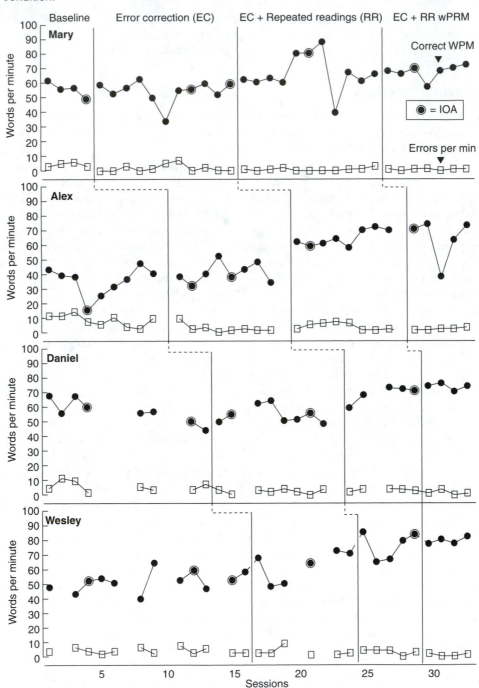

**Table 10-2**
Mean Number of Words Read Correctly and Incorrectly (Errors) per Minute by Each Student in Each Condition

| Student | Baseline | | Systematic Error Correction | | Systematic Error Correction plus Repeated Readings | | Condition 3 with Previously Read Material | |
|---|---|---|---|---|---|---|---|---|
| | Correct | Errors | Correct | Errors | Correct | Errors | Correct | Errors |
| Mary | 56.00 | 4.25 | 54.36 | 1.64 | 67.00 | 0.82 | 68.29 | 0.71 |
| Daniel | 35.78 | 9.00 | 41.38 | 3.38 | 66.00 | 4.33 | 64.80 | 2.80 |
| Alex | 57.38 | 5.38 | 55.13 | 2.25 | 69.60 | 3.40 | 74.50 | 1.50 |
| Wesley | 52.17 | 3.5 | 63.83 | 2.83 | 77.40 | 3.00 | 81.00 | 0.75 |

An important limitation of our investigation is that we did not formally assess social validity (measuring consumer satisfaction). It would have strengthened the investigation if we had interviewed the students to determine their opinions of the intervention and their own performance. Formally interviewing the mentor teacher to determine her opinions of the project and whether she would continue to use the intervention would have provided us with important information as well. However, it is important to note that the teacher did comment on several occasions that the children involved in this project were making great gains in their reading performance and functioning better in the classroom.

## Sharing the Findings

Once the research team has discussed and synthesized the results of the investigation, they must find ways to disseminate what they learned. Disseminating the findings of classroom research can be extremely rewarding to all participants in the classroom research project. Results of classroom research can be disseminated by coauthoring a paper for the purpose of publication in a professional journal; submitting a proposal for a national, state, or local conference; or presenting the project and findings to other teachers in the school district at scheduled staff development meetings. Because the participants have devoted a great deal of time to this project, they should be generously rewarded with recognition for their efforts. In addition to receiving recognition through publications and presentations, the participating mentor teachers may be rewarded with a teaching or service award, credit for professional development activities, travel money to attend a national conference, or release time to collaboratively develop future research projects.

We began disseminating the findings of our research by sending a memo that summarized the project and results to the school board, the superintendent of the school district, and the administrator of the mentor teacher's school. Our local newspaper also published an article about this project after being contacted by one of the university faculty members. Additionally, we presented this research at one international and one state conference, and we published this research in a special education journal. The student teachers were very enthusiastic about participating in the conference presentations and coauthoring the publication.

## Following Up

Once a collaborative classroom research relationship has been established between the university and local school district, the stage is set for continuing and extending research with other student and mentor teachers. For example, mentor teachers involved in research projects may volunteer to supervise other student teachers interested in participating in classroom research. One way to obtain more student teacher volunteers may be to ask the former student teacher researchers to present their projects to new preservice teachers. This may inspire other student teachers to volunteer to participate in collaborative research projects. One of the student teachers who participated in our project asked to meet with one of the university faculty members to plan another research project in her own classroom.

The university researchers and mentor teacher may begin making plans for the next project. Other university faculty members and graduate research assistants may also be interested in becoming involved with collaborative research projects within the school district. Collaborative classroom research between the university and local schools might eventually take the place of some traditional staff development activities, significantly contribute to changes in classroom practice, and comply with the mandates of the No Child Left Behind Act (2001). An important area for future research is to assess the extent to which collaborative research actually improves the likelihood that teachers will use evidence-based procedures in the classroom.

## OBSTACLES

In this chapter we have described how collaborative classroom research with mentor and student teachers might be conducted. We have also given some examples of the difficulties that may be faced at each stage of such projects. In this section we provide more information about some of the obstacles research teams may encounter.

The greatest obstacle was the time delay that resulted from having to obtain school district and human subjects review board permissions. One suggestion for dealing with this obstacle is to begin the steps for obtaining permission a

couple of months prior to the student teaching experience. Alternatively, university faculty could initiate a collaborative agreement between a school district and university that would require only one approval or an agreement that projects consisting of validated practices not considered "experimental" do not require IRB permission. Another option would be to avoid obtaining permission by designing action research projects considered to be typical classroom practice and have them be applied, for the most part, by the mentor teacher. Although this would eliminate widespread dissemination, it would allow for teacher-to-teacher sharing and might increase the likelihood that student and mentor teachers would use validated practice in the future.

For mentor teachers, involvement in a research project certainly takes more time than is required for typical student teacher mentoring. In our case, this concern was exacerbated by the fact that our project was implemented at the end of the school year. Many classroom research projects are implemented at the end of the school year because of time delays related to planning and waiting for necessary permission. The mentor teacher in our project was exceedingly busy with end-of-the-year responsibilities, not the least of which were individualized education program (IEP) meetings. This circumstance somewhat limited her day-to-day involvement in decision making and most certainly curtailed her involvement in data collection. Finding ways to reward mentor teachers for any time they are willing to invest should be a priority. This will increase the likelihood of future participation.

Research involvement also requires more time of student teachers. Although we substituted some research activities for some of the written assignments ordinarily required of student teachers, they still invested extra time. For example, they completed many research-related activities outside of the school day, including such tasks as attending team meetings and preparing research materials. One student teacher continued to collect data for 2 weeks after the student teaching experience had ended. To say that not all student teachers would be willing put in that much extra time is an understatement. This underscores the importance of voluntary participation in the project. It is important to note that real-life circumstances may limit a volunteers' intended involvement. For example, one student teacher got married, moved to a new home, and began applying for teaching positions immediately after graduation. She was thus unavailable for data analysis and for writing proposals and manuscripts.

University faculty should also expect to devote more time and effort than would ordinarily be required for student teacher supervision. For the project to run smoothly, more field visits and more contact with mentor and student teachers will be needed. Given that most student and mentor teachers lack research experience, much more coaching and support will be required. University faculty who have not recently spent much time in classrooms must be prepared to be reminded of all the things that can go wrong with the implementation of research. In addition to the 8-week wait to obtain approval, the things that can and did go wrong in our project included abrupt changes in school and classroom schedules and data collection sessions interrupted or lost due to announcements on the intercom, field trips, school assemblies, and student or teacher absences. Having said all this, the advantages for faculty far outweigh the disadvantages. For us, perhaps the foremost of those advantages was witnessing the student teachers' sense of accomplishment. This gave us more hope that what we preach will be actually practiced.

## CONCLUSION

If well conducted, collaborative research projects may be costly in terms of time and labor. However, the benefits gained from involvement in classroom research may prove to be well worth the efforts of the mentor teachers, student teachers, and university faculty. Ideally, these projects will result in professional growth and recognition and have lasting effects on individual teacher practice. Of course, the goal of highest priority for all educators is to effect positive changes in student performance. To attain that goal, teachers must be able to make accurate judgments regarding the effectiveness of particular instructional practices. Collaborative classroom research is one way to ensure that such judgments are in fact sound.

## REFERENCES

Abbott, M., Walton, C., Tapia, Y., & Greenwood, C. R. (1999). Research to practice: A "blueprint" for closing the gap in local schools. *Exceptional Children, 65,* 339–352.

Carnine, D. (1997). Bridging the research to practice gap. *Exceptional Children, 63,* 513–522.

Cooper, J. O., Heron, T. E., & Heward, W. L. (1987). *Applied behavior analysis.* Upper Saddle River, NJ: Prentice Hall/Merrill.

Cuban, L. (1993). The lure of curricular reform and its pitiful history. *Phi Delta Kappan, 75,* 182–185.

Fuchs, D. F., & Fuchs, L. S. (2001). One blueprint for bridging the gap: Project PROMISE (Practitioners and researchers orchestrating model innovations to strengthen education). *Teacher Education and Special Education, 24,* 304–314.

Gersten, R., Morvant, M., & Brengelman, S. (1995). Close to the classroom is close to the bone: Coaching as a means to translate research into practice. *Exceptional Children, 62,* 56–67.

Gersten, R., Vaughn, S., Deshler, D., & Schiller, E. (1997). What we know about using research findings: Implications for improving special education practice. *Journal of Learning Disabilities, 30,* 466–476.

Greenwood, C. R., & Abbott, M. (2001). The research to practice gap in special education. *Teacher Education and Special Education, 24,* 276–289.

Greenwood, C. R., Delquadri, J., & Bulgren, J. (1993). Current challenges to behavioral technology in the reform of schooling: Large-scale, high-quality implementation and sustained use of effective instructional practices. *Education and Treatment of Children, 16,* 401–440.

Greenwood, C. R., & Maheady, L. (2001). Are future teachers aware of the gap between research and practice and what should they know. *Teacher Education and Special Education, 24,* 333–347.

Joyce, B., & Showers, B. (1995). *Student achievement through staff development* (2nd ed.). White Plains, NY: Longman.

Kaestle, C. F. (1993). Research news and comment: The awful reputation of education research. *Educational Researcher, January–February,* 23–31.

Lieberman, A., & Miller, L. (1991). *Teachers—Their world and their work: Implications for school improvement.* New York: Teachers College Press.

Malouf, D. B., & Schiller, E. P. (1995). Practice and research in special education. *Exceptional Children, 61,* 414–424.

Purvis, J. R., & Tice, T. A. (1996). *Making staff development work.* Jackson, MS: The Southern Education Consortium.

Sindelar, P. T., & Brownell, M. T. (2001). Research to practice dissemination, scale, and context: We can do it, but can we afford it? *Teacher Education and Special Education, 24,* 348–355.

U.S. Department of Education. (2002). No Child Left Behind Act of 2001. http://www/ed.gov/offices/OESE/esea/index.html.

Viadaro, D. (1994). The great divide: The gap between research and practice is wider in education than in other fields, such as medicine and business. *Teacher Magazine, October,* 22–24.

Wood, F. H., & Thompson, S. R. (1993). Assumptions about staff development based on research and best coaching. *Journal of Staff Development, 14,* 52–57.

## STUDY QUESTIONS AND FOLLOW-UP ACTIVITIES

1. What experience have you had participating in collaborative classroom research? Describe the research and your particular role. How might you implement future collaborative research based on ideas presented in this chapter? If you have not participated in collaborative classroom research in the past, describe some potential collaborative opportunities you could develop to begin doing so.

---

Study questions and follow-up activities prepared by Michele M. Nobel and Donna M. Villareal.

2. Gather information about the human subjects review board process at your university, college, or school district. On the basis of the information you gather, design an informative presentation you could give to novice researchers to educate them on the review board process at your institution.

3. Teaching idea magazines, such as *The Mailbox,* are widely used across the country and disseminate information suggested by readers. These magazines include many reproducible pages and lesson plans that can be implemented quickly and easily. However, the strategies and ideas presented in such magazines are not always based on research that identifies effective teaching practices. On the other hand, research journals provide data on effective teaching practices, but are not as easily accessible to teachers as the idea magazines. How can research journals compete with the easily accessible, but not empirically validated, teacher magazines? What are some strategies you would suggest that research journals adopt for increasing the awareness and availability of research journals for teachers?

4. With the current demands on teachers' time, some teachers might argue they just don't have time to engage in collaborative research with university personnel. Assume you are a student or faculty member at a university who would like to begin a collaborative relationship with a school or teacher. Design a presentation that illustrates to the school faculty and administrators the benefits of such activities and how the collaborative relationship might actually save teachers time in the long run.

5. Should collaborative research be a requirement for all preservice teachers? Discuss the benefits and challenges of implementing such a requirement into already packed preservice teacher-training programs.

6. Should collaborative research participation be a requirement for teachers to renew their teaching licenses? Discuss the implications of such a requirement as well as the potential obstacles for creating this standard as a requirement.

7. Should the role of faculty advisors include not only advising their assigned students but also participating jointly in collaborative research with

their advisees? Discuss the strengths and weaknesses of such an arrangement.

8.  Working in a small group of three to six individuals, create a scenario for implementing classroom-based research. Describe the classroom setting and the research participants. Assign roles to each group member (e.g., classroom teacher, teaching assistant, preservice teacher, university graduate student, university professor). Alternatively, if the membership of the class allows, divide into groups so that each group consists of university students, professors, and classroom teachers. Complete the following activities as a group:

    a.  Develop a potential collaborative study. Script a scenario in which you meet to define the research questions and goals of the study. Members should be prepared to introduce themselves and discuss their interest in the project and the ways they could contribute to the study.

    b.  Clarify the roles and tasks of each member of the group in the form of a written agreement.

    c.  List your research questions and specify the independent and dependent variables. Provide an explanation and rationale for how data will be collected and recorded for the variables of interest. Each member of the group should be prepared to report on one of these aspects to the larger group.

    d.  In clear and unambiguous language, describe the procedures for baseline and treatment conditions.

    e.  Identify the research design you will use to analyze the data and to answer your research question(s).

    f.  Measuring the social validity of interventions and procedures relates to the effectiveness of implementation. Plan for determining the social validity of your collaborative study before, during, and after intervention.

### CHAPTER 11

# The Hawthorne Country Day School
## A Behavioral Approach to Schooling

*Christopher S. McDonough*    *Tina Covington*    *Sayaka Endo*
*Deborah Meinberg*    *Trina D. Spencer*    *David F. Bicard*

## HISTORY OF THE HAWTHORNE COUNTRY DAY SCHOOL

The Hawthorne Country Day School (Hawthorne) is a 501(c)3 not-for-profit school approved by the New York State Education Department to serve students with disabilities. The majority of the students served (70%) are diagnosed with autism or pervasive developmental disorder, but the school also serves students diagnosed with mental retardation, Asperger's syndrome, Prader–Willi syndrome, speech–language impairment, multiple disabilities, and other health impairment. The main school campus is located in Westchester County, New York, 15 miles north of New York City. The main campus serves 142 children with disabilities ages 3 to 21. The Hawthorne Manhattan Annex in Harlem, New York, serves 30 children with autism ages 5 to 8. Hawthorne also operates a home-based early intervention program for toddlers ages 18 months to 3 years.

Children and adults with severe developmental disabilities have been educated on the Hawthorne campus in Westchester since the 1920s; the school was first known as the Avery Training School and then as the Margaret Chapman School. Both of these were residential schools for children and adults with disabilities. Since the spring of 2001, the school has been a day school. In 1977 Eileen Bisordi, then educational director at the Margaret Chapman School, became the executive director of the school and its parent organization, Bradhurst Corporation (now the Hawthorne Foundation, Inc.) One of the key strategic initiatives she took on, and perhaps the most enduring, was her decision to use applied behavior analysis as a tool for the measurement and change of student and teacher behavior. To that end, in 1981 she enlisted Dr. R. Douglas Greer, a professor of education and psychology at Columbia University, as a consultant. Over the course of the next two decades, Dr. Greer and scores of his master's and doc-

We express thanks to Doug Greer, Janet Twyman, Bill Heward, and Carl Cheney for their mentorship.

toral students from Columbia, along with the Margaret Chapman School staff, developed a model of schooling called the Comprehensive Application of Behavior Analysis to Schooling (CABAS).[1] The Margaret Chapman School was the first CABAS school. Although Hawthorne is no longer a CABAS school (as of July 2001), the systems approach founded by Dr. Greer continues to develop at the school.

Children are referred to Hawthorne from the committee on special education or preschool special education in each child's home school district. Early intervention students are referred from the Westchester County Department of Health. Approximately 50% of the students at the school come from the New York City schools, and 50% come from school districts in Westchester County. Students come from a wide range of socioeconomic backgrounds, with the majority (70%) coming from poor or working class families. Approximately 35% of the students are White, 32% are African American, 26% are Hispanic, and 7% are Asian/Pacific Islander. The student population is 80% male. Hawthorne services include instruction in small self-contained classes (six to eight students with one teacher and two to four assistants) throughout the year and for 6 weeks in the summer; lunch; physical education; speech–language, occupational, and physical therapy; and parent education. Hawthorne is publicly funded, and all services are free of charge to families.

The primary funding sources for the school are the school districts that place children at the school, the New York State Department of Education, the Westchester County Department of Health, the federal government, and charitable contributions. The New York State education department regulates the school and sets tuition rates. At present, the annual cost of the program per child is about $31,000.

Teachers and teaching assistants at the school are recruited through advertisements in local newspapers, at local colleges that have teacher preparation programs, and through word of mouth. To be eligible for a teaching position, a candidate must have New York State teacher certification in special education, which requires a minimum of a bachelor's degree. To be eligible for a teaching assistant position, a candidate must have at least an associate's degree. Although we prefer to hire teachers with a background in applied behavior analysis, this is not a prerequisite for employment. We prefer to hire teachers with little or no teaching experience if they do not have a background in applied behavior analysis. This is because candidates with less teaching experience are less likely to have developed teaching practices that conflict with the training in applied behavior analysis they will receive at Hawthorne.

The current funding structure at Hawthorne, which is determined by the New York State education department, makes it impossible for Hawthorne to compete with regional public schools in terms of teacher salary. This affects our ability to recruit and retain skilled employees. In all categories (teachers, teaching assistants, support staff, and administration) salaries at Hawthorne are less than the lowest salaries in regional public schools. For example, according to the Office of Negotiations Clearinghouse for Putnum/Northern Westchester, in the 2001–2002 school year the lowest regional starting salary for a public school teacher with a bachelor's degree and no experience, for a 10-month (September–June) contract, was $32,764. The regional average was $39,918. Hawthorne's starting 12-month salary (September–June, plus 6 weeks in July and August) for a teacher with a bachelor's degree and no experience was $32,500. In addition, the public school teacher benefits package often includes full medical and dental insurance coverage and admittance to the New York State Teachers' Retirement System (which includes retirement, disability, and death benefits to public school teachers and adminis-

---

[1]The research validating CABAS was not conducted exclusively at the Margaret Chapman School. For the most complete description of the research validating CABAS and the history of its development, see Greer (2002).

trators in New York State). At Hawthorne, teachers pay for 33% of their medical and dental insurance and are denied access to the New York State Teachers' Retirement System.[2] In sum, Hawthorne employees are asked to work longer and for less money with students who present some of the most complex learning challenges. This presents a significant challenge to overcome with respect to our commitment to provide a quality education for our students. In broad terms, a behavioral approach to schooling provides a heuristic method of inquiry through which we can fulfill this commitment.

## WHAT IS A BEHAVIORAL SCHOOL?

In general, schooling involves an *outcome* (what to teach) and a *process* (how to teach). School outcomes address what students learn at school. For most students outcomes are measured in terms of scores on standardized achievement tests, the number of college-bound seniors, and graduation rates. For some students with disabilities, success is measured in terms of increased independence, employability, and how much treatment and ongoing care costs taxpayers. The schooling process deals with how school outcomes are achieved—specifically, with the philosophy and corresponding methods used by the school to achieve state and national outcomes.

A behavioral school is one in which the outcomes and the process of schooling are informed by behavioral science, and behavior analytic methods are used to achieve predefined learning objectives. Learning objectives are the acquisition of functional skills relative to the baseline or entry-level skill of a learner. Functional skills are ones that promote success for the learner, whether that learner is a student, a parent, a teacher, a teaching assistant, support

personnel, or a behavior analyst. The achievement of functional learning objectives is referred to as an outcome, and a behavioral school adheres to behavior science to maximize learner outcomes.

At Hawthorne we take a systems approach to all aspects of the school. A systems or *cybernetic* approach is one in which "all of the roles of the consumers and professionals are interrelated in terms of the science of behavior. The management and analysis of all the components are tied to an analysis of the interrelated consequences of the behaviors of all parties involved" (Greer, 2002, p. 295).[3] A cybernetic system is self-correcting. By design, it adapts based on the data entered into the system and the goals of the system. At Hawthorne the goal of the system is to maximize learning outcomes for all parties involved in the system. With behavior science informing the learning process, we believe we have the necessary and sufficient criteria for maximizing the learning outcomes for the students, parents, and staff at Hawthorne.

## WHY TAKE A BEHAVIORAL APPROACH TO SCHOOLING?

We offer two simple and related reasons why we take this approach to schooling. First, and most important, the pragmatic assumptions and scientific approach espoused by applied behavior analysis (ABA) are effective. There is a rich literature of over 30 years of effective, replica-

---

[2]The decision to bar our teachers and teachers in schools like ours from the state teachers' retirement system is made by the state of New York.

[3]The term *cybernetic* (Greek in origin, meaning "steersman" and related to the Greek word for "govern") was first used in 1947 by Norbert Wiener to describe the ways in which aspects of a system (or scientific discipline) interact with respect to how predictions are made, goals are defined, action is taken to meet stated goals, and feedback is used to improve overall system effectiveness (Pangaro, 2000). Furthermore, theorists in the field of computer science describe "feedback loops" and "real-time enterprise computing" as self-correcting systems and align closely with the cybernetics movement (see Malone, 2002).

ble, single-subject research to draw from in applied behavior analysis, much of it published in journals such as the *Journal of Applied Behavior Analysis, Behavioral Disorders,* and the *Journal of Behavioral Education,* to name a few. The characteristics that make ABA so effective were outlined early in its history by Baer, Wolf, and Risley (1968). Among the most important of these characteristics is the fact that ABA is designed to be effective because the procedures are derived from the basic principles that affect behavior with focus on the development of functional, socially significant skills. Other aspects of applied behavior analysis that we believe are important include the following:

- *Scope.* Applied behavior analysis is effective for all students, regardless of age or skill level.

- *Accountability.* Learning problems are treated as instructional challenges, not student failures.

- *Technical framework.* A standard for continuous measurement and a standard set of terms allow for efficient, unambiguous communication between instructors and with parents.

At Hawthorne we maximize student progress by replicating instructional activities and tactics whose effects have been systematically investigated through scientific research and published in refereed journals and books.

Along with the procedures derived from ABA (e.g., Cooper, Heron, & Heward, 1987) we also employ Direct Instruction (e.g., Becker & Carnine, 1981). Hawthorne uses these teaching methods because the largest body of valid research available backs them. The best example of the validity of these methods comes from Project Follow Through, which was the largest controlled longitudinal study designed to investigate effective teaching practices in the history of American education (Adams, 1995). From 1968 to 1976, Project Follow Through compared different teaching models associated with different philosophies and learning theories (behavioristic, cognitive, and psychodynamic) to control groups at dozens of school sites around the country and across thousands of children at risk for academic failure. The results clearly indicated that Direct Instruction, classified as a behavioristic teaching approach, produced the best outcomes for students across a wide array of skills, including language, reading, spelling, math, and problem solving (Stebbins, St. Pierre, Proper, Anderson, & Cerva 1977). The only other approach that achieved positive results for students was ABA. Thus, we believe the behavioral approach to schooling is the only responsible choice a school can make for its students. Given the results of Project Follow Through and the clear and robust history demonstrating the effectiveness of ABA in education, the more difficult and troubling question is why do we *not* take a behavioral approach to schooling[4]

Our learning history, which shaped and continues to shape our behavior, is the second reason we take the behavioral approach to schooling. We received our graduate training in the behavior analysis programs at Columbia University (under the direction of Professor R. Douglas Greer), the Ohio State University (under the direction of Professor William L. Heward), and the Utah State University (under the direction of Professor Carl Cheney). All but one of us also spent several years training with Dr. Janet Twyman at the Fred S. Keller School in Yonkers, New York (Twyman, 1998). In short, we have trained for years to apply the science of behavior to schooling. Considering that we were trained by highly skilled behavior scientists who have devoted their careers to the education of students with disabilities and their teachers, it should come as no surprise that we are doing what we were trained to do. On the contrary, it would be surprising if we did not attend to valid

---

[4]See Watkins (1995) for an excellent review of Project Follow Through and a discussion about why the results of this billion-dollar experiment have failed to improve the learning process for the vast majority of American children.

research findings and use them to maximize learner outcomes.

The primary learner group at Hawthorne is the student group. Secondary learner groups include parents, teachers, teaching assistants, support staff, and administrators. In a behavioral school, outcomes for these secondary learner groups are linked in measurable ways to outcomes for students. The ways outcomes for these learner groups are linked to outcomes for students at Hawthorne is the focus of the remainder of this chapter.

## STUDENTS IN A BEHAVIORAL SCHOOL

### Instructional Activities

Instructional activities are the various individual educational programs for each student. Table 11-1 shows examples of instructional activities used with students at Hawthorne. Instructional activities are sequenced systematically throughout the day. For example, James (age 10), is taught to greet peers and teachers and to engage in a morning routine (e.g., take off his jacket, give a communication book to teacher, etc.) using naturalistic teaching methods (see Table 11-1 for reference). Later he is taught verbal behavior, academic skills, and social skills during group training and through one-on-one discrete trial training using direct instruction and fluency-building activities. In addition, this student also engages in independent play using an activity schedule, and incidental verbal behavior training is used throughout the day to promote generality.

### Instructional Tactics

Instructional tactics are the methods used during instructional activities. To help students learn target skills, teachers and teacher assistants are trained to use various types of instructional tactics. Table 11-2 gives examples of some of the instructional tactics used at our school. For a thoroughly compiled list of instructional tactics derived from the behavior analytic research, see

**Table 11-1**
Examples of Instructional Activities Used at Hawthorne and Some of Their References

| Instructional Activities | References |
| --- | --- |
| One-on-one discrete trial training | Lovaas, 1981 |
| Naturalistic teaching methods | Koegel, O'Dell, & Koegel, 1987; McGee, Morrier, & Daly, 1999; Sundberg & Partington, 1999 |
| Group instruction | Heward, 1994 |
| Verbal behavior training | Greer, 2000; Michael, 1988; Partington & Bailey, 1993 |
| PECS | Bondy & Frost, 1994 |
| Direct instruction | Becker & Carnine, 1981; Engelmann & Bruner, 1988 |
| Group play | Dunlap, 1997 |
| Peer interaction | Goldstein, Kaczmarek, Pennington, & Shafer, 1992 |
| Activity schedules | McClannahan & Krantz, 1999 |
| Computer-based instruction | Dube, Iennaco, Rocco, Kledaras, & McIlvane 1992; McDonough, 2000; McDonough & Shimizu, 2002 |
| Toilet training | Foxx & Azrin, 1973 |
| Vocational training | Heward, 2003 |
| Precision teaching/fluency | Binder, 1996; Lindsley, 1996; Johnson & Layng, 1994, 1996 |
| Behavior management | Kerr & Nelson, 2002 |

**Table 11-2**

Examples of Instructional Tactics Used at Hawthorne and Some of Their References

| Instructional Tactics | References |
| --- | --- |
| Establishing/motivating operations | Michael, 1982, 1988; Sundberg, 1993 |
| Token economy | Alberto & Troutman, 2003; Tyler, 1967 |
| Prompting | Cipani & Spooner, 1994 |
| Self-management | Cooper, Heron, & Heward, 1987, in press; Bolstad & Johnson, 1972 |
| Positive reinforcement | Martin & Pear, 2003 |
| Planned ignoring/attention | Kerr & Nelson, 2002; Paine, Radicchi, Rosellini, Deutchman, & Darch, 1982 |
| Strategies to promote generalization | Cooper et al., 1987, in press; Stokes & Baer, 1977 |
| Schedules of reinforcement | Cooper et al., 1987, in press |
| Time delay | Godby, Gast, & Wolery, 1987 |
| Peer tutoring | Delquadri, 1984; Greenwood, Delquadri, & Hall 1989; Miller, Barbetta, & Heron, 1994 |
| Stimulus control procedures | Cooper et al., 1987, in press; Dube, McIlvane, MaGuire, Mackay, & Stoddard, 1989 |
| Shaping | Cooper et al., 1987, in press |
| Time-out | Foxx, 1982; Nelson & Rutherford, 1983 |

Greer (2002, pp. 103–105). For definitions and landmark references for many of the basic tactics used in applied behavior analysis, see Cooper, Heron, & Heward (1987, in press).

## Measurement

Continuous measurement is a fundamental process at Hawthorne. We measure student progress continuously and consider the daily, weekly, and annual measures we take in two ways: as measures of student progress and as measures of instructor effectiveness. That is, when a student is not making progress, instruction is not effective, and when instruction is not effective, the instructor must make changes based on an analysis of student data (usually presented graphically). By linking student progress to instructional effectiveness as a fundamental component, we have tied student progress inextricably to teacher progress.

At Hawthorne we take a contextualistic view of measurement: All measurement is construed within the framework of the learning environment or context in which it occurs. The learning context describes specific antecedent and consequent events functionally related to the occurrence of the behavior that we seek to improve. Various terms have been used to describe this context: discrete trials, learning trials, instructional trials, three-term contingency trials, A-B-C, learn units, frames, and learning frames. Some subtle conceptual differences exist among these terms, and certain terms are used more in some settings than in others. At Hawthorne we use the term *instructional trial* to describe the basic unit of analysis. The instructional trial is defined as an interaction, within a given learning context, between a student and a teacher, a group of students and a teacher, or a student and instructional materials. The vehicle used to increase targeted student behavior within the learning context is direct, systematic reinforcement.

### Daily Measures

When students engage in instructional activities, accuracy (correct and total responses to instructional trials) is recorded continuously. Rate measures (i.e., number of responses per unit of time) are also taken frequently. Teachers and teaching assistants graph these data each day. Graphs give a visual learning picture that promotes accurate and frequent data analysis. When analyzing graphs to solve instructional problems, we follow the decision-making protocol described in Greer, 2002 (pp. 58–80; 106–112).

### Weekly Measures

In addition to the daily measures, we also take summary weekly measures of the instructional trials received by each student. During the first few weeks of the school year, these data should be sharply ascending. If the trend stabilizes (i.e., stops ascending), performance is enhanced by linking increases in instructional presentations to teacher modules, which are in turn linked to teacher remuneration. Figure 11-1 is an example of instructional trials received by a student. Measures are also taken on the average number of instructional trials needed to meet a learning objective (e.g., instructional trials divided by learning objectives met). This represents an *efficiency ratio*. For example, if a student met 5 learning objectives in a week and received 500 instructional trials, the efficiency ratio would be 100/1 (500/5) or simply 100. The goal is to lower efficiency ratios so students require few instructional trials to meet learning objectives. As Figure 11-2 represents, a changing criterion design is used to increase instructional efficiency. As with increasing instructional trials, teacher remuneration is linked with lowering efficiency ratios. The combined effect is an increase in both the quantity and the quality of instruction.

### Annual Measures

Because measurement is taken each day and each week for each student, instructional decisions are rarely based on annual measures. That is, because teachers are measuring student progress continually, annual outcomes are highly predictable. Nevertheless, criterion-referenced assessments (e.g., PIRK—Greer, McCorkle, & Twyman, 1996; ABLLS—Partington & Sundberg 1998) are used to evaluate student progress annually. In addition, our students have started to participate in statewide standard assessments, which will be discussed later in this chapter.

**Figure 11-1.**

Correct and total instructional trials received per week for one student for a year.

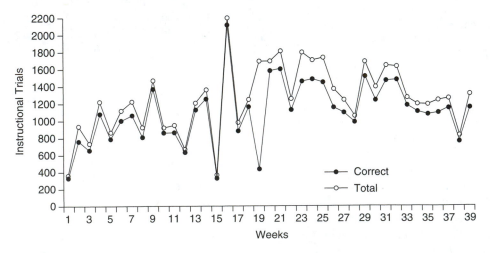

**Figure 11-2.**
A changing criterion design used to decrease the learning efficiency ratio for a student. The efficiency ratio is the mean number of instructional trials needed to meet one learning objective. This is calculated by dividing instructional trials by learning objectives achieved.

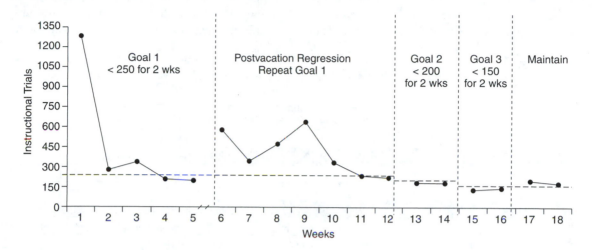

A secondary and perhaps more relevant function of annual criterion-referenced assessment is as a curriculum guide. When a student first enters the school, we use a criterion-referenced assessment to inventory the students' strengths and weaknesses (i.e., what skills the student has and does not have), which serves as a baseline measure of the student's entry-level skill. When the inventory is completed, the teacher has a blueprint for instruction for the coming weeks, months, and year. At the end of the year, the inventory is taken again as a way to verify the instruction that has occurred throughout the year and to plan for the next year.

## TEACHER TRAINING IN A BEHAVIORAL SCHOOL

The term *teacher* is used here to describe a group of learners that includes teachers (who usually hold bachelor's or master's degrees in special education) and teaching assistants (who hold or are working toward associate's or bachelor's degrees in special education, psychology, or a related field). Although there are differ-

ences in training related to the level of education, the amount of responsibility, and the prerequisite skills of the learner, the basic process is the same. Teacher training at Hawthorne includes three interconnected elements: direct teacher observations, personalized system of instruction (PSI) modules and course work, and teacher/supervisor meetings.

### Direct Teacher Observation

A basic assumption at Hawthorne is that the most influential aspect of the learning context is the behavior of the teacher. As noted earlier, the vehicle used to increase student behavior is direct, systematic reinforcement provided by a teacher within a specified learning context. This learning context is determined by and includes the teacher, moment to moment, throughout the school day. This is why direct, frequent, and systematic supervision of teachers working in and designing the learning context, by board-certified behavior analysts (BCBA), is a critical component of the Hawthorne program.

In 1992 Ingham and Greer found that when supervisors increased direct observations of teachers and gave specific feedback about teachers' behavior, the frequency and accuracy of instructional trials increased, and this resulted in an increase in the number of accurate student responses. Based on this research, direct observations at Hawthorne record the rate and the accuracy of teacher presentations in relation to the responding of the students. In addition, direct observations track things such as the schedule of reinforcement, the number of contingent praise statements made to students, and the number of contingent praise statements

**Figure 11-3.**
Hawthorne Country Day School Direct observation measurement form.

Hawthorne Country Day School
Direct observation measurement form

| Observer: | | | | Student: | | | | Sch. R+/Pref. Items: | | | |
|---|---|---|---|---|---|---|---|---|---|---|---|
| | | | | | | | | Deliver and mand level: | | | |
| Teacher: | | | | Program: | | | | Materials ready?　　　Y/N | | | |
| Date: | | | | Short-term objective (tactic): | | | | | | | |
| | | | | | | | Previous data trend:　　Ascend/Descend/Stable/Variable | | | | |
| Time elapsed:　　Decimal: | | | | Interprogram Latency: | | | Recommendation　Continue/Intervene | | | | |

| | | Target behaviors (+/−) | | | Mands (+/−) | | | Collateral R+ | | | |
|---|---|---|---|---|---|---|---|---|---|---|---|
| IT # | Ant. | Resp. | Cons. | IT | Mand | Cons. | IT | Target student | Non-contingent | Other students | Comments |
| 1 | | | | | | | | | | | |
| 2 | | | | | | | | | | | |
| 3 | | | | | | | | | | | |
| 4 | | | | | | | | | | | |
| 5 | | | | | | | | | | | |
| 6 | | | | | | | | | | | |
| 7 | | | | | | | | | | | |
| 8 | | | | | | | | | | | |
| 9 | | | | | | | | | | | |
| 10 | | | | | | | | | | | |
| 11 | | | | | | | | | | | |
| 12 | | | | | | | | | | | |
| 13 | | | | | | | | | | | |
| 14 | | | | | | | | | | | |
| 15 | | | | | | | | | | | |
| 16 | | | | | | | | | | | |
| 17 | | | | | | | | | | | |
| 18 | | | | | | | | | | | |
| 19 | | | | | | | | | | | |
| 20 | | | | | | | | | | | |
| # Correct: | | | | | | | | | | | |
| # Error: | | | | | | | | | | | |
| Number per minute correct IT: | | | | | Num. per min Collateral R+ target students | | | | | | |
| Number per minute incorrect IT: | | | | | Num. per min Collateral R+ other students | | | | | | |

made to other students in the instructional setting. The direct observation form also provides room for the behavior analyst supervisor to give specific written feedback. An example of the Hawthorne direct observation form is shown in Figure 11-3.

The goal of the direct observation is to help shape the teaching repertoire of the teacher. This includes the teacher's ability to (a) deliver scripted curricula accurately during one-to-one and small group instruction, (b) record data reliably and graph it accurately and in a timely manner, (c) manage collateral classroom events while delivering instruction to students one on one, and (d) use a technical vocabulary to describe teaching procedures and analyze the effectiveness of instructional activities and tactics. The data collected from direct observations are reviewed with each teacher, graphed, and displayed. Teacher behavior is shaped through a changing criterion design. At first, goals target the accuracy of instructional presentation. Once accuracy is high, the rate of instructional presentation becomes the target. Goals are cumulative. For example, the first goal may be 10

consecutive direct observations with no errors in teacher presentation. When this goal is met, goals will shift and focus on the rate of instructional presentation while maintaining accuracy. The terminal objective is to maintain a target rate and accuracy across several observations and several different programs with several different students. Figure 11-4 is an example of a changing criterion design used to increase the accuracy and rate of instructional presentations for a new teacher.

## PSI Modules and Course Work for Teachers

The second essential component of teacher training is the PSI modules and course work. At Hawthorne we use a model of training first developed by Greer and colleagues (Albers & Greer, 1991; Greer, McCorkle, & Williams, 1989; Ingham & Greer, 1992; Keohane, 1997; Selinske & Greer, 1991). Based on Fred S. Keller's (1968) personalized system of instruction (PSI), teacher modules are individualized and designed to be self-paced. Teacher modules are a set of goals

**Figure 11-4.**
An example of a changing criterion design used to increase the accuracy and speed of instructional trials presented to students by a new teacher.

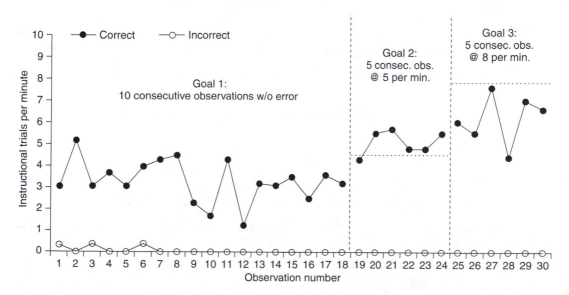

that reflect the needs of the students in the teacher's class. Designed by board-certified behavior analysts, the modules serve as a set of performance goals that specify objectives to increase each teacher's technical vocabulary (i.e., verbal behavior), teaching skills (i.e., behavior shaped by the contingencies available during instruction with students), and knowledge of instructional tactics. To teach a technical vocabulary, teacher modules include readings, quizzes, SAFMEDS (Say All Fast for a Minute Each Day Shuffled; Graf, 1994), and public presentations. To teach teaching skills, the behavior analysts who supervise the program relate module objectives to their direct observations. To learn instructional tactics, teachers practice ana-

lyzing student learning and instructional problems one on one with the behavior analyst supervisor, and they read relevant research articles and pass quizzes. The completion of a set of five modules results in a monetary raise for teachers, so a motivational contingency is attached to increasing teacher expertise in applied behavior analysis. These concepts have been tested and found to be an essential part of a behavioral school (Greer, McCorkle, & Williams, 1989; Lamm & Greer, 1991). An example of an introductory module for a teacher with no experience using applied behavior analysis as a teaching method is shown in Figure 11-5.

The majority of our new teachers come to Hawthorne without any knowledge of or expe-

**Figure 11-5.**
Example of one PSI module for a new teacher.

**Reading**

Using your attention to manage student behavior (Paine, 1983).

Measurement: 90% accuracy on quiz

Date completed _____ BCBA signature _____

**SAFMEDS**

Behavior, response, environment, stimulus, operant behavior, contingency, behavioral consequence, behavior change procedures, positive reinforcement, negative reinforcement

**Measurement:**

Graph SAFMEDS # correct/incorrect per minute.

Two consecutive observations of timing with 10 correct definitions given aloud and zero incorrect per minute.

Oral quiz by BCBA (BCBA gives definition, candidate gives term; candidate gives practical example of each term)

Date completed _____ BCBA signature _____

**Contingency-Shaped Behavior**

1. Zero occurrences of coersive/punitive practices across three 5-minute observations

2. While maintaining #1, use positive attention to manage behavior employing components (moving and scanning) and characteristics (if/then rule, use names, descriptive, convincing) of effective praise

Measurement: three 5-minute observations by a behavior analyst

rience with behavior science. Therefore, we offer in-house university-level classes taught by a special education certified, PhD-level BCBA, staff-development coordinator. Currently we are in the process of negotiating with a local college to have some of these classes affiliated with a degree program. This will make formal course work in applied behavior analysis more easily available to our staff (i.e., our teachers take the courses on site) and more attractive (i.e., training counts toward a degree).

Course work is individualized so that training begins at the teacher's current level of expertise as determined by a pretraining assessment and progresses in a hierarchical manner from there. The behaviors to be learned are defined objectively and broken down into manageable modules. Relevant teacher behavior is continually measured, and completion of modules is linked to their remuneration. Teachers are first trained to understand the elements of the learning context and how changes in these elements, and changes to the instructional setting in general, occasion learning. We want our teachers to view themselves as designers of learning environments. This is critical because teachers who are not taught to look to the environment as the source of instructional problems may be more likely to hypothesize that problems result from intractable internal mechanisms of the student, rather than analyzing and solving the problem. Second, teachers are provided with a repertoire of research-proven teaching tactics from which to make instructional decisions. The more tactics a teacher knows, the more likely the teacher will be to make effective instructional decisions. Third, teachers are trained to use a technical vocabulary (i.e., verbal behavior), which enables them to read research, learn about effective tactics, and discuss and write about student progress and the operations of teaching and learning. Coupled with the PSI modules and course work, teachers are closely supervised and trained in classroom situations to apply the tactics by behavior analyst supervisors.

## Classroom Meetings

The third component of teacher training is classroom meetings. Classroom meetings are held biweekly and include all members of the instructional team—the classroom teacher, teaching assistants, and the BCBA supervisor. The agenda of the meeting is dictated by the needs of the students in the class based on an analysis of the data. The outcome is a set of written goals and time lines for goal completion, which serves as a task-analyzed self-management tool for each member of the instructional team. These meeting minutes are typed and handed out to all members of the team as well as the school principal. The results are graphed as the percentage of goals met and posted outside of each classroom.

The meeting minutes reflect the immediate needs of the students in the class, and the PSI training modules and course work reflect the needs of the teachers and students in the class. As a result, there is a high degree of overlap between the immediate needs of the students in the class and the immediate teacher training needs as outlined in each teacher's PSI modules and course work. The result is that teachers (a) reduce the immediate instructional problems of their students, (b) increase their skill at implementing applied behavior analysis, and (c) receive increased remuneration as a result of the previous two results. This is precisely what we mean by a systems approach to behavioral schooling: *Teacher behavior is systematically linked to student progress.* An example of biweekly meeting minutes is shown in Figure 11-6.

## THE ROLE OF THE BEHAVIOR ANALYST IN A BEHAVIORAL SCHOOL

In addition to the many administrative roles played by behavior analysts (e.g., program development, human resources functions, regulatory compliance, student intakes, fiscal considerations, etc.), behavior analysts are responsible for the research, development, and

Goals carried over:

1. Mary—Increase your collateral praise to three per minute for one 5-minute observation.

2. Mary—Complete 100% of goals.

82% goals met: Sarah—100%, Stewart—100%, Mary—3/5 (60%)

New goals:

1. Sarah—Set up a time with me to review modules.

2. Sarah—Get 100% D.O. agreement across three programs and two staff members.

3. Sarah—Take the tactics quiz.

4. Sarah—Present a "challenging" graph at the next meeting (two completed).

5. Sarah—Set up a time for Theresa to get agreement on interval programs for your modules.

6. Sarah—Review two student books by 8/7 and correct any graphing errors.

7. Stewart—Read module on reinforcers and work on completing.

8. Stewart—Arrive to work on time and leave at scheduled time for 9/10 days.

9. Mary—Present a challenging graph at the next meeting.

10. Theresa—Agreement on whole/partial interval w/Sarah (one with 95% accuracy on whole).

11. Theresa—Class observation on planned ignoring (one completed).

% of goals met: /14 = _____%

**Figure 11-6.**
Example of biweekly classroom meeting minutes.

revision of curricula for students and teachers. We require our behavior analysts to have a minimum of a master's degree in behavior analysis and certification by the Behavior Analyst Certification Board. The school principal and staff development coordinator are required to have PhDs in behavior analysis and certification by the Behavior Analyst Certification Board. They work closely with the behavior analysts, who supervise the various components of the overall school program (e.g., early intervention, preschool, elementary, parent education, etc.) to ensure effective training.

At Hawthorne a PSI module system is used to structure the ongoing training of behavior analysts. An example of PSI modules for a behavior analyst supervisor is shown in Figure 11-7. The most critical feature of these modules is that remuneration for behavior analysts is directly linked to remuneration for teachers. That is, behavior analysts do not get a monetary raise until the teachers they supervise and train get a raise. As noted earlier, increases in teacher remuneration depend on their skill as teachers (i.e., their knowledge and ability to implement applied behavior analysis), measured through module completion, which is linked to student success. As a result, behavior analysts are "brought into the loop" of the system: Student progress is a function of teacher effectiveness, and teacher effectiveness is a function of behavior analyst effectiveness.

The variables we consider critical measures of behavior analyst effectiveness are schoolwide measures of (a) the number of instructional trails presented to students, (b) the efficiency ratio for instructional trials presented to students, and (c) the number of direct observations completed by behavior analysts, including the percentage of observations in which the teacher presented instruction flawlessly. These variables are measured weekly. Additional measures (reported annually) include the cumulative number of objectives met by students and the number of modules completed by teachers.

Board-certified behavior analyst: modules 1–5

Modules 1–3: Teacher training

1. Write modules 1–5 for two teachers, two teaching assistants, and four behavior analyst assistants (a total of 40 modules across eight employees).

2. Mentor all eight employees through modules 1–5 until each has earned a raise.

Module 4: direct program supervision for six classrooms

1. Biweekly classroom meetings (cc minutes to principal)

2. Goal attainment graphed by teacher and posted

3. Goal attainment built into teacher modules

4. Minimum of 20 direct observations per week in these classrooms for six consecutive weeks

5. Observation of group direct instruction at least once a week per classroom for 6 consecutive weeks. Includes written feedback and suggestions. Notes filed in the teacher meeting file along with the goal attainment graph w/goals derived from this feedback.

Module 5: Professional development

Conference presentation—Using self-editing script to teach preschoolers addition

College course work—Verbal behavior seminar, fall 2001, Columbia U. (Minimum B+)
College course work—Doctoral seminar, spring 2002, Columbia U. (Minimum B+)
Theoretical Paper: Relational Frame Theory

**Figure 11-7.**
Example of supervisor modules.

## PARENT EDUCATION IN A BEHAVIORAL SCHOOL

Parents are among the most important teachers their children will ever have. Two important things happen when parents are taught to apply behavioral principles and techniques with their children: The training of new behaviors occurs in the natural environment, and the parents' methods of training become in sync with those used at school, creating stimuli common to both settings (Stokes & Baer, 1977).

Because the job of teaching and facilitating generalization is so important, parents must also become learners. In general, parent training involves any intervention with parents designed to change a child's behavior. Similar to a related service (i.e., speech, occupational, and physical therapies), parent education supplements the school program, providing children with an enhanced education. For example, it has been used to increase spontaneous speech in children with autism (Charlop-Christy & Carpenter, 2000), increase appropriate play (Eyberg, 1988), and help manage disruptive behavior (Danforth, 1998). Often parent training is the primary service provided to a family or child (Baker, 1996). More and more, however, training for parents is integrated into the services provided to families of children with developmental disabilities. Lovaas's Young Autism Project involved parents taking a key role in delivering instruction to their children (Lovaas, 1987). Similarly, the CABAS system includes parent education as an essential part of the students' education (Greer, 1996).

Parent training at Hawthorne is used to increase learning opportunities for students and to promote generalization. Generality of behavior change is durable over time, appears in a variety of settings, or spreads to other behaviors (Baer et al., 1968). Generality is a fundamental dimension of ABA and is especially important when evaluating behavioral programs. Therefore, it is also critical that a school that uses the strategies and tactics of ABA offer a program devoted to the generalization of behavior. Parent education, as a component of a behavioral school system, seeks to fulfill this requirement.

At Hawthorne, the parent educator is a BCBA who has expertise in working with parents and families. Although participation in the parent education program is voluntary, it is strongly encouraged. Participation is offered in a variety of formats to suit the needs and interests of each family, from PSI modules to group instruction. The goal is to provide parents with the knowledge and skills necessary to adapt what they learn to any and every necessary situation or behavior. In other words, the behavior change seen in the parent generalizes to different situations.

Throughout the year a graph of weekly and cumulative points received by parents for meeting predefined learning objectives for working with their child is publicly posted at the school to display progress within the point system. These points are used at the parent education auction held at the end of the year. At the auction, parents use their points to silently bid for donated items such as gift certificates to restaurants, trips, toys, and baby-sitting. Although not meant to be the primary motivation for participation in parent education, the auction serves as a terrific incentive and celebrates the parents' hard work.

Another event that recognizes parents' dedication to their children's education is the parent education poster session. Similar to what is seen at a professional conference, each parent has the opportunity to present a poster. Throughout the year, parents target skills to teach their children. For the parent education poster session, they are encouraged to choose a skill they have worked on with their child and display the results of their efforts with a brief description of the methods. The poster session provides an opportunity for parents, staff, and friends of the school to view parent and student accomplishments and praise success.

## IS BEHAVIORAL SCHOOLING EFFECTIVE?

Figures 11-8 through 11-11 compare results for the school across 10 to 12 years in four areas: (1) instructional trials presented to students (Figure 11-8), (2) the learning efficiency ratio (Figure 11-9), (3) direct observations (Figure 11-10), and (4) cost per learning objective achieved (Figure 11-11).

Figure 11-8 shows the mean number of instructional trials received per student per day in

**Figure 11-8.**
The mean number of instructional trials received per student per day in language and academic instruction. This is calculated by dividing annual instructional trials for all students by annual instructional days (e.g., *n* students enrolled per year × *n* days of instruction per year = instructional days).

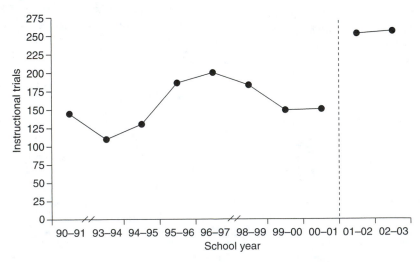

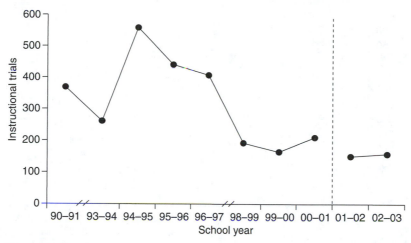

**Figure 11-9.**
Schoolwide efficiency ratio across years. This is calculated by dividing all instructional trials received by students in the year by all learning objectives achieved by students in the year.

the areas of language and academic literacy. This number is calculated by multiplying the total number of school days in the year by the number of students enrolled at the school and dividing that number into the total number of instructional trials recorded for the year. Language and academic literacy includes verbal behavior training, reading, writing, math, science, social studies, social skills, problem solving, self-management, and stimulus discrimination skills across a variety of materials (e.g., simple and conditional discriminations with colors, shapes, etc.). Data are reported for 10 years from the 1990–1991 school year through the 2002–2003 school year. Data were not available for three years: 1991–1992, 1992–1993, and 1997–1998. These breaks in time are indicated by hatch marks on the x-axis of the graph. For the

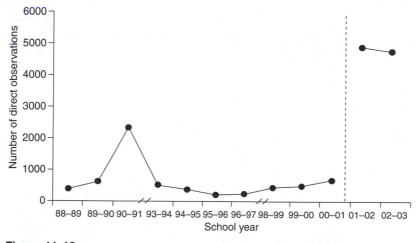

**Figure 11-10.**
The total number of direct observations completed per year by behavior analyst supervisors.

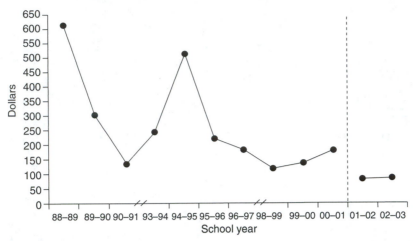

**Figure 11-11.**
The cost per learning objective achieved by students. This is calculated by dividing the total tuition costs in the year for all students (e.g., *n* students enrolled × *n* dollars per student per year) by the number of learning objectives achieved by all students in that year.

1990–1991 school year through the 2000–2001 school year (8 years), the data are variable with a mean of 156 and a range of 110 to 200 instructional trials per student per day. For the two years of data after the phase change line, the data are relatively high and stable, with a mean of 252 instructional trials per student per day in the 2001–2002 school year and a mean of 254 in the 2002–2003 school year.

Figure 11-9 shows the mean number of instructional trials needed for a student to meet one learning objective. We call this an efficiency ratio, and the overall goal is to get this ratio as low as possible. The mean efficiency ratio is calculated by dividing the total number of instructional trials in a year by the total number of learning objectives achieved by students in that year. Data are reported in the same manner and across the same years as in Figure 11-8. For the 1990–1991 through 2000–2001 school years, the data are variably descending (mean: 324, range: 559–164). For the last 2 years reported (2001–2002 and 2002–2003), the data are relatively low and stable (147 and 151, respectively).

Figure 11–10 shows the total number of direct observations completed by behavior analyst supervisors per year. Data are reported for 12 years, going back to the 1988–1989 school year but missing the same 3 years of data noted previously. For the first 10 years reported (1988–1989 through 2000–2001), the number of direct observations ranged widely, from 171 (1995–1996 school year) to 2,365 (1990–1991 school year). The mean number of direct observations per year for the first 10 years reported was 571. For the last 2 years (2001–2002 and 2002–2003), the number of direct observations conducted per year jumped up sharply to 4,972 and 4,830, respectively.

Figure 11-11 shows the cost per learning objective met by students each year over 10 years. This cost is calculated by summing the tuition received by the school to educate all students in a year (number of students × annual tuition for one student) and dividing it by the total number of learning objects met by students in that year. For the first 10 years, the data are highly variable with an overall descending trend (mean: $266 per objective, range: $612–$121 per objective). For the last 2 years, the data are relatively low and stable ($84 and $88 per objective for 2001–2002 and 2002–2003, respectively).

Significant changes are evident in the last 2 years of reported data (2001–2002 and 2002–2003). The phase change line in Figures 11-8 through 11-11 indicates changes that we believe have positively affected the results for the school from that point forward. These changes include the following:

1. *Addition of board-certified behavior analysts.* From June 2001 to September 2003, the school went from 0 to 12 board-certified behavior analysts on staff. Of course, there were skilled and knowledgeable behavior analysts working at the school prior to the 2001–2002 school year. However, these individuals were affiliated with the CABAS model and left when the CABAS affiliation ended after the 2000–2001 school year.

2. *Increased use of direct observations.* A heavy emphasis has been placed on increasing contact time between teachers and behavior analysts within the classroom setting since July 2001.

3. *Classroom meetings.* The third component of the teacher training system at Hawthorne consists of biweekly classroom meetings (described previously). The agenda of the meeting is dictated by the needs of the students based on an analysis of the data. The outcome is a set of written goals that serves as a task-analyzed self-management tool for each member of the instructional team.

These measures are interrelated within a behavior analytic framework. We view change in terms of objective measures of the behavior of students, teachers, and behavior analysts. By linking these learner groups together systematically and measuring progress continually, we learn how the goals of the different learner groups interact. When we know how the goals

of these learner groups interact, the system becomes more predictable and we know what actions to take to improve the overall system.

If a school is a self-correcting system with socially valid goals, then it is, by definition, effective. Goals for students at Hawthorne are derived from (a) criterion-referenced assessments and (b) individualized education programs (IEP), which are drawn up for each student by the committee of special education (which includes teachers, parents, administrators, and other individuals familiar with the student) within the student's home school district. These goals are tailored to fit the needs of each student and linked to the New York State education department learning standards.

One measure of external validity is standardized testing. How do our students compare to other students in New York State on tests of math, language arts, science, and so forth? Until recently, we could not answer this question because our students were considered exempt from testing and excluded from the testing process. However, as a result of changes in education law in recent years, a few of our students have begun to participate in standardized New York State assessments. In addition, an alternate New York State assessment has been designed for students with the most severe learning delays and is currently being piloted in schools around the state.

In the 2001–2002 school year, one Hawthorne fourth-grader took the New York State assessment in English/language arts and math. He scored in the 10th percentile in English/language arts and in the 25th percentile in math. In 2002–2003 the same student took the fifth-grade social studies assessment and scored in the 50th percentile. In 2002–2003 one eighth-grader took the eighth-grade social studies assessment. He scored in the 25th percentile. In 2002–2003 two ninth-graders took the New York State regents exam in physical setting/earth science. Both students passed the exam and are now preparing for the 10th-grade biology regents exam. What's most remarkable is that these regents exam students were not allowed to take the exam at Hawthorne. We had to make arrangements for them to take the exam at a local public high school—a completely unfamiliar setting with completely unfamiliar faces. Their success is an excellent example of skill generality.

## CONCLUSION

In this chapter we have outlined our ongoing work to put the principles and procedures of behavior science to work to improve the lives of all the people associated with Hawthorne. We view the school environment—the students, parents, teachers, and supervisors of our school—as a living behavioral system in which a change in one affects all others. However, we believe it is important to mention that although our approach is unabashedly behavioral, it is *a* behavioral approach, not *the* behavioral approach. There are a small number of other behavioral schools located throughout the country, such as the Bay School, the ABC School, and the STARS School in California; the Morningside School in Washington; the Juniper Gardens Children's Project in Kansas; the Kennedy Krieger School in Maryland; the Princeton Child Development Center and the Alpine Learning Center in New Jersey; and the Judge Rutenberg Center and the Fred S. Keller School in New York, to name a few. All of these schools are using and developing their own models based on behavioral science. Unfortunately, it has been our experience that many parents and laypeople have come to misconstrue a particular method or procedure as the only valid way to practice ABA. We hope that this problem is diminished by the efforts of the Association for Behavior Analysis, the Behavior Analysis Certification Board, sound scientific research, and by time. We encourage anyone interested in effective treatment for autism and many other disabilities to visit the following Web sites:

- Association for Behavior Analysis (http://www.abainternational.org)
- Association for Science in Autism Treatment (http://asatonline.org)
- Behavior Analysis.Com (http://www.behavioranalysis.com)
- Behavior Analysis Certification Board (http://www.bacb.com)
- Cambridge Center for Behavioral Studies (http://www.behavior.org)
- Hawthorne Country Day School (http://www.hawthornecountryday.org)
- Kennedy Krieger Institute (http://www.kennedykrieger.com)

Finally, the publication of Lovass and colleagues' landmark research (Lovaas, 1987), augmented by Cathrine Maurice's *Let Me Hear Your Voice* (Maurice, 1994), has generated a great deal of interest in behavior analysis in general and ABA in particular, especially with parents of children diagnosed with autism. We hope this trend continues and expands to other areas of education from gifted programs to general education. If this happens, a behavioral systems approach to schooling will not be so rare.

## REFERENCES

Adams, G. (1995). Project Follow Through and beyond. *Effective School Practices, 15*. Retrieved July 7, 2003, from http://darkwing.uoregon.edu/~adiep/ft/adams.htm.

Albers, A. E., and Greer, R. D. (1991). Is the three-term contingency trial a predictor of effective instruction? *Journal of Behavioral Education, 1,* 337–354.

Alberto, P. A., & Troutman, A. C. (2003). *Applied behavior analysis for teachers* (6th ed.). Upper Saddle River, NJ: Merrill/Prentice Hall.

Baer, D. M., Wolf, M. M., & Risley, T. R. (1968). Some current dimensions of applied behavior analysis. *Journal of Applied Behavior Analysis, 1,* 91–97.

Baker, B. L. (1996). Parent training. In J. W. Jacobson & J. A. Mulick (Eds.), *Manual of diagnosis and professional practice in mental retardation* (pp. 289–299). Washington, DC: APA Books.

Becker, W., & Carnine, D. (1981). Direct instruction: A behavior theory model for comprehensive educational intervention with the disadvantaged. In

S. Bijon (Ed.), *Contributions of behavior modification in education* (pp. 1–106), Hillsdale, NJ: Erlbaum.

Binder, C. (1996). Behavioral fluency: Evolution of a new paradigm. *The Behavior Analyst, 19,* 163–197.

Bolstad, O. D., & Johnson, S. M. (1972). Self-regulation in the modification of disruptive classroom behavior. *Journal of Applied Behavior Analysis, 5,* 443–454.

Bondy, A., & Frost, L. (1994). PECS: The picture exchange communication system. *Focus on Autistic Behavior, 9,* 1–9.

Charlop-Christy, M. H., & Carpenter, M. H. (2000). Modified incidental teaching session: A procedure for parents to increase spontaneous speech in their children with autism. *Journal of Positive Behavior Interventions, 2* (2), 98–112.

Cipani, E. C., & Spooner, F. (1994). *Curricular and instructional approaches for persons with severe disabilities.* Boston: Allyn and Bacon.

Cooper, J. O., Heron, T. E., & Heward, W. L. (1987). *Applied behavior analysis.* Upper Saddle River, NJ: Merrill/Prentice Hall.

Cooper, J. O., Heron, T. E., & Heward, W. L. (in press). *Applied behavior analysis* (2nd ed.). Upper Saddle River, NJ: Merrill/Prentice Hall.

Danforth, J. S. (1998). The outcome of parent training using the Behavior Management Flow Chart with mothers and their children with oppositional defiant disorder and attention-deficit hyperactivity disorder. *Behavior Modification, 22,* 443–473.

Delquadri, J. C. (1984). Teacher versus peer mediated instruction: An ecobehavioral analysis of achievement outcomes. *Journal of Applied Behavior Analysis, 17,* 521–538.

Dube, W. V., Iennaco, F. M., Rocco, F. J., Kledaras, J. B., & McIlvane, W. J. (1992). Microcomputer-based programmed instruction in identity matching to sample for persons with severe disabilities. *Journal of Behavioral Education, 2,* 29–51.

Dube, W. V., McIlvane, W. J., MaGuire, R. W., Mackay, H. A., & Stoddard, L. T. (1989). Stimulus class formation and stimulus-reinforcer relations. *Journal of the Experimental Analysis of Behavior, 51,* 65–76.

Dunlap, L. L. (1997). *An introduction to early childhood special education.* Boston: Allyn and Bacon.

Engelmann, S., & Bruner, E. (1988). *Reading mastery I.* Chicago: Science Research Associates.

Eyberg, S. (1988). Parent-Child Interaction Therapy: Integration of traditional and behavioral concerns. *Child & Family Behavior Therapy, 10,* 33–46.

Foxx, R. M., (1982). *Increasing behaviors of severely retarded and autistic persons.* Champaign, IL: Research Press.

Foxx, R. M., & Azrin, N. H. (1973). *Toilet training persons with developmental disabilities.* Harrisburg, PA: Help Services Press.

Godby, S., Gast, D. L., & Wolery, M. (1987). A comparison of time delay and system of least prompts in teaching objective identification. *Research in Developmental Disabilities, 8,* 283–306.

Goldstein, H., Kaczmarek, L., Pennington, R., & Shafer, K. (1992). Peer-mediated intervention: Attending to, commenting on, and acknowledging the behavior of preschoolers with autism. *Journal of Applied Behavior Analysis, 25,* 289–305.

Graf, S. A. (1994). *How to develop, produce and use SAFMEDS in education and training.* Youngstown, OH: Zero Brothers Software.

Greenwood, C. R., Delquadri, J. C., & Hall, R. V. (1989). Longitudinal effects of classwide peer tutoring. *Journal of Educational Psychology, 81,* 371–383.

Greer, R. D. (1996). The education crisis. In M. Mattaini & B. Thyer (Eds.), *Finding solutions to social problems: Behavioral strategies for change* (pp. 113–146). Washington, DC: APA Books.

Greer, R. D. (2000). *Teaching operation for verbal behavior.* Unpublished manuscript.

Greer, R. D. (2002). *Designing teaching strategies.* New York: Academic Press.

Greer, R. D., McCorkle, N., & Twyman, J. S., (1996). Preschool inventory of repertoires for kindergarten. *Fred S. Keller School Curriculum* [Unpublished].

Greer, R. D, McCorkle, N., & Williams, G. (1989). A sustained analysis of the behaviors of schooling. *Behavioral Residential Treatment, 4,* 113–141.

Heward, W. L. (1994). Three "low-tech" strategies for increasing the frequency of active student response during group instruction. In R. Gardner III, D. M. Sainato, J. O. Cooper, T. E. Heron, W. L. Heward, J. Eshleman, & T. A. Grossi (Eds.), *Behavior analysis in education: Focus on measurably superior instruction* (pp. 283–320). Pacific Grove, CA: Brooks/Cole.

Heward, W. L. (2003). *Exceptional children: An introduction to special education* (7th ed., pp. 576–621). Upper Saddle River, NJ: Merrill/Prentice Hall.

Ingham, P., & Greer, R. D. (1992). Functional relationships between supervisors' observations of teachers in observed and generalized settings. *Journal of Applied Behavior Analysis, 25,* 153–164.

Johnson, K. R., & Layng, T. V. J. (1994). The Morningside model of generative instruction. In R. Gardner, D. M. Sainato, J. O. Cooper, T. E. Heron, W. L. Heward, J. W. Eshleman, & T. A. Grossi (Eds.), *Behavior analysis in education: Focus on measurably superior instruction* (pp. 173–197). Pacific Grove, CA: Brooks/Cole.

Johnson, K. R., & Layng, T. V. J. (1996). On terms and procedures: Fluency. *The Behavior Analyst, 19,* 281–288.

Keller, F. S. (1968). Good-bye, teacher. . . . *Journal of Applied Behavior Analysis, 1,* 79–89.

Keohane, D. (1997). *A functional relationship between teachers' use of scientific rule governed strategies and student learning.* Unpublished Ph.D. dissertation, Columbia University, New York.

Kerr, M. M., & Nelson, C. M. (2002). *Strategies for addressing behavior problems in the classroom* (4th ed.). Columbus, OH: Merrill/Prentice Hall.

Koegel, R. L., O' Dell, M. C., & Koegel, L. K. (1987). A natural language teaching paradigm for nonverbal autistic children. *Journal of Autism and Developmental Disorders, 17,* 187–200.

Lamm, N., & Greer, R. D. (1991). A systematic replication of CABAS I Italy. *Journal of Behavioral Education, 1,* 427–444.

Lindsley, O. R. (1996). The four free-operant freedoms. *The Behavior Analyst, 19,* 199–210.

Lovaas, I. O. (1981). *Teaching developmentally disabled children: The me book.* Austin, TX: Pro-Ed.

Lovaas, I. O. (1987). Behavioral treatment and normal educational and intellectual functioning in young autistic children. *Journal of Consulting and Clinical Psychology, 55* (3), 3–9.

Malone, M. (2002, October 7). Welcome to feedback universe. *Forbes,* pp. 21–25.

Martin, G., & Pear, J. (2003). *Behavior modification: What it is and how to do it* (7th ed.). Upper Saddle River, NJ: Prentice Hall.

Maurice, C. (1994). *Let me hear your voice: A family's triumph over autism.* New York: Ballentine Books.

McClannahan, L. E., & Krantz, P. J. (1999). *Activity schedules for children with autism: Teaching independent behavior (topics in autism).* Bethesda, MD: Woodbine House.

McDonough, C. S. (2000). *A procedure used to incorporate computer technology and programmed instruction into a preschool curriculum.* Paper presented at the 26th annual convention of the Association for Behavior Analysis, Washington, DC.

McDonough, C. S., & Shimizu, H. (2002). *Teaching young children with developmental disabilities to*

*point and click with a computer mouse.* Paper presented at the 28th annual convention of the Association for Behavior Analysis, Toronto, Canada.

McGee, G. G., Morrier, M. J., & Daly, T. (1999). An incidental teaching approach to early intervention for toddlers with autism. *Journal of the Association for the Severely Handicapped, 24,* 133–146.

Michael, J. (1982). Distinguishing between the discriminative and motivational functions of stimuli. *Journal of the Experimental Analysis of Behavior, 37,* 149–155.

Michael, J. (1988). Establishing operations and the mand. *Analysis of Verbal Behavior, 6,* 3–9.

Miller, A. D., Barbetta, P. M., & Heron, T. E. (1994). START tutoring: Designing, training, implementing, adapting, and evaluating tutoring programs for school and home settings. In R. Gardner III, D. M. Sainato, J. O. Cooper, T. E. Heron, W. L. Heward, J. Eshleman, & T. A. Grossi (Eds.), *Behavior analysis in education: Focus on measurably superior instruction* (pp. 265–282). Pacific Grove, CA: Brooks/Cole.

Nelson, R. O., & Rutherford, R. B. (1983). Timeout revisited: Guidelines for its use in special education. *Experimental Education Quarterly, 3,* 56–67.

Paine, S. C., Radicchi, J., Rosellini, L. C., Deutchman, L., & Darch, C. B. (1982). *Structuring your classroom for academic success.* Champaign, IL: Research Press.

Pangaro, P. (2000). Cybernetics (definition). [on line] http://www.pangaro.com/published/cyber-macmillan.html.

Partington, J. W., & Bailey, J. S. (1993). Teaching intraverbal behavior to preschool children. *Analysis of Verbal Behavior, 11,* 9–18.

Partington, J. W., & Sundberg, M. L. (1998). *The assessment of basic language and learning skills: An assessment, curriculum guide, and tracking system for children with autism or other developmental disabilities.* Danville, CA: Behavior Analysts.

Selinske, J. E., & Greer, R. D. (1991). A functional analysis of the comprehensive application of behavior analysis to schooling. *Journal of Applied Behavior Analysis, 24,* 107–117.

Stebbins, L. B., St. Pierre, R. G., Proper, E. C., Anderson, R. B., & Cerva, T. R. (1977). *Education as experimentation: A planned variation model* (Vol. IV-A: *An evaluation of Follow Through*). Cambridge, MA: Abt Associates.

Stokes, T. F., & Baer, D. M. (1977). An implicit technology of generalization. *Journal of Applied Behavior Analysis, 10,* 349–367.

Sundberg, M. L. (1993). The application of establishing operations. *The Behavior Analyst, 16,* 211–214.

Sundberg, M. L., & Partington, J. W. (1999). The need for both discrete trial and natural environment language training for children with autism. In P. M., Ghezzi, W. L. Williams, & J. E. Carr (Eds.), *Autism: Behavior-analytic perspectives.* Reno, NV: Context Press.

Twyman, J. S. (1998). The Fred S. Keller School. *Journal of Applied Behavior Analysis, 31,* 695–701.

Tyler, V. O. (1967). Application of operant token reinforcement of academic performance of an institutionalized delinquent. *Psychological Report, 21,* 249–260.

Watkins, K. (1995). Follow Through: Why didn't we? *Effective School Practices, 15.* Retrieved July 7, 2003, from http://darkwing.uoregon.edu/~Adiep/ft/watkins.htm.

## STUDY QUESTIONS AND FOLLOW-UP ACTIVITIES

1. Discuss the potential benefits and limitations in the use of the direct observation form in Figure 11-3. Have you ever used a form like this? If you were supervising teachers, would you use such a form? Why or why not?

2. Discuss the potential benefits and risks of requiring beginning teachers to complete PSI modules. List some benefits to having the teachers understand and respond to technical behavioral vocabulary.

3. What are the similarities between the processes used to teach the teachers and those used to teach the students at Hawthorne?

4. Select a process (e.g., how to teach) from those referenced in Tables 11-1 and 11-2 and choose a target behavior that is measurable (outcome).

   a. Clearly, concisely, and completely define your behavioral objective.

   b. Specify how you might measure this behavior in reference to the process you have selected.

   c. Discuss how you would evaluate the outcome.

5. The authors describe students and staff/parents as primary and secondary learner groups, respectively. Suggest some tertiary learner groups (e.g., community members) who could enhance the generality of student outcomes. Outline a plan for how you would program for generalization of student outcomes with the participation of this group. Develop some suggestions for incentive programs for tertiary learner groups that are similar to the incentives offered to staff and parents.

6. Discuss how a behavioral schooling system is self-correcting. What are the necessary components of a self-correcting system?

7. Assume that you are a behavior analyst supervisor at the Hawthorne Country Day School. You are in the process of conducting interviews for teaching positions. Devise a series of activities that you and other supervisors could employ during interviews that include (a) opportunities for one-on-one discussion between interviewees and interviewers and (b) classroom observations that involve interactions with current teachers and students. Describe the specific behaviors that you would be looking for from interviewees, and indicate how you would summarize each interviewee's performance as it relates to his or her likelihood of being hired. Discuss why the behaviors you selected are important for promoting student success at Hawthorne.

8. The authors explain many different components of a behavioral systems approach, including teacher training and compensation, meetings, data collection, and parent education. Explain some potential obstacles to applying a behavioral systems approach in a public school. Must *all* of the components the authors described be implemented to produce a self-correcting system? Explain your answer, and its implications.

9. The authors write that "although our approach is unabashedly behavioral, it is *a* behavioral approach, not *the* behavioral approach." Explain why this is an important issue to highlight in a chapter on behavioral schooling. Discuss the differences between the science of behavior and

---

Study questions and follow-up activities prepared by Susan M. Silvestri and Renée K. Van Norman.

any particular behavioral approach. See Hawthorne's Web site, www.hawthornecountryday.org/overview, for helpful information written by the staff at the school.

10. Is it necessary for teachers to espouse the philosophy of behaviorism (in addition to demonstrating verbal, contingency-shaped, and instructional tactic problem-solving behaviors) to be effective teachers? Why or why not?

11. Discuss the issue of teaching as an art versus teaching as a science as it relates to teacher training at Hawthorne. In what areas, if any, is the school's scientific approach lacking? In what ways is it an improvement on traditional approaches to teacher training?

12. Extend the description of PSI and the examples of teacher modules to develop a set of modules

within all three areas—verbal behavior, contingency-shaped behavior, and problem solving with instructional tactics—to address skills outside of working directly with students in classrooms. Examples of other skills include student intake assessment and evaluation, working with parents, preparing for and participating in district meetings, interacting with supervisors, and training aides.

13. Given the issues the authors discuss regarding the salary structure at Hawthorne, propose some additional incentive systems for teachers beyond salary increases that may promote and maintain student success at this school.

14. Discuss how Baer, Wolf, and Risley's (1968) seven dimensions of ABA are illustrated in the Hawthorne approach to schooling.

### CHAPTER 12

# Behavioral Systems Analysis and Higher Education

*Richard W. Malott*

## PROLOG

I suggest that we behavior analysis college professors should practice what we preach, that we should apply behavior analysis, organizational behavior management (OBM), and behavioral systems analysis to our university instruction. I suggest that we college professors apply to what we do most (teaching) the approaches and philosophy we know works everywhere else—behavior analysis and all it implies.

Furthermore, I suggest that what works for teaching behavior analysis works for teaching everything else, from philosophy to physics to fine art to football. And what works for teaching at a university works for teaching everywhere else, from preschool to postgraduate refresher courses, though the logistics will vary from setting to setting (Moran & Malott, 2005).

However, it takes a lot of work to apply behavior analysis to anything, including higher education. Therefore, we all have a strong tendency to argue covertly against the applications in our own area, getting off the hook by explaining to ourselves why these effortful innovations won't really work in our own specific settings and why the less effortful, more expedient status quo is really best. But it's more fun and more productive to covertly come up with ways we could get around the obvious obstacles to implementing a high percentage of these instruction-enhancing suggestions. You might even find it fun and useful to make a running list of applications you could make, as you read this chapter. (So, why don't you grab a piece of paper and a pencil right now. Or maybe you already have them at hand.)

---

If you would like a copy of the PowerPoint presentation on which this chapter is based or details of the relevant instructional and systems technology described in this chapter, please go to DickMalott.com. You can also find some of the references in this chapter at DickMalott.com where you can read them online or download them.

## CRITIQUE

### A.D. 1950

*Fred R. Malott, MD:   The practice of medicine wouldn't be so bad if it weren't for the damn patients.*

### A.D. 1965

*Prototypical business manager.   The practice of management wouldn't be so bad if it weren't for the damn workers.* Labor and management are usually at war. (Frequently implied by participants in organizational behavior management workshops at the University of Michigan for business managers from around the country.)

### A.D. 1970

*OBM (organizational behavior management) safety consultant:   Workers injure themselves so they can get insurance benefits.*

*Behaviorman:   OBMers, please don't blame the victims.*

### A.D. 1975

Western Michigan University faculty organizes to form its first labor union.

*Irate WMU professor:   The people in the administration are basically bad human beings.*

*Behaviorman:   Come on, man, they're just faculty members, like you and me, only they happened to have been promoted to administration.*

*Irate WMU professor:   No, it takes a certain type of nasty personality to become a university administrator.* Then, as a single organism, the faculty grabbed picket signs and marched around the administration building singing "We Shall Overcome."

Here is my point: The faculty is usually at war with the administration *and* the students. The faculty feels that teaching wouldn't be so bad if we poor faculty members weren't caught between a lazy, incompetent, psychopathic administration and a lazy, incompetent, psychopathic student body, neither of whom appreciates how hard we faculty members work and how wonderful we really are.

Still not convinced? Need some more of those hard-core scientific data? Here they come. (See Figures 12-1 and 12-2.)

### A.D. 1980

**Figure 12-1.**
Prototypical professor.

### A.D. 1985

**Figure 12-2.**
Famous behavior analyst meets Behaviorman.

*Behaviorwoman:   Behavior analysts, please don't blame the victim. The reason they don't study is that you haven't arranged effective performance-management contingencies to support their studying.*

### A.D. 2000

*New WMU psychology faculty member:  The grad students at WMU are a bunch of whiners. When I assign them a few dozen books to read, they complain. Not like when I was in grad school.*

*Charles Darwin:  Like there's been a major genetic drift in the 5 years since you got your PhD.*

*Behaviorman:  New PhDs, please don't blame the victims.*

The point: Even behavior analysts fail to appreciate B. F. Skinner's dictum: The subject is always right.

If the students aren't pressing the lever the way we think they should, it's our fault, not theirs. There's no such thing as a dumb or lazy rat. And there's no such thing as a dumb or lazy student. There are only dumb and lazy professors. (Or is it possible that professors are no dumber or lazier than their students and the lab rats? Behaviorman wonders to himself. [For an elaboration of this mea culpa, see the addendum to this chapter.])

### A.D. 2002

The following is from an article by a distinguished behavior analyst in the WMU faculty union newsletter:

Today's students aren't serious about their education. All they care about is their new surround-sound entertainment centers, in their lavishly furnished, upscale apartments, and their new sports cars. To support their decadent lifestyles, they work at outside jobs 20 to 40 hours per week. The result is they have neither the time nor the energy to study, and they fall asleep when they do manage to make it to class.

I disagree with this article. I've done a lot of academic and career counseling with WMU undergrads, and I often find very serious students. If they work full-time, it's because they must, in order to go to school. If it weren't for table waiting and bartending jobs, half of our students couldn't afford to go to school. These working students often take full-time course loads and still do great work at school and get excellent grades. And only rarely do they fall asleep in class, in spite of the chronic state of sleep deprivation most serious students suffer.

### 335 B.C.

*Aristotle:  The new generation is not nearly as good as the earlier generations.*

I disagree with Aristotle. The older and younger generations are usually at war. And the older generation has been dissing the younger generation for at least 2,400 years. If, for the last 2,400 years, each generation were worse than the previous, by now we'd all be sitting on tree limbs and picking cooties, not writing and presenting all those scholarly papers at wonderful behavior analysis conferences.

*Behaviorwoman:  Older gen, please stop blaming the victims.*

Now, just a little more of those hard-core scientific data (see Figure 12-3):

### Today

**Figure 12-3.**
Faculty's favorite comment and inferences.

*Behaviorwoman: Self-righteous indignation is one of our biggest reinforcers. Professors get a cheap thrill from being indignant about half their students failing the midterm.*

*Behaviorman: I get a cheap thrill from being indignant about professors failing half their students and then blaming those students.*

## RECOMMENDATIONS

Let's shift from critique to recommendations. Remember Skinner's dictum: The organism is always right. Therefore, the students are always right. The students you have to work with are the students you have to work with. So design your educational systems (curriculum and instructional technology) to accommodate your students' entering repertoires and values. Your semester's goals should be that your students learn as much about your subject as is humanly possible and also that they love your subject (e.g., behavior analysis).

Let me rephrase that: Your semester's goals are that your students *acquire as many subject-related skills* as is humanly possible and that they love your subject.

The less we talk about learning and the less we talk about education and the more we talk, think, and teach in terms of skills training, the more successful we will be in helping our students acquire a functional and lasting repertoire. We should think of ourselves as running a trade school, even though that trade involves complex, subtle, higher-order skills. But we should not think it easy to train complex, subtle, higher-order skills.

These issues lead to three behavior analysis models: the skills training model of education, the performance management model of task accomplishment, and the three-contingency model of performance management.

## Skills Training Model of Education

The philosophy behind the skills training model is well expressed in a message from a Chinese fortune cookie: *Education that does not lead to action is wasted.* I find it helpful to look at education in terms of skills training. In other words, we conceive of education as preparing students to do something they could not do before, for example, the skillful use of behavior analysis to understand and work with issues in basic research, professional applications, and everyday life (Brethower & Smalley, 1998).

The skills training model of education has four components: (a) concept and principles training, (b) strategy training, (c) knowledge teaching, and (d) appreciation enhancing.

### Concept and Principles Training

Concepts and principles are the basic building blocks of verbal and intellectual skills (e.g., the concept of the reinforcer and the principle of reinforcement; Shimamune & Malott, 1994). Markle (1990) and Tiemann and Markle (1978) described an effective technology of concept training involving the training of students to discriminate between carefully chosen examples and nonexamples of concepts. I add to that the training of students to generate original examples of those concepts and also principles.

### Strategy Training

As students master the concepts and principles, they also need to learn how to combine those concepts and principles in ways that will help them interact more effectively with the world of basic research, professional applications, and everyday life. Tiemann and Markle (1978) used the term *strategy* to label these functional combinations of concepts and principles (e.g., the strategy used to analyze a complex behavioral interaction or the strategy used to design an effective performance management program).

### Knowledge Teaching

To understand the concepts, principles, and strategies and be able to apply them in various settings, students need to know a set of examples of each concept, principle, and strategy—if possible, in the variety of settings they are currently encountering and will encounter after graduation. Often, the best understood and most easily remembered examples are those coming from the students' current professional and everyday lives. These examples constitute the student's immediate-access database for that discipline.

### Appreciation

To use a course's concepts, principles, strategies, and database, students must appreciate their value and utility. Both Mager (1984) and Gilbert (1996) addressed this issue.

## Traditional Knowledge-Imparting Model of Education

Some courses primarily teach concepts and strategies (e.g., mathematics). However, most courses teach knowledge, the database, the discipline's content and facts, and the examples (e.g., psychology). Although some knowledge-oriented courses may explicitly teach concepts and principles, unfortunately, most courses leave it to the students to infer those underlying concepts and principles. Moreover, almost all courses leave it to the student to infer the strategies of application. I suspect that the systematic application of the skills training model, although intellectually difficult and time consuming, will improve most, if not all, university courses. Therefore, as teachers, our semester's goals should be that our students become eager, skilled practitioners of our discipline. That's a big task for students, which leads to another model.

## Performance Management Model of Task Accomplishment

The five steps to accomplishing any big task are as follows:

1. Divide the big task into a series of small tasks.
2. Specify exactly what each small task is and how to accomplish it.
3. Set frequent deadlines for the tasks.
4. Monitor the task accomplishment.
5. Provide small but significant outcomes for each monitored task.

These steps comprise the performance management model of task accomplishment, and I will apply them to classroom instruction later in this chapter. We also use this model to help students complete theses and dissertations (Garcia, Malott, & Brethower, 1988). Incidentally, this model applies not only to tasks in education but also to motor skills training (e.g., sports), OBM, self-management, behavioral medicine, and clinical interventions (Malott & Suarez, 2004).

This approach is not without its detractors, however (see Figure 12-4).

**Figure 12-4.**
Professor Tradition meets Behaviorwoman.

*Well, I certainly manage to teach my behavior analysis classes and prepare my scholarly papers, without procrastination.*

*So I have no sympathy for procrastinating students.*

*Show me a person who says she doesn't procrastinate,*

*and I'll ask for inter-observer reliability.*

*Professor Tradition: Unnecessary coddling. Just tell the little brats what they're supposed to do and toss them out of school if they don't do it. We already have too many weak sisters in our field; we don't need any more.*

*Behaviorwoman:    Ninety percent of the professional behavior analysts don't get their Association for Behavior Analysis presentation proposal in until 5 days before the deadline. Seventy percent don't get their papers finished until they're at the ABA conference. And 60% should have spent at least 20 more hours preparing their papers. But, no doubt, you are the exception, Professor Tradition.*

## Three-Contingency Model of Performance Management

Why does procrastination reign supreme across the land? The three-contingency model of performance management explains why we procrastinate and how we can prevent it (Malott, 1989; 1993, October; 2002, May; in press; Malott & Garcia, 1991). We procrastinate because the outcomes of our task-related behavior are too small or too improbable to reinforce that behavior. The delay of the outcomes is irrelevant. (For the rationale behind this controversial de-emphasis of the role of delay of outcomes, see the addendum to this chapter and Malott & Suarez, 2004.)

### *Contingency 1: The Ineffective Natural Contingency*

Suppose a student has a course assignment due one month from now (e.g., an exam or a term paper). Will he start working on the assignment right now? To answer this, we need to consider the ineffective, natural contingency operating on his starting to work on the assignment. (See the contingency in the top diagram of Figure 12-5.) It is an ineffective avoidance contingency: The

**Figure 12-5.**
The three-contingency model of performance management.

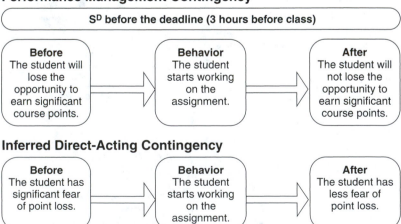

### Ineffective Natural Contingency

| **Before** The student will be a few minutes closer to class without some preparation. | **Behavior** The student starts working on the assignment. | **After** The student will not be a few minutes closer to class without some preparation. |

### Performance Management Contingency

S^D before the deadline (3 hours before class)

| **Before** The student will lose the opportunity to earn significant course points. | **Behavior** The student starts working on the assignment. | **After** The student will not lose the opportunity to earn significant course points. |

### Inferred Direct-Acting Contingency

| **Before** The student has significant fear of point loss. | **Behavior** The student starts working on the assignment. | **After** The student has less fear of point loss. |

student's working on the assignment will avoid his getting a few minutes closer to class without some preparation done. The before condition is an aversive stimulus or condition. The aversiveness of the condition (stimulus) of not having some preparation done on his assignment is conditional (dependent) on the amount of time before the class for which that assignment is due. Therefore, the closer the student gets to the due date, the more aversive becomes the condition of not having done some preparation. And the more aversive that before condition, the greater the reinforcement of escaping that aversive condition and avoiding an even more aversive condition by starting to work on the assignment. But with a month to go before the assignment is due, getting a few minutes closer to that distant time with no preparation (or no new preparation) is not very aversive. For most students, it's not aversive enough to motivate them to start work on the assignment (after all, they can always start working on the assignment a few minutes from now, or a few minutes after that, or a few minutes after that, etc.). So the student procrastinates. Thus, this natural contingency is ineffective because the differences between the before and after conditions are too small to reinforce the avoidance response.

*Professor Tradition: That's a nice academic analysis, my good man, but I still have no sympathy for the procrastinating student. I always manage to get my lectures prepared in time for class.*

*Behaviorwoman: And you always start preparing enough ahead of time that you end up with the high-quality lecture you had desired? Maybe, but I doubt it.*

If this ineffective, natural avoidance contingency is so pervasive, how do students—or professors, for that matter—manage to get anything at all done? Why don't we all procrastinate on everything to the point of no return? Because, eventually, the student gets close enough to the due date that being just a few minutes closer

without some preparation will be fairly aversive. Now, the decrement in aversiveness from the before to the after condition in the natural contingency is large enough to support the avoidance behavior of starting to work on the assignment. The natural avoidance contingency becomes effective. But often the before condition does not become aversive enough soon enough, and the student does not have enough time left to prepare adequately before the due date. The student's preschool behavioral history determines how close to the deadline he or she must get before the proximity becomes aversive enough to evoke the escape behavior of working on the assignment, which in turn may help the student avoid the missed deadline (Malott, 2002).

But, again, this approach is not without its detractors (see Figure 12-6).

Now, let's apply the three-contingency model of performance management to the prevention of procrastination.

### Contingency 2: Effective Performance Management Contingencies

Recall that the performance management model of task accomplishment consists of five steps to accomplishing any big task:

*Step 1:* *Divide the big task into a series of small tasks.* Suppose the big task is reading and

**Figure 12-6.**
Professor Traditional meets Contingency Man.

studying a textbook for a midterm and final exam. The professor might divide the textbook into single-chapter assignments.

*Step 2: Specify exactly what each small task is and how to accomplish it.* The professor might provide a set of detailed study objectives for each chapter—for example, *be able to define the following terms; be able to classify and give original examples of the following terms; be able to compare and contrast the following concepts; be able to describe the rationale, procedure, and results of the following experiment.*

*Step 3: Set frequent deadlines for the tasks.* The professor might give a quiz on a new chapter at each class meeting.

*Step 4: Monitor the task accomplishment.* Of course, the professor would then administer and evaluate those quizzes.

*Step 5: Provide small but significant outcomes for each monitored task.* Contingent on each quiz score, the students could earn a few points that count toward the final course grade.

This performance management effort results in the second contingency shown in Figure 12-5, the effective performance management contingency, also an avoidance contingency: By starting to work on the assignment, the student avoids losing the opportunity to earn the course points.

At first glance this contingency might look like an analogue to a reinforcement contingency, in which starting to work on the assignment produces the delayed reinforcer of course points or at least the delayed reinforcer of the opportunity to earn the course points. But the imposition of the deadline drastically changes the contingency. With the deadline, if the student does not start to work soon enough to finish the assignment (e.g., 3 hours before class), he will lose the opportunity to earn 100% of the course points, an analogue to avoidance of the loss of a reinforcer.

Thus, the deadline acts as our aversive control savior and comes to our rescue; without the

deadline and the resultant aversive control, the student would be in procrastination land forever. Without the deadline, the resulting analogue to a reinforcement contingency would be too tolerant of procrastination. Deadline-induced analogue avoidance contingencies keep our world in its orderly orbit. (For more details of this analysis, see Malott & Suarez, 2004.)

By *analogue contingencies,* I mean indirect-acting contingencies in which the outcome is too delayed to reinforce or punish the behavior; outcomes delayed by as much as 60 seconds after the response are probably too delayed to reinforce or punish that response (Snycerski, Laraway, Byrne, & Poling, 1999; Sutphin, Byrne, & Poling, 1998). Although some contingencies with delayed outcomes are effective in controlling our behavior, they are effective only when we know the rules describing those contingencies. I call such effective, delayed-outcome contingencies *analogue contingencies* (Malott, 1989, 1993). For example, suppose the student knows that if he starts studying 3 hours before class, he will avoid losing the opportunity to earn a good grade. The outcome is too delayed to reinforce that avoidance response, yet this rule-governed analogue to an avoidance contingency will probably control the student's behavior. It may work like this: The student states the rule describing the performance management contingency as such, "If I don't start studying by 3 hours before class, I won't have enough time to do the assignment and I'll lose the opportunity to earn a good grade." This statement creates a conditional, learned, aversive warning stimulus—being within 3 hours of class time and not studying. The student can immediately attenuate this aversiveness by starting to study—a direct-acting escape contingency (Malott, 1998; Malott & Suarez, 2004).

It is not that we couldn't, in theory, control assignment preparation with direct-acting reinforcement contingencies; but, in fact, we usually do not. Of course, if the student were deprived of food and we gave him a bite of food every time he read a paragraph or rehearsed a definition, then we could readily get a high rate of assignment preparation with simple reinforcement contingencies. But that ain't going to happen.

In addition, I think it is important to distinguish between what I call *instrumental* reinforcers and *instrumental* aversive conditions on the one hand and what I call *hedonic* reinforcers and *hedonic* aversive conditions on the other hand. Instrumental reinforcers are reinforcers that are only of value in that they are instrumental in our obtaining some other valued reinforcer. Hedonic reinforcers are of value in their own right. Access to a water fountain is instrumental in (a necessary prerequisite to) obtaining a drink of water. Therefore, access to the water fountain is only a reinforcer when we are deprived of water so that water is a reinforcer and access to the water fountain will be useful (instrumental) in our obtaining that reinforcer. However, the smile of a passing stranger is a hedonic reinforcer in that it is a reinforcer, even though we know that this particular smile from this particular passing stranger will not be instrumental in our obtaining some other valued reinforcer.

The learned reinforcers, as well as the unlearned reinforcers, in the Skinner box seem to be hedonic reinforcers and not mere instrumental reinforcers. Because most basic research involves hedonic reinforcers (e.g., unlearned reinforcers), we should be cautious about extrapolating from basic research with these powerful reinforcers to applications with more tenuous, tentative instrumental reinforcers such as tokens, points, and grades.

With the delayed delivery of those instrumental reinforcers or the delayed opportunity to earn them, we have analogues to reinforcement contingencies. Such analogue reinforcement contingencies result in procrastination and poor student performance (Malott, 1986).

### Contingency 3: The Direct-Acting Contingency

A theoretical question remains. The effective performance management contingency does control behavior, and it does so even though it is only a delayed analogue to an avoidance contingency, rather than a direct-acting avoidance contingency in which the outcome is immediate enough to reinforce the response. But note that this sort of performance management contingency works only if the person knows the rule that describes that contingency. The question is, How does knowing the rule make that contingency effective?

I think control by such a performance management contingency is indirect. It depends on the actual statement of the rule describing the contingency; for example, *If I don't start studying now, I will get a bad grade*. This rule statement creates a conditional aversive condition—proximity to the deadline *without* having started to study.

This *conditional* aversive stimulus, being close to the deadline, is *conditional* in that it is maximally aversive only if the student has not started studying. The student can escape this conditional aversive stimulus by starting to study, and the resultant, immediate reduction in the aversiveness reinforces that escape response. In other words, the combination of proximity to the deadline and the stimuli arising from not studying is aversive, but the combination of proximity to the deadline and the stimuli arising from actually studying is not aversive (see Figure 12-7).

The notion of a *conditional aversive stimulus* or *conditional aversive condition* is important in that it makes it clear that an aversive stimulus has at least two components (in our example, proximity to the deadline and not studying). The maximum adversiveness of this stimulus or condition is conditional (dependent) on both components being present—both being close to the deadline and not studying. Being far from the deadline and not studying or being near to the deadline and studying are not as aversive as being near the deadline and not studying. So, starting to study when the student gets near the deadline is supported by an effective, direct-acting escape contingency because starting to study reduces the aversiveness of that condition,

**Figure 12-7.**
Example of a direct-acting escape contingency.

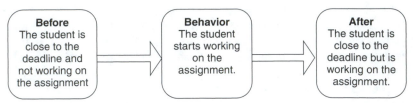

| **Before** The student is close to the deadline and not working on the assignment | **Behavior** The student starts working on the assignment. | **After** The student is close to the deadline but is working on the assignment. |

even though the mere proximity to the deadline itself may retain some aversiveness.

I am suggesting that the main function of the rule describing the performance management avoidance contingency is that it establishes the aversiveness of this direct-acting escape contingency. Without the rule, *If I don't start studying now, I will get a bad grade,* getting close to the deadline and not studying would not be an aversive condition that would support the escape behavior of starting to study. The combination of the performance management avoidance contingency and the resulting direct-acting escape contingency forms something akin to the classic two-factor escape/avoidance contingencies.

This deadline-proximity-study contingency exists. It is an inference that it is an effective escape contingency that reinforces studying. In other words, it is an inference that the before condition is an aversive condition for the student and that there is a sufficient difference in the aversiveness between the before and after conditions to reinforce the escape response of starting to work on the assignment. But, I infer that if the indirect-acting, rule-governed, analogue-to-avoidance performance management contingency is effective, it must be because of this escape contingency.

I think it is important to examine, as we just did, the details of the conditional aversive before condition that motivates the escape behavior (working on the assignment). The terminology coming from this fine-grained conceptual analysis, however, is somewhat awkward. I find it handier simply to use the commonsense term *fear* to label that aversive

before condition (see the bottom contingency diagram in Figure 12-5). However, methodological behaviorists uncomfortable with the fear terminology but otherwise comfortable with the three-contingency model are, of course, free to use the more specific conditional aversive stimulus terminology.

As I mentioned earlier, I believe that how close students get to the deadline before starting to work is a function of their early behavioral histories. We can understand that better in terms of the inferred, direct-acting escape contingency of Figure 12-5. Students differ greatly in terms of how close they must get to the deadline before they start studying. I suggest that this means that students differ greatly in terms of how close the deadline must get before fear kicks in, before the conditional stimulus of proximity to the deadline and not working on the assignment becomes sufficiently aversive. And I suggest that this difference among students is a function of differences in their early behavioral histories, differences in parental role modeling and direct parental intervention.

For example, if Mama gets into a panic when she has not started working on a task, even though she is a long way from the deadline, this analogue pairing of aversive panic and a distant deadline will cause distant deadlines to become aversive to the child. But more to the point, suppose Mama also panics and starts shouting at the child or merely gets subtly critical of the child or starts making dire predictions of failure when the child has not started working even though the deadline is still distant. Then, even when the deadline is distant, that pairing of aversiveness with not working will have a major impact on the child that will last throughout the person's college life and the rest of his or her adult life. That person will begin to fear failure earlier than many of his or her compatriots and will thus begin working on assignments or other projects much earlier than others will. As a result, that person will be much more successful as a student and as a professional than his or her compatriots will be. But such success has a price—a life much fuller of fear of failure (again, for more details, see Malott, 2002).

Thus, we have seen how the three-contingency model of performance management offers an explanation of procrastination and the prevention of procrastination. We prevent procrastination by adding performance management contingencies, which are necessary for those of us who have not been raised by appropriately hysterical parents (Malott, 2002).

## THE BEHAVIOR ANALYSIS TRAINING SYSTEM: AN EXAMPLE OF A BEHAVIORAL SYSTEMS APPROACH TO HIGHER EDUCATION

We have just looked at three behavioral models relevant to higher education. The skills training model of education provides the rationale for the selection of the educational objectives and curricula. The performance management model of task accomplishment helps students do what they need to do to acquire those skills and accomplish those educational objectives. The three-contingency model of performance management helps us implement the performance management model correctly.

Building on those three models, there is a wider educational context to which we can apply behavior analysis—a systems-wide approach. This behavioral systems approach consists of two components: organizational behavior management and behavioral systems analysis. Most of the details of this behavioral systems approach to higher education have been previously described (Heward, 1994; Jackson &

Malott, 1994; Malott, 1984, 1993; Malott, Vunovich, Boettcher, & Groeger, 1995). Therefore, I will only briefly summarize some of those details, illustrating them with examples from the behavior analysis training system and adding a little enrichment.

Over the last 40 years, my students and I have developed four different "major" instructional systems. Sometimes these systems run concurrently, but usually I get bored with one after 5 or 10 years and feel guilty because I have not been doing enough writing and publishing. Then I hand off the instructional system to colleagues or close it down so I can create my own publish-or-perish academic monastery. But then I feel guilty again, this time because I am not training enough students; so I get an idea for a great new instructional system that will clearly save the world. But the new system turns out to be only a minor variation of the previous ones, which is fine with me because I think the previous ones were good enough.

I call my current and probably final system the behavior analysis training system (BATS). We have designed BATS to teach behavior analysis and behavioral systems analysis to undergraduate and graduate students who are my advisees at WMU. We started BATS around 1990 with three MA students and one PhD student, when I realized I had already broken my vow never to be the advisor to any more grad students and instead just teach a few nondemanding undergrad courses and concentrate on my writing. In 2004 there were 3 PhD student advisees, 20 MA student advisees, and 25 BA honors-thesis students in BATS.

The main goal of BATS is to produce and professionally place as many well-trained behavior analysts as possible at the BA, MA, and PhD levels. We divide this main goal into two subgoals.

One subgoal of BATS is to train undergrads in the principles of behavior, the principles of organizational behavior management (OBM) and behavior systems analysis, the general applications of those principles, and the specific skills of discrete trial training with preschool autistic children. We accomplish this with three sequential undergrad courses that are teaching the equivalent of about 400 students per year (because many of the students take all three courses, the number of different students is about 200).

The other subgoal of BATS is to train at a more advanced level the BA, MA, and PhD student members of the BATS teaching team. These more advanced students master more advanced levels of the principles of behavior, the principles of OBM and behavior systems analysis, the general applications of those principles, the specific skills of discrete trial training with preschool autistic children as well as the skills of training and managing other populations with behavior problems, and specific OBM and behavior systems analysis skills. To a large degree, these advanced undergrad and grad students achieve this mastery by helping to improve and manage BATS: They teach the undergrad courses, supervise and provide adjunct services to those courses, and run BATS and the various BATS components, which I will describe later in this chapter.

We are effective in achieving these two subgoals to the extent that we accomplish another subgoal—that BATS be an exemplary system, an exemplary organization, illustrating the best of OBM and behavior systems analysis, a place where we practice what we preach about using behavior analysis to help build a better world. When we started BATS, we achieved perhaps 15% of that goal of being an exemplary system—15% reality, 85% pipe dream. Over time we have reversed those percentages; now we are about 85% of being an exemplary system (OK, maybe only 80%).

For years I taught OBM and behavior systems analysis in regular courses and had about as much success as I would have had if I had been teaching roller-skating by the lecture method. The only way I have been able to teach OBM and behavior systems analysis so that it seeps into the souls of students is to intensely immerse them in OBM/behavior systems analysis systems such as BATS. After a year or two in BATS, many, maybe most, students acquire to an impressive level an OBM/behavior systems analysis world view and OBM/behavior systems analysis skills.

## Organizational Behavior Management

By OBM (organizational behavior management), I mean setting up procedures that effectively manage the behavior of people in organizations (Malott, Malott, & Shimamune, 1993; Malott, Shimamune, & Malott, 1993). The people in or served by BATS are the students in our undergrad courses, the MA students teaching those courses, the advanced MA and PhD students supervising those courses, the undergrad and grad students managing subsystems that serve the undergrad and grad students, and the CEO—me. For BATS, OBM entails using the performance management model of task accomplishment along with the three-contingency model of performance management.

All of this is based on a strong commitment to the avoidance of victim blaming (my earlier blaming of the college professor victims notwithstanding). So, if people within our system are failing to do the tasks they are supposed to do, we try not to blame them. Instead, we analyze the existing contingencies and implement performance management systems and performance management contingencies to support the desired performance more effectively. Unfortunately, that's neither as easy nor as emotionally gratifying as victim blaming, but it's much more effective in eliciting the desired performance.

We have already discussed performance management contingencies to support studying for quizzes. We also have found it necessary to implement contingencies for class attendance because the quiz contingencies are not enough for a few students, even though they must be in class to take the quizzes. Students who have more than three absences from our 30 semesterly class meetings automatically have their final grade reduced by half a letter grade. This prevents all but about 2% of our students from drifting into a lower grade than they wanted because they had unintentionally slept in a few too many times.

At the MA teaching assistant level, we have found that the TAs do not read the TA procedure manual as reliably as they need to because the natural contingencies are insufficient. So rather than throw a conniption fit about what a bunch of unconscientious TAs this new generation of grad students is, we implemented review quizzes on the TA manuals. On the other hand, the natural contingencies usually support the TAs' reviewing the day's assignment they will be teaching, so we have not needed to add a performance management contingency for that.

In hierarchical organizations, performance frequently falls apart at the top because the CEO reports to no one (even, it would seem, when there is a board of directors). BATS is no different. So I hereby vow that, starting with the new semester, I, as CEO of BATS, will tighten up the performance management contingencies on my own BATS performance (I already have tight performance management contingencies on other areas of my life; Malott, in press).

## Specific Behavioral Systems Analysis Interventions

In much the same spirit as avoiding victim blaming, in BATS we also try to avoid complaining about things that are not happening the way they should. If things aren't right, inside or outside of BATS, then we must design and implement a subsystem to make them right. This approach has resulted in many subsystems within BATS; here are a few:

### GRE Prep Course

One of our goals is to place as many students into graduate school as possible. But a major problem was that too many students were not getting into the grad school of their choice be-

cause of their low GRE scores. This was even true of excellent students, those getting the top grades in our courses and those with well-earned, high GPAs. So, we implemented an elective GRE prep course that was mainly a performance management program. Typically, the students would get points toward their grade in the GRE course for doing the hard work of spending the necessary 100 to 150 hours studying standard GRE prep books. This study would raise their GRE scores an average of 100 points (Groeger & Malott, in press; Miller, Goodyear-Orwat, & Malott, 1996; Vunovich, 1996).

### Behavioral Academic Career Counseling (BACC)

Another problem with placing our BA graduates in grad schools and jobs is that they had no idea what opportunities were available and how to achieve those opportunities. So, I started giving a lecture each semester on grad schools and jobs and how to get into grad school and find jobs. At the end of each lecture, I would invite the students to set up a BACC appointment with me for personalized counseling. Maybe one or two of 50 students would accept my invitation. So I instructed the TAs to explicitly set up BACC appointments with me for the top students in their seminar sections. They came, they appreciated, and they got into grad school.

As is my tendency, I faded out of most of the BACC appointments. Now the TAs for the undergrad seminars do the BACC counseling. To encourage the students to make appointments with the TAs, we give them 10 optional activity points that they can substitute for participation in some required course activity. Now over half the students have BACC appointments, and they evaluate the appointments as being quite valuable.

Students should not need an individualized appointment because not only do I give the lecture but all that material is in the last chapter of one of the texts used in our course, *Principles of Behavior* (Malott & Suarez, 2004), but the fact is that most students do need one-on-one counseling sessions. They should not need a special, individualized invitation for the counseling session, but most of them do. And they should not need the optional activity points for attending, but most of them do. We try not to get too hung up on *should;* instead, we try to focus on what it takes to achieve our goals. And what it takes consists of providing high-quality training in behavior analysis to as many students as possible and making sure those students end up in positions in which they can make good use of that training (those positions can be in behavior-analysis-informed graduate programs or in jobs requiring behavior analysis skills). That exemplifies our goal-directed systems approach.

### Behavioral Research Supervisory System

The biggest problem grad students face is completing their theses and dissertations in a timely manner or completing them at all. By the time students reach the end of their PhD program, they should have sufficient time management skills that they would not have trouble completing writing projects, not even projects as big as a dissertation; but most grad students do not have those time management skills. The truth is, most of their faculty advisors do not have those time management skills either. The truth is, I do not have those time management skills. So, instead of blaming the victims, we implemented another subsystem, the behavioral research supervisory system (BRSS), to solve the problem by using the previously described performance management model of task accomplishment and the three-contingency model of performance management (Garcia & Malott, 1988; Garcia, Malott, & Brethower, 1988). BRSS effectively supports the research and writing of all BATS students; this includes undergraduate honors theses, MA projects, MA theses, and PhD dissertations. Almost all students produce quality products in a timely manner, a rarity without BRSS or the equivalent.

### Welcome Wagon

Many of the crucial subsystems, components, and procedures of BATS are a result of grad student initiatives. A grad student identifies a prob-

lem, proposes a solution, and implements that solution. Often, although I think there is no problem or the solution will not work, I allow them to give it a try. And often I am wrong; the student saw a problem or an unrealized need and the solution did work. Last year Melinda Sota, a new MA student from St. Cloud University, identified a problem and proposed to develop a solution. The problem is the lost, "freshman-like" feeling new grad students from other schools have when they come to WMU as my advisees (and probably as the advisees of any faculty member in any grad school). Melinda developed the BATS Welcome Wagon, a set of information that is useful to students considering entering our program and useful to them once they are here. In addition, she set up a sort of big brother, big sister program in which advanced grad students adopt and mentor incoming grad students.

### Super-A

Many of our subsystems are designed not so much to fix a problem but rather to enrich our current educational/training system. For example, I noticed that in our basic principles course a reasonable percentage of elite students were performing much better on their daily quizzes than was needed to achieve our 92% criterion for an A. I thought we should recognize this accomplishment and provide an incentive for other students wishing to stretch themselves out a bit. So we set up the Super-A program. Students who meet the requirements for a Super-A can sign up next semester for a one-credit course that automatically gives them an A, as a delayed reinforcer for their accomplishment. To complete the Super-A program, the student must earn an A in the regular course and earn 500 optional activity points (about 50 hours' worth of work) for other activities and accomplishments that semester. They earn 40 points for each cumulative quiz percentage point above 92%; they also earn points by attending special Super-A lectures and doing self-management projects. About 25% of our students are now earning Super-A's.

### A Letter to Mom and Dad

Another enrichment component is the Letter to Mom and Dad project. About the only things Mom and Dad receive from the university are tuition bills and a certain amount of perplexity about just what their child is studying, especially if their child is studying behavior analysis. So, our TAs get the names and addresses of the top-performing two or three students in each course section and write letters of congratulations to their parents, which both the TAs and I sign. Those top two or three students are excellent, serious, hard-working students who deserve that little bit of special recognition and whatever praise will now bounce off Mom and Dad. And because those super-students did not invent themselves (they are a result of excellent child rearing and nurturing by excellent, serious, hard-working parents), their parents also deserve a little recognition and the opportunity for some bragging rights on their kids. In addition, Mom and Dad may now be a little more supportive of the super-kid who is thinking about going to grad school to study behavior analysis (whatever that is). Maybe being a lawyer or a doctor is not the most important thing after all.

## General Behavior Systems Approaches

In the previous section we looked at specific examples of a behavior systems approach. In this section we will look at more general behavior systems strategies that underlie those specific examples.

### Goal-Directed Systems Design

Goal-directed systems design is the specification of the goals a system is to accomplish and the design of that system so all its components lead to the accomplishment of those goals (Malott & Garcia, 1987). Most systems have no clear goals and are not explicitly designed; instead, they evolve as a result of historic tradition and momentary expedience. That especially describes most systems in higher education, from the level of the course, to the department, to the college.

In BATS we try to practice goal-directed systems design. We try to design each component of each course and each supporting subsystem so that they will all help us achieve our ultimate goal. That goal is saving the world with behavior analysis by training as many behavior analysts as well as we can and helping them find positions in which they can save the world using their behavior analysis and behavior systems analysis skills, along with their very effective social skills.

### Continuous Quality Improvement

In implementing a goal-directed systems design, we must continually monitor and evaluate that system and all its components, down to the most minute, to determine if all those subsystems and components are contributing to the mission of the system—in the case of BATS, saving the world with behavior analysis. Often, we find that the components are not functioning quite as well as planned. So after the negative evaluation, we must recycle; we must redesign the component or subsystem, reimplement, reevaluate, and so on, until it is working as it should or at least as well as we can get it to work (we are not able to solve all of our problems).

This continuous quality improvement is a fascinating process because it points to so many things that should work but do not until they are revised. The evolution of our behavioral academic career counseling subsystem is an excellent example of this, as we discussed earlier.

The greatest amount of our continuous quality improvement efforts are devoted to our instructional materials—the texts (Bosch, 2001; Suarez, 2001), homework, computer-based instruction, study objectives, and quizzes. If 20% or 30% of our students miss a quiz question, something is wrong. At times even we find it hard not to blame the victim because reducing the error rate can be frustrating. But our performance management contingencies are sufficiently effective that we can reasonably assume that our students are studying and doing the best they can. In that case, the errors are not their fault; they are ours. Then we examine, with an eye toward revision, the quiz question itself, the relevant study objective, and the relevant homework and text material. We make the changes that seem appropriate. We implement the revised component the next semester. We revaluate. And we recycle until we have fixed the problem or run out of solutions.

Occasionally, we conclude that it is too much sugar for a cent. For example, we might have one high-error-rate quiz question based on one study objective and one paragraph of text. But after recycling several times, it looks as though we would need to expand the paragraph to an entire chapter because the concept is much more difficult than we had anticipated. In such cases, we may conclude that the concept is not crucial enough to justify that much course time, so we either eliminate it or put it in an optional advanced enrichment section at the end of the relevant chapter.

Most professors revise their instructional material from semester to semester, but my observation is that most simply blame the students for poor quiz performance and then proceed to update their lectures. Those updates are designed more to keep up with the latest developments in their field than to improve the effectiveness of their instruction. I have known few professors who engage in the sort of molecular, continuous quality improvement described here. Therefore, I think few professors realize how difficult the concepts they are teaching are for sincere, conscientious, hard-working students to learn. I also think that few professors realize the difficulty of simply communicating to other people (e.g., students) because they have not systematically assessed the success of their communication efforts. They may also attribute communication failures to low student motivation. In fact, sometimes I even find myself asking, "How can those undergrads be so thick as to not understand this concept?" And then my grad student TAs are apt to say, "We don't understand the concept either." Oh, yes, don't blame the victim. Often a difficult concept is really a concept that has problems with internal logic consistency or runs into too many gray areas when it is applied.

Also, as part of our continuous quality improvement, we ask the students to evaluate anonymously each of my lectures, in absolute terms, in comparison to typical university lectures and to other course activities. Although my lectures usually compare favorably to typical university lectures, they often compare unfavorably to the structured seminars my grad students conduct. In these structured seminars, the students review the day's textbook chapter and the day's structured homework; in addition, each student presents a transparency in each class with a contingency diagram illustrating his or her original example of the concept they have studied that day (Malott, Vunovich, Boettcher, & Groeger, 1995). The students evaluate highly these structured seminars in which they can actively practice talking and doing behavior analysis, receive feedback about the accuracy with which they are using the concepts and principles, and thereby improve their behavior analytic skills. Much to my disappointment, they prefer actively participating in these structured seminars to passively listening to me talk and do behavior analysis, even though I illustrate the concepts and principles with dazzling PowerPoint slide shows that are big hits at behavioral conferences. Therefore, most classes are devoted to structured seminars rather than my lectures and PowerPoint presentations.

One final comment about our continuous quality improvement: We evaluate almost every detail of a very large instructional system. That means that our evaluations and fixes are rough and ready, at best. Our primary goal is to get this large system functioning as effectively as possible, and our primary method is to try to continually improve as many aspects of that system as we can. My observation of our efforts and most other applications of continuous quality improvement is that it is rarely possible to evaluate these efforts in a way that will make such evaluations publishable in journals with primary concern for methodological rigor. Instead, we note problems suggested by confusions in the seminars and homework, student questions and complaints, quiz performances, and student social validity evaluations on anonymous questionnaires. Then we try to fix the problem based on our behavior analytic educated guesses. We then evaluate our fixes the next semester. In other words, this is real-world R&D (research and development), not scholarly research. But it is real-world R&D, not scholarly research that most behavior analysts do, even those with PhDs; therefore, working in BATS provides our students with very appropriate job skills (Malott, 1992a, 1992b). Of course, it is possible to do methodologically rigorous, publication-level research within such educational systems (Bacon, Fulton, & Malott, 1982; Dean, Fulton, & Malott, 1983; Rollofson, & Malott, 1972; Sundberg, Ober, Wysocki, Malott, 1978; Welsh, Malott, & Kent, 1980; Yaber & Malott, 1993); however, usually the goals of such research are more to disseminate information about a specific aspect of a specific instructional technique than to continuously improve the quality of the setting in which that research is conducted.

## CONCLUSIONS AND IMPLICATIONS

What I advocate (and therefore, what I do; or is it the other way around?) is that college and university faculty in all disciplines and teachers at all levels not be teachers of courses but, instead, be instructional systems designers and managers. Our job is not to present subject matter, but to help students acquire complex, subtle skills and values. Such an approach makes little, if any, use of lectures; instead, it involves designing and implementing learning opportunities in the form of readings, homework, seminars, quizzes, and practica.

Such an approach requires much more work than traditional teaching. But one solution is to give a large number of grad students and even undergrad students an opportunity to help with the analysis, design, implementation, evaluation, and recycling of the training system. In so doing, the undergrad students in the courses get much better training, and the undergrad and

grad students helping with the system get even better training. (Peer instruction has proven valuable for all parties involved, even in grade school [Greenwood et al., 1987].)

Although the system requires much effort, it can be more cost effective than traditional approaches to teaching. For example, BATS has very few paid assistants. Instead, students who are receiving academic credit, for which they pay, do most of the work. And although the system is labor intensive in terms of graduate TAs to run the individual seminars, the system is not labor intensive in terms of faculty time. The system takes much faculty time, but doubling the number of students the system serves only slightly increases the amount of needed faculty time.

Finally, a training system such as BATS is a populist meritocracy. There is room for almost everyone to participate and contribute and benefit, and those students with exceptional skills have the opportunity to really stretch out, to really develop, hone, and demonstrate those skills. I am impressed with the number of undergrad and grad students who, when given a chance in the right context, turn out to be very proactive, responsible, dedicated, creative, personable behavior analysts/behavior systems analysts/managers/trainers/therapists/people. As a result, I have great love and respect for our students. We all work toward achieving our goal, even though we know we never will achieve it (see Figure 12-8).

**Figure 12-8.**
Our goal.

## ADDENDUM
## A DIALOGUE ON RESPONSIBILITY
## IN HIGHER EDUCATION*
*Richard W. Malott and Nancy A. Neef*

### This Chapter
"If the students aren't pressing the lever the way we think they should, it's our fault, not the students' . . . . there's no such thing as a dumb or lazy student."

*Neef:*  Sure there is. I was once one myself ("dumb" in the sense of having a limited repertoire—which, after all, is why I was a student—and "lazy" in the sense that there was a lot other than studying that competed for my attention). If I had known at the time that I was a "victim" and could hang the blame for that state of affairs on my professors, I might have sued for big bucks (or at least filed a grievance for that B grade on an exam, given that it was my professor's fault I had to suffer the indignity of less than a Super-A for it). But, alas, *responsibility* for helping to improve a situation and *fault* for the situation that needs improving are not the same thing.

*Malott's reply:*  On the one hand, I think you are taking me too literally. And on the other hand, why not. Just as it is a good general rule for the operant conditioner not to blame the rat's failure to learn to press the lever on its dumbness and laziness, it is also a good general rule for the professor not to blame the student's failure to learn the intricacies or even the rudi-

---

*Editors' Note: Nancy Neef was one of the reviewers of the original version of this chapter. Nancy constructed her review as a dialog with the author, in which she responded to various statements in the paper. The author responded by inserting his reactions to Reviewer B (as Nancy at that time was known to him). With the consent of both participants, we have unmasked Reviewer B and are publishing their interaction as an addendum to the chapter.

ments of behavior analysis on his or her dumbness and laziness. Only neophyte operant conditioners excuse their own teacher or trainer failure by blaming the pupil or victim, but I frequently observe even experienced behavior analysis professors excusing their own failures by blaming the student; in fact, I occasionally catch myself doing that.

However, if I had been writing this chapter for college students, I would have emphasized what they could do to manage their own study behavior so that they could succeed in spite of the suboptimal instruction typical of most courses in most universities, even many behavior analytic courses. I am, however, pleased to acknowledge that many behavior analysts are much more knowledgeable about, and much more conscientious in their use of, effective instructional technology than is the average professor. But I am still saddened by our frequent failure to practice what we preach.

Also, I think the professor who puts effort into using good behaviorally based performance management technology and good behaviorally based instructional technology in his or her course will have students who learn a lot more than will the professor who tries to get the students to more effectively manage their academic behavior, regardless of whether those efforts at student improvement are behaviorally based or merely the traditional exhortation that the students should be responsible adults. I have seen no convincing evidence that even we behavior analysts have the technology to make such personality changes in adults. We are much better at changing the current contingencies governing adult behavior than we are at changing the values and self-management repertoires of adults.

### This Chapter
"There are only dumb and lazy professors."

*Neef:* That seems conceptually inconsistent with the "don't blame the victim" theme; if the "subject is always right," doesn't that apply to everyone, including professor-species?

Similarly, a reader might say, "There are no dumb and lazy professors, only dumb and lazy authors who resort to calling professors dumb and lazy," but that would fail to acknowledge that the author's statement is a reflection of his reinforcement history. Maybe the statement was meant only to remind professors of its implications with respect to students, but I wonder if insults are really the best way to promote receptivity to the message. If "practicing what we preach" is what is being advocated, I don't think such statements are examples of it (I'm quite sure the author doesn't preach the use of sarcastic and derogatory statements as a behavior change strategy for students).

*Malott's reply:* Of course I am being conceptually inconsistent; that's the joke. Of course the behavior of us professors and, yes, us authors, is merely a product of our behavioral histories and the current contingencies, and we are no more to be blamed than are our students. And, yes, I was trying to bring closer to home the point that we should not blame the students for our failure to arrange effective performance management and instructional systems.

Having failed to find any way that will promote more than lip-service receptivity to this message and more than I'm-too-busy excuses for not implementing effective behavioral technology, I am guilty of letting my "natural" tendency toward sarcasm and irony out of the bottle.

### This Chapter
"The students are always right. The students you have to work with are the students you have to work with."

*Neef:* True, and it serves us to be reminded of it. But the power of that excellent message is diluted in the way it is delivered. My attention was diverted from the truth and usefulness of the point to what I found not to be true or useful about the context for the point. Examples: My colleagues (here and at other institutions), like the professors I had, do practice what they teach. They do not always have the luxury of relying on students to do most of the work for academic credit as with BATS because the students' programs (especially those with licensure requirements) are intensive as it is, and many students do not have the financial resources to pay for the additional credit hours. If my colleagues are among the "ninety percent of the professional behavior analysts [who] don't get their Association for Behavior Analysis presentation proposal in until 5 days before the deadline," it is probably because they are helping students with *their* presentations and proposals while managing numerous other responsibilities. Their "thrills" aren't "cheap" and are associated with students succeeding, sometimes at the expense of a great deal of effort. Yes, we occasionally lapse into complaints about the few students who don't succeed (actually, the complaints are more lament than indignation), but given that we do not have unlimited resources and time (nor perhaps the technology) to remedy the histories of some students, it would not be productive to demean and assign guilt to faculty members for those occasional failures. Sometimes members of the administration and the student body do appreciate "how wonderful we faculty members really are and how hard we work," but to the extent that they don't, et tu, Brutus?

*Malott's reply:* Yes, many behavior analytic professors do make effective use of behavior analysis in their university teaching. And, yes, there are program constraints on the extent to which advanced students can be involved in teaching beginning students. But many more behavior analytic professors make little effective use of behavior analysis and expend little effort in trying to work within program constraints to provide opportunities for involvement to their advanced students that will benefit both those students and the beginning students.

I wish our deadline brinkmanship on submitting our proposals was because we were devoting so much of our time to effective teaching. But my point is not that professors don't work hard. Many do, although often their hard work is directed more at furthering their research careers and not at being optimally effective teachers. Even when it is directed at teaching, their hard work may be more consumed by traditional instructional technologies (e.g., lectures) than by behavioral technology. However, my informal observation is that, even without heavy-duty publish-or-perish contingencies, and even without heavy commitments to helping students get their ABA proposals written, we professors often have a strong tendency toward procrastination, just as our students do in suboptimally structured learning environments. Therefore, we should hesitate to criticize them when they are poorly prepared for our classes. Instead, we should try to provide them with optimally structured learning environments.

Of course I agree that we professors get very rich thrills from our students' successes. I find my students' passing their PhD orals as emotionally rewarding as I do watching them get married. But in saying, "Professors get a cheap thrill by being indignant about half of their students failing the midterm," my point was that many professors find it automatically, emotionally reinforcing to be indignant about their students' failures; this lets those professors off the hook for having failed to provide the students with the support and structure they need.

Of course we are sometimes appreciated, except at contract negotiation time. And, of course, my behavior is as controlled by cheap emotional thrills as is the next professor's—unfortunately.

### This Chapter

Your "goals should be that your students . . . love behavior analysis."

*Neef:* Again, true, and it serves us to be reminded of it. We say someone loves something when, in a free operant situation, the person typically chooses to engage in it. For example, we determine that a person loves jazz when, given multiple alternatives and all else being equal, he chooses to play jazz. But I don't see much reflection of that goal or outcome in the manuscript as it pertains to behavior analysis. Instead, the focus is on the faculty member's arrangement of "decrements in aversiveness" with respect to "the avoidance behavior of starting to work on the assignment." Presumably, procrastination would be less of a problem with assignments that students "loved."

*Malott's reply:* Would that it were true, but I think life and behavioral contingencies are much more complex than that. For example, I really love reading your criticism of my manuscript. And I love even more replying to it. Yet your critique has been lying around on my hard drive, unanswered, for 2 months. And when do I choose to work on it? Only when I have drifted so far beyond the deadline that further procrastination will result in certain professional humiliation, complete alienation of my highly valued OSU friends and colleagues, and the loss of the opportunity for this chapter to be published.

Yes, part of my failure to work on this manuscript is because I have been finishing up other manuscripts that were even further behind the deadline. But, unfortunately for my self-respect, that is not the whole story. I had a 2-week between-semester break set aside to work on these delinquent manuscripts. But what did I do? I worked on other, lower priority tasks, surfed the Web, downloaded MP3 files (among other things), and watched a few DVDs. Was it because I love these other activities more? Not really. I think it was because they are easier, less psychologically and intellectually effortful.

But now that the hounds of failure are snapping at my heels with sufficient proximity that I am breaking out into a cold sweat and finally starting to work on this chapter, I love working on this chapter. The fact that my starting it, and even my maintaining it, is a result of aversive control does not detract in the slightest from the pure emotional and intellectual joy of typing these words.

Furthermore, even if I did love watching DVDs more than the intellectual activity of writing this chapter, the fact that I am now doing this writing as a result of avoidance contingencies still does not detract from the value of the emotional and intellectual reinforcers contingent on my writing.

This is consistent with our student evaluations saying that the students greatly appreciate the way our frequent quizzes cause them to make frequent, thoughtful contact with our instructional materials and that they love the instructional materials and consequently that they love behavior analysis. Yes, love can be a major fallout of aversive control when the aversive avoidance contingencies are reasonably arranged so that they are not too aversive and success is probable.

### This Chapter

Behaviorman: ". . . we can use performance management to get rid of most of the student's procrastination, and some of our own too."

*Neef:* That depends on how procrastination is conceptualized. It seems to me that it is not absolute (as Behaviorman suggests), but relative. For example, when I am working on tasks that are due on Monday, I am by definition not working on tasks that are due on Tuesday and Wednesday. Given that I am responsible for many tasks every day, procrastination (in the sense of putting off work on a task that has a later deadline to work on one that has an earlier deadline) is inevitable. The commitments-to-time ratio usually leaves little, if any, margin for working on tasks much before the respective due dates, and it is a constant balancing act. From this perspective, planned procrastination *is* effective performance management, rather than something that *can be prevented by* effective performance management.

This applies to many of our students as well. Most of my colleagues practice the five steps to accomplishing any big task that you list (e.g.,

administering weekly quizzes over single-chapter assignments). That's the problem—when students are devoting time to studying for one class, they cannot be simultaneously studying for another, and as a result of the performance contingencies we've arranged, the faculty are all in competition for that time. (Maybe that's the real problem in need of behavior systems analysis.) To prepare for the classes they have on Tuesday, students must put off preparing for the class they have on Wednesday, and so on. If all of us arrange weekly quizzes, students will still postpone (procrastinate) studying for our quizzes until the last day. Procrastination is rarely a matter of doing nothing versus doing something, but a matter of which tasks are delayed in order to perform others.

That being said, I realize that my colleagues do not present a very representative sample of the approaches used by faculty in other courses and that procrastination is a big problem. In fact, our university newspaper recently featured the "discovery" of a decade of research by a faculty member in another department that undergraduate students often procrastinate working on their assignments and therefore are at risk of not doing well. He exhorted students not to procrastinate. I think he would benefit from the information in this manuscript.

*Malott's reply:* Yes, we are all trying to do more than we have time to do—we professors, our grad students, and many of our undergrad students. Furthermore, we are all our own worst enemies, often taking on more tasks than we have time for and sometimes eagerly searching for more tasks even though our plates are already overflowing. But even with overflowing plates, I find that we often fail to use our time as effectively as we might. And even among those with overflowing plates, I find considerable variability among my colleagues as to how close they must get to the deadline before they start working on a task. In other words, I suspect that many of the 5% who get their ABA proposals in well ahead of time do so in spite of their having as many important competing contingencies as do the 95% of us who wait until the last moment or the moment after. Again, my point has not been to criticize my colleagues' self-management skills, but rather to criticize the frequent failure of empathy for the students that I observe among my colleagues.

### This Chapter

". . . we try to fix the problem based on our behavior analytic educated guesses. We then evaluate our fixes the next semester. In other words, this is real-world R&D (research and development), not scholarly research."

*Neef:* There is a great deal of research on schedule performance that is relevant to the issues addressed by this manuscript (especially the problems of student procrastination); I would have found it very helpful if some connection were made to those findings. "Real-world R&D" is great, but the "guesses" can be more "educated" (thereby limiting some of the trial and error) if they make use of what is known.

*Malott's reply:* On the contrary, I think that there is essentially no research on schedule performance that is relevant to the issues addressed by this manuscript, unfortunately. Here is why:

> *Grandma's Wisdom:* The problem with today's generation is they cannot delay their gratification.
> *Basic Research:* Let us operationalize (danger) Grandma. She means that we do not "choose" (danger) larger delayed reinforcers. Instead, today's generation "chooses" smaller immediate reinforcers. And we've proven it with pigeon research. But we can establish "self-control" (danger) by "fading" in delays for larger reinforcers.
> *Bridging Research:* "ADHD" (danger) kids show "impulsivity" (danger). "ADHD" (danger) kids "choose" the immediate reinforcers, although those reinforcers are smaller, of lower quality, and less frequent. "ADHD" (danger) kids are more influenced by "immediacy of reinforcement" (dan-

ger). But we can establish "self-control" (danger) by "fading" in delays for larger reinforcers.

*Malott:* I think operationalization of everyday terms is dangerous. Operationalizing everyday terms buys everyday face validity for our esoteric research. But operationalization does not eliminate the mentalistic and free-willist connotations of those words (e.g., *ADHD, impulsivity, choose, self-control*). Operationalization causes the reification and thus the creation of hypothetical constructs (explanatory fictions) such as impulsivity and self-control.

I think Grandma's view of self-control is wrong. So is the basic researcher's and the bridging researcher's approach to self-control. The basic and bridging research is excellent methodologically. However, I think the presumed relation between basic and bridging research is often nonexistent. Basic animal research uses direct-acting contingencies of reinforcement, with the reinforcer delayed less than 60 seconds. Of course, it is done with nonverbal subjects. However, bridging research often uses indirect-acting contingencies of reinforcement, with the reinforcer delayed up to 24 hours, and it is done with verbal subjects who frequently have received verbal instructions. Usually in these cases, the behavior is directly controlled by contingencies induced by rule-governed analogues to reinforcement contingencies, not the direct-acting reinforcement contingencies themselves.

Here is what I think is wrong with the Grandma/researcher theory: Yes, today's generation and ADHD kids cannot delay gratification. And, yes, they are controlled only by direct-acting contingencies with fairly immediate outcomes. But that's also true of Grandma and the researchers. No one ever escapes the tyranny of immediate outcomes, although superficially some occasionally seem to do so.

Let me support my argument with obvious, contrary, hypothetical examples: Suppose you had a normal preverbal kid and you wanted to condition his glancing toward a doll. Each time he glanced, you gave him a sip of milk, but 30 minutes after each glance. No way will glancing be conditioned, even if the kid is not ADHD. No one ever escapes the tyranny of immediate outcomes.

Suppose I wanted to condition your glancing at me. Each time you glanced at me, I gave you a sip of highly desired, expensive booze, but 30 minutes after each glance. No way will your glance be conditioned, even though you are not ADHD, unless you figured out the rule describing the delayed-outcome contingency. No one ever really escapes the tyranny of immediate outcomes, not even sophisticated behavior analysts.

Grandma and the researchers all believe what I call the myth of poor self-control—poor self-control occurs because immediate outcomes control our behavior better than delayed outcomes do. Let me support my argument that this is a myth with more obvious, although clearly hypothetical, examples selected to intuitively prove that delay doesn't matter much:

- The smoker will definitely die a painful, lung cancer, cardio death next month if she takes one more puff.

- The obese, slothful couch potato will definitely have the body of (Brad Pitt/Brittney Spears—user selects) next month if he or she works out one hour today.

- The ADHD kid will get a lifetime subscription to *Spiderman* comics starting next month if he studies continuously for 2 hours today.

- Sam Speeder will definitely be killed one month from now (do not ask why) if he speeds in his pickup unbuckled and drunk today.

I suggest that if these people believed the rules describing those contingencies, the rules would undoubtedly control their behavior. Why? Because the people know the rules, and the rules describe contingencies with outcomes that are sizable and probable. The delay will not matter much.

On the other hand, consider these everyday examples of "poor self-control":

- Tracy speeds unbuckled and drunk because the probability is too low that he will get in trouble.

- The sloth fails to exercise because each hour of exercise produces only a small benefit, although the benefits accumulating over hundreds of hours are significant.

- The smoker smokes because one more puff produces only a small harmful effect, although the harmful effects accumulating over hundreds of packs are significant.

This is what I consider to be the truth about "poor self-control": Rules that are easy to follow describe outcomes that are both sizable and probable. The delay is not crucial. Rules that are hard to follow describe outcomes that are either too small (although often of cumulative significance) or too improbable. The delay is not crucial.

Therefore, I think there is little relation between basic/bridging research on schedules or self-control and the real world to which those results are often overextrapolated. Why? Operant research studies contingencies with delayed outcomes. Real-world "self-control" problems usually result from contingencies with small but cumulative outcomes or improbable outcomes, and the delay is essentially irrelevant. On the other hand, I suggest that the implied rule-governed behavior model of "self-control" is theoretically rigorous and loaded with practical significance. Of course, I could be wrong; this is only my humble opinion.

To the tune of "Brother, Can You Spare a Dime," here's a little number I call "Brother, Can You Paradigm":

Once I built a model
it was scorned by all;
it wouldn't toe the party line.
Once I built a model,
that was all.
Brother, can you paradigm?

So much to cover,
so against the grain,
and so little time.
So much to cover,
it strains the brain.
Brother, shift the paradigm.

The analysis of self-control described in this chapter is based on Malott (2002) and is elaborated in Malott and Suarez (2004).

*Neef:*  I like Malott's approach to higher education, if not his approach to guilt tripping. In fact, I am a beneficiary of his educational approach given that he was one of my most influential professors (for which I am grateful). So if he takes exception to any of my comments, "don't blame the student (reviewer) . . . ."

*Malott's reply:*  I wish I and my instructional systems could take even the smallest credit for this thoughtful, insightful, informed review, but I fear our impact is much too transient. Instead I suspect the repertoire that produced this excellent review is much more a result of Neef's preschool and post-WMU experiences.

# REFERENCES

Bacon, D. L., Fulton, B. J., & Malott, R. W. (1982). Improving staff performance through the use of task checklists. *Journal of Organizational Behavior Management, 4,* 17–25

Bosch, S. (2001). Making of a textbook on behavior analysis and autism: A behavior analytic approach. Unpublished doctoral dissertation, Western Michigan University, Kalamazoo.

Brethower, D., & Smalley, K. (1998). *Performance-based instruction: Linking training to business results.* San Francisco: Jossey-Bass/Pfeiffer and Washington, DC: International Society for Performance Improvement.

Dean, M. R., Fulton, B. F., & Malott, R. W. (1983). The effects of self-management on academic performance. *Teaching of Psychology, 10,* 77–81.

Garcia, M. E., & Malott, R. W. (1988). Una solucion al fenomeno "todo menos tesis y disertacion." *Revista Intercontinental de Psicologia y Educacion, 1,* 205–216.

Garcia, M. E., Malott, R. W., & Brethower, D. (1988). A system of thesis and dissertation supervision: Helping graduate students succeed. *Teaching of Psychology, 15,* 186–191.

Gilbert, T. F. (1996). *Human competence: Engineering worthy performance* (3rd ed). Amherst, MA: HRD Press.

Greenwood, C. R., Dinwiddie, G., Bailey, V., Carta, J. J., Dorsey, D., Kohler, F. W., Nelson, C., Rotholz, D., & Schulte, D. (1987). Field replication of classwide peer tutoring. *Journal of Applied Behavior Analysis, 20,* 151–160.

Groeger, C., & Malott, R. W. (in press). Preparation for the GRE. *Journal of Behavioral Education.*

Heward, W. L. (1994). Three "low-tech" strategies for increasing the frequency of active student responses during group instruction. In R. Gardner, D. M. Sainato, J. O. Cooper, T. E. Heron, W. L. Heward, J. Eshleman, & T. A. Grossi (Eds.), *Behavior analysis in education: Focus on measurably superior instruction* (pp. 283–320) Pacific Grove, CA: Brooks/Cole.

Jackson, M., & Malott, R. W. (1994). Helping high-risk black college students. In R. Gardner, D. M. Sainato, J. O. Cooper, T. E. Heron, W. L. Heward, J. Eshleman, & T. A. Grossi (Eds.), *Behavior analysis in education: Focus on measurably superior instruction* (pp. 349–363). Pacific Grove, CA: Brooks/Cole.

Mager, R. F. (1984). *Developing attitude toward learning* (2nd ed.). Belmont, CA: Lake.

Malott, R. W. (1984). In search of human perfectibility. In W. L. Heward, T. E. Heron, D. S. Hill, & J. Trap-Porter (Eds.), *Focus on behavior analysis in education* (pp. 218–245). Columbus, OH: Charles E. Merrill.

Malott, R. W. (1986). Self-management, rule-governed behavior, and everyday life. In H. W. Reese & L. J. Parrott (Eds.), *Behavioral science: Philosophical, methodological, and empirical advances* (pp. 207–228). Hillsdale, NJ: Erlbaum.

Malott, R. W. (1989). The achievement of evasive goals: Control by rules describing contingencies that are not direct-acting. In S. C. Hayes (Ed.), *Rule-governed behavior: Cognition, contingencies, and instructional control* (pp. 269–322). New York: Plenum.

Malott, R. W. (1992a). Should we train applied behavior analysts to be researchers? *Journal of Applied Behavior Analysis, 25,* 83–88.

Malott, R. W. (1992b). Follow-up commentary on training behavior analysts. *Journal of Applied Behavior Analysis, 25,* 513–515.

Malott, R. W. (1993). A theory of rule-governed behavior and organizational behavior management. *Journal of Organizational Behavior Management, 12,* 45–65.

Malott, R. W. (1993, October). The three-contingency model applied to performance management in higher education. *Educational Technology, 33,* 21–28.

Malott, R. W. (1998). Performance management and welfare reform: The three-contingency model of performance management applied to welfare reform. *Behavior and Social Issues, 8,* 109–140.

Malott, R. W. (2002). What OBM needs is more Jewish mothers. *Journal of Organizational Behavior Management, 22,* 71–87.

Malott, R. W. (2002, May). *Everything you know about self-control is wrong.* Acceptance talk at the SABA awards ceremony of the Association for Behavior Analysis, Toronto, Canada.

Malott, R. W. (in press). Self-management. In M. Hersen (Ed.), *Encyclopedia of behavior modification and cognitive behavior therapy. Volume One: Adult clinical applications.* Thousand Oaks, CA: Sage.

Malott, R. W., & Garcia, M. E. (1987). A goal-directed model approach for the design of human performance systems. *Journal of Organizational Behavior Management, 9,* 125–159.

Malott, R. W., & Garcia, M. E. (1991). The role of private events in rule-governed behavior. In L. J. Hayes & P. Chase (Eds.), *Dialogues on verbal behavior* (pp. 237–254). Reno, NV: Context Press.

Malott, R. W., Malott, M. E., & Shimamune, S. (1993). Comments on rule-governed behavior. *Journal of Organizational Behavior Management, 12,* 91–101.

Malott, R. W., Shimamune, S., & Malott, M. E. (1993). Rule-governed behavior and organizational behavior management: An analysis of interventions. *Journal of Organizational Behavior Management, 12,* 103–116.

Malott, R. W., & Suarez, E. W. (2004). *Principles of behavior* (5th ed.). Upper Saddle River, NJ: Prentice Hall.

Malott, R. W., Vunovich, P. L. Boettcher, W., & Groeger, C. (1995). Saving the world by teaching behavior analysis: A behavioral-systems approach. *The Behavior Analyst, 18,* 341–356.

Markle, S. M. (1990). *Designs for instructional designers* (3rd ed.). Champaign, IL: Stipes.

Moran, D. J., & Malott, R. W. (Eds.). (2005). *Empirically supported educational methods.* San Diego, CA: Elsevier.

Miller, J. M., Goodyear-Orwat, A., & Malott, R. W. (1996). The effects of intensive, extensive, structured study on GRE scores. *Journal of Behavioral Education, 6* (4), 369–379.

Pavlov, I. P. (1927/1928). *Lectures on conditioned reflexes* (W. H. Gantt, Trans.). New York: International.

Rollofson, R. L., & Malott, R. W. (1972). An empirical evaluation of student-led discussion. *Psychological Reports, 30,* 531–535.

Shimamune, S., & Malott, R. W. (1994). An analysis of concept learning: Simple conceptual control and definition-based conceptual control. *The Analysis of Verbal Behavior 12,* 67–78.

Snycerski, S., Laraway, S., Byrne, T., & Poling, A. (1999). Acquisition of lever-press responding with delayed consequences in rats: Is a minute too long? *Mexican Journal of Behavior Analysis, 25,* 341–350.

Suarez, E. T. (2001). *A behavioral systems analysis of textbook quality improvement.* Unpublished doctoral dissertation, Western Michigan University, Kalamazoo.

Sundberg, C., Ober, B., Wysocki, T., & Malott, R. W. (1978). An examination of the effects of remediation on student performance in a PSI psychology course. *Journal of Personalized Instruction, 3,* 93–97.

Sutphin, B., Byrne, T., & Poling, A. (1998). Response acquisition with delayed reinforcement: A comparison of two-lever procedures. *Journal of the Experimental Analysis of Behavior, 69,* 17–28.

Tiemann, P. W., & Markle, S. M. (1978). *Analyzing instructional content: A guide to instruction and evaluation.* Champaign, IL: Stipes.

Vunovich, P. L. (1996). *Fluency training on quantitative skills tested by the graduate record examination*. Unpublished doctoral dissertation, Western Michigan University, Kalamazoo.

Welsh, T. M., Malott, R. W., & Kent, H. M. (1980). The use of behavioral contracting to eliminate procrastination in a PSI course. *Journal of Personalized Instruction, 4,* 103.

Yaber, G. E., & Malott, R. W. (1993). Computer-fluency training: A resource for higher education. *Education and Teaching of Children, 16,* 306–315.

## STUDY QUESTIONS AND FOLLOW-UP ACTIVITIES

1.  What are your reactions to B. F. Skinner's dictum, "The subject is always right"? One may support the idea that if environmental contingencies have not been adjusted, an organism will not behave accordingly, thus "there's no such thing as a dumb or lazy rat." However, Ivan Pavlov described four basic "types" of dogs: sanguine dogs were strong, lively, and active; melancholic dogs were slow and depressed; choleric dogs were unstable and impetuous; and phlegmatic dogs were inert and slothful (Pavlov, 1927/1928). Do you believe there are "dumb (slow) and lazy (depressed) students and professors" or only melancholic dogs?

2.  Consider how the skills training model of education applies to your current teaching. Use this model to outline how you might improve the organization and delivery of your instruction.

3.  Use the performance management model of task accomplishment to help you complete an assignment, manuscript, project, or presentation. You will need to (1) divide the big task into a series of small tasks, (2) specify exactly what each small task is and how to accomplish it, (3) set frequent deadlines for those tasks, (4) monitor task accomplishment, and (5) provide small but significant outcomes for each monitored task.

4.  Write a mock debate between Professor Tradition and Behaviorwoman in which they discuss behavior analytic approaches to college teaching.

5.  Using one of Malott's approaches to training students, diagram not only an example and nonexample, but also an original example of the three-contingency model of performance management that will help you generate ideas for decreasing self-procrastination or student procrastination. Warning: Stay away from Professor Tradition. Let Behaviorwoman act as your guide.

6.  Malott mentions that during a 2-week break, instead of working on delinquent manuscripts, he surfed the Web, downloaded MP3 files, and watched a few DVDs. He believes that he did so not because he loves these activities more, but because "they are easier, less psychologically, intellectually effortful." Do you feel the research on choice making, such as someone choosing a low-quality reinforcer over a high effort-task, is applicable to the debate between Malott ("there is essentially no research on schedule performance") and Neef ("there is a great deal of research on schedule performance")?

7.  List two or three subsystems (e.g., the behavioral research supervisory system) that could improve your current graduate program. Discuss how the subsystems could be implemented and evaluated.

8.  Continue the dialogue between Malott and Neef. Using Neef's comments as an example, select two or three statements from the chapter and write an insightful and informed response to each statement. Write reactions to these responses based on Malott's perspective.

9.  Will you complete these discussion questions without a deadline or do you need "the deadline-induced analogue avoidance contingencies that keep our world in its orderly orbit"? What contingencies are in place to support your completion of these questions?

---

Study questions and follow-up activities prepared by Summer J. Ferreri and Charles L. Wood.

# PART IV

## Perspectives on the Current and Future Functions of Behavior Analysis in Education

Chapter 13     Inclusion and Applied Behavior Analysis: Mending Fences and Building Bridges
*Ilene S. Schwartz*

Chapter 14     Building Behaviors versus Suppressing Behaviors: Perspectives and Prescriptions for Positive Schoolwide Behavior Change
*Lloyd D. Peterson* and *Laura Lacy-Rismiller*

Chapter 15     Plato's Allegory of the Cave Revisited: Disciples of the Light Appeal to the Pied Pipers and Prisoners in the Darkness
*Timothy E. Heron, Matthew J. Tincani, Stephanie M. Peterson,* and *April D. Miller*

Chapter 16     The Effects of "Behavior-Speak" on Public Attitudes toward Behavioral Interventions: A Cross-Cultural Argument for Using Conversational Language to Describe Behavioral Interventions to the General Public
*Amos Rolider* and *Saul Axelrod*

Chapter 17     Applied Research: The Separation of Applied Behavior Analysis and Precision Teaching
*John O. Cooper*

Chapter 18     The Detrimental Effects of Reward Hypothesis: Persistence of a View in the Face of Disconfirming Evidence
*Judy Cameron*

Chapter 19     Reasons Applied Behavior Analysis Is Good for Education and Why Those Reasons Have Been Insufficient
*William L. Heward*

### CHAPTER 13

# Inclusion and Applied Behavior Analysis
## Mending Fences and Building Bridges

*Ilene S. Schwartz*

Often, when discussing what comprises a high-quality education for children with disabilities, professionals who advocate inclusive education and applied behavior analysts are on opposite sides of the proverbial fence. This is difficult for many of us with expertise on both sides of the fence who believe that an effective educational program for all children with disabilities must include the best of inclusive education and applied behavior analysis. Encouraging behavior analysts and inclusion advocates to work together may be more difficult than it sounds, even though many researchers and teachers have strong credentials in both camps. Many members of both groups have strong (often negative) opinions about the other, often based on misinformation and little or no actual contact.

We must actively build bridges between these two groups of strong advocates for positive student outcomes. But, as engineers have learned from years of experience, many complex elements must be considered when building a bridge, and going forward without having a well-developed plan can lead to disaster. To build a structurally sound bridge between inclusive education and applied behavior analysis, we need to understand the basics of both. We also need to identify some of the areas in which both groups may have blundered in practice and suggest strategies to improve outcomes for all students.

The purpose of this chapter is threefold. First, I will define inclusive education and applied behavior analysis using seminal writings from both fields. Then, I will identify a series of frequent missteps I have observed on the part of inclusion advocates and behavior analysts and suggest strategies to improve our practice. Finally, I will present an outcome framework for describing results of inclusive education that may help behavior analysts and other educators to work together to plan and implement the best possible education for all children.

## WHAT IS INCLUSIVE EDUCATION?

Inclusion is one of those topics that engenders strong opinions and often conflicting, incomplete, or incorrect definitions. In fact, even in the field of special education there are strong divided views about what counts as inclusive education and whether inclusion is the most effective way to educate children with disabilities (e.g., Kauffman & Hallahan, 1993; Vaughn & Schumm, 1995). Some question whether children with mild disabilities have suffered from the "illusion of inclusion" (Kauffman & Hallahan, 1993), and others continue to point to inclusion as a matter of civil rights (Turnbull & Turnbull, 1998).

For the purpose of this chapter an inclusive program is defined as one that *provides educational intervention to students with and without disabilities in a common setting and provides appropriate levels of instruction and support to meet the needs of all students.* Part of this support includes teacher training and support, curriculum modification, and accommodations at school to ensure that children with disabilities receive high-quality instruction using evidence-based instructional strategies. Even with this definition we need to remember that, as Allen and Schwartz (2001) stated, "Inclusion is not a set of strategies or a placement issue. Inclusion is about belonging to a community—a group of friends, a school community, or a neighborhood" (p. 4). This part of the definition reminds us that inclusion is not just a school issue. It is an issue about choice, lifestyle, community, and friends that does not end when the school bell rings, on the last day of school in June, or when a child ages out of special education. Inclusive education is a commitment that we make to children with disabilities and their families to help them live a life in which they accomplish their goals, achieve their dreams, and create a lifestyle with which they are satisfied.

Unlike mainstreaming, integration, and other attempts at educating children with disabilities in the least restrictive environment, successful inclusion assumes that modifications and adaptations to the general education curriculum will be necessary to accommodate the needs of students. Students do not earn their way into inclusion or need to keep up with the material to maintain their placement. In inclusive schools, children are placed in general education classrooms with their chronologically age-matched peers, and supports are added to ensure the success of all. As Stainback and Stainback (1990) stated:

> Inclusion means providing all students within the mainstream appropriate educational programs that are challenging yet geared to their capabilities and needs as well as any support and assistance they and/or their teachers may need to be successful in the mainstream. But an inclusive school also goes beyond this. An inclusive school is a place where everyone belongs, is accepted, supports, and is supported by his or her peers and other members of the school community in the course of having his or her educational needs met. (p. 3)

## WHAT IS APPLIED BEHAVIOR ANALYSIS?

Applied behavior analysis (ABA) is "the science in which procedures derived from the principles of behavior are systematically applied to improve socially significant behavior to a meaningful degree and to demonstrate experimentally that the procedures employed were responsible for the improvement in behavior" (Cooper, Heron & Heward, 1987, p. 14). ABA is not used only in education or with people with disabilities. It also has uses in industrial safety, environmental causes, sports coaching, and business, as well as in education. As Baer, Wolf, and Risley (1968) stated in their seminal article outlining the current dimensions of ABA, "Applied research is constrained to examining behaviors which are socially important, rather than convenient for study. It also implies that behavior analysts should study those behaviors in their usual social setting rather than a 'laboratory' setting" (p. 92).

These definitions embody the core of what makes ABA an important, unique, and somewhat controversial academic discipline. It is important because it attempts to solve problems that affect the quality of life for many individuals; it is unique because it cares about what those consumers think of the intervention and the outcome; and it is somewhat controversial because it acknowledges that, regardless of the objective evaluation data, a program that consumers do not like has an increased likelihood of failure (Schwartz & Baer, 1991).

The preceding definition of ABA is contrary to the commonly held perception, especially in the special education community. Many educators view ABA as discrete trial teaching, with the discipline consisting of little more than an adult sitting knee to knee with a child with autism in a distraction-free setting, providing mass trials of decontextualized teaching. Many professionals and members of the general public view ABA as a mechanistic, robotic, teacher-directed, authoritarian way to teach. Viewing ABA as a "self-examining, self-evaluating, discovery-oriented research procedure" (Baer et al., 1968, p. 91) that embraces a contextual world view (Baer, Wolf & Risley, 1987; Morris, 1997) is not a mainstream interpretation of ABA. However, it is the accurate way to view it.

Nothing in the definition of inclusive education or ABA would interfere with professionals from these disciplines working together. In fact, the two disciplines share many philosophical tenets. Both believe that all children can learn and deserve a high-quality education. Both believe that the intervention must be effective and acceptable; that is, it must have a high degree of social and ecological validity. Finally, both believe in the importance of instruction taking place in natural contexts. Although studying the core writings of the two disciplines does not turn up major areas of disagreement, in practice much contention often exists between behavior analysts and inclusion advocates. Perhaps by examining some of the blunders both sides have made we will learn how to build a bridge across these differences.

## INCLUSION MISSTEPS

Although there are excellent examples of inclusive programs across the country (see Odom, 2002, for examples of preschool programs, and Grenot-Scheyer, Fischer, & Staub, 2001, for examples of programs across the age range), some program practices being implemented in the name of inclusion are neither inclusive nor good practice under any circumstances. Implementing high-quality inclusive programming requires more than a philosophy or verbal behavior. (Although these components may be necessary, they are certainly not sufficient.) Implementing a high-quality inclusive program requires all the instructional expertise that a high-quality segregated special education program requires. In addition, it requires that teachers be able to work collaboratively with other adults, understand and appreciate the general education curriculum and the school's culture, and be flexible. I address some of the most common missteps that I have observed in so-called inclusive programs in the following sections.

## Assuming That "Being There" Is Enough

One of the axioms of inclusive education is that children with disabilities will learn appropriate skills and behaviors by spending time with their typically developing peers. Although being a member of a group and participating in normalized settings is important (see the later section on the outcome framework), being there is just not enough.

At this point in the evolution of mainstreaming, integration, and inclusion, we have about 40 years of research on the topic. The first report of planned inclusion was published by K. Eileen Allen and her colleagues in 1964 (Allen, Hart, Buell, Harris, & Wolf, 1964). One of the most robust findings that these 40 years of research has yielded is that if you put a child with disabilities and a child without disabilities in a room together without any specialized programming, you will most likely get a child with disabilities and a child without disabilities who are in the same room, but who are not interacting (Odom & Brown, 1993).

To achieve true social interaction and integration, we need to plan for it (Sandall & Schwartz, 2002). An important part of this planning process is to figure out what type of supports are needed by the child with disabilities, the child(ren) without disabilities, and the adults who work in the environment and how to provide those supports. If we want inclusion to work, we need to figure out the most appropriate environment for inclusion, what we expect the children with and without disabilities to do, the expectations for the adults, and whether those expectations are appropriate. Inclusion is an active process; "being there" implies that it is a passive process.

## "Dumping" Rather Than Planning

I experience the following story, or some version of it, more often than I would like to admit. I meet a general education teacher at a social gathering, and she asks me what I do. When I say that I teach special education and do research in inclusion, she shakes her head in disgust and says, "inclusion does not work." She goes on to explain that her one experience with inclusion consisted of a student with a disability being placed in her classroom with no advanced planning and no ongoing support. At this point I explain that she did not experience inclusion; rather, she experienced dumping, and I agree that dumping does not work.

Dumping seems more prevalent in some areas than inclusion. Inclusion involves teamwork and planning. Inclusion requires that all participants, including the general education teacher, be involved in program planning, implementation, and evaluation. Inclusion requires that if training for the adults in the setting is required (e.g., the general education teacher, paraprofessionals), it be done before the child is placed in the setting. Inclusion requires ongoing consultation and support as needed to all members of the team. Inclusion means that if a child with learning disabilities is in a general education classroom, she receives the type of explicit instruction needed to ensure that she is making meaningful academic progress. Inclusion is not a last-minute decision. It is a process, and it

takes time and commitment to implement it with integrity.

## Not Individualizing to Meet Students' Needs

One of the basic tenets of special education is individualization. Our discipline and the federal law both declare individualization as a core principle. We often forget this, however, when we plan for inclusion. Time and again, parents come to IEP meetings requesting that their child be educated in an inclusive setting and are told, "our district does not do that," "your child does not have the right set of skills," or "we can do inclusion, but not at your neighborhood school because it is not our inclusive school."

Decisions made at IEP meetings, including placement, should be based on students' needs, not existing district programs or what has happened in the past. Educational practices should be based on the research and tailored to meet the individual needs of students. High-quality inclusive practices must be student centered; that is, they must address the priorities identified by the student and family and provide adequate support and instruction so that the student makes meaningful progress toward those priorities.

## Overusing Instructional Assistants

Parents of children with disabilities in inclusive schools often advocate for one-on-one instructional assistants for their children. They seem to be under the impression that more adult attention is better. Therefore, in many inclusive schools, the adults who interact most often with students with disabilities are instructional assistants. This results in the majority of instruction for our most challenging students being provided by the people in the school with the least amount of training. Many of these instructional assistants have received little or no training and may have no experience working with children with disabilities when they begin. These assistants, who are most often kindhearted to the students, unwittingly reinforce inappropriate behaviors, interfere with potential interactions with peers, systematically teach students to be dependent on adults, allow students to escape from demands, and often complete the assignments for the students. At the same time, the teacher observes that the student is happy, sometimes engaged, and docile (cf. Winett & Winkler, 1972) and turns her attention to the other 20-something students in her class.

## Focusing on Activities Rather Than Objectives

In many inclusive classrooms there is an emphasis on fitting in with the ongoing activity, rather than focusing on addressing specific objectives. This focus on objectives often results from a lack of cohesive planning by the IEP team, including the instructional assistant. For example, if the activity is journal writing and no planning has been done, the instructional assistant may hand-over-hand prompt the child to write a sentence, rather than allowing the child to work independently on his objectives of tracing shapes, appropriate pencil grasp, and beginning at the top of the paper and working to the bottom. By not outlining the students' objectives in an activity matrix (Sandall & Schwartz, 2002), the IEP team ensures that these objectives will be lost in the flurry of often-changing classroom activities.

## Underestimating the Effectiveness of Explicit Instruction

Teaching works. The No Child Left Behind legislation requires educators to use evidence-based instructional practices in our public schools. Luckily, the special education literature is full of instructional strategies with evidence of their effectiveness. Although our discipline has validated many strategies to teach many students many different skills, these strategies are often not used in or even acknowledged in inclusive classrooms. Rather than focusing on how to teach a specific skill or behavior, the team fo-

cuses on how to feign normality during every part of the day. Some teachers resist adding extra supports for children with disabilities because they think it is not fair to the typically developing children. It is important to remember that being fair does not mean treating everyone the same—it means striving for equally meaningful outcomes. Providing different types or amount of instruction does not interfere with inclusion—it is the essence of inclusive education. All programs should provide all students and their teachers with the types and amount of support they need to be successful.

## Assuming That Sitting Quietly Is an Appropriate Alternative to Participation

Children learn by doing. Participation (i.e., taking part in the activity) is an essential component of learning what the activity is teaching. Although ensuring the full participation of all students in the class on the same activity is not the goal of inclusive classrooms, participation (with support as necessary) in a meaningful activity is. One key to facilitating a meaningful level of participation is to use appropriate curriculum modifications and adaptations. For example, if the children in the class are reading silently, the children with disabilities could be listening to the book (or a similar book) on tape. If the children are working on creative writing, the children with disabilities could either be answering questions about a story, drawing, or dictating a story.

Another key to facilitating participation is to have a thorough knowledge, both conceptual and practical, of instructional strategies to teach important skills including on-task behavior. Teachers in inclusive classrooms must have the tools necessary (i.e., instructional strategies) to teach children to work independently, to participate in group activities, and to be active members of the classroom. By using the appropriate levels of prompting and reinforcement (e.g., token systems), teachers can facilitate high levels of engagement in classroom activities or in adapted, but similar, activities.

## Always Attending to the Squeaky Wheel

The Oberti decision (*Oberti v. Borough of Clementon School District,* 1993) states that "inclusion is a right, not a privilege." Although that is the opinion of the court, in reality, inclusion is often a privilege. Those children whose parents advocate voraciously or show up at the IEP meeting with an attorney (or both) are included. Other children, who may present the same way both educationally and behaviorally but whose parents do not know that they have the right to question the school's decision, are placed in segregated classes. For inclusive education to achieve its full potential, educators must work with all children and families to provide equal access to all opportunities.

## ABA MISSTEPS

### Assuming That "Being There" Is Not Important

Many behavior analysts discount the importance of context and experience. Many believe that where and when instruction occurs is not important. Therefore, some behavioral programs may purposefully exclude children from the mainstream "until they are ready" (cf., Lovaas, 1987; Maurice, Green & Luce, 1996), whereas others advocate removing children from class to accommodate therapists, regardless of the classroom schedule. Being a member of a classroom group can facilitate important learning opportunities and developmental outcomes (Schwartz, Staub, Gallucci, & Peck, 1995). Behavior analysts should not assume that explicit instruction is more important than the incidental learning that can occur during ongoing classroom routines and activities. We must ensure that students in inclusive classrooms have opportunities to participate in important ongoing classroom activities and routines and receive the explicit instruction they need to make meaningful progress toward their educational goals.

## Writing Ridiculous Objectives

Many families with children with autism have behavioral consultants working with them to run home programs. When these consultants attend IEP meetings or work with the school teams, one of the major areas of conflicts is objectives or target behaviors. Behavior analysts often write objectives that are contextually irrelevant or developmentally inappropriate or have ridiculous criteria. Following are some examples that I have seen on real IEPs written by board-certified behavior analysts:

- Assessing coloring by requiring that a 6-year-old nonverbal child with no functional communication or functional play skills make 70 strokes a minute on the page.

- Evaluating a child's knowledge of emotions by counting how many pictures depicting different emotions she can label a minute, despite the fact that she does not demonstrate appropriate affect with her peers.

- Spending valuable instructional time on systematic reading institution with a 3-year-old who has no play or social interaction skills, even if the child shows an interest in letters, numbers, and books.

- Teaching a 4-year-old complex cognitive skills rather than working on simple play or independence skills.

If behavior analysts are going to have an impact on what goes on in public schools, one of the first steps is to learn how to work collaboratively with school personnel and families to identify important target skills and objectives. We need to identify behaviors that are developmentally appropriate, are chronologically age appropriate, and make sense within the social context of the school.

## Focusing on the *How* of Teaching Rather Than on the *What*

Applied behavior analysts have developed a large and diverse toolbox of instructional strategies. These strategies can be used to teach people with varied strengths and require an array of skills and behaviors. As a field, however, we have focused on developing teaching strategies rather than worrying about what skills are being taught. This trend of focusing on the *how* rather than the *what* of teaching is evident in the *Journal of Applied Behavior Analysis (JABA)*. In the 2001 volume of *JABA* (Vol. 34), only 44% of the research articles addressed functional behaviors (Schwartz, 2003). This is an alarming trend for a discipline that was developed to apply behavior principles to socially important behaviors. As we work with educators to facilitate high-quality inclusion for students with disabilities, we must address functional, socially valid, and educationally relevant behaviors. Interestingly, these behaviors may be more challenging to teach because they may be less discrete and occur in more complex environments.

## Not Valuing Other Disciplines

Although behavior analysis is the discipline most often associated with evidence-based instructional strategies and effective strategies to decrease challenging behaviors, many other disciplines can make meaningful contributions to educational programming in inclusive schools. These disciplines include, but are not limited to, speech–language pathology, occupational therapy, reading specialists, mainstream psychology, general education, and mainstream special education. Professionals from these disciplines can provide essential assessment information, identify functional target behaviors, and suggest intervention strategies. Although some of these strategies may not be well validated, behavior analysts can work with these professionals to collect evaluation data. Following are two examples of how this might work.

Social stories are an intervention strategy developed by a speech–language pathologist to help children with autism and related disorders be more successful in socially complex situations by clarifying the expectations and helping them understand the perspective of others (Gray

& Gerard, 1993). Although social stories are hugely popular (a search on the Internet search engine Google turns up 5,470 hits on this entry), there is very little empirical data about this intervention. One of the few high-quality studies evaluating social stories was completed by behavior analysts and published in *JABA* (Thiemann & Goldstein, 2001). In this study, a multiple baseline design was used to evaluate social stories along with other visual support strategies to facilitate social interaction in a public school setting. This study is an excellent example of how behavior analysts can use behavioral methodology to evaluate strategies developed by other disciplines.

Another example of a class or intervention strategy that is not backed by a strong empirical base is that of sensory-based techniques, which are most often recommended by occupational therapists. Although professionals who recommend these strategies often base their work on a conceptual framework much different from that of behavior analysis, behavioral techniques can be used to assess the effectiveness of these interventions. For example, Schilling and her colleagues (Schilling, Washington, Billingsley, & Deitz, 2003) used an A-B-A-B withdrawal design to evaluate the use of therapy balls with children with ADHD. In this study they demonstrated that on-task behavior and work production increased when children sat on therapy balls instead of chairs in the classroom during language arts instruction.

## Conducting FBAs in Laboratories to Develop Treatments for Behaviors That Occur in Classrooms

Functional behavior assessment (FBA) is now standard practice in special education; in fact, it is mandated by the 1997 revision of the Individuals with Disabilities Education Act (IDEA). The integration of FBA into the educational mainstream is one of the most recent examples of contributions of applied behavior analysis in our society. Although the way most public school teachers implement FBAs is a far cry from how Iwata and his colleagues originally described them (Iwata, Dorsey, Slifer, Bauman, & Richman, 1994), they retain the original purpose of attempting to identify the variables that may be motivating or maintaining challenging behavior.

In many situations, especially when the challenging behavior is severe or persistent, public schools ask behavior analysts to conduct the FBAs. In the best of all situations, behavior analysts work with school personnel to implement the FBA in the school context. In far too many situations, however, behavior analysts remove children from school and conduct these assessments in the laboratory. Not only do these FBAs have low instructional utility, but they also violate one of the basic tenets of applied behavior analysis: the importance of context (Baer, Wolf, & Risley, 1987).

## DEFINING OUTCOMES FOR ALL CHILDREN

Schwartz and her colleagues attempted to address the need to define important outcomes for children participating in inclusive education through a 5-year, federally funded longitudinal investigation of children with severe disabilities in inclusive settings (Schwartz, et al., 1995). The primary objective of that project was to find a way to describe the important outcomes that children achieved in inclusive settings. The data were collected by spending many hours observing children in classrooms, talking to teachers and parents, and interviewing typically developing peers. These observations resulted in the development of a framework that has proved to be a useful way to describe such observed outcomes. The outcome framework consists of three interrelated domains: membership, relationships, and knowledge/skills (Schwartz, 2000; see Figure 13-1). The intervention and learning that takes place in these domains is set in a context of valued activities and routines with an emphasis placed on active participation in meaningful, culturally relevant, interesting

settings. This outcome framework is particularly helpful because it captures the outcomes that are meaningful to educators and parents while at the same time describing what children are learning and doing in a holistic manner, without the constraints imposed by traditional developmental and educational domains. What has been most rewarding about this framework is that the domains apply equally to children with and without disabilities and have been used by both general and special education teachers.

Further, this model suggests that each of the outcome domains (membership, relationships, and skills) is affected by the others in a bidirectional manner. That is, changes in skills will also affect relationships and membership. Although this is a fairly traditional view, the model also suggests that changes in relationships affect skills and membership and that changes in membership affect skills and relationships. These last two interdependencies have received little thought or attention in our professional literature. This imbalance of professional attention is evident when one compares the amount of literature devoted to teaching children skills as opposed to teaching children about membership. In addition to understanding these bidirectional influences, understanding the framework also depends on understanding what is meant by *membership, relationships,* and *skills.*

### Membership

Membership refers to how the child is accepted into and participates in groups. The term *membership* also is used to indicate the child's sense of belonging to the social fabric of the group. Membership can be achieved through participation in either formal (e.g., circle time) or informal (e.g., playing on the playground) activities. Direct measures of memberships are still in the development stages (Garfinkle & Schwartz, 2002; Staub, 1998); however, membership can be informally assessed by looking for any accommodations that are made to facilitate the

**Figure 13-1.**
Community of practice: participation in valued routines, rituals, and activities.

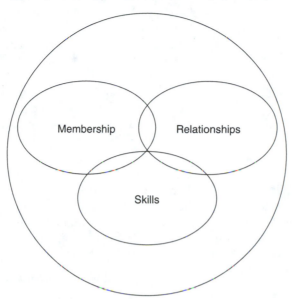

participation of a child (e.g., changes in the rules of a game on the playground to give a child with a disability an extra turn) in classroom activities and overt symbols of membership (e.g., a cubby or mailbox in a classroom). Membership also can be measured by observing teacher-designed groups in the classroom (e.g., literacy groups, snack groups); student-designed groups in and out of the classroom (e.g., play groups, student-initiated project groups); activities in which the entire class participated as one group (e.g., class meetings); activities in which the entire school participated as one group (e.g., assemblies); and outside-of-school activities (e.g., scouts, sports teams, activities at churches or synagogues).

Children without disabilities help to make children with disabilities welcome members of classrooms and other groups easily and often without adult assistance. Many parents of young typically developing children attending inclusive early childhood programs realize early on that their children do not even realize that some children in their classrooms are "different." I have heard children tell their parents that one of their classmates talks with his hands (i.e., uses sign language) or talks with pictures (i.e., picture-exchange communication system), but I have never heard a child say that a classmate has a developmental delay. Children do, however, understand when others are not treated in a fair manner. For example, Schnorr (1990) asked first-graders without disabilities about a child with Down syndrome who spent part of the day in their classroom. They were quick to point out that he was not a true member of their class because he did not have a mailbox, was allowed to color while other children had to work, and did not have an envelope to receive valentines during their party on February 14. Clearly these 6-year-olds were aware of the signs of membership and had suggestions for their teacher about what could be done to help Peter participate more fully.

The lessons learned by making accommodations for students with disabilities to participate in educational and community activities may be among the most salient positive outcomes for typically developing students in inclusive schools. Staub and Peck (1995) identified five potential benefits of inclusion for students without disabilities that can all be linked to facilitating membership:

1. Reduced fear of human differences accompanied by increased comfort and awareness
2. Growth in social cognition
3. Improvements in self-concept
4. Development of personal principles
5. Warm and caring friendships

## Relationships

Whereas the domain of membership refers to the interactions a child has with groups of peers, the domain of relationships focuses on interactions with individual peers. Unlike traditional discussions of social interactions, in which interactions and responses are usually counted, the goal of focusing on relationships is to evaluate a more complex interaction than can be described by focusing solely on initiations and responses. Thus, the domain of relationships refers to a broad range of behaviors and complex interpersonal interactions. A child may form relationships with peers in all the different environments in which she spends time. Further, relationships can be categorized as follows: play/companionship (e.g., children who choose to play together during free time); helper (e.g., a child who assists a peer); helpee (e.g., a child who receives help from a peer); peer (e.g., two children who may be walking next to each other during a transition and interact, but may not choose to interact given a free choice situation); and conflictual (e.g., children arguing over the rules of a game or over taking turns with a preferred material). Children with successful relationships have interactions with many children and these interactions occur across the different categories of this domain.

The importance of developing social relationships during childhood is well documented in the literature (e.g., Hartup, 1996; Howes, 1988). Examples of the types of relationships that children with and without disabilities develop in in-

clusive classrooms are also easily available in the literature (e.g., Grenot-Scheyer et al., 2001; Kishi & Meyer, 1994; Murray-Seegart, 1989; Peck, Donaldson, & Pezzoli, 1990; Staub, 1998; Staub & Peck, 1995). Staub, Schwartz, Gallucci, and Peck (1994) described four friendships between children with and without disabilities that developed in an inclusive elementary school. All four sets of friends displayed a range of relationships; that is, they were observed in episodes of play, helping each other, and sometimes having and resolving conflicts. What was extremely interesting to their teacher, parents, and the researchers was the scope of the positive impact these relationships had on the children without disabilities. One mother described her sixth-grade son's relationship with a classmate with severe disabilities in this way:

> Aaron's friendship with Cole is a caring, teaching relationship. I get the feeling that Aaron wants to let Cole experience the things he has experienced. He gets a lot of joy from being able to do that. (Staub et al., 1994, pp. 318–319)

## Knowledge/Skills

Knowledge/skills is the most traditional of the three outcome domains and is the most familiar to school psychologists and special educators. Of the three outcome domains, knowledge/skills is also the easiest to quantify. As such, this domain requires less explanation than the previous domains. We conceptualize the knowledge/skills domain to include social communication skills, academic skills, cognitive skills, motor skills, adaptive skills, and so forth. These are the traditional domains of schooling—the reading, writing, and arithmetic. Interestingly, however, this domain is currently under much political scrutiny. The current political landscape is calling for more accountability in this domain, although there is little agreement about how to measure success or what it means to succeed.

One of the most persistent myths about inclusion is that the presence of children with disabilities interferes with the academic achievement of typically developing children. There is absolutely no data to support this contention (Staub & Peck, 1995). There is also documentation of typically developing children who benefit academically from accommodations and modifications made with children with disabilities in mind, participating in tutoring programs as either tutors or tutees, and smaller class size.

To be successful in school and society, children need to learn skills; however, although knowledge and skills are necessary for success, they are insufficient to constitute a complete set of desirable outcomes. When planning or evaluating a comprehensive educational program for all children, all three domains—membership, relationships, and skill—must be considered. Together these three domains provide a holistic and community-based view of meaningful outcomes for all children in inclusive schools. Educators must be prepared to create a physical and social environment that supports growth and learning across all three domains.

## CONCLUSION

The time is right for applied behavior analysts and advocates for inclusive education to work together to build the bridge that will help to provide high-quality educational opportunities for all children. In fact, the consumers of our work—parents of children with disabilities, general education teachers, and special education teachers—are calling for this collaboration. These people understand the value of consultation and of the contributions that both behavior analysts and inclusion advocates can make to the free and appropriate education of children with disabilities. These consumers may turn out to be the foundation of the bridge we build across these disciplines. Both behavior analysts and advocates of inclusive education bring important contributions to the construction site. Behavior analysts bring the instructional strategies and research methodologies to evaluate the effectiveness and efficacy of these strategies. Inclusion advocates bring with them the under-

standing of the general education curriculum and the social context of schooling. Together we can form a team that will help all students become full members of their schools and classrooms, develop meaningful relationships with their peers, and acquire meaningful and functional skills and knowledge.

## REFERENCES

Allen, K. E., Hart, B., Buell, J., Harris, F., & Wolf, M. (1964). Effects of social reinforcement on isolated behavior of a nursery school child. *Child Development, 35,* 511–518.

Allen, K. E., & Schwartz, I. S. (2001). *The exceptional child: Inclusion in early childhood education.* Albany, NY: Delmar.

Baer, D. M., Wolf, M. M., & Risley, T. R. (1968). Some current dimensions of applied behavior analysis. *Journal of Applied Behavior Analysis, 1,* 91–97.

Baer, D. M., Wolf, M. M., & Risley, T. R. (1987). Some still current dimensions of applied behavior analysis. *Journal of Applied Behavior Analysis, 20,* 313–327.

Cooper, J. O, Heron, T. E., & Heward, W. L. (1987). *Applied behavior analysis.* Columbus, OH: Merrill.

Garfinkle, A. N., & Schwartz, I. S. (2002). Peer imitation: Increasing social interactions in children with autism and other developmental disabilities in inclusive preschool classrooms. *Topics in Early Childhood Special Education, 22* (1), 26–38.

Gray, C., & Gerard, J. D. (1993). Social stories: Improving responses of students with autism with accurate social information. *Focus on Autistic Behavior, 8* (1), 1–10.

Grenot-Scheyer, M., Fischer, M., & Staub, D. (2001). *At the end of the day: Lessons learned in inclusive education.* Baltimore: Brookes.

Hartup, W. W. (1996). The company they keep: Friendships and their developmental significance. *Child Development, 67,* 1–13.

Howes, C. (1988). Peer interaction of young children. *Monographs of the Society of Research in Child Development, No. 217.* Chicago: University of Chicago.

Iwata, B., Dorsey, M., Slifer, K., Bauman, K., & Richman, G. (1994). Toward a functional analysis of self-injury. *Journal of Applied Behavior Analysis, 27,* 197–209.

Kauffman, J. M., & Hallahan, D. P. (1993). *The illusion of full inclusion*. Austin, TX: Pro-Ed.

Kishi, G. S., & Meyer, L. H. (1994). What children report and remember: A six-year follow-up of the effects of social contact between peers with and without severe disabilities. *Journal of the Association for Persons with Severe Handicaps, 19,* 277–289.

Lovaas, O. I. (1987). Behavioral treatment and normal educational and intellectual functioning in young autistic children. *Journal of Consulting and Clinical Psychology, 55,* 3–9.

Maurice, C., Green, G., & Luce, S. (Eds.). (1996). *Behavioral interventions for young children with autism: A manual for parents and professionals*. Austin, TX: Pro-Ed.

Morris, E. K. (1997). Some reflections on contextualism, mechanism, and behavior analysis. *Psychological Record, 47,* 529–542.

Murray-Seegart, C. (1989). *Nasty girls, thugs, and humans like us: Social relations between severely disabled and nondisabled students in high school*. Baltimore: Brookes.

*Oberti v. Borough of Clementon School District*. WL 178480 (3rd Circ. NJ 1993).

Odom, S. L. (2002). *Widening the circle: Including children with disabilities in preschool programs*. New York: Teachers College Press.

Odom, S. L., & Brown, W. H. (1993). Social interaction skills interventions for young children with disabilities in integrated settings. In C. A. Peck, S. L. Odom, & D. Bricker (Eds.), *Integrating young children with disabilities into community programs: Ecological perspectives on research and implementation* (pp. 39–64). Baltimore: Brookes.

Peck, C. A., Donaldson, J., & Pezzoli, M. (1990). Some benefits adolescents perceive for themselves from their social relationships with peers who have severe handicaps. *Journal of the Association for Persons with Severe Handicaps, 15,* 241–249.

Sandall, S. R., & Schwartz, I. S. (2002). *Building blocks for teaching preschoolers with special needs*. Baltimore: Brookes.

Schilling, D., Washington, K., Billingsley, F., Deitz, J. (2003). Classroom seating for children with attention deficit hyperactivity disorder: Therapy balls versus chairs. *American Journal of Occupational Therapy, 57* (5), 534–541.

Schnorr, R. F. (1990). "Peter? He comes and goes": First graders' perspectives on a part-time main-stream student. *Journal of the Association for the Persons with Severe Handicaps, 15,* 231–240.

Schwartz, I. S. (2000). Standing on the shoulders of giants: Looking ahead to facilitating membership and relationships for children with disabilities. *Topics in Early Childhood Special Education, 20* (2), 123–128.

Schwartz, I. S. (2003). Social-validity assessments: Voting on science or acknowledging the roots of applied behavior analysis? In T. Stokes & K. Budd (Eds.), *A small matter of proof: The legacy of Donald M. Baer*. Reno, NV: Context Press.

Schwartz, I. S., & Baer, D. M. (1991). Social-validity assessments: Is current practice state-of-the-art? *Journal of Applied Behavior Analysis, 24,* 189–204.

Schwartz, I. S., Staub, D., Gallucci, C., & Peck, C. A. (1995). Blending qualitative and behavior analytic research methods to evaluate outcomes in inclusive schools. *Journal of Behavioral Education, 5* (1), 93–106.

Stainback, W., & Stainback, S. (1990). *Support networks for inclusive schooling: Interdependent integrated education*. Baltimore: Brookes.

Staub, D. (1998). *Delicate threads: Friendships between children with & without special needs in inclusive settings*. Brookline, MA: Woodbine House.

Staub, D., & Peck, C. A. (1995). What are the outcomes of nondisabled students? *Educational Leadership,* 36–40.

Staub, D., Schwartz, I. S., Gallucci, C., & Peck, C. A. (1994). Four portraits of friendship at an inclusive school. *Journal of the Association for Persons with Severe Handicaps, 19,* 314–325.

Thiemann, K. S., & Goldstein, H. (2001). Social stories, written text cues, and video feedback: Effects on social communication of children with autism. *Journal of Applied Behavior Analysis, 34,* 424–446.

Turnbull, H. R. III, & Turnbull, A. P. (1998). *Free and appropriate public education* (5th ed.). Denver: Love.

Vaughn, S., & Schumm, J. S. (1995). Responsible inclusion for students with learning disabilities. *Journal of Learning Disabilities, 28* (5), 266–270, 290.

Winett, R. A., & Winkler, R. C. (1972). Current behavior modification in the classroom: Be still, be quiet, be docile. *Journal of Applied Behavior Analysis, 5,* 499–504.

# STUDY QUESTIONS AND FOLLOW-UP ACTIVITIES

1. List three benefits of collaboration between applied behavior analysts and advocates of inclusive education. What are some of the disadvantages, if any, of such collaboration?

2. Walden Elementary is a school within a large school district. Currently, special education services are provided primarily in resource rooms and self-contained classrooms. You have been appointed as a consultant, with the primary responsibility of conducting a needs assessment of the delivery of special education services and proposing a shift to an inclusion model. Outline the various steps you would take to complete this task.

3. In a small group, brainstorm ideas on how you would teach children in your classroom about membership. Elaborate on one of the ideas and briefly write how you would implement such an intervention.

4. In your opinion, if the school does not have a behavior analyst on board, then who should be responsible for conducting a functional behavior assessment, and why?

5. As mentioned by the author, the *Oberti* decision states that "inclusion is a right, not a privilege." Do you consider it to be a right or a privilege? Provide reasons for your stance.

6. Select one target skill within the three domains of the outcome framework described by the author. Provide the (a) rationale for choosing the skill, (b) proposed intervention, (c) dependent measures, (d) data collection procedures, and (e) appropriate research design.

7. How do you view ABA? How was your opinion of ABA shaped (by people in the field, books, or other resources)?

8. Outline a plan for professionals in the field of ABA providing ways in which they can improve the public's view of their profession. Who would be the target audience, and how would one reach that audience?

9. The author suggests that many parents do not know how, or aren't able, to influence educators' decisions regarding the services their child receives at school (e.g., inclusion). What do you believe are the most important skills parents should possess to obtain educational opportunities for their children? How would you teach parents to be advocates for their children?

10. If you were a parent with a child needing special education services, would you want your child to be a part an inclusive program? If inclusion is implemented properly (i.e., as the author suggests), are there any drawbacks to this approach? Consider how the benefits and disadvantages (if any) of inclusion would affect your child's education.

11. The author noted that "many of these instructional assistants have received little or no training and may have no experience working with children with disabilities when they begin." Are you concerned that the person with the most training (i.e., the teacher) spends less time with the child with disabilities than the person with the least training (i.e., the instructional assistant)? What would you propose as a solution?

12. The author mentioned that "behavior analysts often write objectives that are contextually irrelevant or developmentally inappropriate or have ridiculous criteria." Many behavior analysts are not trained as teachers; thus, do you think that someone certified as a behavior analyst is qualified to write IEPs? If so, explain what qualifies someone to write IEPs. If not, give a description of the type of training a behavior analyst should undergo before writing objectives.

13. Provide an example of the ideal inclusive educational setting, assuming parents of children with disabilities, general and special education teachers, advocates of inclusion, and applied behavior analysts were all part of a positive collaboration effort.

Study questions and follow-up activities prepared by Summer J. Ferreri and Shobana Musti-Rao.

### CHAPTER 14

# Building Behaviors versus Suppressing Behaviors
## Perspectives and Prescriptions for Schoolwide Positive Behavior Change

*Lloyd D. Peterson*     *Laura Lacy-Rismiller*

What does it mean to implement schoolwide positive behavior change, and what do school administrators hope to achieve through such change? Of course district officials want their students to perform better, especially on the "high-stakes tests" that states are now mandating. In addition, they want their students to behave better—to act in an appropriate, socially acceptable manner. They also likely want their schools to be positive, nurturing places for students. However, district administrators must realize that positive change in students' behavior cannot occur by providing the same failed interventions with different names. There must be a paradigm shift, from the top down, in the way educators deal with disruptive or inappropriate school behaviors—a shift away from behavior management strategies that attempt to suppress inappropriate behaviors, toward behavior management strategies that build appropriate behaviors.

In this chapter we provide a brief overview of past and present behavior change programs. Some of these programs focus on inappropriate student behavior as an opportunity to suppress inappropriate behaviors, and others focus on inappropriate student behavior as an opportunity to build appropriate behaviors. In addition to this overview, we will present our conceptualization of the structure of schools, areas we view as important to consider prior to and during schoolwide positive behavior change programs, and finally a case example of a schoolwide positive behavior change program.

## OVERVIEW OF PAST AND PRESENT BEHAVIOR CHANGE PROGRAMS

Aggressive and violent behaviors committed by children and adolescents have reached epidemic proportions (Koop & Lundberg, 1992; Rutherford & Nelson, 1995). Furthermore, less severe forms of problem behavior, such as defiance and noncompliance, are also on the rise (Walker, Colvin, & Ramsey, 1995). As a result of the impact these behaviors are having on U.S. school systems, educational literature is permeated with calls for schools to "get tough" on problem behaviors (e.g., "Elements of an Effective Disciplinary Strategy," 1995–1996).

To meet these disciplinary needs created by their students, many schools are instituting "no nonsense" strategies that are intended to punish disruptive behavior. For example, one school in Franklin, Tennessee, implemented a Saturday School program, in which students engaged in physical labor, academic work, and counseling within a "detention" atmosphere (Winborn, 1992). Though this may have been an attempt at an alternative to suspension and expulsion, it was primarily based on a punitive model—a model in which the focus was on suppressing inappropriate behaviors rather than building appropriate behaviors.

Another alternative to suspension and expulsion with which schools are experimenting is in-school suspension (Collins, 1985). In-school suspension generally consists of a room located within the school building or on the school grounds to which students who engage in inappropriate behavior are sent for a period of time (i.e., 3 hours, 3 days). In a survey administered to 200 Missouri high school principals (with 159 responses) to determine which disciplinary measures were perceived as most effective, 88% of the respondents reported that they used in-school suspension (Billings & Enger, 1995). Another survey administered to 365 Michigan high school principals reported that in-school suspension and school probation were the most frequently used disciplinary measures in both suburban and urban schools (Adams, 1992). Similar to the program implemented by the Franklin, Tennessee, school, in-school suspension is based on a punitive model—a model similar to time-out the focus of which is suppressing inappropriate behaviors by removing students from something they may have found desirable (being with other students) rather than building appropriate behaviors.

Although administrators are "cracking down" on disruptive behavior by implementing zero tolerance policies and punishment-oriented consequences, some researchers suggest that these methods only exacerbate the problem (Lewis & Sugai, 1999; Mayer, 1995; Sugai & Horner, 2001). Schools may be so quick to implement consequences intended to punish disruptive behavior that they fail to recognize the effects these consequence may have on their students. Such contingencies may actually set the stage for aggression, violence, vandalism, and escape (Azrin, Hake, Holz, & Hutchinson, 1965; Berkowitz, 1983; Hutchinson, 1977; Mayer, 1995). In fact, Mayer (1995) suggested that such contingencies may further contribute to disruptive behavior in the school:

> The resultant specific occurrences of punishment and extinction (e.g., disapproving comments, academic task errors, and a lack of recognition for either student or staff effort) appear to serve as setting events that evoke aggression, attendance problems (escape), and other antisocial behaviors. It appears, then, that a punitive school discipline environment is a major factor contributing to antisocial behavior problems. (p. 474)

In a meta-analysis of over 500 studies on juvenile delinquency, Lipsey (1992) found that preventing and treating problem behavior using structured approaches have shown the most promise. In an effort to further define such "structured" approaches, Horner, Sugai, and Horner (2000) outlined several key practices of schools with "effective disciplinary systems" (p. 20). These schools

1. invest in *prevention* of disruptive behavior,
2. establish efficient systems for identifying and *responding to at-risk youth early,*
3. build the capacity for highly intense *interventions with the small number of students* with chronic problem behaviors, and
4. *collect and use information* about student behavior to guide ongoing improvement. (p. 20, italics added)

Several educational researchers suggest that schools use positive programs when addressing problem behavior rather than emphasizing procedures intended to punish problem behavior (Goldiamond, 1974; Goldstein, Sprafkin, Gershaw, & Klein, 1980; Lewis & Sugai, 1999; Mayer, 1995; McGinnis & Goldstein, 1984; Schwartz & Goldiamond, 1975). Goldiamond, (1974) and Schwartz and Goldiamond (1975) suggested a more positive approach to intervention for problem behavior that emphasized increasing positive or desirable behaviors rather than targeting unwanted or undesirable behavior. This can be accomplished by (a) choosing behaviors to be strengthened rather than choosing behaviors to reduce; (b) analyzing whether these behaviors are in the student's existing repertoire; (c) identifying a method of providing instruction and reinforcement for teaching these behaviors if they are not in the student's existing repertoire; and (d) choosing reinforcers to increase and maintain the desirable behaviors. To make this shift from focusing on suppressing behavior to focusing on building behavior requires a change in how schools operate; thus, the structure of schools must be considered.

## STRUCTURE OF SCHOOLS

### Faculty, Staff, and Administration

Schools can be conceptualized as inverted pyramids (see Figure 14-1). At the top of this inverted pyramid are students. The only reason schools exist is for students to gain knowledge and skills, which will help them become productive members of our society. The teachers are found directly under the students. The sole purpose for teachers being in the school is to help students gain knowledge and skills and become productive members of our society. Before beginning class sessions or school meetings, teachers should ask themselves, How will this benefit the students? After ending class sessions or meetings, they should ask themselves, How did/will this benefit the students? If teachers cannot identify benefits to students, they should question why they are engaged in the activity.

**Figure 14-1.**
Conceptualization of the organization of a school.

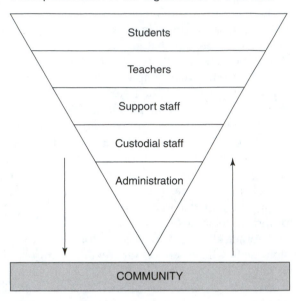

Support staff (paraprofessionals, secretaries) can be found below the students and teachers on the inverted pyramid. The support staff's purpose is to support the teachers so they can do their jobs. Next comes the custodial/maintenance staff, whose sole purpose for being in the school is to keep the building and grounds clean and functional. They maintain the physical structure of the building so the others (i.e., teachers and support staff) can perform their jobs. Finally, administrators are at the bottom of this inverted pyramid. Their sole purpose is to support everyone else above them to ensure that the custodians, support staff, and teachers can all do their jobs and that students gain the knowledge and skills that will help them become productive members of our society.

### Community

The plane the inverted pyramid in Figure 14-1 balances on is the community. When we conceptualize school systems as inverted pyramids, we see what a precarious balancing act schools must maintain. If schools move in a certain direction without first communicating to the community about this move (so the community can shift simultaneously with the schools), the pyramid will tumble, and the schools are at risk for failure. The same can be said for a community shifting without first communicating to schools which direction it is moving in and how this move will benefit the schools and the community. Clear communication between schools and the community (and vice versa) must be maintained.

## Students

Students are found at the top of the inverted pyramid, but they also constitute a structure of their own. We view the school as having three tiers of students, or circles within a circle (see Figure 14-2). The largest circle encompasses all the students of the school. Within that large circle is a smaller circle of students who are at risk for school failure. And within the smaller circle is the smallest circle of students who are what we call "at intervention." These students in the smallest circle are no longer at risk for school failure; they are already failing and need remediation.

**Figure 14-2.**
Three-tier model of schoolwide intervention.

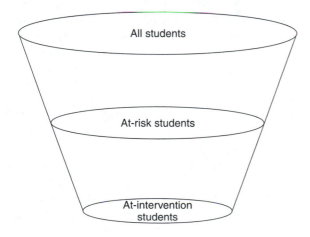

Interventions that address the needs of all the students in the school must be implemented if schoolwide positive behavior change is to be effective. A schoolwide plan that does not address the needs of the students at risk or at intervention is likely to fail because, knowingly or unknowingly, the behaviors of these students will undermine the planned interventions. Research indicates that students at various skill levels will respond differently to behavior change interventions (Horner & Sugai, 2002; Sugai et al., 2000; Walker et al., 1996). A major goal of the schoolwide positive behavior change program presented in the next section was to implement an intervention that could be effective across the various skill levels of students.

## IMPORTANT CONSIDERATIONS FOR SCHOOLWIDE POSITIVE BEHAVIOR CHANGE

Many interventions can be implemented to help bring about schoolwide positive behavior change. The following nine key points are important to consider when planning schoolwide positive behavior change:

1. Available funds
2. Available trained personnel
3. Teacher training
4. Teaching desirable behaviors to students
5. Rewarding/reinforcing desirable student behavior
6. A three-tier approach—schoolwide, at-risk, at-intervention
7. Community involvement
8. Commitment of the school administration
9. Improved academic program and teaching methodologies.

Each of these nine points will be discussed within the context of the case example described in the following section.

## CASE EXAMPLE OF SCHOOLWIDE POSITIVE BEHAVIOR CHANGE PROGRAM

The schoolwide interventions discussed here were implemented in a middle school in rural Utah. The school had 252 students of a variety of heritages. The racial (tribal) makeup of the school was 52% Americans of Northern European heritage and 48% Americans of North American Indian heritage (approximately 7% were Ute and approximately 41% were Navajo). This school had concerns and problems similar to those of many other schools throughout the United States. A great many of the students were from families with low socioeconomic status (SES). Approximately 65% of the students qualified for free or reduced lunch. Historically, the school had difficulty recruiting and retaining teachers. And, as with many schools in the nation, racial and tribal prejudices and tension affected how the students interacted with each other, school personnel, and the community as a whole.

Although no quantitative data were kept on the number of fights, suspensions, expulsions, and so forth, the year prior to this schoolwide intervention, anecdotal reports by parents, community members, teachers, and staff indicated that fights between students of different races and tribes occurred almost weekly; parents worried about sending their children to the school fearing they would be hurt by other students; police were called to the school nearly twice per week; and in-school suspension, school suspension, and expulsion were used as the major means to address inappropriate student behavior.

### Funds

In considering what interventions to implement, we first had to address the issue of funding and how much we were willing to invest. This school, as with most schools, had few funds available for an extensive intervention package. Because of this limited funding, we chose inter-

ventions that were cost efficient both in monetary value and time. The total expenditures for this year-long intervention were less than $1,800. Of this total, $1,000 came from a picnic fund that the school had historically earmarked for a year-end picnic for the students, and $400 was contributed through the DARE program. Only $400 came from previously uncommitted school funds. No additional funds were needed.

### Trained Personnel

The principal, who was hired specifically to bring about schoolwide change in the social behavior of the students, had previously conducted other schoolwide positive behavior change interventions. He had a doctoral degree in special education and educational leadership, and his doctoral studies had focused on behavior analysis and its application to schoolwide positive behavior change.

### Teacher Training

The principal provided minimal training to the half-time vice principal and school counselor. This training consisted of acquainting them with a list of social behavior skills that would be taught to specific students in the building (see Peterson, Peterson, & Lacy, 2002, for a description of 12 of these skills). This training took approximately 2.5 hours. Minimal training was provided for the teachers. Because part of this intervention consisted of students learning to apologize to their teachers for their misconduct, teacher training consisted only of teaching the teachers to accept apologies from their students by saying an affirmative (i.e., "Okay," "Welcome back to the classroom," etc.). This training took approximately 1 hour. More in-depth training was provided for two paraprofessionals who had previously been employed by the school to supervise the in-school suspension room. Instead of supervising in-school suspension, the paraprofessionals were reassigned to teaching social skills. Their instruction consisted of teaching them how to deliver a structured social skill lesson to a small group of students (see Peterson, Peterson, & Lacy, 2002, for a description of these lessons). This training took approximately 10 hours. All the training took place during school hours. Thus, no additional training funds were needed.

## Teaching Desirable Behaviors

As discussed previously, lasting schoolwide positive behavior change occurs by building desirable behaviors rather than attempting to suppress undesirable behaviors. Perhaps the most radical change in this school was when the principal removed the in-school suspension room and replaced it with an intensive services (IS) room. Rather than coming to an in-school suspension classroom to sit for long periods of time either with nothing to do or with some academic work that was either "busy work" or too difficult for the students, the children now came to the IS room to build social behaviors. When a teacher asked a student to leave the classroom because of an inappropriate social behavior, the student first came to the main office. An administrator (typically the principal, but sometimes the vice principal or counselor, who had been trained by the principal) met the student in the office to determine what skill deficit the student displayed to result in a referral to the office. Based on that, the administrator determined what social skill the student would work on while in the IS room. Then the student was escorted to the IS room, where a paraprofessional provided the student with a lesson on the skill identified by the administrator.

For example, a frequent reason students were sent out of a classroom at this school was for not following instructions (noncompliance). When the student arrived in the office for this reason, the administrator typically identified *following instructions* as the skill the student needed to practice in the IS room. Upon arrival in the IS room, the student was presented with a structured lesson on the steps of how to follow

instructions (see Peterson, Peterson, & Lacy, 2002, for a description of the teaching procedures). When the student demonstrated acquisition of this skill, he or she was then taught how to apologize. When the student demonstrated acquisition of both skills, an administrator was called, and the student performed the steps of the target social skill and practiced apologizing in the presence of the administrator. If the student performed each skill satisfactorily with the administrator, the administrator escorted the student back to class. The administrator asked the teacher to step into the hallway, where the student was prompted to apologize to the teacher for the previous behavior. If the apology was done appropriately (i.e., following the steps of apologizing), the teacher replied with an affirmative and the student returned to the classroom.

The teachers had previously been taught by the principal that when a student apologized correctly they were not to reprimand the student. They were told that this was not the time to "grind an ax" with the child because such behavior on the part of the teacher might serve to punish appropriate apologizing. The principal stressed to teachers that from a student's perspective apologizing was very difficult. In such situations, the student could be viewed as being a turtle. As you know, a turtle never gets anywhere in life unless he sticks his neck out. In this case, when apologizing, the student was sticking his or her neck out, demonstrating an appropriate behavior that he or she may have never done in the past. The principal stressed to teachers that this was no time to chop off the student's head. It was a time to reinforce appropriate behavior and get the student back in class. Thus, teachers were specifically taught to accept appropriate apologies and admit the student back into the classroom. If a student's apology was done incorrectly (i.e., the student did not follow the steps correctly), the administrator escorted the student back to the IS room for more training (this happened only once throughout the entire year).

**Table 14-1**
Number of Student Visits, Percentage of Total Students, and Percentage of Total School Population Visiting the IS Room

| Number of Visits | 1 | 2 | 3 | 4 | 5 | 6 | 7 | 8 | 9 | 10 | 11 | 12 | 13 | 14 | 15 | 17 | 21 | Total |
|---|---|---|---|---|---|---|---|---|---|---|---|---|---|---|---|---|---|---|
| Number of Students | 54 | 34 | 22 | 11 | 7 | 2 | 4 | 2 | 3 | 2 | 2 | 1 | 1 | 1 | 1 | 1 | 1 | 149 |
| Percentage of Total Student Visits | 36 | 23 | 15 | 7 | 5 | 1 | 3 | 1 | 2 | 1 | 1 | 1 | 1 | 1 | 1 | 1 | 1 | 100 |
| Percentage of Total School Population | | | | | | | | | | | | | | | | | | 59 |

Throughout the school year, a total of 149 different students visited the IS room. Nearly 60% of these students visited the IS room only once or twice. Only 8% of the total student body came more than five times, and each time they came, they had the opportunity to demonstrate the acquisition of a desirable social skill (see Table 14-1).

This system differed significantly from the typical in-school suspension procedure that had been in place prior to the institution of the IS room. Instead of spending several hours or multiple days in in-school suspension, students typically spent less than 2 hours in the IS room. In fact, most students were ready to be returned to their classrooms in 30 minutes or less, but because of other duties, the administrators were not always available at that time to return the student to the classroom. Of course, when the IS room was first instituted, a few students required more time (e.g., 1 to 3 hours) the first couple of times they visited, but students who returned frequently to the IS room spent less time with each visit (see Table 14-2). They came to the IS room, demonstrated the acquisition of desirable social skills, and went back to their classrooms where they belonged, with professional teachers who taught the students skills they needed to become productive members of our society.

Under the previous program of in-school suspension, parents whose children were given in-school suspension sometimes complained that their children were not getting an appropriate education or that the school was simply punishing their children. They questioned what the school was doing to help their children. However, with the IS room, the students received

**Table 14-2**
Average Time (per hour) Students Stay in IS Room and Number of Social Behaviors Taught

| Month | Aug | Sept | Oct | Nov | Dec | Jan | Feb | Mar | Apr | May |
|---|---|---|---|---|---|---|---|---|---|---|
| Average Time in IS Room (in hours) | 1.15 | 1.3 | 1.73 | 0.98 | 1.17 | 0.97 | 0.86 | 0.85 | 0.5 | 0.68 |

one-on-one or small group instruction on skills that would benefit them not only during their school years, but for the rest of their lives. Throughout the school year, 20 different social skills were taught to the students for a cumulative total of 1,152 times (see Table 14-3). Many parents commented that they now saw the school as educating their children rather than punishing them.

The training that occurred in the IS room was an intervention that addressed the behaviors not

**Table 14-3**

Number of Times Each Social Behavior Was Taught During the School Year

| Social Behaviors Taught | Total Times Taught |
|---|---|
| How to apologize | 447 |
| How to make a decision | 243 |
| How to follow instructions | 194 |
| How to resist peer pressure | 107 |
| How to avoid trouble with others | 35 |
| How to respond to teasing | 20 |
| How to set a goal | 18 |
| How to disagree appropriately | 14 |
| How to know and express your feelings | 11 |
| How to make a request | 10 |
| How to stay out of fights | 9 |
| How to act positively toward others | 7 |
| How to resolve conflicts | 7 |
| How to accept no for an answer | 6 |
| How to accept conse- quences and feedback | 6 |
| How to deal with someone else's anger | 6 |
| How to deal with an accusation | 6 |
| How to get a teacher's attention | 4 |
| How to stand up for a friend | 1 |
| How to give negative feedback | 1 |

only of students at risk or at intervention, but of all students in the school. It was a cost-efficient method that produced schoolwide positive behavior change. The paraprofessionals were no longer working to suppress behaviors; they were now working to build behaviors.

## Rewarding Desirable Behaviors

Although the IS room was a critical component of the schoolwide behavior change package, the principal implemented additional interventions for little or no cost that were important to the success of the program. In addition to teaching desirable behaviors, administrators and teachers must have rewards and reinforcers in place to maintain those behaviors over time. The principal in this school implemented several reward programs to "catch students being good."

One of these programs rewarded students for keeping the school clean and in good condition. Historically, a sum of $1,000 from the school's budget was designated for the year-end school picnic. In the past, the students were told that the fund was for their year-end picnic, but for each school violation, a fine would be administered and the fine would come out of the picnic fund. The amount of money remaining in the fund at the end of the school year was the amount of money the students had for their picnic. At the end of the school year prior to the schoolwide positive behavior change interventions, the fund had been reduced to $335. This type of system can be referred to as a response cost procedure, which is designed to punish target behaviors (Cooper, Heron, & Heward, 2005). Although response cost procedures can be effective in suppressing specific target behaviors, they have many disadvantages. That is, they do not teach new, more desirable behaviors. In addition, response cost procedures—which are intended to punish problem behavior—are subject to all of the potential problems associated with punishment procedures. For example, such procedures may cause increases in other undesirable behaviors, they may cause aggression, and they may trigger counter control responses in children (Alberto & Troutman, 2003).

The principal wanted the focus of this school to be a reward system for building desirable behaviors. So, instead of fining inappropriate behavior, the reward-based intervention awarded the students with $5.55 ($1,000 divided by 180 school days) for each day that the students kept the school clean and used appropriate social skills. That is, if they walked through the hallways, spoke using acceptable voice volume and language, exhibited courteous behavior to others, and took care of the school building and fixtures, they earned $5.55 for their end-of-the-year picnic. Every morning at the beginning of the school day, the principal announced over the school intercom whether the money had been earned the previous day and what the current balance was in the picnic fund. The principal also posted a bar graph in the main entrance hallway to depict the amount earned to date. This chart was updated weekly. Interestingly, when the system was changed from a punishment-based system to a reward-based system, there were only 2 days all year that the money was not earned. One day one particular student's behavior was so outstanding that his behavior earned double the daily amount. At the end of the school year, the balance in the picnic fund was $994.55. This was a far larger sum than the previous year's balance of $335, and thus the school picnic was far grander than it had been in the past.

One might ask what a student could do that was so noteworthy as to earn double the amount of money available per day. The three grades in this building (sixth, seventh, and eighth) ate lunch at separate times. During the sixth-grade lunch, a drape in the cafeteria was pulled off the wall. The principal went to each of the four sixth-grade classrooms and spoke with the students about how disappointed he was in this behavior and how the students would not earn the picnic fund money for that day. In the last of the four classrooms, a student stood up and—in front of the entire class—said,

"I did it." Though he had made a mistake in judgment during the lunch period, he was certainly displaying integrity at that moment. As a result of this exemplary behavior, the principal decided to award the entire school double the daily money for the school picnic. It was announced to the whole school that, because a student had had such integrity as to come forth and admit he had made a mistake, his behavior earned the school double the normal amount for the day. Interestingly, the principal reported that he could see in the faces of this student's fellow classmates that they were proud of his demonstrated honesty. As a result, other students repeated this type of appropriate behavior throughout the year. The student and school body could have been punished for the original inappropriate behavior, but the occasion arose to reward appropriate behavior, and that is what the principal did. He took the opportunity to build desirable behaviors.

The second intervention for rewarding desirable behavior was increasing the praise available for appropriate social behavior. This was done by instituting praise notes (Embry, 1997). The praise notes were 4 1/4- by 5 1/2-inch pieces of two-part NCR paper. The following headings were on the praise notes, with blank lines for students or teachers to write in the comments.

- Presented to:

- What behavior you did:

- Presented by:

- Why that behavior was important to me:

Students or teachers could fill out a praise note for a student. After doing so, the individual giving the praise note presented the original copy to the recipient and placed the NCR copy in a box kept in the administrative office. On Monday mornings, the principal held a drawing during which time two or three praise notes were randomly selected from the box. The winners (the recipients as well as the presenters) were announced during morning announcements and presented with small prizes such as pencils, erasers, candy bars, and so on. Then all of the praise notes collected in the box during the past week were put up on a bulletin board in the main hallway for the following week. This allowed students, teachers, and visitors to the building an opportunity to read them.

Twice per year (at Christmas break and just before the end of school) a schoolwide assembly was held for a grand prize drawing of the praise notes. At each of these assemblies, three push scooters were presented to students. Two drawings were held: one for praise notes from students and one for praise notes from teachers. For the drawing of praise notes from students, one scooter went to the student who received the praise note and one scooter went to the student who gave the praise note. For the drawing of praise notes from teachers, one scooter was awarded to the student who received the praise note. Because the school did not have enough money for all these scooters, the principal approached the police officers in town who were affiliated with the DARE program. As a result, the police officers contributed funds for five of the six scooters.

A brief discussion of praise is warranted here. All too often praise is treated like a four-letter word—something that should not be said and, if said, should not be said very often. Why teachers would not want to praise student achievement is a mystery, given that student achievement is the goal of good teaching. This does not mean that praise should be given randomly. As Dale Carnegie (1936) stated in his book *How to Win Friends and Influence People,* "neither proffer nor receive cheap praise." When students demonstrate the achievement of desirable behavior, sincere, warranted, meaningful praise should be given lavishly.

When the praise notes intervention first began, now and then a praise note would be submitted that was inappropriate or insincere. When this occurred, the note was discarded and no mention was made of it. Only appropriate praise notes were eligible for the drawings and

posting on the bulletin board. The few inappropriate praise notes ceased to be given. The students appeared so excited about the possibility of earning a weekly prize or a scooter and seeing their praise notes posted on the bulletin board that they often went out of their way looking for opportunities to praise one another.

The third intervention for rewarding appropriate behavior was related to school assemblies. Historically, because of student disruptive and inappropriate behavior, this school rarely had student assemblies. In fact, they had never had a sports assembly. Believing that assemblies can be useful for building positive schoolwide behavior change and because the students requested more assemblies, the principal agreed to have them. However, the principal used these assemblies as rewards for students' appropriate behaviors and as a means to give recognition for student achievements. Thus, during the year of the schoolwide positive behavioral interventions, the school had numerous assemblies for each of the following:

- Golden Panther Awards (these awards were known by the name of the school mascot)
- Year-end academic and social awards
- Heritage Days
- Sports
- Music (school concerts)

Because most readers are probably familiar with sports, music, and year-end award assemblies, we will briefly describe the Golden Panther Awards and Heritage Days.

The Golden Panther Awards were given each quarter during the school year. Near the end of each quarter, each teacher was prompted by the principal to submit the names of two students who he or she thought were exemplary. *Exemplary* was not defined as *A* students only. Instead, *exemplary* was defined as students who were trying hard to do well in school. The principal compiled the names of all the students nominated and sent this list to all the teachers. The teachers were told to review the list and cross off the name of any student they believed shouldn't be on the list. If just one teacher crossed off the name of any student for any reason, that student's name was removed from the list. Thus, this was a very difficult award to achieve. Students who were nominated and whose names were not crossed off the list by any teachers were winners of the Golden Panther Award.

The parents of the winners were notified of their child's accomplishment and that an assembly in honor of that accomplishment was held. Interestingly, a large number of parents took off work just to be present at these awards assemblies. They often came dressed in their finest clothes and brought other members of the family (children, grandparents, etc.). They brought cameras and took pictures during and after the assembly.

At the assembly, the winning students were called to the stage and presented with a Golden Panther certificate (suitable for framing), a Golden Panther personal identification card (which, when presented, allowed them to be first in the lunch line and first to come to and leave assemblies, functioned as a library and hall pass, and gained them free admission to any school event) and a Golden Panther candy bar (this was a Snickers bar wrapped in golden paper with the listed ingredients of courtesy, integrity, perseverance, self-control, and indomitable spirit—the school's tenets). At the end of the assembly, the award recipients and their parents were invited to the cafeteria for cookies and punch with the principal. Students and their parents loved this award (and the total cost was only $50).

Heritage Days assemblies were brought about to address the racial and tribal unrest that had occurred in the past at the school. A Heritage Day was held for each of the four "tribes" that made up the school population: Celtic, Navajo, Ute, and Danish. An assembly was held on each of four Heritage Days, and community members from the honored heritage came to the school to give presentations to the student body. The idea was that if students were given the chance to see not only the unique things that made each of their cultures different, but also the many things that they all shared as part of the overall American culture, acceptance of each other would increase. It appeared to work; incidences of inappropriate behaviors related to racial or tribal differences were virtually eliminated. After these assemblies, students appeared to recognize that they had far more in common than not.

## A Three-Tier Approach

The interventions discussed earlier did in fact address the needs of students within each of the three tiers. The IS room was for all students across the school. Sure, the typically developing students, the ones from the larger student population, never were sent to the IS room or, if sent, came only once or twice. Those students who were at risk may have come one to five or six times before their behaviors improved to the extent that they were not sent back for more training. Students at intervention came 1 to 20 times. But each time students were in the IS room they had the opportunity to practice positive social behaviors that would benefit them not only in school, but for the rest of their lives. The IS room was an intervention that was quite inexpensive and addressed the individual needs of all three tiers of students.

The other interventions were more global in nature. Although they were not designed to meet each student's individual needs, they had the potential to affect the behaviors of all the students across all the tiers. Many students from the at-risk tier participated in the praise notes, and one student from the at-intervention tier was elected as a student government representative. After being elected, her behavior changed completely; she never again was sent to the IS room or the office. All the students participated in the assemblies and school fair. No undermining of the intervention program occurred because the interventions benefited all students.

## Community Involvement

This low-cost schoolwide change package did not require any parent or community training. However, the principal did implement several activities to assist the parents and community members in becoming more aware of and involved in the interventions that were occurring in the school. First, the principal created a volunteer parents' organization. This consisted of one or two parents' volunteering to assist a teacher at times when extra help was needed. This help took the form of accompanying classes on field trips, helping with bigger class projects, and so on.

Second, the principal formed a parent advisory board. This board consisted of five parents, two teachers, and the school administrators. The board met once per month to discuss issues related to the school. Though the board did not set policy, they did get to influence the decisions made by the school administrators.

Third, the principal established weekly lunches with parents. Each week 10 parents were invited to have lunch with the principal. The parents and principal sat at tables on the cafeteria stage while students ate lunch at tables on the main floor. Each week parents from a different grade level were invited to attend the lunch. As mentioned earlier, students from each of the three grades (sixth, seventh, and eighth) ate at separate times. So, for example, parents of sixth-grade students were invited to eat lunch with the principal during the sixth-grade lunch period. The principal paid for their lunches, and the parents and principal ate the same lunch as the children ate. Historically, the school had purchased lunches for teachers who performed lunch duty. However, the principal reworked the paraprofessionals' schedules so that paraprofessionals performed lunch duty as part of their jobs. Because teachers were no longer used as lunch monitors, the funds that had bought the teachers' lunches were now used for the parents' lunches. These lunches were opportunities for the principal and parents to interact and have discussions about what was occurring at the school and what parents would like to see occur at the school. It brought parents into the school for positive, nonthreatening interactions.

Finally, another method for getting the community more involved in the school was opening up the school to community members. Community members often came by the school and asked permission to use the gymnasium or library for some event. The principal made sure to say yes whenever feasible. He viewed the school as a community asset, and in this case the community was invited to come and share in that asset. The principal let the community know that the school was there for them and that the school administration supported the community. This brought more community members into the school and got them involved in the school. Community members became more aware of the needs of the school and what an important role the school played in the community.

## Administration Involvement

Although the interventions described were not expensive, they did require a fair amount of commitment, time, and effort by the school administration. This was especially true for the IS room intervention because all the students first went to the office, where the administrator decided what social skills the students needed to learn. Then, when the student demonstrated acquisition of the social behavior, the administrator once more was called on to escort the student back to class. One advantage of this time-consuming system was that the school administrators were aware of the problem behaviors occurring in the school.

These interventions required support not only from the school administration, but also from the district administration and school board members. In this case, the principal was not supported by the district administration, and he eventually left for another position. As a result, the interventions he started did not continue after he left.

To achieve maximum effectiveness, interventions like these must be in place for longer periods of time so that teachers, students, the district administration, and the community can observe the long-term benefits. When only one individual (in this case, the principal) is responsible for such change, the change does not tend to last when that individual leaves the district. If interventions such as these are to have the chance at continued implementation, district administration and school board support is necessary. They must hire and retain teachers and other school staff who are committed to the intervention's continued success.

## Improved Academic Program and Teaching Methodologies

Because this positive behavior change program lasted only 1 year, there was not enough time to bring about a significant change in the curriculum. However, some changes to teaching methodologies did occur. Though one particular teacher stated that she did not believe in praising students for doing well, the majority of the other teachers increased their praise of positive student behavior. By the end of the year, 2 of the 28 teachers were averaging more than one praise statement per minute during class time. That was a major advancement. More than half of the teachers were actively pursuing structured teaching methods that helped keep their students actively engaged in learning. These teachers were beginning to approach student learning from a belief of learning by trial and success, not trial and error. Not only were their students experiencing success with learning, but also, because they were actively engaged in learning, the students had no time to display inappropriate behaviors. Yes, having students actively en-

gaged in learning may be the best classroom management tool of all.

## CONCLUSION

When attempting to create schoolwide positive behavior change, administrators and teachers must give all students in the school opportunities to participate in the interventions that will help to facilitate behavior change (Horner & Sugai, 2002; Sugai et al., 2000; Walker et al., 1996). The interventions described in this chapter addressed each of the three tiers of students within the school. Disruptive behaviors were decreased by focusing on building and rewarding behaviors that would be of benefit to the students not only during school, but throughout their lives (Goldiamond, 1974; Schwartz & Goldiamond, 1975). Although this program collected data on behaviors, these data were not collected within a scientific design. Rather, they were collected to help guide the interventions and indicate whether the interventions appeared to be of benefit to the students, the school, and the community.

In one short year many good, positive changes occurred within this school. Praise from student to student, teacher to student, and student to teacher increased; attendance increased; and expulsions and fights decreased. The atmosphere of the school became one of peace and scholarship. At the end of the year, the local police chief commented that the police had been called to the school only twice all year, whereas in the previous year the police averaged two calls per week. To top it all off, for the first time in the history of the school district, the students of this school achieved the highest scores in the district on the year-end tests. Yes, we can bring about both social and academic schoolwide positive behavior change.

We will leave you with a couple of thoughts. We have heard it said many times that schools are not a business and cannot be run like one. But schools are a business. In many counties throughout the nation, the school district is the biggest employer and biggest business around.

Schools need to be run like businesses. They need to strive to create the best product they can, and they need to be held accountable for the product they produce. Schools need to continue searching for ways to build positive student behaviors, both academic behaviors and social behaviors. Schools need to look at inappropriate behaviors as opportunities to teach, not opportunities to suppress. Remember, our job as teachers is not to suppress undesirable behaviors; our job is to build desirable behaviors. We are not behavior suppressors, we are behavior builders; we are teachers. Yes, our schools are a business, and the product they produce is the future of America.

# REFERENCES

Adams, A. T. (1992). *Public high schools: The uses of rehabilitative and punitive forms of discipline: A final report.* Washington, DC: Office of Education Research and Improvement.

Alberto, P. A., & Troutman, A. C. (2003). *Applied behavior analysis for teachers* (6th ed.). Upper Saddle River, NJ: Merrill/Prentice Hall.

Azrin, N. H., Hake, D. G., Holz, W. C., & Hutchinson, R. R. (1965). Motivational aspects of escape from punishment. *Journal of the Experimental Analysis of Behavior, 8,* 31–34.

Berkowitz, L. (1983). Aversively stimulated aggression: Some parallels and difference in research with animals and humans. *American Psychologist, 38,* 1135–1144.

Billings, W. H., & Enger, J. M. (1995, November 8–10). *Perceptions of Missouri high school principals regarding the effectiveness of in-school suspension as a disciplinary procedure.* Paper presented at the annual meeting of the Mid-South Educational Research Association, Biloxi, MS.

Carnegie, D. (1936). *How to win friends and influence people.* New York: Simon and Schuster.

Collins, C. G. (1985, April). *In-school suspensions.* Paper presented at the annual meeting of the Council for Exceptional Children, Anaheim, CA.

Cooper, J. O., Heron, T. E., & Heward, W. L. (2005). *Applied behavior analysis* (2nd ed.). Upper Saddle River, NJ: Merrill/Prentice Hall.

Elements of an effective disciplinary strategy. (1995–1996). *American Educator, 19* (4), 24–27.

Embry, D. D. (1997). Does your school have a peaceful environment? Using an audit to create a climate for change and resiliency. *Interventions in School and Clinic, 32* (4), 217–222.

Goldiamond, I. (1974). Toward a constructional approach to social problems: Ethical and constitutional issues revised by applied behavior analysis. *Behaviorism, 2,* 1–85.

Goldstein, H. P., Sprafkin, R. P., Gershaw, N. J., & Klein, P. (1980). *Skillstreaming and the adolescent: A structured learning approach to teaching prosocial skills.* Champaign, IL: Research Press.

Horner, R. H., & Sugai, G. (2002, April). *Overview of positive behavior support.* Paper presented at the convention of the Council for Exceptional Children, New York.

Horner, R. H., Sugai, G., & Horner, H. F. (2000). A schoolwide approach to student discipline. *The School Administrator, 57,* 20–23.

Hutchinson, R. R. (1977). By-products of aversive control. In W. K. Honig & J. E. R. Staddon (Eds.), *Handbook of operant behavior* (pp. 415–431). Upper Saddle River, NJ: Prentice Hall.

Koop, C. E., & Lundberg, G. (1992). Violence in America: A public health emergency: Time to bullet back. *Journal of the American Medical Association, 267,* 3075–3076.

Lewis, T. J., & Sugai, G. (1999). Effective behavior support: A systems approach to proactive schoolwide management. *Focus on Exceptional Children, 31* (6), 1–17.

Lipsey, M. W. (1992, October). *The effects of treatment on juvenile delinquents: Results from meta-analysis.* Paper presented at the HIMH meeting for potential applicants for research to prevent youth violence, Bethesda, MD.

Mayer, G. R. (1995). Preventing antisocial behavior in the schools. *Journal of Applied Behavior Analysis, 28* (4), 467–478.

McGinnis, E., & Goldstein, A. P. (1984). *Skillstreaming the elementary school child: A guide for teaching prosocial skills.* Champaign, IL: Research Press.

Peterson, S. M., Peterson, L. D., & Lacy, L. (2002). *Dealing with students who challenge and defy authority.* Austin, TX: Pro-Ed.

Rutherford, R. B., & Nelson, C. M. (1995). Management of aggressive and violent behavior in the schools. *Focus on Exceptional Children, 27* (6), 1–15.

Schwartz, A., & Goldiamond, I. (1975). *Social casework: A behavioral approach.* New York: Columbia University Press.

Sugai, G., & Horner, R. (2001). School climate and discipline: Going to scale. Paper presented at National Summit on the Shared Implementation of IDEA. Washington, DC, June 23, 2001.

Sugai, G., Sprague, J. R., Horner, R. H., & Walker, H. M. (2000). Preventing school violence: The use of office referrals to assess and monitor schoolwide discipline interventions. *Journal of Emotional and Behavioral Disorders, 8,* 94–101.

Walker, H. M., Colvin, G. M, & Ramsey, E. (1995). *Antisocial behavior in the school: Strategies and best practices.* Pacific Grove, CA: Brooks/Cole.

Walker, H. M., Horner, R. H., Sugai, G., Bullis, M., Sprague, J. R., Bricker, D., & Kaufman, M. J. (1996). Integrating approaches to preventing antisocial behavior patterns among school-age children and youth. *Journal of Emotional and Behavioral Disorders, 4,* 193–256.

Winborn, J. D. (1992, November). *A study of the effectiveness of a Saturday school in reducing suspension, expulsion, and corporal punishment.* Paper presented at the annual meeting of the Mid-South Educational Research Association, Knoxville, TN.

## STUDY QUESTIONS AND FOLLOW-UP ACTIVITIES

1. Many school districts have responded to increases in disruptive behavior by implementing zero tolerance policies. Assume that you are the teacher of a student who was expelled for carrying Tylenol in her purse while on school property. Given that you disagree with this expulsion, what information would you share with the principal, school district administrators, and board members in an effort to eliminate or refine zero tolerance policies?

2. The authors point out that many schools are quick to implement consequences that are intended to punish disruptive behavior. What are some possible reasons teachers and administrators are so quick to implement punitive procedures (i.e., discuss the principle of negative reinforcement as it relates to the teacher or administrator)?

3. Horner, Sugai, and Horner (2000) described several key practices of schools with effective disciplinary systems. If you were the principal of a school, name some specific programs or steps you would implement to develop an effective disciplinary system in your building.

4. The authors focus on increasing positive or desirable behaviors rather than targeting negative or unwanted behaviors. Assume that you are part of an intervention assistance team and a student has been referred for excessive talk-outs and frequent out-of-seat behavior. Design an intervention that focuses on increasing appropriate behavior rather than decreasing the undesirable behavior (talk-outs and out-of-seat behavior).

5. Students at risk or at intervention often undermine the effectiveness of schoolwide interventions. Describe how this might happen and provide specific examples of interventions that may be implemented to address these concerns.

6. In the schoolwide discipline program described in this chapter, teachers are instructed to accept their students' apologies and admit them back into their classrooms. This can be a difficult thing to do for teachers who believe that disruptive students should be lectured or scolded for their transgressions. What are some other possible variables that may affect the success of a schoolwide intervention, and how could those threats to procedural integrity be avoided?

7. Design a course on classroom management for preservice teachers that includes the principles and procedures described in this chapter. List critical objectives that you would want your preservice teachers to master to demonstrate an understanding of the importance of reinforcing appropriate classroom behavior.

8. Collecting and using information about student behavior to guide future instruction is an integral part of a teacher's responsibility to improve student social and academic achievement. However, data collection is typically an area of weakness for many classroom teachers (i.e., they have not been properly trained or they "don't have time" to collect data). What are some ways to support teachers in collecting data and using those data to guide their instruction?

### CHAPTER 15

# Plato's Allegory of the Cave Revisited
## Disciples of the Light Appeal to the Pied Pipers and Prisoners in the Darkness

*Timothy E. Heron*  
*Stephanie M. Peterson*

*Matthew J. Tincani*  
*April D. Miller*

To paraphrase Dickens (1859), education faces the best of times and the worst of times. Although mounting research has documented an increasing array of effective curricula and teaching methods (Gardner et al., 1994; Kame'enui, Carnine, Dixon, Simmons, & Coyne, 2002; Lloyd, Forness, & Kavale, 1998; Wolery & Shuster, 1997), a growing number of vocal opponents are challenging these strategies as being inhumane, perfunctory, ill conceived, or outright dangerous to the psychological health and educational well-being of children (e.g., Gallagher, Heshusius, Iano, & Skrtic, 2004; Heshusius, 1991; Kohn, 1993; Poplin, 1988 ).

In the wake of national reform debates, it is not surprising to see one educational philosophy pitted against another, leaving well-intended practitioners who seek solutions to systemic educational problems in a quandary. Not knowing exactly which philosophy to embrace or whom to believe, teachers, parents, and administrators fall prey to novel, untested, and ill-defined instructional ideas and methods that promote antiscientific and/or constructivist

viewpoints that supposedly teach the "whole" child and reject behavior analytic approaches as restrictive, mechanistic, or punishing (Heshusius, 1982, 2004; Kohn, 1993). As test scores plummet, real achievement levels decrease, and frustration grows, the chorus of dissatisfaction from teachers and parents is joined by politicians who scurry to enact remedies to fix the "leaky roof" (Kame'enui, 1994), adding to teacher and parent confusion about what and whom to believe.

Plato's "The Allegory of the Cave" (4 B.C.E./ 2002) may provide a metaphor for the status of many educational practitioners today. This allegory portrays a cave in which prisoners are chained in the dark in front of a parapet (see Figure 15-1). The parapet, from which the puppeteers tell their stories to the prisoners, is lit from behind. As a result, the prisoners can see only shadows—representations of what the puppeteers dangle from behind—but never the real objects themselves. Because of the way they are chained and oriented, the prisoners are not provided with firsthand knowledge of

**Figure 15-1.**
Plato's allegory showing the prisoners chained to their seats, showmen on the parapet displaying books, a fire to backlight the books, and the cave entrance leading to the sunlight. *(Courtesy of Michael Plummer)*

reality, only the representations of that reality as revealed by those in control. Occasionally, a prisoner escapes from his chains, climbs to the cave entrance, and sees the light. At this point, the prisoner achieves knowledge and truth because he is no longer dependent on those on the parapet to deliver information. Instead, he is free to seek out information from original sources and to draw his own conclusions rather than relying on the representations of truth previously presented. However, only a few prisoners ever escape their tight chains and, once freed, fewer risk returning to the cave to help others escape their bonds of illusion.

We suggest that Plato's allegory, written in 4 B.C.E. can be applied to the status of educational practitioners in the 21st century. In this "revised" allegory, the prisoners can be viewed as a metaphor for teachers and practitioners who have fallen prey to novel, untested, and ill-

defined instructional ideas and are shackled by their chains. The puppeteers can be viewed as a metaphor for those theorists or philosophers who champion antiscientific instructional ideas and who hold practitioners in the chains of darkness. The light, of course, can be viewed as a metaphor for science—"a set of methods designed to describe and interpret observed or inferred phenomena, past or present, and aimed at building a testable body of knowledge open to rejection or confirmation" (Shermer, 2002, p. 18). The light (i.e., science) allows one to see the truth and to gain knowledge. Those prisoners who have escaped the darkness and who have seen the light can be viewed as a metaphor for those who apply the scientific method to evaluate educational theories and practices.

This chapter examines Plato's "The Allegory of the Cave" within the context of the present-day discussion on educational practice. In addition, we discuss several key and distinguishing elements of behavior analysis that serve as candles in the dark and that can guide practitioners to select effective interventions. Our discussion includes exemplars of field-tested, tried-and-true effective methodologies. Finally, we appeal to pied pipers and practitioners alike to see the light (i.e., use the scientific method) and to adopt "best practice" standards when considering school or home-based educational procedure (Peters & Heron, 1993).

## THE REVISED ALLEGORY

In our view, Plato's original allegory serves as an excellent metaphor to describe present circumstances in education. In our revised allegory, the chained prisoners are now teachers (see Figure 15-2).[1] The chains that bind them to their current, failed teaching practices consist of their own educational backgrounds that did not prepare them properly, their lack of formal preparation to analyze instructional methods critically and to be able to apply experimental criteria to determine best practice (Peters & Heron, 1993), an antiscientific climate in schools (Heward, 2003), an educational culture that switches from method to method even in the presence of improved student performance (Van Houten, 1984), and a culture that seemingly relishes process in favor of product (Gallagher et al., 2004). Hence, the teachers in the allegory are chained rigidly to their seats, doomed to

---

[1]Although in our revised allegory, the teachers are chained, any practitioner who is locked into failed practice might be substituted.

**Figure 15-2.**
The revised allegory showing teachers chained to their seats, pied pipers broadcasting misleading statements, the escape path for teachers, and a teacher returning to the cave to assist others. *(Courtesy of Michael Plummer)*

**Figure 15-3.**
Misleading content projected on the cave wall.
*(Courtesy of Michael Plummer)*

view shadowy illustrations of what is real while multiple showmen on the parapet—the present-day pied pipers—are all too eager to dangle misleading, or what Kame'enui (1994) reminded us is "not even wrong," information relative to what is occurring with respect to student performance before their glazed-over eyes (e.g., "Reinforcement is bribery," "Use whole language," "Try discovery learning and invented spelling") (Heward, 2003; Kame'enui, 1994) (see Figure 15-3). The objects that the showmen hold out as being authentic include unvalidated or fuzzy educational methods (e.g., whole language, invented spelling), trade and college-level textbooks that provide inaccurate or misleading educational statements related to basic and fundamental principles (Cooke, 1984), and mis-

stated or unsubstantiated positions (e.g., Heshusius, 1982).

The teachers are trapped and shackled by their chains. Their prior educational histories and current practices consist largely of viewing the shadow objects. It's no wonder that after a steady diet of seeing attractive, but illusionary, images, practitioners are not able to discern real, experimentally tested, best practices approaches that are advanced by behavior analysts from the blurry proposals advanced by the pied pipers (Heward, 2003; Lloyd et al., 1998; Peters & Heron, 1993). Indeed, they lack what Carl Sagan (1996) described as a "Baloney Detection Kit," a toolbox that contains the conceptual instruments for skeptical thinking. As Sagan stated, "if [a] new idea survives examination by the tools in our kit, we grant it warm, although tentative, acceptance. . . . The question is not whether we *like* the conclusion that emerges out of a train of reasoning, but whether the conclusion *follows* from the premise or starting point and whether that premise is true" (p. 210). Practitioners would be better served if they used the scientific approach as a candle in the dark to lead them beyond the quagmire of educational pseudotheories and philosophies (what they see now on the cave wall) to the light at the cave entrance.

As it stands, teachers fall victim to highly touted propositions supposedly designed to improve children's performance by using such methods as new math, whole language, and invented spelling. With respect to the latter, Dixon used poignant sarcasm to make the point that poor spellers do quite well under conditions of invented spelling; they get all the words wrong (personal communication, October 2, 2003).

Still, not all teachers are victimized all of the time. Perhaps because of their continued frustration with failed approaches, hearing whisperings of new ideas that circulate beyond the parapet, or recognizing at last that the emperor has no clothes, a teacher may free herself from her chains, climb to the cave entrance, and reach the knowledge that awaits in the light. We would echo Plato's position that after acquiring

**Figure 15-4.**
Teachers crossing paths during an escape from and return to the cave. *(Courtesy of Michael Plummer)*

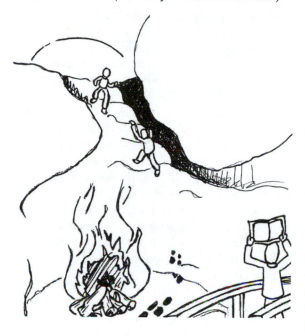

the wisdom and knowledge in the light, the teacher needs to return to the depths of the cave to help other prisoners overcome their chains and escape as well (see Figure 15-4).

## APPLIED BEHAVIOR ANALYSTS AS DISCIPLES WHO HAVE SEEN THE LIGHT

At the outset, it might seem arrogant to claim that behavior analysts are the only disciples to see the light. Of course, this is not the case. However, what separates behavior analysts from other philosophers and theorists, and certainly from prophets on the parapet, is their reliance on the basic attitudes and tenets of science: determinism, empiricism, parsimony, scientific manipulation, and philosophic doubt (Cooper, Heron, & Heward, in press). Coupling these tenets with the guiding philosophy that decisions relative to educational practice must be

supported by data—not opinion and testimonials—serves as a basis for self-regulated skepticism that provides the candlepower for parsimonious explanations of student performance in and outside of classrooms.

In short, behavior analysis has developed a considerable technology of effective instruction, focusing on preintervention strategies (Murdick & Petch-Hogan, 1996), classroom management practices (Cipani, 1998), social skills instruction (Gumpel & Frank, 1999), academic and psychomotor skills (Seabaugh & Schumaker, 1994; Ward, Smith, Makasci, & Crouch, 1998), language development (Bondy & Frost, 1994), and health and safety skills (Utley, Reddy, Delquadri, Greenwood, Mortweet, & Bowman, 2001) among a number of other research areas (cf. Sulzer-Azaroff & Gillat, 1990). There is a growing—and robust—literature that demonstrates that behavior analysis interventions produce consistently positive outcomes for students, their teachers, and their parents (Heward, 2003). Further, if practices are properly programmed, these outcomes are much more likely to be repeatable, maintained over time, and generalized to nontrained settings.

Sadly, much of this technology has been condemned by the pied pipers on the parapet as being simplistic, mechanistic, inhumane, or oxymoronic (e.g., Gallagher et al., 2004; Kohn, 1993). For instance, Kohn (1993) contrasted rewards and punishment in curious terms: "In respects major and minor, rewards and punishments are fundamentally similar" (p. 50). Later, he claimed:

A reward, by definition, is a desired object or event made conditional on having fulfilled some criterion: only if you do this will you get that. . . . The whole point is to control people's behavior, and the most effective way to do this is to describe what will be given to them if they comply—or done to them if they don't comply. For this very reason, the possibility of ending up without the reward, which makes the process essentially punitive, is always present. The stick is contained in the carrot. (p. 53)

In taking this position, however, Kohn failed to grasp the actual definition of reinforcement (Skinner, 1953), and in transmitting misleading and inaccurate information from the parapet did double damage. For instance, he claimed that rewards and punishers are fundamentally the same. In fact, (a) rewards are not synonymous with reinforcers, and (b) rewards function in quite opposite ways from punishers. Reinforcers are defined as stimuli that follow a behavior contingently and have the effect of increasing the future frequency of that response class of behaviors under certain stimulus conditions (Cooper et al., in press). By definition, reinforcers clearly *increase* behavior. Punishment, by definition, is applied to *reduce* or *suppress* behavior by either presenting or removing stimuli following that behavior (Cooper et al., in press). Cooper and colleagues (in press) further indicated that reinforcers and punishers are determined by their functions. If a future response class of behavior increases in frequency because of the presentation of the stimulus subsequent to the behavior, then positive reinforcement can be claimed. If the response class of behavior decreases or is suppressed, then punishment has occurred. Reinforcement and punishment, as defined by their respective functions, produce exactly the opposite phenomena in practice to what Kohn claimed. They are simply not similar.

In addition to misstating the functional definitions of reinforcement and punishment, Kohn missed the entire point of the principles of reinforcement and punishment. Reinforcement and punishment occur all the time, whether such consequences are "programmed" (i.e., planned for) or not. Like the laws of physics, behavioral principles are simply observations of human phenomena. That is, the law of gravity states that objects released from a height above the ground fall perpendicular to the ground. This law may not be to our liking, especially when we accidentally drop a piece of Grandma's best china, but the fact is, the premise is true. Similarly, when a consequence follows a behavior, and the behavior occurs again more frequently in the future, then reinforcement has occurred. In some cases, this principle may not be to our liking, but that does not change the fact that the principle holds. For example, if a child acts out and her teacher becomes upset, turns three shades of red, and reprimands the child, and in the future the child's acting-out behavior increases, then the act of reprimanding the child has served to reinforce acting-out behavior. Although the teacher certainly never intended to reinforce such behavior, reinforcement still occurred.

More disturbingly, Kohn suggested that reinforcement is designed to *control* people's behavior using context that connotes a dark and sinister event. In making such claims, he missed the point about the underlying purpose of reinforcement-based interventions—to increase the future frequency of targeted appropriate, socially acceptable behaviors and to bring the individual into closer contact with other reinforcers. Behaviors initially selected for change are those that are socially significant (Baer, Wolf, & Risley, 1968) and that bring the individual into closer contact with other natural reinforcers in the environment. For example, teaching an individual appropriate workplace behaviors (e.g., social skills, money-handling skills, reading skills) using programmed reinforcement contingencies may help that individual maintain employment so that he or she will contact the natural contingencies of working (i.e., receiving a paycheck).

Poplin (1988) is another example of a pied piper who misrepresents behavior analysis. In her view, the holistic/constructivist approach takes the high ground by confidently asserting that "people are always learning" and asserting with equal confidence that such is not the case for those who follow behavior analysis precepts. Speaking of the attitudinal differences between philosophies, she stated (incorrectly):

> This is incompatible with the myriad manipulation techniques that are used to force, coerce, or cajole students to learn what others want them to learn. These behavior management systems are developed to assure that students' behaviors are

controlled while "learning" is forced down passive, uninterested throats. (p. 410)

In both the Kohn and Poplin examples, to state that rewards (sic) are punishers or that behavior analysts do not believe that children are always learning misses the mark. The contrary is actually true. Behavior analysts believe that students are always learning within an environment that shapes their behavior through reinforcement, extinction, generalization, and punishment contingencies. In a behavior analytic view, learning is dynamic. Pied pipers who miss this distinction—and worse, who misrepresent this view to the public—are at best disingenuous, misguided, and not even wrong (cf. Kame'enui, 1994).

## KEY CONTRIBUTIONS OF BEHAVIOR ANALYSIS TO EFFECTIVE INSTRUCTION

Through rigorous experimentation, behavior analysts have discovered many truths regarding how to select, implement, and evaluate instructional strategies that are effective, individualized, and humane. These truths are based on the tenets of science. We further believe that behavior analysts hold at least six candles that can lead our metaphorical teachers out of the darkness to the cave entrance and to higher levels of truth and wisdom. In our view, these candles represent the key contributions of behavior analysis to effective instruction. They include the focused recognition of data-based decision making, alterable variables, repeated practice, active student responding, instructional efficiency, and social validity.

### Data-Based Decision Making

A critical tool in a teacher's "Baloney Detection Kit" (Sagan, 1996) is the quantification of the phenomenon in question. A "show me" attitude is essential to evaluate claims regarding the effectiveness of instruction. That is, evidence sup-

porting the claim that instruction was effective must be presented. Such evidence should have some numerical basis to discriminate well between effective and ineffective practices. Vague, qualitative information, such as anecdotal reports that "Johnny seems to be reading much better lately," allow for too many interpretations to be useful. "Without corroborative evidence from other sources, or physical proof of some sort, ten anecdotes are no better than one, and a hundred anecdotes are no better than 10. Anecdotes are told by fallible human storytellers" (Shermer, 2002, p. 48). The use of public evidence open to close scrutiny can help teachers avoid making subjective errors in judgments in instruction. Thus, data-based decision making sets the occasion for effective instruction because it employs frequent (i.e., daily) and direct (i.e., tallies or counts of observed behaviors) measurement of student behavior (Heward, 2003). Bushell and Baer (1994) stated it best:

> Our general thesis is that close, continual contact with relevant outcome data is a fundamental, distinguishing feature of applied behavior analysis. Close continual contact with relevant outcome data ought to be a fundamental feature of classroom teaching as well (p. 7).

Data-based decision making ensures that the assessment and evaluation elements of student performance are noted and that growth, plateaus, or lapses in student progress can be acted on quickly. That is, such data are used to provide the formative and summative context for making necessary changes to instruction. Although we concede that many teachers face challenges during their day that may have their roots in the child's home situation, disability, poverty level, and so forth, teachers must come to believe that they are capable of changing some aspects of the students' school-based environment, especially as it relates to their instruction. Student performance data are the key that informs teaching practices. The data drive decisions along an educational continuum from most to least intrusive intervention approaches.

Conversely, if teachers believe that students are unteachable, that the students, especially those with disabilities, are likely to discover their own knowledge, or that student progress can be determined intuitively, then little progress will likely occur.

## Alterable Variables

The second author taught a college-level methods course attended by teachers of students with emotional and behavioral disorders. On the first day of class he asked, "Why do your students misbehave?" Their responses spoke to issues of poverty, poor home life, past teachers' mistakes, and psychiatric problems. The teachers did not, however, view the students' behavior as a function of their *current* teaching practices. Instead, most believed that the students' misbehavior was caused by variables *outside* of their classrooms and *beyond* their control (e.g., the students were born that way or their performance was low because they were poorly motivated). Perhaps what these despairing teachers were experiencing could best be termed explanatory fiction—that is, a circular way of viewing the cause and effect of a situation. Specifically, the teachers' explanations for poor motivation are just another way of describing the behavior (i.e., poor student performance). Vargas (1977) provided a behavior analytic perspective on explanatory fiction:

> Explanatory fictions are of no help to the teacher. Being told that a student doesn't work enthusiastically *because* he or she is not motivated does not tell the teacher what to change. We are no closer to a solution if we are told to motivate Johnny than we were when we knew we had to get him to work harder. In practice, explanatory fictions are worse than no help. Too often they put the blame on the student, thus discouraging the teacher from looking at the environment for the real causes of the problem. (p. 20)

The candle that a behavior analyst holds to light the way would shift the teacher's attention from the student's socioeconomic status, family upbringing, or cultural differences as a cause for poor performance, to specific environmental conditions in the classroom that the teacher *can* alter (e.g., preteaching, teaching, and postteaching strategies). Teachers who modify their mode of presentation (i.e., how they *present* information to students) or the expected mode of student response (i.e., verbal versus written versus motoric; individual versus group arrangements) have made the transition to examining environmental variables that they can alter and that do make a difference. In making this shift, those teachers are more likely to set the occasion for appropriate student responses, and they are in a better position to reinforce them when they do occur.

## Repeated Practice

In addition to data-based decision making, effective teachers occasion many opportunities for students to practice acquired and emerging skills (Heward, 1994). As many special educators know, repeated practice has been out of vogue in general education for some time. In an era of heuristic learning in which the overarching philosophy is that students discover and construct their own schemas (Heshusius, 1982), drill and practice protocols are unfortunately looked on with disdain. Indeed, many preservice teachers hear from the parapet that repeated practice ruins students' intrinsic motivation to learn and sets the occasion for student misery. Kohn (1997) provided yet another example of the work of the puppeteers when he stated: "A sour 'take your medicine' traditionalism goes hand in hand with drill-and-skill lessons (some of which are aptly named 'worksheets') and a reliance on incentives to induce students to do what they understandably have no interest in doing" (p. 2).

However, repeated drill and practice is a necessary component of effective learning. Perhaps this is why music teachers, physical education teachers, and athletic coaches continue to view repeated practice as an essential component of learning. These professionals design repeated practice of musical scales, motor movements, and offensive or defensive movements because they know the value that these lessons provide to their learners.

## Active Student Responses (ASR)

Students learn best by doing, a tenet championed from the time of John Dewey to the present day. Active responses are those that are observable and countable and that include error correction responses as well (Barbetta, Heron, & Heward, 1993; Heward, 1994). Strategies that evoke high ASR include, among others, peer tutoring, choral responding, and response card methods. High-ASR approaches have been demonstrated repeatedly to produce better learning outcomes than instructional strategies that promote low ASR (Barbetta et al., 1993; Narayan, Heward, Gardner, Courson, & Omness, 1990). A clear advantage of high ASR is that every trial produces a correct response. The more trials that are correct, the more reinforcement and feedback are delivered. Increased levels of reinforcement and feedback produce sustained learning.

Narayan and colleagues (1990) compared a traditional hand-raising condition with a response card condition on fourth-graders' rate of active responding and quiz performances in social studies. Results showed that active student responding was significantly higher when the response card condition was in effect than when hand-raising was used. Specifically, students answered slightly fewer than 2 questions per 20-minute lesson under hand-raising conditions, but almost 30 questions per 20-minute lesson under response card conditions. Further, student performance on quizzes favored the response card condition. Narayan and colleagues, extrapolating these data to a 180-day school year, suggested that upward of 5,000 additional opportunities to respond can be achieved.

Heward (1994) summed up the situation quite well with respect to the affect of ASR when he stated:

> Increasing active student response in the classroom will not in itself turn education into a discipline guided by scientific decision making, but it is one way that classroom teachers can put themselves in touch with the immediate consequences of their efforts. When instruction is designed around high-ASR activities, not only is it hard for students to passively attend, it is equally difficult for teachers to avoid direct and daily feedback on the effectiveness of their teaching. (p. 316)

## Instructional Efficiency

Efficiency is another candle that behavior analysts hold for those willing and able to grasp it. Efficiency is an important dimension of instructional effectiveness. Efficient teaching produces desired learning outcomes in as few trials as possible, while carefully considering the transfer of stimulus control from instructional stimuli to the natural environment (Grunsell & Carter, 2002). Efficient procedures allow teachers to present more learning trials and lessons within an allocated instructional period. Efficient procedures are desirable because they save time, resources, and money without sacrificing student learning. In short, instructionally efficient procedures improve students' rate of learning (Narayan et al., 1990), set the occasion for teachers to provide individualized attention to students who may have special needs, and establish the focus on relevant data for instructional decision making (Bushell & Baer, 1994). That is, if students are not making reasonable and consistent progress toward instructional aims, the teaching tactic is changed, combined with a more robust strategy, or abandoned altogether.

## Social Validity

The sixth, and perhaps the most personalized, of the candles that behavior analysts have to offer relates to social validity. In their seminal article on the current dimensions of applied behavior analysis, Baer and colleagues (1968) stressed that functionally effective behavioral teaching techniques produce outcomes of "practical value." Stated differently, the degree of behavior change produced by an intervention should be directly useful to the individual as well as to significant others in the environment. Functionally effective teaching not only improves the behavior targeted for intervention, but also increases the student's quality of life in socially significant ways (Baer, Wolf, & Risley, 1987). Socially significant outcomes include enhanced peer relationships; higher scores and grades; and improved independence in school, at home, and in the community. Therefore, although effectiveness data serve as a solid benchmark in their own right, teachers can also look beyond student performance data to determine the impact of instruction on students' lives.

The teachers in chains who hear the siren call of the pied pipers might think to ask the following questions when considering whether to accept the alluring instructional procedures they recommend: (a) Are the procedures effective? Do they produce important learning gains that students, teachers, parents, and administrators notice? (b) Do the procedures allow for instruction accommodation if the student does not make progress? (c) Are the procedures "user friendly"? and (d) Will teachers continue to implement them if they are not required to do so by administrators?

Questions relevant to the issue of social validity are these: Is the student in a less restrictive environment as a result of this intervention and is the student more integrated into school, home, or general community settings as a result of an intervention? A yes response to these questions provides assurance that instruction is making a measurable difference in the student's life. The key to social validity for the behavior analyst is subjecting these questions to scientific examination.

Contrary to what Kohn (1993) and Poplin (1988) believe, behavior analysts are deeply interested in meaningful outcomes that improve the whole individual and the quality of life of that individual. A compelling statement by Hawkins (1984)—a parent of an adult-aged daughter with severe disabilities—makes this point:

> The definition of the "meaningfulness" of a behavior change will thus be one that refers to the functionality of that behavior for someone. In the case of severely and profoundly retarded persons, I think the "someones" who are by far the most important are the student himself, and if he or she lives at home, members of the immediate family. (p. 284)

## THE CONTINUUM OF EFFECTIVE INSTRUCTION PRACTICE

Being effective does not mean that teachers are limited to a restricted set of instructional alternatives. A continuing misrepresentation of behavior-analytic-oriented teaching methods is that they embrace only "scripted" instruction.[2] On the contrary, behavior analysis has provided educators with a number of functional and effective teaching strategies that can be categorized into three main areas: teacher-directed (e.g., Carnine, Silbert, Kame'enui, & Tarver, 2004; Heward, 1994; Stein, Carnine, & Dixon, 1998), peer-mediated (e.g., Miller, Barbetta, & Heron, 1994; Wright, Cavanaugh, Sainato, & Heward, 1995), and semi-independent and independent (Bryant & Seay, 1998; Rieth & Semmel, 1991) approaches. Teacher-directed approaches include such practices as direct instruction (Carnine et al., 2004) and active student response methods (Heward, 1994). In peer-mediated approaches the students themselves are the pri-

---

[2]Although many Direction Instruction (capital *D*, capital *I*) programs use scripted lessons, they are by no means the only type of lesson that embraces a direct instruction (lowercase *d*, lowercase *i*) approach. Scripted lessons used within the context of DI relate to explicit instruction in which lessons are sequenced based on skill acquisition. Explicit instruction is not synonymous with rote, mechanical lessons that students must endure.

mary agents of instructional delivery (Barbetta et al., 1993). Tutoring systems in academic and specialized content areas (Heron, Welsch, & Goddard, 2003; Miller et al., 1994) serve as outstanding, well-researched examples of peer-mediated approaches. Finally, semi-independent and independent approaches involve student self-delivery of instruction, using computers (Rieth & Semmel, 1991) or other forms of assistive technology. These strategies pass the litmus test for effectiveness because they meet or exceed the standards required by best practice (Peters & Heron, 1993).

We recommend teacher-directed, peer-mediated, and independent strategies for several reasons. First, students have a fundamental right to effective instruction (Barrett et al., 1991). That is, students are entitled to programs that are individualized; provide sufficient opportunity to practice skills; offer differential consequences for academic and social progress and errors; generate effectiveness data; and provide teachers with the necessary support, feedback, and reinforcement from administrators. The use of this trilogy of strategies provides for this multicomponent instruction for children. More important, these strategies meet the spirit and intent of the *Daubert* standard, a standard upheld by a Supreme Court ruling (*Daubert v. Merrell Dow Pharmaceuticals, Inc.,* 1993) that specifies that practitioners must use reliable, state-of-the-art, field-tested strategies when working with students. To meet the *Daubert* standard, students must have the benefit of instructional approaches that are valid and reliable, not merely available and convenient. Second, practitioners can use the strategies with confidence, recognizing that if they implement them correctly, they will achieve positive outcomes. Finally, these strategies provide a useful road map when designing fun, balanced, innovative, and well-articulated teacher-directed, peer-mediated, or independent lessons.

Of course, the arrangement that the teacher configures will depend on the nature of the learning task, the students' prior knowledge and history with the content, the expected modes of presentation and response, and the student's individualized education program (IEP) goals. It is within the context of these empirically based, field-tested, and validated approaches that we make the following appeals to the pied pipers and the prisoners.

## CONCLUSION

We offer five direct appeals. First, we appeal to the pied pipers to read the *original* sources of behavior analysis literature (e.g., Baer et al., 1968; Holland & Skinner, 1961; Michael, 1993; Skinner, 1938, 1953) and recognize what these scholars and researchers say with respect to basic principles and procedures. Misrepresentations are far less likely if the sound educational positions advanced by these scholars are discussed and addressed accurately.

Unfortunately, general education textbooks that misconstrue basic principles and procedures of behavior analysis to unsuspecting audiences still abound. As Kame'enui (1994) stated, "the educational tools themselves (e.g., textbooks, computer programs) are rarely systematically field-tested. Untested and ineffective tools discriminate most harshly and insidiously against low performers—those who are already victims of education's leaky roof" (p. 158). While Kame'enui was referring to textbooks that children read and the ultimate disservice they render to students with special needs in public schools, his point could also apply to college-level texts and the teachers-in-training who read them. By holding these misleading representations as examples for the *prisoners,* an implicit conspiracy of untruth is sustained—bestowing an unwarranted light of authenticity where really only shadow exists. When more shadow than substance is displayed on the wall of the cave, no one gains. With respect to publishing continuing misinformation, we would ask that pied pipers revisit Oliver Cromwell's admonition: "I beseech you . . . think it possible you may be mistaken."[3]

Second, we appeal to those on the parapet to adopt a scientific method based on observation, hypothesis testing, data collection, analysis, prediction, and control, which has served our culture well in terms of discriminating what's right, what's wrong, and what's not even wrong (Heward, 2003; Kame'enui, 1994). We recognize that many educators have slipped into an antiscientific mode in the past decade and have accepted educational fads and fictions for verifiable truths. As Heward (2003) stated:

> In recent years, the general lack of interest in applying the results of research to classroom practice has been replaced in some education circles by a distinct distrust of empirical research altogether . . . some dismiss objective evidence as irrelevant to the issue at hand; others simply invent data to support their viewpoint. (p. 199)

Third, we suggest that teachers and other practitioners work to free themselves from their chains. Of course, this will take great effort and strong leadership. Vocal opposition may occur along the way (Heron, 1997). The journey to the top of the cave is difficult. However, once teachers have seen the light of effective instructional practice, they will also note improved student performance.

Fourth, we encourage the pied pipers, and those prisoners still in chains, to listen to those escapees who have returned from the top of the cave. They have seen the light and they have knowledge to offer. Over the past 30 years, an impressive body of research literature on effective teaching practices has been generated and has withstood the test of peer review, replication, and rigorous intellectual scrutiny (Forness, Kavale, Blum, & Lloyd, 1997; Gardner et al.,

1994; Gersten 1998; Kame'enui et al., 2002; Lloyd et al., 1998; Wolery & Shuster, 1997). This research has also met the *Daubert* standard and federal legislation regulations (e.g., the No Child Left Behind Act of 2001, P.L. 107–110). At the very least, the pied pipers have the obligation to preservice and inservice educators—those still chained—to consider carefully what they have to say now that they have returned after seeing the light. In effect, our appeal is to the pied pipers to consider applying philosophic doubt.

Finally, we appeal to the special education and behavior analysis community to remember that effective change takes time, energy, persistence, and an effective task analysis of the problem. As Baer (1987) stated:

> When I have an effective interim reinforcer, and I know the correct task analysis of this problem, long problems are simply those in which the task analysis requires a series of many behavior changes, perhaps in many people, and although each of them is relatively easy and quick, the series of them requires not so much effort as time, and so is not arduous but merely tedious. (pp. 336–337)

Perhaps by maintaining our focus on children, we will eventually prevail, and research-driven, teacher-directed, peer-mediated, and independent approaches will be used more regularly in schools. Having been released from their chains, our colleagues may see the light of effective practice and ultimately shun the misleading and shadowy images that the pied pipers display. In shedding their chains, they are likely to enjoy the clearer and brighter vision of empirically based truth. Their students, and indeed our entire society, will be the better for it.

---

## REFERENCES

Baer, D. (1987). Weak contingencies, strong contingencies, and many behaviors to change. *Journal of Applied Behavior Analysis, 20,* 335–337.

Baer, D. M., Wolf, M. M., & Risley, T. R. (1968). Some current dimensions of applied behavior analysis. *Journal of Applied Behavior Analysis, 1,* 91–97.

---

[3]Attribution: Oliver Cromwell (1599–1658), British parliamentarian general, Lord Protector of England. letter, August 3, 1650, to the General Assembly of the Scottish Kirk (Thomas Carlyle, 1845).

Baer, D. M., Wolf, M. M., & Risley, T. R. (1987). Some still-current dimensions of applied behavior analysis. *Journal of Applied Behavior Analysis, 20,* 313–327.

Barbetta, P. M., Heron, T. E., & Heward, W. L. (1993). Effects of active response during error correction on the acquisition, maintenance, and generalization of sight words by students with developmental disabilities. *Journal of Applied Behavior Analysis, 26,* 111–119.

Barrett, B. H., Beck, R., Binder, C., Cook, D. A., Engelmann, S., Greer, R. D., Kyrklund, S. J., Johnson, K. R., Maloney, M., McCorkle, N., Vargas, J. S., & Watkins, C. L. (1991). The right to effective education, *The Behavior Analyst, 14* (1), 79–82.

Bondy, A., & Frost, L. (1994). The picture exchange communication system. *Focus on Autistic Behavior, 9,* 1–19.

Bryant, B. R., & Seay, P. C. (1998). The technology-related assistance to Individuals with Disabilities Act: Relevance to individuals with learning disabilities and their advocates. *Journal of Learning Disabilities, 31* (1), 4–15.

Bushell, D., Jr., & Baer, D. M. (1994). Measurably superior instruction means close, continual contact with the relevant outcome data. Revolutionary! In R. Gardner, III, D. M. Sainato, J. O. Cooper, T. E. Heron, W. L. Heward, J. Eshleman, & T. A. Grossi (Eds.), *Behavior analysis in education: Focus on measurably superior instruction* (pp. 3–31). Monterey, CA: Brooks-Cole.

Carlyle, T. (Ed.), (1845). *Oliver Cromwell's lectures and speeches: with elucidations.* New York: Wiley & Putman.

Carnine, D., Silbert, J., Kame'enui, E. J., & Tarver, S. (2004). *Direct instruction reading* (4th ed.). Upper Saddle River, NJ: Merrill/Prentice Hall.

Cipani, E. D. (1998). *Classroom management for all teachers. Eleven effective plans.* Upper Saddle River, NJ: Merrill, an imprint of Prentice Hall.

Cooke, N. L. (1984). Misrepresentations of the behavioral model in preservice teacher education textbooks. In W. L. Heward, T. E. Heron, D. S. Hill, & J. Trap-Porter (Eds.), *Focus on behavior analysis in education* (pp. 197–217). Columbus, OH: Merrill.

Cooper, J. O., Heron, T. E., & Heward, W. L. (in press). *Applied behavior analysis* (2nd ed.), Columbus, OH: Merrill/Prentice Hall.

*Daubert v. Merrell Dow Pharmaceuticals, Inc.,* 509 U.S. 579 (1993).

Dickens, C. (1859). *A tale of two cities.* London: Chapman & Hall.

Forness, S. R., Kavale, K. A., Blum, I. M., & Lloyd, J. W. (1997). Mega-analysis of meta-analyses: What works in special education and related services. *Teaching Exceptional Children, 29* (6), 4–9.

Gallagher, D. J., Heshusius, L., Iano, R. P., & Skrtic, T. M. (2004). *Challenging orthodoxy in special education: Dissenting voices.* Denver, CO: Love.

Gardner, R., III, Sainato, D., Cooper, J. O., Heron, T. E., Heward, W. L., Eshleman, J., & Grossi, T. A. (Eds.), (1994). *Behavior analysis in education: Focus on measurably superior instruction.* Monterey, CA: Brooks-Cole.

Gersten, R. (1998). Recent advances in instructional research for students with learning disabilities: An overview. *Learning Disabilities Research & Practice, 13,* 162–170.

Grunsell, J., & Carter, M. (2002). The behavior change interruption strategy: Generalization to out-of-routine contexts. *Education and Training in Mental Retardation and Developmental Disabilities, 37* (4), 378–390.

Gumpel, T. P., & Frank, R. (1999). An expansion of peer tutoring paradigm: Cross-age peer tutoring of social skills among socially rejected boys. *Journal of Applied Behavior Analysis, 32,* 115–118.

Hawkins, R. P. (1984). What is "meaningful" behavior change in a severely/profoundly retarded learner: The view of a behavior analytic parent. In W. L. Heward, T. E. Heron, D. S. Hill, & J. Trap-Porter (Eds.), *Focus on behavior analysis in education* (pp. 282–295). Columbus, OH: Merrill.

Heron, T. E. (1997, May). *In defense of leadership: Or whales are only harpooned when they surface.* Paper presented at the Association for Behavior Analysis Conference, Chicago, IL.

Heron, T. E., Welsch, R. G., & Goddard, Y. (2003). Applications of tutoring systems in specialized subject areas: An analysis of skills, methodology, and results. *Remedial and Special Education, 25,* 288–300.

Heshusius, L. (1982). At the heart of the advocacy dilemma: A mechanistic world view. *Exceptional Children, 49,* 6–13.

Heshusius, L. (1991). Curriculum-based assessment and direct instruction: Critical reflections on fundamental assumptions. *Exceptional Children, 57,* 315–328.

Heshusius, L. (2004). The Newtonian mechanistic paradigm, special education, and contours of alternatives: An overview. In S. Danforth & S. D. Taff (Eds.), *Crucial readings in special education* (pp. 80–95). Upper Saddle River, NJ: Pearson.

Heward, W. L. (1994). Three "low tech" strategies for increasing the frequency of active student response during group instruction. In R. Gardner, D. Sainato, J. O. Cooper, T. E. Heron, W. L. Heward, J. Eshleman, & T. A. Grossi (Eds.), *Behavior analysis in education: Focus on measurably superior instruction* (pp. 283–320). Monterey, CA: Brooks-Cole.

Heward, W. L. (2003). Ten faulty notions about teaching and learning that hinder the effectiveness of special education. *Journal of Special Education, 36* (4), 186–205.

Holland, J. G., & Skinner, B. F. (1961). *The analysis of behavior: A program for self-instruction.* New York: McGraw-Hill.

Kame'enui, E. J. (1994). Measurably superior instructional practices in measurably inferior times: Reflections on Twain and Pauli. In R. Gardner, D. Sainato, J. O. Cooper, T. E. Heron, W. L. Heward, J. Eshleman, & T. A. Grossi (Eds.), *Behavior analysis in education: Focus on measurably superior instruction* (pp. 149–159). Monterey, CA: Brooks-Cole.

Kame'enui, E. J., Carnine, D. W., Dixon, R. C., Simmons, D. C., & Coyne, M. D. (Eds.). (2002). *Effective teaching strategies that accommodate diverse learners* (2nd ed.). Upper Saddle River, NJ: Merrill/Prentice Hall.

Kohn, A. (1993). *Punished by rewards: The trouble with gold stars, incentive plans, A's, praise, and other bribes.* Boston: Houghton Mifflin.

Kohn, A. (1997). Students don't 'work'—they learn. *Education Week,* September 3, 1997. http://www.alfiekohn.org/teaching/edweek/sdwtl.htm.

Lloyd, J. W., Forness, S. R., & Kavale, K. A. (1998). Some methods are more effective than others. *Intervention in School and Clinic, 33* (4), 195–200.

Michael, J. (1993). *Concepts and principles of behavior analysis.* Kalamazoo, MI: Society for the Advancement of Behavior Analysis.

Miller, A. D., Barbetta, P., & Heron, T. E. (1994). START tutoring: Designing, training, implementing, and adapting tutoring programs for school and home settings. In R. Gardner, D. Sainato, J. O. Cooper, T. E. Heron, W. L. Heward, J. Eshleman, & T. A. Grossi (Eds.), *Behavior analysis in educa-*

*tion: Focus on measurably superior instruction* (pp. 265–282). Monterey, CA: Brooks-Cole.

Murdick, N. L., & Petch-Hogan, B. (1996). Inclusive classroom management: Using preintervention strategies. *Intervention in School and Clinic, 31* (3), 172–176.

Narayan, J. S., Heward, W. L., Gardner, R., Courson, F. H., & Omness, C. K. (1990). Using response cards to increase student participation in an elementary classroom. *Journal of Applied Behavior Analysis, 23,* 483–490.

Peters, M., & Heron, T. E. (1993). When the best is not good enough: An examination of best practice. *Journal of Special Education, 26* (4), 371–385.

Plato. (4 B.C.). The allegory of the cave. In *The Republic,* Book VII (Translated by S. Marc Cohen, 2002). http://faculty.washington.edu/smcohen/320/cave.htm.

Poplin, M. (1988). Holistic/constructivist principles of the teaching/learning process: Implications for the field of learning disabilities. *Journal of Learning Disabilities, 21,* 401–416.

Rieth, H. J., & Semmel, M. L. (1991). Use of computer-assisted instruction in the regular classroom. In G. Stoner, M. R. Shinn, & H. M. Walker (Eds.), *Interventions for achievement and behavior problems* (pp. 215–239). Washington, DC: National Association of School Psychologists.

Sagan, C. (1996). *The demon-haunted world: Science as a candle in the dark.* New York: Ballantine Books.

Seabaugh, G. O., & Schumaker, J. B. (1994). The effects of self-regulation training on the academic productivity of secondary students with learning problems. *Journal of Behavioral Education, 4* (1), 109–133.

Shermer, M. (2002). *Why people believe weird things: Pseudoscience, superstition, and other confusions of our time.* New York: W. H. Freeman/Owl Books.

Skinner, B. F. (1938). *The behavior of organisms: An experimental analysis.* New York: Appleton-Century-Crofts.

Skinner, B. F. (1953). *Science and human behavior.* New York: Macmillan.

Stein, M., Carnine, D., & Dixon, R. (1998). Direct Instruction: Integrating curriculum design and effective teaching practices. *Intervention in School and Clinic, 33* (4), 227–234.

Sulzer-Azaroff, B., & Gillat, A. (1990). Trends in behavior analysis in education. *Journal of Applied Behavior Analysis, 23,* 491–496.

Utley, C. A., Reddy, S. S., Delquadri, J. C., Greenwood, C. R., Mortweet, S. L., & Bowman, V. (2001). Classwide peer tutoring: An effective teaching procedure for facilitating the acquisition of health education and safety facts with students with developmental disabilities. *Education and Treatment of Children, 24,* 1–27.

Van Houten, R. (1984). Setting up performance feedback systems in the classroom. In W. L. Heward, T. E. Heron, D. S. Hill, & J. Trap-Porter (Eds.), *Focus on behavior analysis in education* (pp. 114–125). Columbus, OH: Merrill.

Vargas, J. S. (1977). *Behavioral psychology for teachers.* New York: Harper & Row.

Ward, P., Smith, S. L., Makasci, K., & Crouch, D. W. (1998). Differential effects of peer-mediated accountability on task accomplishment in elementary physical education. *Journal of Teaching in Physical Education, 17,* 442–452.

Wolery, M., & Shuster, J. W. (1997). Instructional methods with students who have significant disabilities. *Journal of Special Education, 31,* 61–79.

Wright, J. E., Cavanaugh, R. A., Sainato, D. M., & Heward, W. L. (1995). Somos todos ayudantes y estudiantes: Evaluation of a classwide peer tutoring program in a modified Spanish class for secondary students identified as learning disabled or academically at-risk. *Education and Treatment of Children, 18,* 33–52.

## STUDY QUESTIONS AND FOLLOW-UP ACTIVITIES

1. Compare and contrast postmodern beliefs about how students learn and what constitutes effective instruction with behavior analytic beliefs. Construct a Venn diagram showing beliefs that overlap versus those that are clearly divergent.

2. Identify empirically based methods or strategies that could be used by teachers who "see the light" to free teachers who are still in chains. What additional considerations should be addressed to increase the probability that teachers once in chains and who now see the light will remain so?

3. Develop a functional plan for parents to set the occasion for teachers to "see the light." Which

strategy do you believe would be more effective: (a) parents encouraging—perhaps even demanding—effective instructional methods administratively, or (b) teachers (such as special educators) employing these techniques in inclusive general education settings, thereby modeling data-based strategies for their colleagues? Give reasons to support your answer.

4. What are the key obstacles to implementing effective instructional methods in schools today? Do these obstacles differ across urban, suburban, or rural districts? How can these obstacles be overcome?

5. What changes need to be made to preservice teacher training programs, housed within colleges of education, to address the multiple issues presented in this chapter (e.g., misrepresentation of basic concepts in the general education literature; antiscientific beliefs)? Do you believe these changes will be implemented in the future? Defend your opinion.

6. Provide your reaction to the following scenario: Ms. Williams has been teaching sixth grade for several years. For the most part, her students have been successful and do well in her class. However, each year there are a few students who struggle to earn a passing grade. In the teachers' lounge, Ms. Williams laments to her colleagues that she wishes she could reach these failing students. One teacher assures Ms. Williams that some children learn at a different rate and her slow learners will improve when they are ready. Another teacher adds that Ms. Williams may not be addressing the correct learning style with her failing students. The teacher claims that the failing students ultimately will be fine. Finally, another teacher pipes in, "You can't reach them all, honey. Don't worry about it." At the next table, a special education teacher shakes her head and contemplates, If these teachers do not help the children this year, who will?

7. Behavior analysts and constructivists examine student lack of progress or school failure from very different perspectives. Provide an analysis of these perspectives and state how behavior analysts might sway constructivists closer to a scientific position (e.g., by looking at alterable variables).

8. Provide your reaction to the following situation: After observing her classroom for the first

Study questions and follow-up activities prepared by Michele M. Nobel and Corinne M. Murphy.

2 weeks of school, a fourth-grade general education teacher in an urban classroom setting noticed that student participation in her classroom activities was low. She decided to do something to increase student participation. She implemented what she called a "positive reinforcement procedure" that included praise statements for hand-raising and other participatory behaviors. After a week of observing the effects of this change, the teacher noted that participation behavior actually decreased. At a meeting with her supervisor, the teacher reported, "I tried a positive reinforcement procedure once, too, but it didn't work for me either. I agree with those who say that rewards actually punish the behavior you're trying to teach."

9. Is there a place for anecdotal evidence in behavior analysis? Compare and contrast anecdotal evidence and single-subject research designs as avenues for promoting applied behavior analysis and direct instruction in schools.

10. How can behavior analysis be used to empower teachers? What part, if any, do the key principles of behavior analysis cited in the chapter play in enhancing this effort?

11. Read textbooks and professional literature written by Kohn, Poplin, and others who hold a constructivist viewpoint (see references in the chapter). Apply the criteria for best practice offered by Peters and Heron (1993) to determine if there is support for the constructivist view.

# The Effects of "Behavior-Speak" on Public Attitudes toward Behavioral Interventions
## A Cross-Cultural Argument for Using Conversational Language to Describe Behavioral Interventions to the General Public

*Amos Rolider*      *Saul Axelrod*

Perhaps nothing has been more frustrating to behaviorists than the fact that the effective interventions they have developed have been met with hostility and apathy by other professionals (Axelrod, 1991, 1996). For example, effective behavioral treatment has been developed for children with autism. Such treatment has been so effective that many children no longer display the behavioral characteristics of autism and therefore are no longer labeled with autism (Lovaas, 1987; Maurice, 1993; McEachin, Smith, & Lovaas, 1993). Rather than embracing such an outcome, many professionals with other educational orientations have claimed that the original classification of autism was flawed and therefore have rejected the outcomes as an indication of effective behavioral treatment (Brandsma & Herbert, 2001). Similarly, when the Follow Through program, a large study aimed at comparing methods of educating children of poverty (Bereiter & Kurland, 1982; Stebbins et al., 1977), found direct instruction and applied behavior analysis (ABA) teaching procedures to be highly effective, educators paid little attention to the outcomes (Tashman, 1994; Watkins, 1996). Teacher preparation programs around the world have rarely taken advantage of the applied behavior analytic technology as it applies to classroom settings (Axelrod, Moyer, & Berry, 1990).

In the last two decades, several behavior analysts have suggested a number of reasons for the lack of acceptance of ABA by the general public and educational professionals in spite of its documented effectiveness (Axelrod, 1996; Bailey, 1991; Binder, 1994; Cooke, 1984; Foxx, 1996; Hickey, 1994; Hineline, 1990). Among the proposed reasons are the large amount of work required to implement behavioral interventions (Axelrod, 1996), the notion that other professionals view behavioral explanations as shallow and limited in their ability to explain complex behaviors (Hineline, 1990), the lack of efforts to communicate the benefits of behavior analysis to nonbehavior analysts (Bailey, 1991; Foxx, 1996), the misrepresentation of behavior analysis terminology in the most frequently used preservice teacher textbooks (Cooke, 1984), and the fact that behavior analysts use the same terminology to explain both adaptive and maladaptive behaviors (Hickey, 1994).

Another reason for ABA's rejection by the general public could be related to the language used by behavior analysts. Many view the technical language behavior analysts use to communicate their interventions as a contributing factor in the failure of educational and therapeutic communities to adopt behavior analytic technology (Bailey, 1991; Binder, 1994; Skinner, 1938; Yulevich & Axelrod, 1983). Historically, the selection of objective, scientific terms served to distinguish behaviorism from the popular mentalism that was used to explain behavior at the time (Skinner, 1938) and was advantageous for the purposes of laboratory research. Yet, terms such as *positive reinforcement, negative reinforcement, extinction,* and *punishment* may have inhibited popular acceptance of behavioral philosophy and application. Binder (1994) suggested that the use of behavioral terminology to communicate with the general literate public is "similar to using engineering jargon to sell cars . . . [it] simply doesn't work" (p. 25). It has been claimed that terms such as *consequences, extinction,* and *contingencies* sound harsh and controlling and contradict modern movements toward "progressive education" and "humanistic psychology" (Yulevich & Axelrod, 1983).

Yulevich and Axelrod (1983) argued that practicing behavior analysts may exacerbate the problem by frequently using the word *punishment* when describing a proposed intervention. The colloquial meaning of punishment is very different from the technical meaning ascribed to the term by behavior analysts. Individuals outside the field of behavior analysis may be unfamiliar with the technical meaning behind the term and may therefore misunderstand a behavior analyst's meaning when this term is used. In fact, Yulevich and Axelrod went so far as to suggest the term *deinforcement* instead of *punishment* to counter this problem.

The problem of terminology has been recognized by a number of scholars throughout the years, most notably by Philip Hineline, who stated in his 1990 presidential address to the Association for Behavior Analysis: "Perhaps the resistance to behavioral interpretations and techniques arises from our forbidding terms, from the misunderstood language of control, or from our eschewal of mentalistic phrasing, as others have suggested." Similarly, Bailey (1991) suggested that the use of technical language restricts our ability to connect with potential consumers in our field.

Rolider, Axelrod, and Van Houten (1998) first examined the differences in reported understanding and acceptance of behavioral treatment descriptions using three different communication styles with two groups of participants. The first group included behavior analysts who were familiar with behavioral analytic terminology. The second group included individuals from the general public who had limited (or no) previous exposure to behavioral terminology. Four behavioral interventions were described, each using three different communication styles. The first style was technical; that is, interventions were described in behavior analytic terminology. The second was a conversational style in which interventions were described without using behavioral terminology. The third was a conversational style with an added statement describing the intended outcomes of the proposed intervention. Questionnaires consisting of four items each with a 5-point Likert-type scale were distributed to all participants to evaluate the acceptability of each of the communication styles. Results indicated that the general public rated behavioral interventions more favorably when they were communicated in conversational style and, specifically, when statements related to the benefits of the interventions were added. The behavior analysts indicated that they were comfortable with the technical style.

One limitation of the study conducted by Rolider and colleagues (1998) was that it included only 40 participants from the general public and 8 behavior analysts. Therefore, the first purpose of the present study was to replicate the 1998 study with a larger number of participants. In addition, the 1998 study was conducted in Canada with English-speaking participants. The second purpose of the present study was to examine whether members of a non-English-speaking culture would demonstrate attitudes toward the applied behavior analytic terminology similar to those of the English-speaking participants in the Rolider and colleagues (1998) study. For purposes of this study, the four behavior interventions and their associated questions used in the Rolider and colleagues study were translated into Hebrew and were given to Hebrew-speaking behavior analysts and the general public in Israel.

## METHOD
## Participants

Two groups of Hebrew-speaking Israeli students participated in the study. Group 1 consisted of 58 women and 26 men for a total of 84 people. All had majored in psychology and education and had graduated from an Israeli liberal arts college within 2 years prior to the study. Their ages ranged from 21 to 34 with a mean of 24. During their studies, all students had taken four courses in applied behavior analysis and participated in at least one behavior analysis field project. Group 2 included 74 Israeli citizens, 48 women and 26 men, with a mean age of 29 and an age range of 24 to 45. All of the participants were unfamiliar with behavioral principles and procedures and included college administrative personnel, health care professionals, business-persons, and maintenance workers who possessed undergraduate degrees or certificates in their respective professions.

## Examples of Descriptions of Clinical Interventions

The following behavioral interventions were described in three styles of communication:

1. Aggression was treated by differential reinforcement of other behavior (DRO) and social reprimand.

2. Social interruption was treated with differential reinforcement of incompatible behavior (DRI) and extinction.

3. Stealing was treated with a token economy and response cost.

4. Self-injurious behavior was treated with momentary movement restraint (Rolider & Van Houten, 1985).

Each of the four interventions was described in technical language, conversational style, or conversational style with a statement of intended outcome.

Following is an example of the *technical* description of the first intervention:

> Benny's displays of aggression will be treated with:
>
> *DRO 15*—On a 15-min interval, in the absence of aggression, a behavior therapist will approach Benny and deliver descriptive praise (e.g., "Benny, you are demonstrating a good pace in your work assignment").
>
> *Reprimand*—Contingent on episodes of aggression, staff will confront Benny, request eye contact, and deliver a firm social reprimand (e.g., "Benny! Look at me! Stop being aggressive immediately! Control yourself!").

Following is an example of a *conversational* description of the same intervention for the same behavior:

> Whenever Benny has difficulty controlling his emotions and he becomes aggressive, we will assist him to overcome his difficulties in the following manner:
>
> First, we will ensure that Benny is provided with encouragement in an orderly manner. We will use a system that allows behavior analysts to acknowledge his success in controlling his emotions at an interval of at least every 15 minutes. Specifically, whenever Benny does not have difficulty with displaying aggression for at least 15 minutes, a behavior analyst will approach him and

acknowledge his success. This high rate of encouragement is important when we first begin to work with Benny because learning emotional control is a very difficult task and we want to provide Benny with the support he deserves and requires in attaining his goals.

Despite our attempts to ensure Benny's success, there may be occasions where he has difficulty controlling his emotions. At these times he may display aggression. On the occasions that Benny displays outbursts of aggression, we will work through the difficult issue with Benny. We will confront Benny and let him know that this type of behavior is not acceptable. The therapist will firmly say to Benny, "Benny! Look at me! Stop being aggressive! Control yourself!" This confrontation will be a difficult time in therapy both for Benny and his therapist, but it is an integral component of assisting him to reach his goals.

An example of a statement of the *intended outcome* that was added to the previous *conversational* description of the intervention follows:

Benny displays serious problems in controlling his emotions and engages in severe outbursts of aggressive behavior. It is important to teach Benny to control his emotions and express himself in a controlled and effective manner so that he may remain in the community. If Benny is able to learn to overcome his difficulties and express himself in appropriate, alternative modes of communication, he will be able to maintain his job and relationship with his family. Benny often feels very depressed after he becomes aggressive and feels hopeless about his inability to control his actions. His family and job are very important to him. Teaching Benny to overcome his emotional–behavioral difficulties will provide him with a strong sense of accomplishment, improve his self-esteem, and substantially increase his life satisfaction.

The second intervention, for social interruption, was treated with differential reinforcement for incompatible behavior and extinction. Following is an example of the *technical* description of the intervention:

When David exhibits interrupting behavior when his parents are justifiably busy conversing with others, the following behavioral intervention will be implemented:

*DRI*—David's behavior that is incompatible with interrupting behavior will be consequated by immediate positive social reinforcement in the form of enthusiastic praise (e.g., "David, I am very proud of the way you are waiting quietly for your mom and allowing her to finish her conversation"). Incompatible behavior is defined as David waiting for an appropriate opportunity to cue his parents with a gesture and then wait for their attention.

*Extinction*—Our analysis has led us to believe that in the past David's interrupting behavior was positively reinforced by his parents' attending to the behavior. Therefore, contingent on interrupting, David's parents will place his interrupting behavior on extinction. They will do so by completely removing any attention directed toward him. This will be accomplished by not providing him with eye contact while continuing in their previous activity whenever he engages in interrupting behavior.

Following is an example of a *conversational* description of the same intervention for the same behavior:

When David has difficulty waiting for his parents' attention when they are conversing with others and justifiably busy, the following treatment will be implemented to assist him in overcoming his difficulty:

**A.** To teach David alternative, appropriate forms of interaction, we will encourage and praise behaviors that do not provide the opportunity for him to interrupt. Specifically, when David waits quietly and politely when his parents are busy conversing with others, we will provide him with enthusiastic social praise (e.g., "David, I am very proud of the way you are waiting quietly for your mom and allowing her to finish her conversation").

**B.** Based on our analysis, we feel that David's interrupting behavior may have been inadvertently supported through the occasional times that his parents directed attention to him when he did interrupt. In relation to this, it is important that we ensure that his interrupting behavior is not promoted through any form of social attention. Thus, when David does interrupt his parents, we recommend that his parents not provide him with any attention, including eye contact. This should be accomplished by his parents continuing with their previous activity and avoiding eye contact with David whenever he does interrupt.

An example of a *statement of intended outcome* that was added to the previous *conversational* description follows:

David is having difficulty waiting patiently whenever he wants to communicate with his parents while they are busy doing something else and cannot attend to him immediately. It is important to teach David to wait patiently for a while for the opportunity to converse with his parents without interrupting them. This is a critical skill to acquire because life will present many situations in which he will be required to wait for attention before he can communicate his needs, desires, and thoughts. Learning to wait and not interrupt will improve his

relationship with his parents and will assist him in similar situations in school and among his friends.

## Questionnaires

After each description, participants were asked to respond to four questions (see Figure 16-1). The first question evaluated the reader's ability to understand how the intervention was to be implemented, based on a 5-point scale. A rating of 1 indicated no understanding, and a rating of 5 indicated very clear understanding. Question 2 referred to the participant's level of comfort and acceptance of the intervention as a means of treatment. Question 3 referred to the participant's perception of the intervention's level of compassion, from being extremely cold and mechanical to being extremely caring and compassionate. In Question 4 the participants were asked to rank the intervention from the perspective of client autonomy and participation in the prescribed treatment.

**Figure 16-1.**
Questions answered by participants of the study after reading descriptions of four interventions in technical, conversational, and conversational plus intended outcome styles.

---

Question 1: Please indicate the degree to which you feel you understand how the treatment will be implemented.

1 = Not at all     2     3 = General understanding     4     5 = Completely understand

Question 2: Please indicate how comfortable you are with the intervention, or how acceptable you feel this intervention is as a means of treatment.

1 = Not at all     2     3 = Somewhat comfortable     4     5 = Completely comfortable

Question 3: Please indicate your perception of this intervention on a continuum of being cold and mechanical to being caring and compassionate.

1 = Cold/mechanical     2     3 = Neither     4     5 = Caring/compassionate

Question 4: Based on the description provided, please indicate the level of participation you feel the treatment allows the individual. Participation includes degree of involvement, opportunity to make choices, and level of overall personal control.

1 = No participation     2     3 = Moderate participation     4     5 = Full participation

---

The four descriptions were listed in random order. The members of the general public and the group of behavior analysts were randomly divided into three groups. One group read technical descriptions of the procedures. The second group read conversational descriptions, and the third group read conversational descriptions along with statements of intended outcome.

## RESULTS

The mean rating for each question was calculated by summing each group of participants' ratings on each question and dividing by the number of ratings obtained.

Figure 16-2 depicts the self-reported level of understanding of the interventions by behavior analysts (striped bars) and the general public (darkened bars). The mean rating for the behavior analysts' understanding of the technical language was 4.3 out of a possible 5.0. The mean

rating for the general public's understanding of the technical language was 1.3. The conversational description resulted in a mean rating of 4.5 for the applied behavior analysts and 3.7 for the general public. When the intended outcome was described, the mean rating for the applied behavior analysts was 4.7 compared with 4.4 for the general public.

The results for the second question, on level of understanding, are shown in Figure 16-3. The mean rating of the technical description by the behavior analysts was 4.9 (striped bars). The mean rating by the Israeli general public of the technical description was 2.1 (darkened bars). The behavior analysts' mean rating of level of comfort with the interventions described in conversational style was 4.8. The general public's rating of level of comfort with the intervention described in conversational style was 3.2. When the intended outcome was added, behavior analysts rated their comfort level as 5.0 as compared with 4.3 for the general public.

**Figure 16-2.**
The Israeli behavior analysts' and general public's ratings of the level of understanding the interventions as presented in three styles of communication.

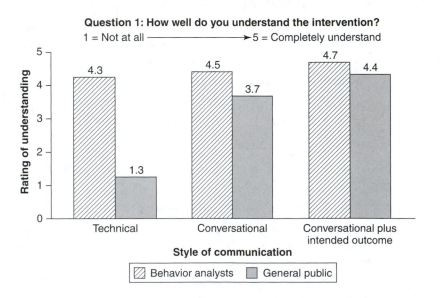

**Figure 16-3.**
The Israeli behavior analysts' and general public's ratings of the level of being comfortable with the interventions as presented in three styles of communication.

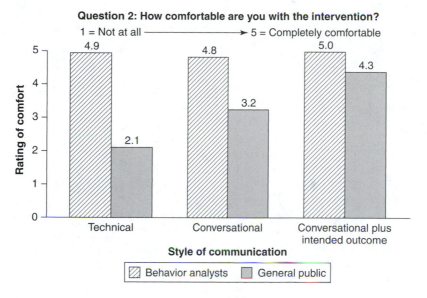

Question 2: How comfortable are you with the intervention?

1 = Not at all ⟶ 5 = Completely comfortable

The fourth question (see Figure 16-5) addressed the degree to which the raters perceived the clients as participants in their treatment. The behavior analysts rated client participation described in technical and conversational styles as 3.1 and in conversational style plus intended outcomes as 3.7. The general public rated client participation described in technical language as 1.4, in conversational style as 2.5, and in conversational style with outcome as 3.3.

Figure 16-6 summarizes the general public's rating results in relation to the first two ques-

Question 3 dealt with the degree to which treatment was perceived as cold and mechanical as opposed to caring and compassionate. Figure 16-4 indicates that the behavior analysts gave an average rating of 4.5 to the technical style, 4.6 to the conversational style, and 4.8 to the conversational style when the intended outcome was provided. The general public rated the level of compassion described in technical language as 1.9, in conversational language as 3.8, and in conversational language with the intended outcome provided as 4.7.

tions (level of understanding and comfort) on the four behavioral procedures. With respect to all recommended procedures, the mean ratings of the group that responded to the technical communication style were less than 2.2, except for the ranking applied to the technical description of token economy plus response cost, which was 3.7 with respect to level of comfort. With respect to the two groups that responded to the conversational and conversational plus intended outcome communication styles, the mean ratings were 2.9 and above for the conversational style and 4.2 and above when intended outcomes were added to the conversational style, except for the ranking applied to the description of the momentary movement restraint (MMR) procedure, which was 3.7.

## CONCLUSION

The results of this study, which was conducted in the Hebrew language with Israeli students, were similar to the results obtained in the Rolider and colleagues (1998) study, which was

**Figure 16-4.**
The Israeli behavior analysts' and general public's ratings of the level of compassion the interventions convey as presented in three styles of communication.

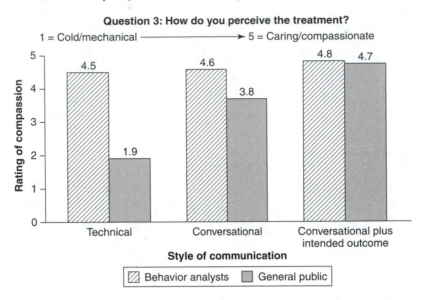

**Figure 16-5.**
The Israeli behavior analysts' and general public's ratings of the level of client participation in the interventions as presented in three styles of communication.

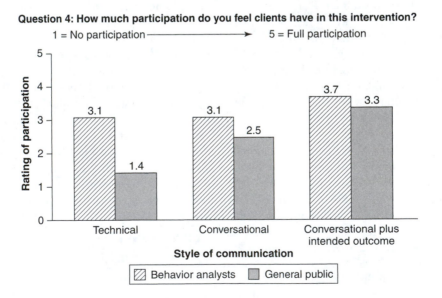

**Figure 16-6.**
The Israeli general public's ratings of the level of understanding of, and being comfortable with, the four behavioral interventions as presented in three styles of communication.

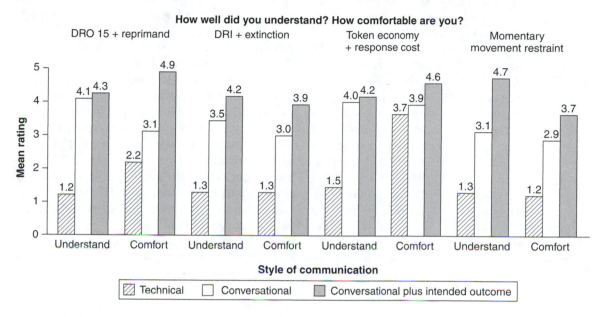

conducted in English with Canadian participants. That is, the general public considered behavioral interventions to be more acceptable and more understandable when written in conversational language, especially when the intended outcomes of the intervention were described. When behavioral interventions were described in more technical jargon, the general public found behavioral interventions to be less understandable and less compassionate. There were no differences in understandability and comfort level across the descriptors for trained behavior analysts, however. The outcomes suggest that the use of technical terminology may decrease the public's understanding of behavior analytic methodology and evoke unfavorable emotional ratings. Across all measures identifying the reader's level of comprehension and feelings of comfort and acceptability, in addition to the level of perceived control, the general public rated descriptions that were communicated in a conversational style more favorably than those explained in the technical style. When a brief outline describing the intended benefits of treatment was added, the ratings were even more favorable. The results also indicate that, regardless of the style used to describe the four interventions, the behavior analysts responded favorably to all the descriptions of interventions.

Although the responses of the Israeli general public were similar to those of the Canadian general public in the Rolider and colleagues (1998) study on most items, it is interesting to note that the Israeli general public responded less favorably to the technical description of all interventions than the Canadian public did. One possible explanation is that some of the behavioral terms may evoke negative emotional responses because of their connection to the history of the Jewish people. For example, the term *extinction* is heavily associated with the Holocaust. These results stress the importance of choosing carefully the words we use when communicating with the public.

Given that the behavior analysts rated all styles of communication highly, technical language may be an appropriate means of discourse when behavior analysts communicate with each other. These outcomes argue in favor of two types of communications—one for the general public and the other for behaviorally trained professionals, as is the case in other fields such as medicine.

For behavior analysts to allow the general population to perceive behavior analytic procedures as cold, mechanical, and controlling is doing their field and themselves a disservice (Rolider et al., 1998). The procedures employed regularly by behavior analysts allow individuals to overcome difficult behavior problems and therefore promote increased self-esteem, self-worth, and overall satisfaction more than many other therapies do. Our findings in this study clearly indicate that, by using nontechnical descriptions to communicate behavioral interventions and by referring to the intended outcomes of the interventions, behavior analysts can promote increased public comfort and acceptance of such interventions. Using conversational language when communicating behavioral interventions to the public is an important factor in placing applied behavior analysis in a well-deserved and esteemed position in the general public's eye.

We realize that the study has limitations. First, it should be noted that this study was conducted with a relatively small group of individuals. Therefore, generalizations regarding the applicability of these findings across populations and even within Hebrew populations should be made with caution. Further replication of this study across cultures and with larger groups of individuals will address this potential limitation in the future.

A second limitation relates to the participants of the study. As we stated in the opening of this article, the use of effective ABA interventions has historically been thwarted by education professionals. Their reasons for rejecting behavioral interventions are not always clear, but our field needs to identify and correct miscommunications and misperceptions if we are ever to gain more widespread acceptance of ABA interventions.

One theory for the lack of acceptance is that technical behavioral terminology and language tend to repel people who have not already been trained in and accepted ABA methodology. This study took a first step at investigating this perceived problem by assessing the general public to see if these individuals would be more receptive to behavioral interventions if the language used to explain those interventions was less technical, more descriptive, and more familiar to them and included an explanation of the intended outcomes. The results show that, indeed, using nontechnical language did make a positive difference in acceptance of ABA interventions by the general public.

It must be noted, however, that the participants in this study were members of the general public, not educational professionals or even consumers (i.e., people who are the recipients of behavioral or other interventions and their families). The next step in this line of research should be to use these two groups of individuals as the subjects of further investigation. We predict that the results of such a study will be similar; however, we realize that other variables may come into play. For example, unlike the general public, education professionals may have been trained to use methodologies (such as a constructivist approach) that are incompatible with ABA interventions. These educators may even have been taught to reject any instructional strategies that follow ABA protocols. Consumers may have had similar experiences and exposures. Therefore, if we are to address the problem of rejection of effective behavior analysis interventions more thoroughly, we will need to replicate the study using education professionals and consumers as the participants.

## REFERENCES

Axelrod, S. (1991). The problem: American education. The solution: Use behavior analytic technology. *Journal of Behavioral Education, 1,* 275–282.

Axelrod, S. (1996). What's wrong with behavior analysis? *Journal of Behavioral Education 6,* 247–256.

Axelrod, S., Moyer, L., & Berry, B. (1990). Why teachers do not use behavior modification procedures. *Journal of Educational and Psychological Consultation, 1,* 309–320.

Bailey, J. S. (1991). Marketing behavior analysis requires different talk. *Journal of Applied Behavior Analysis, 24,* 445–448.

Bereiter, C., & Kurland, M. (1982). A constructive look at Follow Through results. *Interchange, 12,* 1–22.

Binder, C. (1994). Measurably superior instructional methods: Do we need sales and marketing? In R. Gardner, III, D. M. Sainato, J. O. Cooper, T. E. Heron, W. L. Heward, J. Eshleman, & T. A. Grossi (Eds.), *Behavior analysis in education: Focus on measurably superior instruction* (pp. 21–31). Pacific Grove, CA: Brooks/Cole.

Brandsma, L. L., & Herbert, J. D. (2001). Applied behavior analysis for childhood autism: Does the emperor have clothes? *The Behavior Analyst Today, 3* (1), 45.

Cooke, N. L. (1984). Misrepresentations of the behavioral model in preservice teacher education textbooks. In W. L. Heward, D. T. E. Heron, D. S. Hill, & J. T. Porter (Eds.), *Focus on behavior analysis in education* (pp. 197–217). Columbus, OH: Merrill.

Foxx, R. M. (1996). Translating the covenant: The behavior analyst as ambassador and translator. *The Behavior Analyst, 19,* 147–161.

Hickey, P. (1994). Resistance to behaviorism. *The Behavior Therapist, 17,* 150–152.

Hineline, P. N. (1990). *Priorities and strategies for this new decade.* Presidential address at the meeting of the Association for Behavior Analysis, Nashville, TN.

Lovaas, O. I. (1987). Behavioral treatment and normal educational and intellectual functioning in young autistic children. *Journal of Consulting and Clinical Psychology, 55,* 3–9.

Maurice, C. (1993). *Let me hear your voice.* New York: Fawcett Columbine.

McEachin, J. J., Smith, T., & Lovaas, O. I. (1993). Long-term outcome for children with autism who received early intensive behavioral treatment. *American Journal on Mental Retardation, 97,* 359–372.

Rolider, A., Axelrod, S. & Van Houten, R. (1998). Don't speak behaviorism to me: How to clearly and effectively communicate behavioral interventions to the general public. *Child & Family Behavior Therapy, 20,* 39–56.

Rolider, A., & Van Houten, R. (1985). Movement suppression, timeout, and undesirable behavior in psychotic and severely developmentally delayed children. *Journal of Applied Behavior Analysis, 18,* 275–288.

Skinner, B. F. (1938). *The behavior of organisms.* New York: Appleton-Century-Crofts.

Stebbins, L. B., St. Pierre, R. G., Proper, E. C., Anderson, R. B., & Cerva, T. R. (1977, April). Abt Associates Report No. AAI-76-196A under USOE Contract No. 300-75-0134.

Tashman, B. (1994, November 15). Our failure to follow through. *Newsday,* p. A36.

Watkins, C. L. (1996). Follow through: Why didn't we? *Effective School Practices, 15* (1), 57–66.

Yulevich, L., & Axelrod, S. (1983). Punishment: A concept that is no longer necessary. In M. Hersen, R. M. Eisler, & P. M. Miller (Eds.), *Progress in behavior modification* (Vol. 14; pp. 355–382). New York: Academic Press.

## STUDY QUESTIONS AND FOLLOW-UP ACTIVITIES

1. Read the Rolider, Axelrod, and Van Houten (1998) study that was designed to communicate behavioral interventions to the general public. Compare the methods and results of the 1998 study with those used in the present study.

2. Choose an experimental study from the *Journal of Applied Behavior Analysis* that evaluated one of the four interventions cited in this chapter. Rewrite the procedure section using a conversational description of the intervention.

3. The authors claim that terms such as *positive reinforcement, negative reinforcement, extinction,* and *punishment* may inhibit popular acceptance of behavior analysis. After reading Cooke (1984), Binder (1992), or others who make a case for the misrepresentation of behavior terms, state your position with respect to the authors' claims.

4. Identify the possible effects of using a conversational communication style to describe an inter-

Study questions and follow-up activities prepared by Corinne M. Murphy and Madoka Itoi.

vention that requires technical precision, accuracy, and explicit description.

5. Draw parallels between the medical profession and behavior analysis with respect to technical language and the general public's understanding of that language. Might the behavior analysis community consider the medical community as a model for future directions regarding the dissemination of behavior analytic principles?

6. What do you consider to be the major limitations of the Rolider and Axelrod study? From a methodological perspective, how might future replications address these limitations?

7. The authors write, "One possible explanation [for the comparatively low rating by the Israeli general public to the technical style] is that some of the behavioral terms may evoke negative emotional responses because of their connection to the history of the Jewish people. For example, the term *extinction* is heavily associated with the Holocaust. Identify other possible reasons for the low ratings by the Israeli general public. Do you agree with the authors' position?

8. Conduct a debate with two contestants focused on the proposition that changing ABA terminology to be more user-friendly and accepted by the general public is a positive step for behavior analysis.

9. In your view would different ratings of intervention acceptability have been obtained if the *function* of the problem behavior (i.e., in the functional analysis sense of that term) was identified and communicated to the participants?

10. Consider the nature of the four interventions described in the study. How might the nature of the interventions have affected the participants' reactions? Would you consider this issue a potential confound in analyzing and interpreting the results?

### CHAPTER 17

# Applied Research
## The Separation of Applied Behavior Analysis and Precision Teaching

*John O. Cooper*

The precursor for this chapter happened in 2001 during the 27th annual convention of the Association of Behavior Analysts, when I visited with a behavior analyst who had made major scientific contributions to the education and treatment of autism. We enjoyed discussing several current topics of interest to behavior analysts. At one point in that conversation, I noted that Catherine Maurice's (1993) book *Let Me Hear Your Voice* had produced an amazing impact on service delivery for children with autism, parents, and applied behavior analysis. Of course, mentioning Catherine Maurice and her accomplishments moved the focus of our conversation to autism.

I am grateful to Mary Salmon, a PhD student in special education and applied behavior analysis at Ohio State, for keyboarding a transcription of my invited address to The Ohio State University's Third Focus on Behavior Analysis in Education Conference, September 2002. I used Mary's transcription of my address as the foundation for this chapter.

I asked later in our conversation, "Have you had an opportunity to attend the presentations by precision teachers who are working with children with autism? I believe the precision teachers have produced some excellent results." The behavior analyst answered, "Yes. I attended several precision teaching presentations at ABA over the last few years. I don't recommend that service providers in autism use precision teaching." "Why is that?" I asked. The behavior analyst continued, "I have yet to see a controlled experiment by precision teachers. The results from precision teaching are not science. In my view, precision teachers are presenting testimonials, much like the advocates for facilitated communication, not controlled scientific evidence. God only knows how many children have been harmed when testimonials such as those offered by precision teachers form the basis for treatment." I immediately had four thoughts, even as we continued our pleasant conversation. I didn't share these four thoughts with the behavior analyst, of course.

My first thought was, Whoa! Over the last 15 years, I have attended at least half of all precision teaching presentations at the annual conventions of the Association for Behavior Analysis. I have found that most precision teachers give data-based presentations, not testimonials, and occasionally videotaped demonstrations of accomplishments accompany the data-based presentations.

My second thought was an audiovisual image. I saw a woman walking down a dirt road. The woman saw a starving man at the side of the road. She stopped, bent down, and put some food in the man's mouth. But the man would not eat because her food was different from what he was accustomed to eating. The food smelled different, it felt different, and it tasted different. The starving man did not take the nourishment offered. "You were hungry. I put food in your mouth, but you did not eat it," said the woman.

My third thought was, How could two experienced scholars and teachers attend the same presentations and leave with totally different understandings?

My fourth thought provided the answer. I knew what produced the different understandings: passion.

Passion, properly channeled and focused, facilitates the development of expert performances and masterful accomplishments. Applied behavior analysts and precision teachers frequently exhibit great passion for their work. These analysts and teachers have produced masterful accomplishments. Occasionally, however, passion becomes so strong that it blocks the consideration of newly discovered knowledge, especially when the discovery occurred using experimental methods that differ from a passionately held belief.

The behavior analyst I spoke with at the convention believed that precision teachers have not validated their findings with controlled experiments. I am reasonably confident that the analyst defined a controlled experiment as a re-search method that compares an individual's performance during the treatment condition against a steady state baseline (i.e., data suggesting the absence of transition or transitory states of behavior) and the scientific manipulation of an independent variable.

In this chapter I present the position that applied behavior analysis (ABA) and precision teaching (PT) ask different experimental questions about behavior, and those different questions necessitate a different set of research methods. The content addresses four points: (a) Researchers can conduct experiments without asking questions about functional relations; (b) ABA is defined by a search for functional relationships; (c) behavior analysis began as an investigation of behavior dynamics, but the focus of ABA became steady state; and (d) PT produces applied research, but it is not ABA.

## RESEARCHERS CAN BE EXPERIMENTAL WITHOUT ASKING QUESTIONS ABOUT FUNCTIONAL RELATIONSHIPS

### Three Levels Of Experimentation: They're All Good

Johnston and Pennypacker (1980) recognized three levels of experimentation: demonstration, correlation, and functional relation. At the level of *demonstration,* the researcher presents an empirical illustration of a discovery, showing that a certain outcome is possible. Johnston and Pennypacker used William Harvey's classic demonstration of blood circulation in 1628 as an example of experimental demonstration (*On the Movement of the Heart and Blood in Animals*). Harvey's demonstration had a profound impact on the future development of medical science.

To continue with instances of experimental demonstrations, Edison in 1877 offered demonstrations of the carbon telephone transmitter. On December 17, 1903, near Kitty Hawk, North Carolina, Orville and Wilbur Wright demonstrated human flight. Bass (2000, May) chaired a symposium on ABA and the Suzuki method of music instruction. This symposium noted the similarities between the principles of behavior that ground ABA and the principles of behavior that guide Suzuki instruction. To close the symposium, a live performance of very young string players provided an empirical demonstration of musical products produced by Suzuki instruction. An audiovisual demonstration of changes in student learning and performance also functions as an empirical demonstration.

At the level of *correlation,* the researcher defines, observes, and measures occurrences of events, showing a correlation between multiple events (i.e., when $X$ occurs, $Y$ occurs). Most researchers seem to undervalue correlation research, including applied behavior analysts. I still recall my first graduate course on statistical analysis and experimental design. For an example of correlation research, my professor used a researcher who reported a high correlation between the mean length of big toes and the amount of precipitation occurring in specific geographic areas of India. Individuals who lived in the geographic area with the most rainfall (precipitation) had longer big toes, on the average, than did people living in areas of India with less rainfall. Still, one experiment does not constitute persuasive evidence. Persuasion develops from using replication logic to establish the reliability and generality of the outcomes. Consider the impact of the discovery if another researcher made a direct replication of the big toe research in India and found that in this one geographic area people did have longer big toes. Then, another researcher discovers in China, just as in India, a high correlation between the mean length of big toes and the amount of precipitation. The generality of the correlation is increased when, in Japan, researchers find the same correlation. In Australia and Brazil, researchers find a similar correlation. Would you be willing, with this degree of reliability and generality, to make a prediction that persons living in Hawaii on the rainy

slopes of Mt. Waialeale on Kauai might have bigger toes on average than the general population in Hawaii? I would.

The correlation between the big toe and precipitation may provide an example of a very silly correlation. Correlation research can become, however, predictive and believable when researchers doing replications accumulate reliable outcomes. The value of correlation findings is that they predict outcomes, and that's what behavioral researchers of all stripes want to do.

Correlation is useful in behavioral research when it is impossible, unethical, or socially unacceptable to manipulate variables. For example, Ebbinghaus (1885; also see Barnes & Pennypacker, 2001) provided major contributions to experimental science in his research on memory at the level of correlation. Ferster and Skinner's (1957) research on patterns of responding under different schedules of reinforcement provides numerous examples of correlation experimentation.

Critics often use *causality* as an argument against correlation research. The critics contend that the researcher has not experimentally shown a causal relation between $X$ and $Y$. The researcher has only shown that when $X$ occurs, $Y$ occurs at some level of probability or confidence. This is true. A scientist, however, can demonstrate a functional relation between an independent variable and the dependent variable with the scientific manipulation of an independent variable, providing more confidence that a "co-relation" exists between $X$ and $Y$ than do experiments at the levels of demonstration and correlation. Even with increased confidence in a co-relation, most scientists do not make causal statements about experimental effects (Johnston & Pennypacker, 1993). That is, the independent variable *caused* an effect on the dependent variable. Gifford and Hayes (1999) noted, "The flame from a match being struck is not more 'caused' by the combustible tip than it is by the rough surface of the area struck, or the oxygen present, or the ambient temperature, or the lack of water on the match" (p. 297).

Johnson and Pennypacker (1993) described it like this:

> In fact, all we ever really know is that two events are related or "co-related" in some way. To say that one "causes" another is to say that one is solely the result of the other. To know this, it is necessary to know that no other factors are playing a contributing role. This is virtually impossible to know because it requires identifying all possible such factors and then showing that they are not relevant. (p. 240)

A third level of experimentation searches for *functional relationships* between an independent variable and a dependent variable. At the level of functional relationship, a behavior analyst repeatedly measures the behavior of interest during alternating sequences of the presence and the absence of the independent variable. The *Journal of Applied Behavior Analysis* (1968–to date) provides many excellent examples of experimental research at the level of functional relations.

Readers should note that ABA does not hold an exclusive franchise for the experimental demonstration of functional relations. Other experimental methods also search for functional relations, such as group comparison research. With the manipulation of an independent variable, the single-case experimental designs and group comparison designs both occur at the functional relationship level of experimentation. Each research method measures the dependent variable in the presence and in the absence of the independent variable.

Researchers who use experimental methods to discover functional relations closely approximate the ideal experimental design. In an ideal experimental design, the behavior of a single subject is measured simultaneously in the presence and absence of the independent variable. All experimental designs compromise this ideal. The ideal experimental design represents an impossible construct. Nature does not allow for the simultaneous presence and absence of an independent variable.

## A SEARCH FOR FUNCTIONAL RELATIONSHIPS: THE DEFINING FEATURE OF APPLIED BEHAVIOR ANALYSIS

I believe that most behavior analysts accept the definition of ABA as presented by Baer, Wolf, and Risley (1968). Baer and colleagues described seven dimensions of an applied behavior analysis: applied, behavioral, analytic, technological, conceptually systematic, effective, and generality. The applied, behavioral, and analytic dimensions provide the foundation for evaluating the quality of the other dimensions. But the analytic dimension provides the cornerstone for ABA and differentiates ABA from other types of applied research.

In the words of Baer and colleagues, "The analysis of a behavior, as the term is used here, requires a believable demonstration of the events that can be responsible for the occurrence or non-occurrence of that behavior" (pp. 93–94). The authors continued their discussion with a description of the "reversal" and "multiple baseline" single-case experimental designs. By selecting these experimental designs, Baer and colleagues advocated for experimental designs that use steady state experimental logic for the analysis. Steady state experimental logic seeks to experimentally produce steady state behavior in all conditions and phases of the experiment (i.e., data suggesting the absence of behavior in transition or transitory states). The steady state logic contributes to experimental designs that make apparent demonstrations of a functional relationship between independent and dependent variables.

Most authors of textbooks on ABA use Baer and colleagues' (1968) "Current Dimensions" article as the basis for defining ABA. Table 17-1 provides a historical progression of ABA textbook definitions of applied behavior analysis,

**Table 17-1**

Historical progression of textbook definitions of applied behavior analysis

| Date | Definition |
| --- | --- |
| 1977 | [Applied behavior analysis is] an intervention derived from the principles of behavior analysis, designed to change behavior in a precisely measurable and accountable manner; restricted to those interventions that include an experimental design to assess treatment effects. (Sulzer-Azaroff & Mayer, p. 511) |
| 1987 | Applied behavior analysis is the science in which procedures derived from the principles of behavior are systematically applied to improve socially significant behavior to a meaningful degree and to demonstrate experimentally that the procedures employed were responsible for the improvement in behavior. (Cooper, Heron, & Heward, p. 14) |
| 1996 | [Applied] behavior analysis is behavior modification in which there has been an attempt to analyze or clearly demonstrate controlling variables of the behavior of concern. (Martin & Pear, p. 391) |
| 2003 | [Applied behavior analysis is the] systematic application of behavioral principles to change socially significant behavior to a meaningful degree. Research tools enable users of these principles to verify a functional relationship between a behavior and an intervention. (Alberto & Troutman, p. 531) |

beyond the "Current Dimensions" article. Each textbook in Table 17-1 defines ABA as a steady state science dedicated to the study of functional relations.

The use of steady state logic has served the physical sciences and applied behavior analysis well. Findings derived from this "classical science" of steady state end points have strong reliability, meaning that additional experimentation usually does not overturn its findings (Davison, 1998).

Unquestionably, the use of steady state baseline logic makes good science. Baer and colleagues guided ABA in technologically brilliant and scientifically sound directions.

## THE EXPERIMENTAL ANALYSIS OF BEHAVIOR BEGAN AS AN INVESTIGATION OF BEHAVIOR DYNAMICS: THE FOCUS OF ABA BECAME STEADY STATE

The experimental analysis of behavior began with the study of behavior dynamics by using response variability to define operant behavior (Skinner, 1938, 1950). Response variability as the subject matter of behavior analytic research addressed not only the change in frequency of behavior, but also the acquisition of behavior, that is, the description and measurement of the transition and transitory states of behavior. "Behavior analysts first sought to understand behavior change (Skinner, 1938), but somehow this goal became obscured by the aesthetics and seeming simplicity of steady-state performance" (Marr, 1992, pp. 249–250). In *Farewell, my LOVELY!* Skinner (1976) lamented the current absence of the analyses of behavior dynamics:

> There is no point in publishing a block of sloping straight lines if the only important fact is the slope; better a point on a graph. But what has happened to the curves that were curves? What has happened to experiments where rate changed from moment to moment in interesting ways, where a cumulative record told more at a glance than could be described in a page? (p. 218)

For almost four decades, Lindsley (e.g., 1964, 1971, 1990, 1991, 1992, 2001a, 2001b) advocated for precision teachers to investigate reproducible patterns of behavior—behavior dynamics. Lindsley encouraged these applied researchers to quantify celeration, frequency bounce, and verge (i.e., the divergence and convergence of frequency bounce) *within* experimental conditions and phases; and frequency jumps, celeration turns, and agility (i.e., learning to learn, quicker learning) *across* experimental conditions and phases.

The first generation of precision teachers conducted applied research without using steady state logic for the analysis (e.g., Gaasholt, 1970; Jordan & Robbins, 1972; *Teaching Exceptional Children,* 1971). These early precision teachers often included different experimental conditions and phases in their research, but not necessarily for a steady state baseline analysis (e.g., Neely 1994; Spence, 2002). Most of the PT research influenced by Lindsley continued with the experimental traditions of Ferster and Skinner's (1957) dynamic research on schedules of reinforcement, rather than the steady state baseline research advocated by Baer, Wolf, and Risley (1968).

Interestingly, some PT research may be drifting from its historical roots toward a melding with ABA research conventions. For example, PT does have a limited history of using ABA research conventions in applied research, including the steady state baseline logic (e.g., Brown, Dunne, & Cooper, 1996; Carroll, McCormick, & Cooper, 1991; DeAngelis, McLaughlin, & Sweeney, 1995; Gregori & McLaughlin, 1996; Smyth & Keenan, 2002). I have also encountered precision teachers who advocate using the research methods as published in the *Journal of Applied Behavior Analysis* (e.g., messages on the Standard Celeration List Serve,[1] conversations at ABA and PT conventions).

I believe that ABA and PT should maintain their unique research traditions. Each approach to research will in its own way contribute to the discovery of new behavior–environment relationships, for the betterment of learners.

---

[1]To subscribe, (1) send an e-mail message to listserv_AT_lists.psu.edu; (2) leave the subject field of the message blank; (3) in the body of the message, type the following: subscribe SClistserv <Your First Name> <Your Last Name>.

## THE SEPARATION OF APPLIED BEHAVIOR ANALYSIS AND PRECISION TEACHING: PT ASKS QUESTIONS ABOUT BEHAVIOR DYNAMICS NOT FUNCTIONAL RELATIONS

What separates ABA and PT? Identifying environmental conditions that control response variability defines the general subject matter of ABA and PT. Both have the goal of predicting and controlling response variability. ABA and PT, however, approach the prediction and control of variability from different perspectives.

ABA strives to produce steady state responding in each experimental condition and phase. Most students of ABA understand the importance of establishing a steady state baseline before introducing the independent variable. Yet, the steady states are not just for baselines. Steady state experimental logic seeks the occurrence of a steady state during all conditions and phases of the experiment (i.e., data suggesting the absence of transition or transitory states).

Conversely, precision teachers strive to find variables that induce transition states (i.e., acquisition, celeration) and other dynamic patterns of behavior change in each experimental condition and phase, but generally avoid demonstrations of steady states.

To my knowledge, no research articles with standard celeration charts (Pennypacker, Gutierrez, & Lindsley, 2003) have appeared in the *Journal of Applied Behavior Analysis* (*JABA*). (Note that without the standard celeration chart, it's not PT.) Earlier in my career I held a conspiracy theory about this; I convinced myself that PT did not appear in *JABA* because of bias on the part of the journal's editors and reviewers. I now believe that bias was not the case. *JABA* has not published standard celeration charts because PT asks different questions about the behavior of individual learners than does ABA, and those different questions necessitate a different set of research methods. Why would the flagship journal of ABA publish applied research from precision teachers, unless that applied research conformed to the stated goals and methodological conventions of ABA? *JABA* by definition dedicates its publications primarily to steady state research and functional relations, not to the prediction and control of dynamic patterns of behavior change.

I understand that early behavior analysts had difficulty publishing their research in mainstream psychology journals. The peer review process blocked the acceptance of behavior analytic research. Why? Behavior analysts addressed different questions and perhaps a different subject matter than mainstream psychologists. What happened? Eventually, the behavior analysts established the *Journal of Experimental Analysis of Behavior* (*JEAB*) (1958–to date).

In its early years, *JEAB* published applied and basic behavior analytic research. Applied researchers, however, began to experience difficulty publishing in *JEAB*. Why? The applied and basic researchers were interested in different questions about behavior. What happened? The applied researchers established the *Journal of Applied Behavior Analysis* (1968–to date), and the discipline of behavior analysis diverged into two mostly independent branches, the experimental analysis of behavior (EAB) and ABA.

A similar sequence of events occurred in PT. Research by precision teachers was not accepted for publication in *JABA*. What happened? Precision teachers established the *Journal of Precision Teaching* (*JPT*) (1980–to date).

The history of the origins of *JEAB, JABA,* and *JPT&C*[2] has convinced me that different subject matters need different journals dedicated to those subject matters. The rejection of PT and the standard celeration chart by *JABA* was not caused by bias; nor was it a denial of or an objection to the accomplishments of PT. PT research just does not fit the experimental conventions of *JABA*. Some of my best friends are thoroughgoing applied behavior analysts who also just love precision teaching. But that affection would not lead to a standard celeration chart being published in *JABA*.

Tom Lovitt (1977) titled one of his books *In Spite of My Resistance . . . I've Learned from Children*. I love the title of that book, and the content is great too. Like Tom, I resisted the separation of ABA and PT. It took me a long time, and a lot of charting, to finally acknowledge that researching PT with steady state logic does not work well because PT addresses the dynamics of behavior, not steady state end points, as does ABA.

## CONCLUSION

Sidman's (1960) greatly respected book, *Tactics of Scientific Research,* emphasized steady state logic in the design of experiments and had a powerful influence on behavior analysis. It exerted so much influence that steady state experimental designs became the standard for behavior analytic research (Davison, 1998; Galbicka, 1992), especially in ABA. Some applied behavior analysts have difficulty accepting, or taking seriously, experiments that do not use steady state experimental logic. Some analysts believe that experiments at the level of demonstration or correlation do not meet the requirements of scientific experimentation, meaning *controlled* steady state baseline experiments. I contend that a belief in the scientific position, passionately held as it is, is just a point of view. Campbell and colleagues (e.g., Campbell & Stanley, 1963; Cook & Campbell, 1979) had a powerful influence on the design of research in the social sciences, as Sidman did in behavior analysis. Campbell and colleagues believed that the single-case experimental analysis with repeated measurement and steady state logic is a quasi-experiment, not a true experiment.

_____

[2]In 1995 the *Journal of Precision Teaching* changed its name to the *Journal of Precision Teaching and Celeration* (*JPT&C*).

In my view, the use of steady state experimental logic makes good science. The use of replication logic without a steady state baseline also makes good science. Perhaps a dispassionate reexamination of the purposes, methods, and analysis techniques of applied science at the level of proof will allow ABA and PT to grow, learn from each other, and eventually develop a more refined and compassionate understanding by and among researchers and students of each discipline.

## REFERENCES

Alberto, P. A., & Troutman, A. C. (2003). *Applied behavior analysis for teachers* (6th ed.). Upper Saddle River, NJ: Prentice Hall/Merrill.

Baer, D. M., Wolf, M. M., & Risley, T. R. (1968). Some current dimensions of applied behavior analysis. *Journal of Applied Behavior Analysis, 1,* 91–97.

Barnes, W. S., & Pennypacker, H. S. (2001). Fluency research: An example from history. *Journal of Precision Teaching & Celeration, 17,* 92–96.

Bass, R. (2000, May). Musical contingencies: Can behavioral and Suzuki educators perform a duet? Parts 1 & 2. International, 26th annual convention of the Association for Behavior Analysis, Washington, DC.

Brown, S. A., Dunne, J. D, & Cooper, J. O. (1996). Immediate retelling's effect on student retention. *Education and Treatment of Children, 19,* 387–407.

Campbell, D. T., & Stanley, J. C. (1963). *Experimental and quasi-experimental designs for research.* Chicago: Rand McNally.

Carroll, C. L., McCormick, S., & Cooper, J. O. (1991). Effects of a modified repeated reading procedure on reading fluency of severely disabled readers. *Journal of Precision Teaching, 8,* 16–26.

Cook, T. D., & Campbell, D. T. (1979). *Quasi experimentation: Design and analysis issues for field settings.* Chicago: Rand McNally.

Cooper, J. O., Heron, T. E., & Heward, W. L. (1987). *Applied behavior analysis.* Upper Saddle River, NJ: Prentice Hall/Merrill.

Davison, M. (1998). Experimental design: Problems in understanding the dynamical common findings from two areas of research. *The Behavior Analyst, 21,* 219–240.

DeAngelis, L., McLaughlin, T. F., & Sweeney, W. J. (1995). Use of error drill, feedback, praise, and fading to increase the legibility of D'Nealian handwriting with two special education students. *Journal of Precision Teaching and Celeration, 13,* 25–34.

Ebbinghaus, H. (1885). *Uber das gedachtnix.* Leipzig, Germany: Duncker & Humbolt. Cited in R. Klatzky (1980), *Human memory: Structures and processes* (p. 275). San Francisco: Freeman.

Ferster, C. B., & Skinner, B. F. (1957). *Schedules of reinforcement.* Englewood Cliffs, NJ: Prentice Hall.

Gaasholt, M. (1970). Precision techniques in the management of teacher and child behaviors. *Exceptional Children, 37,* 129–135.

Galbicka, G. (1992). The dynamics of behavior (Editorial). *Journal of the Experimental Analysis of Behavior, 57,* 243–248.

Gifford, E. V., & Hayes, S. C. (1999). Functional contextualism: A pragmatic philosophy for behavioral science. In W. O'Donohue & R. Kitchener (Eds.), *Handbook of behaviorism* (pp. 285–327). New York: Academic Press.

Gregori, A., & McLaughlin, T. F. (1996). The effects of praise, error drill and assisted reading on oral reading. *Journal of Precision Teaching and Celeration, 13,* 23–27.

Johnston, J. M., & Pennypacker, H. S. (1980). *Strategies and tactics of human behavioral research.* Hillsdale, NJ: Erlbaum.

Johnston, J. M., & Pennypacker, H. S. (1993). *Strategies and tactics of behavioral research* (2nd ed.). Hillsdale, NJ: Erlbaum.

Jordan, J. B., & Robbins, L. S. (1972). *Let's try doing something else kind of thing.* Arlington, VA: Council for Exceptional Children.

Lindsley, O. R. (1964). Direct measurement and prosthesis of retarded children. *Journal of Education, 147,* 62–81.

Lindsley, O. R. (1971) Precision teaching in perspective: An interview. *Teaching Exceptional Children, 3,* 114–119.

Lindsley, O. R. (1990). Our aims, discoveries, failures, and problem. *Journal of Precision Teaching, 7,* 7–17.

Lindsley, O. R. (1991). Precision teaching's unique legacy from B. F. Skinner. *Journal of Behavioral Education, 2,* 253–266.

Lindsley, O. R. (1992) Precision teaching: Discoveries and effects. *Journal of Applied Behavior Analysis, 25,* 51–57.

Lindsley, O. R. (2001a). Celeration and agility for the 2000's. *Journal of Precision Teaching & Celeration, 17,* 107.

Lindsley, O. R. (2001b). Do times two, then go for four, or more: Precision teaching aims for the 21st century. *Journal of Precision Teaching & Celeration, 17,* 99–102.

Lovitt, T. C. (1977). *In spite of my resistance . . . I've learned from children.* Columbus, OH: Merrill.

Marr, M. J. (1992). Behavior dynamics: One perspective. *Journal of the Experimental Analysis of Behavior, 57,* 249–266.

Martin, G., & Pear, J. (1996). *Behavior modification: What it is and how to do it* (5th ed.). Upper Saddle River, NJ: Prentice Hall.

Maurice, C. (1993). *Let me hear your voice.* New York: Fawcett Columbine.

Neely, M. D. (1994). Camelot's first-grade reading pilot: Report of performance and learning effects from three years of SBG's World of Reading with the '93 class enhanced by SRA's Reading Mastery, Fast Cycle I/II and precision teaching. *Journal of Precision Teaching, 11,* 36–58.

Pennypacker, H. S., Gutierrez, A., & Lindsley, O. R. (2003). *Handbook of the Standard Celeration Chart.* Gainesville, FL: Xerographics.

Sidman, M. (1960). *Tactics of scientific research.* New York: Basic Books.

Skinner, B. F. (1938). *The behavior of organisms.* New York: Appleton-Century-Crofts.

Skinner, B. F. (1950). Are theories of learning necessary? *Psychological Review, 52,* 193–216.

Skinner, B. F. (1976). Farewell, my LOVELY! *Journal of the Experimental Analysis of Behavior, 25,* 218.

Smyth, P., & Keenan, M. (2002). Compound performance: The role of free and controlled operant components. *Journal of Precision Teaching & Celeration, 18,* 3–15.

Spence, I. (2002) Reducing the time required by dyslexic readers to become fluent: A comparison of two approaches. *Journal of Precision Teaching & Celeration, 18,* 2–9.

Sulzer-Azaroff, B., & Mayer, G. R. (1977). *Applying behavior-analysis procedures with children and youth.* New York: Holt, Rinehart and Winston.

*Teaching Exceptional Children* (Spring, 1971). Arlington, VA: The Council for Exceptional Children.

## STUDY QUESTIONS AND FOLLOW-UP ACTIVITIES

1. Compare and contrast the defining features of applied behavior analysis (ABA) and precision teaching (PT). Which dimensions of ABA, as described by Baer, Wolf, and Risley (1968), are represented in PT?

2. Discuss the advantages and disadvantages of a separation of ABA and PT.

3. Compare and contrast data-based outcomes and testimonial outcomes. In what ways are both important?

4. Give an example of demonstration, correlation, and functional relations. How are these related, and how do they differ?

5. Steady states and behavior dynamics are valuable in the analysis of behavioral research. Discuss the benefits and limitations of each.

6. Use a set of frequency data to construct a line graph with an add–subtract scaled vertical axis (used in ABA). Plot the same data on a Standard Celeration Chart (multiply–divide scale used in PT). Compare and contrast your visual analysis of the ABA graph and Standard Celeration Chart.

7. Discuss your reaction to Cooper's statement, "The ideal experimental design represents an impossible construct. Nature does not allow for the simultaneous presence and absence of an independent variable."

8. Prepare a mock debate in which you act as an editor of a new behavioral journal. You and your co-editors can't agree on the journal's focus and mission. Discuss your rationale for including or excluding ABA or PT research in the new journal.

Study questions and follow-up activities prepared by Gwen Dwiggins and Charles L. Wood.

### CHAPTER 18

# The Detrimental Effects of Reward Hypothesis
## Persistence of a View in the Face of Disconfirming Evidence

*Judy Cameron*

Western culture emphasizes individualistic values. This is especially true in North America, where self-determination, pulling oneself up by the bootstraps, freedom of the individual, taking responsibility for oneself, pursuing personal interests, exploring one's inner creative potential, and so on, are highly valued ideals. As a result of these values, a prominent view in Western society is that people are most effective and most happy when they are in control of their own behavior. Many educators put forward this outlook. Coming from this perspective, there is a concern in the educational and psychological literature that strengthening performance with external rewards or reinforcement causes the unpleasant experience of being controlled by others. The argument is that external rewards serve to reduce a person's self-determination and intrinsic motivation. Over the past 30 years, the notion that rewards destroy intrinsic motivation has become widely accepted in educational settings. Consequently, many teachers are reluctant to use incentive systems in their classrooms.

The view that external rewards are harmful receives support from the literature in social psychology as well. Over the past few years, our research team has conducted a series of reviews and analyses of this literature (Cameron, Banko, & Pierce, 2001; Cameron & Pierce, 1994, 2002; Eisenberger & Cameron, 1996). Our research shows that reward has no inherent negative property. Our analyses indicate that the argument against the use of rewards is an overgeneralization based on a narrow set of circumstances. The purpose of this chapter is to describe the experimental literature that led to the view that rewards are harmful and to provide a summary of what the evidence indicates about when to use (or not use) external rewards. Although the evidence does not support the contention that external rewards are detrimental, many researchers, writers, and practitioners continue to espouse the negative effect view. Thus, a final aim of this chapter is to examine why this position continues to be upheld in the face of disconfirming evidence.

# RESEARCH ON REWARDS AND INTRINSIC MOTIVATION

Research on rewards and intrinsic motivation was initiated in the early 1970s. At the time, several researchers were interested in the relation between different sources of human motivation, specifically, intrinsic versus extrinsic motivation. People are said to be intrinsically motivated when they do an activity for its own sake, rather than for any extrinsic reward (Deci, 1975). In contrast, extrinsically motivated behaviors are those in which an external controlling factor can be readily identified. For example, if people solve puzzles, play games, or paint pictures for no obvious external reason, they are said to be intrinsically motivated. On the other hand, students who study hard to obtain high grades, employees who work extra hours for pay, and children who do their homework to please their parents are said to be extrinsically motivated.

There are difficulties with the intrinsic/extrinsic distinction (e.g., see Bandura, 1986; Dickinson, 1989; Flora, 1990). The term *intrinsic motivation* is defined by the absence of obvious external factors such as extrinsic rewards. Although many human behaviors appear to occur in the absence of any obvious or apparent extrinsic consequence, they may, in fact, be a result of past consequences, or they may be due to anticipated future benefits. From this perspective, intrinsically motivated behavior is simply behavior for which appropriate controlling stimuli have yet to be specified. In other words, when we do not know why a person engages in a particular activity, we infer intrinsic motivation. Thus, the motives for engaging in many activities get categorized as intrinsic motivation. As a result, behavior due to distant, hidden, or obscure external causes gets mistakenly labeled as intrinsically motivated.

In spite of these conceptual difficulties, the terms *intrinsic motivation* and *extrinsic motivation* are frequently used, and a large body of research has focused on the effects of extrinsic rewards on behavior that was previously thought to have been maintained by intrinsic motivation.

In the 1950s and 1960s, the view was that intrinsic motivation and extrinsic motivation were independent. Some theorists assumed that intrinsic and extrinsic rewards were additive and combined to increase overall performance and motivation (e.g., Porter & Lawler, 1968; Vroom, 1964). In terms of work, the view was that the highest motivation to perform would occur in a system in which jobs were interesting and challenging and in which the employee was extrinsically rewarded for performance (e.g., with pay, recognition, promotion). That is, productivity and satisfaction would be highest when intrinsic motivation was supplemented with extrinsic incentives.

The notion that extrinsic rewards could be harmful to overall motivation was raised in the late 1960s by the psychologist DeCharms (1968). DeCharms speculated that intrinsic and extrinsic motivation may not be additive and that external rewards might actually interfere with intrinsic motivation. He suggested that external rewards would change people's perceptions about the causes of their behavior. If people were rewarded for engaging in activities, they would begin to see themselves as doing the activity for the reward rather than for interest and enjoyment. In this way, DeCharms suggested, external rewards would undermine intrinsic motivation.

The hypothesis that extrinsic rewards could disrupt an individual's intrinsic motivation has been highly influential in social psychology and education, leading many researchers to investigate the relationship between external rewards and intrinsic motivation. Since the early 1970s, more than 140 studies have been conducted on this topic. Two early experiments on the topic (Deci, 1971; Lepper, Greene, & Nisbett, 1973) set the stage for the dozens of studies that followed; in addition, these two studies continue to be the most cited examples of the negative effects of reward. Based on these early experiments, the detrimental effect hypothesis gained wide public acceptance. Given this wide acceptance, it is informative to examine these two early experiments.

## Deci's Original Experiment (1971)

In Deci's (1971) original study, 24 college students fulfilling a course requirement were presented with a puzzle-solving task called the Soma puzzle. The Soma puzzle (a commercial puzzle composed of seven different shapes that can be fitted together to form an infinite variety of configurations) was chosen because the college students indicated high interest in it. The study was made up of three 1-hour sessions over a 3-day period. Twelve students were assigned to an experimental group; the other twelve, to a control group. During each session the participants were individually taken to a room and asked to work on the Soma puzzles to reproduce various configurations that were drawn on a piece of paper. Four puzzles were presented in a session, and the students were given 13 minutes to solve each one. In the second session only, experimental participants were told that they would receive one dollar for each puzzle solved. They were paid for each puzzle solved within the 13-minute time limit prior to the third session. The control group was not offered or given any money.

In the middle of each session, the experimenter made an excuse to leave the room for 8 minutes. The participants were told that they could do as they pleased but were not told when the experimenter would return. The puzzles, three magazines, and an ashtray were available in the room. During the 8-minute periods, the experimenter observed the participants through one-way glass and recorded the time that each individual spent engaged on the Soma task.

The amount of time spent on the task during the free-choice periods was taken as one measure of intrinsic motivation (specifically, the measure was called "free-time" intrinsic motivation and was calculated as the difference in time on task between the third session and the first session). A second measure of intrinsic motivation was the participants' self-reported interest (a questionnaire measure of task interest given at the end of the third session).

In accord with the detrimental effect hypothesis, Deci proposed that reward (money) would decrease subsequent intrinsic motivation and that there would be a statistically significant difference between the experimental and control groups on the free-time measure. Deci's findings indicated that the rewarded group spent less free time playing with the puzzles than the non-rewarded group ($p < .10$). However, the difference did not meet the alpha .05 level of statistical significance recognized by most social scientists. No significant differences were found between the two groups on the second measure of intrinsic motivation, the self-reports of task interest. Participants who had received a reward reported as much interest in the Soma task as the control participants.

Thus, Deci's initial study on the topic of rewards and intrinsic motivation showed no difference between the reward group and the control group on the task interest measure. And, although a small difference between the two groups on the free-time measure was found, this difference was not statistically significant at the .05 level. In other words, Deci's findings did not support the detrimental effect hypothesis. Nonetheless, this experiment is still cited today as groundbreaking evidence for the negative effects of reward and reinforcement on intrinsic motivation. Based on his findings, Deci (1971) claimed that "if a person is engaged in some activity for reasons of intrinsic motivation, and if he begins to receive the external reward, money, for performing the activity, the degree to which he is intrinsically motivated to perform the activity decreases" (p. 108).

## Lepper, Greene, and Nisbett's Study (1973)

One of the best known and most cited studies on the detrimental effects of reward on behavior was conducted by Lepper, Greene, and Nisbett (1973) at Stanford University. In this study, nursery school children were observed during a free-play period to determine their initial interest in a drawing activity. Two observers sat behind a one-way glass and recorded the amount of time each child was engaged in drawing. Those children who spent the most time on the task were selected as participants for the experiment and randomly assigned to one of three conditions. Children in the "expected-reward" condition were offered a good player award when they drew with magic markers, children in the "unexpected-reward" group received the award but were not told about it beforehand, and "no-reward" participants did not expect or receive an award.

In a subsequent free-play session, children who were promised an award (expected-reward group) spent significantly less time drawing than the other two groups. Furthermore, the expected-reward group spent less time drawing in the postexperimental session than they had in the initial session (preexperimental free-play session). The unexpected-reward and no-reward groups did not significantly differ from each other; both groups showed slight increases in time spent drawing from preexperimental to postexperimental sessions.

Based on the findings, Lepper and his colleagues concluded that their results provided "empirical evidence of an undesirable consequence of the unnecessary use of extrinsic rewards" (Lepper et al., 1973, p. 136). It is curious that they arrived at this conclusion considering that *the children in the unexpected-reward condition spent more time on the task during the postexperimental free-play period than the children in either the expected-reward or the control group.* Because unexpected rewards and expected rewards are both reward conditions, the conclusion that these results demonstrate the negative effects of reward is simply not correct. Children in the unexpected-reward and expected-reward groups received the same reward; what differed was whether the reward was promised beforehand. That is, the promises made must have produced the results. Thus, the

experiment actually showed that promises of reward (telling children that they would receive a reward for doing the activity), not reward per se, reduced time on task. Nonetheless, the findings of the Lepper and colleagues (1973) study are frequently cited in journal articles and introductory psychology textbooks as evidence that extrinsic rewards and reinforcement undermine intrinsic interest in a task.

## Subsequent Experiments on Rewards and Intrinsic Motivation

Although the findings from the early studies were weak, they were taken as support for the view that rewards have negative effects on people's performance and interest. Because of the implications for business, education, and the psychology of motivation, the early findings led to a great deal of research on the topic. The majority of the research has been conducted using between-groups designs similar to the studies conducted by Deci (1971) and Lepper and colleagues (1973).

In a typical between-groups experiment, people are presented with an interesting task (e.g., solving puzzles, drawing pictures, or playing word games) for which they receive praise, money, candy, gold stars, and so forth. A control group performs the activity without receiving a reward. Both groups are then observed during a nonreward period in which they are free to continue performing the task or to engage in some alternative activity (free-choice period). The time participants spend on the target activity during this period (free time), their performance on the task during the free-choice session, and/or their expressed interest in the activity are used as measures of intrinsic motivation. If participants in the reward group spend less free time on the activity, perform at a lower level, or report less task interest than those in the nonreward group, reward is said to undermine intrinsic motivation.

Some behavioral researchers have noted problems with the between-groups design studies. One of the criticisms is that researchers employing such a design often refer to their reward manipulation as a reinforcement procedure. Behavioral psychologists make an important distinction between the terms *reinforcement* and *reward*. *Reinforcement* is defined by its effect on behavior. A reinforcer is an event that has been shown to increase the frequency of the behavior it follows. A reward, however, is defined socially. Rewards are stimuli that are assumed to be positive events, but they have not been shown to strengthen behavior. In most studies on intrinsic motivation, researchers have not demonstrated that the events used as rewards increased the frequency of the behavior studied. That is, the rewards used in the studies may not have been positive events for all the participants involved.

Critics (e.g., Feingold & Mahoney, 1975; Mawhinney, 1990) have also pointed out that the procedures used in the between-groups studies do not involve the repeated presentation of rewards over time. In educational environments, rewards are usually presented over a period of time, and as proficiency in a task increases, the rewards are gradually faded out. In contrast, in the typical reward and intrinsic motivation experiment, the procedure involves a single reward delivery followed by a single assessment of intrinsic motivation without reward.

To address these concerns, five studies have used a within-subject repeated measures design to investigate the rewards and intrinsic motivation issue (Davidson & Bucher, 1978; Feingold & Mahoney, 1975; Mawhinney, Dickinson, & Taylor, 1989; Skaggs, Dickinson, & O'Connor, 1992; Vasta, Andrews, McLaughlin, Stirpe, & Comfort, 1978). In the within-subject design, participants serve as their own controls. Each participant engages in a task for a number of sessions with and without reward. Measures such as time on task or rate of performance are taken over each session in a baseline phase before the presentation of reward. Reward procedures are then implemented for repeated sessions and, finally, reward is withdrawn and rate of performance is

assessed on repeated occasions. A difference in rate of performance between baseline and post-reinforcement phases is used as an index of an increase or decrease in intrinsic motivation.

All of the five studies employing a within-subject design reported that participants' performance on the task during the postreward phase either exceeded or remained at the same level as performance in the prereward sessions. In other words, when a within-subject, repeated measures procedure was used, there was no evidence for a decremental effect of reward.

One important advantage of the within-subject design for this research topic is that the researcher can determine whether the rewards used are actual reinforcers—that is, whether behavior increases during the reinforcement phase. Statements can then be made about the effects of "reinforcement," rather than "reward." In addition, the repeated use of reward followed by extended task performance without reward is more characteristic of the natural environment than the typical short-term experimental procedure used in the between-groups designs.

Unfortunately, many researchers in education and psychology do not accept within-subject designs as true experiments. Critics argue that the results are limited because too few participants are investigated and no-reward control groups are omitted (e.g., Deci, Koestner, & Ryan, 1999). Instead, those who advocate the detrimental effects of reward hypothesis rely on evidence from between-groups designs. In fact, 145 of the 150 studies on rewards and intrinsic motivation have been conducted using between-groups designs.

## META-ANALYTIC REVIEWS OF THE RESEARCH

My interest in this topic began in the early 1990s. Throughout my readings as a graduate student, I continually encountered statements denouncing the use of extrinsic rewards in educational settings. When I began to examine the large body of experimental research (between-groups designs) that was cited to support these statements, I expected to find a robust set of research findings that showed the strong negative effects of reward. Instead, as I delved into the topic, I discovered a mixed set of results. That is, in some studies extrinsic rewards reduced intrinsic motivation; other studies reported positive effects of reward; still others showed no effects. Although the results were not at all clear-cut, many textbooks, journal articles, and magazines endorsed the view that rewards are predominantly harmful.

What was clear to me, after my reading of the research literature, was that a great deal of overgeneralization was going on based on scant evidence. In other words, conclusions were being drawn that misrepresented results reported in the experimental literature and that went well beyond the scope of the findings. I decided that another study was not needed. What was needed was a way to organize and make sense of the literature. In collaboration with other researchers, I used the technique of meta-analysis as a way to integrate and review the findings. This work culminated in a number of reviews that we have published on the topic (Cameron & Pierce, 1994; Cameron et al., 2001; Eisenberger & Cameron, 1996). What follows is a brief description of meta-analysis and a summary of our main findings.

Meta-analysis is a statistical technique for combining the results from a large number of studies on the same topic (for a technical discussion, see Hedges & Olkin, 1985). It involves the statistical analysis of a large collection of results from individual studies; the purpose is to integrate the findings. In our most recent meta-analysis on rewards and intrinsic motivation (Cameron et al., 2001), 145 between-groups studies were included (within-subject studies were not included because they do not present data in a form necessary for meta-analysis). For each study in which a rewarded group was compared to a control group on measures of intrinsic motivation, effect sizes (standardized differences between experimental and control

groups) were determined. (For a detailed and technical description of our analyses, see Cameron et al., 2001.)

Overall, our meta-analyses indicate that negative effects of reward are limited. Specifically, negative effects have been observed only under the following conditions:

- *The activity is of initial high interest.* Using rewards with low-interest activities does not produce a negative effect.

- *The delivery of reward is stated beforehand. That is, participants have to be told that they will receive a reward.* Unexpected rewards do not produce a negative effect.

- *Rewards are material or tangible.* Verbal praise does not produce a negative effect.

- *The reward contingency is loose or vague.* Rewards given for success or for meeting a performance criterion do not produce a negative effect.

- *The reward is delivered only once over a single reward session.* Repeated delivery of rewards does not produce a negative effect.

- *Intrinsic motivation is indexed by measures of time, performance, or interest following the withdrawal of reward.* Measuring intrinsic motivation during the rewarded period does not produce a negative effect.

- *Intrinsic motivation is assessed only once following the removal or rewards.* Repeated measures of performance and interest show no negative effects following the removal of reward.

Our analyses also indicate that in several of the studies rewards produced positive effects on measures of people's intrinsic motivation. These findings are particularly interesting in light of the fact that most of the studies on this topic were designed to detect negative effects. Specifically, positive effects are found under the following conditions:

- *Rewards are given to participants for engaging in low-interest tasks.*

- *Rewards involve positive feedback or praise (on both high- or low-interest tasks).*
- *Tangible rewards are given to participants for engaging in high-interest tasks, and the rewards are tied to successfully achieving various standards of performance.*

Based on our findings, it is clear that there is no pervasive negative effect of reward. In addition, the laboratory circumstances necessary to produce negative effects require an unusual combination of conditions that would rarely be found in everyday life. Further, the evidence indicates that rewards increase performance and motivation under many circumstances.

## Practical Implications of Our Findings

Our analyses indicate that on tasks of low initial interest, extrinsic rewards can be used to increase motivation and performance. On a practical level, this finding suggests that rewards can be used to shape performance, build skills, and cultivate interest in an activity that students have not yet found appealing.

A negative effect was detected in our analyses when the task was of high initial interest, when the rewards were tangible and offered beforehand, and when the rewards were delivered without regard to success on the task or to any specified level of performance. In a classroom situation, if a student has high interest in a particular subject—say, a history course—and receives the same grade regardless of performance, interest in history could deteriorate. The student may be less likely to spend time reading history both during the course and following its conclusion.

To avoid poor performance in educational settings, teachers and administrators need to consider the basis on which they allocate rewards, recognition, and advancement. Our meta-analyses indicate that when people are praised or given positive feedback for their work, task interest and performance increase. When tangible rewards (e.g., grades, scholarships) are made contingent on success or on meeting a performance standard, motivation is also enhanced. These findings suggest that rewards should be given to students when they achieve specific goals or standards.

In many practical settings, the reward contingencies are not clearly related to those examined in the intrinsic interest studies conducted in the laboratory. A student may have to meet a performance standard, set rather low, to avoid failing a course. In other school settings, students may have to achieve increasingly challenging standards to receive rewards. Systematic research is needed concerning the effect of stringency of the standard on intrinsic motivation. As well, in many settings the magnitude of reward is often a continuous function or step-function of performance; that is, the greater the performance, the greater the reward. These situations differ from the typical laboratory use of an all-or-none performance standard to study reward. Sliding scales of reward and performance, frequently used in everyday life, need to be experimentally investigated because they may have strong beneficial effects on intrinsic interest. As Perone (2003) pointed out, research is also needed that assesses how reward contingencies foster behavior that is in the long-term interest of the individual.

## PERSISTENCE OF THE DETRIMENTAL EFFECT OF REWARD HYPOTHESIS

The early studies by Deci (1971) and Lepper and colleagues (1973) did not produce evidence of a generalized negative effect of reward. And, when all studies on the topic are considered, the negative effect remains highly circumscribed. In other words, the evidence indicates that rewards are not inherently harmful; in fact, rewards produce positive effects in many situations. Nonetheless, the view that rewards reduce people's intrinsic motivation is frequently put forward in psychology and education textbooks (e.g., Kohn, 1993; Sansone & Harackiewicz, 2000), journal articles (e.g., Deci et al., 1999; Lepper, Keavney, & Drake, 1996), and the popular media. This view continues to be held in high regard today.

In 1999 Deci and his colleagues reported their own meta-analysis of the rewards and intrinsic motivation literature (Deci et al., 1999). Their results were organized in terms of cognitive evaluation theory, a popular theoretical account of how rewards have detrimental effects. Even based on this theoretical orientation, their findings indicated that not all rewards are harmful. Nonetheless, Deci and his colleagues concluded that rewards have pervasive negative effects on intrinsic motivation. Deci continues to promote this position today as the following statement from his Web site indicates: "Tangible extrinsic rewards reliably undermine intrinsic motivation . . . and, interestingly the most detrimental reward contingency involves giving rewards as a direct function of people's performance" (http://www.psych.rochester.edu/SDT/cont_reward.html). This statement runs in direct contrast to the most recent research findings that indicate that, when people are offered tangible rewards based on achievement of performance standards, their intrinsic motivation is maintained or enhanced.

Given that the evidence does not support the detrimental effects of reward hypothesis, why does this view persist? One answer to this question may lie in an examination of the historical context in which studies on rewards and intrinsic motivation were instigated.

## HISTORICAL CONTEXT OF THE REWARDS AND INTRINSIC MOTIVATION LITERATURE

Research on rewards and intrinsic motivation began in the early 1970s. At that time, many varieties of behaviorism were being taught in North American colleges and universities. At the same time, other schools of thought such as hu-

manism and cognitive psychology began to emerge. Psychologists and educators found themselves engaged in disputes over the best way to understand human nature. Humanists and behaviorists debated the role of the environment and the control of human behavior. Cognitive psychologists argued that the human mind is the agent of causation and that behavioral principles must be flawed. Within this context of a broader debate among humanists, cognitivists, and behaviorists, the research on rewards and intrinsic motivation originated.

## The Humanist versus Behaviorist Perspective

The humanist movement in psychology arose during the 1950s and 1960s as a reaction to both psychoanalysis and behaviorism. Humanists view people as naturally self-determined, good, and willful. To humanists, the goal of individuals is to become self-actualized (to become aware of one's true feelings and to be unconditionally accepted by others). Humanists typically have strong negative reactions to behaviorism and especially to Skinner's (1971) ideas. They believe that Skinner opposed the concepts of free will, purposeful action, self-actualization, and inner meanings of self. In fact, Skinner provided an account of freedom, purpose, and the self in behavioral terms (Skinner, 1953, 1974). The major point of disagreement was that humanists believed in "autonomous man" as the guiding force in human behavior. Skinner rejected the individual as a causal agent. He argued that human behavior changes the environment, and these changes in turn influence and select subsequent human conduct. Skinner believed that only by acknowledging the role of the environment will humans be able to shape behavior that is creative, meaningful, and self-fulfilling.

In terms of education, the behavioral view is that structured classrooms and planned intervention by teachers are necessary for successful learning. From the behavioral perspective, control is inevitable. Rather than allow student behavior to be controlled by unplanned contingencies, educators can motivate students with the systematic application of positive reinforcement. From the humanist perspective, any form of control is viewed as negative. Humanists advocate for unstructured classrooms and minimal teacher involvement.

The humanist view had a strong impact on education in the 1960s and 1970s. This was the time of the open classroom, nongrading of students, and so on. The idea was that students would bloom on their own and find their own inner potential. From this perspective, rewards were seen as sources of control, and humanists argued that any form of control had negative implications for self-actualization. It was within this context that researchers began to investigate the negative effects of rewards. The claim that rewards lessen a person's intrinsic motivation was a logical extension of the humanist thesis for education.

## The Cognitive versus Behavioral Perspective

The rise of cognitive psychology is another historical force contributing to the debate about rewards and intrinsic motivation. From the cognitive view, human behavior results from underlying cognitive processes that are much like information processing by computers. The causes of behavior lie within a person and the person's cognitive representations of the world, not within contingencies of reinforcement. Cognitive psychologists emphasize the person as the source of causation and self-determination.

From the cognitive perspective, external rewards are harmful because they change people's cognitive representations. More specifically, rewards shift a person's attributions (conclusions people make about where their behavior comes from) of control from the person to the environment, undermining perceptions of self-determination. This change in attribution results

in less intrinsic motivation for activities for which the person was rewarded.

The notion of cognitive representations of actions and outcomes is in contrast to the modern behavioral view that began with B. F. Skinner (Skinner, 1953; 1978). From a behavioral perspective, remembering, thinking, and feeling are not seen as cognitive processes that direct behavior but rather as private behaviors of an individual. To the behaviorist, these private events do not explain behavior but are, in fact, more behavior to be explained. The explanation of both private behaviors and overt actions rests on an analysis of the biology of the species and the contingencies of reinforcement encountered by individuals over their lifetimes.

The 1970s was a period of great debate between cognitive and behavioral psychologists. Many writers of the cognitive persuasion claimed that a cognitive revolution was taking place and that behavioral techniques and principles were faulty (e.g., MacKenzie, 1977; Palermo, 1971; Schwartz, Schuldenfrei, & Lacey, 1978). It is within this context that researchers began to claim that rewards and reinforcement destroyed people's intrinsic motivation.

## CONCLUSION

By the 1960s and 1970s, differences in focus among cognitivists, humanists, and behaviorists led advocates of the different perspectives to debate and criticize each other's position. Skinner's strict determinism and his emphasis on the environment as the primary source of control roused a great deal of controversy. It ran contrary to the basic belief in free will held by most North Americans and led several psychologists to put forth a position of humans as willful and self-determining. It was during this period of rivalry and unrest that the research designed to show the negative effects of reward/reinforcement on intrinsic motivation was instigated.

Given the pervasive influence of cognitive psychology and of humanism in education, research examining the effects of rewards and reinforcement on intrinsic motivation was timely and relevant. As well, since most of the criticisms aimed at behaviorism were based on logical argument rather than experimental findings, the time was ripe to produce research evidence demonstrating negative effects of reinforcement. Research showing the detrimental effects of rewards was viewed by many as an attack on the principle of reinforcement (the very heart of behaviorism) and had widespread implications for behavioral technology.

Within this context Deci (1971) and Lepper and colleagues (1973) conducted and interpreted their early studies. However, the results of those studies were weak and inconclusive. Meta-analyses of dozens of subsequent studies also indicate negligible detrimental effects of reward. Nonetheless, the findings have frequently been used to discredit the behavioral view and, in general, reinforcement theory. A historical analysis of this literature suggests that overgeneralizations and misinterpretations of the studies were a result of the fervor of the times (a fervor to overthrow behaviorism) rather than a careful analysis of the data. A careful examination of the studies shows that the literature on rewards and intrinsic motivation has not resulted in a discrediting of behavioral theory, specifically, the principle of reinforcement. Instead, what has resulted is a literature that points to conditions in which a negative effect of promised reward will occur and, inadvertently, to several conditions in which positive effects of rewards will occur.

Had the studies on rewards and intrinsic motivation been conducted in another time or place, with different dominant psychological views, the findings may have been interpreted in a different light. In other words, the conclusions drawn from the findings need to be understood in the context of the strong values of individualism and freedom. Ironically, as Skinner (1953) pointed out, values are a question of a culture's reinforcement contingencies. Thus, an answer to why many continue to argue that rewards are harmful may not be resolved by more experi-

ments on the effects of rewards on people's intrinsic motivation; instead, the answer may lie with an experimental analysis of values.

## REFERENCES

Bandura, A. (1986). *Social foundations of thought & action: A social cognitive theory*. Upper Saddle River, NJ: Prentice Hall.

Cameron, J., Banko, K. M., & Pierce, W. D. (2001). Pervasive negative effects of rewards on intrinsic motivation: The myth continues. *The Behavior Analyst, 24,* 1–44.

Cameron, J., & Pierce, W. D. (1994). Reinforcement, reward and intrinsic motivation: A meta-analysis. *Review of Educational Research, 64,* 363–423.

Cameron, J., & Pierce, W. D. (2002). *Rewards and intrinsic motivation: Resolving the controversy*. Westport, CT: Bergin and Garvey, Greenwood.

Davidson, P., & Bucher, B. (1978). Intrinsic interest and extrinsic reward: The effects of a continuing token program on continuing nonconstrained preference. *Behavior Therapy, 9,* 222–234.

DeCharms, R. (1968). *Personal causation*. New York: Academic Press.

Deci, E. L. (1971). Effects of externally mediated rewards on intrinsic motivation. *Journal of Personality and Social Psychology, 18,* 105–115.

Deci, E. L. (1975). *Intrinsic motivation*. New York: Plenum Press.

Deci, E. L., Koestner, R., & Ryan, R. M. (1999). A meta-analytic review of experiments examining the effects of extrinsic rewards on intrinsic motivation. *Psychological Bulletin, 125,* 627–668.

Dickinson, A. M. (1989). The detrimental effects of extrinsic reinforcement on "intrinsic motivation." *The Behavior Analyst, 12,* 1–15.

Eisenberger, R., & Cameron, J. (1996). The detrimental effects of reward: Myth or reality? *American Psychologist, 51,* 1153–1166.

Feingold, B. D., & Mahoney, M. J. (1975). Reinforcement effects on intrinsic interest: Undermining the overjustification hypothesis. *Behavior Therapy, 6,* 357–377.

Flora, S. R. (1990). Undermining intrinsic interest from the standpoint of a behaviorist. *The Psychological Record, 40,* 323–346.

Hedges, L. V., & Olkin, I. (1985). *Statistical methods for meta-analysis*. Orlando FL: Academic Press.

Kohn, A. (1993). *Punished by rewards*. Boston: Houghton Mifflin.

Lepper, M. R., Greene, D., & Nisbett, R. E. (1973). Undermining children's intrinsic interest with extrinsic reward: A test of the "overjustification" hypothesis. *Journal of Personality and Social Psychology, 28,* 129–137.

Lepper, M. R., Keavney, M., & Drake, M. (1996). Intrinsic motivation and extrinsic rewards: A commentary on Cameron and Pierce's meta-analysis. *Review of Educational Research, 66,* 5–32.

MacKenzie, B. D. (1977). *Behaviorism and the limits of the scientific method*. Atlantic Highlands, NJ: Humanities Press.

Mawhinney, T. C. (1990). Decreasing intrinsic "motivation" with extrinsic rewards: Easier said than done. *Journal of Organizational Behavior Management, 11,* 175–191.

Mawhinney, T. C., Dickinson, A. M., & Taylor, L. A. (1989). The use of concurrent schedules to evaluate the effects of extrinsic rewards on "intrinsic motivation." *Journal of Organizational Behavior Management, 10,* 109–129.

Palermo, D. S. (1971). Is a scientific revolution taking place in psychology? *Science Studies, I,* 135–155.

Perone, M. (2003). Negative effects of positive reinforcement. *The Behavior Analyst, 26,* 1–14.

Porter, L. W., & Lawler, E. E. (1968). *Managerial attitudes and performance*. Homewood, IL: Irwin-Dorsey.

Sansone, C., & Harackiewicz, J. M. (Eds.). (2000). *Intrinsic and extrinsic motivation: The search for optimal motivation and performance*. San Diego CA: Academic.

Schwartz, B., Schuldenfrei, R., & Lacey, H. (1978). Operant psychology as factory psychology. *Behaviorism, 2,* 229–254.

Skaggs, K. J., Dickinson, A. M., & O'Connor, K. A. (1992). The use of concurrent schedules to evaluate the effects of extrinsic rewards on intrinsic motivation: A replication. *Journal of Organizational Behavior Management, 12,* 45–83.

Skinner, B. F. (1953). *Science and human behavior*. New York: Macmillan.

Skinner, B. F. (1971). *Beyond freedom and dignity*. New York: Knopf.

Skinner, B. F. (1974). *About behaviorism*. New York: Knopf.

Skinner, B. F. (1978). Why I am not a cognitive psychologist. In *Reflections on behaviorism and society*. Upper Saddle River, NJ: Prentice Hall.

Vasta, R., Andrews, D. E., McLaughlin, A. M., Stirpe, L. A., & Comfort, C. (1978). Reinforcement effects on intrinsic interest: A classroom analog. *Journal of School Psychology, 16,* 161–168.

Vroom, V. (1964). *Work and motivation*. New York: Wiley.

---

## STUDY QUESTIONS AND FOLLOW-UP ACTIVITIES

1. Define the terms *reward* and *reinforcement*. Give an example of each. How are they similar, and how are they different? Discuss whether the difference in definition between *reward* and *reinforcement* is important in examining the research on the detrimental effects of reward hypothesis.

2. Some theorists have suggested that intrinsic and extrinsic motivations are independent of each other, whereas other theorists have suggested that there are additive effects of intrinsic and extrinsic motivation. Explain the difference between the "independent" and "additive" effects of intrinsic and extrinsic motivation, and provide an example of each.

3. Explain the advantages and disadvantages of the experimental designs used by Deci (1971) and Lepper and colleagues (1973) to evaluate the effects of rewards on subsequent behavior.

4. Explain how the experimental designs used by Davidson and Bucher (1978), Feingold and Mahoney (1975), Mawhinney and colleagues (1989), Skaggs and colleagues (1992), and Vasta and colleagues (1978) differed from those used by Deci (1971) and Lepper and colleagues (1973) to evaluate the effects of rewards on subsequent behavior. Discuss the strengths and limitations of these designs in evaluating this question.

5. Explain what meta-analysis is and how it differs from the research designs used by the authors listed in Questions 3 and 4. What is the purpose of meta-analyses? Identify other areas of education in which meta-analyses of data sets would be useful for addressing the problems and issues faced by researchers and practitioners.

---

Study questions and follow-up activities prepared by Natalie J. Allen and Madoka Itoi.

6. Summarize the humanistic perspective of psychology. How does it contrast with behavioral perspective in relation to the research on rewards and intrinsic motivation? What aspects are common to the humanistic and behavioral perspectives? Give two examples from the literature to support your answers.

7. Summarize cognitive perspective psychology. How does it contrast with behavioral perspective in reference to the research on rewards and intrinsic motivation? What aspects are common to the cognitive and behavioral perspectives? Give two examples from the literature to support your answers.

8. The author suggests that an experimental analysis of cultural values might be beneficial to the understanding of the effects of reward on intrinsic motivation. Identify a research question related to this issue. Provide a brief overview of the experimental methods that might be used to answer the question. Specifically, your proposal should address the dependent and independent variables and the experimental design you would use to conduct the analysis.

9. Suppose you are a new teacher in a school building and are eager to get your classroom management system up and running. You mention something to a colleague about the things you will be doing in your classroom and she replies, "Oh, I don't use rewards; I have heard they are harmful and I don't want my students to get hooked on praise and rewards." How would you respond to this comment, given the literature review presented in this chapter?

10. Given the results of the meta-analysis conducted by Cameron and colleagues (2001), how would you implement a rewards-based classroom management system that would avoid the potential negative effects and capitalize on the positive effects of rewards? How would you promote that system to your colleagues and administrator?

# Reasons Applied Behavior Analysis Is Good for Education and Why Those Reasons Have Been Insufficient

*William L. Heward*

I count myself among those who believe that the widespread, competent application of behavior analysis can help create a better world. Applied behavior analysis's pragmatic, natural science approach to discovering environmental variables that reliably influence socially significant behavior, and its approach to developing a technology to take practical advantage of those discoveries, offers humankind its best hope for solving many of its problems.

One of the most important challenges facing U.S. society today is improving the effectiveness of public education. For more than four decades, researchers have provided powerful demonstrations of how applied behavior analysis (ABA) can promote learning in the classroom. In spite of this evidence, however, behavior analysis is, at best, a bit player in our country's efforts to reform education.

## THE KNOWLEDGE-TO-PRACTICE GAP

The experimental analysis of behavior (EAB), a basic research program begun by B. F. Skinner in the 1930s and continuing today, has revealed fundamental principles that describe functional relations between behavior and some of the variables that influence it (e.g., reinforcement, extinction) (Keller & Schoenfeld, 1950; Skinner, 1938). The branch of behavior analysis that would later be called applied behavior analysis took root in the mid-1950s and early 1960s when researchers began applying the basic principles discovered in the operant laboratory with children and adults (e.g., Ayllon & Michael, 1959; Baer, 1960, 1962; Bijou, 1957, 1958; Lindsley, 1956). Classroom applications of behavior principles soon followed, from which were derived teaching procedures such as contingent teacher praise and attention (Hall, Lund, & Jackson, 1968), token reinforcement (Birnbrauer, Wolf, Kidder, & Tague, 1965), curriculum design (Becker, Englemann, & Thomas, 1975), and programmed instruction (Bijou, Birnbrauer, Kidder, & Tague, 1966; Markle, 1962). The strategies and techniques for reliably improving student performance developed by those early applied behavior analysts provided the foundation for contemporary behavioral approaches to curriculum design, instructional methods, classroom management, and the generalization and maintenance of learning.

By the mid-1970s hundreds of reports of the positive and reliable effects on student learning that could be achieved by behaviorally inspired curriculum design and instruction were available in the form of journal articles (e.g., *Journal of Applied Behavior Analysis,* 1968–1975) and chapters in edited books (e.g., O'Leary & O'Leary, 1972; Ramp & Hopkins, 1971; Ulrich, Stachnik, & Mabry, 1974). In fact, demonstrations of the effectiveness of behavioral interventions published in peer-reviewed publications in the 1960s and 1970s were so numerous and widespread that Baer and Bushell (1981) proclaimed more than 20 years ago that "applied behavior analysis has been visible and available to education for nearly two decades" (p. 260).

Figure 19-1 illustrates one way to conceptualize the knowledge-to-practice gap in education. Examples of current knowledge and technology—basic principles and behavior change strategies discovered through EAB and existing technology of teaching developed through ABA—are shown in the middle column. The left-hand column demonstrates that behavior analysis's knowledge of "how behavior works," even at the level of fundamental principles, is incomplete, as is the technology of teaching derived from those principles. We know relatively little about certain aspects of teaching and learning, and additional research is needed to clarify, extend, and fine-tune the knowledge we do have. Thus, a significant knowledge gap exists between what we understand relatively well and what we understand poorly or not at all (illustrated by the distance between the middle and left-hand columns in Figure 19-1).

Closing the knowledge gap is a large and worthy task. However, I believe that the more pressing (and possibly larger) gap we must close is the one between what research has discovered about effective instruction and what is practiced in the majority of classrooms. This knowledge-to-practice gap is illustrated by the space between the middle and right-hand columns in Figure 19-1. Observational studies of classroom practice consistently report that the education received by many U.S. students does not take advantage of existing knowledge about effective instruction.

Of course, we cannot state with certainty that the gap between the current knowledge of teaching and learning and classroom practice is larger than the gap between current knowledge and a complete understanding of human behavior. Measuring the distance between two things is impossible when the location of one of them is unknown, and we simply do not know, and may never know, how much we do not know. What is quite certain, however, is this: The distance between what is known about effective education and what takes place in far too many classrooms is wide, and it is deep. "The separation between research and application in education can be characterized not merely as a gulf but as an abyss" (Sidman, 1994, p. 532).

The scope and depth of the gap between the useful knowledge generated by behavioral research and classroom practice has caused many behavior analysts to lament and decry the gap's existence, to discuss and analyze possible reasons for it, and to suggest ways to shrink it (e.g., Axelrod, 1991, 1992; Baer & Bushell, 1981; Bailey, 1991; Binder, 1994; Carnine, 1992, 1997, 2000; Dietz, 1994; Fowler, 1994; Greer, 1983, 1991; Hall, 1991; Heward & Cooper, 1992; Kohler & Strain, 1992; Lindsley, 1992; Skinner, 1984; Stone, 1994). These authors provided insights into the nature and varied causes of the knowledge-to-practice gap, and they suggested numerous empirically supported and conceptually sound strategies for reducing the gap. This chapter is an effort to extend that discussion. I identify a dozen attributes of ABA that make it especially well suited to contribute to the improvement of education. I also identify characteristics of ABA and those of contemporary educational philosophy and society that impede the widespread acceptance and adoption of behavioral practices in the classroom.

**Figure 19-1.**
**Existing Knowledge vs. Classroom Practice.** Although the gap between existing knowledge about how to change behavior and a complete understanding of "how behavior works" is significant, the gap between currently available knowledge and classroom practice may be larger. (EAB = experimental analysis of behavior; ABA = applied behavior analysis)

| Incomplete and Missing Knowledge | | Current Knowledge and Technology | | Current Practice in Many Classrooms |
|---|---|---|---|---|
| • Private events<br>• Generalization and maintenance of learning<br>• Complex schedules of reinforcement<br>• Indirect acting contingencies<br>• Delayed consequences<br>• Contingency adduction<br>• Behavioral cusps<br>• Collateral effects<br>• Equivalence relations<br>• Behavioral contrast<br>• Respondent-operant interactions<br>• ?<br>• ?<br>• ?<br>• ?<br>Etc. | ⇐ Knowledge Gap ⇒<br>⇐ Knowledge Gap ⇒<br>⇐ Knowledge Gap ⇒ | *Basic Principles and Behavior Change Procedures (EAB)*<br>• Reinforcement<br>• Punishment<br>• Extinction<br>• Stimulus control<br>• Stimulus generalization<br>• Shaping<br>• Chaining<br>• Etc.<br>*Technology of Teaching (ABA)*<br>• Contingent praise<br>• Response prompts<br>• Transferring stimulus control (e.g., time delay)<br>• Embedding motivating operations<br>• Programmed instruction<br>• Positive behavior supports<br>• Interspersal training<br>• Self-monitoring<br>• Programming for generalization<br>• Etc. | ⇐ Practice Gap ⇒<br>⇐ Practice Gap ⇒<br>⇐ Practice Gap ⇒ | • Poorly defined learning objectives<br>• Low rates of active student responding<br>• Infrequent teacher praise<br>• Unsystematic use of instructional feedback<br>• Instructional materials with faulty stimulus controls that enable students to be "right for the wrong reason"<br>• Illogical sequences in curriculum materials create unnecessary errors<br>• Indirect teaching<br>• Slow-paced instruction<br>• Infrequent use of fluency-building activities<br>• On-task behavior valued more than productivity<br>• Emphasis on building self-esteem over achievement<br>• Instructional decisions seldom based on direct and frequent measurement of student performance<br>• Train-and-hope predominant "method" of programming for generalization<br>• Etc. |

# TWELVE REASONS ABA IS GOOD FOR EDUCATION

Thinking about the defining dimensions of ABA (Baer, Wolf, & Risley, 1968, 1987), the characteristics of ABA-inspired lesson plans and instructional strategies, and the documented effects on student achievement when those teaching plans and strategies are systematically applied has led me to conclude that ABA is good for education for the following reasons:

1. ABA is meaningful.
2. ABA is effective.
3. ABA is focused.
4. ABA is broadly relevant.
5. ABA is self-correcting.
6. ABA is accountable.
7. ABA is public.
8. ABA is doable.
9. ABA is replicable.
10. ABA is empowering.
11. ABA is optimistic.
12. ABA knows motivation.

## ABA Is Meaningful

Teachers use behavioral instructional materials and methods to help students learn how to do things that matter, such as read stories and textbooks, write complete sentences and letters, solve arithmetic problems, state social studies facts, apply science concepts, and get along with their classmates (and teachers!). Other approaches to education are also interested in teaching students things that matter, but ABA is explicit about its dedication to do so. The word *applied* in the term *applied behavior analysis* signals ABA's commitment to affecting improvements in socially significant behavior (Baer et al., 1968, 1987). The fact that behavioral interventions are sometimes used to change student behaviors that have little or no educational significance (cf., Bannerman, Sheldon, Sherman, &

Harchik, 1990; Winett & Winkler, 1972) does not negate the fact that, when properly implemented, ABA is all about meaningful learning.

## ABA Is Effective

What works in education? Hundreds of published, peer-reviewed research studies show that ABA-derived curricula and instruction work. This large and continually growing body of research includes studies ranging in size from true single-subject studies with one participant to Project Follow Through, in which thousands of children participated in the largest experiment ever conducted that compared the effectiveness of educational methods. Many of these studies have found behavioral techniques to be not just effective, but measurably superior to methods most often used in classroom.

A bibliography of edited books on behavior analysis in education is shown Figure 19-2. This bibliography provides a representative overview of the breadth of the development of behavioral research and application education from the 1970s to the present. Chapters include literature reviews, original research studies across a wide range of students and curriculum areas, conceptual papers, program descriptions, and discussions of professional issues such as teacher training.

An athlete who repeatedly displays winning performances while stating or otherwise displaying his or her confidence in playing well is sometimes referred to as a player who is "really good and knows it." In a similar way, ABA is effective and knows it. ABA's confidence is the product of experimental control. The "knows it" is ABA's *analytic* dimension (Baer et al., 1968, 1987). ABA not only demonstrates its effectiveness, but it also provides (and indeed insists on) experimental "proof" of functional relationships between the interventions it recommends and educationally significant outcomes.

> Because [ABA is] a data- and design-based discipline, we are in the remarkable position of being able to prove that behavior can work in the way that our technology prescribes. We are not theoriz-

**Figure 19-2.**
Applications of behavior analysis in education: A bibliography of edited collections spanning four decades.

Becker, W. C. (Ed.). (1971). *An empirical basis for change in education.* Chicago: Science Research Associates.

Bijou, S. W., & Ruiz, R. R. (1981). *Behavior modification: Contributions to education.* Hillsdale, NJ: Erlbaum.

Brigham, T. A., Hawkins, R., Scott, J. W., & McLaughlin, T. F. (Eds). (1976). *Behavior analysis in education.* Dubuque, IA: Kendall/Hunt.

Crandall, J., Jacobson, J., & Sloane, H. (Eds.). (1997). *What works in education* (2nd ed.). Cambridge, MA: Cambridge Center for Behavioral Studies.

Gardner, R., III, Sainato, D., Cooper, J. O., Heron, T. E., Heward, W. L., Eshleman, J., & Grossi, T. A. (Eds.). (1994). *Behavior analysis in education: Focus on measurably superior instruction.* Monterey, CA: Brooks-Cole.

Heward, W. L., Heron, T. E., Hill, D. S., & Trap-Porter, J. (Eds.). (1984). *Focus on behavior analysis in education.* Columbus, OH: Merrill.

Heward, W. L., Heron, T. E., Neef, N. A., Peterson, S. M., Sainato, D. M., Cartledge, G., Gardner III, R., Peterson, L. D., Hersh, S. B., & Dardig, J. C. (Eds.). (2005). *Focus on behavior analysis in education: Achievements, challenges, and oppor-*

*tunities.* Upper Saddle River, NJ: Prentice Hall/Merrill.

Neef, N.A., Iwata, B.A., Horner, R. H., Lerman, D. C., Martens, B. K., Sainato, D. M. (Eds.) (2004). *Behavior analysis in education* (2nd ed.). Lawrence, KS: Society for the Experimental Analysis of Behavior.

O'Leary, K. D., & O'Leary, S. (1972) *Classroom management: The successful use of behavior modification.* New York: Pergamon.

Ramp, E. A., & Hopkins, B. (Eds.). (1971). *A new direction for education: Behavior analysis 1971, Vol. 1.* Lawrence, KS: University of Kansas.

Ramp, E. A., & Semb, G. (Eds.). (1975). *Behavior analysis: Areas of research and application.* Upper Saddle River, NJ: Prentice Hall.

Thoresen, C. E. (Ed) (1972). *Behavior modification in education.* Chicago: National Society for the Study of Education.

Ulrich, R., Stachnik, T., & Mabry, J. (Eds.). (1974). *Control of human behavior (Vol. 3), Behavior modification in education.* Glenview, IL: Scott, Foresman.

West, R. P., & Hamerlynck, L. A. (Eds.). (1992). *Designs for excellence in education: The legacy of B. F. Skinner.* Longmont, CO: Sopris West.

ing about how behavior *can* work; we are describing systematically how it *has* worked many times in real-world applications, in designs too competent and measurement systems too reliable and valid to doubt. Our ability to prove that behavior can work that way does not, of course, establish that behavior *cannot* work any other way: we are not in a discipline that can deny any other approaches, only in one that can affirm itself as knowing many of its *sufficient* conditions at the level of experimental proof. . . . Our subject matter is behavior change, and we can specify some *actionable* sufficient conditions for it. It is illuminating to ask all alternative approaches whether they can specify even some actionable and sufficient conditions for behavior change of the sort necessary to the solution of educational problems, and can do so at the level of proof. (D. M. Baer, per-

sonal communication, October 21, 1982, emphasis in original)

## ABA Is Focused

Like "smart bombs" that can be programmed to seek and destroy specific targets, behavioral assessment, analytic, and intervention tools can be used to find and repair specific instructional problems. In other words, ABA can be focused to yield a "smart analysis" at the individual student, classroom, school-building, or district level, or the level at which any student contacts the curriculum. For example, systematic assessment and the application of reinforcers can reduce motivational problems (e.g., Alber & Heward, 1996; Northrup, 2000), and analyses of the task or skill to be learned or the student's relevant prerequisite skills can improve the efficiency of lessons for all students (e.g., Becker, 1992; Dixon, 1991) as well as for individual students (e.g., Neef, Nelles, Iwata, & Page, 2003). The functional analysis of maintaining contingencies can lead to effective interventions for problem behaviors (O'Neill, Horner, Albin, Sprague, Storey, & Newton, 1997) and instructional materials that promote students learning (e.g., Twyman, Layng, Stikeleather, & Hobbins, 2005; Vargas, 1984).

## ABA Is Broadly Relevant

ABA is an approach[1] with broad relevance for education. The applicability and effectiveness of behaviorally based educational interventions have been demonstrated across learners, curriculum content, instructional arrangements, and settings. The peer-reviewed, experimental research literature shows that ABA-based interventions have been successful with students of all ages; students of widely different ability levels; students from diverse cultural, ethnic, and linguistic backgrounds; students from poor, middle-income, and wealthy families; and students enrolled in urban, suburban, and rural school districts. ABA-based interventions have increased student achievement, often markedly, in basic tool skills, in standard academic content subjects, and in social skills. ABA-based interventions have been effective in all types of instructional arrangements (teacher-led whole class and small group instruction, collaborative learning groups, peer tutoring arrangements,

---

[1]In many respects, it is a misnomer to refer to "the ABA approach." Although ABA offers educators a collection of teaching techniques whose effectiveness has been empirically validated, it does not prescribe any particular instructional method. ABA includes a philosophy, a set of principles from which situation-specific educational interventions with a high probability of success can be derived, and—most important—a data-driven method for continually evaluating the effectiveness of those interventions.

and individual learning) and everywhere teachers want to help students: in the classroom and in the lunchroom, on the playground and on the bus, in the band room and in the gym.

## ABA Is Self-Correcting

If students are not learning, then something about the way they are being taught ought to be changed so that learning does occur. Although most educators would agree with this precept in principle, in practice they do not often follow it. When teachers do not collect direct and frequent measures of student performance to verify the effects of instruction, they are prone to two mistakes: (1) continuing ineffective instruction when no real learning has occurred (e.g., perhaps the teacher believes a certain type of intervention is effective) and (2) discontinuing an effective program of instruction because subjective judgment finds no improvement (e.g., without objective measures it is difficult to discern that a student's reading rate has increased from 70 words per minute to 80 words per minute).

Direct and frequent measurement is the foundation and most important component of ABA in education. Such measurement enables teachers to detect their successes and, equally important, their failures so that they can make changes that will turn failure into success (Bushell & Baer, 1994; Greenwood & Maheady, 1997).

> Our technology of behavior change is also a technology of behavior measurement and of experimental design; it developed as that package, and as long as it stays in that package, it is a self-evaluating enterprise. Its successes are success of known magnitude; its failures are almost immediately detected as failures; and whatever its outcomes, they are attributable to known inputs and procedures rather than to chance events or coincidences. (D. M. Baer, personal communication, October 21, 1982)

## ABA Is Accountable

ABA's focus on environmental variables that reliably influence learning and that can be acted on yields a form of accountability and responsibility that is good for education. Behaviorally oriented educators focus on what Bloom (1980) called "alterable variables," things that both make a difference in student learning and can be affected by teaching practices. Alterable variables include factors such as the selection of curriculum content and instructional examples; the amount of time allocated for instruction; whether instructional materials call for a recognition or recall response; the sequence of activities within the overall lesson; the pacing of instruction; how often students actively respond during instruction; whether, how, and when students receive praise or other forms of reinforcement for their efforts; and the way errors are corrected.

Gambrill (2003) described ABA's sense of accountability, as well as its self-correcting nature, very well.

> Applied behavior analysis is a scientific approach to understanding and behavior in which we guess and critically test ideas, rather than guess and guess again. It is a process for solving problems in which we learn from our mistakes. Here, false knowledge and inert knowledge are not valued. (p. 67)

Behavior analysts do not, as many believe, deny or discount the influence of genetic, societal, cultural, and familial factors on learning. Behavior analysts do, however, recognize three problems with viewing genetic and sociocultural factors as primary determinants of student learning: (1) These factors are usually beyond teachers' control, (2) teachers can positively affect student learning with alterable variables in spite of the presence of such factors, and (3) deferring to such factors reduces educators' sense of responsibility for providing effective instruction. Just as disability labels are often used to "explain" special education students' failure to learn (e.g., "Brandon has not learned to read *because* he has a learning disability"), educators frequently identify inherent student traits (e.g., low intelligence, faulty cognitive processes, poor intrinsic motivation) and/or socioeconomic, cultural, and familial factors as underlying causes of students' low achievement. Although factors over which teachers have no control do indeed influence student learning, they can also serve as an excuse for failing to provide effective instruction, shifting accountability for the lack of learning from teachers and schools.

## ABA Is Public

Everything about ABA is visible and public, explicit and straightforward. It is an honest, roll-up-your-sleeves and get-to-work approach that demands a commitment to specific learning outcomes, a desire to intervene in a systematic and consistent way, a commitment to measure and record the results of the intervention, and a willingness to let the data guide the next move. ABA entails no ephemeral, mystical, or metaphysical explanations; there are no hidden treatments; there is no magic. The visible nature of ABA should be highly valued in a profession such as public education, whose goals, methods, and outcomes are of interest to and the responsibility of many constituencies: the public at large, families, students, teachers, administrators, and school board members.

## ABA Is Doable

In the majority of ABA classroom studies, the students' regular teacher implemented the intervention. This is a highly valuable feature of behavioral research because it demonstrates the pragmatic element of most ABA interventions. Although "doing ABA" requires far more than learning to administer a few simple procedures, it is not prohibitively complicated or arduous. As many teachers have noted, implementing behavioral strategies in the classroom—especially the continual assessment of the relationship between student learning and instruction through close, continual contact with relevant outcome data (a.k.a., 3CROD; Bushell & Baer 1994)—might best be described as good old-fashioned hard work.

## ABA Is Replicable

No matter how powerful its effects are in any given study, a teaching method will be of little value if practitioners are unable to replicate it. The development of a replicable technology of teaching has been a defining characteristic and continuing goal of ABA from its very beginning (Baer et al., 1968). Interventions that cannot be replicated with sufficient fidelity to achieve desired outcomes are not considered part of the technology. Behavioral strategies are replicable and teachable to others. As Baer and Bushell (1981) noted, the behavioral approach could easily be copied and used by others because it is "public, clear, and relatively simple to understand, imitate, . . . well-articulated at the level of principle, and even fairly well-endowed with recipe at the level of technique" (p. 260).

## ABA Is Empowering

ABA provides educators with real tools that work. Knowing how to do something and having the tools to do it instills in teachers a sense of confidence in their abilities and helps them tackle difficult teaching challenges.

## ABA Is Optimistic

The environmental view promoted by behaviorism is essentially optimistic; it suggests that (except for gross genetic factors) all individuals possess roughly equal potential. Rather than assuming that individuals have some essential internal characteristic, behaviorists assume that poor outcomes originate in the way the environment and experience shaped the individual's current behavior. Once these environmental and experiential factors are identified, we can design prevention and intervention programs to improve the outcomes. . . . Thus, the emphasis on external control in the behavioral approach . . . offers a conceptual model that celebrates the possibilities for each individual. (Strain, et al., 1992, cited by Strain & Joseph, 2004, p. 58)

A sense of optimism, expressed by the question "Why not?" has been a central feature of ABA and has had an enormous impact on its development from its earliest days. Why can't we teach a person who does not yet talk to talk? Why shouldn't we go ahead and try to change the environments of young children so that they will display more creativity? Why would we assume that this person with a developmental disability could not learn to do the same things that many of us do? Why not try to do it?

ABA is an optimistic approach to the difficult task and heavy responsibility of teaching in three fundamental ways. First, direct and continuous measurement enables teachers to see small improvements in student performance that they would otherwise overlook (and therefore not reinforce and, as a result, the student may not repeat). Second, the more a teacher successfully uses behavioral strategies with positive outcomes (and positive outcomes are the most common result of behaviorally based interventions), the more optimistic the teacher becomes about the prospects for future success. Third, the published literature provides many examples of ABA's success in teaching students who had been considered unteachable. ABA's continual record of achievements evokes a feeling of optimism that future developments will yield solutions to teaching challenges that are currently beyond existing technology.

Some of us have ignored both the thesis that all persons are educable and the thesis that some persons are ineducable, and instead have experimented with ways to teach some previously unteachable people. Those experiments have steadily reduced the size of the apparently ineducable group relative to the obviously educable group. Clearly, we have not finished that adventure. Why predict its outcome, when we could simply pursue it, and just as well without a prediction? Why not pursue it to see if there comes a day when there is such a small class of apparently ineducable persons left that it consists of one elderly person who is put forward as ineducable. If that day comes, it will be a very nice day. And the next day will be even better. (D. M. Baer, as cited in Heward, 2003, p. 497)

## ABA Knows Motivation

> There are three important things to remember about education. The first one is motivation, the second is motivation, and the third is motivation. (Terrell Bell, U.S. Secretary of Education)

If the former secretary of education is correct, then ABA knows at least three important things about education. If ABA knows anything about learning, it is how to increase students' motivation to participate. Positive reinforcement is "the most basic and essential feature of applied behavior analysis" (Northup, Vollmer, & Serrett, 1993, p. 534) behavior analysis. ABA has developed a body of practical knowledge that helps educators identify reinforcers, create motivating operations to increase the momentary effectiveness of reinforcers (Michael, 2000), schedule reinforcement, shift from contrived to naturally occurring reinforcers, and so on. Skillful application of reinforcement is necessary for learning to occur at optimal rates.

## WHY ABA HAS HAD A LIMITED IMPACT ON EDUCATION

The 12 reasons ABA is good for education make it sound like a Boy Scout: trustworthy, loyal, helpful, friendly, courteous, kind, obedient, and so on. After considering this impressive list of positive attributes, one might reasonably exclaim, Wow! What's not to like about ABA? It is all good for education. But, as ESPN college football analyst Lee Corso says, "Not so fast, my friend!" The following list of reasons may help to explain why ABA has not had anywhere near the impact and influence on education that its positive characteristics suggest that it should:

1. ABA's basic assumptions about the purpose and process of education are incompatible with the views of many educators.
2. ABA's data do not interest educators.
3. ABA's data do not matter because educational decisions are seldom informed by data on student learning.
4. ABA's empirical pragmatism is antithetical to education's retreat from objective science.
5. ABA seems too simplistic.
6. Other approaches promise more.
7. ABA's use of reinforcement goes against current beliefs in education.
8. ABA is an easy mark for criticism.
9. Some teachers view ABA as a threat to their creativity and independence.
10. ABA places the responsibility for student learning on teachers and schools.
11. Implementing behavioral approaches yields too little reinforcement for teachers.
12. Behavioral educators have insufficient understanding and control of the contingencies that govern the adoption and maintenance of effective practices.
13. ABA has yet to prove its value to the students about whom society cares most.
14. Improving education is not an urgent mission for society.

### ABA's Basic Assumptions about the Purpose and Process of Education Are Incompatible with the Views of Many Educators

ABA makes two basic assumptions about education: (1) that teachers should identify desired learning outcomes, and (2) that teachers should plan and deliver instruction to help students achieve those outcomes. Both assumptions, as straightforward and logical as they may seem, are at odds with the views of many educators today. According to the "child-centered, constructivist" perspective that currently dominates many teacher preparation programs in schools of education today, teachers should not determine learning outcomes for their students, and methods of explicit instruction hamper rather than aid student learning. Advocates of the constructivist/holistic viewpoint contend that "the task of schools is to help students develop new meanings in response to new experience rather than to learn the meanings others have created" (Poplin, 1988a, p. 401). It is said that predetermined learning objectives and lesson plans limit students' freedom and encourage passivity:

> Students' minds are allowed very little freedom when specific psychological processes, academic skills, and cognitive strategies are structured for them. . . . The more structured the curriculum, the more passive become our students. (Poplin, 1988a, p. 395)

According to this view, standard curricula and preset lesson plans are unnecessary, irrelevant, and boring to students and teachers. Predetermined learning objectives require teachers to be a "sage on the stage" who coerces students to learn knowledge and skills that others have decided are important but that may have no meaningful context for them. These educators say that teachers should act as a "guide on the side" who encourages children to construct their own meanings from materials and activities. When a constructivist model is fully applied, students determine what and how much they will learn.

> From a holistic, constructivist perspective, all children simply engage in a process of learning as much as they can in a particular subject area; how much and exactly what they learn will depend upon their backgrounds, interests, and abilities. (Stainback & Stainback, 1992, p. 72)

If there is no corpus of knowledge and skills that all children should learn, then it follows that there is little point in attempting to determine beforehand how to teach. As Gallagher (2004) explained, "prediction and control of the education environment [are] neither possible nor desirable, and teaching is the context-bound act of making meaning" (p. 23). If learning is considered the process by which students construct their own knowledge, then ABA's most valuable contributions to education—strategies and techniques of explicit instruction that reliably achieve specific changes in student behavior—are both irrelevant and undesirable.

## ABA's Data Do Not Interest Educators

Richard Foxx (1996) began his presidential address at the annual convention of the Association for Behavior Analysis by describing a recurring nightmare in which he woke up each morning to a newspaper headline that read, "Behavior analysis reported today that they could cure apathy. No one, however, has shown any interest" (p. 147). With respect to education, Foxx's bad dream reveals an unfortunate reality: Much of what ABA has to offer has engendered little interest from educators.

The kind of data obtained by ABA to verify and illustrate the effectiveness of its techniques may be a contributing factor in education's nearly wholesale apathy toward behavioral approaches to curriculum design and instruction (Landrum, 1997). ABA does not target and measure many of the things educators consider important, at least in the way educators typically conceptualize and talk about those things.

> [S]uppose a whole language (WL) advocate offers as evidence of the effectiveness of WL some carefully collected data showing that children who have spent the school year in a WL classroom report that they like to read and they enjoy the WL activities. At the same time, a supporter of explicit instruction (EI) presents graphs showing sharply increasing rates of correctly read words per minute (WPM) by children who had participated in EI over the course of the school year. The WL person thinks it blasphemy and bad practice to measure an out-of-context variable like WPM and that the EI proponent misses the whole point of reading. The EI person, in turn, sees the fact that children say that they like to read and enjoy the WL activities as positive information, but cannot accept it as evidence that the children actually do read or that WL had anything to do with their reading. In cases like this, neither party's data matter because they do not represent a canon of proof considered meaningful by the other party. (from Heward, 2003, p. 199)

Another reason for education's apathy may be that most of ABA's evidence has been obtained with a research model not widely accepted in education and the so-called social sciences. ABA's "single–subject" research designs featuring repeated measures of the behavior of individual students in the presence and absence of independent variables are considered "quasi-experimental" research with little or no external validity (Campbell & Stanley, 1966; Johnston & Pennypacker, 1986).

## ABA's Data Do Not Matter Because Educational Decisions Are Seldom Informed by Data on Student Learning

ABA's value as a self-correcting, data-driven approach to instruction does not matter at the classroom level because most teachers do not take direct and frequent measures of student performance and then use those data as the basis for instructional decisions. Even special education teachers, who by law (i.e., the Individuals with Disabilities Education Act, IDEA) and training know the importance of and have learned procedures for collecting and using student performance data, seldom do so systematically. Although 75% of the 510 special education teachers in one survey agreed that it is "important" to frequently collect student performance data, the majority indicated that they most often used anecdotal observations and subjective measures to determine whether students were meeting IEP objectives, and 85% said they "never" or "seldom" collected and charted student performance data to make instructional decisions (Cooke, Heward, Test, Spooner, & Courson, 1991).

Evidence of effectiveness also appears to play little or no role when school districts make decisions to adopt curricula and instructional approaches. Unlike most professions in which practitioners' tools are thoroughly field-tested to ensure that they are effective and reliable before they are implemented on a widespread basis, education has a long history of adopting new curricula and teaching methods with little or no evidence of effectiveness (Grossen, 1998; Spear-Swerling & Sternberg, 2001). Ideology, dogma,

folklore, fashion, fad, convenience, and personal preference have had greater influence on theory and practice in education than have the results of scientific research (Carnine, 1992; Gersten, 2001; Jacobson, Mulick, & Foxx, in press; Sarnoff, 2001; Vaughn & Damann, 2001).

> In all areas of medicine and engineering, practitioners keep up with research publications in order to make use of new discoveries. . . . I know of no service area except education in which practitioners habitually disregard fundamental research. (Sidman, 1994, p. 532)

Indeed, policy makers in education almost seem to make a special effort to disregard data on effectiveness. Project Follow Through (PFT) remains the most perplexing and tragic example of U.S. education's inability and unwillingness to use the results of scientific evidence to improve educational outcomes for children. PFT was a carefully designed federally sponsored experiment that compared the effectiveness of 22 different models for teaching low-income children in the primary grades. The models included Piagetian-based approaches, open classroom models, discovery learning approaches, models based on building self-esteem, and two behaviorally based models. PFT was the largest experiment on education ever conducted and involved thousands of children in 51 sites ranging from inner-city districts in New York City and East Saint Louis to tiny rural areas such as Flippin, Arkansas. The results were significant and unambiguous: The two behavioral models were at or near the top on every achievement variable measured in the study (Abt Associates, 1973, 1977; Bock, Stebbins, & Proper, 1996). Interestingly, the Direct Instruction model that focused on improving children's reading, math, and language skills also produced the *highest* scores on measures of children's self-concept—higher even than the models designed to help children feel good about themselves (Watkins, 1997).

The federal government created the Joint Dissemination Review Panel (JDRP) and National Diffusion Network (NDN) to validate and disseminate effective educational practices to the nation's schools. In 1977 the sponsors of the various Follow Through models submitted their programs to the JDRP for review. Watkins (1996) described how the JDRP's decision that "effectiveness" should be broadly interpreted effectively neutered the government's worthy intentions to use the results of scientific research to improve educational practice.

> [A]ccording the JDRP, the positive impact of a program need not be directly related to academic achievement. In addition, a program could be judged effective if it had a positive impact on individuals other than students. As a result programs that had failed to improve academic achievement in Follow Through were rated as "exemplary and effective." And once a program was validated, it was packaged and disseminated to schools through the National Diffusion Network. (p. 61)

As a result of this policy decision, schools were unable to distinguish programs that had proven their effectiveness by raising children's academic achievement from programs that had produced little (and in some cases even negative) effects on achievement. Some programs were officially labeled "exemplary and effective" on the basis of factors such as the extent to which teachers liked to use them.

The education community's lack of interest in objective evidence has not been limited to the PFT debacle 30 years ago. A large-scale review by the American Institutes for Research of the 24 most adopted schoolwide reform models found that only three of the models (Direct Instruction, Success for All, and High Schools That Work) had "strong evidence" of positive effects on student achievement (Olson, 1999).

## ABA's Empirical Pragmatism Is Antithetical to Education's Retreat from Objective Science

Educational research has undergone a so-called paradigm shift from its traditional emphasis on quantitative measures of clearly specified variables to a preference for qualitative data. Quali-

tative data take the primary form of narratives or scripts that are produced by researchers, study participants, and people external to the study who review the original scripts and then construct their own narrative accounts of the events. Scriptwriters are encouraged to construct "thick, rich descriptions" of events during the study and their experiences with and perspectives about those events.

According to Creswell and Miller (2000), three "paradigm assumptions," or world views, provide the framework for qualitative research: postpositivism, a constructivist perspective, and critical theory. These world views provide qualitative researchers with pluralistic, open-ended, and contextualized perspectives to "uncover the hidden assumptions about how narrative accounts are constructed, read, and interpreted" (p. 126). For more information on how the validity and usefulness of qualitative data are determined, see Tierney and Twombly (2000).

An increasing number of educators contend that science is an antiquated and mechanistic approach to knowledge generation based on a misguided empiricism of arbitrary variables that no longer fits the more sophisticated, postmodern understanding of teaching and learning. Supporters of this view believe that research methods predicated on the "untenable assumptions of the empiricist paradigm" (Gallagher, 2004, p. 23) should be replaced with the qualitative, narrative-based methods of deconstruction and discourse (e.g., Gallagher, 1998, 2004; Danforth, 1997; Elkind, 1998; Heshusius, 1982, 1986, 2004; Iano, 2004; Lather, 1992, 1993; Poplin, 1988b; Skrtic, Sailor, & Gee, 1996).

Gallagher (2004), an advocate for the virtues of postmodernism, conceded that when we set out to teach a child to read we would like to know beforehand if our methods will be effective. However, she stated that "applying the scientific method to the study of teaching fails to accomplish this goal" (p. 15). According to Gallagher,

> If we believe that things simply are the way they are, there can be no responsibility for them, and

likewise no possibility for changing them. If we understand that our knowledge about the world is a construction, our thinking becomes altered dramatically. Rather than thinking in terms of "this is reality," we being to think in terms of "this is the way we have constructed reality." Subsequently, we begin to realize that what we construct we can deconstruct and reconstruct, and that we have the responsibility for doing so when "the way things are" has undesirable consequences. (p. 13)[2]

The motivation behind many educators' wholesale undervaluing of the scientific method and quantitative data in favor of the qualitative discourse of postmodernism may be understandable. However, the logic behind it is flawed, and the consequences of it are severe.

After waiting patiently for more than half a century for the "scientific approach" to produce an effective and reliable technology of education, it should surprise no one that practitioners and the public have little faith that educational research will come to the rescue. But the research methods most often used in education have not matched the subject matter studied. The application of statistical inference and one-time measurement was doomed to failure in education, a field in which the most important questions are about human behavior. Teaching and learning are behavioral phenomena

whose scientific analysis requires investigative methods suited to the individual and dynamic nature of the subject matter. It is a classic and tragic case of throwing the baby out with the bath water. (Heward & Cooper, 1992, p. 358)

## ABA Seems Too Simplistic

When the subject matter we seek to understand is complex and has proven difficult to predict and control, complex and profound explanations may seem necessary.[3] Compared to the "deep understanding of pedagogy" promised by authors of more "enlightened and holistic world views," behavior analysis's description of teaching and learning as interlocking, three- and four-term contingencies does appear, at least on the surface, to be simplistic and mechanistic. It is true that many who describe behavior analysis as simplistic base their judgments on inaccurate and superficial knowledge of the science. Nevertheless, when it comes to telling an interesting story about teaching and learning, terms such as *response prompt* and *stimulus control* are no match for *spirals of knowledge* (Poplin, 1988a) and *multiple intelligences* (Gardner, 1993).

Elaborate theories of teaching and learning suggest an aura of profundity and intellectual sophistication, which may be another reason they are favored over more parsimonious explanations. Apparent profundity is well represented in contemporary education literature by writers

---

[2]While I do not claim to know what Gallagher means by this passage, it appears that she may be suggesting the following: (1) If you do not believe or do not like what you detect in the physical world, that is OK because (2) whatever you have detected is your own construction of reality, and that is OK because (3) if you do not like the reality you have constructed, just make up alternative constructions until you arrive at a meaning that pleases you. The implication of Gallagher's position for research, like that of so many other postmodern authors, seems to be this: There is no longer any need to conduct those artificial, manipulative, and cumbersome experiments; we can just talk about things in a never-ending process of construction, deconstruction, and reconstruction. As for classroom practice, I confess complete confusion as to how such a linguistic and epistemological muddle will help anyone learn how to teach a child to read.

[3]Some authors contend that human behavior is so complex and unique in each instance that any attempt to discover its governing principles is a fool's errand doomed to failure and irrelevancy. For example, Cziko (1989) gave the following explanation for the unpredictability of human behavior: First, no two people are exactly alike. In contrast to things in the physical world, such as molecules of oxygen, for which lawlike generalizations are possible, people differ in ways that make them unpredictable. Second, because people possess consciousness and can change their minds at any given moment, human behavior is an inherently novel and creative process with infinite meanings.

espousing postmodernism, deconstructivism, and critical theory (e.g., Brantlinger, 1997; Danforth, 1997; Elkind, 1998; Gallagher, Heshusius, Iano, & Skrtic, 2004; Lather, 1992; Smith, 1999). The dense and at times impenetrable language used by many of these authors has produced a "very popular form of know-nothingism that does considerable mischief, particularly in higher education" (Kauffman, 2002, p. 14), where the mantra of postmodernism, deconstructivism, and critical theory is daily fare for students enrolled in teacher preparation programs.

## Other Approaches Promise More

High-sounding phrases such as *authentic assessment, teaching for deep understanding, holistic teaching, critical thinking skills, self-regulated learning,* and *integrated curriculum* promise more—more meaningful student learning and a more sophisticated role for the teacher—than do terms such as *choral responding, guided practice,* and *error correction.* It is understandable that a teacher (or principal, school board member, parent, or student) might view the use of "brain-based learning activities to unlock a child's emerging literacy" as more important than the use of "repeated reading to increase the number of words read correctly per minute."

ABA offers education a set of teaching techniques whose effectiveness has been demonstrated in numerous classroom studies, a set of fundamental principles about teaching and learning from which additional techniques with a high probability of success can be derived, and a method for systematically and continually evaluating the effectiveness of both the previously demonstrated and the newly derived techniques every time they are applied. Although ABA's offer is a very good one, many educators view it as severely limited. The kinds of knowledge and skills targeted in many behavioral studies may contribute to the perception held by

many educators that behavioral techniques are only relevant for simple and routine skills.

> Programmed learning and task analysis do lend themselves to certain limited kinds of practices that are technical, routinelike, and the relatively closed-ended, such as tying knots, buttoning shirts, washing clothes, and operating machines. But programmed learning and task analysis do not have much to offer for most of the educational curriculum. (Iano, 2004, p. 238)

Another drawback of ABA is that its most effective techniques tend to be structured, fast-paced, and demanding and require regular daily application (Lindsley, 1992). In addition to promising to help students learn more than "rote, closed-ended, splinter skills," most other approaches promise teachers greater flexibility in planning and conducting instruction. As mentioned previously, the absence of scientifically sound data showing the effectiveness of these other approaches does not matter to many in education.

Education's reluctance to use science as its primary tool for discovering and verifying effective practices has made it highly susceptible to the widespread adoption of curriculum and instruction "methods" based on ideology, dogma, personal preference, and testimonials (Carnine, 1992, 2000). The education of students with disabilities has been a particularly fertile ground for fads and miracle treatments (cf., Jacobson, Mulick, & Foxx, in press; Maurice, 1993, 2000; Rooney, 1991).

## ABA's Use of Reinforcement Goes Against Current Beliefs in Education

The systematic use of positive reinforcement—ABA's most thoroughly developed and generally useful tool for teachers—is anathema to some educators today. Increasingly, teachers read and hear that using "extrinsic motivators," such as token reinforcement, activity rewards, and verbal praise, is an artificial and ineffective approach to improving student learning that harms students in the long run by damaging their "intrinsic motivation."

Freelance writer Alfie Kohn (1993) has become the most prominent voice of the anti-praise and rewards campaign. Kohn has achieved widespread popularity (and many speaking fees) by traveling around the country speaking to educators on the dangers of using praise and rewards with students. Kohn tells teachers of the negative effects of "extrinsic motivators" in the classroom. For example, in "Five Reasons to Stop Saying 'Good Job!'" Kohn (2001a) informed teachers that praising and rewarding students for their accomplishments manipulates children, creates praise junkies, steals their pleasure, causes children to lose interest, and reduces achievement. Kohn's contentions about the harmful effects of praise and positive reinforcement on children, however, stand in stark contrast to the extensive research literature showing the positive benefits of such practices (see Cameron, 2005; Kratochwill & Stoiber, 2000; Wolery, 2000). As Strain and Joseph (2004) noted, the "planned use of positive reinforcement is antithetical to [Kohn's pejorative description of the practice as] blurted-out judgments, slathered-on praise, knee-jerk tendencies, and evaluative eruptions" (p. 58, words in brackets added).

It would be wonderful if all students came to school prepared to work hard and to learn for so-called intrinsic reasons. The ultimate "intrinsic motivator" is success itself (Skinner, 1984)—using new knowledge and skills effectively enough to enjoy control over one's environment, such as solving a never-before-seen algebra problem or reading a murder mystery with sufficient accuracy and endurance to find out who did it. But it is naive and irresponsible for educators to expect students with limited skills and a history of academic failure to work diligently and happily without positive consequences. Contingent teacher praise and other "extrinsic motivators," such as points toward a grade or slips of paper as entries in the classroom weekly lottery, are proven methods for helping students to at-

tain the performance levels that will enable them to contact the naturally existing reinforcement "contingencies of success."

## ABA Is an Easy Mark for Criticism

ABA's focus on observable and measurable learning objectives, the straightforward nature of its instructional methods, and its scientific ancestry make it vulnerable to criticism. Certainly no educational theory, model, or approach is above criticism. Researchers, practitioners, participants, and consumers should continually and critically evaluate the appropriateness, effectiveness, practicality, and cost–benefit ratios of all educational approaches. However, some of the most frequently voiced criticisms of behavioral techniques in education have nothing to do with those important issues.

ABA's practice of targeting measurable behaviors is often criticized from the perspective that isolating any skill for explicit instruction renders the skill trivial. For example, Heshusius (1982) poked fun at an IEP objective that called for a girl to smile when entering the classroom 4 out of 5 days. ABA translates educational problems into behaviors to be changed. Sound, carefully considered translations result in educationally significant teaching objectives. "Arbitrary translations can easily be foolish translations, and subsequent behavior-change programs aimed at foolish targets are rendered foolish themselves" (D. M. Baer, personal communication, October 21, 1982). Designing a teaching program to increase the frequency of the girl's "smiling behavior" could very well have been foolish and trivial. If, however, smiling more often when she entered the classroom made the girl's peers more likely to interact with her and as a result increased the girl's opportunities for language development and making friends, her teachers were wise to target "smiling behavior" for instruction.

The explicit, structured nature of behavioral teaching methods, which strike some educators as mechanistic, boring, and too much like work, is frequently criticized. For example, even though research shows that drill and practice is a consistently effective teaching method (e.g., Swanson & Sachse-Lee, 2000), teachers are told that drill and practice dulls students' creativity and interest and produces only rote memorization.[4]

> The educational crisis we are allegedly facing has occurred under a "drill-and-skill," test-driven system in which students are treated as passive receptacles rather than active learners. . . . A sour "take-your-medicine" traditionalism goes hand in hand with drill-and-skill lessons (some of which are aptly named "worksheets"). (Kohn, 1998, pp. 197, 212)

Of course, just as meaningless learning objectives can be targeted, so can behavioral teaching techniques such as drill and practice be conducted in ways that render them pointless, a waste of time, and frustrating for children.

ABA's scientific heritage remains a favorite target of critics. It is still common to read in books and journal articles for educators that behavioral approaches are not valid or are abhorrent for use with children because the principles on which those approaches are based were discovered in laboratory research with animals. In the *Handbook on Effective Instructional Strategies,* published by the Institute for Evidence-Based Decision-Making in Education, Friedman and Fisher (1998) explained the following "facts" about reinforcement as revealed by a "review of the research":

> Fundamental laws of reinforcement were derived by psychologists, ranging over time from Pavlov to Skinner, who did research using food to shape the behavior of captive starved lower animals. Such laws are as applicable to shaping the behavior of lower animals today as they ever were. And the laws appear to be applicable to mentally retarded and young children as well. . . . More mentally competent humans are not as habit bound and are not as prone to be conditioned to react in a particular way to a particular prompt or stimulus.
>
> Another reason laws of reinforcement have limited generalizability is because the captive lower animals used in traditional reinforcement research are placed in highly confining environments, which severely restrict their movements and choice. . . .
>
> [L]aws of reinforcement derived from rewarding starved lower animals with food are not generalizable to human learning environments in free countries because it is illegal to starve human learners.
>
> Moreover, the laws of reinforcement are derived from conditioning individual animals one at a time, not from conditioning groups of animals. . . . It is not only unwarranted, but impractical as well, for teachers to administer reinforcement to a class of students.
>
> In conclusion, "laws of reinforcement" are generalizable to the conditioning of single captive starved lower animals and mentally retarded and very young human students, but not beyond. Therefore, they do not qualify as generalizations of human instruction when the objective is academic achievement. (pp. 233–234)[5]

As if denying the relevance of the basic principles of behavior to teaching and learning—which is akin to claiming that gravity affects some objects, but not in my classroom—is not silly enough, Heshusius (2004) contended that the basic operant principles do not even hold for "self-respecting" animals.

---

[4]The word *rote* is frequently used to demean the outcomes of just about any behavioral teaching technique, regardless of whether the technique is designed to produce rote learning (which is not the point of this footnote). I sometimes wonder when, and on what empirical and conceptual bases, education decided that knowing things by rote is undesirable. *Rote* means to do something in a routine or fixed way, to respond automatically by memory alone, without thought. Although it is important to debate what things are most useful to commit to memory, every educated person knows many things by rote. Rote is good.

[5]To summarize what Friedman and Fisher (1998) told educators: (1) Reinforcement is ineffective with school-age students who are not mentally retarded; (2) for reinforcement to work, children would have to be treated like starved rats who have no choice but to respond to the only thing provided in their deprived environments; and (3) should you still be crazy enough to consider using reinforcement in the classroom, be reminded that it is illegal to starve children in a free country.

The courses in behavior theory and research I had to take also were based entirely on the application of control techniques and formula to people. The reductionistic simplicity that characterized what I had to learn in these theories astonished me. I could not believe that academics actually used these methods, which, after all, were taken directly from experiments with laboratory animals (which is not the same as "animals." They are two different species. No self-respecting rats or pigeons would voluntarily—out of *self-organization*—engage in what their laboratory counterparts, half starved and isolated, can be "taught" to do). (p. 173, emphasis in original)

It is a short distance, conceptually and linguistically, from the explanations of what "research shows" about reinforcement by writers such as Friedman and Fisher (1998) and Heshusius (2004) to Coles's (1998) description of the awful outcomes that await children who are "subjected" to the direct instruction model.

"[D]irect instruction" pedagogy might be successful literacy education for some educators and parents, but it is an abomination to others. Within its standards, [DI] might "work," but who would want his or her child's early education to: discourage participation in initiating and creating written-language activities; discourage experience making choices and solving problems; discourage exploration of multiple views on stories read; discourage experience developing, expressing, and contesting a viewpoint; constrict emotions in learning experiences; constrict creativity in written language; and assume a "dog eat dog" outlook? These are hardly qualities to help children understand their own thoughts and emotions, feel secure about themselves, be creative, assess accurately the views of others, care about others, understand the world, and make sound judgments. (p. 38)

Even though rhetoric like this has no resemblance to the positive results of research on the use of reinforcement with schoolchildren (e.g., Kratochwill & Stoiber, 2000) or studies evaluating the effects of explicit, skills-based instruction on academic and social outcomes (e.g., Gersten, 1992; Watkins, 1997; Weisberg, 1994), this kind disinformation and misinformation about behav-

iorally based instruction continues to find a voice and a wide audience in educational publications. For example, Kohn's (2001a) "Five Reasons to Stop Saying 'Good Job!'" article appeared in *Young Children,* a professional journal received by more than 100,000 early childhood educators.

"There is too much at stake" (Sarason, 1990, p. 133) to sit on the sidelines and let the wacky and harmful intentions of writers such as Kohn go unchallenged. I believe that misinformed attacks on applied behavior anlaysis or any measurably superior teaching practice, regardless of its theoretical foundation, should be met head on in each of the media and forums in which they appear. "Words have the power to incite, comfort, inflame, sooth, excite, calm, prejudice, and assuage. In effect, they set the occasion for behavior" (Foxx, 1996, p. 147). Fortunately, many authors whose thinking about and recommendations for educational practice are guided by science have responded to refute misconceptions and give an accurate account of topics such as methods of curriculum organization and explicit instruction (e.g., Dixon & Carnine, 1992; Heron & Kimball, 1988; Tarver, 1998), teachers' use of praise and reinforcement (e.g., Cameron, 2005; Maag, 2001; Strain & Joseph, 2004), and behaviorism as a guiding philosophy for education (Heward & Cooper, 1992; Kimball, 2002).[6]

---

[6]Some behaviorists believe that responding to ill-informed attacks on behavior analysis is a mistake because doing so provides attention that might "reinforce" the attacker's behavior, and that simply ignoring the attack might help "extinguish" the behavior. However, that any reactions by behavior analysts would function in any significant way as reinforcement for the critics' behavior is a huge conceptual leap and a practical unlikelihood. That aside, the purpose of attempts to give accurate accounts of behavior analysis is not to try to change the behavior of the critic, but to reach the critic's audience and provide current and future teachers with opportunities to consider alternative descriptions of how learning occurs and what they can do to enhance it (Gambrill, 2003).

## Some Teachers View ABA as a Threat to Their Creativity and Independence

As Lindsley (1992) noted, the teaching techniques that behavioral researchers have found most effective in raising student achievement feature structured curriculum content, standard techniques for presenting instructional material and providing feedback to students, and frequent student practice with opportunities to develop fluency. Such techniques are fast-paced, demanding, and require consistent application on a daily basis. Structured curricula and instructional methods that must be consistently applied, however, run counter to the beliefs held by many teachers that developing one's own "style" of instruction and being creative are keys to their effectiveness as educators.

A popular phrase in education today is that "there are as many ways of teaching as there are teachers" (Kohn, 1999, p. 2). Indeed, a popular assignment in many preservice teacher education courses requires each future teacher to develop his or her own "theory of pedagogy." Some educators contend that behavioral strategies cause a teacher to become little more than a semiskilled technician who has learned to perform a collection of tasks (Darling-Hammond, 1985), someone whose role is to deliver scripted lessons. "One must then ask: What makes a teacher a teacher? After all, any reasonably intelligent person can follow a script" (Gallagher, 2004, p. 22). Some teachers feel that teaching the same way day after day becomes boring, and that they have the right to change their approach to teaching when they get "tired of doing it the same way" (cf., Purnell & Claycomb, 2001).

Teachers are told that their profession is an art, not a science, and that not only is it permissible to teach in different ways from time to time, but such change is good for students. Adding variety to instructional activities and materials to make lessons more interesting and fun is one way teachers frequently try to be creative. Although creativity is highly valued in the arts, in many other professions it is considered counterproductive, if not harmful. Patients do not want doctors to perform surgery creatively, passengers do not want pilots to fly planes creatively, and investors do not want accountants to do math creatively. To do so would risk the lives and livelihoods of consumers and would constitute unnecessary risk-taking with outcomes that are too important. For these same reasons, creativity for the sake of trying something different is counterproductive in education. Creative, inconsistent teaching methods are actually the opposite of evidence-based teaching methods.

Teacher creativity will always have an important place in the classroom, but the need and direction for that creativity should be guided and subsequently evaluated by students' achievements, not the whims of teachers (Heward & Silvestri, in press).

## ABA Places the Responsibility for Student Learning on Teachers and Schools

Although accountability can be viewed as one of ABA's strongest virtues, not all educators are comfortable accepting responsibility for students' achievement. As Gambrill (2003) noted, the public, transparent nature of behavior analysis can be threatening to those who prefer to base decisions on authority-based criteria.

Kohn (2001b) encouraged teachers to resist "the accountability fad," smugly claiming that scores on achievement tests may be the "least significant results of learning." The fact that any given test may not measure important learning outcomes does not mean that "authentic learning" cannot be objectively assessed. Outcomes that are not measurable are not observable. If students are only "taught" unobservable skills, how will we, or they, know if they have learned anything?

As Usher and Edwards (1994) pointed out, in the gobbledygook "world view" of postmodernism that rejects the existence of physical reality other than one's construction of it, the truth is an amorphous, your-version-is-as-good-as-mine concept in which responsibility for student learning is impossible.

> The significant thing is that in postmodernity uncertainty, the lack of a center, and the floating of meaning are understood as phenomena to be celebrated, rather than regretted. In postmodernity, it is complexity, a myriad of meanings, rather than profundity, the one deep meaning, which is the norm. (p. 10)

What about the students who are victims of ineffective instruction? Is their lack of achievement just another of the myriad meanings to be expected? Is their lack of progress an "uncertainty" or "floating of meaning" to be celebrated? Perhaps hiding behind the "abstract, obscurant prose" (Shattuck, 1999, p. 79) that is passed off for humanistic educational reform is easier than taking a stand and being responsible for the difficult and often unglamorous work of providing systematic instruction.

## Implementing Behavioral Approaches Yields Too Little Reinforcement for Teachers

In spite of poorly designed curricula and unsystematic instructional practices, the majority of students learn at reasonable rates and get along with others well enough to be passed from grade to grade without causing too many concerns (Baer & Bushell, 1981). Because pretests are seldom administered to determine what students already know prior to instruction, education takes credit for teaching all of the knowledge and skills students demonstrate at the end of the grading period or school year. For example, Taylor and Frye (1988) found that 78% to 88% of fifth- and sixth-grade average readers could pass pretests on basal comprehension skills before those skills were covered in the basal reader. The average readers were performing at approximately 92% accuracy on the comprehension skills pretests. So, it is possible that a significant portion of what many students know or can do may not have resulted from the instruction to

which they were exposed. Nevertheless, the students' achievement may function as "reinforcement" for the use of poorly designed curricula and unsystematic teaching methods. And if most students are doing "just well enough," teachers are insufficiently motivated to use more vigorous instructional methods on a consistent basis.

To produce optimal results, behavioral strategies must be implemented on a consistent basis. The fact that behavioral teaching methods require diligent, hard work does not, in itself, keep teachers from applying them.[7] But if a new technique that requires diligent application does not produce immediate and strong results, teachers may not continue to use it. One problem with behavioral strategies is that they often produce delayed outcomes that must accumulate over time for maximum effects.

The naturally occurring contingencies in the classroom pose another obstacle to the use of behavioral techniques by working against teachers' systematic use of contingent praise and positive attention. Natural contingencies tend to select the use of reprimands and other negative means of managing student behavior.

> Teachers are more likely to notice and pay attention to a disruptive student than a student who is working quietly and productively. . . . Disruptive behavior is aversive and usually evokes teachers to respond immediately so disruptive behaviors will cease. Paying attention to students when they are behaving inappropriately (e.g., "Carlos, you need to sit down right now!") may be negatively

---

[7]Teachers work very hard every day, perhaps too hard in some ways. One way that many teachers work too hard and inefficiently is trying to score and give feedback on students' papers. Self-scoring by students, on the other hand, would give students contact with the correct answer and provide more immediate feedback and active engagement with the instructional content. Self-scoring also frees up teacher time that can be used for other instructional tasks such as lesson planning, grading student products they may not be able to self-evaluate, and working with individual students.

reinforced by the immediate cessation of the inappropriate behavior (e.g., Carlos stops running around and returns to his seat), thereby increasing the future likelihood of the teacher paying attention to student disruptions.

The effects of reprimanding a child who misbehaves are immediate—the negative reinforcement we receive in the form of cessation of the annoying behavior effectively and naturally teaches us to punish one another. But the effects of verbal praise are usually delayed, making it difficult for us to learn how to use praise. These naturally occurring contingencies are so pervasive that Foxx (1992) has suggested that praising one another be considered "an unnatural act" for humans. The natural contingencies of the typical classroom undermine frequent teacher praise and strengthen reprimanding behavior. Few teachers have to be taught to reprove student misbehavior, but many need help increasing their frequency of praising student behaviors. (Alber & Heward, 2000, p. 178)

## Behavioral Educators Have Insufficient Understanding and Control of the Contingencies That Govern the Adoption and Maintenance of Effective Practices

Although applied behavior analysts have a reasonably good understanding of the principles for designing effective educational interventions, they understand less well the systemic metacontingencies that control the adoption and sustained implementation of behavioral methods, especially at the level of school- and districtwide applications. For applied behavior analysis to make its optimal contribution to education, much more attention and resources will have to be devoted to research on the adoption and retention of effective practices. More than 20 years ago, Baer and Bushell (1981) called this the "next problem."

Behavior analysis has done enough research and been applied enough in the schools to see that the problem is not to learn more about how to conduct schools. Assuredly, a great deal more can be learned, but enough has been learned already to transform a great deal of education practice with great assurance of desirable outcomes. If that is not happening, then research should be shifted to a different behavioral arena: the one in which the findings of social science are implemented by a society. That, too, is a behavioral problem, and a behavioral science should have some head start on analyzing it. Doing so is the next problem. (p. 268)

For more in-depth discussions of this important topic from a variety of behavioral perspectives, see Baer, 1987, 1992; Carnine, 2000; Greenwood and colleagues (1992); Johnston (2000); Kohler and Strain (1992), and Malott (2005).

## ABA Has Yet to Prove Its Value to the Students about Whom Society Cares Most

The majority of ABA's clearly demonstrated accomplishments have been with students who live in poverty, students with developmental disabilities, and students who display emotional and behavioral problems. The 40-plus-year collaboration between ABA researchers and individuals with disabilities has yielded many important benefits. First and foremost has been the direct benefit to the participants themselves. Students whose learning is dependent on effective instruction are in most need of the help that ABA can provide. Second, students with limited repertoires, challenging behavior, and a penchant for displaying only the forms of behavior within the stimulus conditions taught in a lesson are experts at revealing flaws in lesson design and delivery. Learners with disabilities have taught us most of what we know about effective instructional design, and they deserve our recognition and thanks for doing so.

Although the outcomes with these learners have been impressive, those outcomes have not had sufficient meaning for society as a whole. Moreover, ABA's heavy involvement with such learners may be responsible in part for the perception of some educators that behavioral approaches are only relevant and appropriate for students with developmental disabilities or behavior problems. There is an inverse correlation between students' ability to learn in the absence of carefully planned, systematic instruction and the likelihood of their participation in an ABA research study. There are literally hundreds of published studies of students with severe and profound developmental disabilities, a still large but smaller number of studies of students with mild disabilities and learning problems, relatively few studies of students in regular education classrooms, and nearly a complete absence of behavioral analysis work with gifted and talented students (e.g., the term *gifted and talented* does not appear in the subject index of the *Journal of Applied Behavior Analysis* through the year 2003). Although ABA has proven to be the best hope for students with disabilities and for poor, disenfranchised, and untaught students, it has yet to prove itself on a large scale with "regular" students. This could be one of the biggest reasons for ABA's relatively small role in education.

## Improving Education Is Not an Urgent Mission for Society

Education may need ABA, but it does not yet want it, and until we are desperate, want usually wins out over need. Lindsley (1992) likened ABA's inability to make it big in education to the story of a roofing company that went out of business in a community in which all the roofs were in disrepair. Home owners said they could not afford roof repairs, yet a new TV satellite dish sat in the front yard of each home. While ABA is offering to clean up wet basements, improve the structural soundness of homes, and repair roofs, the customers want new entertainment centers.

Well over two decades have passed since Baer and Bushell (1981) suggested that significant improvements in educational reform are

unlikely unless and until doing so becomes an "urgent social mission." Until society insists that public education do better than "just well enough," there will continue to be "more talk, argument, proposal, and politics than research-based development" (p. 262). If and when society becomes truly desperate and makes improving education an "urgent mission," the need to know will outweigh the need to believe (Heward & Cooper, 1992), and ABA's good stuff will be wanted as well as needed.

## RECONCILING THE OPPOSING REASONS

ABA can help improve the effectiveness of education. As a partner in education and a contributor to its improvement, ABA has a lot to recommend it. ABA is meaningful, effective, focused, accountable, and replicable. ABA is not the only valid and worthwhile way of understanding teaching and learning. ABA does, however, have a proven track record of producing interventions with robust effects, and education is poorer without the contributions of ABA. Unfortunately, many educators perceive ABA as a largely irrelevant approach based on a mechanistic world view and an overly simplistic theory. Although some educators recognize ABA as a source of techniques for managing behavior problems, the consensus in education is that ABA has limited application to curriculum and instruction.

Education is one of the most distressing examples of the disconnect between the great potential of behavior analysis for doing good in the world and its application in society—a discrepancy that has caused many behaviorists to lament:

> Why aren't *they* (government and community leaders, educators, business people, etc.) using our good stuff more often? Can't *they* see that it will help them to _____ (the choices seem nearly endless: make our streets safer, teach every

child to read and play cooperatively, provide more jobs and increase productivity, etc.)? (Heward & Malott, 1995, p. 69)

This chapter is an effort to help behavior analysts see why many educators do not consider ABA a particularly useful approach. If the reasons stated herein for ABA's value to—and lack of adoption by—education are on the mark, many of ABA's strengths are also its weaknesses: ABA's predisposition for explicit instruction of carefully defined skills is considered out-of-context teaching; ABA's emphasis on direct and frequent measures of student performance is thought to obscure authentic learning, if not prevent it altogether; ABA's requirements of procedural fidelity and repetition are regarded as threats to teachers' independence and creativity; ABA's use of reinforcement is thought to have detrimental effects on students, and so on. ABA's fundamental assumptions about learning, the principles from which its strategies are derived, the teaching techniques it recommends, and its approach to evaluating outcomes resemble a fistful of square pegs that do not fit into the round holes of education.

How can the differences between what ABA has to offer and what education wants be reconciled? The short answer is, I don't know. A full discussion of this important question is beyond the scope of this paper. However, ABA has taught us that accurate, functional assessment of a problem greatly increases the likelihood of designing effective solutions. Although I have suggested that some of the reasons working against the adoption of behavioral practices in education are practically misguided, logically faulty, and/or unsupported by scientific data, those reasons exist nonetheless. With apologies to the postmodernists, the impediments to better educational practice cannot be "deconstructed" away.

Virtually all of the behavioral analysts in education whose work I have read are pragmatic realists. They are fully aware that the impediments to the adoption of effective instructional prac-

tices are significant. They also understand that some of those impediments are due to shortcomings in ABA's knowledge and accomplishments. Numerous behavior analysts have brought the conceptual and empirical tools of their science to bear on the complex problem of educational reform, and their thoughtful analyses have provided the basis for much of this chapter. Anyone interested in how the knowledge-to-practice gap in education might be reduced should consider the pragmatic and social implications of implementing the various solutions found in this body of literature.

Other ways in which those who want to help ABA play a more influential role in education include contributing to research on the adoption of effective instructional practices, spreading the good story of ABA, remaining optimistic, and attempting to reinforce all efforts by teachers and schools to implement evidence-based educational practices.

## Develop a Technology of Adoption

At the present time, there are no easy-to-copy, complete behavior analytic solutions to the problems of education. Too often the solutions ABA offers education are what Baer (1992) called "one-legged stools"—partial remedies to what must be a four-legged program of reforming American education (p. 78). Until ABA can offer education more than one- or two-legged stools for its complex problems, the discipline will likely remain a minor player in educational reform. ABA's limited knowledge about and nearly nonexistent technology for ensuring the adoption and sustained maintenance of effective instructional practices in schools are almost certain to be one of the missing legs on the school reform stool.

Although ABA has produced a scattered research literature on factors that influence the adoption and sustained use of instructional practices by teachers and schools, such studies represent a very small fraction of behavioral

research in education. Most behavior analytic research in education consists of discovery-
oriented studies designed to demonstrate the
effectiveness of various curricular and instructional arrangements. Perhaps this is because
researchers believe that discovery-oriented research is more glamorous or is held in higher
regard by university promotion and tenure com-
mittees. I have heard some academicians state
that, before an investigator can conduct meaningful research on the dissemination and adoption of a science-based educational strategy, he
or she must first be heavily involved in fundamental research designed to discover and analyze the functional variables and principles of
the strategy. I disagree.

Limiting research on dissemination and adoption to the small circle of investigators involved
in the original discovery process is an inefficient
and unnecessarily slow way to turn scientific
discovery into technological applications. Consider Henry Ford and the automobile. Ford did
not invent the internal combustion engine, nor
did he design and build the first reliable automobile.[8] His contributions were in the areas of
mass production (the assembly line) and marketing the automobile that made it affordable,
accessible, and desirable to the public (a Model
T in everyone's favorite color, black). If you
don't think that research on making an already
"proven" instructional practice accessible to and
used by classroom teachers is as valued or recognized as the research that discovered, developed, and fine-tuned the practice, consider this:
Everyone knows who Henry Ford was, but very
few of us can name the person who invented
the internal combustion engine that made the
car possible.

Developing an effective technology of adoption will require the combined and sustained efforts of many behavioral researchers and school
practitioners working together. It will require
not just more and better applied research, but
also more and better applied practice (Johnston,
1996, 2000; Moore & Cooper, 2003). A positive
sign for the future of education would be a sizable number of young behavior analysts dedi-
cating their research careers to studying the
adoption and sustained use of evidence-based
strategies. ABA in education could surely use a
Henry Ford or two.

## Keep Telling Our Story

As Foxx (1996) states, every behavior analyst
has been entrusted with a covenant to do everything possible to ensure the survival and success
of the science. Behavior analysis must be promoted, not because it is "the right way," but
because doing so offers society a scientific approach to human affairs—in this instance, to
one of society's most important responsibilities:
education—that is "unrivaled in its effectiveness" (p. 147).

Although the effective discussion and advancement of any science requires a technical
language consisting of terms with precise and
limited meanings, the scientific language of behavior analysis limits its attractiveness and accessibility to many educators and the public in
general (e.g., Axelrod, 1992; Bailey, 1991; Foxx,
1996; Lindsley, 1992; Neuringer, 1991). As Baer
(2005) noted, using the connotational vocabulary of the everyday vernacular to describe principles and practices that are best explained (and
properly delimited) by the denotational language of science is tricky business. But doing so
is essential for ABA to achieve a meaningful degree of acceptance and use by society.

Insisting on technical language regardless of
our audience increases the likelihood that potential converts, supporters, and allies will be
put off, turned off, and punished for their attempts to communicate and participate. Behavior

---

[8]Reliability (like validity and everything else in the
cosmos) is a relative concept. The early cars worked
often enough and safely enough to meet the travel
contingencies of their time.

analysis must describe what it has to offer education in the language of the larger culture as that language is reflected in educational practice. Instead of avoiding words like *critical thinking* and *self-regulated learner,* behavior analysts should help teachers identify and apply alterable variables that will make their goals for students a reality (Fowler, 1994; Schwartz, 2005).

Behavior analysts have been translating their work for audiences without technical background for more than 30 years, and we must continue to do so. Early examples of "translating the covenant" for parents include *Parents Are Teachers* (Becker, 1971), *Toilet Training in Less Than a Day* (Azrin & Foxx, 1974), and *Sign Here: A Contracting Book for Children and Their Families* (Dardig & Heward, 1976). Just a few of the many excellent recent examples of effectively disseminating behavior analysis to teachers include *Teach Your Children Well* (Maloney, 1998), *Don't Shoot the Dog! The New Art of Teaching and Training* (Prior, 1999), *Preventing School Failure: Tactics for Teaching* (Lovitt, 2000), *How to Improve Classroom Behavior* series (e.g., Heron, Hippler, & Tincani, 2002; Milchick, 2002; Peterson, Peterson, & Lacy, 2003), and the *Tough Kid* books and materials (Rhode, Jenson, & Morgan, 2003; Rhode, Jensen, & Reavis, 1998).

## Maintain a Realistic Optimism

Given that most of the fundamental strategies of ABA have been "visible and available to education" for decades (Baer & Bushell, 1981, p. 260), the size and protracted nature of the knowledge-to-practice gap is especially frustrating. However, before we behavior analysts blame education for its slowness in adopting our great discoveries, or blame our own ineptness at disseminating the technological innovations made possible by those discoveries, we should recognize that long lags between scientific discoveries and their widespread application by society are the rule, not the exception. Although I am not suggesting that patience is a virtue in this case and that time is of no concern, those out to reform education with behavior analysis should realize that education is not alone in its slowness to put important research findings into practice.[9]

There are reasons to remain optimistic. One such reason is the continued progress within ABA to design curriculum and instructional practices with ever-increasing effectiveness (e.g., see numerous chapters in this volume and other recent titles shown in Figure 19-2). The growing number of behavioral educators and school programs provides another reason for optimism. Although behavior analysts make up only a tiny percentage of professionals in education, there are more behaviorally oriented teachers and teacher education programs today than ever before (e.g., Alber & Nelson, 2005; Maheady, Harper, & Mallette, 2005; Webber, 2005), and there are more schools employing thoroughgoing

---

[9]Rogers (1995) described numerous cases of very long lags between scientific discoveries and their adoption by society. In 1601 an English sea captain, James Lancaster, conducted an experiment that showed the effectiveness of lemon juice in preventing scurvy. The problem of scurvy was severe and widespread at the time, and one might have expected the British navy to follow up on this important discovery. Nearly 150 years later. it did. In 1747 James Lind, a British navy physician who knew of Lancaster's results, carried out another citrus fruit and scurvy experiment with the crew of the HWS *Salisbury.* Lind found that scurvy patients who ate citrus fruit were cured in a few days. In spite of this clear evidence, it was another 48 years before the British navy, in 1795, required that no ship could leave port for a long voyage without lemons on board. Although scurvy on navy ships was immediately wiped out, it took 70 more years before the British Board of Trade adopted a similar policy in 1865 and eradicated scurvy in the merchant marine. Let's hope that the needless intellectual scurvy caused by the neglect of effective instructional practices can be eradicated in less time than it took the British government to put fruit on its sailing ships.

behavioral systems that can serve as models for administrators and program developers (e.g., Johnson & Layng, 1994; McDonough et al., 2005). Additional hope that ABA may have an increased role in education is found in federal legislation such as the No Child Left Behind act and the Reading First grants, which emphasize explicit instruction and data-based accountability.

## Keep Nibbling

The best advice I have heard about how each of us might help close the knowledge-to-practice gap in education comes from Fred Keller, who recently described himself as the "oldest living behaviorist in the world" (Keller, 1992, p. 1). He delivered the advice while talking with a group of graduate students in one of my seminars at Ohio State. One of the students asked Professor Keller how behavioral educators could best promote and advocate for effective instruction in the schools. He replied:

> I guess the best advice I ever heard was offered by a friend of mine, Burrhus Skinner . . . someone asked him what we can do to promote better education. Skinner was silent for a moment, then he said, "Well, I guess we just keep nibbling." I take that to mean to keep on working in a small way, keep on promoting good things. When you see something good taking place, reinforce it if you can. When you see something going in the right direction, praise it. Anytime you see a model school that looks as if it's applying good behavioral principles, give it your support. Every time you hear of somebody doing something good, drop him or her a line and say, "Thank you very much for what you're doing." I believe the process is something like shaping. Don't expect many big changes to take place. There's not going to be a revolution. But maybe, if we all keep on nibbling, we can change education. I don't know of any other way. (F. S. Keller, as cited in Heward & Dunne, 1993, p. 343)

As they have so many times in the past, Keller and Skinner offer us wise counsel. When we see a teacher or school doing something good, we should try to reinforce it. We should not make the mistake of thinking that a teacher's or school's effort must meet the technical rigor and conceptual purity expected of a study published in the *Journal of Applied Behavior Analysis* before we recognize it as "behavioral" and worthy of our support and attention. Doing so will cause us to miss many opportunities to make inroads, friends, and partnerships. Such an approach could easily put behavior analysis in a can't-see-the-forest-for-the-trees situation in which we do not recognize effective applications of behavioral strategies because we are looking for them by formal characteristics instead of by their function. An example is failing to recognize an effective application of programming generalization because the procedure is described as a "cognitive learning strategies" approach. Such a mistake is akin to a fundamental error that Skinner (1953) warned us about half a century ago: defining an operant by its topography instead of its function.

The primary goal of behavior analysts working in education should not be getting education to do more and better ABA; our goal should be helping education do better. Although increasing the number of educators who value ABA would be good, our focus needs to be on improving education. We must remember that it is the product (student achievement and learning), not the process (and certainly not what that process is called) that is most important.

Because ABA is ultimately all about the analysis of function, ABA is ideally suited to help discover and refine educational practices that will produce improved learning. This is the essence of applied behavior analysis and the most important reason it is good for education.

## REFERENCES

Abt Associates, Inc. (1973). *Education as experimentation: Evaluation of a planned variation model.* Report No. AAI-74-13. Cambridge, MA.

Abt Associates, Inc. (1977). *Education as experimentation: A planned variation model* (Vol. IV). Cambridge, MA.

Alber, S. R., & Heward, W. L. (1996). "GOTCHA!" Twenty-five behavior traps guaranteed to extend your students' academic and social skills. *Intervention in School and Clinic, 31,* 285–289.

Alber, S. R., & Heward, W. L. (2000). Teaching students to recruit positive attention: A review and recommendations. *Journal of Behavioral Education, 10,* 177–204.

Alber, S. R., & Nelson, J. S. (2005). Collaborating with pre-service and mentor teachers to design and implement classroom research. In W. L. Heward, T. E. Heron, N. A. Neef, S. M. Peterson, D. M. Sainato, G. Cartledge, R. Gardner III, L. D. Peterson, S. B. Hersh, & J. C. Dardig (Eds.), *Focus on behavior analysis in education: Achievements, challenges, and opportunities* (pp. 173–187). Upper Saddle River, NJ: Prentice Hall/Merrill.

Axelrod, S. (1991). The problem: American education. The solution: Use behavior analytic technology. *Journal of Behavioral Education, 1,* 275–282.

Axelrod, S. (1992). Disseminating effective educational technology. *Journal of Applied Behavior Analysis, 25,* 31–35.

Ayllon, T., & Michael, J. (1959). The psychiatric nurse as a behavioral engineer. *Journal of the Experimental Analysis of Behavior, 2,* 323–334.

Azrin, N. H., & Foxx, R. M. (1974). *Toilet training in less than a day.* New York: Simon & Shuster.

Baer, D. M. (1960). Escape and avoidance response of preschool children to two schedules of reinforcement withdrawal. *Journal of the Experimental Analysis of Behavior, 3,* 155–159.

Baer, D. M. (1962). Laboratory control of thumbsucking by withdrawal and representation of reinforcement. *Journal of the Experimental Analysis of Behavior, 5,* 525–528.

Baer, D. M. (1987). Weak contingencies, strong contingencies, and many behaviors to change. *Journal of Applied Behavior Analysis, 20,* 335–337.

Baer, D. M. (1992). The reform of education is at least a four-legged program. *Journal of Applied Behavior Analysis, 25,* 77–79.

Baer, D. M. (1993). To disagree with Meyer and Evans is to debate a cost-benefit ratio. *Journal of the Association for Persons with Severe Handicaps, 18,* 235–236.

Baer, D. M. (2005). Letters to a lawyer. In W. L. Heward, T. E. Heron, N. A. Neef, S. M. Peterson, D. M. Sainato, G. Cartledge, R. Gardner III, L. D. Peterson, S. B. Hersh, & J. C. Dardig (Eds.), *Focus on behavior analysis in education: Achievements, challenges, and opportunities.* Upper Saddle River, NJ: Prentice Hall/Merrill.

Baer, D. M., & Bushell, D., Jr. (1981). The future of behavior analysis in the schools? Consider its recent past, and then ask a different question. *School Psychology Review, 10* (2), 259–270.

Baer, D. M., Wolf, M. M., & Risley, T. R. (1968). Some current dimensions of applied behavior analysis. *Journal of Applied Behavior Analysis, 1,* 91–97.

Baer, D. M., Wolf, M. M., & Risley, T. R. (1987). Some still-current dimensions of applied behavior analysis. *Journal of Applied Behavior Analysis, 20,* 313–327.

Bailey, J. S. (1991). Marketing behavior analysis required different talk. *Journal of Applied Behavior Analysis, 24,* 445–448.

Bannerman, D. J., Sheldon, J. B., Sherman, J. A., & Harchik, A. E. (1990). Balancing the right to habilitation with the right to personal liberties: The rights of people with developmental disabilities to eat too many doughnuts and take a nap. *Journal of Applied Behavior Analysis, 23,* 79–89.

Becker, W. C. (1971). *Parents are teachers.* Champaign, IL: Research Press.

Becker, W. C. (1992). Direct instruction: A twenty-year review. In R. P. West & L. A. Hamerlynck (Eds.), *Designs for excellence in education: The legacy of B. F. Skinner* (pp. 71–112). Longmont, CO: Sopris West.

Becker, W. C., Englemann, S., & Thomas, D. R. (1975). *Teaching 2: Cognitive learning and instruction.* Chicago: Science Research Associates.

Bijou, S. W. (1957). Patterns of reinforcement and resistance to extinction in young children. *Child Development, 28,* 47–54.

Bijou, S. W. (1958). Operant extinction after fixed-interval schedules with young children. *Journal of the Experimental Analysis of Behavior, 1,* 25–29.

Bijou, S. W., Birnbrauer, J. S., Kidder, J. D., & Tague, C. (1966). Programmed instruction as an approach to teaching of reading, writing, and arithmetic to retarded children. *The Psychological Record, 16,* 505–522.

Binder, C. (1994). Measurably superior instructional methods: Do we need sales and marketing? In R. Gardner, D. Sainato, J. O. Cooper, T. E. Heron, W. L. Heward, J. Eshleman, & T. A. Grossi (Eds.), *Behavior analysis in education: Focus on measur-*

*ably superior instruction* (pp. 21–31). Monterey, CA: Brooks-Cole.

Birnbrauer, J. S., Wolf, M. M., Kidder, J. D., & Tague, C. (1965). Classroom behavior of retarded pupils with token reinforcement. *Journal of Experimental Child Psychology, 2,* 219–235.

Bloom, B. S. (1980). The new direction in educational research: Alterable variables. *Phi Delta Kappan, 61,* 382–385.

Bock, G., Stebbins, L., & Proper, E. C. (1996). Excerpts from the Abt reports: Descriptions of the models and the results. *Effective School Practices, 15* (1), 10–16.

Brantlinger, E. (1997). Using ideology: Cases of non-recognition of the politics of research and practice in special education. *Review of Educational Research, 67,* 425–459.

Bushell, D., Jr., & Baer, D. M. (1994). Measurably superior instruction means close, continual contact with the relevant outcome data: Revolutionary! In R. Gardner III, D. M. Sainato, J. O. Cooper, T. E. Heron, W. L. Heward, J. Eshleman, & T. A. Grossi (Eds.), *Behavior analysis in education: Focus on measurably superior instruction* (pp. 3–10). Monterey, CA: Brooks/Cole.

Cameron, J. (2005). The detrimental effects of reward hypothesis: Persistence of a view in the face of disconfirming evidence. In W. L. Heward, T. E. Heron, N. A. Neef, S. M. Peterson, D. M. Sainato, G. Cartledge, R. Gardner III, L. D., Peterson, S. B. Hersh, & J. C. Dardig (Eds.), *Focus on behavior analysis in education: Achievements, challenges, and opportunities* (pp. 304–315). Upper Saddle River, NJ: Prentice Hall/Merrill.

Campbell, D. T., & Stanley, J. C. (1966). *Experimental and quasi-experimental designs for research.* Chicago: Rand-McNally.

Carnine, D. (1992). Expanding the notion of teachers' rights: Access to tools that work. *Journal of Applied Behavior Analysis, 25,* 13–19.

Carnine, D. (1997). Bridging the research to practice gap. *Exceptional Children, 63,* 513–521.

Carnine, D. (2000). *Why education experts resist effective practices: Report of the Thomas B. Fordham Foundation.* Washington, DC: Thomas B. Fordham Foundation.

Coles, G. (1998, December 2). No end to the reading wars. *Education Week, 18* (14), 52, 38.

Cooke, N. L., Heward, W. L., Test, D. W., Spooner, F., & Courson, F. H. (1991). Student performance data in the special education classroom: Measurement and evaluation of student progress. *Teacher Education and Special Education, 13,* 155–161.

Creswell, J. W., & Miller, D. L. (2000). Determining validity in qualitative inquiry. *Theory Into Practice, 39* (3), 124–130.

Cziko, G. A. (1989). Unpredictability and indeterminism in human behavior: Arguments and implications for educational research. *Educational Researcher, 18* (3), 17–25.

Danforth, S., (1997). On what basis hope? Modern progress and postmodern possibilities. *Mental Retardation, 35,* 93–106.

Dardig, J. C., & Heward, W. L. (1976). *Sign here: A contracting book for children and their families.* Kalamazoo, MI: Behaviordelia.

Darling-Hammond, L. (1985). Valuing teachers: The making of a profession. *Teachers College Record, 87,* 210.

Dietz, S. (1994). The insignificant impact of behavior analysis in education: Notes from a Dean of education. In R. Gardner, D. Sainato, J. O. Cooper, T. E. Heron, W. L. Heward, J. Eshleman, & T. A. Grossi (Eds.), *Behavior analysis in education and public policy: Focus on measurably superior instruction* (pp. 33–41). Monterey, CA: Brooks-Cole.

Dixon, R. C. (1991). The application of sameness analysis to spelling. *Journal of Learning Disabilities, 24* (5), 285–291, 310.

Dixon, R. C., & Carnine, D. W. (1992). A response to Heshusius' "Curriculum-based assessment and direct instruction: Critical reflections on fundamental assumptions." *Exceptional Children, 58,* 461–463.

Elkind, D. (1998). Behavioral disorders: A perspective. *Behavioral Disorders, 23,* 153–159.

Fowler, S. A. (1994). Behavior analysis in education: A necessary intersection. In R. Gardner, D. Sainato, J. O. Cooper, T. E. Heron, W. L. Heward, J. Eshleman, & T. A. Grossi (Eds.), *Behavior analysis in education and public policy: Focus on measurably superior instruction* (pp. 367–372). Monterey, CA: Brooks–Cole.

Foxx, R. M. (1992, November). Comments during teleconference seminar: Contemporary issues in special education. Columbus, OH: The Ohio State University.

Foxx, R. M. (1996). Translating the covenant: The behavior analyst as ambassador and translator. *The Behavior Analyst, 19,* 147–161.

Friedman, M. I., & Fisher, S. P. (1998). *Handbook in effective instructional strategies: Evidence for decision-making*. Columbia, SC: Institute for Evidence-Based Decision-Making in Education.

Gallagher, D. J. (1998). The scientific knowledge base of special education: Do we know what we think we know? *Exceptional Children, 64,* 493–502.

Gallagher, D. J. (2004). Entering the conversation: The debate behind the debates in special education. In D. J. Gallagher, L. Heshusius, R. P. Iano, & T. M. Skrtic (Eds.), *Challenging orthodoxy in special education: Dissenting voices* (pp. 3–26). Denver, CO: Love.

Gallagher, D. J., Heshusius, L., Iano, R. P., & Skrtic, T. M. (2004). *Challenging orthodoxy in special education: Dissenting voices*. Denver, CO: Love.

Gambrill, E. (2003). Science and its use and neglect in the human services. In K. S. Budd & T. Stokes (Eds.), *A small matter of proof: The legacy of Donald M. Baer* (pp. 63–76). Reno, NV: Context Press.

Gardner, H. (1993). *Multiple intelligences: The theory in practice*. New York: Basic Books.

Gersten, R. (1992). Passion and precision: Response to curriculum-based assessment and direct instruction: Critical reflections on fundamental assumptions. *Exceptional Children, 58,* 464–467.

Gersten, R. (2001). Sorting out the roles of research in the improvement of practice. *Learning Disabilities Research and Practice, 16,* 45–50.

Greenwood, C. R., & Maheady, L. (1997). Measurable change in student performance: Forgotten standard in teacher preparation? *Teacher Education and Special Education, 20,* 265–275.

Greenwood, C. R., Carta, J. J., Hart, B., Kamps, D., Terry, D., Delquadri, J. C., Walker, D., & Risley, T. (1992). Out of the laboratory and into the community: Twenty-six years of applied behavior analysis at the Juniper Gardens Children's Center. *American Psychologist, 47,* 1464–1474.

Greer, R. D. (1983). Contingencies of the science and technology of teaching and pre-behavioristic research practices in education. *Educational Researcher, 12,* 3–14.

Greer, R. D. (1991). L'enfant terrible meets the educational crisis. *Journal of Applied Behavior Analysis, 25,* 65–69.

Grossen, B. (1998). What is wrong with American education? In W. M. Evers (Ed.), *What's gone wrong in America's classrooms?* (pp. 23–47). Stanford, CA: Hoover Institution Press.

Hall, R. V., Lund, D., & Jackson, D. (1968). Effects of teacher attention on study behavior. *Journal of Applied Behavior Analysis, 1,* 1–12.

Hall, R. V. (1991). Behavior analysis in education: An unfulfilled dream. *Journal of Behavioral Education, 1,* 305–316.

Heron, T. E., & Kimball, W. H. (1988). A behavioral commentary on Poplin's discussion of the reductionistic fallacy and holistic/constructivist principles. *Journal of Learning Disabilities, 21,* 425–428.

Heron, T. E., Hippler, B. J., & Tincani, M. J. (2002). *How to help students complete classwork and homework assignments*. Austin, TX: PRO-ED.

Heshusius, L. (1982). At the heart of the advocacy dilemma: A mechanistic worldview. *Exceptional Children, 49,* 6–11.

Heshusius, L. (1986). Paradigm shifts and special education: A response to Ulman and Rosenberg. *Exceptional Children, 52,* 461–465.

Heshusius, L. (2004). From creative discontent toward epistemological freedom in special education: Reflections on a 25-year journey. In D. J. Gallagher, L. Heshusius, R. P. Iano, & T. M. Skrtic (Eds.), *Challenging orthodoxy in special education: Dissenting voices* (pp. 169–230). Denver, CO: Love.

Heward, W. L. (2003). Ten faulty notions about teaching and learning that hinder the effectiveness of special education. *The Journal of Special Education, 36* (4), 186–205.

Heward, W. L., & Cooper, J. O. (1992). Radical behaviorism: A productive and needed philosophy for education. *Journal of Behavioral Education, 2,* 345–365.

Heward, W. L., & Dunne, J. D. (1993). A teleconference with Professor Fred S. Keller. *The Behavior Analyst, 16,* 341–345.

Heward, W. L., & Malott, R. W. (1995). How the happy few might become the competent many. *The Behavior Analyst, 18,* 69–71.

Heward, W. L., & Silvestri, S. M. (in press). The neutralization of special education. In J. W. Jacobson, J. A. Mulick, & R. M. Foxx (Eds.), *Fads: Dubious and improbable treatments for developmental disabilities*. Hillsdale, NJ: Erlbaum.

Iano, R. P. (2004). The tale of a reluctant empiricist. In D. J. Gallagher, L. Heshusius, R. P. Iano, & T. M. Skrtic (Eds.), *Challenging orthodoxy in special education: Dissenting voices* (pp. 231–249). Denver, CO: Love.

Jacobson, J. W., Mulick, J. A., & Foxx, R. M. (Eds.). (in press). *Fads: Dubious and improbable treatments for developmental disabilities*. Hillsdale, NJ: Erlbaum.

Johnson, K. R., & Layng, T. V. J. (1994). The Morningside Model of generative instruction. In R. Gardner III, D. M. Sainato, J. O. Cooper, T. E. Heron, W. L. Heward, J. Eshleman, & T. A. Grossi (Eds.), *Behavior analysis in education: Focus on measurably superior instruction* (pp. 173–197). Monterey, CA: Brooks/Cole.

Johnston, J. M. (1996). Behavior analysis and the R&D paradigm. *The Behavior Analyst, 23,* 141–148.

Johnston, J. M. (2000). Distinguishing between applied research and applied practice. *The Behavior Analyst, 19,* 35–48.

Johnston, J. M., & Pennypacker, H. S. (1986). Pure versus quasi-behavioral research. In A. Poling & R. W. Fuqua (Eds.), *Research methods in applied behavior analysis* (pp. 29–54). New York: Plenum Press.

Kauffman, J. M. (2002). *Education deform: Bright people sometimes say stupid things about education*. Lanham, MD: The Scarecrow Press.

Keller, F. S. (1992, October). *Friends and foes of educational reform*. Paper presented at the First International Conference of Behaviorism and the Sciences of Behavior, Guadalajara, Mexico.

Keller, F. S. (1992, December 3). Comments during teleconference seminar: Contemporary issues in special education. Columbus, OH: The Ohio State University.

Keller, F. S., & Schoenfeld, W. N. (1950). *Principles of psychology: A systematic text in the science of behavior*. New York: Appleton-Century-Crofts.

Kimball, J. W. (2002). Behavior-analytic instruction for children with autism: Philosophy matters. *Focus on Autism and Other Developmental Disabilities, 17* (2), 66–75.

Kohler, F. W., & Strain, P. S. (1992). Applied behavior analysis and the movement to restructure schools: Compatibilities and opportunities for collaboration. *Journal of Behavioral Education, 2,* 367–390.

Kohn, A. (1993). *Punished by rewards*. Boston: Houghton Mifflin.

Kohn, A. (1999). *The schools our children deserve: Moving beyond traditional classrooms and "tougher standards."* Boston: Houghton Mifflin.

Kohn, A. (2001a). Five reasons to stop saying "Good job!" *Young Children, 56* (5), 24–28.

Kohn, A. (2001b, September 26). Beware of the standards, not just the tests. *Education Week*. Retrieved December 9, 2002, from http://www.alfiekohn.org/teaching/edweek/botsnjtt.htm.

Kratochwill, T. R., & Stoiber, K. C. (2000). Empirically supported interventions and school psychology. *School Psychology Quarterly, 15,* 233–253.

Landrum, T. J. (1997). The data don't matter. *Journal of Behavioral Education, 7,* 123–129.

Lather, P. (1992). Critical frames in education research: Feminist and post-structural perspectives. *Theory Into Practice, 33,* 86–99.

Lather, P. (1993). Fertile obsession. Validity after poststructuralism. *The Sociological Quarterly, 34,* 673–693.

Lindsley, O. R. (1956). Operant conditioning methods applied to research in chronic schizophrenia. *Psychiatric Research Reports, 5,* 118–139.

Lindsley, O. R. (1992). Why aren't effective teaching tools widely adopted? *Journal of Applied Behavior Analysis, 25,* 21–26.

Lovitt, T. C. (2000). *Preventing school failure: Tactics for teaching* (2nd ed.). Austin, TX: PRO-ED.

Maag, J. W. (2001). Rewarded by punishment: Reflections on the disuse of positive reinforcement in education. *Exceptional Children, 67,* 173–186.

Maheady, L., Harper, G. F., & Mallette, B. (2005). Developing, implementing, and maintaining a responsive educator program for preservice general education teachers. In W. L. Heward, T. E. Heron, N. A. Neef, S. M. Peterson, D. M. Sainato, G. Cartledge, R. Gardner III, L. D. Peterson, S. B. Hersh, & J. C. Dardig (Eds.), *Focus on behavior analysis in education: Achievements, challenges, and opportunities* (pp. 139–153). Upper Saddle River, NJ: Prentice Hall/Merrill.

Maloney, M. (1998). *Teach your children well*. Cambridge, MA: Cambridge Center for Behavioral Studies.

Malott, R. W. (2005). Behavioral systems analysis and higher education. In W. L. Heward, T. E. Heron, N. A. Neef, S. M. Peterson, D. M. Sainato, G. Cartledge, R. Gardner III, L. D. Peterson, S. B. Hersh, & J. C. Dardig (Eds.), *Focus on behavior analysis in education: Achievements, challenges, and opportunities* (pp. 211–236). Upper Saddle River, NJ: Prentice Hall/Merrill.

Markle, S. M. (1962). *Good frames and bad: A grammar of frame writing* (2nd ed.). John Wiley & Sons.

Maurice, C. (1993). *Let me hear your voice: A family's triumph over autism*. New York: Fawcett Columbine.

Maurice, C. (2000). The autism wars. In W. L. Heward (Ed.), *Exceptional children: An introduction to special education* (6th ed., pp. 496–497). Upper Saddle River, NJ: Merrill/Prentice Hall.

McDonough, C. S., Covington, T., Endo, S., Meinberg, D., Spencer, T. D., & Bicard, D. F. (2005). The Hawthorne Country Day School: A behavioral approach to schooling. In W. L. Heward, T. E. Heron, N. A. Neef, S. M. Peterson, D. M. Sainato, G. Cartledge, R. Gardner III, L. D. Peterson, S. B. Hersh, & J. C. Dardig (Eds.), *Focus on behavior analysis in education: Achievements, challenges, and opportunities* (pp. 188–210). Upper Saddle River, NJ: Prentice Hall/Merrill.

Michael, J. (2000). Implications and refinements of the establishing operations concept. *Journal of Applied Behavior Analysis, 33,* 401–410.

Milchick, S. L. (2002). *How to help students follow directions, pay attention, and stay on-task.* Austin, TX: PRO-ED.

Moore, J., & Cooper, J. O. (2003). Some proposed relations among the domains of behavior analysis. *The Behavior Analyst, 26,* 69–84.

Neef, N. A. Iwata, B. A., Horner, R. H., Lerman, D. L., Martens, B. A., & Sainato, D. S. (Eds.) (2004). *Behavior analysis in education* (2nd ed.). Lawrence KS: Society for the Experimental Analysis of Behavior.

Neef, N. A., Nelles, D. E., Iwata, B. A., & Page, T. J. (2003). An analysis of precurrent skills in solving mathematics story problems. *Journal of Applied Behavior Analysis, 36,* 21–34.

Neuringer, A. (1991). Humble behaviorism. *The Behavior Analyst, 14,* 1–13.

Northrup, J. (2000). Further evaluation of the accuracy of reinforcer surveys: A systematic replication. *Journal of Applied Behavior Analysis, 33,* 335–338.

Northrup, J., Vollmer, T. R., & Serrett, K. (1993). Publication trends in 25 years of the *Journal of Applied Behavior Analysis. Journal of Applied Behavior Analysis, 26,* 527–537.

O'Leary, K. D., & O'Leary, S. (1972). *Classroom management: The successful use of behavior modification.* New York: Pergamon.

Olson, L. (1999). Researchers rate whole-school reform models. *Education Week, 28* (23), 1, 14–15.

O'Neill, R., Horner, R., Albin, R., Sprague, J., Newton, J. S., & Storey, K. (1997). *Functional assessment and program development for problem behavior* (2nd ed.). Monterey, CA: Brooks/Cole.

Pennypacker, H. S., & Hench, L. L. (1997). Making behavioral technology transferable. *The Behavior Analyst, 20,* 97–108.

Peterson, S. M., Peterson, L. D., & Lacy, L. (2002). *Dealing with students who challenge and defy authority.* Austin, TX: PRO-ED.

Peterson, S. M., Peterson, L. D., & Lacy, L. N. (2003). *How to deal with students who challenge and defy authority.* Austin, TX: PRO-ED.

Poplin, M. S. (1988a). Holistic/constructivist principles of the teaching/learning process: Implications for the field of learning disabilities. *Journal of Learning Disabilities, 21,* 401–416.

Poplin, M. S. (1988b). The reductionistic fallacy in learning disabilities: Replicating the past by reducing the present. *Journal of Learning Disabilities, 21,* 389–400.

Prior, K. (1999). *Don't shoot the dog! The new art of teaching and training* (rev. ed.). New York: Bantam.

Purnell, S., & Claycomb, C. (2001). *Implementing reform: What Success for All teaches us about including students with disabilities in comprehensive school restructuring.* Alexandria, VA: National Association of State School Boards of Education.

Ramp, E. A., & Hopkins, B. (Eds.). (1971). *A new direction for education: Behavior analysis 1971, Vol. 1.* Lawrence, KS: University of Kansas.

Rhode, G., Jensen, W. R., & Morgan, D. P. (2003). *The tough kid new teacher kit.* Longmont, CO: Sopris West.

Rhode, G., Jensen, W. R., & Reavis, H. K. (1998). *The tough kid book: Practical classroom management strategies.* Longmont, CO: Sopris West.

Rogers, E. M. (1995). *Diffusion of innovations* (4th ed.). New York: Free Press.

Rooney, K. J. (1991). Controversial therapies: A review and critique. *Intervention in School and Clinic, 26,* 134–142.

Sarason, S. B. (1990). *The predictable failure of school reform. Can we change course before it's too late?* San Francisco: Jossey-Bass.

Sarnoff, S. K. (2001). *Sanctified snake oil: The effect of junk science on public policy.* Westport, CT: Praeger.

Shattuck, R. (1999). *Cando and perversion: Literature, education and the arts.* New York: Norton.

Sidman, M. (1994). *Equivalence relations and behavior: A research story.* Boston: Author's Cooperative.

Simpson, R. L. (2001). ABA and students with autism spectrum disorders: Issues and considerations for effective practice. *Focus on Autism and Other Developmental Disabilities, 16,* 68–71.

Skinner, B. F. (1938). *The behavior of organisms: An experimental analysis.* New York: Appleton-Century.

Skinner, B. F. (1984). The shame of American education. *American Psychologist, 39,* 947–954.

Skrtic, T. M., Sailor, W., & Gee, K. (1996). Voice, collaboration, and inclusion: Democratic themes in educational and social reform initiatives. *Remedial and Special Education, 17,* 143–157.

Smith, P. (1999). Drawing new maps: A radical cartography of developmental disabilities. *Review of Educational Research, 69,* 117–144.

Spear-Swerling, L., & Sternberg, R. J. (2001). What science offers teachers of reading. *Learning Disabilities Research and Practice, 16,* 51–57.

Stainback, S., & Stainback, W. (Eds.). (1992). *Curriculum considerations in inclusive classrooms: Facilitating learning for all students.* Baltimore: Brookes.

Stone, J. E. (1994). Developmentalism's impediments to school reform: Three recommendations for overcoming them. In R. Gardner III, D. M. Sainato, J. O. Cooper, T. E. Heron, W. L. Heward, J. Eshleman, & T. A. Grossi (Eds.), *Behavior analysis in education: Focus on measurably superior instruction* (pp. 57–72). Monterey, CA: Brooks/Cole.

Strain, P. S., & Joseph, G. E. (2004). A not so good job with "Good job." *Journal of Positive Behavior Interventions, 6* (1), 55–59.

Strain, P. S., McConnell, S. R., Carta, J. J., Fowler, S. A., Neisworth, J. T., & Wolery, M. (1992). Behaviorism in early intervention. *Topics in Early Childhood Special Education, 12,* 121–142.

Swanson, H. L., & Sachse-Lee, C. (2000). A meta-analysis of single-subject-design intervention research for students with LD. *Journal of Learning Disabilities, 38,* 114–136.

Tarver, S. G. (1998). Myths and truths about Direct Instruction. *Effective School Practices, 17* (1), 18–22.

Taylor, B. M., & Frye, B. J. (1988). Pretesting: Minimize time spent on skill work for intermediate readers. *The Reading Teacher, 42* (2), 100–103.

Tierney, W. G., & Twombly, S. (Guest Eds.). (2000). Getting good qualitative data to improve educational practice. *Theory Into Practice, 39* (3), 122–192.

Twyman, J. S., Layng, T. V. J., Stikeleather, G., & Hobbins, K. A. (2005). A non-linear approach to curriculum design: The role of behavior analysis in building an effective reading program. In W. L. Heward, T. E. Heron, N. A. Neef, S. M. Peterson, D. M. Sainato, G. Cartledge, R. Gardner III, L. D. Peterson, S. B. Hersh, & J. C. Dardig (Eds.), *Focus on behavior analysis in education: Achievements, challenges, and opportunities* (pp. 55–68). Upper Saddle River, NJ: Prentice Hall/Merrill.

Ulrich, R., Stachnik, T., & Mabry, J. (Eds.). (1974). *Control of human behavior* (Vol. 4). Glenview, IL: Scott, Foresman.

Usher, R., & Edwards, R. (1994). *Postmodernism and education: Different voices, different words.* London: Routledge.

Vargas, J. S. (1984). What are your exercises teaching? An analysis of stimulus control in instructional materials. In W. L. Heward, T. E. Heron, D. S. Hill, & J. Trap-Porter (Eds.), *Focus on behavior analysis in education* (pp. 126–141). Columbus, OH: Merrill.

Vaughn, S., & Damann, J. D. (2001). Science and sanity in special education. *Behavioral Disorders, 27,* 21–29.

Watkins, C. L. (1996). Follow through: Why didn't we? *Effective School Practices, 15* (1), 57–66.

Watkins, C. L. (1997). *Project Follow Through: A case study of contingencies influencing instructional practices of the educational establishment.* Cambridge, MA: Cambridge Center for Behavioral Studies.

Webber, J. (2005). Teaching ABA to preservice personnel: A cooperative field-based approach. In W. L. Heward, T. E. Heron, N. A. Neef, S. M. Peterson, D. M. Sainato, G. Cartledge, R. Gardner III, L. D. Peterson, S. B. Hersh, & J. C. Dardig (Eds.), *Focus on behavior analysis in education: Achievements, challenges, and opportunities* (pp. 154–172). Upper Saddle River, NJ: Prentice Hall/Merrill.

Weisberg, P. (1994). Helping preschoolers from low-income backgrounds make substantial progress in reading through Direct Instruction. In R. Gardner III, D. M. Sainato, J. O. Cooper, T. E. Heron, W. L. Heward, J. Eshleman, & T. A. Grossi (Eds.), *Behavior analysis in education: Focus on measurably superior instruction* (pp. 115–129). Monterey, CA: Brooks/Cole.

Winett, R. A., & Winkler, R. C. (1972). Current behavior modification in the classroom: Be still, be quiet, be docile. *Journal of Applied Behavior Analysis, 5,* 499–504.

Wolery, M. (2000). Recommended practices in child-focused interventions. In S. Sandall, M. E. McLean, & B. J. Smith (Eds.), *DEC recommended practices* (pp. 34–38). Longmont, CO: Sopris West.

Wolf, M. M. (1978). Social validity: The case for subjective measurement or how applied behavior analysis is finding its heart. *Journal of Applied Behavior Analysis, 11,* 203–214.

## STUDY QUESTIONS AND FOLLOW-UP ACTIVITIES

1. The author states 12 reasons why ABA is good for education. Rank those reasons in terms of influence and importance.

2. What reasons why ABA is good for education would you add or delete to the author's list? Provide empirical and conceptual support for each reason you add or delete.

3. The author states 14 reasons why ABA is not well accepted in education. Rank those reasons in terms of pervasiveness, influence, and difficulty to counteract.

4. What reasons why ABA is not well accepted in education would you add or delete to the author's list? Provide empirical and conceptual support for each reason you add or delete.

5. For each entry on your revised list of reasons why ABA is not well accepted in education, describe the relative importance of the following factors with respect to strengthening or combating it: political, economic, philosophical, practical, and scientific.

6. Describe how naturally existing contingencies of reinforcement and punishment select against the use of and advocacy for behavioral procedures by classroom teachers. How do naturally existing contingencies select against advocacy and support for behavioral procedures by administrators, school board members, and politicians?

7. Choose one of the reasons stated by the author for why ABA is not well accepted in education and find a journal article or other published source in which that reason is examined. Identify the points made by the author(s) and describe

how you would respond in an effort to make a case for the use of behavioral techniques.

8. Identify a cause or issue that became an "urgent social mission" in the United States (e.g., eradicating polio, landing on the moon) and describe the social, economic, political, or other factors responsible for that cause's achieving "urgent mission" status. Compare and contrast the cause you analyzed with improving education and describe what would have to happen for improving education to become an urgent social mission.

9. Why do you think applied behavior analysis is more widely accepted in special education than in regular education?

10. What can you do to increase ABA's positive impact on education?

11. Ineffective instruction is especially destructive for children who come to school with limited resources. How would the universal use of well designed, systematic curriculum and instruction impact the current and future lives of these children?

12. How would the universal use of well designed, systematic curriculum and instruction impact the current and future lives of children who come to school with well developed language abilities, social skills, and cognitive repertoires?

13. Debate with a classmate the pros and cons of two opposing reasons from the lists presented by the author (e.g., ABA emphasizes explicit instruction on discrete skills vs. teaching discrete skills obviates authentic learning). Summarize the results of your debate in a form useful to classroom teachers, administrators, school board members, and parents.

14. Identify three to five books, articles, or Internet resources that present behavioral strategies to educators very effectively. Summarize the common features of those materials and describe how those features might be applied to presenting another behavioral strategy to teachers.

15. Identify an instructional strategy that has significant research evidence to support its widespread

---

Study questions and follow-up activities prepared by Michele A. Anderson and Corinne M. Murphy.

application in schools but that has limited acceptance and use in schools. Try to identify features
of the strategy that work for and against its adoption by teachers. Outline a research program that
might be pursued to increase educators' adoption and sustained use of the strategy.

16. Describe three to five specific things that you
can do to increase the acceptance and use of evidence-based curriculum and instructional tools
by public schools.

# Name Index

Abbot, M., 173, 174, 175
Abbot, R., 91
Adams, A. T., 253
Adams, G., 191
Adams, M. J., 69, 70, 72, 84
Adelinis, J. D., 127
Ager, C., 127
Ainslie, G. W., 132
Aitken, T. A., 131
Alber, S. R., 320, 335, 339
Albers, A. E., 197
Alberto, P. A., 155, 160, 161, 193, 260, 299
Albin, R. W., 98, 160, 321
Allen, K. E., 240, 241
Anderson, J., 98
Anderson, L. T., 26
Anderson, R. B., 191, 283
Andrews, D. E., 308
Apple, C., 126
Ard, W. R., Jr., 128
Asher, K. N., 91
Atwater, J. B., 103
Avery, D. L., 26
Axelrod, S., 139, 237, 283, 284, 317, 338
Ayllon, T., 129, 316
Azrin, N. H., 129, 192, 253, 339

Bacon, D. L., 227
Baer, D. M., 3, 4, 5, 22, 30, 42, 43, 97, 191, 193, 201, 210, 240, 241, 246, 272, 273, 275, 276, 277, 278, 298, 300, 303, 316, 317, 319, 321, 322, 323, 325, 330, 335, 336, 337, 338, 339
Bagnato, S. J., 104
Bailey, J. S., 192, 283, 284, 317, 338
Bailey, V., 227
Baker, B. L., 201
Bambara, L. M., 127
Bandura, A., 305
Bannerman, D. J., 126, 127, 130, 319
Barbetta, P. M., 193, 275, 276, 277
Barbetti, V., 90
Barkley, R. A., 132
Barnes, W. S., 297
Barrett, B. H., 277
Barrett, S., 96
Barriga, A., 90
Bass, R., 297
Bauman, K. E., 43, 246

Beck, R., 277
Becker, W. C., 191, 192, 316, 320, 321, 339
Beland, L., 91
Bell, L., K., 127
Bereiter, C., 283
Berg, W. K., 125, 129, 131
Berkowitz, L., 253
Berry, B., 283
Berry, D. L., 125
Bettelheim, B., 36
Bicard, D. F., 132, 340
Biglan, A., 91
Bijou, S., 3, 316, 320
Billings, W. H., 253
Billingsley, F., 245
Binder, C., 192, 277, 283, 284, 293, 317
Binder, L. M., 132
Birnbrauer, J. S., 26, 316
Blanko, K. M., 304, 309
Bloom, B. S., 85, 322
Blough, D. S., 62
Blum, I. M., 278
Blumenthal, A., L., 127
Bock, G., 326
Boettcher, W., 221, 226
Boffa, J., 127
Bolstad, O. D., 193
Bondy, A. S., 20, 192, 271
Borden, S. L., 83
Bosch, S., 42, 225
Bowditch, C., 90
Bower, B., 70, 72
Bowman, L. G., 129
Bowman, V., 271
Brandsma, L. L., 283
Brantlinger, E., 329
Braun, D., 69, 76, 85
Bredekamp., S., 105
Brengelman, S., 173
Brennan, L., 40
Brethower, D., 214, 215, 224
Bricker, D., 94, 255, 264
Brigham, T. A., 320
Bristol, M., 6
Brown, D., 96
Brown, F., 126
Brown, K. A., 125, 129, 131
Brown, S. A., 300
Brown, W. H., 241
Brownell, M. T., 173
Brownowski, J., 55, 56

Bruner, E., 192
Bryant, B. R., 276
Bucher, B., 308, 314
Budd, K. S., 3
Buell, J., 241
Bulgren, J., 98, 174
Bullis, M., 94, 255, 264
Bumgarner, M., 127
Burton, A. W., 104
Bushell, D., Jr., 4, 273, 275, 317, 321, 322, 323, 335, 336, 339
Butterworth, T., 91
Byrne, T., 218

Cameron, J., 237, 304, 309, 330, 332
Campbell, D. T., 301, 326
Carnegie, D., 261
Carnine, D. W., 85, 91, 93, 154, 175, 191, 192, 267, 276, .317, 326, 329, 332, 335
Carpenter, M. H., 201
Carr, J. E., 128
Carroll, C. L., 300
Carta, J. J., 103, 104, 105, 106, 108, 110, 111, 113, 114, 116, 227, 323, 335
Carter, M., 275
Cartledge, G., 320
Catalano, R. F., 91
Cataldo, M. F., 3, 4
Catania, A. C., 128
Cavanaugh, R. A., 276
Cerva, T. R., 191, 283
Champlin, S. M., 127
Chard, D., 75
Charlop-Christy, M. H., 201
Chen, R., 83
Chiang, B., 72, 110
Christian, W. P., 26
Cipani, E. C., 193, 271
Clarke, S., 127
Claycomb, C., 333
Cline, G., 104, 106, 108, 113, 115, 116
Cohen, D., 6
Cohen, J., 96
Cohen, N., 105
Cohen, S., 36
Cole, C., 69, 76, 85, 96
Cole, C. L., 125
Coles, G., 332
Collins, C. G., 253
Colvin, G., 90, 91, 96, 154, 252
Comfort, C., 308

Contrucci, S. A., 128, 131
Conway, T., 8300
Cook, D. A., 58, 277
Cook, T. D., 301
Cooke, N. L., 270, 283, 293, 326
Cooper, J. O., 164, 168, 178, 191, 193, 237, 240, 259, 267, 271, 272, 278, 299, 300, 317, 320, 328, 332, 336, 338
Cooper, L. J., 125, 131
Corah, N. L., 127
Corsi, L., 126
Costello, J., 6
Courson, F. H., 275, 326
Covington, T., 340
Coyne, M. D., 69, 85, 267
Crandall, J., 320
Creswell, J. W., 327
Crosland, K., 127
Crouch, D. W., 271
Cuban, L., 139, 173
Cziko, G. A., 328

Daly, P., 164, 168
Daly, T., 192
Damann, J. D., 326
Danforth, J. S., 201
Danforth, S., 327, 329
Darch, C. B., 193
Dardig, J. C., 320, 339
Darling-Hammond, L., 140, 333
Davidson, P., 308, 314
Davis, C. C., 112
Davis, P. K., 128
Davis, S. D., 120, 121
Davison, G. C., 127
Davison, M., 299, 301
Day, M. D., 125, 131, 133
Dean, M. R., 227
DeAngelis, L., 300
DeCharms, R., 305
Deci, E. L., 127, 305, 306, 307, 308, 310, 311, 313, 314
Deitz, S. M., 139, 154, 158, 317
DeLeon, I. G., 128
Delquadri, J., 98, 174, 193, 271, 335
Denckla, M., 6
Denckla, M. B., 83
Deno, S. L., 71, 72, 106, 108, 110, 121
dePerczel, M., 127
Deshler, D., 174
Deutchman, L., 193
Devine, D. A., 127
Dickens, C., 267
Dickey, C., 96
Dickinson, A. M., 305, 308, 314
Didow, S. M., 112
Dietz, J., 245
Dinwiddie, G., 227
DiPietro, E. K., 26
Dixon, M. R., 132
Dixon, R. C., 85, 267, 277, 321, 332

Donaldson, J., 238
Doran, J., 90
Dorsey, D., 227
Dorsey, M., 246
Dorsey, M. F., 43
Dube, W. V., 192, 193
Dunlap, G., 91, 92, 98, 127
Dunlap, L. L., 192
Dunn, S., 104, 119
Dunne, J. D., 300, 340
Dwyer, K. P., 91
Dyer, K., 127

Ebbinghaus, H., 297
Ebey, T., L., 127
Ebmeier, H., 148
Eckberg, T., 6
Eckerman, C. O., 112
Edwards, G. L., 26
Edwards, R., 333
Eikeseth, A., 41
Eisenberger, R., 304, 309
Eldevik, S., 41
Elkind, D., 327, 329
Embry, D. D., 260
Endo, S., 132, 340
Engelmann, S., 192, 277
Enger, J. M., 253
Englemann, S., 316
Eshleman, J., 267, 278, 320
Espin, C. A., 71
Eyberg, S., 201

Farmer-Dougan, V., 127
Faw, G. D., 128
Fein, D., 40
Feingold, B. D., 308, 314
Fenske, E. C., 26, 40, 41, 44
Fernald, P. S., 127
Fernandez, E. R., 96, 97
Ferster, C. B., 132, 297, 300
Fischer, M., 241, 248
Fisher, J. R., 41
Fisher, S. P., 331, 332
Fisher, W. W., 125, 128, 129, 131
Flora, S. R., 305
Foorman, B. R., 83, 84
Ford, V., 65
Forness, S. R., 267, 270, 278
Forsheim, D., 96
Forsyth, P., 148
Fovel, J. T., 164
Fowler, S. A., 4, 317, 323, 339
Fox, L., 98
Foxx, R. M., 32, 192, 193, 326, 329, 332, 335, 338, 339
Frank, R., 271
Frey, K., 91
Friedman, L. N., 127
Friedman, M. L., 331, 332
Frischmeyer, P., 125, 131

Frost, L. A., 20, 192, 271
Frye, B.J., 334
Fuchs, D. F., 173
Fuchs, L. S., 71, 72, 73, 110, 121, 173
Fuentes, F., 26
Fulton, B. J., 227
Fuqua, W., 42
Furlong, M. J., 91

Gaasholt, M., 300
Galand, B., 91
Galbicka, G., 301
Gallagher, D. J., 267, 269, 271, 325, 327, 329, 333
Gallucci, C., 244, 246, 248
Gambrill, E., 322, 332, 333
Garcia, M. E., 215, 216, 224, 225
Gardner, H., 328
Gardner III, R., 267, 275, 278, 320
Gardner, W. I., 125
Garfinkle, A. N., 246
Garrison, M., 155, 161
Garvan, C., 83
Gast, D. L., 193
Gatchel, R. I., 127
Gee, K., 327
Geer, J. H., 127
Gerard, J. D., 245
Gershaw, N. J., 253
Gersten, R., 173, 174, 278, 326, 332
Gifford, E. V., 297
Gilbert, M. B., 65, 91
Gilbert, T. F., 64, 91, 215
Gillat, A., 271
Glass, D. C., 127
Godby, S., 193
Goddard, Y. L., 76, 83, 277
Goff, G. A., 131
Goldiamond, I., 56, 57, 58, 59, 60, 63, 65, 254, 264
Goldstein, A. P., 254
Goldstein, H., 192, 245, 254
Gomez, A., 127
Good, R. H., 69, 72, 73, 74, 75, 76, 79, 82, 85, 109, 121
Good, R. L., 105
Goodyear-Orwat, A., 223
Gordon, R., 26
Gorman-Smith, D., 91
Gottfredson, D. C., 91
Gottfredson, G. D., 91
Gottschalk, J. M., 129
Graf, S. A., 198
Graff, R. B., 129
Gray, C., 245
Green, C. W., 128
Green, G., 32, 40, 41, 244
Green, L., 132
Greene, D., 305, 306, 307, 310, 313
Greenwood, C. R., 98, 103, 104, 105, 106, 108, 113, 114, 115, 116, 119,

140, 141, 143, 173, 174, 175, 193, 227, 271, 321, 335
Greer, R. D., 189, 190, 192, 193, 195, 197, 201, 277, 317
Gregori, A., 300
Grenot-Scheyer, M., 241, 248
Gresham, F., 91
Grimm, L. G., 127
Groeger, C., 221, 223, 226
Grossen, B., 326
Grossi, T. A., 267, 278, 320
Grossman, D. C., 91
Gruba, J., 109
Grunsell, J., 275
Guerra, N. G., 91
Gumpel, T. P., 271
Gutierrez, A., 300

Hagopian, L. P., 129
Hake, D. G., 253
Hall, R. V., 139, 154, 193, 316, 317
Hall, S., 96
Hallahan, D. P., 240
Halperin, S., 129
Hamerlynck, L. A., 320
Hamlett, C. L., 71, 73
Handleman, J. S., 26, 40
Handler, M. W., 91
Hanley, G. P., 128, 131
Harackiewicz, J. M., 311
Harchik, A. E., 126, 127, 130, 319
Harding, J., 129
Haring, T. G., 127
Harn, B. A., 69, 76, 85
Harper, G. F., 141, 142, 144, 155, 339
Harris, F., 241
Harris, S. L., 26, 40
Harrison, C. D., 128
Hart, B., 107, 241, 335
Hartup, W. W., 248
Haug, C., 140
Haughton, E. C., 59
Hawkins, J. D., 91
Hawkins, R. B., 276, 320
Hawkins, W. E., 90
Hayes, L. J. 132
Hayes, S. C., 297
Hedges, L. V., 309
Heins, J. M., 130
Henry, D., 91
Herbert, J. D., 283
Heron, T. E., 76, 83, 91, 178, 191, 193, 237, 240, 259, 267, 269, 270, 271, 272, 275, 276, 277, 278, 282, 299, 320, 332, 339
Hersh, S. B., 320
Heshusius, L., 267, 269, 270, 271, 327, 329, 330, 331, 332
Heward, W. L., 4, 32, 80, 178, 191, 192, 193, 221, 237, 240, 259, 267, 269, 270, 271, 272, 273, 274, 275, 276,

277, 278, 299, 317, 320, 323, 325, 326, 328, 332, 333, 335, 336, 337, 339, 340
Hickey, P., 283, 284
Hieneman, M., 91, 92, 98
Higbee, T. S., 128
Hill, D. S., 320
Hill, K. G., 91
Hineline, P. N., 283, 284
Hines, C. V., 144
Hippler, B. J., 339
Hobbins, K. A., 55, 64, 321
Hoffman, C. C., 91
Holland, J. G., 277
Holubec, E. J., 158, 163, 170
Holz, W. C., 253
Hopkins, B., 317, 320
Horner, H. F., 253
Horner, R. H., 91, 92, 94, 96, 97, 125, 127, 128, 131, 133, 154, 160, 253, 255, 264, 320, 321
Hosp, M., 71, 72
Houk, J. L., 129
Howard, L., 155, 161
Howell, K., 71, 72
Howes, C., 248
Howey, K., 144
Huber, M., 144
Hughes, M., 97
Hutchins, M. P., 128
Hutchinson, R. R., 253
Hybl, L. G., 91
Hyman, I. A., 90

Iano, R. P., 267, 269, 271, 327, 329
Ingham, P., 195, 197
Iwata, B. A., 43, 127, 128, 129, 131, 246, 320, 321

Jackson, D., 316
Jackson, M., 221
Jacobs, A. L., 130
Jacobson, J. W., 40, 45, 326, 329
Jahr, E., 41
Jefferson, G., 72
Jenkins, J. R., 71, 72
Jensen, W. R., 339
Johnson, D. W., 158, 159, 162, 163, 170
Johnson, H., 159, 162
Johnson, K. R., 63, 64, 65, 192, 340
Johnson, R. T., 158, 163, 170
Johnson, S. M., 193
Johnston, J. M., 56, 296, 297, 298, 326, 335, 338
Jordan, J. B., 300
Joseph, G. E., 323, 330, 332
Joyce, B., 173
Juel, C., 73, 74

Kaczmarek, L., 192
Kaestle, C. F., 174

Kagan, S. L., 104, 105
Kallen, R., 6
Kame'enui, E. J., 69, 70, 72, 73, 74, 75, 76, 79, 82, 85, 91, 93, 109, 267, 270, 273, 276, 277, 278
Kaminski, R. A., 73, 74, 79, 82, 105, 106, 108, 109, 110, 111, 121
Kamps, D., 335
Kanfer, F. H., 127
Karnes, M., 141, 142, 144, 155
Karoly, P., 127
Karp, H., 62
Kartub, D. T., 96
Katzir-Cohen, T., 69
Kauffman, J. M., 154, 240, 329
Kaufman, M. J., 94, 255, 264
Kavale, K. A., 267, 270, 278
Keenan, M., 300
Kellam, S. G., 90
Keller, F. S., 197, 316, 340
Kelly, S. Q., 129
Kennedy, C. H., 127
Kent, H. M., 227
Keohane, D., 197
Kerr, M. M., 192, 193
Kidder, J. D., 316
Kilpatrick, D., 129
Kimball, W. H., 332
Kishi, G. S., 248
Kitchner, P., 56
Kledaras, J. B., 192
Klein, N., 126
Klein, P., 254
Klingner, J., 97
Knoster. T., 98
Koegel, L. K., 192
Koegel, R. L., 127, 192
Koespsell, T. D., 91
Koestner, R., 308, 311
Kogan, J. S., 127, 129
Koger, F., 127
Kohler, F. W., 26, 139, 154, 227, 317, 335
Kohn, A., 126, 267, 271, 272, 273, 274, 276, 311, 330, 331, 333, 334
Koop, C. E., 252
Kosanic, A. Z., 119
Kosterman, R., 91
Kraemer, H., 6
Krantz, P. J., 26, 40, 41, 42, 44, 192
Kratochwill, T. R., 330, 332
Kristoff, B., 26
Kromrey, J. D., 144
Kuntz, S., 104, 106, 108, 113, 115, 116
Kurland, M., 283

Lacerenza, L., 83
Lacey, H., 312
Lacy, L. N., 256, 257, 339
Lamm, N., 198
Lancioni, G. E., 125

Landrum, T. J., 325
Lankester, L. D., 130
Laraway, S., 127, 128, 218
Latham, G., 97
Lather, P., 327, 329
Lathin, D., 127
Lawler, E. E., 305
Laying, M. P., 65
Layng, T. V. J., 55, 62, 63, 65, 192, 321, 340
Leach, D. J., 26
Lee, S., 154
Leew. S. V., 112
Lehmann, J., 96
Leitschuh, C., 104, 106, 108, 113, 114, 115, 116
Lennaco, F. M., 192
Lepper, M. R., 305, 306, 307, 310, 313, 314
Lerman, D. C., 127, 320
Levin, L., 41
Lewis, T. J., 91, 92, 94, 253, 254
Lewis-Palmer, T., 91, 94, 96
Liaupsin, C., 91, 92
Libby, M. E., 129
Liberman, A. M., 69, 85
Liberman, I. Y., 69, 85
Lieberman, A., 173
Lindamood, P., 83
Lindberg, J. S., 131
Lindsley, O. R., 63, 192, 299, 300, 316, 317, 329, 333, 336, 338
Linebarger, D. L., 113, 114, 116
Linn, R. L., 140
Lipsey, M. W., 253
Liu, P., 91
Lloyd, J. W., 267, 270, 278
Lochner, D. G., 129
Loeber, R., 91
Logue, A. W., 132
Longton, J., 96
Lonigan, C. J., 105
Lord, C., 6
Lovaas, O. I., 6, 21, 23, 24, 25, 27, 28, 32, 35, 39, 44, 192, 201, 244, 283
Lovett, M. W., 83
Lovitt, T. C., 301, 339
Luce, S. C., 32, 244
Luiselli, J. K., 91
Lund, D., 316
Lundberg, G., 252
Lutz, M. N., 130
Luze, G. J., 104, 106, 108, 113, 114, 115, 116, 119

Maag, J. W., 332
Mabry, J., 317, 320
Mace, F. C., 130
Mackay, H. A., 193
MacKenzie, B. D., 312
Mager, R. F., 59, 215
Maglieri, K. A., 128

MaGuire, R. W., 193
Maheady, L., 140, 141, 142, 143, 144, 155, 173, 174, 175, 321, 339
Mahoney, M. J., 308, 314
Maisel, E., 127
Makasci, K., 271
Mallette, B., 141, 142, 144, 155, 339
Mallott, R. W., 155, 211, 214, 215, 216, 217, 218, 221, 222, 223, 224, 225, 226, 227, 234, 236, 335, 337
Malone, M., 190
Maloney, M., 339
Malott, M. E., 222
Malouf, D. B., 174
Manthey, S., 132
Marchand-Martella, N. E., 127
Markle, S. M., 58, 59, 63, 64, 214, 316
Marr, M. J., 299
Marston, D., 72
Martella, R. C., 91, 127
Martens, B. K., 129, 320
Martin, G., 193, 299
Mason, S. A., 127
Maurer, R., 6
Maurice, C., 31, 32, 39, 206, 244, 283, 295, 329
Mauro, B. C., 130
Mawhinney, T., C., 308, 314
Mayer, G. R., 90, 91, 253, 254, 299
Mayer, J. A., 130
Mayer, L. S., 90
Mazur, J. A., 125, 128
Mazur, J. E., 132
McAllister, J. R., 103
McClannahan, L. E., 26, 40, 41, 42, 44, 192
McComas, J. J., 125, 129, 131
McConnell, S. R., 103, 105, 106, 108, 110, 111, 120, 121, 323
McCorkle, N., 194, 197, 198
McCormick, S., 56, 300
McDonough, C. S., 192, 340
McDowell, J. J., 126
McEachin, J. J., 21, 283
McEvoy, M. A., 105, 108, 110, 111, 120, 121
McGee, G. G., 42, 127, 192
McGinnis, E., 254
McIlvane, W., 6, 192, 193
McLaughlin, A. M., 308
McLaughlin, T. F., 300, 320
Meinberg, D., 340
Meisles, S. J., 103
Messick, S., 72
Metzler, C. W., 91
Meyer, L. H., 248
Meyer, L. S., 41
Michael, J., 127, 128, 192, 193, 277, 316, 324
Middleton, S. G., 128
Millard, T., 125, 131
Miller, A. D., 193, 237, 276, 277

Miller, D. E., 104
Miller, D. L., 327
Miller, J. M., 223
Miller, L., 173
Miller, M. S., 130
Minshew, N., 6
Mirkin, P. K., 71, 72, 110
Moats, L. C., 74
Monty, R. A., 127
Moore, E., 105
Moore, J., 338
Moran, D. J., 211
Morrier, M. J., 192
Morris, E. K., 241
Morrison, D. C., 130
Morrison, E., 90
Morrison, G. M., 91
Morrison, R. L., 91
Mortweet, S. L., 271
Morvant, M., 173
Moyer, L., 283
Mulick, J. A., 326, 329
Munk, D. D., 125
Murdick, N. L., 271
Murray, A., 119
Murray-Seegart, C., 248

Nakasato, J., 97
Narayan, J. S., 275
Neckerman, H. J., 91
Neef, N. A., 130, 132, 236, 320, 321
Neisworth, J. T., 104, 111, 120, 323
Nelson, C., 227
Nelson, C. M., 91, 92, 154, 192, 252
Nelson, J. R., 91
Nelson, J. S., 339
Nelson, L., 96
Nelson, R. O., 193
Nersesian, M., 96
Neuman, S. B., 56
Neuringer, A., 338
Newcomer, L. L., 91
Newell, S., 90
Newton, J. S., 128, 160, 321
Nisbett, R. E., 305, 306, 307, 310, 313, 314
Nolet, V., 71, 72
Northrup, J., 320, 324
Nowinski, J. M., 125

O'Connor, K. A., 308
O'Connor, R., 83
O'Dell, M. C., 192
O'Leary, K. D., 317, 320
O'Leary, S., 317, 320
O'Neill, R. E., 160, 321
O'Reilly, M. F., 125, 129, 154
Ober, B., 227
Odom, S. L., 241
Olkin, I., 309
Olson, L., 327
Omness, C. K., 275

Osher, D., 91
Oswald, K., 91, 94

Paine, S. C., 193
Palermo, D. S., 312
Pangaro, P., 190
Parsons, M. B., 127, 128
Partington, J. W., 192, 194
Paul, J. L., 144
Pavlov, I. P., 236, 331
Pear, J., 193, 299
Peck, C. A., 128, 244, 246, 247, 248, 249
Peck, S. M., 125, 129, 131
Pennington, R., 192
Pennypacker, H. S., 56, 296, 297, 298, 300, 326
Perlmuter, L. C., 127
Perone, D. C., 90
Perone, M., 310
Petch-Hogan, B., 271
Peters, M. T., 91, 269, 270, 282
Peterson, L. D., 237, 256, 257, 320, 339
Peterson, R. L., 90
Peterson, S. M., 237, 256, 257, 320, 339
Pezzoli, M., 248
Piazza, C. C., 128, 129, 131
Pierce, W. D., 304, 309
Plato, 268, 270
Platt, J. R., 56
Poling, A., 127, 128, 218
Pond, R. V., 107
Ponti, C. R., 91
Poplin, M. S., 267, 272, 273, 276, 325, 327, 328
Popper, K. R., 56
Porac, J., 127
Porter, L. W., 305
Pratt, A., 83
Preator, K. K., 103
Priest, J. S., 105, 107, 110, 111, 120, 121
Prior, K., 339
Proper, E. C., 191, 283, 326
Purnell, S., 333
Purvis, J. R., 173
Putnam, R. F., 91

Rachlin, H., 132
Radicchi, J., 193
Rainville, B., 127
Ramp, E. A., 317, 320
Ramsey, E., 90, 154, 252
Rashotte, C. A., 83
Ray, B. A., 62
Reavis, H. K., 339
Rebok, G. W., 90
Reddy, S. S., 271
Reid, D. H., 127, 128
Remich, M. L., 128, 131
Renzaglia, A., 128, 154
Repp, A. C., 125
Reuf, M., 91, 92
Reynolds, J., 127

Rhode, G., 339
Richman, D., 125, 129, 131
Richman, G. S., 43, 246
Rieth, H. J., 276
Risley, T., 3, 335
Risley, T. R., 107, 127, 191, 201, 210, 240, 241, 246, 272, 276, 277, 278, 298, 300, 303, 319
Rismiller, L. L., 237
Rivara, F. P., 91
Robbins, B., 90
Robbins, J. K., 62
Robbins, L. S., 300
Rocco, F. J., 192
Rogers, E. M., 339
Rolider, A. 237, 284, 285, 289, 291, 292, 293
Rollofson, R. L., 227
Rooney, K. J., 329
Rosales-Ruiz, J., 42
Rose, E., 83
Rosellini, L. C., 193
Rosenkoetter, S., 105
Rosselli, H., 144
Rotholz, D., 227
Ruiz, R. R., 320
Rummel, J. E., 129
Rusby, J. C., 91
Rutherford, R. B., 193, 252
Ryan, R., 308, 311

Sachse-Lee, C., 331
Sadler, C., 96
Safran. S. P., 91, 94
Sagan, C., 270, 273
Sailor, W., 91, 92, 327
Sainato, D. M., 267, 276, 278, 320
Salvia, J., 71
Sandall, S. R., 241, 243
Sansone, C., 311
Sarason, S. B., 332
Sarnoff, S. K., 326
Scanlon, D. M., 83
Scheinkopf., S., 26
Scheuermann, B., 164
Schiller, E. P., 174
Schilling, D., 245
Schnorr, R. F., 247
Schoenfeld, W. N., 316
Schon, D., 144
Schuldenfrei, R., 312
Schulte, D., 227
Schumaker, J. B., 271
Schumm, J. S., 240
Schwartz, A., 254
Schwartz, B., 312
Schwartz, I., 103, 240, 241
Schwartz, I. S., 237, 241, 243, 244, 245, 246, 248, 264
Schweitzer, J. B., 132
Scott, J. W., 320
Scott, T., 91, 92, 96

Scott, T. M., 154
Scriven, M., 63
Seabaugh, G. O., 271
Searle, J. R., 70, 81
Seay, P. C., 276
Selinske, J. E., 197
Semb, G., 320
Semmel, M. L., 276
Shade, D., 130
Shafer, K., 192
Shattuck, R., 334
Shaywitz, S., 69, 70, 85
Shearer, D. D., 26
Sheinkopf, S. J., 40
Sheldon, J. B., 126, 127, 130, 319
Sherman, J. A., 3, 126, 127, 130, 319
Shermer, M., 268, 273
Shevin, M., 126
Shimamune, S., 214, 222
Shimizu, H., 192
Shinn, M. R., 71, 72, 73
Shore, B. A., 127
Shore, R., 40
Showers, B., 173
Shulman, L. S., 144
Shuster, J. W., 267, 278
Sidman, M., 56, 62, 63, 301, 317, 326
Siegel, B., 26, 40
Sigman, C., 132
Sigman, M., 6
Silbert, J., 276
Silvestri, S. M., 333
Simeonsson, R. J., 75, 77, 82
Simmons, D. C., 69, 72, 73, 74, 75, 76, 79, 85, 109, 267
Simmons, D. S., 82
Sindelar, P. T., 173
Singer, J. E., 127
Sipay, E. D., 83
Skaggs, K. J.,
Skiba, R. J., 90
Skinner, B. F., 272, 277, 284, 297, 299, 300, 311, 312, 316, 317, 320, 330, 331, 340
Skrtic, T. M., 267, 269, 271, 327, 329
Slavin, R. E., 140
Slifer, K., 246
Slifer, K. J., 43
Sloane, H., 320
Small, S. G., 83
Smalley, K., 214
Smith, P., 329
Smith, R. G., 127
Smith, S., 73, 82
Smith, S. B., 73
Smith, S. L., 271
Smith, T., 21, 41, 283
Smyth, P., 300
Snycerski, S., 127, 128, 218
Spear-Swerling, L., 326
Specter, M., 34

Spence, M., 6
Spencer, T. D., 340
Spooner, F., 193, 326
Sprafkin, R. P., 254
Sprague, J. R., 91, 94, 154, 160, 255, 264, 321
Sprick, R., 155, 161
St. Pierre, R. G., 191, 283
Stachnik, T., 317, 320
Stainback, S., 240, 325
Stainback, W., 240, 325
Stanley, J. C., 301, 326
Stanovich, K. E., 73
Staub, D., 241, 244, 246, 247, 248, 249
Stebbins, L. B., 191, 283, 326
Stein, M., 276
Steiner. V. G., 107
Sternberg, R. J., 326
Stirpe, L. A., 308
Stoddard, L. T., 193
Stoiber, K. C., 330, 332
Stokes, T. F., 43, 97, 193, 201
Stokes, T., 3
Stone, J. E., 317
Storey, K., 160, 321
Stotland, E., 127
Strain, P. S., 26, 139, 154, 317, 323, 330, 332, 335
Strikeleather, G. 55, 56, 65, 321
Strong, S. R., 127
Suarez, E. W., 215, 216, 218, 223, 225, 234
Sugai, G., 91, 92, 94, 96, 97, 154, 253, 254, 255, 264
Sulzer-Azaroff, B., 91, 132, 271, 299
Sunberg, C., 227
Sunberg, M. L., 192, 193, 194
Sutphin, B., 218
Swanson, H. L., 331
Swartz, J., 96
Sweeney, W. J., 300

Tague, C., 316
Tapia, Y., 174
Tarver, S., 276
Tarver, S. G., 332
Tashman, B., 283
Taylor, B. A., 41
Taylor, B. M., 334
Taylor, L. A., 308, 314

Taylor-Greene, S., 96
Terry, D., 335
Test, D. W., 326
Thiemann, K. S., 245
Thomas, D. R., 316
Thompson, D., 56
Thompson, S. R., 173
Thoresen, C. E., 320
Tice, T. A., 173
Tiemann, P. W., 58, 59, 214
Tierney, W. G., 327
Tincani, M. J., 237, 339
Todd, A. W., 91, 94, 96, 154
Tolan, P., 91
Torgesen, J. K., 69, 83, 84
Trap-Porter, J., 320
Troutman, A. C., 155, 160, 161, 193, 260, 299
Turnbull, A. P., 91, 92, 240
Turnbull, H. R. III, 91, 92, 240
Twombley, S., 148, 327
Twyman, J. S., 55, 63, 64, 65, 191, 194, 321
Tyler, V. O., 193

Ulrich, R., 317, 320
Usher, R., 333
Utley, C. A., 271

Van Houten, R., 269, 284, 285, 289, 291, 292, 293
Vargas, J. S., 274, 321
Vasta, R., 308
Vaughn, B. J., 127
Vaughn, S., 97, 174, 240, 326
Vellutino, F. R., 83
Viadero, D., 174
Vogel, J. M., 130
Vollmer, T. R., 129
Vroom, V., 305
Vunovich, P. I., 221, 223, 226

Wacker, D. P., 125, 129, 131
Wagner, R. K., 83
Waldron-Soler, K. M., 127
Walker, D., 103, 105, 106, 108, 110, 111, 113, 114, 116, 335
Walker, H., 90, 94
Walker, H. M., 154, 252, 255, 264
Wallin, J. U., 79, 62

Walton, C., 174
Ward, P., 271
Ward, S. M., 104, 119
Warren, S., 112
Washington, K., 245
Watkins, C. L., 283, 326, 327, 332
Watson, J., 96
Webber, J., 164, 339
Weisberg, P., 332
Welsh, R. G., 277
Welsh, T. M., 227
Wenig, B., 126
West, R. P., 320
White, R., 127
Whitehurst. G. J., 105
Wickham, D., 91, 92
Wilcox, B., 91, 92
Williams, G., 197, 198
Williams, K. R., 91
Wilson, D., 127
Winborn, J. D., 253
Winett, R. A., 243, 319
Winkler, R. C., 243, 319
Winterling, V., 127
Wolery, M., 193, 267, 278, 323, 330
Wolf, M., 3, 69, 241
Wolf., M. M., 108, 191, 201, 210, 240, 241, 246, 272, 276, 277, 278, 298, 300, 303, 316, 319
Wood, C. L., 4
Wood, F. H., 173
Wright, J. E., 276
Wright, R. M., 127
Wright, S., 127
Wysocki, T., 227

Yaber, G. E., 227
Yoder, P. J., 112
Yopp, H. K., 73
Youngs, P., 140
Ysseldyke, J., 71
Yulevich, L., 284

Zalenski, S., 26, 40, 41, 44
Zdanowski, D. M., 132
Zhou, L., 131
Zimmerman, I. L., 107
Zins, J. E., 76, 83, 91
Zuckerman, M., 127

# Subject Index

A-B-C, 193
ABC School, 206
Abell Foundation, 140
ABLLS, 194
Accountability
  cooperative learning and, 163
  environmental variables and, 321–322
  in the knowledge/skills domain, 248
  professional, 140
  of teachers and schools, 333–334
Accreditation, 140, 143–147
Active learning, autistic children and, 41
Active student response (ASR), 275, 276
Administrators, positive behavior supports (PBS) and, 92, 97
Agency for Health Care Policy and Research (AHCPR), 37
Agility, 299–300
Alpine Learning Group, 32, 39, 206
Analysis
  and effectiveness of ABA, 8
  nonlinear, 62–63
  systemic, 63
  topical, 63
Applied behavior analysis (ABA)
  as an educational treatment for children with autism, 3–29
  behavioral schools and, 188–209
  choice and, 125–133
  contributions to effective instruction of, 273–276
  curriculum design and, 55–67
  higher education and, 211–236
  inclusion and, 239–250
  individual growth and development indicators (IGDIs) and, 103–124
  lack of acceptance of, 283–285
  and precision teaching (PT), 295–303
  preservice personnel and, 139–171
  reading risk assessment and, 69–88
  reasons for limited impact of, 324–336
  strengths of, 319–324
  and technologies of effective instruction, 271–272
Applied research, 173, 295–303
Assessment. See Evaluation
Assessment of preference, role of choice in, 128
Association for Behavior Analysis, 206
Association for Science in Autism Treatment (ASAT), 32, 37–38
Attention deficit hyperactivity disorder (ADHD), 132
Authentic assessment, 329
Autism
  applied behavior analysis and, 3–29
  early intensive behavioral intervention for, 31–46

  Hawthorne Country Day School and, 188–209
  parent training and, 201–202
Autism Society of America (ASA), 33, 34, 37
Aversive stimulus, 219
Avery Training School, 188

BACC (behavioral academic career counseling), 223–224
BATS (behavioral analysis training system), 221–222, 224, 227
Bay School, 206
BCBA (board-certified behavior analyst), 195–200
Behavioral momentum, 24, 28
Behavioral psychology, 312
Behavioral schools, 188–209
Behavior Analyst Certification Board, 38, 200, 206
Behavior change. See also Problem behavior
  for autistic children, 32–39
  distrust of, 35
Behavior dynamics, versus steady state, 299–300
Benchmark instructional recommendation, 77, 79
Bethel School District, Oregon, 70, 82–83, 85–86
Biological intervention, for autistic children, 33
Bradhurst Corporation, 188
BRSS (behavioral research supervisory system), 224
Budgets
  institutional support and, 149, 256
  and positive behavior supports (PBS), 90, 92

CABAS (Comprehensive Application of Behavior Analysis to Schooling), 189, 201
Cambridge Center for Behavioral Studies, 38
Case studies, preservice teacher training and, 145–146
Causality, 297–298
Cause. See Functional analysis
Celeration, 299–300
Chaining, 11
Child/centered constructivist view, 324
Choice, intervention planning and, 125–133
Choral responding, 275, 329
Civil rights, inclusion and, 240
Classwide Peer Tutoring, 141, 145
Cognitive psychology, 311, 312
Collaboration
  in applied research, 173–185
  within the field of behavior, 45
  between the public and private sectors, 45–46
Communication
  autistic children and, 7–8, 33, 34, 36
  of benefits of behavior analysis, 283–285
  with caregivers and parents, 104, 263
  between schools and community, 255

Community, schoolwide positive behavior change and, 255, 263
Component skills, 59
Composite skills, 59
Comprehension, as a critical skill in reading, 59
Comprehensiveness, in behavioral treatment, 42
Comprehensive School Reform, 140
Computer-based learning, for reading, 55–66
Concepts, 214
Conditional aversive stimulus, 219
Conditional discrimination
    autistic children and, 41
    nonlinear analysis and, 62
Confidence, in inferences, 56
Constructionist worldview, 327
Constructivist/holistic view, 324–325
Contingencies
    analogue, 218
    cooperation and, 159, 161–162
    direct-acting, 219–221
    effective, 218
    effective performance management, 217–221
    reinforcement, 218
Contingent restraint, autistic children and, 10
Continuous quality improvement, 225–227
Cooperative groups
    limitations of, 168, 170
    preservice personnel training and, 141, 158–164
Core programs, 77
Correlation, in experimentation, 296–298
Criterion-referenced assessment, 194, 205
Critical theory, 327, 329
Curriculum-based method (CBM), 71, 73
Curriculum design. *See* Instructional design
Cusps, behavioral changes as, 42
Cybernetic approach, 190

Data
    collaborative research project and, 181, 182
    decision-making based on, 273–274
    evaluation and, 44
    positive behavior supports (PBS) and, 94, 95, 97
    preservice teacher training case studies and, 145–146
    preventing problem behavior and, 253
    qualitative *versus* quantitative, 325–328
    on teacher candidates, 140
*Daubert v. Merrell Dow Pharmaceuticals, Inc.,* 277
Decoding, 74
Deconstructivism, 329
Deinforcement, 284
Demonstration, in experimentation, 296–297
Detention, 253
Developmental testing. *See* Evaluation
Differential reinforcement, 12
Direct instruction, 191, 276, 283, 326, 327, 332
Discipline, positive behavior supports (PBS) and, 90–99
Discrete trial training (DTT)
    as applied behavior analysis, 241
    autistic children and, 8, 10–11, 24–25, 41
    in behavioral schools, 193
    training university students in, 222

Discrimination, conditional, 41
Diversity, cooperative groups and, 162–163
Dolphin therapy, autistic children and, 33, 34
Drugs, for behavioral intervention, 33
Dumping, 242
Dynamic Indicators of Basic Early Literacy Skills (DIBELS), 73–86

Early Childhood Research Institute on Measuring Growth and Development, 73
Early Head Start, 103
Early Intensive Applied Behavior Analysis model, 33
Early intervention. *See* Intervention
Education, lack of interest in reform of, 336
Effective behavior support (EBS), 154
Efficiency, 194, 275
Emotions, autistic children and, 14
Empowerment, 34, 323
Entry behavior, 61
Error correction, 61, 329
Errorless teaching, autistic children and, 12, 15, 24, 28
Escape/avoidance contingency, 220
Evaluation
    ABA and, 6
    criterion-based, 60, 72, 194
    data-based, 44
    developmental testing as, 63–64
    discrete trial training (DTT) and, 11
    field testing as, 64
    formative, 63, 71, 108
    by observations, 71
    ongoing assessment and, 173
    and standardized testing, 205–206
    summative, 108
Evidence-based practice. *See also* Data
    No Child Left Behind and, 69, 84, 90, 173
    policies for, 140
    positive behavior supports (PBS) and, 92–94
Experimental analysis of behavior (EAB), 301, 316
Experimental control, 178
Experimental design, 178
Explanatory fiction, 274
Extinction, 155, 273
Extrinsic *versus* intrinsic motivation, 304–314, 329–330

Facilitated communication, 33, 34, 36
Fading, 11, 12, 24, 28
Falsifiability, 56, 81
Families. *See* Parents and families
Field testing. *See* Evaluation
Fiscal resources. *See* Budgets
Fluency
    as a critical skill in reading, 59
    and oral reading fluency (ORF), 71–73
    partial attainment of, 109–110
Frames, 193
Fred S. Keller School, 206
Frequency bounce, 299
Frequency jumps, 299–300
Full attainment/mastery, 110
Functional analysis, autistic children and, 27, 33

Functional behavioral assessment (FBA), 154, 155, 245–246
Functional relation
  in applied behavior analysis, 298–299
  in experimentation, 296, 298
Functional skills, 190

General education
  mainstream, 245
  preservice, 139–171
Generalization, 12, 33, 43, 201, 273
General outcome measurement. *See* Measurement
Get tough policies, 90, 252–253
Gifted and talented, behavioral analysis and, 336
Goal-directed systems design, 225
Goals, in instructional design, 59
Graphemes, 59, 74
Graphic organizers, 141, 145
GRE prep course, 223
Groups, membership in, 246–248
Growth *vs.* mastery, 109
Guided notes, 141, 145
Guided practice, 329

Hawthorne Country Day School, 188–209
Headsprout, 55–66
Head Start, 103
Hedonic reinforcers, 219
Higher education
  faculty collaborative research project and, 173–185
  and preservice general education, 140–141
  responsibility in, 228–234
  using behavioral systems analysis in, 211–227
High Schools That Work model, 327
Holistic/constructivist philosophy, 272
Humanism, 311–312

Identifiability, of reading risk, 81–82, 105
Impulsivity, 132
Incentives. *See* Reinforcement; Rewards
Incidental learning
  autistic children and, 11, 24, 28, 33, 41
  inclusion and, 244
Incidental Teaching and Responsive Interaction, 107
Inclusion
  applied behavior analysis and, 239–250
  schoolwide positive behavior supports (PBS) and, 90–99
Independence skills, behavioral research and, 141
Indicated level of prevention, 77, 80–81
Individual growth and development indicators (IGDIs), 103–124
Individualization
  autistic children and, 10, 28, 41–42
  inclusion and, 242
  problem behaviors and, 92, 96
Individualized Education Program (IEP), 15, 205, 242, 243, 277, 326
Individualized Family Service Plans (IFSPs), 115
Individuals with Disabilities Education Act (IDEA), 6, 90, 245, 326
Infants and toddlers, individual growth and development indicators (IGDIs) and, 103–124

Inferences, 56
Initial sound fluency (ISF), 73–74, 79, 82
In-school detention, 90
In-school suspension, 253, 257, 258–259
Institutionalization, autistic children and, 6, 24
Institutions of higher education (IHE). *See* Higher education
Instructional activities, 192
Instructional assistants, 242–243
Instructional design, nonlinear approach to, 55–66
Instructional tactics, 192–193, 243, 244–245
Instructional trials, 193
Instrumental reinforcers, 219
Integrated curriculum, 329
Integration, inclusion and, 240
Intelligence quotient (IQ), autistic children and, 13
Intensity, of ABA program for children with autism, 11–12, 40–41
Intensive instructional recommendation, 77, 80–81
Intensive services (IS) room, 257–259
Interdependence
  cooperative learning, 158
  models of, 159
  promoting, 163–164
Internet, instructional programs on, 55–66
Intervention
  for autistic children, 31–46
  early, 40, 253
  for infants and toddlers, 103–124
  intensive, 40–41
  quality of, 41
Intrinsic *versus* extrinsic motivation, 304–314, 329–330
Invented spelling, 270

Joint Dissemination Review Panel (JDRP), 326–327
Judge Rutenberg Center, 206
Juniper Gardens Children's Project, 206

Kennedy Krieger School, 206
Key skill elements. *See* Skills
Knowledge/skills outcome, 246, 248–249
Knowledge teaching, 215
Knowledge-to-practice gap, in behavior analysis, 316–318

Learning channels, 59
Learning frames, 193
Learning objectives, 190
Learning trials, 193
Learn units, 193
Letter naming fluency (LNF), 79, 82
Letter to Mom and Dad Project, 225
Literacy, behavioral research and, 141
Lovaas studies, 21, 35, 36, 38, 201, 206

Maine Administrators of Services for Children With Disabilities, 37
Mainstreaming
  autistic children and, 9–10
  inclusion and, 240
Margaret Chapman School, 188

Measurement
    contextual, 193–195
    criterion-based, 104, 115, 118
    general outcome, 71, 108–119
    intervention results for infants and toddlers, 103–124
    normative-based, 104
    norm-referenced, 72
    positive behavior supports (PBS) and, 94
    terminal skill, 110
    validation testing as, 64
Medicaid, funding treatment of autistic children by, 5–14
Medical necessity, as criterion for treatment of autistic chil-
        dren, 5–6, 9, 23–24
Membership, 246–248
Mentors, 173–185
Meta-analysis, of research on effects of rewards, 308–312
Metal detectors, 90
Motivation
    extrinsic *versus* intrinsic, 304–314
    importance of, 323
Multi-gated assessment model (MGAM), 147
Multiple baseline across students, 178

National Alliance for Autism Research (NAAR), 38
National Council for the Accreditation of Teacher Educa-
        tion (NCATE), 140, 143–147
National Diffusion Network (NDN), 326–327
Naturalistic teaching, 28
New math, 270
No Child Left Behind, 69, 84, 90, 173, 243
Nonlinear analysis, 62–63
Nonlinearity, in instructional design, 57–65
Nonsense word fluency, 74–75, 82
Norm-referenced measurement, 72
N-term contingency, 24
Numbered Heads Together, 141, 145

*Oberti v. Borough of Clementine School District,* 244
Objectives, 190, 244
Occupational therapy, 245
Operant conditioning, 36, 155
Optimism, 323, 339–340
Oral language, reading readiness and, 105
Oral reading fluency (ORF), 71–73
Organizational behavior management, 221–223
Outcome indicator, 108
Outcomes, 190, 246–249

Pair Tutoring Program, 142, 146–147
Parents and families
    of autistic children, 6–8, 34
    instructional assistants and, 242–243
    positive behavior supports (PBS) and, 95, 96
    schoolwide positive behavior change and, 262, 263
    training and education of, 42–43, 201–202
    understanding of early intervention measures by, 104,
        111–112
Parsimony, of inferences, 56
Partial attainment, 109
Partner pairings, 141
Peer collaboration, 141

Peer instruction, 227, 276
Peer review, in publishing, 301
Peer tutoring, 275, 277
Performance management model of task accomplishment,
        215–221
Personality, autistic children and, 14
Personalized system of instruction (PSI), 197–198
Pharmacological intervention, for autistic children, 33
Phenomenology *versus* behaviorism, 70
Phonemes, 59, 74
Phoneme segmentation fluency (PSF), 73–74, 82
Phonics, 59, 70
Phonological awareness, 73–74
Picture-exchange system (PECS), 20
Pinpoints, of learning behavior, 59
PIRK, 194
Play testing, individual growth and development indicators
        (IGDIs) and, 113–115
Play therapy, autistic children and, 35
Positive behavior support (PBS), 90–100, 154
Postmodernism, 327–328, 329
Postpositivism, 327
Practice
    criticism of, 331
    guided, 63, 329
    repeated, 274–275
Praise, 260–261, 329
Precision teaching (PT), 295–303
Preference assessment, 11
Preintervention strategies, 271
Premack principle, 24
Preschool Language Scale, 107–108
Prevention
    of disruptive behavior, 253–254
    of failure in reading, 69–86
    model of, 75–86
    schoolwide positive behavior supports (PBS)
        and, 90–99
Princeton Child Development Center, 206
Principles, 214
Probation, 253
Problem behavior
    autistic children and, 43–44
    behavioral research and, 141
    and positive behavior supports, 90–99, 252–281
    prevention of, 253
    punitive models to deal with, 253
Process, of schooling, 190
Process of responsive instruction (PIRR), 143
Professional accountability, 140
Professional development, 96, 97–98
Professional educational unit (PEU), 143
Project Follow Through, 191, 283, 319, 326–327
Psychoanalysis, intervention based on, 33
Psychology, mainstream, 245
Psychophysical indicator response methodology, 60
Punishment
    autistic children and, 43
    *deinforcement* as a term for, 284
    preservice personnel training in, 155, 156
    for problem behavior, 252–253

and reinforcement, 272
schoolwide, 90–91

Random assignment, in Lovass studies, 22–23, 25–26
Reading
    computer-based learning program for, 55–66
    prevention of failure in, 69–86
    school readiness and, 105
Reading First Initiative, 69, 90
Reading specialists, 245
Reflective and Responsive Educator (RARE) program,
    141–147
Reform, lack of interest in, 336
Reinforcement. *See also* Rewards
    criticism of, 329–330
    differential, 12
    to facilitate participation, 243–244
    hedonic, 219
    importance of, 324
    as increasing/suppressing behaviors, 272
    instructional trials and, 193
    instrumental, 219
    positive behavior supports (PBS) and, 90–99
    preservice personnel training in, 155, 156
    role of choice in, 128–130, 131
    scheduling, 12
    of schoolwide positive behavior, 259–262
Relationships, 246, 248
Repetition
    of practice, 274
    *versus* practice, 63
Replication, 56, 323
Research. *See also* Lovaas studies
    on adoption and retention of effective practices, 335
    autism and, 45
    behavioral services and, 141
    between-groups design of, 307–308
    on choice in educational settings, 127–128
    collaborative classroom project for, 173–185
    meta-analysis and, 308–311
    prevention and, 84–85
    and the research-to-practice gap, 174–175, 316–318
    training for preservice personnel in, 155
    within-groups design of, 307–308
Resource interdependence, 159
Response cards, 141, 145, 275
Response cost
    autistic children and, 43
    procedure for, 259
Response deprivation methods, 24
Responsive Educator Program (REP), 140
Rewards
    cooperation and, 159, 161–162
    and intrinsic *versus* extrinsic motivation, 304–314
    and punishments, 271–273
    research on detrimental effects of, 305–308
    schoolwide positive behavior change and, 259–262
    teaching autistic children and, 18–21
Risk
    prevention of, 83–84
    quantification of, 69–86

Robot training, ABA as, 33, 241
Role interdependence, 159

Safe Schools, 90
SAFMEDS (Say All Fast for a Minute Each Day), 198
Saturday School, 253
Schools
    accountability of, 333–334
    behavioral, 188–209
    and communication with community, 255
    detention in, 90
    intensive services (IS) room in, 257–259
    probation in, 253
    punishment strategies in, 90–91
    readiness for, 103, 105
    schoolwide positive behavior change and, 255–266
    schoolwide positive behavior supports (PBS) and, 90–99
    structure of, 254–255
    suspension in, 253, 258–259
Science, use in developing instructional programs, 55–56
Scientifically based reading research (SBRR), 69, 77
Security, 90
Selected level of prevention, 77, 79–80
Self-actualization, 311
Self-assessments, positive behavior supports (PBS) and, 97
Self-control, 131–132
Self-correction, 321–322
Self-delivery, of instruction, 277
Self-destructive behavior, 9, 11–13
Self-regulation, 105, 329
Self-stimulation, autistic children and, 11–13
Shaping, 11, 12, 28
Skills
    behavioral research and, 141
    component, 59
    composite, 59–60
    and key skill elements, 108, 109–110, 112
    and skills training model of education, 214–221
    social, 114, 163
Social competency, reading readiness and, 105
Social stories, 245
Social validity, 108, 275–276
Soma puzzle, 306
Special education, 8, 155–171, 245
Special needs students
    autism and, 3–47
    choice and, 131, 132
    inclusion and, 239–250
    and the Pair Tutoring Program, 142
    success of ABA with, 3–47
Speech-language pathology, 245
Speech professionals, autistic children and, 7–8
Standards, teaching, 140
STARS School, 206
Steady state, in applied behavior analysis, 299–301
Stimulus control, 11, 12, 28
Stimulus equivalence, 24, 28
Strategic instructional recommendation, 77, 79–80
Strategy, training in, 214
Student teachers. *See* Teachers, preservice
Success for All model, 327

Super-A, 224
Superposition, 24
Surveillance cameras, 90
Suspension
    in-school, 253, 257, 258–259
    out-of-school, 90
Systemic analysis, 63
Systems approach, 190

Target behavior, 57. *See also* Objectives
Task interdependence, 159
Teachers
    accreditation of, 140
    criticism of ABA by, 333
    discrete trial training (DTT) and, 8–9, 10–11
    as mentors, 173–185
    positive behavior supports (PBS) and, 92, 97
    preservice
        collaborative classroom research and, 173–185
        general education programs for, 139–171
    reinforcement for, 334–335
    special education teachers and ABA, 8–9
    training of (*See* Training)
Teaching
    for deep understanding, 329
    holistic, 329
    strategies for, 276–277
Teams
    collaborative research and, 175–185
    preservice personnel training and, 158–159
Teamwork, positive behavior supports (PBS) and, 94, 95, 97
Technology, and positive behavior supports (PBS), 93
Terminal behavior, 57
Terminal skill attainment, 110
Terminology, of behavior analysis, 282–285, 338–339
Testing. *See* Evaluation

Three-contingency model of performance management, 216
Three-term contingency, 24
Time-out, 43, 253
Toddlers. *See* Infants and toddlers
Topical analysis, 63
Toys, individual growth and development indicators (IGDIs) and, 113–115
Train and hope approach, 97–98
Training
    of parents and families, 42–43, 201–202
    of school personnel, 256
    skills training model of education, 214–221
    of teachers, 45, 173, 195–199, 256–257
Transformation, 24
Treatment validity, 104, 119
Tutoring, 275, 277

Universal level of prevention, 77, 79
University. *See* Higher education
University of Minnesota Institute for the Research on Learning Disabilities (IRLD), 71

Validation testing. *See* Evaluation
Variables, alterable, 274
Verbal behavior, 39
Verge, 299
Verifiability, 81
Victim blaming, avoidance of, 222–223
Vitamin therapy, autistic children and, 33
Vocabulary
    as a critical skill in reading, 59
    technical, 198

Whole language, 70, 270

Zero tolerance, 90, 253